SISTERHOOD, FEMINISMS AND POWER

SISTERHOOD, FEMINISMS AND POWER:

FROM AFRICA TO THE DIASPORA

EDITED BY
OBIOMA NNAEMEKA

Africa World Press, Inc.

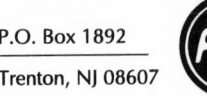

| P.O. Box 1892 | | P.O. Box 48 |
| Trenton, NJ 08607 | | Asmara, ERITREA |

Africa World Press, Inc.

P.O. Box 1892
Trenton, NJ 08607

P.O. Box 48
Asmara, ERITREA

Copyright © 1998 Obioma Nnaemeka

First Printing 1998

Book and cover design: Jonathan Gullery

This book is composed in New Baskerville and American Typewriter

Library of Congress Cataloging-in-Publication Data

Obioma Nnaemeka.
    Sisterhood, feminisms and power: from Africa to the diaspora /
edited by Obioma Nnaemeka.
        p.   cm.
    Papers presented at an international conference on Women in Africa
and the African Diaspora (WADD), held July 13–18, 1992 in Nsukka,
Nigeria.
    Includes bibliographical references and index.
    ISBN 0-86543-438-7 (cloth : alk. paper). -- ISBN 0-86543-439-5
(pbk. : alk. paper)
    1. Feminism- - Africa- - Congresses. 2. Women- - Africa- -Congresses.
3. Women, Black- - Congresses. I. Nnaemeka, Obioma, 1948-
HQ1788.S57   1997
305.42'096–dc21

                                                        97-19965
                                                          CIP

In memory of
Ezihe "Adanma" Afigbo
Catherine Bicknell
Edith Ihekweazu
Chuma Ijomah
Audre Lorde
Flora Nwapa
'Zulu Sofola
who saw the beauty in difference
and lived it

When something stands, something stands beside it.
(Igbo proverb)

The sky is vast enough for all birds to fly without colliding.
(Yoruba proverb)

One head cannot go into counsel.
(Ashanti proverb)

*Knowledge is like a baobab tree: no one can
encompass it with both hands.*
(Ewe proverb)

CONTENTS

II. WOMEN ORGANIZING FOR CHANGE

III. WEAVING OUR LIVES: THE PERSONAL IS POLITICAL

IV. POSTSCRIPT

V. FORUM

VI. APPENDIX

ACKNOWLEDGEMENTS

I AM MOST GRATEFUL TO ALL **WAAD** CONFERENCE participants, especially Flora Nwapa, Ama Ata Aidoo, and 'Zulu Sofola, for accepting my invitation and making "Nsukka '92" memorable. My profound gratitude also goes to our sponsors, particularly the MacArthur Foundation, the Swedish International Development Authority (SIDA), the Swedish Agency for Research Cooperation with Developing Countries (SAREC), the International Development Research Center (IDRC), Ottawa, Canada, ECOWAS, UNESCO, and Nigerian Merchant Bank, Lagos, whose generous gifts made it possible for many African participants to attend. Many thanks to the University of Nigeria, Nsukka, for hosting the conference. I am most grateful to C. Achufusi, the Director of Akulue Hospital, Nsukka, for providing free medical services for conference participants. A hearty Odidama *deme* to Obiora Udechukwu for designing the beautiful WAAD logo on the front cover of this volume.

My former school, the College of Wooster, Wooster, Ohio, deserves a special recognition. The College of Wooster gave me two of my best years in the profession and saw the beginning of the WAAD project. I owe a lot of gratitude to the College, especially Dean Yvonne Williams for her usual warmth, unwavering support, and sisterhood, as well as her willingness to extend to me postage and photocopying privileges during the critical initial stages of the project. My indebtedness to my colleagues and diaspora sisters, Annetta Jefferson and Martha Banks, for their caring spirit and sisterhood. My heart-felt gratitude goes to our secretaries at The College—Dale Catteau, Ardis Gillund, and Carol Boreman—for their immense kindness and patience. Without Wooster, WAAD would not have happened and for that, and much more, I remember The College with fondness. I am equally grateful to my current school, Indiana University at Indianapolis, for supporting me in my work. My profound gratitude also goes to Amy Jones, Wanda Porter, Cynthia Randolph, Billi Brown, and Nancy Worthman for providing secretarial support and to Lizzy Egwu for proofreading. Special thanks go to my assistant, Uzoamaka Maduka, for her patience, generosity, loyalty, and hard work in helping to put the proceedings together.

Words cannot fully express the gratitude I owe members of the organizing committee, country and regional representatives, city and institutional representatives (Nigeria) and, particularly, the local planning committee at Nsukka under the able leadership of Edith Ihekweazu and Julie Okpala, for working tirelessly in support of the project. Julie remained unflappable throughtout the difficult WAAD project and I thank her from the bottom of my heart for being a pillar of strength and teaching me patience. Words cannot fully express my indebtedness to the members of the local organizing committee who, for lack of space, I cannot name individually. They all worked tirelessly under most difficult circumstances to put the conference together; they were the backbone of the entire operation and I thank them most sincerely. The governments of Anambra and Enugu States, Nigeria, gave us their full support. The conference was enriched by the participation of the Better Life Programs of Enugu and Anambra States under the directorship of the wives of the governors of both states—Dorothy Nwodo and Njideka Ezeife. My sincere thanks go to the governments and Better Life Programs of both states. I am grateful to Joy Orah, Monica Eze, and Chi Okafor for making our meeting with the wife of the governor of Enugu State possible.

For his unalloyed support and persistent encouragement, I sincerely thank Michael Mbabuike, who never wavers in his belief that I have something worthwhile to contribute. To Emmanuel Obiechina and Chimalum Nwankwo I say a big *dalu* for keeping me focused on Igboland. Special thanks to Armand and Madeleine Renaud for their encouragement and goodwill which date back to my graduate school days. I thank Susan Geiger for many years of friendship, laughter, and lengthy discussions on Africa. Jude Akudinobi continues to keep me abreast of new publications in the field and I thank him and his wife, Amaka, for their support and friendship. My gratitude to Peter Hitchcock for long-standing intellectual exchanges and, in this instance, my admiration for his courage, as the lone white man represented in this volume, in standing firm amidst women in Africa and the African Diaspora as they agree and disagree.

I thank the following for the permission to republish some of the contributions to the volume: Bedford Publishers for "Africana Womanism" (Clenora Hudson-Weems), Sheffield Academic Press for "North American Feminisms and Global Feminisms: Contradictory or Complementary?" (Angela Miles), Ama Ata Aidoo for "African Woman Today," *Agenda* for "The Nigerian Conference Revisited" (Lumka Funani), and "The Nigerian Conference" (Fidelia Fouché), *Sage: A Scholarly Journal on Black Women* for "The First International Conference on Women in Africa and the African Diaspora: A View from the USA" (Deborah Plant), and Jonathan Ball Publishers for Annemarie Hendrikz's poem, "For Marion Sparg." Audre Lorde's verses cited in "Postscript" (page 374) are reprinted with permission from "Uses of Anger: Women Responding to Racism" in *Sister Outsider: Essays and Speeches* by Audre Lorde ©1984, published by The Crossing Press, Freedom, Calif. (800-777-1048).

Throughout the difficult WAAD project, I was very fortunate to be surrounded by extraordinary friends—Uche Amazigo, Nikki Johnson, Susan Geiger, Florence Achonu, Chuma Ijomah, Janet Spector, Carolann Dickinson, Sholanda Jefferson, Lehn Benjamin, Charlie Sugnet, Joy Ijomah, Kathleen Mullaney, Betty Owsley, Catherine Bicknell, and Donna Blacker—whose love, collegiality, loyalty, and unwavering support buoyed me and for that, I am most grateful. My "rainbow coalition" of friends affirms my faith in the possibilities of global sisterhood. I am proud of and grateful to the entire Obidiegwu family for always being there for me. Finally, my most profound gratitude goes to my two wonderful sons, Ike and Uche (tireless workers and my greatest supporters), whose love and laughter are rare gifts; whose lives have enriched mine in profound ways.

INTRODUCTION: READING THE RAINBOW[1]

OBIOMA NNAEMEKA

To see Africa as a continent of people—just people, not some
strange beings that demand a special kind of treatment.
If you accept Africans as people, then you *listen* to them.
They have their preferences.
—Chinua Achebe
(emphasis added)

We are making our voices heard. May the world stop to *listen*.
—Nahid Toubia (emphasis added)[2]

MORE THAN ANY OTHER VOLUME THAT I HAVE EDITED,
Sisterhood, Feminisms, and Power is unique in its demands and its difficulty in that it mandates editorial distance. The search for meanings leads not only to what the contributions say—ideas, conflicts,
agreements, cross-fertilization, etc.—but also, and more importantly, *how* they *speak* their truth. The power of the contributions
lies in their manner of *speaking*. For example, as I read 'Zulu Sofola,
I *hear* her lament the impotence (what she calls "dewomanization")
of the so-called modern, Western-educated African woman *vis-à-vis*
her rural, illiterate counterpart :

In light of the relevance, power, and effectiveness of the illiterate, "traditional" African women, one wonders why the

Western-educated African women of the new order are ineffective, always timidly and indecisively stepping behind the
men and periodically making weak scratches at issues of
importance, while their non-literate counterparts would
always march out in full force and achieve unbelievable successes.... Quite often, when one hears the Western-educated African woman speak in a demeaning manner about her
illiterate, rural, "traditional" counterpart, one cannot help
but pity the former for her false sense of importance and
delusion of grandeur. It never occurs to her that while she
parrots the phrase, "what a man can do, a woman can do
better," her illiterate counterpart asserts: "what a woman can
do, a man cannot do." While she quotes the European saying, "Behind every successful man is a woman," her illiterate counterpart affirms: "The strength of a man is in his
woman," or "A soldier with a mother does not die at the war
front." While she conceives of herself as someone to be seen
not heard; her illiterate counterpart says: "If the *Ada* (daughter) says that a day-old chick is a hen, so it is." While she
hangs on to a wicked and bestial husband, her illiterate
counterpart throws such a husband off in the spirit of the
following proverb: "The burden of a husband is carried on
the wife's shoulder, not on her head; she quickly drops it
when it becomes too unbearable." (63)

In Sofola's text, I hear not only her voice but the voices of women
I have come to know in my village of Agulu; women who would plant
their feet firmly on the ground and with arms akimbo look any one
(men included) in the eye and speak their mind without batting an
eye-lid. The power of similar voices in the volume holds the editorial pen in abeyance, and preserving that power poses a great challenge to the editorial process.

Faced with the task of maintaining a balanced distance between
alienation and over- identification, I wrestle with the unscriptable
factor that Richard Wright calls perspective:

Perspective is that part of a poem, novel, or play which a
writer never puts directly upon paper. It is that fixed point
in intellectual space where a writer stands to view the struggles, hopes and sufferings of his people. There are times
when he may stand too close and the result is blurred vision.
Or he may stand too far away and the result is a neglect of
important things. (*Black Aesthetics*, 341)

As editor, I have tried as much as possible to respect the distance mandated by the contributions without moving so far away as to lose sight of important details. Hence, from a measured distance, I shall in this introduction focus on three broad and recurrent areas: (1) feminism/womanism debates; (2) research/documentation questions; (3) African Continent/African Diaspora relationships.

Aware that on many issues (feminism, for example) the contributors do not speak with one voice, this introduction attempts to delineate the convergences and affinities as well as tease out the differences and paradoxes for a better understanding of the complex web of issues raised in the volume. The issue of authority and agency that is addressed in some of the contributions can be examined in light of the arguments made in Peter Hitchcock's paper on the Arab Women's Solidarity Association (AWSA) and the politics of voice. Hitchcock's examination of the the difficulty (or even impossibility) of simultaneously articulating the terms "Arab" and "woman" veers not towards the theory of the subject but to the history of AWSA as it is embedded in the history of post-World War II Egyptian politics, from Nasser to Mubarak; a history that throws the challenge of articulating "a notion of political constituency that does not cancel itself out with the subtleties of sliding signifiers." A similar difficulty arises in the articulation of the category "African feminist," not only in the African continent but as it is complicated by the African diaspora question. What emerges from listening to the African women in this volume is not the necessity or desirability of a monolithic, representative political voice, but the eagerness to recognize and promote a common ground while respecting the nuances that make the emergence of a monolith impossible.

Sisterhood, Feminisms, and Power engages the conflicts in feminism, among other issues. However, the volume focuses less on the transcending of difference and more on the challenges of living successfully with contradictions, less on the obliteration of difference (an impossible task!) and more on allowing difference to be and in its *being* create the power that energizes *becoming*. The book speaks of feminism in the plural (feminisms) within Africa and between Africa and other continents because it is mindful of the multiplicity of perspectives and the need for accommodation. As my ancestors philosophized: *adiro akwu ofu ebe enene nmanwu* (One does not stand in one spot to watch a masquerade). As with the dancing masquerade, vantage points shift and one must shift with them for the maximization of benefits. In their exploration of the relationships among sisterhood, feminisms, and power, the contributions to this volume argue for the power of sisterhood that resides in the recognition and respect of the pluralism of *feminisms*. The volume underscores the power of African women to work with patri-archal/cultural structures that are liberating and ennobling while challenging those that are limiting and debilitating. It focuses on what African women are doing with/to patriarchal and cultural structures, and decenters but keeps in view the ever pervasive litany (particularly in Women's Studies) of what patriarchy is doing with/to African women. *Sisterhood, Feminisms, and Power* evokes the power, not the paralysis, of African women; it accounts for their tri-umphs amidst obstacles without underestimating the gravity of the impediments or failing to advocate vigorously for removal of such.

In addition to examining the faces of feminism and conflicts in feminism, *Sisterhood, Feminisms, and Power* focuses on who or what plays a role in shaping African women's lives. Aware of the impor-tance of a thorough assessment of the relationship among the gath-ering, construction, and dissemination of knowledge, *Sisterhood, Feminisms, and Power* examines the nature and modalities of infor-mation-gathering and dissemination as well as the gender, feminist, institutional, and global politics that undergird such undertakings.

Although the papers in this volume are grouped in sections, they actually defy categorization by virtue of their border crossings and search for dialogue. For example, Ifeyinwa Iweriebor's paper on her involvement in the formative years of Women in Nigeria (WIN)—a Nigerian feminist organization that is ideologically rad-ical in a socially transformative sense—is a personal perspective that allegorizes collective consciousness and engagement and weaves together practical and theoretical imperatives. The first three sec-tions of this volume, respectively, can be titled simply the theoreti-cal, the practical, and the personal, although the papers therein cross boundaries by revealing not only points of resistance and dif-ference but also marks of affinity and convergence. The "Forum" section provides the space for participants at the first internation-al conference on Women in Africa and the African Diaspora (WAAD) to debate the controversial issues that erupted at the con-ference—from race and gender issues to theoretical and cultural questions framed in the context of feminist and global politics and debated in the context of shifting subjectivities and border cross-ings. My engagement with the contributions will reflect these bor-der crossings as well.

The nature, politics, and crises of feminism as well as related research problems are extensively discussed in Section One, which

focuses primarily on epistemological, theoretical, and methodological questions. The diverse positions on feminism raise a crucial question: Can one be a feminist in isolation? African women's
claims about feminism call into question the theory/praxis dichotomy in feminist engagement. They interrogate the essentialism of
home politics, the exclusions of standpoint intransigence, and the
potential (or real) chaos of postmodernist indeterminacy; indeed,
they shatter the comfort of "home politics" to allow the unfolding
of a true political gesture—an *engagement* in the Sartrean sense of
the word. It seems to me that for African women, *to be or think feminist is to act feminist.*

The feminist spirit that pervades the African continent is so
complex and diffused that it is intractable. Not too long ago, a colleague asked me to provide a framework for African feminism as
articulated by African feminists. My off-the-cuff response was: "the
majority of African women are not hung up on 'articulating their
feminism;' they just do it."[3] In my view, it is *what* they do and *how*
they do it that provide the "framework;" the "framework" is not carried to the theater of action as a definitional tool. It is the dynamism
of the theater of action with its shifting patterns that makes the feminist spirit/engagement effervescent and exciting but also
intractable and difficult to name. Attempts to mold "African feminism" into an easily digestible ball of pounded yam not only raise
definitional questions but create difficulties for drawing organizational parameters and unpacking complex modes of engagement.
In this regard, it will be more accurate to argue not in the context
of a monolith (*African feminism*) but rather in the context of a pluralism (*African feminisms*) that captures the fluidity and dynamism
of the different cultural imperatives, historical forces, and localized
realities conditioning women's activism/movements in Africa—
from the indigenous variants to the state-sponsored configurations
in the postcolonial era.[4] The inscription of *feminisms* in the title of
this volume underscores the heterogeneity of African feminist thinking and engagement as manifested in strategies and approaches
that are sometimes complementary and supportive, and sometimes
competing and adversarial. The differences and conflicts among
African feminisms notwithstanding (Sofola, Aina, Nwapa, Fester,
Iweriebor, Aidoo, and Chukukere), there exist common features
and shared beliefs that undergird them. It is in recognition of this
commonality and for convenience that I will, in this instance, use
the term in the singular—*African feminism.* Furthermore, it is also
for convenience that an English word—*feminism*—is used to cap-

ture the intractable spirit of an engagement that speaks literally
thousands of different languages across the African continent. The
argument for the pluralism of African feminism is equally applicable to Western feminism, although one can glean common features
in Western feminisms against which African feminisms argue.

A major flaw of feminist attempts to tame and name the feminist spirit in Africa is their failure to define African feminism *on its
own terms* rather than in the context of Western feminism. Such a
contextualization of African feminism argues in effect that African
feminism is what Western feminism is not. In other words, that
African feminism establishes its identity through its resistance—it
is because it *resists*. It is to the most recurrent and contentious areas
of disagreement and resistance—radical feminism, motherhood,
language, sexuality, priorities, (gender) separatism, and universal-
ism—that I now turn.

First, resistance is raised against radical feminism—African feminism is not radical feminism. Second, resistance is directed towards
radical feminism's stridency against motherhood—African feminism neither demotes/abandons motherhood nor dismisses maternal politics as non-feminist or unfeminist politics. Third, the
language of feminist engagement in Africa (collaborate, negotiate,
compromise) runs counter to the language of Western feminist
scholarship and engagement (challenge, disrupt, deconstruct, blow
apart, etc.)—African feminism challenges through negotiation and
compromise.

Fourth, there is resistance to Western feminism's inordinate and
unrelenting emphasis on sexuality (*human* sexuality, to be more precise) that conditions, for example, the nature, tone, spectacle, and
overall *modus operandi* of Western feminist insurgency against female
circumcision in Africa and the Arab world.[5] Flora Nwapa's identification, in her contribution to this volume, of what is radically feminist in her *oeuvre* is revealing. Criticisms of Nwapa's works—often
concentrating on *Efuru, Idu, One is Enough,* and *Women Are
Different*—have always looked at gender relations and human sexuality in them for feminist agenda and insurgency. However, Nwapa
does not turn to these works for what she considers her truly auda-
cious gesture from a feminist standpoint; she turns instead to the
one work that is rarely discussed in feminist criticism of her *oeuvre*—
her *Cassava Song and Rice Song.* In the mock epic, "Cassava Song,"
Nwapa engages in a daring and subversive undertaking by dethron-
ing the Igbo icon of masculinity—the yam:

The Cassava tuber is accessible to both the rich and the poor in many parts of Nigeria and Africa. Cassava is planted by women, unlike yam, the "King of all Crops," that is planted by men. Every year in Igboland, the New Yam Festival is observed. New yam is not eaten until this festival is performed. But, is there a festival for Cassava? No. In "Cassava Song," the various uses of cassava are enumerated to show that *she* deserves to be celebrated and sung like the yam.... Cassava is enthroned above yam and cocoyam—above all other foodstuff. Cassava is woman. Yam is man.(94)

Nwapa's use of the "epic" style (the first and only time such a style appears in her *oeuvre*) for "Cassava Song" underscores the importance of her feminist agenda in the work—as it were, she elevates her daring feminist gesture to epic proportions. In "Cassava Song," Nwapa goes for the ultimate effrontery as she challenges the Igbo cultural hierarchy by unseating the icon of masculinity and promoting the ascendancy of the unsung icon of femininity (cassava) in order to reclaim the complementarity and parity that are inscribed in Igbo cosmology ("*she* deserves to be celebrated and sung like the yam"). The obsession with *human* sexuality in feminist analyses of Nwapa's works excludes "Cassava Song" and, consequently, averts the revelation of the feminist gesture that Nwapa herself claims.

Fifth, there are disagreements between African feminism and Western feminism over priorities. The much bandied-about intersection of class, race, sexual orientation, etc., in Western feminist discourse does not ring with the same urgency for most African women, for whom other basic issues of everyday life are intersecting in most oppressive ways. This is not to say that issues of race and class are not important to African women in the continent (not in the face of racial conflicts from Algeria and Kenya to Zimbabwe [ex-Rhodesia] and South Africa). Rather, I argue that African women see and address such issues first as they configure in and relate to *their own lives and immediate surroundings*. To go to a remote village in Africa and round up a group of women who have no clean water to drink, no food to eat, and have never seen a different race of humans, and theorize/preach to them the feminist framework of intersection of race, class, etc., is nothing but feminism in futility. Such an intervention can have meaning only when the women are convinced that they lack food and clean water because they belong to a particular category of humans.[6] Sixth, African feminism resists the exclusion of men from women's issues; on the contrary, it invites men as partners in problem solving and social change.[7]

Finally, there is resistance to the universalization of Western notions and concepts. One occurrence in Africa that has captured the Western feminist imagination is the 1929 Igbo Women's War. The different interpretations of the war are instructive. Some feminist scholars who claim human rights as a feminist issue dismiss the Igbo Women's War as a non-feminist uprising because, according to them, it was motivated not by the demand for gender equality but by economic considerations. However, it is important to recall that when the Igbo woman who started the uprising was asked the number of people and livestock in her compound by the colonial agent who came to her home, she shouted back at him to go and count his own people—and the rest is history. Such a question in an environment where the counting of human beings is taboo constitutes a human rights violation (the woman felt that her humanity was violated). That this culturally unacceptable interrogation may not qualify for a Western notion of human rights violation does not make it less so for this woman. If the war has elements of resistance to human rights violation as well as affirmation of cultural nationalism *in the eyes of the people who fought it*,[8] then we have to rethink not only the contours and naming of human rights, in general, but also the feminist/non-feminist debate about the Igbo Women's War.

The universalization of Western notions of sexual harassment poses problems in cultures where human touch is more prevalent and admissible. An understanding of human interaction and social etiquette in such cultures will certainly have implications for the rethinking of the globalization of Western notions of personal space and what constitutes sexual harassment. It is therefore important to emphasize that what constitutes sexual harassment in an office in Washington, D. C. or London may not be regarded as such in a farm in an African village. Some African and Middle-eastern immigrants in the West have faced serious legal troubles for touching their children "improperly." In actuality, *some* of the *specifics* of the allegations in some high-profile cases of sexual harassment in the West will not compel women farmers in some African village to drop their hoes and march in "feminist solidarity" to the seat of Government in a far-away capital city they have never visited and would probably not visit in their lifetime. In an environment where holding hands or throwing one's arms around someone else's shoulders does not carry the same sexual baggage as it does in other places, it would be senseless for feminists in that environment to raise a battle cry each time cross-gender touching occurs in the work place. Probably, the human touch that prevails—holding hands, etc.—contributes to holding certain societies together. Must those societies jettison what holds them together because some feminists somewhere have declared such acts "unacceptable"? I don't think so. If human touch helps to hold certain societies together, shouldn't imploding/disintegrating societies where human touch is suspect at best and anathema at worst try what seems to be holding other places together?

All the different types of resistance and disagreement noted above contribute towards defining and explaining African feminism. However, what is crucial is *how* they are contextualized.To meaningfully explain the phenomenon called African feminism, it is not to Western feminism but rather to the African environment that one must refer. African feminism is not reactive, it is proactive. It has a life of its own that is rooted in the African environment. Its uniqueness emanates from the cultural and philosophical specificity of its provenance. African feminism's valorization of motherhood and respect for maternal politics should not be pitted against the demotion of motherhood/maternal politics by radical feminism in the West; rather these traits should be investigated in the context of their place and importance in the African environment. The same argument goes for the language issue raised above. The language of African feminism is less a response to the language of Western feminism and more a manifestation of the characteristics (balance, connectedness, reciprocity, compromise, etc.) of the African worldview as demonstrated in the encoding in many African languages of gender-neutral third-person-singular pronouns as well as words whose etymologies are mindful of gender neutrality and balance (Sofola). Equally revealing and pertinent are the different inscriptions of body parts in African and European languages respectively. For example, unlike the English language that inscribes body parts in order to reinforce individualism, separatism, conflict, and opposition ("on the one hand, on the other hand"), Igbo language inscribes body parts to highlight reciprocity and contact zones (*aka nni kwọ aka ekpe, aka ekpe akwọ aka nni*/As the right hand washes the left hand, the left hand washes the right hand).[9] Furthermore, African feminism's resistance to gender separatism is less a reaction against Western feminism and more a manifestation of the cross-gender partnership that is a prominent and time-tested feature of African cultures[10]—a partnership that is reinforced by colonialist and imperialist threats.

To a large extent, some contributors to this volume wrestle with understanding and explaining African feminism without having Western feminism (at least, not too much of it) on their mind. The different perspectives on feminism—African feminism/womanism (Aina, Aidoo, Sofola, Chukukere, Iweriebor), Africana womanism (Hudson-Weems), and North American and global feminisms (Miles)—raise crucial questions, one of which is "What is feminism?" African women's different positions on feminism, emanating as they do from different perceptions of feminism and differing assessments of the impact of "modernity," lead some (Aidoo, Sofola, Chukukere) to assert that feminism (the feminist spirit, at least) is indigenous to the continent and others (Aina) to claim that feminism in Africa is still in its infancy.

Some contributors' interrogation of the relationship between feminism and Africa/African women produce subversive readings that unpack dichotomies, such as urban/rural, male/female, and powerful/powerless, by emphasizing affinities and border crossings. For example, Ifeyinwa Iweriebor's interrogation of the urban/rural split as basis for measuring privilege and comfort evokes what I consider to be the dilemma, and indeed tragedy, of much of contemporary urban Africa where basic amenities that mark urban living (such as pipe-borne water, electricity, and telecommunication services) are either nonexistent or so dilapidated as to leave urban dwellers—victims of urbanization exacerbated by massive rural exodus with attendant rapid urban population growth—as deprived as their compatriots in the rural areas. On the one hand, the urbanites like their rural counterparts are deprived of such modern amenities and, on the other hand, they are denied the serenity (environmental, at least) that mark rural life. In a sense, the situation of the urbanites as victims of rural living in a deteriorating urban setting makes the separate naming of "urban" and "rural" increasingly more difficult. Sofola brings up for scrutiny the powerful/powerless grid that authorizes the masculinization of power in Western feminist discourse. Through a concept she calls "dewomanization," Sofola attempts to account for the more marginalized and less relevant so-called modern African woman. So, while Western feminist discourse articulates disempowerment in the context of "emasculation," Sofola responds to the same process with a terminology, "dewomanization," that locates power and agency in womanhood.

Diverse views about the nature of power locate power differently in gender analysis. While a zero-sum matrix and a winner-take-all reasoning govern the articulation of power in Western feminist discourse, African feminism defines power as an item that is negotiable and negotiated; it assesses power not in absolute but in *relative* terms—in terms of power-sharing and power ebb and flow. While Western feminist discourse emphasizes the power grabbing that reinforces individualism, African feminist discourse foregrounds the power-sharing that underscores community and humane living as encapsulated in many African proverbs. For example, the Igbo proverbs—*ife kwulu, ife akwudebie* (When something stands, something stands *beside* it) and *egbe belu, ugo belu* (May the hawk perch and may the kite perch)—point to a theology of contiguity and a *horizontal* power matrix that emphasize accommodation, sharing, interdependence, and negotiation.

The Igbo dual-sex institutions of shared authority and power are extensively discussed by Kamene Okonjo, 'Zulu Sofola, Flora Nwapa, and Sabine Jell-Bahlsen.[11] Jell-Bahlsen's study of the water priestesses of the Oru-Igbo shows how the inscription of power-sharing created the space for women to acquire ritual and political powers that cut across the (spi)ritual and human worlds. In agreement with Sofola and Okonjo, Jell-Bahlsen asserts that the erosion of women's power was caused by the intrusion of foreign systems with different gender orientation and new paradigms of power organization:

> The ritual and political involvement of women in general and of female priesthood and leadership in particular was an important aspect of precolonial Igbo society that was not recognized during colonial times. Because the male elders of a lineage act as its visible agents, they were recognized as the lineage's representatives. Because vital female rituals are highly secretive and exclusive, male elders commonly appear to outsiders as the dominant agents in charge of resource management, preservation of the custom, maintenance of social order, religious practices, and mediation between human and spirit worlds.... The non-recognition of female priesthood and other expressions of female leadership relegated women to the background. Women's power is further eroded by the imposition of Christian and Islamic values and the lack of attention to African indigenous religious beliefs and practices. Moreover, Western-style structural inequalities and elitism in contemporary African societies and economies continue to erode previously established positions of power held by women. (109-110)

Power-sharing, complementarity, accommodation, compromise, negotiation, and inclusiveness form the foundation of African feminism. In an essay entitled "African Feminism: A Worldwide Perspective," Filomina Chioma Steady emphasizes the inclusive and complementary thrust of "African patterns of feminism":

> For women, the male is not "the other" but part of the human same. Each gender constitutes the critical half that makes the human whole. Neither sex is totally complete in itself to constitute a unit by itself. Each has and needs a complement, despite the possession of unique features of its own. Sexual differences and similarities, as well as sex roles, enhance sexual autonomy and cooperation between women and men, rather than promote polarization and fragmentation. Within the metaphysical realm, both male and female principles encompass life and operate jointly to maintain cosmological balance. (8)

Steady's views about patterns of feminism in Africa are well taken. However, it will be useful to assess them in the context of a critique of African patriarchy and the negotiations women are compelled to make within it, particularly in light of the arguments made by Olabisi Aina, who sees them "[as] a rather complex knot to untie" (76), and Ifeyinwa Iweriebor, who affirms that African feminism "is integrationist rather than separatist," but also insists that "any objective assessment of the modern women's movement in Nigeria has to be based on its own realities, and not that of the past or of other countries or *a priori* assumptions" (303).

Sofola's examination of the etymologies of man/woman, male/female (English), *nwa-oke/nwa-nyi* (Igbo), and *okunrin/obirin* (Yoruba) as well as her analysis of social power structures among the Yoruba and Igbo west of the Niger, corroborate Steady's views as well as Kamene Okonjo's earlier research on the inscription of gender complementarity and cooperation in the African landscape. Studies of African female institutions—*umu ada, umu inyemedi* or *ikpoho idunu* (Nwapa, Sofola, and Okonjo) and *iyalode* [12]—and the power that lies in them show that some African societies emphasize (or at least, formally create space for) the relevance of women; relevance that is accentuated by each woman's industriousness and achievement.

In this volume, many of the arguments for the power and/or loss of power of African women are framed in historical and generational contexts. Aidoo, Sofola, and Chukukere trace a long history of African women's individual and collective activism and achievements as well as their insurgency against internal and external oppressive systems. On a more personal level, Iweriebor attributes her feminist consciousness to a long lineage of women in her family—from her female ancestor to whom her family owes the salutation "Ogbuefi" to her maternal grandmother who protests her multiple roles by remarking acidly to her husband "I am the cook, steward and washerman. And you want me also to be the missus" (298). Flora Nwapa notes that she was inspired by the strong, powerful, socially relevant women who were part of the landscape of Igboland where she grew up and to whom she paid homage in her works by reinscribing them in African literature after a long history of marginalization by Nigerian male writers:

> I was inspired by the women around me when I was growing up. These women were not like Jagua Nana, Amope, Miss Mark or Ebiere [female characters in the works of African male writers]. They were solid and superior women who held their own in society. They were not only wives and mothers but successful traders who took care of their children and their husbands as well. They were very much aware of their leadership roles in their families as well as in the churches and local government.... In my first two novels, I tried to recreate the experiences of women in the traditional African society....the two novels (I hope!) give insight into the resourcefulness and industriousness of women which often made them successful, respected, and influential people in the community. In these two novels, therefore, I tried to debunk the erroneous concept that the husband is the lord and master and the woman is nothing but his property. I tried to debunk the notion that the woman is dependent on her husband. The woman not only holds her own, she is astonishingly *in*dependent of her husband. So while some Nigerian male writers failed to see this power base, this strength of character, this independence, I tried in *Efuru* and *Idu* to elevate the woman to her rightful place. (92-93)

If strong, powerful, activist, independent, and socially relevant women populate African history and traditional cultures, how does one explain the contemporary pathetic, despondent, hungry, helpless and dependent women enshrined in photojournalism? Whose creations are they? How does one explain the current image of the African woman as dilemma?

> She is breeding too many children she cannot take care of,
> and for whom she should not expect other people to pick
> up the tab. She is hungry, and so are her children. In fact,
> it has become a cliché of Western photojournalism that the
> African woman is old beyond her years; she is half-naked;
> her drooped and withered breasts are well exposed; there
> are flies buzzing around the faces of her children; and she
> has a permanent begging bowl in her hand. (39)

The contemporary African woman is a creation of historical and
current forces that are simultaneously internally generated and
externally induced (Aidoo, Sofola)—from indigenous sociocultural structures and foreign influences (Westernization, Christianity,
and Islamization) to "apparent lack of vision or courage in the leadership of the post-colonial period" (42). As noted by Okonjo, Jell-
Bahlsen, and Sofola, the intrusion of foreign influences created
situations whereby dual-sex systems of power sharing were replaced
with unilinear, male-centered power systems that not only marginalized women but also set the stage for the intensification and erup-
tion of gender conflicts.

Furthermore, the negative image of the African woman is partly created and promoted by the Western media and—tragically—
internalized, reproduced, and disseminated by Africans themselves,
as epitomized in Werewere Liking's acerbic but pertinent and long-
overdue critique of African filmmakers:

> For us, what constitutes the indescribable but quite percep-
> tible weakness of most African films is this kind of incoher-
> ence inherent to African film-makers' ignorance of their own
> traditions, of the true history of their peoples, and hence of
> their most profound aspirations. The only image they rep-
> resent of Africa is the impoverished one they've been
> taught—the world-view of others. And this is the only thing
> they should be ashamed of, because they are not doomed to
> such ignorance and lethargy, or worse, to the servility that
> keeps them in that condition. The image of Africa that the
> world consumes today is so pathetic that it can only be viewed
> with condescension, even by those who pay the production
> costs, whatever their motivations. What should shame them
> even more is the way they associate their inner poverty and
> servility with the image of an entire continent. (172)

Contrary to the claim by Aidoo, Sofola, and Chukukere that feminism is indigenous to the African environment, Aina asserts that feminism is still in its infancy on the continent, due to the contradictions and complexities of African cultures, cultural allegiances, and overall resistance to the extreme radicalism of Western feminism with, among other things, its insurgency against motherhood and extreme emphasis on sexuality. She also ascribes the slow rise of feminism on the continent to the lack of "feminist consciousness" among most African women, and worse still, their lack of "[consciousness] of the reality of their social situation":

> The present state of feminism in Africa needs proper reappraisal if the emancipatory nature of feminism is to be achieved. First, not only do grassroots women lack appropriate conceptual definition of feminism, there is a general lack of trust between rural grassroots women and the elite women who are mostly in the cities.... It thus becomes difficult for such Western trained women to identify appropriately with grassroots women and organize them politically.... Although some women within the academy and few political reformists have started to build feminist consciousness across the continent through feminist research and political programs, a lot remains to be done.... A major task facing the growth of feminism in the continent is how to appropriately bridge the gap which now exists between the few elite who are concerned with feminist struggles on the one hand and, on the other hand, the non-feminist conscious elites and the grassroots women, both of whom are in large majority. The future of feminism on the continent depends on how the few feminist conscious female elites and these other groups of women (especially the women at the grassroots)... come together to fight for democratic rights. (82-83)

The contributors' divergent views, ranging from urban/rural split to disagreements on the nature and politics of feminism, are primarily due to their different perceptions of feminism and power. It will, therefore, be useful to examine Aina's position in the context of the issues raised by the other contributors (particularly Sofola, Aidoo, Nwapa, and Iweriebor).

The contributors generally agree on many of the fundamental arguments that undergird the debates about the place of African women/African feminism in the overall feminist agenda. For example, they agree that due to different worldviews, cultural imperatives, and priorities between the West and Africa, feminism in Africa and feminism in the West have followed and will follow different paths. They also agree that radical Western feminism has no place and usefulness for African women and has in fact created problems by hindering African women from overtly laying claims to feminism and the feminist agenda. Furthermore, many of the contributors (Bryant, Fester, Aina, Maholtra, Chukukere, etc.) emphasize the need for cooperation between academic feminists and activists, particularly in an environment where the elitism and arrogance of Western-educated women breed distrust and alienation. However, for the feminist agenda to move forward, contributors seem to disagree on the source of power and appropriate leadership. While Aina attributes what she sees as the slow pace of feminism in Africa to the fact that "grassroots women lack appropriate conceptual definition of feminism," and argues that "a full-fledged feminism cannot emerge in Africa....unless African women at the grassroots abandon their present position as silent partners to become active partners of the movement" (85), Sofola and others argue that the power lies with the grassroots women and not the elite, Western-educated women who are "dewomanized" (disempowered) and unlikely to provide the appropriate leadership; suggesting, in effect, that grassroots women are not "silent partners" (as the title of Aina's paper claims) but *silenced* partners.

The disagreement between the two camps seems to run along generational and academy/activism lines. The older and activist African women favor African traditional cultures as empowering for women and harboring strong, relevant women endowed with leadership abilities, while the younger academicians—who seem to emphasize such concerns as human rights, racism, sexual harassment, motherhood, etc., *as seen, prioritized, and articulated by the West*—see the leadership of the feminist movement in Africa as the prerogative of academic and elite women: "the growth of feminism in Africa differed from those of the West. For example, while the women's movement in the West began as a political movement and gradually emerged as an intellectual discourse, the reverse is the case in most African States. In Africa, feminist consciousness has been left to a few elite women, who are mostly in academia" (79). It will be useful to read Aina's assertion in the context of the views expressed by Sofola, Aidoo, Nwapa, and Jamiila Chipo Cushnie.[13]

Furthermore, arguing that "a full-fledged radical feminism has failed to emerge on the African continent up till now despite the long history of female resistance to destructive socio-political systems" (72), Aina asserts that the past struggles of African women (from the 1929 Igbo Women's War and other mass movements in Nigeria to demonstrations against taxation and continent-wide liberation struggles) were not feminist because they were not specifically aimed at ending gender inequalities in the traditional structure. Aina's definition of what constitutes feminist engagement marks a long-standing disagreement in feminist circles about the scope of feminist engagement. Echoing other feminist scholars and activists, two Indian feminists assert that

> Many of us believe that everything in the world concerns women because everything affects us. Since feminists seek the removal of all forms of inequality, domination and oppression through the creation of a just social and economic order, nationally and internationally, all issues are women's issues. There is and has to be a women's point of view on all issues and feminists seek to integrate the feminist perspective in all spheres of personal and national life. Women must therefore take a position on everything whether it is nuclear warfare, war between two countries, ethnic and communal conflict, political, economic and development policies, human rights and civil liberties or environmental issues. (Bhasin and Khan, 1986: 12)[14]

The difference between the school with broader definition of feminist engagement (Bhasin and Khan) and the one with the narrower definition (Aina) accounts for the disagreement among African feminists regarding the nature of feminism and the source of feminist leadership. With reference to another context, it was in fact the restriction of the definition of feminist struggle to gender issues (gender as sex) that opened the floodgate of resistance by women of color to Western feminism as dominated by white, middle-class women, forcing it to think in terms of the intersection of differences—sex, race, class, ethnicity, etc.—between and within genders; or, more specifically, compelling it to rethink the complicity of race, class, and other categories of difference in constructing "gender." Furthermore, the narrow definition of feminist struggle insists, for example, on distinguishing between engaging as a "woman" and engaging as a "mother" or "wife." In their discussion of the backlash against feminism in the United States in the 1980s and 1990s, Leslie Wolf and Jennifer Tucker (1995) argue that:

> One of the legacies of these years was a subtle shift in defin-
> ing "women's issues." The feminist vision of these issues as
> a constellation of concerns for ending structures of domi-
> nance and advancing women's equality and empowerment
> began to disappear. It was replaced by a nonfeminist vision
> of work and family issues that continued to define women
> primarily through their roles as mothers and wives.... This
> undermined feminist demands for real transformation in
> the cultures of the workplace and the home. (448)

The claim that the fight for economic independence, for preservation of family interests, or against imperialism and colonization
are not feminist struggles is debatable. The dismissal of maternal
politics[15] as nonfeminist politics on the grounds that maternal politics entails engaging as a mother and not as a woman fails to recognize that one is a mother because one is a woman. Some mothers
who are changing their individual situations in particular and gender relations and societal structures in general through maternal
politics may sometimes find it difficult to make a distinction between
fighting as a mother and fighting as a woman.

Sometimes, the dilemma facing African feminists who are working for change is having to choose between conducting their struggles in such a way as to suit definitions of "feminist struggles" and
understanding/respecting their environment and carrying out
their struggles in such a way as to achieve desired results:

> For example, when informed that some state governments
> had refused to implement the Federal Government policy
> of giving housing allowances to married women public ser-
> vants, Ifeyinwa Nzeako, National President of the Nigerian
> National Council of Women's Societies, rather than quar-
> rel about the gender inequality of fringe benefits, issued a
> statement pointing out that this policy hurt the family,
> depriving it of the adequate space that could be provided
> with the benefit of two incomes. (305)

Should Nigerian women abandon strategies and rules of engagement that work for them and have produced desired results simply
because such moves do not qualify for the "feminist" label? I wonder. Furthermore, Julia Wells's study of maternal politics by black
women in South Africa demonstrates that motherism (in spite of
its ephemerality in instances), whether as manifested in the activities of mothers of the Plaza de Mayo in Argentina or the long his-

tory of anti-pass campaigns by black mothers in South Africa, has contributed to promoting social change.

In my view, to fully account for the complexity of feminism and women's situation in Africa today, it will be necessary to provide a meeting ground for the divergent views expressed above in order to allow their specific and collective "truths" to produce a better understanding of the issues at stake—"truths" about Africa's past/present and other binaries such as urban/rural and male/female. For example, one can extol Africa's past without romanticizing it by downplaying or totally ignoring gender inequalities in an environment where women's power/empowerment is institutionalized, authorized, and enforced within patriarchal boundaries. As Aina rightly points out, it is equally important to thoroughly examine and account for the contradictions in the assumed, egalitarian power structures in Africa "where men and women might be hierarchically related to each other in certain reciprocal statuses but not in others" (77).

In discussions of African women's power and/or powerlessness, it is misleading to argue along precolonial and postcolonial lines by exaggerating women's power in either of the two time periods. It may be more accurate to discuss women's power in *relative* terms by showing the ways in which the intervention of the colonial period created a situation where the earlier *relatively* powerful positions held by women were *further* eroded by the introduction of new power paradigms and opportunities for acceding to power that are rooted in gender politics. So, *relatively* speaking, some of women's earlier power was eroded, but at the same time new avenues to power were created from which women are not totally shut out but to which they are denied equal access with men. This way of thinking *relatively* should also apply to the assessment of the origins of the problems of postcolonial Africa. Africa should not place the blame for all of its problems *entirely* at the doorstep of the West. Africa must also look inwards for what ails her.

While lauding the power invested in traditional female institutions like the *umuada* (daughters of the clan), one must gauge critically both the use and abuse of that power, particularly in the promotion of woman-on-woman violence. In order to create a better understanding of these intra-gender relationships and unequal power relations, it may be more useful to replace the male/female dichotomous power paradigm with what Patricia Hill Collins calls the "matrix of domination"[16] that focuses on the nexus of interlocking systems of oppression where oppressor/oppressed positions

shift. Although the institution of daughters of the clan serves to protect the interests of women in their natal and matrimonial homes,
the *formal* maintenance of hierarchies among women creates the
potential for woman-on-woman violence and abuse: "At the top of
the female arm [of governance] is the Institution of Daughters; for
wives, there is the Institution of Wives....though the line of *Umuada*
(Institution of Daughters) is stronger than that of the Institution of
Wives, *Ndi Inyemedi* or *Ikpoho Idunu*" (56). For example, many scholars and activists[17] have documented the status of widows (women
as wives) in some African communities—a situation so appalling
that a radical intervention is urgently needed. The perpetrators of
the widows' sad plight are *women* (the *umuada,* for example) just as
circumcisers are *women.* The oppression of women as wives (widows) is not surprising, given the culturally sanctioned formalization
of hierarchies among women (daughters over wives). However,
African women must rethink the hierarchies and "privileges" that
subtend the perpetration and perpetuation of woman-on-woman
violence as daughters grow up to become wives and widows. The
issue of women as agents of patriarchal violence against women in
Africa needs urgent attention.[18]

In assessing gender relations in Africa, it is equally important to
emphasize the danger subtending the unexamined exaggeration of
gender complementarity that masks real and insidious gender
inequalities and conflicts, particularly in racist and imperialist contexts. The primacy of racial and ethnic loyalties in such contexts fore-
closes the urgency of a critical look at tensions in intra-group
relations (gender relations, in particular). Pamela Ryan's study of
Caesarina Kona Makhoere's *No Child's Play* underscores not only the
use of a prohibited activity—singing in prison—as a sign of protest
but also black women's reluctance to break ranks with abusive black
men "out of sympathy for their plight under white domination and
out of a common loyalty to the struggle (201)." Caesarina
Makhoere's excuses for her father's betrayal that landed her in
prison are not too different from those made by abused women who
are reluctant to press charges against their abusive husbands (Aina).

Clenora Hudson-Weems proposes "Africana womanism" as an
antidote to the limitations of African feminism and Black feminism
as conceptual and analytical tools for examining the lives of black
women:

Neither an outgrowth nor an addendum to feminism,
Africana womanism is not Black feminism, African feminism,

or Walker's womanism that some Africana women have come to embrace. *Africana womanism is* an ideology created and designed for all women of African descent. It is grounded in *African* culture and, therefore, it necessarily focuses on the unique experiences, struggles, needs, and desires of Africana women. It critically addresses the dynamics of the conflict between the mainstream feminist, the Black feminist, the African feminist, and the Africana womanist. The conclusion is that Africana womanism and its agenda are unique and separate from both white feminism and Black feminism; moreover, to the extent of naming in particular, Africana womanism differs from African feminism. Clearly there is a need for a separate and distinct identity for the Africana woman and her movement. (155)

Hudson-Weems rejects African feminism and Black feminism by asserting that they, unlike Africana womanism, are both aligned with white, middle-class feminism: "It becomes apparent, then, that neither the term Black feminism nor African feminism is sufficient to label women of such complex realities as Africana women, particularly as both terms, through their very names, align themselves with feminism (151)." Hudson-Weems's argument about terminology/ naming is well taken.[19] However, it seems to me that my earlier comment regarding the pitfalls of explaining African feminism in the context of Western feminism may be applicable here. There is a lot to be gained by arguing for Africana womanism *on its own terms* rather than in the context of white, middle-class feminism— arguing, in effect, that Africana womanism is what white, middle-class feminism is not. Hudson-Weems's focus on the definition and scope of African feminism and Black feminism is an important one. However, one can argue that the deficiency of African feminism and Black feminism respectively in addressing the full range of black women's experience arises more from their relationship one to the other than their relationship to white, middle-class feminism, particularly in view of the fact that "African" in this context refers to those on the continent exclusively and "Black" refers to people of African descent in the diaspora (the United States, in particular).[20] Hudson-Weems argues for an Africana womanism that is grounded in African culture. African feminism argues for similar cultural grounding; its deficiency (in a global/diasporic context) lies in its failure to include the African diaspora. It seems to me that a workable, culturally relevant, and mutually beneficial symbiosis of

African feminism/womanism and Black feminism/womanism will address the African Continent/African Diaspora issue and ultimately have a wider appeal for women of African descent. In this regard, the terminology—Africana womanism—has the potential of capturing the African Continent/African Diaspora inclusiveness that should be encouraged.

While Hudson-Weems presents a monolithic feminism (white and middle-class) against which Africana womanism argues, Angela Miles cautions against the homogenization of feminism and chooses instead to emphasize the pluralism of feminism (*feminisms*) both in North America and globally. Like Chandra Mohanty who argues against monoliths such as "Third World feminism" and "Western feminism,"[21] Angela Miles notes that "feminisms in North America, like feminisms everywhere, are enormously diverse (163-4)." However, she identifies two main tendencies in North American feminisms: (1) The assimilationist tendency that challenges women's exclusion without interrogating hierarchical structures and paradigms of power—a tendency that would in all likelihood use such structures and paradigms when so privileged. (2) The transformative tendency that argues for gender equality as it revalorizes women by recognizing and affirming the value of women's differences from men[22]—a tendency that emphasizes not sameness but the respect for and appreciation of difference. Transformative feminism argues for a rethinking of "progress," "development" and overall North/South relations. It challenges the giver/receiver, researcher/researched paradigms of unequal relations that govern North/South debates and engagement by replacing them with a more reciprocal, equitable, and dialogic vision of the North and the South as respectively harboring givers and receivers as well as mutually reinforcing communities of learners. Miles focuses on the interaction, collaboration, and mutual education among transformative feminists in national, regional, and global contexts:

> Transformative feminists from all parts of the world challenge the dominations of class, race, and colonialism as well as gender; they present feminist perspectives on the whole of society and not just selected "women's issues"; and they reject the assumptions and value judgments underlying the "modernization" project which is being imposed by the West to the detriment of the whole of nature and most of the world's people in all regions. Transformative feminists everywhere share the view that the existing world system is in cri-

sis on all levels in all parts of both "third" and "first" worlds and that this is reflected in ecological, economic, social, cultural, and ethical breakdowns. This system is neither sustainable nor desirable. The unequal, competitive, profit-based, individualistic market relations at its core are exploitative and destructive.... Today, "first world" feminist criticisms of patriarchal industrial "progress," growth, production, consumption, and profit parallel "third world" feminist criticisms of "development" guided by the same profit-centered, instrumental values. Transformative feminists all over the world not only resist the worst consequences of modernization and "development," but work towards totally different, equal, cooperative, life-sustaining, communal forms of social and economic organization.... These shared values and visions mean that "third world" feminists can expect significant support from transformative Western feminists in their resistance to the destruction being imposed on their communities in the name of "modernization" and "development," and that transformative feminisms in the West will be significantly broadened and strengthened by these links. (165-7)

Such a transformative view of women's engagements worldwide differs markedly from the "unequal discourse of development that shapes and contains WID (Women in Development) and GAD (Gender and Development)"(168) and masks the existence of transformative feminism/feminists in developed countries by its exclusion of autonomous feminist movements. Global feminisms, as a transformative gesture that is rooted in a dialectical feminist politics, recognize the commonality of struggle at the intersection of local realities. Transformative feminism, like Africana womanism, argues for connections. Africana womanism argues for links between Africa and the African diaspora; transformative feminism champions the creation of global linkages across racial, ethnic, and national boundaries.

The research/activism or theory/practice axis on which hinges women's engagement globally is vigorously debated in this volume (Bryant, Aina, Fester, and Kasente) not only in terms of the tenuous nature of the binaries but the urgent need to assert and promote their interaction and mutuality. Many of the research and documentation questions in the volume are raised in the context of the authority and authenticity of the researcher *vis-à-vis* the researched and their impact on research outcome. Often, as was the case at the WAAD conference, the issue of authenticity is argued in terms of identitity politics or professionalism. Ros Posel argues against two of the major issues raised in the critique of white women researching black women's lives—legitimacy (do they have the right?) and objectivity (will they be biased due to their own historical and cultural realities?)—on the basis of incommensurability and what de Reuck calls "radical conceptual solipsism" (i. e., "the only proper subject of my own investigation is myself").[23] In this debate, Posel locates authenticity not in identity politics but in professionalism—i. e., professions have research guidelines and methodologies as well as institutions, mechanisms, and bodies (journals, conferences, etc.) for ensuring the transmission of professional values:

> [C]ritical self-reflection alone, without submitting one's conclusions to the scrutiny of the relevant professional body, cannot guarantee the elimination of what is "merely personal" or "arbitrary." What is, therefore, required is to elucidate the professional and intellectual values to which historians subscribe and which provide the basis for adjudication of such accounts.... All historians, irrespective of their point of view, are bound by what Edmiston calls the value of rationality, that is "the shared standard to which appeal is made in all methodological criticism".... All historians share certain professional standards for determining the accuracy and reliability of their sources.... The maintenance and transmission of these values are ensured by teaching bodies as well as by professional institutions such as journals, lectures and congresses.... Within that model, communicative symmetry involves the rational examination of arguments and the shared recognition of the authentic right of all to take part in that dialogue as full and equal partners. [24]

However, some on the other side of the debate argue for "equal access" and against the danger posed by the politics of publishing as well as economic, racial, gender, institutional, and other locational politics.[25] Authority and legitimacy that are based on professional exigencies are as problematic as those that are anchored in identity politics. A little over a decade ago, Audre Lorde, arguing against the decision of a women's magazine to publish only prose "saying that poetry was a less 'rigorous' or 'serious' art form," called attention to the material conditions that draw women of color

to poetry writing and would ultimately have excluded them from
being published in the women's magazine:

> Over the last few years, writing a novel on tight finances, I
> came to appreciate the enormous differences in the mate-
> rial demands between poetry and prose. As we reclaim our
> literature, poetry has been the major voice of poor, work-
> ing class, and Colored women. A room of one's own may be
> a necessity for writing prose, but so are reams of paper, a
> typewriter, and plenty of time. The actual requirements to
> produce the visual arts also help determine, along class
> lines, whose art is whose. In this day of inflated prices for
> material, who are our sculptors, our painters, our photog-
> raphers? When we speak of a broadly based women's cul-
> ture, we need to be aware of the effect of class and economic
> differences on the supplies available for producing art.
> (*Sister Outsider*, 116)[26]

Deborah Kasente's more specific examination of research problems
in a national (Ugandan) context raises questions about the relationship between information gathering and information dissemination. To a large extent, information becomes relevant when it is
dissseminated and more so when it is disseminated in an easily accessible and usable form. Kasente identifies the major problem of gender research in Uganda as the inaccessibility of research findings
to policy-makers and the researched for whom these findings are
of particular importance. Individual research projects and results
are neither coordinated and organized nor professionally documented for current and future users. Many of the research findings
are in the form of unpublished theses and papers [27] whose retrieval
would entail a wild goose chase from academic institutions to towns
and villages where the authors work or live—a time-consuming and
financially debilitating undertaking that will certainly discourage
many well-intentioned and determined knowledge seekers, particularly in Africa where such tasks are very difficult to accomplish.
The concern expressed by Audre Lorde and others regarding material conditions as impediments to knowledge production and creativity is an important one.

    While Kasente's paper focuses on the gap between research and
activism, Dé Bryant proposes to bridge the research/activism,
town/gown, research/researched dichotomies through what she
calls "participatory research"—a strategy employed in two projects
she conducted in Benton Harbor, a predominantly black commu-

nity in southwest Michigan. Bryant's intervention package for community development replaces the pervasive top-down pyramid model in development work, that places a handful of "experts" at the apex, with a network model that establishes a horizontal interaction between the researcher and the researched, between the "interventionists" and the community in which the intervention occurs, thereby encouraging a more diffused flow of information, expertise, and power. Bryant's work, though conducted at a local level, has national and cross-national applicability and relevance. In actuality, it embodies some of the elements of Angela Miles's international focus on the transformative agenda of global feminisms.

Writing about research and activism during the apartheid regime in South Africa, Gertrude Fester shows how the research and documentation problems noted by Kasente are exacerbated in situations of war, crisis, and liberation struggle:

> As a woman activist for more than a decade in a period of extreme state repression, violence and intense mass action, I knew there was no way that even the most realistic program of action could be adhered to. Activities that had to be sacrificed because of responses to crises included education and training programs and a task whose urgency was apparent to us and yet we never succeeded in executing—the documentation of our struggle. Very seldom could we be pro-active; our activities were largely reactive. (224)

Fester also notes that given the political climate in South Africa under apartheid which left hardly anyone untouched, it is tenous, at best, to make the academy-versus-activism distinction, as "many women interviewed saw themselves as combining the two extremes." (223) As an activist/researcher herself, Fester is well-placed to assess the complex task of bridge-building between the academy and activism that is made difficult by the entrenched suspicion on both embankments, as is the case in the urban/rural binary noted earlier (Aina, Sofola). Some of the suspicion emanates from the inability of the over-researched and over-interviewed women—usually poor, black, and/or rural—to see how the research and interviews have improved their lives as Mama Holo, a veteran woman activist from the South African township of Nyanga, complains about yet another interview by a particular academic: "She keeps on interviewing me and writing more and more books and she buys more pillows. And I still live in the same hovel. Nothing's changed for me" (226). Nevertheless, according to Fester, Pamela Ryan, and other activists and scholars from South Africa, such suspicions have not prevented South African women from forming multiracial alliances and organizations (such as the National Coalition for the Women's Charter) for common causes. Betty Welz's account of the participation of white women in *Umkhonto We Sizwe*, the ANC Army of Liberation, explains in greater detail the persistence, despite threats and reprisals, of multiracial alliances for social change in South Africa.

While recognizing the contributions that some academicians have made in effecting social change, Fester reserves her strongest criticism for "opportunistic, feminist academics and intellectuals" (226) who join grassroots organizations without either making their skills available to such organizations or acknowledging the organizations in their publications. The work of these academicians "who have used the study of less privileged women for economic and professional advancement [without] challenging the status quo"[28] (226) is nothing short of "academic colonialism" in the sense that the academicians (mostly white and middle-class women) are often the researchers while poor, black women are the researched: "At the moment there is a wealth of data about black women and very little about white women"(227). One can conclude that for a complete and more balanced documentation of the power/oppression of women in South Africa to emerge, the sharing of resources must be intensified, the material conditions that impede black women from writing their experiences must be lifted, and the documentation of the experiences of white women, as oppressors and oppressed, must be pursued more vigorously.

To promote a more inclusive engagement, space and time must be provided for the participation of marginalized groups (mostly poor, black, and illiterate). P. L. Maholtra emphasizes the importance of the form ("user-friendly") of research documentation and the widening of the clientele for research dissemination:

> In addition to popularizing research findings for the use of women in the wider society, it is hoped that women researchers and professors within the academy can also reach out and share some of their new frontiers of knowledge on societal processes and gender issues with colleagues in schools and adult education as well as in teacher training colleges. It is hoped that in this manner the message of social justice and gender equity can begin to be incorpo-

rated into teaching materials and spread to new generations. (195) [29]

Fester anchors her own recommendation on the need for more attention to be focused on the language question, particularly the investment in patience, accommodation, and time it requires:

> Our meetings are often long, as it is imperative that we use translators. To facilitate broad participation, members are encouraged to speak in the language that they are most comfortable in. As English, Xhosa, and Afrikaans are spoken in our region we would, therefore, use these three languages simultaneously. Meetings are often lengthened by repeated explanations, which we do not find problematic as we feel it is important for members to understand the issues discussed. It is because of these practices that many women, who were shy and without confidence initially, now participate actively. Many women leaders on being interviewed about their political growth, admitted that their training ground was in the women's organizations. (225)

Equally relevant to the widening of the field of participants in social transformation processes is the need to encourage the use of "oral tradition" in meetings and conferences to enable illiterate women to *speak their truth* unmediated. Such oral deliveries should be videotaped and/or audio-taped, transcribed and included as part of meeting records and conference proceedings. Again, this is a difficult, time-consuming task, but the benefits far outweigh the time investment.

In my view, many of the issues raised above with regard to research, conferencing, documentation, and the dissemination of information point to the need for funding agencies to pay more attention to post-conference activities in terms of fund allocation. It is neither efficient nor sufficient to invest most or all conference funding solely in the organizing and running the conference itself, nor is it very useful to produce proceedings that are either not in a user-friendly form or that cannot be disseminated in any form due to lack of funds. A good portion of conference funding should be earmarked for crucial post-conference follow-ups and undertakings such as the preparation of important items of the proceedings in a user-friendly form—e.g., paraphrasing into layman's terms as well as translation into local languages—for productive use by grassroots women and policy-makers alike.

While focusing on a wide range of issues—from theory and practice to methodology and organizational questions—some of the
contributors (Hudson-Weems, Sofola, Banks, Aina, Opara,
Geathers, Braxton, Plant) call attention to a very important issue—
the relationship between African Continent / African Diaspora and
the need to strengthen it through education, information and
resource sharing as well as intellectual and cultural exchanges.[30]
The story of Jamiila Chipo Cushnie-Mnyanga—a remarkable,
Jamaican-born activist who journeyed to Africa in search of a
home—is instructive. Although the marginalization this strong
woman from the islands faced in her new and long-sought-after
home (Tanzania) did not break her fighting spirit, it points to the
urgent need to address the Continent/Diaspora question. There
has always been and always will be yearnings on both sides of the
Atlantic for reconnections that are sometimes manifested in movements and theories (from Négritude and Black Consciousness to
Afrocentricity and Africana Womanism) and sometimes in practice
(like the fascinating Ajanaku Sisterhood experiment in Memphis,
Tennessee).

The establishment of the Ajanaku social family, with its three
branches of Brotherhood, Sisterhood, and Childrenhood, underscores the yearning on the western side of the Atlantic to reconnect
with the ancestral home by transplanting or simulating conditions
and concepts—such as the importance of community, respect for
elders, complementarity, negotiation, acceptance of all children
without stigma of illegitimacy,[31] etc.—in which societies in the ancestral home are rooted. The failure to sustain the Ajanaku "family-
hood" over a longer period of time would seem to be due primarily
to factors in the environment in which this communal experiment
itself was rooted: (1) an environment of dizzying mobility and domi-
ciliary changes, and (2) an environment that customarily devalues
Africa, African cultures, and African peoples:

> One sister mentioned that she never felt the issue of skin
> color was resolved even though it was consciously addressed
> in the Sisterhood. Another sister felt that darker-skinned
> children suffered color discrimination in the process from
> members who had not internalized the beauty of African
> features and, consequently, favored lighter-skinned ones. It
> was difficult to hear a person outside the community ask
> those with lighter skin tones, "Why do you mess up yourself
> with those nappy dreadlocks?" but tragic when a member

of the family reflected this same attitude.... One sister said she had learned that the very people who laugh the loudest at your "strangeness" will admit after having a chance to know you that they are working on their own acceptance of African culture. For example, a woman at her job had asked her to take down her dreadlocks and change her hairstyle but she refused. By the next year, this same woman divulged that she might try wearing dreadlocks if only her boss would let her. (344-5)

The Africa Continent/African Diaspora question, however, will not be resolved by the universalization of the black experience grounded in positions taken on either side of the Atlantic. Rather, it will be better and more meaningfully addressed through a serious commitment to forging *intellectual and cultural linkages* and constructing *economic bridges*[32] that are grounded in the recognition and appreciation of the commonality of origin and the divergences wrought by historical imperatives.

The WAAD logo that graces the cover of this book captures the dispora question in its telling of the story of a moving away. The black woman in a boat reminds us of the tragic, inhuman history that split our *ọfọ*[33] and walked away with one half. The African diaspora, half of our *ọfọ*, is a symbol of life. The black woman in the boat is neither sitting nor lying down, her head is not bowed, her knees are not bent: she is standing. She stands tall in all her power, majesty, elegance, and beauty, defiantly proclaiming that *ọfọ never dies*. All boats do not move in the same direction; some move away, others move back; some move away and move back retracing the same trajectory. Boats are metaphors for the congruence of beginnings and endings. The meaningful interchange that occurs with the crisscrossing of our boats, journeys, and destinies will keep our *ọfọ* whole and alive. In many ways, *Sisterhood, Feminisms, and Power* points to the complexity, paradox, and possibilities of difference. It marks locations of isolation and broken dreams that challenge us to seek strength and solidarity along the broken lines of contact zones. Above all, *Sisterhood, Feminisms, and Power* paints in broad strokes the beautiful symphony of colors that can only be forged in the crucible of mutual respect. The volume points us to the possibilities of the rainbow.

NOTES

1. I thank Helen Mugambi, Pamela Smith, and Susan Andrade, who read an earlier version of this introduction and made useful suggestions.

2. The remarks by Achebe are from an interview with Bill Moyers (see Moyers 1989:335); those by Toubia are from her *Women of the Arab World* (London: Zed Press, 1988).

3. When the fight for supremacy among feminists, womanists, and Africana womanists (mostly from the United States and Europe) erupted at the first international conference on Women in Africa and the African Diaspora (see Obioma Nnaemeka, pp. 351 ff. in this volume), one Nigerian participant said to me: "This [controversy/rhetoric] is not what we came here for." When I asked her what we came there for, she responded *"Nne, ka emebe emebe"* (My sister, let's get into action/let's do something).

4. See Obioma Nnaemeka, "Development, Cultural Forces and Women's Achievements in Africa," *Law and Policy* (forthcoming).

5. In Africa, private parts are still private and not appropriate subjects for dinner discussions, unwarranted public spectacle, and definitely not the usual subject for cinematography. See also Obioma Nnaemeka, "Urban Spaces, Women's Places: Polygamy as Sign in Mariama Bâ's Novels" in Obioma Nnaemeka, ed., *The Politics of (M)Othering: Womanhood, Identity and Resistance in African Literature* (London: Routledge, 1997), for a discussion of the focus on sexuality in feminist debates about polygamy.

6. See Domitila Barrios de Chungara, *Let Me Speak!* (New York: Monthly Review Press, 1978). In her testimony, Domitila, a remarkable activist from Bolivia, repeatedly criticized the "outsiders" (mostly Western-educated Bolivians) who came to speak to her and other miners/miners' wives for "not speaking [their] language." Domitila's criticism should not be taken literally in view of the fact that the "outsiders" spoke to the miners in the local dialect. Domitila spoke figuratively, meaning that the "outsiders" did not level with them in that they failed to frame the issues in a way that made sense to the miners. The same charge could be levelled against feminist interventionists in Africa on behalf of grassroots women—they do not speak the language (à la Domitila) of grassroots women.

7. At the WAAD conference, some foreign participants complained endlessly about the presence of male participants—they complained about men presenting papers and about a man delivering one of the three keynote addresses (the other two keynote speakers were women). African women made it clear that they had no problems with the presence of male participants many of whom are dedicated activists and serious scholars with strong record of publication in Women's Studies.

8. See Adiele Afigbo, "Women in Nigerian History," in Martin Ijere, ed., *Women in the Nigerian Economy* (Enugu: Acena Publishers, 1991), 37.

9. The French say *"d'une part, d'autre part"* (on the one hand, on the other hand). While the English insist that you "put your best foot forward" ("best" as if you have more than two!) the Igbo say that *ike bu nkukota nkukota* ("The buttocks keep touching each other"[i.e. as you walk]). I first heard this saying at a wedding in my village when an old man hand-

ed it down to the newlywed couple as an advice that underscores the need for and benefits of cooperation, interdependence, and complementarity). While the English say "an eye for an eye, a tooth for a tooth," the Igbo say *welu ile gi gua eze gi onu* ("Use your tongue to count your teeth")—a proverb that urges you to figure things out for yourself: it is impossible for your tongue to count your teeth *one at a time*; as it touches one tooth, it touches the adjacent tooth/teeth as well.

10. See Kamene Okonjo, "The Dual-Sex Political System in Operation: Igbo Women and Community Politics in Midwestern Nigeria," in Nancy J. Hafkin and Edna G. Bay, eds., *Women in Africa: Studies in Social and Economic Change* (Stanford, Calif.: Stanford University Press, 1976), pp. 45-85. See also essays (in this volume) by Nwapa (pp. 89 ff.), Sofola (pp. 51 ff.), and Jell-Bahlsen (pp. 101 ff.).

11. Ibid.

12. See Bolanle Awe, "The Iyalode in the Traditional Yoruba Political System," in Alice Schlegel, ed., *Sexual Stratification: A Cross-Cultural View* (New York: Columbia University Press, 1977), pp. 144-159.

13. Jamiila Chipo Cushnie-Mnyanga makes an interesting comparison between her grandmother (older generation, but more feminist and socially conscious) and her mother (younger generation and less socially conscious).

14. Cited in Angela Miles in this volume (172). Miles also works with this broader definition of feminist engagement.

15. See Julia Wells's paper, pp. 251 ff. in this volume, for discussion of maternal (motherist) politics/motherism.

16. See Patricia Hill Collins, *Black Feminist Thought* (Boston: Unwin Hyman, 1990), pp. 225-228.

17. See *Proceedings of the First International Conference on Women in Africa and the African Diaspora: Bridges across Activism and the Academy*, Vol. IX, Nsukka, Nigeria, July 13-18, 1992, for the following essays: Eunice E. Adiele, "Widowhood Practices in Igboland: An Examination of the Role of Christian Churches" (pp. 49-62); Adiele Afigbo, "Widowhood Practices in Africa: A Preliminary Survey and Analysis" (pp. 63-94); Uche Azikiwe, "Widowhood Practices in Nigeria: The Case of Afikpo Community" (pp. 205- 216); and Vol. X for Christiana E. E. Okojie, "Widowhood Practices and Sociocultural Restrictions on Women's Behavior in Edo and Delta States of Nigeria" (pp. 175-197).

18. Many participants (mostly young African academicians and activists) at the WAAD conference raised the issue of woman-on-woman abuse and insisted that it be placed on the agenda for future WAAD meetings.

19. It is equally important to note that the use of the word "feminism" does not necessarily mean the endorsement of white, middle-class feminism. African feminism argues against white, middle-class, liberal feminism. "Feminism," as used to capture women's engagement in demanding and creating an equitable society, is an English word that speaks different languages worldwide. If women in different societies have to name their struggle in their own language, "womanism" will be as alien and inappropriate as "feminism" in an African village where English is not spoken. In my view, the usage of feminism or womanism in the

plural—*feminisms* or *womanisms*—points to (at least in the English-speaking world) both the necessity and expedience of a terminology that captures women's engagement and at the same time recognizes variations of the same theme.

20. See Obioma Nnaemeka in this volume (p. 378 and notes no. 27 and 28 on pp. 384-5) for comments about the restrictive usage of "African" and "Black."

21. See Chandra T. Mohanty, "Introduction" in Chandra Mohanty, Ann Russo, and Lourdes Torres, eds., *Third World Women and the Politics of Feminism* (Bloomington: Indiana University Press, 1991).

22. See also 'Zulu Sofola, pp. 51 ff. in this volume.

23. Ros Posel, "'Alien Researchers?' White Feminists Writing about the Past of Black Women," in *Proceedings of the First International Conference on Women in Africa and the African Diaspora: Bridges across Activism and the Academy*, Nsukka, Nigeria, July 13-18, 1992, Vol. II, p. 393.

24. Ibid., pp. 397-98.

25. See Fester (pp. 215 ff.) and Ryan (pp. 197 ff.) in this volume. In addition, see "Forum" for comments by various contributors, particularly Lumka Funani, Fidelia Fouché and Maria Olaussen.

26. Another black woman writer, Miriam Tlali of South Africa, echoes similar views in a 1988 interview with Cecily Lockett: "It [writing a novel] needs a long time and you have to think about it. And you have to dream about it and black women do not have time to dream....you have to have material, you have to have typewriters, you have to read a lot. That also means that you have to have a lot of time," in Craig Mackenzie and Cherry Clayton, ed., *Between the Lines* (Grahamstown: National English Literary Museum, 1989), p. 71. Simone de Beauvoir also explores the relationship between material conditions and the production of art in her essay, "Women and Creativity," in Toril Moi, ed., *French Feminist Thought* (London: Basil Blackwell, 1987), pp. 17-32.

27. The fact that the majority of the papers used by Kasente herself are unpublished makes the point for the need to have research findings in a form that is easily accessible to a wide audience. The wealth of information in the papers she consulted will most likely remain inaccessible to people beyond her immediate environment.

28. See also Pamela Ryan, pp. 197 ff. in this volume.

29. Maholtra's recommendation is a sound one. Women's issues and development issues should not be exclusively a "higher education" issue; they should be part of the educational system at all levels. The same argument could be made in the case of multicultural education in the United States. It grew out of higher education and stayed there for a long time (too long, in fact) before the importance of making it available at the elementary and secondary levels was acknowledged and implemented.

30. See also Obioma Nnaemeka, pp. 351 ff. in this volume for comments on the strengthening of the Continental and Diasporic relationship.

31. See Protus Kemdirim, pp. 443 ff. in this volume.

32. See Rubin Patterson, *Foreign Aid after the Cold War: The Dynamics of Multipolar Economic Competition* (Trenton, N.J.: Africa World Press, 1997).

33. *Ofo* is a potent staff that symbolizes the land and the ancestors.

WORKS CITED

Adiele, Eunice E. "Widowhood Practices in Igboland: An Examination of the Role of Christian Churches." *Proceedings of the First International Conference on Women in Africa and the African Diaspora: Bridges across Activism and the Academy.* Nsukka, Nigeria, July 13-18, 1992, Vol. IX: 49-62.

Afigbo, Adiele. "Women in Nigerian History." *Women in the Nigerian Economy.* Ed. Martin Ijere. Enugu: Acena Publishers, 1991. 22-40.

—— "Widowhood Practices in Africa: A Preliminary Survey and Analysis." *Proceedings of the First International Conference on Women in Africa and the African Diaspora: Bridges across Activism and the Academy.* Nsukka, Nigeria, July 13-18, 1992, Vol. IX: 63-94.

Awe, Bolanle. "The Iyalode in the Traditional Yoruba Political System." In *Sexual Stratification: A Cross-Cultural View,* ed., Alice Schlegel. New York: Columbia University Press, 1977. 144-159.

Azikiwe, Uche. "Widowhood Practices in Nigeria: The Case of Afikpo Community." *Proceedings of the First International Conference on Women in Africa and the African Diaspora: Bridges across Activism and the Academy.* Nsukka, Nigeria, July 13-18, 1992, Vol. IX: 205-216.

Bhasin, Kamla, and Nighat Said Khan. *Some Questions about Feminism and Its Relevance in South Asia.* New Delhi: Kali for Women Press, 1986.

Barrios de Chungara, Domitila. *Let Me Speak!: Testimony of Domitila, a Woman of the Bolivian Mines,* trans., Victoria Ortiz. New York: Monthly Review Press, 1978.

Collins, Patricia Hill. *Black Feminist Thought.* Boston: Unwin Hyman, 1990.

de Beauvoir, Simone. "Women and Creativity." In *French Feminist Thought,* ed., Toril Moi. London: Basil Blackwell, 1987. 17-32.

Liking, Werewere. "An African Woman Speaks out against African Filmmakers," trans., Christopher Winks. *Black Renaissace/Renaissance Noire* 1.1 (1996): 170-177.

Lorde, Audre. *Sister Outsider.* Trumansburg: Crossing Press, 1981

Mackenzie, Craig and Cherry Clayton, ed., *Between the Lines.* Grahamstown: National English Literary Museum, 1989.

Mohanty, Chandra, Ann Russo and Lourdes Torres, ed. *Third World Women and the Politics of Feminism.* Bloomington: Indiana University Press, 1991.

Moyers, Bill. *A World of Ideas.* New York: Doubleday, 1989.

Nnaemeka, Obioma. "Urban Spaces, Women's Places: Polygamy as Sign in Mariama Bâ's Novels." In *The Politics of (M)Othering: Womanhood, Identity and Resistance in African Literature,* ed., Obioma Nnaemeka. London: Routledge, 1997.

"Development, Cultural Forces, and Women's Achievements in Africa." *Law and Policy* (forthcoming).

Okojie, Christiana E. E."Widowhood Practices and Sociocultural Restrictions on Women's Behavior in Edo and Delta States of Nigeria." *Proceedings of the First International Conference on Women in Africa and the African Diaspora: Bridges across Activism and the Academy.* Nsukka, Nigeria, July

13-18, 1992, Vol. X: 175-197.

Okonjo, Kamene. "The Dual-Sex Political System in Operation: Igbo Women and Community Politics in Midwestern Nigeria." In *Women in Africa: Studies in Social and Economic Change*, ed., Nancy J. Hafkin and Edna G. Bay. Stanford, Calif.: Stanford University Press, 1976. 45-85.

Patterson, Rubin. *Foreign Aid After theCold War: The Dynamics of Multipolar Economic Competition*. Trenton, NJ: Africa World Press, 1997.

Steady, Filomina Chioma. "African Feminism: A Worldwide Perspective." In *Women in Africa and the African Diaspora*, ed., Rosalyn Terborg-Penn, Sharon Harley, and Andrea Benton Rushing. Washington, DC: Howard University Press, 1987.

Toubia, Nahid. *Women of the Arab World*. London: Zed Press, 1988.

Wolfe, Leslie R. and Jennifer Tucker. "Feminism Lives: Building a Multicultural Women's Movement in the United States." In *The Challenge of Local Feminisms*, ed., Amrita Basu. Boulder: Westview Press, 1995. 435-462.

Wright, Richard. "Blueprint for Negro Writing." In *The Black Aesthetics*, ed., Addison Gayle, Jr. New York: Doubleday, 1971.

I
FRAMING THE ISSUES

THE AFRICAN
WOMAN TODAY

AMA ATA AIDOO

> In most countries of Africa whole sectors of the economy,
> such as internal trade, agriculture, agro-business
> and health care are in the hands of women.
> — *West Africa* (September 9-15, 1991)

IT MIGHT NOT BE FAIR TO BLAME AS WELL-INTENTIONED
an event as Bob Geldof's *Band Aid*,[1] which was staged to raise awareness of the plight of drought victims in Ethiopia, and even raise
funds for them, but there is no doubt that, ever since, the image of
the African woman in the mind of the world has been set: she is
breeding too many children she cannot take care of, and for whom
she should not expect other people to pick up the tab. She is hungry, and so are her children. In fact, it has become a cliché of
Western photojournalism that the African woman is old beyond her
years; she is half-naked; her drooped and withered breasts are well
exposed; there are flies buzzing around the faces of her children;
and she has a permanent begging bowl in her hand.

This is a sorry pass the daughters of the African continent have
come to—especially when we remember that they are descended
from some of the bravest, most independent, and most innovative
women this world has ever known. We speak of the Lady Tiy of Nubia
(ca. 1415-1340 B. C. E.), the wife of Amenhotep III and the mother
of Akhenaton and Tutenkhamen, who is credited, among other
achievements, with leading the women of her court to discover make-

up and other beauty-enhancing processes. Her daughter-in-law was the incomparable Nefertiti, a black beauty whose complexion was far superior to the alabaster with which she is now willfully painted. Again from the pharaonic era, we evoke Cleopatra, about whom "more nonsense has been written...than about any African queen...mainly because of many writers' desire to paint her white. She was not a white woman. She was not a Greek..." says John Henrik Clarke with the impatience of painstaking scholarship.[2] According to C. W. King, of Julius Caesar, Mark Antony, and Cleopatra, the last was "the most captivating, the most learned, and the most witty." Among the many languages she spoke fluently were "Greek, Egyptian, Latin, Ethiopian, and Syrian." Yet Shakespeare, heralding Western racism, could only dismiss Cleopatra as a "strumpet."[3]

COLLISIONS

Modern Africa came into collision with Europe with the journey of Vasco da Gama from Portugal southward to find Asia. He passed what became known to the West as the Gold Coast (Ghana) in 1492, and the Cape of Good Hope in 1496. Since then Africa has never known peace. First there was the slave trade. Then the end of the slave trade was celebrated with the conquest and colonization of Africa in the mid-nineteenth century. From then on, various Western groups considered Africa their happiest hunting ground. The energies of the people, the wealth on and in the land, everything that could be taken was taken by European powers with complete abandon. The people resisted to the best of their abilities. But it could not have been an even match, since one side fought with spears or bows and arrows, while the other used guns.

Less known is that in response to Europe's insistence on conquering the continent, Africa over five centuries produced countless women soldiers and military strategists, many of whom died in the struggles. A famous example was Nzingha (1582-1663), who tried to prevent the Portuguese from overrunning Angola. She died without achieving her objective, but only after showing them what she was made of. For their part, the Portuguese demonstrated that they had not come to Africa on a mission of chivalry. They fought Nzingha with uncompromising viciousness. When she suffered serious setbacks in 1645-1646, they captured her younger sister Fungi, beheaded her, and threw her body into the river.

In fact, in precolonial times, fighting women were part of most African armies, a well-known example being the all-female battalions of Dahomey (ancient Benin, early nineteenth century), who sought to protect their empire against invaders and internal treachery. The Nzingha/Portuguese pattern was to be repeated in several areas of the continent over the next three centuries. In the last years of the nineteenth and early twentieth centuries, Yaa Asantewaa, queen of the Asante (Ashanti, Ghana), led an insurrection against the British. Although her armies were defeated, "it is safe to say that she helped to create part of the theoretical basis for the political emergence of modern Africa."

True, all of these women were reigning monarchs who found it relatively easy to organize armies against foreign occupation. But history is also replete with accounts of insurgencies organized by women from nonmonarchial traditions. One example is the Igbo women of Eastern Nigeria, who in the 1920s so successfully harassed the British that the colonial administration had to move its headquarters from Calabar to Lagos. Around the same time in Rhodesia (Zimbabwe), Mbuya Nehanda (Nyakasikana) was accused of fomenting an insurgency against the British. In the end, the conquerors decided that the only way to get rid of this frail woman was to hang her. And they did.

STRUGGLES FOR INDEPENDENCE

After the Second World War, many women stayed in the forefront of the agitation for independence. Some, like General Muthoni (of the Mau Mau Rebellion) became guerrilla leaders whom the enemy feared even more than the male insurgents. Others, like Mrs. Ramsome-Kuti of Western Nigeria, were mainly nationalists of bourgeois and petit-bourgeois backgrounds. But then, so were the majority of the men who were their companions in such struggles.

Today, we know that the story of South Africa's fight against the institutionalized horrors of conquest would be different if women had not been prepared to get actively involved. And they paid the price. They were killed, maimed, incarcerated, and exiled. For instance, Sibongile Mkhabela was a student leader at the time of the Soweto riots. The only woman charged in the June 7th (1978) trials, she was jailed for three years and then banned after serving the sentence. Countless others like Winnie Mandela, Albertina Sisulu, and Zodwa Sobukwe survived the hounding of their men, only later to show an awesome readiness to assume leadership with all the sacrifices such decisions entailed.

Given such a heroic tradition, it is no wonder that some of us regard the docile, mendicant, African woman of today as a media creation. But if she does exist, she is a result of the traumas of the last five hundred years' encounter with the West, the last one hundred years of colonial repression, the current neocolonial disillusionment, and a natural environment that is now behaving like an implacable enemy.

In 1992, the African woman must cope with a "structural adjustment program" imposed by the International Monetary Fund (IMF) and the World Bank that is removing subsidies from her children's education, from health care, from food. Transportation to and from vital areas of her life have either broken down or never existed. In 1992, there is a drought and the world is phenomenally hot. And the African woman has already given up on the season's crops. She is now wondering whether there will be enough water to last her and her children through this year for drinking, for cooking nonexistent food, and to keep the body minimally clean. In 1992, the African woman is baffled by news of a "plague that has come to end all human hopes."[4] And she is afraid that she and her children might not survive this disease whose origins no one seems to know, and for which there is yet no cure.

Africa is the second largest continent, covering an area of over thirty million square kilometers. In spite of centuries of exploitation by its conquerors, it is still, potentially, the richest piece of earth in the world, with 60 percent of all known exploitable natural resources. And in spite of the vicious propaganda about an African population explosion, Africa is not the most populous place on this earth. China is. In fact, given its size, and its current population of around five hundred million, the continent is *underpopulated*.

BURDENS AND RIDDLES

Three major historical factors have influenced the position of the African woman today: indigenous African societal patterns; the conquest of the continent by Europe; and the apparent lack of vision, or courage, in the leadership of the postcolonial period. "Leadership" in this context does not refer to the political leadership exclusively, but to the entire spectrum of the intellectual, professional, and commercial elites in positions to make vital decisions on behalf of the entire community.

From ancient times, the majority of societies around the world were either matrilineal or patrilineal. It is now clear that most African societies were matrilineages lasting millennia, from the

prepharonic period all the way down to a micronation like the
Akans of Ghana. What changed the pattern in some areas were,
first, Islam, and, later, Christianity, since both religions were profoundly patriarchal in orientation. The African societies that
retained vestiges of their matrilineages were also ones that met both
Islam and Christianity with the greatest resistance. These areas—
for instance, coastal West Africa—are also where one finds some of
the least oppressed women.

Today, it is not at all easy to imagine the *coastal* West African
woman bearing with any equanimity even the thought of the heavy
black veil, the burden of purdah, circumcision, infibulation, and so
forth. But even for the West African Moslem woman, the veil is no
more than a couple of meters of an often pretty gossamer fabric.
This she normally and winsomely drapes over the back of her head
and her shoulders. Indeed, the effect of this type of veil is to make
its wearers look more attractive and decidedly unhidden. In this,
West African women seemed to have more in common with Islamic
women in faraway places like the Indian peninsula and the rest of
Asia than with their sisters to their immediate north.

What seems to separate the woman "south of the Sahara" from
the Arab-Islamic woman of the north is not so much the latter's
"closeness to Europe" and "civilization," as the former's relative freedom to create herself, economic and political dynamics permitting.
But then, according to Nawal El Saadawi, "There are many misconceptions (in the West) about the identity, character and diversity of Arab women." This Egyptian writer asserts that although the
North African Islamic-Arab woman is veiled and circumcised, to
know nothing more than that about her "borders on racism." Maybe
African women share more commonalities than we are aware of.

In any case, some tenets presumed to be "Islamic" may not
sound so strange to women in Southern Africa who have had nothing to do with Islam. For instance, in precolonial Zimbabwe as well
as in colonial Rhodesia, the woman was regarded as a permanent
minor, first her father's ward, then her husband's. If she outlived
her husband, then as a widow she became the ward of some male
in either her husband's home or her own home. Sometimes a
woman became a ward of her own son(s)! This meant that she could
never own property or be granted a bank loan. The situation was
so bad that in 1982 a conscientious and sensitive ZANU (PF) government (in Zimbabwe) attempted a corrective measure by passing the Legal Age of Majority Act. This law stipulated that at age
eighteen a young woman became an adult, with all the attendant

rights and privileges. To a certain extent, African women are some sort of riddle. This is because, whether formally educated or not, whether "traditional" or "modern," they do not fit the accepted notion about them as mute beasts of burden. And they are definitely not as free and equal as African men (especially those with formal education) would have us believe. In fact, they fall somewhere between those two concepts.

To some West African men, the way West African women struggle to be independent "is really quite bad." They think that "these women are all over the place." Wherever men meet, you can be sure to hear jokes and stories about women, all of which are supposed to show how "terrible" we are. One solid piece of "advice" any growing boy is likely to pick up along the coast of West Africa is: "Fear women." And if there really is a Fon (Gabon) proverb that translates as "Woman is the root of all evil, only our souls can save us (from her)," then women have been in trouble for a long time in Africa!

The colonial period did not help women either. It is true that some of the "civilizing" missions did not want their policies to run counter to any patterns in the "natives" that were tolerant of women's development. So they gave a few girls some opportunities for formal education. Some of the girls' secondary schools in the area go as far back as 1837. But the missions came with their own ideas as to how females should be educated to be "proper women." While the boys in colonial elite schools were prepared to go to England to become professionals (mostly lawyers), girls in the equivalent schools were taught needlework and needlepoint, crochet, and baking. This was to make sure that they became wonderful wives and great mothers. And many turned out exactly as programmed. Only a few women, usually form either royal or *nouveaux riches* families, benefitted from formal education. For the great majority of West African women, colonialism meant unmitigated suffering.

A few women managed to squeeze some advantages out of the neocolonial era, and excelled in areas where women would not normally be expected to. I emphasize "few," because educational policies in Africa have never been democratic. Today, the pyramid is a symbol of what is happening to young women in the educational systems of West Africa; a massive base and a needle-thin top. At the primary levels, girls and boys get equal or almost equal opportunities to enter the system; but by the time a given age group gets to the universities, the ratio of girls to boys is as low as 1:10 or worse. Apart from the impossibly poor environments, this situation is a result of a number of negative forces in young women's lives, such as becoming pregnant and getting expelled from school (while the offending male, whose identity no one cares to know, is left free[5]) or receiving discouraging career counsel from sexist teachers and school authorities, from schoolmates, and from well-meaning but reactionary relatives.[6]

HIGH-POWERED TOKENS

Given the chance, a number of young women show their independence and courage in choosing careers and in most cases perform brilliantly, but women in high-powered positions are still hostages to tokenism. Certainly as "tokens" many of them have attained the top of their professions. Some even got there as early as other women from some of the most technologically advanced regions of the world. Thus, for a long time some countries in Africa have produced women doctors, lawyers, judges, university lecturers, and professors. There have been women in "rarified" professional areas such as imaginative writing, publishing, geology, architecture, engineering, transportation ownership and management, and music conducting. When we talk of African women today, we speak of over two hundred million people, some of whom are commercial airline or air-force pilots, engineers (electrical and mechanic), primary and secondary school teachers, telephone operators, and nurses. These professional African women are the exception rather than the rule—but Africa is not alone in this; the marginalization of women in certain professions is a worldwide phenomenon.

However, there is one group of women almost peculiar to West Africa. These women, popularly known as "market women" or "market mammies," are in trade and commerce. But of course, not all of them actually work from the markets, although the great majority do. Their activities range from gem dealing and high finance to "petty" trading. Therefore, their workplaces also range from highly sophisticated modern office complexes to the pavements of the cities where their kiosks stand.

For these women, "the market" is both a business arena and a home away from home. From early morning when they occupy their stalls they conduct both their commercial business and their business as homemakers, including the day's cooking for husband and children. Indeed, many people who grew up in urban areas (e.g., in Ghana, Nigeria, Togo, and Benin) could confirm that much of the time they went after school straight to the market to be with their mothers. The market was where they ate lunch and supper, did their homework, and had their baths from buckets and bowls. Such people recall, often with a great deal of nostalgia, that during the weekday, home was the market; a house was only for sleeping in. Meanwhile, these women make money to feed, clothe, and educate their children, and sometimes support their men.

For most West African women, work is a responsibility and an obligation. This idea is drummed into us from infancy. We never have had to fight for the "right to work"—a major concern of early Western feminists. In West Africa, virtually no family tolerates a woman who doesn't work. Consequently, there are not many homes in the region today—not even in traditionally Islamic areas—in which girls are discouraged from having ambitions of their own on the premise that they will marry and be looked after by men.

Yet, Africa's women farmers may get the rawest deal of all.[7] Although it may now be fashionable to admit that women have been the backbone of the continent's agriculture, such recognition is a very recent trend. Earlier on, their existence was not even acknowledged (governments, for example, hardly mentioned women in agricultural policies). So, to the deprivation of being invisible to policymakers was added the burden of constant poverty, of working on the farm from sunup to sundown and then coming home to take on dozens of other roles.

DEBATING FEMINISM

Currently, the debate about African women and feminism is quite heated. It is common to hear feminism dismissed as a foreign ideology, imported into Africa to ruin good African women. It is also easy, and a trap we all fall into occasionally, to feign a lack of interest in this discourse, or to airily maintain that "we don't need feminism" because we had strong women for antecedents. Many of us have declared at one time or another that African women were feminists long before feminism. Certainly from the male camp, the chorus is that African women do not need feminism. Even though in many modern African states grown-up women are expected by their in-laws and others in authority generally to crawl on their knees to offer food and other services to their husbands, most men still maintain that in their country, "women are not oppressed, there are roles which women and men have to play"—including crawling, obviously. The latest and most interesting front in the discourse was opened by Alice Walker, when she proposed that we substitute the term "womanist" to describe the particular concerns of women of African descent.

When people ask me rather bluntly every now and then whether I am a feminist, I not only answer yes, but I go on to insist that every woman and every man should be a feminist—especially if they believe that Africans should take charge of African land, African wealth, African lives, and the burden of African development. It is not possible to advocate independence for the African continent without also believing that African women must have the best that the environment can offer. For some of us, this is the crucial element in our feminism.

On the whole, African traditional societies seemed to have been at odds with themselves as to exactly what to do with women. For although some of them appeared to doubt gender and biology as bases for judging women, in the end they all used gender and biology to judge women's capabilities. Otherwise, how was it that men ruled by proxy for women from those nations, like the Akan of Ghana, among whom inheritance and succession, and therefore power, were vested in the matrilineage and not the patrilineage?[8]

Some of us are convinced of something else: that much of the putting down of women that educated African men indulge in and regard as "African culture" is a warmed-up leftover from colonization. European colonizing men (especially Victorians) brought with them a burden of confusion; first about their own women, and then about other women—all of which was further muddled up by the colonizers' fantasies about the sexual prowess of both African men and women.

In the meantime, no one wants to hear African women discuss their own problems. In Harare, a journalist recently wrote an incredible outburst that began with "Women, women, women, will they ever stop moaning?" He then went on to ask "whether (our) women will ever stop weeping to find solutions to their problems so they won't weep again?" He ended by declaring grandly that "it serves no purpose trying to convince each other that women are oppressed. *There are better issues to focus on*"[9] (emphasis mine). A full comment on this piece could make a sizable book.

One way to appreciate some of the contradictions in the position of African women today is to adopt a bifocal mode of looking at them. One view would be from inside their own environments. This would reveal that in relation to their men, they were just as badly off as women everywhere. But viewed from outside (internationally) the picture changes somewhat. "For years, some of us have been struggling to get the world to look at the African woman properly. Hoping that with some honesty it would be seen in actual fact, vis-à-vis the rest of the world, the position of the African woman has not only *not* been that bad but in some African societies....she had been far better off than the others"[10]—and this would include the self-congratulatory West.

This much is evident about the majority of the African women today, from the Cape of Good Hope to Cairo: they live in the rural areas and urban shanties of the continent; they have had only the most minimal education or none at all; they are married, monogamously or polygamously; they have had between two and six children; they are involved in peasant farming and petty trading; their lives are ruled locally by men who speak in languages they do not understand and from abroad by alien men who speak languages they have no hope of understanding.

All this should be enough to make the African woman want to fold her arms, keel over, and just die. However, she is doing anything *but* that. She is still pushing. The African woman today is a real heiress of her past. We need to intensify our struggle. For instance, instead of letting ourselves be "lulled into a false sense of security through tokenism and processes of 'defeminization,' which in most cases are prerequisites for performing certain functions, [we need to be able to challenge]....gender and class oppression, imperialism and exploitation [and seek]....access to policy-making positions, legal reforms, equal rights in education, employment and credit facilities."[11]

In the meantime, if, like men around the world, African men harbor any phobias about women moving into leadership positions, then they had better get rid of such phobias quickly. After all, men have monopolized leadership positions in Africa over the last five hundred years and still overwhelmingly do. If they alone could save us, they would have done so by now. But instead, every decade brings us grimmer realities. It is high time African women moved onto center stage, with or without anyone's encouragement. Because in our hand lies, perhaps, the last possible hope for ourselves and for everyone else on the continent.

NOTES

1. Sometimes also referred to as *Live Aid*, the concert organized by Geldof in 1985 galvanized the world. Among the honors Geldof received were an honorary knighthood bestowed by the Queen of England and the 1986-1987 Third World Prize. The Western media fell all over itself paying him well-deserved homage, calling him "Santa Bob," "Sir Bob," and "St. Bob."

2. See, among others, Cheikh Anta Diop, *Cultural Unity of Negro Africa* (1980); Ivan Van Sertima, ed., *Black Women In Antiquity* (1981), and any of the volumes in *The Journal of African Civilizations* series by the latter.

3. In Act One of *Antony and Cleopatra*, Shakespeare was unbelievably crude about Cleopatra. But then the Bard's racism is a great source of acute embarrassment. See *The Tempest*, *The Merchant of Venice*, and *Titus Andronicus*.

4. Line from my poem entitled "These Days: II."

5. The story is so heartbreaking that no aspect of it bears telling. *The Herald* (Harare, Feb. 20, 1992) reports the most terrifying example of this to have come to the continent's notice in recent times. In an incident between boys and girls in a co-educational secondary school in Kenya that left *"19 female students dead,"* and during which, according to doctors, *"71 girls were raped," "only two schoolboys were charged with the offense!!!"* (emphasis added). Some of us keep talking about the problem, albeit to deaf ears. For example, "Profile: Remember Tomorrow—A Conversation with Ama Ata Aidoo," by Sarah Modebe, *Africa World Review* (October 1990); *African Woman* (Autumn 1991).

6. One stock piece of advice to a young schoolgirl who plans on having higher education is that she should be careful lest she never find a husband. The harm done by such "advice" is never lessened by the advisor's "good intentions" or by the bromide that "men are scared of smart women."

7. According to Anthony Yudeowei of West Africa Rice Development Association, "over 80 percent of the small holder rice farmers of West Africa are women."

8. Of course, this shows why it is dangerous to assume that because a society is matrilineal, it is also a matri*archy*. Certainly, the Akans are a prime example of a people with a matrilineal base and an obvious patriarchal superstructure.

9. Cephas Chitsaka in the *Sunday Mail* (November 24, 1991).

10. Quotation from my letter to Mineke Schipper to explain my chagrin at the title and subtitle of her book, *Source of All Evil—African Proverbs and Sayings on Women*.

11. See *West Africa* (3-9 February, 1992), p. 176. Bisi Adeleye-Fayemi was reacting to a letter from K. Asare in a previous issue of the weekly. From my rather brief experience as the Ghana Minister of Education (January 1982-June 1983), I fully endorse the view that in order to function as tokens, women defeminize. But then, either way, we are rendered ineffective, because on the one hand we alienate the public and on the other our male colleagues refuse to take us seriously.

WORKS CITED

Adeleye-Fayemi, Bisi. *West Africa* (3-9 February, 1992):176.

Chitsaka, Cephas. *Sunday Mail* (November 24, 1991).

Diop, Cheikh Anta. *Cultural Unity of Black Africa*. Intro. John H. Clarke. Chicago: Third World Press, 1978.

Modebe, Sarah. "Profile: Remember Tomorrow—A Conversation with Ama Ata Aidoo." *Africa World* Review (October 1990), London; *African Woman* (Autumn 1991), London.

Schipper, Mineke. *Source of All Evil—African Proverbs and Sayings on Women*. Chicago: Ivan R. Dee, 1991.

Shakespeare, William. *Antony and Cleopatra*. Cambridge: Cambridge University Press, 1950.

The Herald (Harare). February 20, 1992.

van Sertima, Ivan, ed. *Black Women in Antiquity*. New Brunswick, N.J.: Transaction Books, 1984.

FEMINISM AND AFRICAN WOMANHOOD

'ZULU SOFOLA

SOMETHING LIKE A WHIRLWIND IS SWEEPING ACROSS OUR planet and this time it is feminine. But it does not bear a female name like those given to hurricanes and tornadoes in the West. It is curious indeed that when the real thing began to happen, minds that used to christen such natural eruptions and turbulence with female names failed to identify this one as a real female turbulence. Just the same, there is no doubt that a wind of change is blowing strong across our human landscape and it is female.

Today, we are gathered here in Nigeria for the WAAD conference that aims at bringing together under one umbrella academics and activists to discuss issues concerning women of African descent—from health, politics, and the economy to culture, religion, and feminism. But when one thinks of how people of African descent have been subverted culturally, psychologically, materially, and intellectually, one wonders whose foreign point of view shall be used at this conference to define African womanhood, diagnose her problems, and suggest a cure. The centrality of the academy in our deliberations notwithstanding, I argue that the academe is not necessarily the right place in the African context to seek knowledge on things pertaining to Africa. In the academe, knowledge and the learning process are foreign in form and content. Consequently, and due to mental blankness caused by years of brainwashing, most educated Africans, male and female, are ill-equipped to discuss the African experience. And for the African woman, there is an added dimension which I refer to as the *de-womanization* of African womanhood.

This paper will focus on the processes and implications of the *de-womanization* of the African woman. Assailed by Western and Arab cultures, she has been stripped bare of all that made her central and relevant in the traditional African socio-political domain. Even though both male and female children of Mother Africa were assailed by the invasion of the male-centered and male-dominated European and Arab cultures, the female suffered the greater damage. For wherever the new alien powers dislodged African men from their previous positions of power, those African men would in turn grab whatever was left of power by dislodging their female counterparts from their own positions of power. As a result, the male managed to carve out a niche in the new dispensation and within it managed to maintain a continuous link with his essence, thus ensuring a stronger sense of self. This demotion of African womanhood has produced the contemporary African women who are to a large extent disoriented, weakened, and rendered ineffective and irrelevant.

It is pertinent at this point to examine the conceptualization of "psyche" in the African worldview. In African cosmology, the psyche is the god-man in the individual which connects the creature to the center of Creative Energy. It is known as the spirit of life, *Mo Ndu* among the Igbo, and *Emi* among the Yoruba. It is the aspect of man that contains in essence all that the created person is and will become on earth. Because it is genderless, it is the element that makes all human beings equal in essence. It is in this regard that Ivan van Sertima notes that "The woman in Africa was not seen as a rib or an appendage, or an afterthought to man, but as his divine equal" (van Sertima 1984: 8). For in essence, where all things began and are determined, both genders are equal before the Supreme Essence. It is instructive to read from Idowu's *Olodumare*, that the essence of *Ori*, the inner principle in the human being, is *Orise*, the "Head Source"—*Olodumare*. This etymological identification of the human personality with Being itself underscores the exalted place that the human being has in the universe. Thus, unlike other creatures, the essence of man's or woman's personality is *Orise*, God (Ehusani 1991:86).

The African worldview underscores the idea that both genders have the same divine source even though each has its own distinctive roles to play in the life of the community. Consequently, the African sees the human society as an organic, holistic reality whose existence and survival can be achieved only through a positive, harmonious social organization in which all the members are relevant and effective. It is this thinking that informs the Yoruba philosophy as found in the *Odu* corpus of *Ifa* in its elaboration of the coming of the first set of human beings from *Ikole-Orun* (heavenly abode) to build human society, *Ikole-Aiye* (earthly abode). According to this mythology, disaster struck when men tried to marginalize the female member of the entourage. When *Orunmila,* the *Ifa* oracular deity, was consulted, it was revealed that the female member had been marginalized. Quickly, the abnormality was rectified and tranquility restored. This is contrary to the European worldview where the woman is shut out because she is conceptualized as inferior and an agent of evil: "Ever since Eve persuaded Adam to taste the forbidden fruit, women had proven to be Satan's most successful weapon against men" (Catafygioutou-Topping 1991:13). Women were therefore permanently relegated by men to a state of subordination and dependence. She was only to be seen, not heard. Patricia Hollis put it more succinctly: "[In Europe and America]The man is intended for the world, woman for the home; man's strength is in the head, woman's in the heart; the man's function is to protect, woman's to soothe and comfort; men must work, and women must weep" (Hollis 1979: 17). And in the Arab culture, even worse woes constitute her story. She is neither to be seen nor heard.

The female as an appendage is evident in the English language. The very words "woman" and "female" derive from masculine nouns—fe*male,* wo*man.* And when it is not necessary to specify her at all, the terms *man* and hu*man* are used inclusively to refer to *both* genders. On the contrary, in African languages, to use Igbo and Yoruba languages as examples, a common denominator is used in the constitution of words that represent male and female. For example, in Igbo, the word for child, *nwa,* is used as a root word—*nwa*-oke, male; *nwa*-nyi, female. In Yoruba, it is *rin*—*Okunrin* (the type that is male), *Obirin* (the type that is female). And to refer to both genders inclusively (human), it is *madu* (Igbo) and *enia* (Yoruba). There is here no hint of the male chauvinism that is enshrined in the English language. The African perception of the gender question is thus more healthy, positive, and allows for a wholesome development of human society. Consequently, the woman has always had a vital place in the scheme of things within the African cosmology, the most relevant to our present discussion being the dual-sex system of socio-political power sharing fully developed by African peoples and based on the following perceptions of womanhood: (1) as the divine equal of man in essence, (2) as a Daughter, (3) as a Mother, (4) as a wife.

These four realities were conceptualized and established within a structured system of co-rulership. Because of the complexity of this system, a table will be required for elucidation; but first, let us take a look at the African world view that makes this system possible and necessary. The world view of the African is rooted in a philosophy of holistic harmony and communalism rather than in the individualistic isolationism characteristic of European thought. The principle of relatedness is the *sine qua non* of African social reality. Relatedness characterizes the African experience of the living person. If one is cut off from his community, one is considered dead (Ehusani 1991: 92). The individual belongs primarily to a context, and within it he/she moves and has his/her being. It is this philosophy that informs African social order and the dual-sex system of socio-political organization which Kamene Okonjo articulated as follows:

> The African woman has not been inactive, irrelevant and silent. Rather, African tradition has seen the wisdom of a healthy social organization where all its citizens are seen to be vital channels for a healthy and harmonious society. Hence the establishment of a dual-sex power structure which is lacking in European and Arab cultures.(45)

The principle of relatedness makes it possible for a society to evolve a socio-political order that gives every member a proper context for participation governed by a check-and-balance mechanism that helps to maintain equilibrium. The co-ruler concept of governance is the most dynamic and pragmatic realization of that philosophy. It is therefore pertinent at this point to examine briefly the co-rulership system of socio-political organization in order to gain an insight into the position and relevance of women in the traditional African system of governance and the positive effect such an arrangement is bound to have on her psyche. The co-rulership concept of governance falls into the following categories:

(1) Monarchy evolved along gender line
(2) Monarchical co-rulership based on the principle of Daughterhood
(3) Monarchy based on the principle of Queen-Motherhood

(4) Authority based on the principle of Priestess/Spirit Medium
(5) Warrior-Queen system based on Daughterhood representative of the throne in the supreme military council of the kingdom
(6) Monarchical co-rulership based on the principle of Woman of the House role of the first wife of the king, *Anasi-Obi* (Igbo); *Olori* (Yoruba)
(7) Co-Rulership system based on constituted roles of heads of female professionals, *Iyaloja* (Yoruba)
(8) Co-Rulership based on the principle of Institution of Daughters, *Umu -Ada* (Igbo), and Institution of Wives, *Otu Inyemedi* (Igbo)

Space constraints will not allow for an examination of each of the categories listed above, but the first category (Monarchy developed along gender line) will be examined. This is necessary, particularly in light of the thorny issue of the political (dis)empowerment of women in the current political landscape of contemporary Africa. The principle of dual-sex political line of power evolved initially from the principle of father and mother of family units, and gained a stronger reinforcement through the principle of man/woman of the house system of governance. According to Okonjo,

> All the Igbo of each political unit to the West of the Niger were subject to two local monarchs, both of whom were crowned and acknowledged heads who lived in palaces and ruled from thrones. The two monarchs were male *obi* who in theory was acknowledged head (father) of the whole community but who in practice was concerned more with the male section of the community and the female *omu* who in theory was acknowledged the mother of the whole community but who in practice was charged with concern for the female section. (47)

This principle is politically organized among the Igbo, west of the Niger and Onitsha, East of the Niger. Beginning from the *Ezinuno* unit, the power structure moves upwards as shown in the table below:

COUNCIL OF GOVERNORS

Ndi Olinzele, composed of the King's *Olinzele* Members and Representatives of *Ndi Olinzele-Omu* headed by the *Eze-Omu.* It is a joint council of both arms and presided over by the king, Obi, as the father of the community.

Male Line of Power and Authority	**Female Line of Power and Authority**
Izuani Town Council (7–10 *Ogbes* level) with *Ogbelani* as Head	*Otu-Omu* Council with the *Eze-Omu* as Head
Diokpa Ogbe (quarters of 4–6 *Idumus*—neighborhood level)	*Isi-Ada Ogbe*
Diokpa Idumu (neighborhood level of 5–10 family compounds)	*Isi-Ada Idumu*
Diokpa Ezinuno (extended family compound level)	*Isi-Ada Ezinuno*

By virtue of the fact that women leave their natal homes for their matrimonial homes, the female arm of governance also incorporates a division that is meant for wives. This is the reason for inscribing at the beginning of the female arm the Institution of Daughters with its supreme head in the person of the eldest and properly enthroned daughter known as the *Isi Ada,* and the Institution of Wives headed by the eldest wife of the extended family—the equivalent of Yoruba *Olori* on the kingship level. Thus the female section has two lines of power, though the line of *Uma-Ada* is stronger than that of the Institution of Wives, *Ndi Inyemedi* or *Ikpoho Idunu,* whose status is dependent on that of the husband.

But the composition of the governing council of each arm—male and female—demonstrates more clearly the reality and significance of the dual-sex power structure:

MALE	FEMALE
Ndi Olinzele	*Ndi Olinzele Omu*
Obi (Head)	*Eze-Omu or Omu* (Head)
Onishe (King Maker)	*Onishe-Omu (Omu* Maker)
Iyese-Onu Ani (Spokesman)	*Iyese-Omu-Onu-Ani* (Spokeswoman)
Odogwu-Isi Aya (Head of the militia)	*Odogwu-Omu-Isi Aya* (Head of the militia)
Uwolo (Representative of the Military Council)	*Uwolo-Omu* (Representative of the Military Council)
Isagba (Representative of the Military Council)	*Isagba-Omu* (Representative of the Military Council)
Chi Obi (King's godfather)	*Nne-Omu* (Official Royal mother)
Ogbelani (Head of *Izuani* Town Council)	*Agbani-Omu* (Head of *Omu*) Intelligence
Isi Okwalegwe (Head of the Police Force)	*Isi-Okwalegwe Omu* (Head of the *Omu* Police Force)
Oga Obi (Public Relations Officer for the King)	*Oga-Omu* (Public Relations Officer for the *Omu*)

It must be stated here that the *Eze-Omu,* the head of the female line of power, is neither the wife nor a relation of the king. She is a duly elected head of that political line of power and with her governing council, *Ndi Olinzele-Omu,* she caters to the interests of the female citizens, controls certain areas of power in the combined central council of the kingdom. In addition to being in charge of some vital aspects of the spiritual life of the kingdom, she is in control of the commercial life of the state, vital in the enthronement and burial ritual ceremonies of royal heirs and other members of the royal family, a priestess and spirit medium, and plays a primary role in ensuring the spiritual health of the kingdom both in war and peace.

Among the peoples of Ijebuland, Owo, and Ondo, there was a variant of the dual-sex system of authority and political power. Among the Ondo in general, and Ile-Oluji in particular, there existed a strongly dichotomized power structure based on gender, each with a political head as ruling monarch, *Oba-Okunrin* (male monarch), and *Oba-Obirin* (female monarch)—note that *oba* is the root wood for both. Consequently, there were two monarchs simultaneously ruling the kingdom, each having his/her own governing council and ruling over his/her own gender-specific citizens, though periodically a joint council would be held to discuss matters of common interest. At one period in their history, there arose a need to merge the two lines of power with an overall head. As should be expected in a patriarchal system, the male line of power became the ceremonial head of the human family and presided over the joint council of both arms of government. A compromise was arrived at stipulating that at the death of the king (*Oba*) a female regent would reign until a new king is enthroned. This is still in practice in contemporary Ile-Oluji. As a result of this new development and compromise in the interest of the community, the following political structure evolved:

OBA (King)

Iwerebfa (The Male Governing Council of High Chiefs)	*Opoji* (The Female Governing Council of High Chiefs)
High Chief *Lisa*	High Chief *Lisa-Lobun*
High Chief *Jumo*	High Chief *Jumo-Lobun*
High Chief *Odunwo*	High Chief *Odunwo-Lobun*
High Chief *Odofin*	High Chief *Odofin-Lobun*
High Chief *Sama*	High Chief *Sama-Lobun*
High Chief *Sasere*	High Chief *Sasere-Lobun*

Directly below this council are the *Ikule* Chiefs, who are mostly male because of its military nature, but it is also within this section that the next and most popularly known female power line in the Yoruba system, the *Iyalode,* exists. For while the Council of High Chiefs integrates both genders, the *Iyalodo* system—where each line of governance has its own Council of Governors headed by the *Oba* (king) and *Iyalode* (female ruler) respectively—reflects the dual-sex structure that exists among the Igbo west of the Niger. Hence the saying that no matter how powerful a king may be, he cannot be an *Omu* or an *Iyalode.*

In the same general line of the Ondo system, the people of Ijebuland have the *Erelu* in the *Osugbo* Council of Governors. There is a female line of power which in combination with the male line of power forms a joint Council of High Chiefs that serves as the Supreme Executive Council of the kingdom, the *Osugbo.* Then

directly below this Council is a Lower House where the *Iyalode* system also prevails. A similar structure existed in Ile-Ife until
European/Arab encroachment destabilized everything. For it was
at the High Chief level that powerful women emerged in their own
right as astute politicians to become *Obas* in the history of the kingdom. The kingdom of Ile-Ife records one Ooni Luwo, an *Oba Obirin*
or female ruler during whose reign the kingdom of Ile-Ife experienced great development. Ooni Luwo's love of African art led her
to tile the palatial grounds in Ile-Ife in a style typical of the period.
Remnants of those tiles have been preserved at Ile-Ife.

And among the Edos of the eleven dynasties of the Ogiso era
and before the advent of the Oranmiyan era with its Yoruba influences, there was also a High Chief level where women had their
power line. It was within that structure of authority and political
power that Emose and Orhorho, two female rulers/*Ogisos* and
astute, powerful politicians emerged as the ruling monarchs in their
own rights. These female monarchs, Ooni Luwo of Ile-Ife and Ogiso
Emose and Ogiso Orhorho of the Benin Empire were all castigat-
ed as wicked by terrified men who strongly resisted females as
monarchs. Fortunately for the men, Europeans and the Arabs with
their philosophy of womens' inferiority arrived on the scene and
succeeded in institutionalizing the superiority of men. Chaos set in
and women were dislodged and made irrelevant, a fact that is now
full-blown in today's European/Arab systems of governance in contemporary Africa where our women have been rendered irrelevant,
ineffective, and completely *de-womanized*.

For it was as active participants in the established, gender-based
power lines, with proper check-and-balance mechanism, that our
traditional heroines in history left their footprints in the sands of
time. One recalls Moremi of Ile-Ife who, as the Iyaloja head of the
King's Market (*Oja Oba*), offered to risk her life to save the devastated people of Ile- Ife; Emotan of Benin who did risk her life as a
spy to save the kingdom of Benin at a very precarious and threatened period in its history; Warrior Queen Amina of Zaria who, as
the daughter represening her father's throne in the Supreme
Military Council of Zazzau, seized control of a weakened kingdom
and expanded it far and wide through her military leadership and
tactical mobilization of warlords and soldiers. The ancient city of
Zaria, built under her leadership, is a testimony to her greatness.
The legacy was further enriched by Warrior Queen Nzingha of the
Jugas who bravely confronted the Portuguese in their bid to seize
Angola; Yaa Asantewa of Ghana (1863–1923), the Queen Mother

who fought fiercely against the British and finally gave her life in a bid to save her people; the Priestess/Spirit- Medium Mbuya Nehenda of Zimbabwe, who mobilized her people (the Shonas) against the invading British but when the Shonas were invaded and was subsequently executed (by hanging) by the British for her resistance to imperial authority; Nefertiti and Hatshepsut of ancient Egypt; Makeda, the Queen of Sheba, who ruled over Ethiopia and Saba with the capital city of her empire at Axum; Queen Dahia Al-Kahina of North Africa, who offered Arab invaders fierce resistance after the fall of Carthage; the powerful Queen Idia of the Benin Empire whose series of successful war exploits in defense of the throne for her son, Oba Esigie of Benin, put an end to the ritual killing of Queen-Mothers during the coronation ceremonies of their sons; and Queen-Mother Mai Idris Alooma of Borno Empire. Included in this long lineage of powerful women was Iyalode Tinubu of Lagos who, with the strong support of Efunsetan Aniwura, the Iyalode of Ibadan, resisted the signing of a treaty that would have written Lagos off as a colony. Unfortunately the treaty was eventually signed after she was betrayed by the Oba of Lagos. Consequently, she chose to die in protest against the damage the men had done by selling their birthright for a mess of pottage.

And in recent history there was the Igbo Women's War of 1929 (named the Aba Women's Riots by the British) waged by ordinary Igbo women against the British colonial administration for introducing taxation; Mrs. Funmilayo Rasome-Kuti who mobilized the Market Women of Abeokuta in the 1940s and successfully got the king of Egbaland to go into exile for some years until things cooled down; Omu-Ako of Issele-Oligbo of Aniocha who, as the head of the Omu Women's Council, took over the traditional government, combined both male and female lines of power, and confronted both warring camps of Federal Nigeria and Biafra in defense of her citizens during the Nigerian Civil War (1967–70). My own paternal aunt, Madam Okwuanyi Okwumabua, was a member of that governing council.

And with the type of African womanhood reflected in the foregoing array of African heroines, one would have expected nothing less from women in the diaspora who themselves were undoubtedly descendants of warrior queens, monarchs, women intelligence spies, economic magnates, and powerful daughters of the land. In the diaspora of the United States of America, the Underground Railway system that got African-American slaves to escape to freedom was led by Mary Bethune and a galaxy of other fearless African

American women. And it had to take another such fearless African-American woman—Rosa Parks—to resist the racial injustice and humiliation in the United States, opening the door to the Revolution of the 1960s that brought Martin Luther King, Jr., and others into prominence. For these reasons we reject the Eurocentric theory that the depletion of Afro-American men during slavery gave their women the opportunity to develop strong female presence and authority (the so-called black matriarchy). We assert that the presence of strong, black women in the African diaspora was due to the African woman's healthy psyche and heritage that they carried over to the new world. It was not brought about by a mere circumstance of being left in charge of the home during slavery. It runs in the blood.

In view of the foregoing analysis, one is terribly disturbed by what has become of the African women of today, particularly those whose psyche has been severely damaged in the process of acquiring Western education with its philosophy of gender bias. The first level of damage was done when the female lines of authority and socio-political power were destroyed and completely eliminated by the foreign European/Arabian male-centered systems of authority and governance. That was the first death blow to our psyche and the beginning of the *de-womanization* of African womanhood. Then, in quick succcession, three of the four realities of African womanhood—her reality as a woman, the equal of a man in essence; her reality as a daughter; and her reality as a mother—were drastically reduced, giving way to the prominence of her reality as a wife (Sudarkasa 1987: 26-29). She became and remained only an extension of her husband, as was/is the case in the Western world, and a mere shadow as in Arab culture. Consequently, she developed an incurable dependence and inferiority complex that had not existed when her active and relevant existence in the other three realities had balanced the fourth reality of wifehood. Gradually, she grew to be irrelevant, ineffective, redundant, and dull, good only as an ornament, a wall flower—if allowed to be by her egocentric, almighty husband. She was rendered completely impotent in matters which her "illiterate, rural counterparts" would have handled with ease and quick dispatch.

The Nigerian scene is particularly pertinent in this regard because sometimes when there was an impasse in conflict resolution and men could not see their way out, the illiterate, rural women would always mobilize themselves according to the particular traditional power-line required and seize the bull by the horn. The

problem would be quickly resolved and men would be enabled to
get back on the saddle once more. During the recent gubernatori-
al election contest in Benin, for instance, the Daughters of Benin
took control of the situation through an organized, traditonal-style
protest march to the government office and forced the decision in
favor of Governor Oyegun.

In light of the relevance, power, and effectiveness of the illiterate, "traditional," African women, one wonders why the Western-
educated African women of the new order are ineffective, always
timidly and indecisively stepping behind the men, and periodically making weak scratches at issues of importance, while their non-
literate counterparts would always match out in full force and
achieve unbelievable successes. The reasons are multifaceted; first,
the male-centered European and Arab systems do not have any
room for any other outside the egocentric self, while the African
traditional system in concept and actualization has room for many
or more; according to a Yoruba proverb, "the sky is always big
enough for all birds to fly without colliding."

Second, there is now only one channel of socio-political power,
and it is male. That again is an error. In traditional Africa there
exists a dual-sex system in theory and in practice from the smallest
family unit to the governing council of the kingdom. Consequently,
both male and female citizens have parallel channels for self-expression, self- realization, and relevance on all levels. It is not a battle-
ground where the woman fights to clinch some of "men's power."
Foreign cultures have both ignited and fueled a perpetual gender
conflict that has now poisoned the erstwhile healthy social order of
traditional Africa. The battle seems hopeless because the male hegemony will not yield anything more than mere tokenism to the
"intruding," aggressive female. The woman in a "male position"
must wear the masculinist, official/professional persona in order
to survive.

Third, women's self-image is also severely damaged because sexist notions of women are taught in schools and portrayed in the
media. And the most devastating image of the woman is that of a
dependent, helpless hanger-on to a man, always behind the man,
seen not heard; obedient and submissive to her husband. With her
Eurocentric notions of marriage the educated African woman clings
to the husband and runs into an emotional flurry whenever her
husband gives her a scare by invoking the possibility of polygamy.
She is disconcerted particularly in view of the fact that the advent
of European and Arab cultures have eroded the power of the

Institution of Daughters that used to help protect daughters in their matrimonial homes. Totally alienated from her culture, she does not even know how polygamy is organized and operated. Instead, she embraces monogamy where the husband is the central focus rather than a shared commodity as in polygamy. The truth of the matter is that the more he is shared, the less central he becomes in the wife's life, and the more central the mother/child dynamic becomes. Consequently, because of this "wifehood" syndrome, the educated African woman spends most of her time panicking over the possibility of rejection or dethronement by her husband, thus making herself less relevant and less effective. This extreme feeling of insecurity tends to make her distrust her fellow women unduly, and makes it difficult for women to close ranks and fight a common enemy. And the educated man is aware of these fears and further exploits them as the women look on helplessly.

Quite often, when one hears the Western-educated African woman speak in a demeaning manner about her illiterate, rural, "traditonal" counterpart, one cannot help but pity the former for her false sense of importance and delusion of grandeur. It never occurs to her that while she parrots the phrase, "What a man can do, a woman can do better," her illiterate counterpart asserts: "What a woman can do, a man cannot do." While she quotes the European saying, "Behind every successful man is a woman," her illiterate counterpart affirms: "The strength of a man is in his woman," or "A soldier with a mother does not die at the war front." While she conceives of herself as someone to be seen not heard; her illiterate counterpart says: "If the *Ada* (daughter) says that a day-old chick is a hen, so it is." While she hangs on to a wicked and bestial husband, her illiterate counterpart throws such a husband off in the spirit of the following proverb: "The burden of a husband is carried on the wife's shoulder, not on her head; she quickly drops it when it becomes too unbearable," or "It is one's child that keeps a wife in the house of a wicked husband."

African women in the academe are being called upon by the theme of this conference to rise to the occasion and make their contributions as activists in this era of global feminisms. My question is, With what are they to make their contributions? They are not well because their psyche has been diseased through the devastating onslaught of European and Arab cultures. In fact, they are the first to deny the existence of the traditional system in our history and the great heroines presented in this paper. And when some of us make bold to speak out, we are jeered at, laughed at, rebuked, and ignored. And when called upon to conduct research and come up with important publications, they reject original research for fear that their husbands might get another wife in their absence. It is easier to stay near the dinner table and collect the crumbs of twisted knowledge and misinformation from the libraries. The situation is bleak because the damage is deep in our psyche. Perhaps this conference has an answer; I have none.

WORKS CITED

Bamgboye, David. *Space Science and National Development: An Inaugural Lecture.* Ilorin: University of Ilorin Press, 1987.

Catafygioutou-Topping, Eva. "Mourning for Hypatia." *The Greek American* 8.10 (March 16, 1991): 13.

Ehusani, G. O. *An Afro-Christian Vision "OZOVEHE."* Washington, D. C.: University Press of America, 1991.

Hollis, Patricia. *Women in Public: The Women's Movement 1850–1900.* London: George Allen and Unwin, 1979.

Okonjo, Kamene. "The Dual-Sex Political System in Operation: Igbo Women in Community Politics in Midwestern Nigeria." In *Women in Africa,* ed., Nancy J. Hafkin, and Edna G. Bay. Stanford, Calif.: Stanford University Press, 1976: 45-58.

Sudarkasa, Niara. "The 'Status of Women' in Indigenous African Societies." In *Women in Africa and the African Diaspora,* ed., Rosalyn Terborg-Penn, Sharon Harley, and Andrea Benton Rushing. Washington, D. C.: Howard University Press, 1987: 25- 42.

van Sertima, Ivan. *Black Women in Antiquity.* New Brunswick, N.J.: Transaction Books, 1984.

AFRICAN WOMEN AT THE GRASSROOTS: THE SILENT PARTNERS OF THE WOMEN'S MOVEMENT

OLABISI AINA

INTRODUCTION

AS A POLITICAL AND IDEOLOGICAL PROJECT FEMINISM AIMS at examining and analyzing women's oppression, thereby exposing the dynamics of male domination and female subordination through history. Feminism as an emancipatory project therefore specifically aims at the total liberation of women from the yoke of tradition expropriated in various dimensions in different historical epochs. According to Gilligan (1982), to understand feminism is to understand the systemic discrimination with which women live every day in a society which recognizes only the male voice as the norm. MacDonald (1989) defines feminism as that which encompasses both a political activism and an academic or theoretical stance, both stressing the lived experience and action of women's lives as crucial to any understanding of the social aspects of humanity and offering a critique of and a remedy for the prevailing male ideology which influences the lives, the ideas, and the physical, emo-

tional, or financial well-being of women. By this definition, two categories of feminists suffice: the activists and the theorists. While
more often than not a feminist in mainstream academia falls into
both camps, a social reformer outside the academy remains to a
large extent a practitioner, even though both often share the same
ideology and goal.

Central to contemporary feminist debates is a growing recognition that sexism, racism, and class exploitation relate in a dialectical way to subjugate women across societies and ethnic groups.
Consequently, distinctions of gender, race, and class are not only
different experiences for different groups of women, they often
impede the pace of building a viable universal sisterhood among
feminists. Contemporary feminist writers are therefore seeking a
more pluralistic approach that recognizes complexities and differences in women's life experiences (Lorde, 1981; Dill, 1983; hooks,
1988). This in itself cannot be achieved without a thorough understanding and a continuous reassessment of different socio-cultural
formations that make for such differences.

Currently, two major goals of feminism have been identified
(see Bunch 1993:249):

(1) The freedom from oppression for women involves not only
     equity, but also the right of women to freedom of choice and
     the power to control their own lives within and outside of the
     home; having control over their lives and their bodies is essen-
     tial to ensure a sense of dignity and autonomy for women.

(2) The second goal of feminism is the removal of all forms of
     inequity and oppression through the creation of a more just
     social and economic order nationally and internationally. This
     means the involvement of women in national liberation strug-
     gles, in plans for national development, and in local and glob-
     al struggles for change.

Relevant to this essay is the task of identifying the path and the goal
of feminism in Africa; the relevance of Western feminism to women's
liberation movements in Africa; and the reasons for the existence of
specific differences in priorities and practice. At the core of this discussion is the fact that, in Africa, most women at the grassroots[1] have
yet to identify with the aims and caprices of modern-day feminism.
They see feminism as elitist and illusory; yet, to be effective agents of
change, African forms of feminism must properly incorporate women
at the grassroots. These are the women who not only constitute the
large majority, but who continue to be the custodians of African tradition. Therefore, the crucial questions addressed in this essay are:

(1) Are the feminist priorities for the West and for the Third World nations necessarily the same (in terms of goals, values, and ideals of feminist struggle)?
(2) Why is it taking so long to eradicate female subordination in the African continent?
(3) Will the feminist path in Africa be the same as that of the West?

FEMINIST GOALS, VALUES, AND IDEALS

Feminism in the West predated the upsurge of radical feminism of the late 1960s. In the United States of America, feminism started as the Woman's Suffrage Movement, led by liberal white women with concerns for the abolition of slavery and for gaining equal rights for all people irrespective of race, class, and sex (Hudson-Weems, 1992). Jaggar and Rothenberg (1993) noted that the feminism of this early period was embarrassingly narrow, representing the interests of white, middle-class women and largely excluding the experience and perspectives of large numbers of women of color. Although issues of race and ethnicity are now gaining more attention in the emerging feminist perspectives, voices of women from many racial and ethnic groups are still to be heard.

Women's subordination worldwide has been described using various analytical frameworks, including biological determinism, liberalism, classical marxism, radical feminism, and socialist feminism. Central to most of these analytical frameworks are the social transformations brought about by modern industrial capitalism in world societies. Thus Jaggar and Rothenberg remarked:

> As the world economic system becomes increasingly integrated and both the privileges and the exploitation of women in Western Europe and North America are tied increasingly tightly to the privileges and exploitation of women around the globe, it becomes ever more important for feminism to think and act globally as well as locally. (xiii)

The two major events of the last years of the eighteenth century in Europe—the French Revolution and the Industrial Revolution—provided a firm base for capitalism. Industrial capitalism, according to Sheila Rowbotham (1976), resulted in the separation of the workplace from the home, thereby producing roles for women as workers distinct from their roles in the family. Thus, Western women became subjected to a double oppression, at home and in the workplace. Subsequently women have faced an unprecedented choice between reproduction (home and children) and production (the ability to participate in the paid labor force). The result of this sudden social transformation and structural alteration has been that production and reproduction are now perceived as parallel (i.e., the domestic versus the public domain, with men as active participants in the public sphere, and women in the domestic sphere).

The biological determinism (i.e., women seen as the weaker sex) and the culturally constructed differences (nature/nurture hypothesis) both influenced social policies and thinking. Thus, in England, for example, women were seen as biologically unsuitable for the rigors of public life and so were not allowed to vote until 1918; to contest elections; to sit in Parliament; or to be employed in the civil service (Mba 1982:3).

Seeing reproduction as a factor to be used to ensure female subordination in the emerging capitalist society, the early radical feminists staged overt shows of liberation—"bra burning," categorizing marriage and childbearing as social responsibilities which the society must pay for, and (at the extreme) a total rejection of motherhood.

Western feminism is currently facing the battle of acceptance both in Africa and in the diaspora. Hudson-Weems (1991) argues that the Western feminist agenda is designed to meet the particular needs of white women. Hudson-Weems sees as "racist arrogance and domination" Western feminism's strategy of placing women's history under white women's history, the latter position being seen as definitive. She therefore opted for the term "Africana Womanism," which is grounded in African culture and "necessarily focuses on the unique experiences, needs and desires of Africana women" (Hudson-Weems 1991:6). Bell hooks wrote that "white women liberationists saw feminism as their movement and resisted any efforts by non-white women to critique, challenge or change its direction" (1993:502). She stated that the few African Americans who joined the struggle at the initial stage became disillusioned after finding out that white women in the movement had little knowledge of or concern for the problems of black women across classes. Furthermore, she argues that feminism in North America was undermined by "the narcissism, greed, and individual opportunism of its leading exponents" who are usually the white upper/middle class women (hooks 1993.) Feminists from the Third World have criticized major feminist theories which are based on the Western historical experience and which have failed to account for the experiences of black women both in Western societies and in the Third World. This background documents the localized nature of Western feminism and its inability to solve women's oppression in the Third World nations, that have witnessed and continue to undergo a unique process of change—colonialism, imperialism, neocolonialism, debt crises, food crises, etc.

Many writers (Mbuende, 1990; Oluwole, 1994) who wrote on the plight of the African woman often saw the subordination of African women as a creation of Western intellectual tradition. According to Oluwole (1994), this is because pre-capitalist African society did not impute values into the natural act of discriminating between phenomena. Afonja (1994), expanding Oluwole's thesis, wrote that "just as being male or female carried no specific disadvantages, production and reproduction, domestic/public, productive labor/domestic labor become completely irrelevant to social system of non-capitalist societies." The implication of this is that feminism may not be relevant to a society of this kind where there was no control of one by the other. The central thesis of Oluwole's work is that we may need to confine discussions of feminism to modern society, which has copied evaluative criteria from Western science.

Therefore, African feminism may be better explained within different historical epochs—precolonial, colonial, and postcolonial. Although the traditional African system provided some degree of security for the female members, there existed some form of oppression within that very system. According to Mbuende (1990:19), "the fact that women were conditioned to do only specific duties have put limitations to self-development." Other factors within traditional African systems documented in support of some form of female oppression include:

(1) the polygynous family arrangement, which gave a male member a certain degree of power as head of the family over his many wives;

(2) widowhood practices which to this day subject women to obnoxious practices—e.g., shaving of heads; drinking water used to wash the corpse of the deceased husband where a wife is suspected as the cause of the husband's death; widows eating from broken plates, sleeping in ashes, etc.;

(3) arranged marriages, where marriages are contracted without the consent of the bride; and child marriage, where a girl of about 9-11 years becomes a victim of rape by the would-be husband (an adult male who can be as old as the girl's father);

(4) inheritance rights which give primacy to male children inheriting from their fathers, while the female children cannot, etc.

Christine Obbo (1980) wrote that ethnographic studies contain information on women as mothers, daughters, sisters, and wives of male informants and power holders, while the voices of the women themselves are mute. Women in such arrangements, she wrote, are seen as merely assisting their men in the quest for power by building strong networks based on visiting and gossiping with relatives in neighborhoods. Obbo further noted that even in matrilineal societies of Africa, while women may have some advantages in certain types of matrilineal systems, there is still no doubt about the political dominance of men. Birgitta Leander noted that a trend in the literature shows that "true matriarchies—societies in which women appear to have had supreme authority in all aspects—have never existed" (1982:9). The precolonial period recorded no major feminist attacks on African traditional social structure, and not until the colonial era did we have recorded cases of women acting as pressure groups to reject many of colonial economic and political policies (Mba, 1982).

From the above, it could be argued that the traditional African structure set the stage for the subordination of women under capitalist imperialism, both structures interacting in a complex way to further oppress African women. In colonial and postcolonial Africa, the subordination of women is seen at different levels—first, male dominance of the traditional patriarchal social structures; second, domination of women as members of the peripheral societies, subordinated to foreign capitalist males of the metropolitan states; and thirdly, subordination of women as members of the underpaid working class and impoverished peasantry.

As the continent of Africa is ravaged by war, drought, poverty, disease, illiteracy, and ignorance, women and children have been known to be its most defenseless victims. Even in postcolonial Africa, many of the African states are still battling with neocolonialism. Lesotho and Swaziland, for instance, are examples of neocolonialism at its worst. McFadden (1990), writing on the conditions of women under the grip of a military dictatorship and unprogressive monarchy in both Lesotho and Swaziland, noted that women remain the "poorest of the poor, the least literate, the most exploited, and the most marginalized of all the social groups in those countries." Even in Botswana, the post-independence wealth "has not led to any changes for women in the political and social spheres either" (McFadden 1990:8). Also in Ethiopia, women under the oppressive feudal and military regimes suffered untold hardship due to inhibitory traditions in the form of superstitions and taboos (e.g., women could not work on the land due to a superstitious belief that if women touched the plough the land would not yield crops; and other obnoxious marriage practices like child marriage, female circumcision, and women's lack of legal right to divorce). However, the strength and determination of Ethiopian women to free themselves from the yoke of tradition and imminent death were seen as they fought the 17-year people's revolutionary war side by side with their men. This is revisiting the past, for, according to Sudarkasa, women in African societies "were literally expected to 'shoulder their own burdens,' and in many contexts, respect and responsibility, as well as rights and privileges, were accorded without reference to gender" (1989:36).

For the African woman, fighting for survival remains a priority in post-independence African states that are facing economic crises. No doubt, this gender condition has further exacerbated gender inequities in postcolonial Africa. This is particularly so where households in an African context are imbued with the values of the Western nuclear family (as against the traditional context in which households function as complex units, with the roles of the individual household members complementing rather than competing). Today, the survival of poor families from the devastating socio-economic situation on the continent depends largely on the strategies adopted by women. African women today are not only engaged in a variety of income-earning and income saving activities for the survival of their families, they have also started to lead protests against tyrannical regimes and inhuman macroeconomic policies such as Structural Adjustment Program.

However, the African woman today is concerned not only with overcoming the problems of foreign domination/rule, but also with the specific, immediate needs of surviving famine, hunger, drought, disease, and war. To be empowered, African women, unlike their Western sisters, are struggling not just to attain political power but also to be empowered by gaining access to a good education and the professions, among other things. Many of the issues which are of concern to the African feminist are often left out of the Western feminist agenda, i.e.:

(1) how to successfully combine her mothering and nurturing roles with her productive roles;
(2) how to make the men appreciate and join her to fight against societal oppressive structures created by both men and women, and not necessarily fighting against men;
(3) how to fight oppressive traditions such as child marriage and

widowhood taboos; and how to retain those traditional structures which are supportive of women (e.g., social safety nets
provided women by the traditional extended family system);

(4)   how to devise coping mechanisms for stable marital relations
(coping with polygyny; mother/sister-in-law taboos and conflicts; inheritance rights; etc.);

(5)   how to build a bridge between the traditional African communal life and the emerging individualistic tendencies of the
modern capitalist relations, etc.

Many of the issues listed above are peripheral to the ideals, values,
and goals of Western feminism, whereas the issue of heterosexuality versus lesbianism/homosexuality is gaining both public and legislative attention in the West. While Western feminism is now faced
with puzzles emerging from these two worlds (lesbianism/homo-
sexuality and heterosexuality), African feminism is only thinking of
social relations within the heterosexual relations. To the latter, issues
of rights for the gays and lesbians are outside its agenda. This is
because for many African societies lesbianism and homosexuality
are nothing but abominations. Contrary to this, some Western feminists see heterosexuality as a political institution which disempow-
ers women, and therefore to be changed (Rich, 1993:158). While
Western feminism exists within a structure which had successfully
broken away from fetters of tradition, African feminism operates
within a framework that sees tradition as inherently part of the present.

THE SLOW PACE OF ACTIVE FEMINISM IN AFRICA

A full-fledged radical feminism has failed to emerge on the African
continent til now despite the long history of female resistance to
destructive socio-political systems. That history has the Nigerian
experience of the popular Igbo Women's War of 1929 (Van Allen,
1976); the mass movement in Nigeria of the Abeokuta Women's
Union (AWU) and demonstrations against flat rate tax of the Egba
women (Mba, 1982); and the overall participation of African women
in liberation struggles against colonial rule and oppressive feudal
and military regimes (e.g., South Africa, Namibia, Angola, Guinea
Bissau, etc.). Sign Arnfred (1988), writing on the implications of
the activities of the Mozambican women in the country's revolutionary struggle, remarked that

before the war, men and women had led separate lives with

a clear division of labor and different rules of conduct. During the war they came together on equal terms as Mozambicans in the struggle against the Portuguese. In this process, gender relations changed. Some women developed a new concept of themselves as women: new aspirations, new goals. (8)

However, fighting a liberation war is quite different from building a nation state and it seems that what the Mozambican women gained during the war years was taken away from them as gender relations returned to the pre-war situation. Thus Arnfred wrote: "men took back what they had lost of patriarchal power...even more than they had" (9).

The dilemma facing a full-fledged development of feminism in Africa makes it appropriate to ask the same question Filomina Steady asked a few years back: "What are the roots of African feminism?" Steady (1987) argued that a major stumbling block to feminism in Africa is the reality of separating gender domination and exploitation inherent in African culture from a double oppression of African women caused by the processes of slavery, colonialism, imperialism, neocolonialism, and apartheid, an act which has often resulted in conflicting assessments of the status of African women.

The conflicting theoretical assumptions about the impact of development on the status of African women has no doubt slowed down the pace of developing a viable feminist orientation in Africa. For example, the proponents of modernization theory consider life in "traditional" societies as limiting women's access to resources, decision-making power, and employment opportunities. According to Susan Tiano (1981), however, modernists wrongly claim that modernization improves women's situation by expanding their occupational choices and by increasing their natural security. From a modernist viewpoint, colonialism is seen as raising the living and educational standards of African women and ultimately freeing women from the drudgery of farm labor and the oppression embedded in African social customs. The orthodox Marxian perspective also joins this debate. Though full gender equality is assumed to be achievable only within the socialist framework, both Marx and Engels, having hypothesized that the demand for female wage labor would free women from dependence on their husbands and from male dominance within the family, thought they were witnessing the beginnings of women's liberation in nineteenth-century capitalist society. Afonja (1994) identified the inappropriateness of

orthodox Marxist concepts in explaining such micro-level processes as intra-household dynamics. A theoretical scheme which sepa-
rates home and work undermines the complex nature of household
economies in the Third World and their relationship to the national economy. This observation is very important because the household is such an important locus of struggle and exploitation.

In Africa, the linkage between theory and practice is compelling. For a long time, the first generation of Africa women with
Western education saw themselves as different and privileged. For
them, life ceases to be village life with its domestic drudgeries. They
aspire to city life, associated with leisure and freedom from tradition and customs. For both men and women, the general mentality changed with the introduction of Western education. For
example, a new mode of thought emerged, which assumed that all
that is "Western" is better than what is "African." The change in
mentality brought about changes in widely different aspects of life—
language, dressing, ways of knowing, etc. The change also affected
societal institutions. More importantly, the changes brought about
by Western civilization created a gap and a division between rural
and urban dwellers and this rural/urban split to a large extent determined relations between women.

The early literature on African women, and subsequently on
social change, generally measured quality of life principally by educational level, access to paid employment, and access to modern
amenities such as hospitals, transportation, pipe-borne water, and
schools. Important to the assumed positive view of the female status is the wave of changes taking place within African societies,
changes such as

(1) reduction in child marriage (as girls are encouraged to go to
     school);
(2) reduced emphasis on virginity (as the phenomenon of "bridal
     night" becomes a thing of the past, and a girl now makes her
     own choice in matters of marriage and career);
(3) the new wave of monogamous marriage amongst the elites is
     also seen positively as a source of status-building for the
     woman.

The major dilemma of the elite women[2] in most African nations is
that they are so protective of the status quo which they believe marriage offers. Educated women tend to marry men who are more
educated than they are. Thereby, such women gain better life styles
and higher social status through their husbands. Traditionally, the
African woman was accorded respect depending on her husband's

social status. This is to say that the status of the majority of women within the indigenous African setting hinged so much on their marital status, except for the very few who became powerful through success in trade, as recorded amongst the Nupes of Northern Nigeria. Women who acquired high social status independent of the men in their lives are easily described and seen in negative terms—witches, prostitutes, free women, etc. Husbands of such women are not only disrespected, they also become objects of gossip in the community. For example, among the Yorubas, local expressions still exist by which husbands of powerful women or successful women are described. Such phrases include *O ti ra ni ye*,[3] *O ti so di didinrin*,[4] and *O hun ma ni iyawo*.[5]

It is important to note that many contradictions exist in the way the status of women is viewed in many African societies. Such contradictions are found in the use of traditional proverbs and idioms. Yusuf (1994) identified age-old Yoruba proverbs which give contradictory views about the position of women in the society. Such contradictory views incite both negative and positive feelings towards the female. Consequently, such contradiction reinforces the cultural suppression of women and at the same time creates for them access to positive self-expression in traditionally male-dominated areas. The African woman is therefore traditionally equipped with tools for challenging repressive traditions, depending upon her own personal ingenuity.

Access to formal education is today seen as a great achievement for women, although many of these women have no feminist consciousness. Some of them are placid towards marital issues. Often the educated African woman does not want to be described in negative terms and she does not want to appear militant even when her personal well-being is at stake because of the fear of losing social respect or facing up to the social disrespect that being unmarried brings. Therefore, many of the elite women for a long time were more concerned with protecting their status quo, than with developing an interest in modern feminist issues which aim at fighting their persistent domination by men and the exertion of patriarchal arrangements. Women who engaged in feminist causes are described variously as "free-women," "the rejects,"[6] or "the been-tos."[7] Thus, a lot of people, especially women, who believe in equal rights for both men and women often shy away from being labeled "feminists" or "women's libber." According to Obadina (1985), the Women's Liberation Movement (WLM) has got itself such a bad name mainly because of the bad reporting from the male-dominated press which focuses on the bizarre and the outrageous aspects of the WLM to the exclusion of its engagement with more important concerns such as the fight for fundamental human rights. Furthermore, this negative impression is due to the direction the Western WLM has taken, a direction which most people assume focuses increasingly on female sexuality and female separateness. It is thus believed that Western feminism appears to have declared a war against the family, thus creating for African feminists the extra burden of including family values on their feminist agenda, in an effort to demonstrate that feminist development could never pose a threat or constitute a contradiction to a cohesive family life.

The first major task has thus been to create a unique platform for African feminism so as to make it more appealing. The need to sometimes create such an appealing platform has sometimes led to the romanticization of the African past. Thus, many African writers attribute the subordination of women to men to the emergence of modern industrial capitalist development in the continent. Such writers failed to critically examine the traditional social structure, which provided the fertile ground for the breeding of foreign values which further encouraged gender inequities. Also, Western concepts such as "public versus domestic domains," and "complementary versus competition" debates which provided dichotomous views of male and female worlds have been found to be inappropriate for understanding the conditions of African women. Human life in Africa is viewed from a holistic rather than a dichotomous and exclusive perspective. For according to Filomena Steady, "for women, the male is not 'the other' but part of the human same. Each gender constitutes the critical half that makes the human whole. Neither sex is totally complete in itself to constitute a unit by itself. Each has and needs a complement, despite the possession of unique features of its own" (8).

To me, the above observation reveals what a complex knot to untie is feminism in Africa, and that the success of feminism there will depend not only on raising the consciousness of women but on how much cooperation women receive from the men in creating a more humane world, i.e., one devoid of gender oppression. When men look at what they gain from the existing patriarchal relations, it is very likely that they will fight tooth and nail against all that feminism stands for, because feminism will change not only their women, but "a part of their total self." This is to say that gender oppression in Africa might be more enduring, though subtle, while the task of feminism in Africa might demand even more ingenuity to make a break through. This leads our discussion to feminist paths and priorities in Africa.

FEMINIST PATHS AND PRIORITIES IN AFRICA

Seeking the root of African feminism in African cosmological past presents different priorities for African feminism, separate from those of the West. For example, contradictions exist within a structure of assumed egalitarian relationship where men and women might be hierarchically related to each other in certain reciprocal statuses but not in others. Sudarkasa (1989) wrote that both contradiction and congruence characterized the status-clusters termed female and male, thereby making it problematic for African societies to consistently stratify status categories, one against the other, but, rather, codify complementarity. An African woman thus finds it difficult to act spontaneously when one of the statuses within the cluster is at stake, for she has to give consideration to the effect of her single act on her other status roles such as wife, sister, mother, daughter, community member, etc. The individual sees himself or herself as a member of a group and possesses more loyalty to the group than to self, even when it means preserving elements of outright subordination of a particular sex, usually the female sex.

Different feminist priorities are therefore created by African social structure. For example, as mentioned earlier, there is the tendency to overplay traditional complementarity in gender roles, to the neglect of inherent traditional subjugation and exploitation of women. Such an approach neglects inherent conflicts in African social structure which have been used to serve the interests of capital. This also explains why legislation against bigamy in most African countries functions only on paper and is hardly enforced. Also, the destructive effects of polygyny are underplayed, even as the society changes from a predominantly subsistence economy to a modern industrial capitalist system. Not only do men and women struggle over the available limited resources, the relationship among the household members become very calculative. With the unique history of racism, colonialism, neocolonialism, and imperialism in Africa, it becomes easy to overlook sexual oppression and to face those other forms of oppression which are seen as demanding more urgent solutions.

Unlike in the West, in most African countries, middle class women for example, do not have to battle over sharing of housework with husbands—or, until recently (due to deepening economic crises), fight over jobs in the labor market. Until recently, the number of educated women were few and they were trained in traditional female occupations such as nursing, teaching, and service jobs. Since women were often not sufficiently trained to compete in managerial and other male-traditional jobs, very few women either showed interest in such jobs/positions or developed consciousness about gender discrimination in the workplace. Also, because of support networks provided by other women (e.g., relatives who live-in to give childcare services or housemaids and nannies eager for employment), the burden of housework and childcare became lighter. Today, this reality is changing. The dreaded "housemaid syndrome" is now gaining public and research attention, as most families can no longer afford the extra expense of keeping a housemaid. Thus, unforeseen hardships now face nursing mothers as they combine reproductive and productive roles. Unlike Western women, African women cannot afford the leisure of being full-time housewives because they face both marital and extramarital social responsibilities. An educated woman could not afford *not* to work because she is responsible not only to her husband but also to her extended family members. Not only would she have to work to pay off debts incurred for training her in school, she is also obliged to train some of the other junior siblings. The realities of colonization, whereby the labor of both men and women was undervalued and underpaid, forced both men and women to work for survival needs. The wage of the husband is never enough to care for the family's subsistence needs, particularly in a society that is inherently polygynous.

The political and economic rights which Western women have been fighting for over decades are guaranteed constitutionally for most African women. For example, the Nigerian Labor Act of 1974 and the 1979 Nigerian Constitution make specific provisions concerning female employment. The Labor Act guarantees the woman both maternity and night-duty protection, while the 1979 Nigerian Constitution (Section 39) guarantees her right to freedom from discrimination, thus making it possible for men and women to have equal access to employment. The problem is not that these laws do not exist; the problem is with full implementation and enforcement. Akpala identified two cases of outright discrimination against women in Nigeria. First is the case of Miss E. F. Sunday, a holder of OND in Mining Engineering who was refused employment as a mining engineer in the Ministry of Mines and Power on grounds that she is a woman. The other case is that involving Miss Idogisit Ntem, a Solicitor General for Akwa Ibom State, who was denied appointment as a Judge by the Advisory Judicial Commission on the grounds that she is a single parent. Also in Namibia, as in many other African states, many outdated colonial legal systems are still unchanged, particularly in areas concerning marriage, divorce, custody and maintenance, and property acquisition. For example, a woman could not own property separate from her husband. The husband has power to make decisions about property without the wife's consent, but the wife cannot make such decisions without her husband's consent. In many cases, a wife can neither purchase property nor obtain bank loans without a male figure. As it is in Namibia so it is in many African states. In Nigeria, policy on income tax is in favor of men. Men, as the presumed breadwinners in the homes, are the ones entitled to child allowance, thus leaving female-headed households at a disadvantage.

In recent times the reality of female subjugation in Africa has become more obvious, while the need for a more radical women's liberation movement becomes a matter of urgency because only such a move could separate female oppression from other forms of oppression facing the continent and trace the root of female oppression in Africa beyond capitalism to traditional patriarchal structures.

FEMINIST SCHOLARSHIP AND THE WOMEN'S MOVEMENT IN AFRICA

Notably, the growth of feminism in Africa has differed from that in the West. For example, while the women's movement in the West began as a political movement and gradually emerged as an intellectual discourse, the reverse is the case in most African states. In Africa, feminist consciousness has been left to a few elite women, who are mostly in academia. Although there are recorded cases of female resistance to some exploitative socio-political systems in the past, these, it is argued, did not aim specifically at changing the inequality in the traditional structure of gender relations (Mba, 1982).

While different women's societies/associations exist within the continent, most of them lack feminist orientation. Women are frequently organized around definite economic, religious, professional, ethnic, and class interests. The most active ones have been the group organized around economic interests: market women associations or those organized around religious interests, that provide immediate material and social benefits as well as emotional support. However, some war-torn countries such as Ethiopia, Namibia, and Mozambique are currently witnessing the emergence of militant women's organizations.

There are many problems that militate against organizing African women. First, the factors which continue to disunite most African countries as national entities are also the forces that make it difficult to organize women. Women continue to be loyal first to their respective ethnic groups and religions before expressing loyalty to gender unity. Another major barrier is the disunity created by language. Ogundipe-Leslie notes that:

> the reactions of the women differ from class to class. Women of the urban working class, the urban poor, and the peasantry have definitely different attitudes. They insist more on their right to work, as they very often have to live within polygynous systems, Islamic religion and traditions. They tend to ignore the biological and emotional oppression they have to endure, in the view that men are incorrigibly polygynous and that women are socially impotent to correct them. They insist only on the right to have their children fathered, sexually and financially while they expect little from men in terms of companionship, personal care and fidelity (245).

The above quote is in agreement with our claim that most African women lack consciousness with respect to the issue of human rights and that women generally focus less on their own personal well-being. For example, what is viewed in the West as wife battering, child abuse, bigamy, etc., is sometimes accepted by women as that enduring part of marriage which should be settled out of court. Sometimes the ability of the women to endure such outright brutality from their husbands determines the type of social respect married women are accorded. Thus, it is not uncommon to see the majority of women taking such abuses as part of motherhood. For example, among the Yorubas, a common phrase of the doting wife and mother is: *titori omo ni mo se njiya*.[8] This notion becomes an enduring fact in a society which gives all rights over children, including child custody, to the father.

Today, the agonies of development are variously felt by African women. Women not only face job discrimination and sex segregation of jobs within the formal labor market, they also face stiff competition from men even in traditional female jobs, particularly within the informal labor market which was traditionally controlled by women. The current economic wars and debt crises globally, particularly those in African states, and the impact of structural adjustment programs on quality of life lay a more rigorous foundation for assessing the relevance of feminist ideals in contemporary African society. Both scholars and reformists are now pressed to solve the problem of poverty in the continent, while many have directly linked the "woman question" with the African crisis (e.g., as in the food crisis).

As in the West, varieties of academic feminism have long existed on the continent, ranging from the conservative approach of the colonial period, the liberal-reformist approach of the nationalist period, and the socialist feminist model of the post-independence era. Although feminist trends are not the same for all African states, the current trends in research have become more radical in their approaches, challenging the epistemological basis of traditional knowledge about gender relations and about established gender myths. Therefore in Africa, within the last fifteen years, research projects on the conditions of African women have gained momentum; courses on women have been introduced at both undergraduate and graduate levels; and a great number of articles focusing on gender relations have been written in national and international journals. In many African states, the National Women's Commission has been established. In 1982, Nigeria witnessed the emergence of a new women's organization, Women in Nigeria (WIN), with Western socialist feminist tendencies. WIN has gained recognition for its major achievement in establishing research/teaching about women using socialist feminist ideology. Ironically, most of the more recent feminist groups tend to be elitist and identify more with their international sisters in Europe and America. Such academic movements hardly identify with women at the grassroots level. Women at the grassroots continue to use traditional structures such as cooperatives and other forms of women organizations to combat the negative effects of the development process in their lives. For the first time in the history of most African states, gender-specific programs are introduced particularly through the help of national governments and development agencies. However, no major attacks have been launched on the existing patriarchal order. Rather, national governments, which most of the time have sustained gender inequality through their policies, and international agencies run mainly by men, ironically tend to be responsible for shaping the direction of change in women's lives.

The present state of feminism in Africa needs proper reappraisal if the emancipatory nature of feminism is to be realized. First, not only do grassroots women lack appropriate conceptual definitions of feminism, there is a general lack of trust between rural grassroots women and the elite women who are mostly in the cities. The grassroots women see the elite women as privileged and opportunistic. Also, in a continent besieged with poverty, grassroots women are more preoccupied with basic economics of living than with sociopolitical issues. To worsen the situation, most of the women in the forefront of feminist engagement share different life experiences from those of the women in the grassroots. Because of their own different social background, urban elite women lack knowledge of village living, and its attendant drudgeries. It thus becomes difficult for such Western trained women to identify appropriately with grassroots women and organize them politically.

Although some women within the academy and few political reformists have started to build feminist consciousness across the continent through feminist research and political programs, a lot remains to be done. The ability of the "First Lady Syndrome" to effectively mobilize African women has been questioned.[9] First is the general criticism levelled against grandiose government programs targeted at grassroots women: such programs, in which there is much waste, not only take a great share of the government budget, but end up not benefiting the majority of the rural women. The Better Life Program for Nigerian Rural Women has been criticized for its lack of coordination, introduction of inappropriate technology to women, and failure to conscientize women toward self-determination. Secondly, it is argued that many of these "First Ladies" lack adequate education, and managerial know-how; thus, they do not often provide the right leadership for women's programs. Thirdly, because of the general political instability in the continent, there is lack of continuity in many of the government programs targeted at women.

It is important however to note the diversity of the continent in terms of culture, political structures, and economic fortunes. All of these create different structures of gender oppression, requiring different treatment. It is therefore not surprising to see women from the socialist states of Africa and those in the war zones being more militant in the struggle against double oppression—male chauvinism and capitalist imperialism.

A major task facing the growth of feminism in the continent is how to appropriately bridge the gap which now exists between the few elite who are more concerned with feminist struggles on the one hand and, on the other, the non-feminist conscious elites and the grassroots women, both of whom are in large majority. The future of feminism on the continent depends on how the few feminist-conscious female elites and these other groups of women (especially the women at the grassroots) become conscious of the reality of their social situation, as well as on their readiness to come together to fight for democratic rights. It appears that many of the existing women organizations are nothing but government megaphones. Only organizations which operate with some detachment from the government can present a more profound resourcefulness in confronting the dilemmas of the precarious, sexist, male-centric world, and moving towards the creation of neither a man's world nor a woman's, but of a *human* world. For example, the Nigerian National Council of Women's Societies has been accused of being more concerned with demonstrating solidarity with the government than with promoting the interests of Nigerian women (Mustapha, 1985).

A more common bond, irrespective of class, religion, and ethnic origins, is today witnessed between women in the war zones of Africa. No wonder, Professor Wangari Maathai, a leading figure in Kenya's civil rights campaign, was one of those beaten unconscious during one of the Kenyan women's protests against the unlawful detention of some political prisoners in Kenya. Also, women in Ethiopia, South Africa, and Mozambique have fought revolutionary wars side by side with their men, creating a bond of trust between those two groups. Hilda (1985), itemizing the contributions of South African women against the collapsed apartheid regime, wrote: "young and angry, old and undefeated, their continuing defense in the face of persecution, torture, and terrible loss, challenges apartheid, destroys myths of female submissiveness and subservience" (110).

A similar situation is witnessed in Nigeria against repressive military rules. The spontaneity with which grassroots women in Southwest Nigeria engaged in public demonstrations to see the demise of the Babangida regime is indicative of the potentiality in female struggles. Ironically, there tends to be a paradigm shift back to "normal" in gender relations *after* the wars, so that the war of gender equality still remains to be fought and won.

To bridge the gap which now exists between men and women, particularly between the female elites and grassroots women, efforts should be intensified to empower the grassroots women whose works, while central to the process of development, yet generally go unappreciated/unrecognized. The first task is to understand the knowledge and practices in the respective local communities in order to know the type of knowledge and practices appropriate for empowering women. This is best done using the participatory approach in which all citizens, particularly women, contribute to the process of change. Secondly, it is important to raise women's consciousness about oppressive structures which are created by men *or* women. Thirdly, efforts should be geared towards making available to women with the least legitimate power the basic ingredients for empowerment—i.e., formal education, control over their own sexuality, critical resources (land, labor, capital, and entrepreneurial skills). Finally, it will be necessary to challenge policies which subordinate women in the society.

The female elites could play a pivotal role in achieving equality for women in the continent if they would focus on (a) forming pressure groups to lobby for legislative changes, (b) carrying out researches which can further unveil problems in "women development" programs, and (c) suggesting appropriate *alternative* development programs for women at the grassroots.

CONCLUSION

Feminism should not stop at mere access to economic independence and social benefits; rather, it should also focus on the psychological development of the total self, whereby women would see themselves as just as capable as men are of changing the world in which they live.

The goals, values, and ideals of feminism remain the same across regions—i. e., liberating the society from dehumanization and repairing the loss of fundamental human rights—even though women are separated as much by class, ethnicity, religion, and other social situations as by geography. This calls for creating different tactics of organizing across groups. However, the path to full feminism in the Third World might not be the same as in the West because of differences in emphasis and priorities. African feminism tends to be broader in scope, far broader than what is conceived by white women as feminist priorities, for African women are concerned not only about sexism, but also they recognize racism as part of their conundrum. African feminists have not only to question concepts and redraw blueprints, they also have to make feminism relevant to the reality of African social formations.

Presently, in most African nations, the modern vision of feminism is still at its infancy, and remains a mere academic exercise. This is because many African feminist writers shy away from activism, for fear of being described as "women-libbers." Consciousness about feminism in Africa has not cut across classes, and grassroots women have often been left out of feminist agenda. The major problem is how to bring together women, within and across national boundaries, to become conscious of their beings and believe that the essence of feminism is to rebuild and not to destroy the society itself.

Finally, some strategies for building an all-inclusive sisterhood both at the national and international levels are hereby identified:

(1)   Identify feminist priorities within nation states. It should be assumed that the nature and context of female subordination differ within and across national boundaries. Therefore, scholars need to identify feminist priorities within contextual—i.e., local—frameworks and prescribe appropriate solutions.

(2)   Despite group differences and interests, a "pan-feminist" awareness should be created among women such that feminist interests could be developed above other group interests.

(3)   Women's groups with feminist interest need to operate with some detachment from the government. This can only be achieved if the government is not the sole source of financial sustenance for such women groups.

(4)   A central question to be asked is: "Can feminist ideals be achieved in Africa without a political movement or a revolution?" For many of the African nations, the answer is "No," although the intensity of such social transformation may differ from one nation-state to the other. This is as a result of differences in the intensity of societal attitudes towards gender-related issues in each nation-state.

Finally, I believe that a full-fledged feminism can emerge in Africa only when there is a merger between activism and the academy, and only when African women at the grassroots level abandon their present position as silent partners to become active partners of the movement. However, to create a global feminist consciousness, I agree with Charlotte Bunch that it is important to have a sense of connectedness among women activists at the grassroots level in the various regions, such that women's oppression in one region of the world becomes the central concern of feminists the world over. In the words of bell hooks, "to be 'feminist' in any authentic sense of the term is to want for all people, female and male, liberation from sexist role patterns, domination and oppression."(507)

NOTES

1. The phrase "women at the grassroots" refers to women of low socio-economic status, particularly the non-literate rural women and the urban poor. Most such women have been denied access to formal education and modern political power.

2. "Elite women" denotes women who have been exposed to and have benefitted from Western education, modern employment, and are themselves sometimes part of the ruling elites. They comprise both the ruling elites (by their own right or by virtue of being married to the male ruling elites) and non-ruling elites with relative economic independence. Because this class is not homogeneous, members' vision of change depends on their vantage position within the structure of power.

3. This phrase literally means that the wife has cast a spell on the husband such that he has lost all control to exert power over his wife.

4. This means that the wife has caused the husband to lose memory, vision and intellect.

5. It means that the specific roles of 'wife' and 'husband' have been interchanged through casting of spell or witchcraft.

6. "Free women," and "the rejects" are used of women who could not marry because no man wants them.

7. "Been-tos" means women who have spent most of their lives abroad and have been totally Westernized.

8. The phrase literally means: "I am (the woman) enduring all the domestic victimizations because of my children."

9. The issue of the central role of female elites in social mobilization was discussed fully in an article published by this author in 1994, "Mobilizing Nigerian Women for National Development: The Role of the Female Elites," *African Economic History* 21 (1993): 1-20.

WORKS CITED

Afonja, Simi. "Gender Relations in Society: Feminist-Materialist Perspectives." Paper presented at the international conference of the Nigerian Philosophical Association (NPA) on Gender Conflict: The African and European Perspectives, Lagos, Nigeria, May 30-June 2, 1994.

Aina, Olabisi. "Mobilizing Nigerian Women for National Development: The Role of the Female Elites," *African Economic History* 21 (1993): 1-20.

Akpala, Ada. "Eradication of Discriminatory Laws and Regulations Affecting Women in the Nigerian Civil Service." Paper presented at the first international conference on Women in Africa and the African Diaspora, Nsukka, Nigeria, July 13-18, 1992.

Arnfred, Signe. "Women in Mozambique: Gender Struggle and Gender Politics." *Review of African Political Economy* 41 (Sept. 1988): 5-16.

Bunch, Charlotte. 1993. "Prospects for Global Feminism." In *Feminist Frameworks*, third edition, ed., Alison M. Jaggar and Paula S. Rothenberg. New York: McGraw-Hill, 1993: 249-252.

Dill, Bonnie T. "Race, Class and Gender: Prospects for an All-Inclusive Sisterhood." *Feminist Studies* 9 (Sept. 1983): 131-150.

Gilligan, Carol. *In aDifferent Voice*. Cambridge: Harvard University Press, 1982.

Hilda, Bernstein. *For Their Triumphs and for Their Tears: Women in Apartheid South Africa*, third edition., London: International Defence and Aid Fund for Southern Africa, 1985.

hooks, bell. *Talking Back: Thinking Feminist, Thinking Black*. Boston,MA: South End Press, 1989.

———. "Black Women and Feminism." *Feminist Frontiers III*, ed., Laurel Richardson and Verta Taylor. New York: McGraw-Hill, 1993: 499-507.

Hudson-Weems, Clenora. "Africana Womanism." Paper presented at the first international conference on Women in Africa and the African Diaspora: Bridges Across Activists and the Academy, Nusukka, Nigeria, July 13-18, 1992.

Jaggar, A. M. and P. S. Rothenberg, ed. "Introduction." *Feminist Frameworks: Alternative Theoretical Accounts of the Relations between Women and Men*, third edition. New York: Mcgraw-Hill, 1993. xi-xviii.

Leander, Birgitta, ed. *Cultures: Dialogue Between Peoples of the World*. Vol.VIII, No. 4. Paris: UNESCO, 1982.

Lorde, Audre. *Sister Outsider*. Trumansburg: Crossing Press, 1981.

MacDonald, Gayle. "Feminist Teaching Techniques for the Committed but Exhausted." *Atlantis* 15.1 (Fall/Autumn 1989): 145-152.

Mba, N. E. *Nigerian Women Mobilised: Women's Political Activity in Southern Nigeria, 1900-1965*. Berkeley: Institute of International Studies, University of California,1982.

Mbuende, Elizabeth. "The Namibian Woman's Plight." *SAPEM* (August 1990): 19-21.

McFadden, Patricia. "The Condition of Women in Southern Africa: Challenges for the 1990s." *SAPEM* (August 1990): 3-9.

Mustapha, A. R. "On Combating Women's Exploitation and Oppression in Nigeria." In *Women in Nigeria Today*, ed., Editorial Committee. London: Zed Books, 1985: 241-246.

Obadina, E. 1985. "How Relevant is the Western Women's Liberation Movement for Nigeria." In *Women in Nigeria Today*, ed., Editorial Committee. London: Zed Books, 1985: 138-142.

Obbo, Christine. *African Women: Their Struggle for Economic Independence*. London: Zed Press, 1980.

Ogundipe-Leslie, Molara. "Women in Nigeria Today." In *Women in Nigeria Today*, ed., Editorial Committee. London: Zed Books, 1985: 119-131.

Oluwole, Sophie B. "Feminism in Africa." Paper presented at the international conference on Feminism in Africa. Lagos, May 30-June 2, 1994.

Rich, Adrienne. "Compulsory Heterosexuality and Lesbian Existence." *Feminist Frontiers III*, third edition, ed., Laurel Richardson and Venta Taylor. New York: McGraw-Hill, 1993: 158-179.

Rowbotham, Sheila. *Hidden from History: Rediscovering Women in History from the Seventeenth Century to the Present*. New York: Vintage Books, 1976.

Steady, F. C. "African Feminism: A Worldwide Perspective." In *Women in Africa and the African Diaspora*, ed., Rosalyn Terborg-Penn, Sharon Harley, and Andrea Benton Rushing. Washington, D. C.: Howard University Press, 1987: 3-24.

Sudarkasa, Niara. "The Studies of Women in Indigenous Africa and the African Diaspora." In *Women in African and the African Diaspora*, ed., Rosalyn Terborg-Penn, Sharon Harley, and Andrea Benton Rushing. Washington, D. C.: Howard University Press, 1987: 25-42.

Tiano, Susan. "The Separation of Women's Remuneration and Household Work: Theoretical Perspectives on Women in Development." *Working Paper No. 2.* Michigan: Office of Women in International Development, Michigan State University, 1981.

Van Allen, Judith. "Aba Riots or Igbo Women's War?: Ideology, Stratification, and the Invisibility of Women." In *Women in Africa: Studies in Social and Economic Change*, ed., Nancy J. Hafkin and Edna G. Bay. Stanford, Calif.: Stanford University Press, 1976: 59-86.

Yusuf, Y. K. "Contradictory Yoruba Proverbs about Women: Their Significance for Social Change." *Nigerian Women and Social Change*, ed., Simi Afonja and Bisi Aina. Ile-Ife: Obafemi Awolowo University Press, 1994.

WOMEN AND CREATIVE WRITING IN AFRICA

FLORA NWAPA

IT GIVES ME GREAT PLEASURE TO DELIVER THIS KEYNOTE address on "Women and Creative Writing in Africa." I think that two factors make it appropriate for me to be so honored: (1) this first international conference on Women in Africa and the African Diaspora: Bridges Across Activism and the Academy, being held here in Nsukka, is convened by one of my brilliant students from the 1960s, Dr. Obioma Nnaemeka; and (2) my capacity as one of the oldest —if not *the* oldest—of women writers in Africa. Let me say right away that I have not quite prepared a keynote address. On Thursday, July 9th, on arrival at the Enugu airport from Amsterdam where I attended the fifth international Feminist Book Fair, I saw the convener, Dr. Obioma Nnaemeka, who told me: "Auntie, you must come. We have already sent you an invitation." I had thought that the conference was to start on July 17th. But first, I had to travel home (Ugwuta) to see my 83-year-old mother and report my safe arrival. The conference opened on Monday and I was here on Monday and Tuesday. So what I am going to share with you today (Wednesday) is the world of my creative writing, not quite put together as I would have wished.

In 1980, a woman journalist with the *Guardian of London* interviewed me and came out with this headline: "Running out of Boredom." You see, I had told her truthfully in the interview that I started writing because when I was a high school teacher, I had too much time on my hands and did not know what to do with it. I am a Capricorn, restless and hard-working. So, I began to write about my school days, a period in my life I look back on with nostalgia; a happy period when I learned and shared with my school mates; a period that saw the beginning of many years of sisterhood. Young, innocent, and trusting, my fellow boarders and I found ourselves in a school where the white missionaries taught us the ethics of the Christian religion. The white missionaries and some of our teachers introduced us to the world of books. We became avid readers, reading everything we could lay our hands on. One day, I stumbled upon a book written by a Nigerian (Cyprain Ekwensi), *When Love Whispers*, the first book written by a non-white person I ever read. Hitherto, all the authors we read were white and dead. The second Nigerian author I read that made a great impression on me is Chinua Achebe, whose *Things Fall Apart* was published in 1958.

As a high school teacher, I began to write about my childhood in the boarding school. Then, one day, the story of Efuru struck me in a most dramatic way as I was driving at a speed of 80 miles per hour along Enugu-Onitsha Road. I got to my destination, borrowed an exercise book and began to write Efuru's story. I wrote chapter one ("They Saw Each Other") and I did not stop until I finished the entire novel. I gave it to Chinua Achebe, who kindly read it and sent it to his publishers, Heinemann Educational Books, London, that published it in 1966. I have become a writer. I asked myself: Do you want to be a writer? I was not sure. Before I could find answers, the critics had taken over: What was Flora Nwapa trying to do in *Efuru?* Did she succeed? The deed had already been done. I have become a writer. I racked my brain trying to figure out what exactly I was trying to do apart from writing the story of Efuru. All my thoughts led me to the African woman.

The woman's role in Africa is crucial for the survival and progress of the race. This is, of course, true of all women across the globe, be they black or white. In my work, I try to project a more balanced image of African womanhood. Male authors understandably neglect to point out the positive side of womanhood, for very many reasons which I will not attempt to discuss in this address. Recent changes in Nigeria—the 1967-1970 civil war, economic changes, and an emphasis on the education of women—have affected men's views about women. Women have started to redefine themselves; they have started to project themselves as they feel they should be presented.

More than anything else, I would like to give examples of the crucial roles that Igbo women play in their communities; for example, the powerful role of women as *Umuada* (all daughters born in a clan, married or not, and wherever they may be) in burial and title-taking ceremonies and in peace-making where they constitute the final court of appeal; the role of women as *Umunwunyeobu* (wives of the clan); women's various roles as priestesses and members of age-grades. Every member of *Umuada* knows where she belongs and what is expected of her. Members possess individual and group power but rarely act individually. No burial or title-taking ceremony is complete without the presence of *Umuada*, and woe betide any daughter who fails to show up in these ceremonies.

Peace-making is an important function of *Umuada, Umunwunyeobu*, and the women's age-grades. When there is a quarrel between husband and wife, parents and children, these groups of women are called upon to make peace. The role of the wives of the clan is very visible and considerable at home in terms of participating and intervening in their husbands' decision-making processes. If the women find out that their husbands are proving difficult and obstinate, they could take a far-reaching stand, the most common being the refusal to cook for or sleep with their husbands.

Priestesses feature prominently in many parts of Nigeria, especially in the riverine areas of the south. They wield tremendous power in many areas, including healing and predicting the future. As women, they mediate between the supernatural and natural worlds, between the divine (deities) and the human. Those of you who have read *Things Fall Apart* will remember Chielo, the mouthpiece of the oracle.

How do African literary texts project women? A few of them have tried to project an objective image of women, an image that actually reflects the reality of women's role in the society. Peter Abraham's *A Wreath for Udoma* and Sembène Ousmane's *God's Bits of Wood* recognize the "full and complete woman" and provide role models for the female readership. There are three prominent female characters in *A Wreath for Udoma*—Lois, Selina, and Maria. All three women are portrayed, not as victims of male subjugation in a patriarchal society, but as full woman-beings who take up their rightful positions in the society. These three women are the real power behind the struggle for independence. In Adebhoy's words, Selina is: "The real power behind us, homeboy. She tells all the women in all the villages what to tell their men, and the men do what the women tell them. Without her, we wouldn't have this party." Also in Ousmane Sembène's *God's Bits of Wood*, the success of the railway workers' strike is the handiwork of the women. They scout for food and water. They fight the police. They march on to Dakar, their sheer number breaking the power of the colonialists. After the strike, the men learned a hard lesson—i. e., never to tackle or undertake any major issues or projects without first consulting the women.

However, Nigerian male writers, such as Chinua Achebe, Cyprain Ekwensi, Wole Soyinka, J. P. Clark, and Elechi Amadi, have all in their earlier works played down the powerful role of women. Unlike Peter Abraham and Ousmane Sembène, Nigerian male writers have in many instances portrayed women negatively or in their subordination to men. Ekwensi's Jagua Nana is a prostitute; Wole Soyinka's Amope is a ceaselessly nagging woman who makes life intolerable for her husband. Achebe's Miss Mark does not hesitate to put her sex appeal to work in order to attain desired objectives. J. P. Clark's Ebiere entices her husband's younger brother into a sexual relationship. The focus has always been on the physical, prurient, negative nature of woman. Woman's subordinate position is redressed (somewhat) in the name given to the heroine of Achebe's *Anthills of the Savanah*, Nwanyibuife ("Woman is Something"—an assertion that women are a force to be reckoned with). The heroine, Beatrice Nwanyibuife, is a liberated and powerful woman, leading one to surmise that she symbolizes perhaps a sudden awakening to the importance of woman-being.

Yes, in African literature, there have been female portraits of sorts presented by men from their own point of view, leading one to conclude that there is a difference between the African male writer and his female counterpart. So what did I do in *Efuru?* In my two heroines, Efuru and Idu, I was inspired by the women around me when I was growing up. These women were not like Jagua Nana, Amope, Miss Mark, or Ebiere. They were solid and superior women who held their own in society. They were not only wives and mothers but successful traders who took care of their children and their husbands as well. They were very much aware of their leadership roles in their families as well as in the churches and local government. The models for Efuru and Idu were there—in real life—for me to exploit. In my first two novels, I tried to recreate the experiences of women in the traditional African society—their social and economic activities and above all their preoccupation with the problems of procreation, infertility, and child-rearing. Apart from exposing the pain, misery and humiliation which childless or barren women suffer in the traditional society, the two novels (I hope!) give insight into the resourcefulness and industriousness of women which often made them successful, respected, and influential people in the community. In these two novels, therefore, I tried to debunk the erroneous concept that the husband is the lord and master and that the woman is nothing but his property. I tried to debunk the notion that the woman is dependent on her husband. The woman not only holds her own, she is astonishingly *in*dependent of her husband.

So while some Nigerian male writers failed to see this power base, this strength of character, this independence, I tried in *Efuru* and *Idu* to elevate the woman to her rightful place. Unlike African male writers, I could overlook neither the safeguards with which custom surrounds the woman in her community nor the weight of women's opinions. I tried to analyze the woman's independent economic position and the power she wields by the mere fact that she controls the pestle and the cooking pots.

Efuru is the story of a beautiful, intelligent, hardworking, wealthy, and childless woman. Thus, both her stature and tragic dimension are carefully established from the very first few chapters of the novel. Yet, in spite of her handicap (childlessness), she attains a very high and respectable position in her community. No one could do anything about the luckless Efuru for she is already the chosen one of the Great Woman of the Lake; she is called late in life to be the priestess of the water goddess. By this choice, Efuru is elevated to a plane higher than that of human beings; she communicates with gods and goddesses. Similarly, in *Idu*, the protagonist, Idu, in the end does not kill herself, she simply dies preferring to join her dead husband in the spirit world.

The woman writer cannot fail to see the woman's power in her home and society. She sees her economic importance both as mother, farmer, and trader. *She writes stories that affirm the woman*, thus challenging the male writers and making them aware of woman's inherent vitality, independence of views, courage, self-confidence, and, of course, her desire for gain and high social status.

In Nigeria and other countries of Africa, there have been tremendous changes in all facets of life which contribute to the continent-wide awareness and rethinking of women's problems and roles in the society. These changes are affecting both men and women in many ways and creative writers are responding to them by recreating meaningfully women's culture and world-view in this age of female awakening and feminist consciousness. It is this new vision of women that I have striven to depict in my novels (*One is Enough, Women are Different, Never Again*) and short stories (*This is Lagos, Wives at War,* and *Cassava Song and Rice Song*). The thread that runs through these works is women's struggles for survival by whatever means as they respond to the tremendous changes in the society.

Cassava Song and Rice Song is an attempt to re-live in poetry the form and themes of English neo-classical poetry by poets such as Alexander Pope and John Dryden. Cassava is elevated to about the same height as, for example, the "lock" of Belinda, the beautiful lady in Alexander Pope's work, *Rape of the Lock*. Cassava is a staple food in Igboland. The Cassava tuber is accessible to both the rich and the poor in many parts of Nigeria and Africa. Cassava is planted by women, unlike yam, the "King of all Crops," that is planted by men. Every year in Igboland, the New Yam Festival is observed. New yam is not eaten until this festival is performed. But, is there a festival for Cassava? No. In "Cassava Song," the many uses of cassava are enumerated to show that she deserves to be celebrated and sung like the yam. In mock heroic style, "Cassava Song" opens with an invocation:

> We thank thee Almighty God
> For giving us Cassava
> We hail thee, Cassava
> The great Cassava

Cassava is personified as a Great Mother, a forgiving mother, more sinned against than sinning. Cassava is given the Divine Redeemer motif; like Christ who goes through suffering, Cassava remains obedient to fire even unto death. Cassava is enthroned above yam and cocoyam—above all other foodstuff. Cassava is woman. Yam is man.

In *Wives at War and Other Stories*, the story, "The Chief's Daughter," tells of the changing role of the woman in the society. A favorite daughter could be made by her father to remain single in order to have children to bear his name and continue the paternal lineage. The Chief's daughter, Adaeze, is about to return from the land of the white people when the story begins. The Chief is bent on not letting her get married. She rejects her father's plans and marries a man of her choice. In *This is Lagos and Other Stories*, "The Child Thief" is a story that depicts the trauma a woman faces when it dawns on her that she cannot have a child. In order to keep her marriage, she employs all kinds of deceit, and finally resorts to stealing a baby from the hospital. Amaka, the heroine of *One is Enough*, finds herself performing tasks considered to be men's jobs.

She becomes a contractor and attains economic independence. Because Amaka sees men as unreliable, she charts her own path to happiness and works hard so as to be in a position to live on her own terms.

Rose, Agnes and Dora in *Women Are Different* reflect their own spirit of liberation. They explode the myth of female passivity and docility and are blazing a new trail in female consciousness. It is true that this new radicalism has come after the women have been victimized and betrayed by their men. Victim of child marriage, Agnes is made to marry a man old enough to be her father; Dora's husband abandons her and her five children; Mark jilts Rose after exploiting her. This is also the experience of Amaka *(One is Enough)*, who, after eight years of a childless marriage, moves to Lagos determined that: "She would find fulfillment. She would find pleasure, even happiness in being a single woman. The erroneous belief that without a husband a woman was nothing must be disproved." In the case of Dora *(Women Are Different)*, her husband returns after a long absence but now she has acquired the strength and economic independence to dictate the terms of their renewed relationship.

The question I would like to ask is why these women become assertive and aggressive only after they have been brutalized or betrayed by their men. Are there no women in Africa today who can hold their own without waiting to be brutalized or betrayed? Are there no women in Africa today who can say:

To hell with men and marriage.
I don't want to have children.
I want to be free to do just as I please.

Perhaps the time has not yet come. Majority of the women in Africa live in the rural area. Many are uneducated, and there are not too many alternatives to being married and having children. The most natural thing for the rural woman is to marry and procreate. Even for us, the educated urbanites, the time has not come. We still have our roots in the rural areas where we were brought up. Our umbilical cord is still buried in the rural environment. We are the very few that are exposed to Western education. We have traveled in Europe and America, yet we are not Europeans and Americans. We are Africans. We have our ways of doing things; things like marriage, divorce, and motherhood. Marriage is a sacred bond that transcends a simple union between a man and a woman; it is a bond between two families. Therefore, a woman or indeed a man cannot divorce at will, but yet within this tradition, divorce is possible, though difficult when children are involved.

An educated Nigerian woman will not take her husband to court if he commits bigamy. It is true that bigamy is committed every day in Nigeria, but even the educated wife would hesitate to take action against her husband *for the sake of her children.* What would it profit the educated wife if her husband, the father of her children, were sentenced to prison on her own account? How does she explain it to her children? How would the society view her action? But it is interesting to note that the so-called rural woman, at least in my own community, has no such inhibitions. This is an area where the educated woman envies her rural sister. Is the latter more liberated in this regard? Some in-depth research is called for. So Dora *(Women Are Different)* goes out of her way to look for her wayward husband, and when he returns after many years, she throws a party to welcome him. She consoles herself with these words: "But I have the whip hand. I am not a fool. Now my children have a father. That's all that matters....and I have a husband. But it is not the same again...What is left now is stark reality and common sense."

African women writers have been accused of dwelling too much on barrenness. They are told by male critics to write on other "more important" themes. What *are* these other important themes? One of the panelists in this conference asked women writers to "project into the future the figure of a female president; fiction may lead to fact." In addition, a panelist said yesterday in his presentation, "Women are not only Africans but also women." True, the life of a man and that of a woman are interdependent. But then the problem that a woman faces in the world is the pain of not being able to bring forth a child from her womb, a feat no man can (yet) perform. The pain is great if she is denied this function and this is why the theme of barrenness is explored by many African writers, particularly the female ones. A wife is more often than not betrayed and abandoned by her husband if she does not have a child. Therefore, the desire to be pregnant, to procreate is an overpowering one in the life of the woman. She is ready to do anything to have a child, be she single or married.

The African woman writer is urged to break new ground by projecting the future of a female president. Does the woman writer live in an environment in which this is possible? My answer is yes. Because women's issues are very much alive in Africa today and various African governments are using women as resources in nation building. And it is left to the creative writers, male and female, to explore this new awareness, this new image of women's sensibilities, possibilities, and realities, and produce works which modern African women can relate to. Having said that, I must quickly add that we must not force issues on fiction. It is true that the woman writer has found a voice, but (one may ask) what kind of voice? Are we heard? Are we not sometimes completely ignored? Here we must thank our feminist sisters at home and abroad (America and Europe) who have made it possible for African critics to notice us. Projecting a female president can be achieved, why not? But she must be there for all to see. Anowa is there, Adah is there, Efuru is out there for all to see. I must reiterate the fact that this is not exclusively the task of African women writers, but also that of the male writers.

My conclusion on this issue of barrenness is that women are what they are because they can give life, they can procreate. So in African societies, when this unique function is denied a woman, she is devastated. But should this be so, all the time, in this day and age? Does this handicap, this childlessness make a woman less woman, less human? I do not think so. Efuru finds fulfillment by becoming the priestess of the water goddess. Therefore, we *should* create characters that are fulfilled and not weighed down by the shackles of marriage and motherhood. But, of course, there are choices; there are choices in the African environment itself. There must be choices because this handicap, childlessness, does not make a woman less a woman or less human.

In my novels, I explore the theme of moral laxity, but this is treated in response to earlier novels written by men where prostitution is always associated with women. Some of the most notable prostitutes are Jagua Nana of Ekwensi's *Jagua Nana*; Simi of Soyinka's *The Interpreters*; and Wanja of Ngugi's *Petals of Blood*. But in my novels there is a reversal of roles—men are the prostitutes. In *Women Are Different*, Chris, Dora's husband, is a male prostitute, kept by a German woman. Ernest, Rose's former boyfriend, goes from one woman to another without finding satisfaction. Mark is a kept man; he lives with Rose whom he exploits by duping her of hundreds of pounds before deserting her. Olu's sexual adventures take him through numerous affairs in several cities but he always goes back to his wife after each affair. In these novels, women have the upper hand; they are more forthcoming and in control. Dora claims that she "has the whip hand" after her husband returns to her. Amaka is in control in her relationship with the Alhaji and the Reverend Fr. Maclaid. The men have lost initiative, always on the move, finding it impossible to settle down anywhere.

Again, I am asserting that a woman is also flesh and blood. She has a heart and soul and she is capable of human feelings. She can stand on her own two feet just as a man can. But I think that women should have an open mind about relationships with men. I also think that women writers should not only have an open mind but create avenues for this openness of mind. Our task should be to exploit elements of our indigenous traditions —such as democracy, tolerance, sharing, and mutual support —in order to achieve our goal. The fact that one man betrays and brutalizes you does not mean that another will do the same. There should be interdependence and some measure of understanding which blossoms to mutual respect and equality. Did I say equality? Yes, because the lives of a man and a woman are interdependent, there must be mutual understanding and respect. The African woman writer has a great responsibility now and in the future, but can she alone champion the cause? A man can portray a powerful heroine as well as a woman can if he sets his mind to it and if he does not feel that portraying a strong heroine makes him less of a man. As earlier pointed out, Peter Abraham and Ousmane Sembène, in their respective novels, gave a truer and more balanced portrayal of the African women.

The Women's Movement inside and outside Africa as well as the various Women's Studies programs in African, North American, and European universities have created awareness among our own African critics. The voice of the African woman writer is being heard, though somewhat inaudibly. A lot still needs to be done. The global recession is causing a lot of havoc in Africa. What cost us one naira to produce ten years ago, costs a hundred now. With the support of our American and European sisters and our men, we (African women) shall succeed.

WORKS CITED

Abrahams, Peter. *A Wreath for Udoma*. New York: Alfred Knopf, 1956.

Achebe, Chinua. *Things Fall Apart*. London: Heinemann, 1958.

——. *Anthills of the Savannah*. New York: Anchor, 1987.

Ekwensi, Cyprain. *When Love Whispers*. Onitsha: Tabansi Bookshop, 1950.

——. *Jagua Nana*. London: Hutchinson, 1961.

Nwapa, Flora. *Efuru*. London: Heinemann, 1966.

——. *Idu*. London: Heinemann, 1970.

——. *This Is Lagos and Other Stories*. Enugu: Nwankwo-Ifejika, 1971.

——. *Never Again*. Enugu: Nwamife, 1975; Trenton, N.J.: Africa World Press, 1992.

——. *Wives at War and Other Stories*. Enugu: Tana Press, 1980; Trenton, N.J.: Africa World Press, 1992.

——. *One Is Enough.* Enugu: Tana Press, 1981; Trenton, N.J.: Africa World Press, 1992.

——. *Women Are Different.* Enugu: Tana Press, 1986; Trenton, N.J.: Africa World Press, 1992.

——. *Cassava Song and Rice Song.* Enugu: Tana Press, 1986.

Pope, Alexander. *Rape of the Lock.* London: Lane, 1902.

Sembène, Ousmane. *God's Bits of Wood,* trans., Francis Price. Garden City, N.Y.: Anchor Books, 1970.

Soyinka, Wole. *The Interpreters.* New York: Africana Publishing Corp., 1972.

wa Thiong'o, Ngugi. *Petals of Blood.* New York: Dutton, 1978.

FEMALE POWER: WATER PRIESTESSES OF THE ORU-IGBO[1]

SABINE JELL-BAHLSEN

THE FACETS OF WOMANHOOD AND EMPOWERMENT IN Africa are subtle, complex, esoteric, and multidimensional; power balance in gender relations differs from the conventional one-dimensional Western paradigm. Therefore, openness to a completely new definition of basic concepts, such as time, divinity, nature, power, etc. is necessary if we are to grasp the modalities for power distribution in African society at the political, village, and household levels, and in gender relations.[2] This paper on priestesses takes a close look at the ethnographic details of one particular culture and a specific location, rather than venture into a comparative overview of priestesses in different societies.[3] Moreover, it will focus on women who hold offices in an African traditional religion, as opposed to Christianity or Islam.[4] At the center of this discussion are priestesses of the Goddess *Ogbuide*, and other local water deities among the Oru-Igbo of southeastern Nigeria with particular emphasis on the town of Orsu-Obodo/Oguta where I lived for one year (1978–1979), and to which I have returned many times since for visits of various lengths. An appreciation of these traditional priestesses' work and of their social and ritual positions may help shed new light on our conceptualization of female power. My discussion of the Water Goddess priesthood connects to the discourse on power, rather than to interpretations of female ritual leadership and Shamanism as merely a form of compensation for the oppressed.[5] With this presentation I hope to demonstrate the validity of cultural strategies developed in Africa that can be regarded as historical alternatives[6] to Western notions of gender relations.

Until recently, the literature about Africa was largely shaped by the ideas of Europeans who have invented their own images of Africa.[7] These notions and images of African peoples, societies, institutions, religious beliefs, and artistic expressions were really concerned not with African identities, but with cultural samples related to European theories, European history, and European political and economic interests and ideas (e.g., Primitive Art).[8] Colonial administrators did not expect (and therefore did not see) women in charge of ritual and political leadership (i.e., female power) in Africa and, consequently, grossly misinterpreted two areas of African culture[9]—"power" and "women."

POWER

Because the conventional literature on Africa is largely either colonial or derived from that experience, it defines precolonial distributions of power in Africa on European terms. European countries themselves were either monarchies or fascist states, or had just gone through chaotic phases of revolutions and wars at the turn of and early in the 20th century. Consequently, European writers of that time projected their own experiences on Africa by viewing African power structures as male-dominated, monolithic, unidirectional, and one- dimensional. These models describe either secular or sacred rulers, autocratic or diffuse power schemes, absolute dominance or anarchy.[10] While these images have served their own political and economic ends, e.g., conquest and "indirect rule," they failed at several important levels:

(1) to realize the importance and value attached to balance in Africa, and especially to the balancing of multiple powers as opposed to the vertical hierarchical power structure that is more prevalent in Western societies;[11]

(2) to account for the multiple dimensions of power and the subtleties of African power-play;

(3) to recognize the deeply democratic and religious nature of precolonial Igbo society, where power was neither absent nor absolute, but constantly negotiated;

(4) to recognize the intangible, immaterial attributes of power; and

(5) to acknowledge the female component of power.

WOMEN

Outside accounts of women in Africa typically follow the same colonial pattern: either describing promiscuous dominators of men, or mutilated near-slaves, helplessly sold or pushed around, and breeding children out of control.[12] The images of victimized African women cherished by foreigners create divisions among Africans, antagonize women against men, aim at assimilation, and above all, serve to justify the imposition of European and American ethics, educational perspectives, leadership goals, goods, etc. on the African continent and her peoples.[13] Moreover, these inventions of Africa and her peoples sharply contrast with a growing body of writings by African women and men,[14] as well as with my own observations and findings during many stays in and around Oguta over the past fifteen years.

THE ORU-IGBO

The Oru are a group of towns along Oguta lake and the rivers Njaba and Urash. They belong to the riverine Igbo—a group that includes Oguta, Onitsha, and Omoko. Oguta is the largest and most prominent of the Oru towns today. Because of their geographical location, the lake and rivers play an important role in the economies of the Oru towns. Before the construction of roads, rivers provided the most important means of transportation, communication, and trading between networks controlled by women. Both the fertility of the fields and the continuous supply of fish depend on the water level. Though not always predictable, the annual flood determines the cycle of the planting season, marked by major festivals. The economic importance of the waters is paralleled by the supreme cultural importance attached in Oru tradition to the volatile gods and goddesses of the lake, rivers, and creeks.

THE WOMAN AS GODDESS IN IGBO COSMOLOGY

The starting point for our discussion is the divine woman in Igbo cosmology. An understanding of the divine aspect of womanhood is a precondition for illuminating the powers of women who are priestesses of African deities. In Igbo cosmology, as in real life, the contributions of women and men are known to be complementary in creation, pro-creation, and ensuring of human existence. Female elements, such as water spirits, have a very special place in Igbo cosmology, not only with regard to the creation and procreation, but

also for the circular flow of time, reincarnation, challenge, and inno-
vation: both— women and water spirits—are perceived as mobile,
fluid, and slippery. They are at the crossroads of the ordinary and
the extraordinary, of spirits and humans, life and death. In this
regard, two important cosmological aspects of womanhood emerge
in Igbo art and literature:

(1) *The complementarity of male and female* for creation, procreation,
growth, and the continuity of life is symbolized in the complementary use of the colors red and white,[15] endless repetition of a snake
or zig-zag-line motif,[16] the imagery of mature female beauty, and the
depiction of a divine pair embodying balance. The Water goddess,
Ava, near Nsukka is believed to give fertility and children. Her shrine
symbolizes the concept of balance, as the Goddess is represented
together with a male in a sculpture representative of the divine pair.
This idea of complementary duality is captured by the Igbo proverb,
"when something stands, something else stands besides it."[17]

(2) *The extraordinary power of women* is encapsulated in the notion
of the supreme mother at the crossroads of life and death.[18] This
power is expressed in white chalk, the color white, and the circular
python. White is the sacred color of the Water Goddess, *Ogbuide.*
The white chalk drawing of a circle by the *Owu Mmiri,* a water priest
and healer in Egbema, symbolizes the python, signaling death, and
representing eternity, circular time, and transition. This image is
also associated with long, uncut hair, uncultivated, natural beauty,
and the theme of a Mother-Water Goddess.[19]

The divine Mother Water-Goddess is imperial in challenging or
confirming one's destiny: she is not only present, but also pivotal
for one's entry into and exit from this world. The divine woman is
believed to be an eternal, intrinsic, and ruling part of our very
nature, our existence, our life course and destiny. In her book, *The
World of the Ogbanje,* Chinwe Achebe[20] outlines Igbo cosmology and
the place in it of *Nne Mmiri* (popularly known as *Mammy Water*), the
divine Mother and Water Goddess.

> The Supreme God responsible for the being of the Igbo peo-
> ple is *Chi Ukwu, Chukwu,* sometimes called *Anyanwu* and lives
> in the sky.... *Chi Ukwu* is so great that it works through the
> agency of many lesser deities to fulfill its purpose. These
> deities are less autonomous, yet function interdependently.
> They are all, in the final analysis, subject to the superinten-
> dence of *Chi Ukwu.* Only three such agents, *Nne Mmiri,* pop-
> ularly known as *Mami Wota, Onabuluwa,* and *Chi* are of

immediate relevance to this study and will be focused on.... *Nne Mmiri* is a female deity with variants of local names, e.g., *Idemili*. She is the mother of a group of water spirit beings who journey to and fro the land of the living and the dead. Her abode and empire is the water. Her life begins and ends there.... With the arrival of Europeans to this part of the world, *Nne Mmiri* became known as *Mami Wota* —a translation which enables the local inhabitants to communicate the existence and exploits of this female deity to foreigners.[21]

The Igbo supreme God is *Chi Ukwu*, or *Chukwu*, the great *chi*. As in many African religions, the supreme Being is beyond shape and gender.[22] *Chukwu* is also known as the God of Destiny. When the yet-to-be-born individual receives her[23] life and personal *chi* from God, she makes a commitment, witnessed by God, about her personal destiny and course of life on earth.

In the Igbo world view outlined by Achebe,[24] the individual must cross a river before entering and exiting this world. Because the concept of time is circular, she must cross a river twice—not only once, as in the crossing of the river *Styx* at death, in ancient Greek mythology. When crossing the river to enter life on earth, the individual is challenged either by the Water Goddess, *Nne Mmiri, Mammy Water,* or by the Earth Goddess of the wild bush, *Onabuluwa*. At this point, the individual's destiny, *akaraka*, and her sacred pact with the supreme God is at stake. The person may either defend her destiny or change its course by forming a pact with the mother Water Goddess. This not only alters one's life and destiny, it also dedicates the person to the Goddess as Her devotee. If the individual later tries to evade both her destiny and the Goddess' claim, by refusing to conform to either her original destiny or the Goddess's demands for the fulfillment of her requirements, he/she may suffer illness, mental derangement, repeated loss of children and/or husbands, and eventually premature death.[25] At death, a person's *chi* returns to the Sky God, *Chi-ukwu*. The individual is eventually reborn, although not with the same *chi*. Before reincarnating, the new person must again confront the Goddess to sort out her destiny. After birth, it must be determined who reincarnated the new born.[26]

The Water Goddess and other associated deities and spirits in Igbo cosmology embody the female element crucial for creation, procreation, birth, life, death, reincarnation, and the perpetual cycle of time. The patriarchal ideology, linear concept of time, power, and inheritance patterns introduced and reinforced in colonial times and today through the agents of imported religious beliefs and practices contradict the precolonial concept of gender.

PATRILINEAGES AND THE DIFFERENT TYPES OF PRIESTHOOD

Igbo society revolves around multifunctional, patrilineal village-kindreds, the *umunna*. But despite these patrilineal structures, women held religious offices just as men. Even those women who did not hold permanent offices played important complementary roles in precolonial ritual activities and continue to do so in many ways. There is a host of priesthood titles and leadership positions available to both men and women. The Western distinction between categories of leadership, e.g. political and religious, does not always conform to the African arrangement where one person can be an elder, a political leader, priest, diviner, healer, artist, spouse, parent, farmer, fisherman, or trader, at different times or simultaneously. Positions can change according to age, situations, and circumstances. Although each person's identity derives from his/her place in the society and is provided personal security within the kinship, nothing can be taken for granted, nothing is permanent. Women who move out of their parental home are particularly mobile, due to the exogamous nature of marriage. The people of Oguta could take political power away from an Obi (male ruler) and endow another lineage with this inherited title;[27] a once-powerful priestess could suddenly be ignored by the town's oldest women by their refusing to ferry her across the lake; women can challenge and change the verdict of the male council of elders in a murder case; and the testimony of a nine-year-old girl can have a decisive impact.[28] Power—political, economic, personal, esoteric, religious, etc.—is negotiated.[29] Even though a person may be entitled to a position through inheritance, the title (male or female) associated with that position must still be achieved by the individual. In addition, for individual achievement and merit to be fully valid, they must be recognized as such by the community. The openness that enables women to acquire important religious positions and the social status associated with it is due, in part, to the general importance attached to achievement, merit, and title taking in Igbo society.

There are four basic types of priesthood and leadership. An outline of these positions will contribute to our understanding of the position and significance of the water priestesses.

(1) *Priesthood and Leadership Based on Kinship*

This form of "part-time" priesthood is inherited and has male and female positions.

The Male Position of *Okpara* or *Ajie*

The lineage's oldest man, the *okpara,* is entitled to serve the lineage's ancestral and other shrines as a consequence of his membership, maleness, and senior rank in the patrilineage, *umunna,* that owns the shrines.[30] These shrines are bound to their owners and located either in a specific compound, a village square, or a particular piece of farm land, river bank, or bush. In addition to the preconditions defined by the ownership of a shrine, the elder must fulfill certain requirements and perform special rites to become fully installed as a titled *ajie.* His wand of office *(ofo),*whose curse is believed to be deadly, symbolizes ancestral authority. While acting as a priest on special occasions, the elder leads a normal life. Because of his religious authority and closeness to the ancestors, the lineage elder can settle conflicts among the men within his compound or lineage. In addition, he may or may not assume judicial and/or political functions in the town's council of elders and beyond. With very few exceptions, this inherited priesthood and accompanying ritual ceremonies, as well as the secular leadership and authority associated with the male titles, are confined in space and limited to a particular lineage, compound, village, or farm shrine.

The Female Position of *Umuada*

The oldest women of a lineage have collective powers paralleling that of the lineage's oldest man. As lineage sisters, the *umuada,* they are endowed with religious and judicial authority. Their activities are largely secret and they mediate between the living and the dead in funeral rites and other serious events on all levels of society.[31] The *umuada* can come to the assistance of any lineage member, male of female, anywhere. Few people, if any, would dare to challenge the *umuada,*whose curse is feared. They settle disputes between lineage daughters wherever they may be. Because these daughters of the clan are married out of their natal lineages into families in the town and beyond, the authority of the *umuada* transcends the confines of compound, lineage, and village. In precolonial times, they wielded political powers.[32] Even today, the *umuada* can intercede with the town's male council of elders on behalf of any (male or female) member of their own lineage.[33]

(2) *Female Priesthood Based on Marital Status*

The *umunwanyi,* the wives of a patrilineage, have an institution paralleling the senior man. The senior woman of a lineage is entitled to lead the other wives of her husband's lineage in ritual; her status is based on seniority by virtue of the length of time she has been married into the group, not on actual age. Like her male counterpart, she acts as a priestess on certain occasions, but otherwise leads a normal life. There are stark contrasts between some of the rituals performed under the leadership of this woman, as opposed to those performed by the male lineage elder. The most striking differences are (a) the secrecy of the female events that strictly exclude men, and (b) the difference in the conceptualization of space. While a male priest serves only one particular shrine at a time (e.g., that of his ancestors) and the rituals performed under his leadership are location- specific, the lineage wives' rituals are mobile. Their priestess leads her group of women on a journey covering a wide area and many shrines.34 In addition to her religious functions, the senior wife is also in charge of settling disputes among the other women married into her husband's lineage. In view of the fact that lineage wives come from different natal lineages, the authority of the senior co - wife, like that of *umuada*, transcends lineage boundaries.

(3) *Female Priesthood Based on Age, the Eze Nwanyi*

The town's oldest woman is the *Eze Nwanyi*, the queen of the women. Together with her assistants, she performs certain highly secretive rituals during the New Year festival, *Agugu*,[35] and also during the New Yam festival, *Omerife*. Due to her religious importance and authority, the *Eze Nwanyi* can be called upon to settle disputes both among women and among men and women on all levels of society. She is called upon to deal with serious conflicts involving women, wife abuse, etc. The *Eze Nwanyi* protects female interests and she can impose fines (e.g., against a husband, who must abide by her decision). Even though the *Eze Nwanyi* has no physical power to enforce decisions, her verdict is binding, as her curse is believed to be deadly.[36] Her sacred power extends to the secular. Her position, power, and authority are independent of her lineage affiliation, and are instead based on religious beliefs, age, and gender. Her position was also a political one in precolonial days, but these political functions were largely destroyed in favor of the male position of the *Eze Igwe* or *Obi* during colonial times.[37] While the *Obi* was on the colonial payroll as a "native ruler," the women's leader, *Eze Nwanyi*, was not and is still not paid.

(4) *Water Priestess, Eze Mmiri, Water Monarch, or Eze Nwanyi, Queen of the Women* [38]

The priesthood of the Water Goddess and her associates comes through possession, vocation, or inheritance. A person can be called into the service of a water deity and be asked to build a shrine for her, irrespective of kinship affiliation. The Water Goddess priesthood through possession is open to both men women, irrespective of kin group affiliation, age, or marital status. Possession or spirit-calling may lead to full-time devotion to the Water Goddess, or to any of her partners or children. The priestess's title is *Eze Mmiri* (Water Monarch) or *Eze Nwanyi* (Female Ruler/Queen of the Women). Both titles are also given to the Water Goddess herself. The water priestess's male counterpart is the *Eze Ugo* (Crowned King) or the *Owu Mmiri* (in Egbema). Not every water priestess necessarily has a male counterpart, or a male assistant, and there are also some male water priests operating on their own. In part because it is full-time and comes about through spirit-calling or possession, this type of priesthood is very powerful and highly regarded. As a sign of her priestly authority, a water priestess can have an *ofo*. This is the only case I have ever encountered in Igboland of a woman holding an *ofo*, the ultimate symbol of authority. A fully titled water priestess also adorns her red cap with a white eagle's feather, symbol of power. The positions of water priestesses have survived the colonial assault. Although their religious titles are contested by the churches, water priestesses are still highly regarded as healers. They often attend to mental problems associated with individual conflicts resulting from the multiple destructions, antagonisms, and losses created by colonial and postcolonial confrontations.

The ritual and political involvement of women in general and of female priesthood and leadership in particular was an important aspect of precolonial Igbo society that was not recognized during colonial times. Because the male elders of a lineage act as its visible agents, they were recognized as the lineage's representatives. Because vital female rituals are highly secretive and exclusive, male elders commonly appear to outsiders as the dominant agents in charge of resource management, preservation of the custom, maintenance of social order, religious practices, and mediation between human and spirit worlds. Against this background, social structuralists, functionalists, and Marxists have all emphasized the gender-based social division of labor and ignored women's ritual and political involvement.[39] The non-recognition of female priesthood and other expressions of female leadership relegated women to the background. In addition, women's power is further eroded by the imposition of Christian and Islamic values and the lack of attention to African religious beliefs and practices.[40] Moreover, Western-style structural inequalities and elitism in contemporary African soci-

eties and economies continue to erode previously established positions of power held by women.

IGBO WOMEN'S RITUAL AND POLITICAL ACTIVITIES DURING COLONIAL TIMES AND BEYOND

M. M. Green[41] gives a vivid account of women's daily lives and ritual activities during colonial times. Green's research was originally
commissioned by the colonial administration after the Igbo
Women's War of 1929. While the colonial regime preferred to refer
to the war as "riots," elderly Igbo women themselves speak of their
"war" (*ogu*).[42] At that time, thousands of women protested the imposition of taxes on women and confronted the colonial resident.
According to one of the few surviving written reports, handwritten
(and, until recently, classified) by the colonial officer then in charge,
over ten thousand nude and unarmed women were gunned down
with machine guns in one incident alone.[43] Although the officer
attests that the women were nude and adorned only with young
palm fronds, he admits ordering his machine gun division to fire
at the women.

In Igboland, young palm fronds traditionally signal ritual activity, spirit involvement, and danger. The women who were shot
apparently acted not only as warriors, but also as ritual specialists—
signaled by the palm fronds—on behalf of the entire population.[44]
Some women who participated in the Igbo Women's War of 1929
are still alive today, and there are several accounts of that event.[45]
However, much information about this atrocious violence against
African women and about their actions is lost because most of the
colonial reports on the Igbo Women's War of 1929 are either "offi-
cially destroyed," or classified until after the year 2000. The surviving victims, participants, and eye witnesses are now at least in their
eighties.

From the few accounts available, it appears that the colonial
administrators were unable to grasp the ritual significance of the
women's political activities. This failure is understandable only
against the background of the Western conceptual distinction
between "political" and "ritual," a distinction that cannot be automatically applied to non-European cultures. When confronting the
Igbo women warriors in 1929, European men could think only of
a profane act of resistance and ignored the war's religious and cultural dimensions. Even today, scholars wonder why the women, and

not the men, went to war against colonial impositions. Obviously, the numerous accounts of the war that focus on the economic impetus for and implications of the war cannot imagine women in charge of a holy war—i.e., a war not only against economic and political oppression, but also against a foreign assault on the entire world view, the religion, cosmology, and spiritual life of a people. Today, some of the women's rituals, such as "Sitting on a Man" described by Van Allen,[46] may be lost, but other female rituals and strategies have survived. But these female ritual activities cannot be categorized in Western terms as either secular or profane. The ritual activities and positions of Igbo women (and men) are multi-functional. Sometimes the political aspect prevails, at other times the esoteric. Religious rituals can respond simultaneously both to health needs and to the requirements of managing the environment and natural resources.[47]

Most important for our current discussion is the fact that despite all the invasion and oppression brought upon Igboland, the ritual activities involving women are still—i.e., to this day—perceived as an intrinsic part of Igbo custom, *omenala* (how things are done on the land) or the laws of the Earth Goddess, and thus critical to ensuring a town's very existence, continuity, life, and prosperity. Two major manifestations of female power are still evident today:

(1) Every important ritual event at the town, village, or household level has a decisive female component. Most of these female rites are highly secretive, easily slipping an outsider's attention. Their secrecy is an indication of their power, spirit involvement, and danger. Male and female ritual activities are markedly different and complementary: e.g., while the women's rites offered to the earth goddess and other farm, water, and bush spirits for the planting season are highly mobile and innovative, the men's performance of rites is more location-specific, limited in space, and conservative.[48] During the town's major festivals, New Year and New Yam, the female elders' rituals, performed in the middle of the night under the leadership of the *Eze Nwanyi*, are pivotal, exclusive, and elusive. Even the more obvious "public" male performances, including a masquerade, cannot take place unless the women do their part. Male and female events follow each other step by step.[49] Once planting has begun, the men of each lineage perform a ritual without their wives for the Earth Goddess at her shrine. The women then perform a daytime ritual that covers many shrines and deities and a vast area of farm land. No male, not even a male child, is allowed to participate. Apart from these special festivals and events, women

ordinarily partake in all rituals at the kin-group, village, and town levels. Like their male counterparts, women act collectively as members of culturally defined, gender-specific bodies such as *umuada* (lineage daughters), *nwanwa* (children of *umuada*), *umunwanyi* or *umuenyi* (wives of the lineage), or age-grades. Whenever an adult or an elder dies, women's ritual importance is displayed and re-enforced during elaborate funeral rites. These events and performances are fiercely contested by the churches.[50]

(2) Some women attain extraordinary ritual and leadership status through spirit-calling. These women, known as "water priestesses," are extremely powerful, respected, and held in awe. A group of followers of the water priestess is called the *Otu Eze Nwanyi* (the queen's group), or *Ndi Mmiri* (water people).

THE WATER PRIESTESS (*EZE MMIRI*) AND HER FOLLOWERS (*NDI MMIRI*)

Mammy Water priests and priestesses can be of any age. Their dedication to ritual leadership and partial celibacy often begins at the time of marriage or younger. Full-time devotion to the Water Goddess differentiates the priestesses who are possessed or spiritually called from those who become (part-time) priestesses or ritual leaders through lineage membership, marital status, or seniority.[51] In addition, the widely recognized water priestesses are also reputable diviners and healers consulted for a wide range of problems including barrenness, emotional problems, lack of fortune, and witchcraft.

There are many female and some male water priests among the Oru. Because of the prominence of women in this position, we will generally use the female term, priestess, although some of our observations can also be applied to men. A successful water priestess draws a large group of followers and supporters. The majority of these followers are women but there are also child-members. Many are former patients of the priestess. They meet regularly every four days (Igbo market week).[52]

A woman may join a group of water worshippers and thereby gain access to special esoteric knowledge and ritual performance for her own personal reasons, or on behalf of her child. This is evident in the following account given by a young mother:

> Three months after the baby was born, his hair started to coil. Each time we tried to comb his hair, he caught fever. He had a big fever. One of his legs and one of his hands

died. We went to a diviner. He told us that the baby should be called *Urash* because he is reincarnated by [the river god] *Urash*. We had failed to call the baby *Urash* and given him another name instead. Therefore, *Urash* wanted to take the baby away from us. When we found out what was wrong with the child, we took him to the water priestess, *Eze Mmiri*. We bought everything she said and offered a sacrifice to *Urash*. From then on, we started calling the baby *Urash*. *Eze Mmiri* treated the baby and he got better. My child's illness made me join *Eze Mmiri's* water society.[53]

By mediating between the human and the spiritual, the water priestess responds to the needs of any villager or stranger who may call on her for help. Cases involving fertility, birth, illness, death, and questions regarding reincarnation and naming[54] are referred to the priests and priestesses of the local waters by diviners. In this highly male/female segregated society, women seem to prefer conferring with women, while men seem to relate better to men. However, a recognized priestess/ diviner/ healer is consulted by many clients, irrespective of gender.

DIVINATION

The Igbo universe is complex; it is inhabited and controlled by various forces including the supreme god, *Chukwu*, a pantheon of lesser divinities and nature spirits, ancestors, and human beings. Some of these forces are more conservative and location- specific, and their representatives aim at preserving and perpetuating local customs. These forces include the ancestors, the supreme Earth Goddess, *Ani/Ala*, and, by extension, the male elders. Other forces and divinities are more innovative, fluid, and challenging; they renew and invigorate custom and tradition: these are the Water Goddess, water spirits,[55] certain nature spirits, and, by extension, water priestesses.

Human beings must constantly negotiate and balance these different forces, powers, and interests in a world that is not always transparent to humans. To make things even more complicated, there are massive changes taking place in the aftermath of the colonial period, due to church interference and other modern political, social, and economic transformations that resulted in the destabilization of the previously established order of things.[56]

A powerful water priestess is also a good diviner. Diviners are mediators between human beings and the spirit world. They interpret the cosmological forces and their signs to their clients and assist them to sort out their lives, cope with individual problems, and deal with questions ranging from the causes of illness, sudden changes of fate, business decisions, partner choice, child naming, and much more. In psychological terms, diviners could be regarded as therapists helping the individual deal with his/her life. The diviner's spiritual involvement and esoteric character endow her with a special position, recognition, and respect in this deeply religious society. The water deities are perceived as volatile and unpredictable, much like contemporary life. Some priestesses serving these forces seem particularly capable of interpreting these challenges and of guiding people in their daily struggles. A priestess's power is mental and psychological, rather than physical. But, as a diviner and a healer, she can have an immediate impact on her client's spiritual and physical well-being. A priestess's personal skill and her client's improvement and success enhance her recognition, social status, and power. Based on her esoteric and practical knowledge and her success, a water priestesse can become a very powerful woman, highly respected not only by her clients, but also by the entire town and beyond.

HEALING

On one level, all physical or mental disorders are regarded as social disorders, caused either by individual spirits or by an imbalance in the "essential unity of personal, social and natural domains of Beings."[57] There is no rigid dividing line between body and mind, physical and spiritual well-being. Though distinct entities, body and mind are merged in life.[58] Healers are at the same time ritual leaders, attending to both the spiritual and the physical needs of their clients. When the personal balance of body and mind is disturbed, a man or a woman may break with social norms, such as marriage arrangements. This anti-social and often destructive behavior is locally interpreted as a form of "mental disorder" requiring healing by a "native doctor." The priests and priestesses of the local water deities are very widely recognized healers, highly successful in treating what we would call mental disorders. A priestess may reconcile an individual with her personal *chi* (her destiny) and with local customs. The healer-priestess channels spirit possessions and thereby heals the individual by restoring her personal balance. The techniques involved in the healing process are complex. These therapies combine artistic expressions, dances, ritual performances, religious beliefs, and psychological and group factors, as well as herbal medicines. A healer-priestess may turn a former patient into

an initiate and apprentice of religious worship and the art of healing. During the course of healing and initiation, the patient regains
her psychic, social, and cosmic balance. An ex-patient may ultimately become a ritual leader.

Individual Vocation to Water Spirit
Worship and Priesthood

A personal crisis—emotional, physical, or social—invariably appears
as a precondition for water spirit involvement, initiation, and ultimately priesthood and healership. This is evident from many interviews and life histories of the priests and priestesses of the Water
Deities,[59] and also from Nigerian literature. The women, Efuru and
Idu, are the main characters, respectively, of two early novels by
Flora Nwapa.[60] Although fictitious, the two characters are inspired
by real-life women of Oguta, Flora Nwapa's home. Efuru at first
revolts against marriage practices prevalent in Oguta,[61] but both
women suffer hardships and emotional pain in the course of their
lives, their marriages, their losses of children and husbands. In
Europe they might be tragic characters. Instead, both women find
compensation, solace, and strength through their devotion to the
Lake Goddess, *Ogbuide*. They become followers of *Ogbuide*, but both
novels end where the heroine's new life begins. Not too surprisingly,
this theme of personal crisis, emotional suffering, and healing as
preconditions for empowerment through the water worship is
echoed in the following personal account of a real priestess, a widely recognized diviner and successful healer :

> Every person has his or her own destiny, *akaraka*, in the world.
> I wedded in the church before *Mammy Water* came to me.
> When I was small, whenever I went to the stream, I saw some-
> body in the water. When I went fishing with my friends, I would
> catch more fish than anyone else. I didn't know why. When I
> went to the water on *Orie* day, I fell down. When I got married,
> my destined husband [the river God], *Urash* came and asked
> me why I left him and married another person.... I saw the
> *Mammy Water* always, even when I was with my husband. I mar-
> ried in the church, but *Urash* seized control of me so that I will
> help the world. My husband spent money on my treatment. I
> did not know what to do. When I was cooking soup for my
> husband, I put salt in the fire and wood in the pot. Every night
> the spirits took me to the bush. They showed me leaves that
> will kill and leaves that will cure. They asked me to do good

not bad. I lost eleven children. But *Chineke* was kind and gave me so many. *Uhammiri [Ogbuide]* and *Urash* you have helped me. I married [another wife] for my husband and she gave me children. I earn money to feed the children.[62]

It is generally believed that it is not easy for a man to be married to a woman possessed by a water spirit. Unknowingly marrying a girl already betrothed to a water deity may even be dangerous. Elechi Amadi's *The Concubine*[63] and many other Nigerian novels and tales tell of extraordinarily beautiful and highly desirable women who are barren, bear children who always die, and bring misfortune or even death to the men who dare marry them. These extraordinary women are believed to be destined not to marry ordinary men, because they "were already married to a water God." On one level, extraordinary women may be perceived as dangerous for men. But they are also highly desirable, often very beautiful, knowledgeable, creative, and successful in business. They are an asset to their husband and may marry additional wives for him, or become founders and heads of their own lineages.[64]

I. M. Lewis and others have suggested that Shamanism and other forms of ecstatic religion are primarily an outlet for the oppressed.[65] Thus, through such cultic involvement, women could attain status equal to men's, play leadership roles, and gain access to power, wealth, or other sources of authority not readily available to women in ordinary life. This would suggest that ritual leadership, possession, and water spirit priesthood primarily compensate a woman for losses and difficulties suffered in life. However, the theory of compensation does not explain a lot of occurrences and activities such as: (1) why Igbo women were in charge of the war in 1929; (2) women's customary ritual involvement on all levels of society; (3) why a woman finds it necessary to join a water society in order to save her child's life; (4) why water spirit possession is explained as a person's destiny, *akaraka,* a concept deeply rooted in Igbo cosmology and religious beliefs (as evidenced in the work of Uchendu, Achebe, and others).

As Flora Nwapa has pointed out,[66] it is difficult for women of all societies to combine the rearing of small children with a business or professional career. In Oguta, the desire to make money through trading (on the one hand) and the desire to raise many children (on the other) may be mutually exclusive, or at least create a lot of pressure on a woman. The same contradiction poses a problem for ambitious women everywhere who want to be successful both professionally and as a mother/wife. While this can easily have dire consequences in a Western setting, water spirit involvement appears as an alternative strategy alleviating pressure and providing empowerment for Oru Igbo women. The worship of the goddess *Ogbuide* provides women (and other innovative and enterprising individuals) with a special space, recognition, and accepted freedom within their own society that transcend ordinary constraints. Some water worshippers reserve their bodies for their deity, practicing sexual abstinence on every fourth day. They also enjoy other privileges, e.g. meeting in the priestess's house to relax in her cool yard and escape their daily chores and other pressures on every fourth day. The water worshippers encourage, reaffirm, and psychologically strengthen each other. Water worshippers may at times appear unusual and behave differently from ordinary citizens, but this is accepted and respected because of their special status gained through religious devotion and group membership.

While empowering individual women, as priestesses, diviners, healers, and successful businesswomen, the priesthood and worship of the Water Goddess has an additional significance for all of Oru society in the sense that it invests the female population with special responsibilities and importance for the management and conservation of the town's environment and natural resources.

COMPLEMENTARITY IN RITUAL LEADERSHIP

As we have already seen, ritual leadership is open to both genders and can be achieved through spirit possession, inheritance, age, or marriage. An uninterrupted installment of the priest and priestesses serving the shrines of the water deities and performing their rituals is imperative. However, not every individual who inherits senior status and the duty to serve a shrine owned by his lineage is inclined or able to take up this post. For example, the *Osimmiri* shrine for the river Niger owned by a particular lineage in Orsu-Obodo is decaying because the person who inherited the responsibility to be its priest is a Christian who refuses to be fully installed. Similar cases are known from other towns. In some instances, the person next in line either became mad or died prematurely. Although the failure to take up an inherited priesthood may have fatal results, it also opens the way for other candidates, especially women. In the case of the *Osimmiri* priesthood, a water priestess is entitled to serve *Osimmiri* because she is chosen by the Goddess and is highly respected by the entire town. This woman is regarded as far more powerful and important than the man who declined the priesthood. In the same town, there are several shrines, priests, and priestesses for the Lake Goddess, *Ogbuide*, who is invoked on all occasions. The man who had inherited Orsu-Obodo's major shrine for *Ogbuide* was crippled by an accident. Although still recognized as her priest, he can no longer travel to his own shrine located just outside of the town, as he normally would, to preform rites on behalf of the villagers. His role is taken over by several water priestesses who have attained their status through vocation, healing, and initiation, and have established their own shrines for the all-important goddess. These priestesses also take worshippers on pilgrimage to the public shrines for the Goddess, *Ogbuide*, and her husband, *Urash*, on the river bank far from town. Due to the non-discriminatory nature and gender flexibility of leadership roles and power acquisition, women are able to accede to positions of authority in the town.

CONCLUSION

The extraordinary status of womanhood inherent in Igbo cosmology ascribes to women not only complementary importance (expressed in mature beauty)[67] but also, awe- inspiring powers (expressed in unconstrained, adolescent beauty). Beauty as power is symbolized by the white eagle feather on a titled person's red cap.[68] Female power is not only complementary to male power, but also pivotal to humanity in creation, procreation, reincarnation and human existence within the circular flow of time. This is expressed in rituals and in the Water Goddess's power to challenge one's human destiny even before one is born.[69]

The divine woman in Igbo cosmology validates female power. This concept contradicts patrilineal ideology, colonial religions, and other super-impositions and male biases promoted by foreign value and belief systems. In the precolonial balancing of powers through ritual and political activities, male and female were deemed powerful and important. Balancing the forces of nature and people was and still is necessary for ensuring the spiritual and physical well-being of men, women, and children. By extension, the post-colonial impoverishment, environmental damage and resulting problems might be ascribed, in part, to the disturbance of this very balance. Some devotees themselves may initially perceive their vocation as a form of hardship caused by personal destiny. As women's leadership positions have been eroded, some may be particularly prone to seek compensation. Water Goddess priesthood may have compensatory functions to some women, especially as a consequence of the deprivations and the loss of political power and self-esteem in missionary and colonial contexts.

Priesthood through possession provides an alternative value system and with it female access to esoteric status and power. As ritual positions could traditionally have a political dimension, water priestesses could assume powers transcending their sacred domain. They can be powerful diviners and skilled healers. Priesthood of the Water Goddess based on water spirit possession balances leadership based on kinship by emphasizing and reinforcing female power. Through alternative strategies for addressing the vital forces of nature, citizens of a rural community, regardless of gender, can gain a great deal of self-esteem and personal fulfillment. Above all, women's ritual leadership is an expression of women's different but complementary status, corresponding to the female powers of the universe. Water priestesses and female leadership confirm precolonial perceptions of gender, attesting to the female powers that are still valuable, vital, and valid today.

NOTES

1.   The Oru-Igbo are a group of Igbo towns in Imo State, Southeastern Nigeria. These towns are located along Oguta lake and the rivers Njaba and Urash. The group includes Oguta, Orsu-Obodo, Ezi-Orsu (Orsu-Ogbaho), Nkwesi, Nnebukwu, Mgbelle and Izombe. The Oru claim to have migrated from Benin more than ten generations ago. The *Atlas of World Cultures: A Geographical Guide to Ethnographic Literature* shows an ethnic group, "Oru" in today's Delta State. However, I am not certain how close the relation between the Oru Igbo of Imo State and the Oru of Delta State is. The Oru, Omoko and Onitsha are the riverine Igbo. They share a common language, Igbo, and basic cultural features with the rest of Igboland. But, the riverine Igbo also have certain cultural peculiarities that differ from other Igbo groups. An example is the institution of the *Eze Igwe*, or *Obi*, a town's sacred king. Linguistically, the Onitsha dialect differs from the Oru dialect. Among the Oru towns, Oguta is their largest and most prominent center today. Its political and economic leadership is due, in part, to the town's location on the lake resulting in early conquest, trading, and administrative advantages. Orsu-Obodo, on the other hand, although disadvantaged today, is the most senior of the Oru towns and recognized by the Oru as their cultural and religious leader, "head," or senior brother. During most of my field research, I was based in Orsu-Obodo, also referred to as Oguta II, in modern administrative terms. David Price, *Atlas of World Cultures: A Geographical Guide to Ethnographic Literature* (Newbury Park, Calif.: Sage Publications, 1990).

2.   In the context of indirect rule and its derivatives, the key question was: "who dominates locally?" Margery Perham, *Native Administration in Nigeria* (Oxford: Oxford University Press, 1962); Lord Lugard, *The Dual*

Mandate in Tropical Africa (London, 1922); Sir Donald Cameron, *The Principles of Native Administration and their Application* (Lagos, 1935). The inquiries and reports on chieftaincy disputes etc. of that time suggest that the colonial administration was preoccupied with that question. Most importantly, they were always looking for the *men* in charge. While it is always easy to find what one wants to find in the first place, it is not so easy to recognize the unsolicited; to acknowledge the unexpected is particularly difficult if is something or somebody elusive, secretive, and highly privileged within her own society, in this case female leadership. For European and American women, the very existence of female power in Africa entails looking up to African women as their mothers and sources of respect and inspiration. The idea of an African mother of all mankind has recently stirred a major debate in anthropology: According to bio-genetic findings by Cavalli-Sforza and Alan Wilson the primordial mother of all of mankind was an East African woman. These findings are debated by other authors who do not support the theory of an African Eve, or out-of-Africa theory—"New Debate Over Humankind's Ancestress: Biologists Insist All Human Lineages Track Back to a Woman in Africa 200,000 Years Ago," *The New York Times*, October 1, 1991; A. Wilson and R. Cann, "The Recent African Genesis of Humans," *Scientific American* 266(1992):22-27; L. L. Cavalli-Sforza, A. Piazza, P. Menozzi, and J. Mountain, "Reconstruction of Human Evolution: Bringing Together Genetic, Archaeological, and Linguistic Data," *Proceedings of the National Academy of Sciences*, USA 85(1988):6002- 6006; *American Anthropologist* 95.1(March, 1993): Contemporary Issues Forum: A Current Controversy in Human Evolution [Contributors include Robert W. Sussman, guest editor, "Overview"; David W. Frayer, Milford H. Wolpoff, Alan G. Thorne, Fred H. Smith, and Geoffrey G. Pope, "Theories of Modern Human Origins: The Paleontological Test"; Alan R. Templeton, "The 'Eve' Hypothesis: A Genetique and Reanalysis"; Leslie C. Aiello, "The Fossil Evidence for Modern Human Origins in Africa: A Revised View"; Michael D. Lemonick, "How Man Began: New Evidence Shows that Early Humans Left Africa Much Sooner than Once Thought. Did 'Homo Sapience' Evolve in Many Places at Once?"] *Time* March 14, 1994, pp. 41-47.

3.   In terms of its specificity, my approach differs from earlier studies of African priestesses, e.g., Iris Berger, "Rebels or Status-Seekers? Women as Spirit Mediums in East Africa." *Women in Africa: Studies in Social and Economic Change*, ed., Nancy J. Hafkin and Edna G. Bay (Stanford, Calif.: Stanford University Press, 1976), pp. 157-181.

4.   I am largely ignoring both Christianity and Islam in my current discussion. Both religions are historically associated with foreign power structures, ascribing a well-known subordinate place to women that contradicts precolonial African religious beliefs and their social manifestations.

5.   I. M. Lewis, *Ecstatic Religion* (London: Routledge, 1971); V. Lanternari, *Religiose Heilsbewegungen unterdruckter Volker* (Berlin/ Germany: Luchterhand, 1960). For re-evaluation of the Hausa Bori possession "cult" within the discourse of power, see Adeline Masquelier,

"Narratives of Power, Images of Wealth: The Ritual Economy of Bori in the Market," *Modernity and its Malcontents: Ritual and Power in Postcolonial Africa*, ed., Jean Comaroff and John Comaroff (Bloomington: Indiana University Press, 1993), pp. 3-4.

6. The idea of looking at African histories in search of historical alternatives was first presented by Stanley Diamond, "Introduction: Africa in the Perspective of Political Anthropology," *The Transformation of East Africa*, ed., Stanley Diamond and Fred Burke (New York: Basic Books, 1966), pp. 3-29.

7. V. Y. Mudimbe, *The Invention of Africa: Gnosis, Philosophy and the Order of Knowledge* (Bloomington: Indiana University Press, 1988).

8. Sally Price, *Primitive Art in Civilized Places*, (Bloomington: Indiana University Press, 1991).

9. I am aware that Africa is a continent with extreme diversity of peoples, societies, and cultures. "African culture" is a generic term, emphasizing common cultural features that unite the continent and differentiate it from others. Clifford questions the very process of "writing culture," but by extension also the very existence of other cultures, identities, and concepts; this would ultimately deny the possibility of communication. James Clifford, *Writing Culture: The Poetics and Politics of Fieldwork* (Berkeley: University of California Press, 1986).

10. Particularly in British social anthropology and functionalist studies, operating in close collaboration with the colonial administration, African societies were dissected according to social structures and functions derived from European models that disregard the multi-functional character of African institutions. As a result, African societies were described either as acephalous or as subjected to autocratic rulers who abused their powers like European patriarchs, monarchs, emperors, or dictators. At a closer look, both extremes deny any power to the African people, ignore their skillful negotiations of power and the multifunctional character of their institutions. These misrepresentations have been used to justify colonial conquest under the guise of *Pax Britannica* and/or postcolonial foreign "guidance" that influence African countries, their leaders and their peoples. The dismissal of African values has historically served, and continues to serve, to elevate European/American values and power structures. F. Fanon, *Les Damnés de la terre* (Paris: François Maspero, 1961); E. Evans-Pritchard, *Social Anthropology* (London: Routledge, 1951); M. Fortes, *The Dynamics of Clanship Among the Tallensi* (London, 1949); M. Fortes and E. E. Evans-Pritchard, *African Political Systems* (Oxford: Oxford University Press, 1978); Lucy Mair, *African Societies* (Cambridge: Cambridge University Press, 1974); *Primitive Government* (London: Penguin, 1970); S. Nadel, *A Black Byzanthium* (Oxford: Oxford University Press, 1942); A. R. Radcliffe-Brown, and D. Forde, ed., *African Systems of Kinship and Marriage* (Oxford: Oxford University Press, 1970); C. K. Meek, *Law and Authority in a Nigerian Tribe* (Oxford: Oxford University Press, 1937); M. G. Smith, *Government in Zazzau*, (Oxford, 1960).

11. Victor Uchendu, *The Igbo Speaking Peoples of Southeastern Nigeria* (New York: Holt, Rinehart & Winston, 1965). For the value and political ideas

attached to negotiating power in Igbo culture and society see E. N. Njaka, *Igbo Political Culture* (Evanston: Northwestern University Press, 1974), p. 14, quoted in Obioma Nnaemeka, "Orality and Writing in Africa: Perspectives on Gender and Power." Paper presented at a Rockefeller seminar held at the Center for Advanced Feminist Studies at the University of Minnesota. April, 1992, pp. 12-13. On the importance of the concept of "balance" in Igbo culture see Chinua Achebe, *Things Fall Apart* (London: Heineman, 1958), cited by Chimalum Nwankwo in Nnaemeka, *ibid.* For the British colonial administration's need and desire to find centralized local power structures see Lord Lugard, op. cit. For an European inspired emphasis and projection of a centralized power monopoly see Ikenna Nzimiro, *Studies in Ibo Political Systems: Chieftaincy and Politics in Four Niger States* (Berkeley: University of California Press, 1972). See also P. C. Dike, *Symbolism and Authority in the Igala Kingdom*, [Ph.D. dissertation] (New York: The New School for Social Research and Nsukka: University of Nigeria, 1977).

12. Visions of African women dominating men are indebted to the notion of matriarchy derived from Bachofen's hypothesis. J. Bachofen, *The Mothers, Myth, Religion and Mother Right* (Stuttgart, Germany, 1861). This early work has led to a confusion in popular belief of matrilineal kinship with a domination of society by women. Evolutionary concepts following Engels's *Origin of the Family, the Private Property and the State* argue for an universal evolutionary development from female domination to male domination. Ortner uses world-wide examples to show that women everywhere are subordinate to men. This view ignores and disqualifies alternative cultural strategies and locates Africa at the bottom of a hypothetical scale where women were once associated with matriarchy, or female dominance of society. This view ignores, for example, the Igbo value of balance, socially, politically and in gender relations, expressed in Igbo culture and described by Achebe, Nnaemeka and others *op. cit.* S. Ortner, "Is Female to Male as Nature to Culture?" *Woman, Culture and Society*, Michelle Zimbalist Rosaldo and Louise Lamphere, ed. Rayna Reiter Rapp and others have contested this view (see Rayna Rapp, ed., *Toward and Anthropology of Women* (New York: Monthly Review Press, 1975). E. Leacock, "Introduction." In F. Engels, *The Origin of the Family, the Private Property and the State* (New York: New World Paperback, 1972). The other extreme is the Western emphasis on African women as victims of their men (as opposed to foreign men), again assigning to African women the bottom of a fictitious value scale and implying the need for foreign liberation, reminiscent of colonial descriptions of "tribal warfare" to justify *Pax Britannica*. The notion of "African women breeding children out of control" is invoked by media reports on Africa emphasizing overpopulation and crying for population control anywhere in the world but at home. See for instance a recent report in the *New York Times*, "Lost Decade Drains Africa's Vitality" (June 19, 1994), pp. 1, 10. This report creates a contradiction by shifting its tone from lamenting Africa's overpopulation on the one hand, to the continent's "retards per capita growth due to losses from the AIDS crisis," on the other. Moreover, when considering that one person in America con-

sumes at least 10 times as much in natural resources as 100 persons in the "third world," the often projected coupling of an overpopulated "third world" with the depletion of the earth's natural resources on the other seems absurd. The Western phobia about African overpopulation also ignores precolonial methods of birth-control—e.g., child spacing and temporary ritual celibacy—disrupted by the churches.

13. These divisions are evident in the current debate on female circumcision/genital mutilation in Africa rekindled by Alice Walker's controversial film, *Warrior Marks*, and her novel, *Possessing the Secret of Joy*. The film and related issues have sparked an intense discussion among women of all continents. Contributors include Obioma Nnaemeka, editor of a forthcoming book on the issue. See also: Anette Fuller-Reynolds's interview of Obioma Nnaemeka, "Female Circumcision: Genital Mutilation or Female Rite of Passage," *The Indianapolis Star*, March 13, 1994; Seble Dawit and Salem Mekuria, "The West Just Doesn't Get It," *New York Times*, December 7, 1993, p. A13; Leslye Obiora and Cheryl Johnson-Odim, "African Female Circumcision: Two Academic Views," *African Newbreed*, April, 1994, p. 10. Assimilation serves to create consumers of foreign goods, another form of subordination, creating new dependencies. See also Pamela G. Schmoll, "Black Stomachs, Beautiful Stones: Soul Eating among the Hausa in Niger," In *Modernity and its Malcontents: Ritual and Power in Postcolonial Africa*, ed., Jean Comaroff and John Comaroff (Chicago: University of Chicago Press, 1993).

14. Alternative views on African women include among others: Chinua Achebe. *Things Fall Apart* (London: Heinemann, 1958); Ifi Amadiume, *Male Daughters. Female Husbands: Gender and Sex in an African Society* (London: Zed Books, 1987); Obioma Nnaemeka, "Bringing African Women into the Classroom? Rethinking Pedagogy and Epistemology," *Borderwork: Feminist Engagements with Comparative Literature*, ed., Margaret Higgonet (Ithaca: Cornell University Press, 1994), pp. 301-318; Niara Sudarkasa, "Female Employment and Family Organization in West Africa," *The Black Woman Cross-Culturally*, Filomina Chioma Steady (Cambridge, Mass.: Schenkma, 1981), pp. 49-64. Catherine Acholonu. "The African Feminist Challenge in Life and Literature." Hitachi Spring Lecture. New York: Manhattanville College, (1991).

15. For a discussion of the color symbolism pertaining to this particular case see Jell- Bahlsen, "Eze Mmiri di Egwu: The Water Monarch is Awesome: Re-considering the Mammy Water Myths," *Queens, Queen Mothers and Priestesses: Case Studies in African Gender*, ed., Flora Kaplan (forthcoming).

16. The symbolism of zigzag line and circle is a common theme in several African cultures. See G. Parrinder, *African Mythology* (London: Paul Hamlin, 1967); Marcel Griaule, *Conversations With Ogotomelli: An Introduction to Dogon Religious Ideas* (London: Oxford University Press, 1965), and "The Dogon of the French Sudan," *African Worlds: Studies in the Cosmological Ideas and Social Values of African Peoples*, ed., Daryll Forde (London: Oxford University Press, 1991). See also Robert F. Thompson's discussion of the Yoruba color symbolism and the concept of *ashe* in *Flash of the Spirit: African and Afro-American Art and Philosophy* (New York: Vintage Books, 1983), pp. 3-11.

17. Quoted by Nnaemeka (1992), *op. cit.*, p.13
18. See, for instance, Chinua Achebe, "The Sacrificial Egg," in *Girls at War and Other Stories* (London: Heinemann, 1972); Chinwe Achebe, *The World of the Ogbanje* (Enugu: Fourth Dimension Publishers, 1987).
19. The association of unkempt and uncut hair, extra-human beauty and a water spirit is also found among the Mende of Sierra Leone. See Sylvia Boone, *Radiance from the Waters: Ideals of Feminine Beauty in Mende Art* (New Haven: Yale University Press, 1986). For a further exploration of hair symbolism in the Igbo context see Sabine Jell-Bahlsen (Flora Kaplan. *op. cit.*) and "Dada-Rasta-Hair: The Hidden Messages of Mammy Water in West Africa," paper presented at the conference on Body Images, University of Amsterdam, Amsterdam/ The Netherlands, 1993).
20. Chinwe Achebe, *The World of the Ogbanje* (Enugu: Fourth Dimension Publishers, 1987).
21. Achebe, *op. cit.*, p.15.
22. Victor Uchendu, *The Igbo Speaking Peoples of South Eastern Nigeria* (New York: Holt, Rinehart & Winston, 1973); G. Parrinder (1967), *op. cit.*; John Mbiti, *African Religions and Philosophy* (Portsmouth, NH: Heinemann, 1990).
23. The same applies to both men and women. I am using the feminine term here when referring to the individual because, from my observation, there are more women than men who worship the Water Goddess.
24. Achebe, *op. cit.*
25. The characters of several Nigerian novels revolve around this theme. See for instance: Elechi Amadi, *The Concubine*, (London: Heinemann, 1966); Flora Nwapa, *Idu* (London: Heinemann, 1970). The same idea of a man causing his own doom by neglecting a prenatal divine pact appears in the documentary film by Sabine Jell-Bahlsen and Georg Jell. *Eze Nwata— The Small King* (1981). In this case, a father had pledged dedication to the Water God, *Urash*, who granted him a son. After the father's death, the son neglected the shrine established by his father and, as a consequence, became mentally deranged until he was healed by a water priestess.
26. Sabine Jell-Bahlsen. "Names and Naming: Instances from the Oru-Igbo," *Dialectical Anthropology* 13 (1988a), pp. 199-207.
27. H. N. Harcourt, "Report of the Commission of Inquiry into the Oguta Chieftaincy Dispute," *Official Document #19* (London: Colonial, 1961).
28. These are random examples encountered during my stays in Orsu-Obodo. See also Sabine Jell - Bahlsen, "Social Integration in the Absence of the State: A Case Study of the Igbo Speaking Peoples of Southeastern Nigeria," Ph. D. dissertation, The New School for Social Research, New York, 1980, and "A Murder Case: Igbo Conflict Settlement," *Dialectical Anthropology* 12 (1988b), pp. 359-366.
29. See also Nnaemeka (1992, op. cit.).
30. Examples of inherited shrines and the priesthood associated with them are the priesthood of the lineage ancestors, of the Earth Goddesses— *Ani/Ala* —of the compound, town, and farm, and the Lake Goddess, *Ogbuide*. But, as we shall see later, the Water Goddess is so important to the Oru that she has many local shrines, priests and priestesses. Only some of these shrines are owned by a lineage, others are owned by indi-

viduals, and still others are public and located far away from town. These
different shrines of the same Goddess are served by different priests and
priestesses.

31. See Jell-Bahlsen (1988b, *op. cit.*), for a description of the intervention of
    Umuada in the trial of people accused of murdering their "brother."
32. J. Van Allen, "'Sitting on a Man': Colonialism and the Lost Political
    Institutions of Igbo Women," *Canadian Journal of African Studies* 6.2
    (1972):165-181. See also M. M. Green, *Igbo Village Affairs* (New York:
    Praeger, 1964).
33. For example, in a murder case. See Sabine Jell-Bahlsen (1988 b., op. cit.)
34. This visual difference between male and female conceptualizations of
    space has been documented on film by Sabine Jell-Bahlsen, *Divine
    Earth—Divine Water. Part II: Sacrifice to the Earth Goddess, Ani* (New York,
    1980).
35. Sabine Jell-Bahlsen, *Owu: Chidi Joins the Okoroshi Secret Society* (1994), is
    a documentary about this festival. The film includes an interview with
    the *Eze Nwanyi* about her role and position in it.
36. This information is based on extensive field observations since 1978 and
    on interviews with Madame Oroko, the oldest woman of Orsu-Obodo,
    Mrs. Ogana, and other elderly women, in 1988, 1989, 1991, 1992, and
    1994.
37. The male title paralleling the *Eze Nwanyi* is the town's male spiritual
    leader, the *Eze Igwe*, or *Obi*. The foundation of this position is primarily
    religious and spiritual, but its political aspect was strengthened by the
    colonial regime for obvious purposes. However, the male position dif-
    fers from the *Eze Nwanyi* vin that the *Obiship* is hereditary within a par-
    ticular lineage (as in type 1, above), while the female title, *Eze Nwanyi*,
    is not confined to inheritance.
38. The Igbo term, *eze* translates into king or monarch in English. But eze in
    combination with *nwanyi*, woman, or with *mmiri*, water, is feminine.
    Thus, *Eze Nwanyi* usually translates as "queen" or "female monarch."
    Eze Mmiri can be translated as "queen of the water," or more neutral, as
    "water monarch."
39. According to these models, men own the land and are in charge of pol-
    itics, law, ritual and other public and esoteric affairs; women, on the
    other hand, are depicted as taking care of subsistence farming and repro-
    duction under the control and direction of men, a view challenged by
    African women in academia, literature, politics, and daily life. See
    Sudarkasa, *op. cit.*; Nnaemeka, *op. cit.*; and Acholonu, *op. cit.*
40. The assault on precolonial African religious views continues. In 1992,
    the beautiful mud sculpture of a divine pair representing the Water
    Goddess, *Ava*, near Nsukka was *beheaded* by fanatic "church people." It
    is also significant to note that an art object so vividly illuminating the
    value of balance in gender relations attracts aggression by members of
    the very churches that have eroded female powers in European societies
    long ago through witch hunting and other oppressive acts. From a series
    of interviews with a young Igbo historian, Felicia Abaronye, in 1992, I
    got the impression that priestesses and their shrines are much more fre-
    quently subjected to these types of aggression.

41. M. M. Green. *op. cit.*
42. S. Rogers (1980), *op. cit.*; Ekwere Akpan and Violetta Ekpo (1988), *op. cit*; Judith Van Allen (1976), *op. cit.* In history, there were African women warriors from Dahomey who constituted a royal army. Stanley Diamond, "Dahomey: A Proto State in West Africa" [Ph. D. dissertation] (New York: Columbia University, 1951); Melville Herskovits, *Dahomey: An Ancient West African Kingdom* (New York: J. J. Augustin Publisher, 1938). An account of Igbo women warriors is found in Catherine Acholonu, *The Igbo Roots of Olaudah Equiano* (Owerri: Totan Publishers, 1989).
43. Great Britain, Colonial Office, *Report of the Aba Commission of Inquiry*, Memorandum by C. T. Lawrence, Appendix III & Quotations of Captain Hanitsch (Lagos, 1930). See also *Report of the Commission of Inquiry appointed to inquire into the disturbances in the Calabar and Owerri Province, Dec. 1929* (Lagos, 1937).
44. Young palm fronds signal ritual dedication, contact with the spirit world, and transition. Uchendu, *op. cit.* The ritual significance of young palm fronds can have multiple expressions, extending to the profane; e.g., in a photograph from the Biafran civil war, we see a man transporting a coffin adorned with young palm fronds warning people to keep off. Today a farmer could tie young palm fronds around his plot for the same purpose. The idea is not restricted to Igboland. When riots were imminent in Lagos after the aborted elections of June 12, 1993, car owners tried to shield their cars with young palm fronds against potential vandalism.
45. Ekwere Akpan O. and Violetta Ekpo, *The Igbo Women's War of 1929: A Popular Uprising in South Eastern Nigeria : A Preliminary Study* (Calabar: The Government Printer, 1988); S. Rogers, "Anti-Colonial Protest in Africa: A Female Strategy Reconsidered," *Heresies* 3.1 (1980):22-25; Judith Van Allen, "'Aba Riots' or Igbo Women's War? Ideology, Stratification, and the Invisibility of Women," *Women in Africa: Studies in Social and Economic Change*, ed., Nancy Hafkin and Edna Bay (Stanford, Calif.: Stanford University Press, 1976). I have met and interviewed some of the women who "went to war" and who are still alive and well in 1994, although they were already adult and had had children in 1929.
46. Judith Van Allen, "'Sitting on a Man': Colonialism and the Lost Political Institutions of Igbo Women." *Canadian Journal of African Studies* 6.2 (1972):165-181. See also Sylvia Leith-Ross, *African Women: A Study of the Ibo of Owerri Province in Nigeria* (New York: Praeger, 1965). It is doubtful if indeed all of these ritual/ political/judicial female institutions are lost. Among the Oru Igbo, for instance, the *Eze Nwanyi* and the *umuada* are still in charge of protecting female interests and settling disputes concerning women. The *Eze Nwanyi* can impose sanctions and fines on both men and women when women's interests are violated.
47. The following two examples concerning public health and the environment serve as illustrations of the vital importance of some of these female rituals: Among the Oru, one does not normally go swimming or catch fish with baskets near the shore before the flooded rivers and the Oguta lake recede after the rainy season. The precise timing is marked by an

extremely secretive ritual in honor of the Water Goddess performed at night by the town's oldest women led by the *Eze Nwanyi*. It is after this ritual has been performed that the water is declared safe for swimming. The safety condition is defined in religious terms, but it also has a health implications because of the prevalence of Schistosomiasis, a water borne disease. Schistosomiasis or Bilharzia, are parasites in the form of tiny worms that enter the human body through the skin after which they multiply and slowly destroy the internal organs. The parasite has a complicated life cycle. Its eggs are discharged by humans back into the water where the parasite's next host is a water snail. The snail needs grassy waters to grow. It flourishes during the flood. At that time swimmers could easily catch the disease. After the rains and the women's secret ritual has been performed, chances of getting the disease are limited. At that time women will also resume the economic activity of fishing with baskets, traditionally a women's prerogative They fish near the water's edge where the fishes breed in the warm shallow waters. If this type of fishing was done year round, the supply of fish would be exhausted by over fishing and prematurely killing the young fish. Again, religious beliefs guarded by the oldest women prevent this from happening. The women's secret ritual contributes to the management and conservation of the natural resources, maintenance of public health, and the equilibrium between supply and demand, and the avoidance of the exploitation and exhaustion of the environment, one of the pillars of the local economy.

48. Sabine Jell-Bahlsen, *Divine Earth—Divine Water, Part 2: Annual Sacrifice to the Earth Goddess, Ani* (New York, 1980). The film documents complementary ritual activities of men and women and their dual spatial arrangements during the annual sacrifices to the Earth Goddess, *Ani*.

49. Sabine Jell-Bahlsen, *Owu: Chidi Joins the Okoroshi Secret Society* (Gottingen, Germany: IWF and Watertown, Mass.: DER, 1994). In this documentary film, the town's oldest woman, the Eze Nwanyi, explains in an interview the complementary but highly secretive ritual power of women.

50. See also Michael Mbabuike and Frank A. Salamone, "The Plight of the Indigenous Catholic Priest in Africa: An Igbo Example" (unpublished manuscript). It is interesting to note how the churches are using the emotionally charged event of a loved one's death to pressurize people to continue their membership and payments to the church in Africa, just as in Europe, where modern urban populations of continental Europe increasingly abandon the church to escape the "church tax" enforced on church members by the internal revenue service. Especially in the rural areas, the churches are trying to prevent people from abandoning the church by using their control of the graveyard as a bargaining chip.

51. Sabine Jell-Bahlsen, *Mammy Water: In Search of the Water Spirits in Nigeria* (Berkeley: University of California Extension Media Center, 1991). The documentary film illustrates the powers, positions, lives and activities of several Mammy Water priestesses and priests, and their followers.

52. The four days of the Igbo market week are: *Nkwo, Eke, Orie,* and *Afo.* Some groups of water worshippers meet only every eight days, every other market week, following the double market week rhythm of *ukwu*

(great) and *nta* (little), e.g. *Nkwo Ukwu, Nkwo Nta.*

53. Interview on film in Sabine Jell-Bahlsen (1991, op. cit.).
54. On the significance of names and naming in Igbo society see H. A. Wieschoff, "The Social Significance of Names Among the Ibo of Nigeria," *American Anthropologist* 43 (1941), pp. 212-222, and Sabine Jell-Bahlsen (1988, *op. cit.*).
55. This opposition corresponds to the Kalabari ideas described by Robin Horton, "African Traditional Thought and Western Science," *Africa* 37 (1967):150-171, 175-181.
56. Chinua Achebe, *Things Fall Apart* (London: Heinemann, 1958).
57. Michael Jackson, "Thinking Through the Body," *Social Analysis* 14 (1983):127-149, quoted by Elisha Renne. "Women, Water, and Plain White Cloth." Paper presented at the American Anthropological Association meeting in Washington, D. C., 1989).
58. The distinction of body and mind is expressed in the Igbo greeting, "*Ahu gi?*" literally "How is your body?" The notion of the togetherness of body and mind is expressed in the notion of the *chi* leaving the body at death.
59. Jell-Bahlsen (1991, *op. cit.*). This documentary film features several interviews and life histories.
60. Flora Nwapa, *Efuru* (London: Heinemann, 1966); *Idu* (London: Heinemann, 1970).
61. In precolonial Oguta, women were circumcised just before marriage, or at the time of their first pregnancy. According to Dr. Ehirim of the Oguta general hospital, circumcision is now partially abandoned, or performed at birth in the hospital, but only as a slight incision (personal communication, 1979). In Flora Nwapa's novel, *Efuru*, Efuru first resists this practice in her husband's home. This resistance marks the beginning of subsequent irregularities in her life.
62. Sabine Jell-Bahlsen (1991, *op. cit.*). Excerpts from this interview with the *Eze Mmiri* of Orsu-Obodo appear in the documentary film.
63. Elechi Amadi, *The Concubine* (London: Heinemann, 1966).
64. Robin Horton, "Types of Spirit Possession in Kalabari Religion," John Beattie and John Middleton, *Spirit Mediumship and Society in Africa* (New York: Africana Publishing Corp., 1969). See also Ifi Amadiume, *Male Daughters, Female Husbands: Gender and Sex in an African Society* (London: Zed Books, 1987).
65. I. M. Lewis (1971, *op. cit.*); Vittorio Lanternari (1960, *op. cit.*).
66. Personal communication, 1987.
67. See also Senghor's poem, "Black Woman," in Michael Mbabuike, *Notes on the Poems of Léopold Sédar Senghor* (Jersey City: Andre's & Co, 1989). The awe-inspiring quality of female beauty is also addressed by Catherine Acholonu, *The Trial of the Beautiful Ones* (Owerri: Totan Publishers, 1988).
68. Chinua Achebe has elaborated on the dual character of power and beauty as it is symbolized by the white eagle's feather adorning titled Igbo elders' caps. *Opening Address* at the African Studies Association Meeting. University of California, Los Angeles, 1984.
69. Achebe (1987, *op. cit.*).

WORKS CITED

Achebe, Chinua. *Things Fall Apart*. London: Heinemann, 1958.

Achebe, Chinwe. *The World of the Ogbanje*. Enugu: Fourth Dimension Publishers, 1987.

Acholonu, Catherine. *The Igbo Roots of Olaudah Equiano*. Owerri: Afa Publications, 1989

——. *The Trial of the Beautiful Ones*. Owerri: Totan Publishers, 1988.

Akpan, Ekwere, O. and Violetta L. Ekpo. *The Igbo Women's War of 1929: A Popular Uprising in South Eastern Nigeria (Preliminary Study)*. Calabar: The Government Printer, 1988.

Amadi, Elechi. *The Concubine*. London: Heinemann, 1966.

Amadiume, Ifi. *Male Daughters, Female Husbands: Gender and Sex in an African Society*. London: Zed Books, 1978.

Beattie, John, and John Middleton, ed. *Spirit Mediumship and Society in Africa*. New York: Africana Publishing Corp., 1969.

Berger, Iris. "Rebels or Status-Seekers? Women as Spirit Mediums in East Africa." In *Women in Africa: Studies in Social and Economic Change*, ed., Nancy J. Hafkin and Edna G. Bay. Stanford, Calif.: Stanford University Press, 1976: 157-181.

Boone, Sylvia. A. *Radiance from the Waters: Ideals of Feminine Beauty in Mende Art*. New Haven: Yale University Press, 1986.

Clifford, James. *Writing Culture: The Poetics and Politics of Fieldwork*. Berkeley: University of California Press, 1986.

Colonial Office (Great Britain). *Report of the Aba Commission of Inquiry*. Memorandum by C. T. Lawrence, Appendix III & Quotations of Captain Hanitsch Lagos, 1930.

——. *Report of the Commission of Inquiry Appointed to Inquire into the Disturbances in the Calabar and Owerri Provinces, December, 1929*. Lagos, 1937.

Comaroff, Jean and John Comaroff, ed. *Modernity and Its Malcontents: Ritual and Power in Postcolonial Africa*. Chicago: University of Chicago Press, 1993.

Evans-Pritchard, E. *Social Anthropology*. London: Routledge, 1951.

Fanon, F. 1961. *Les Damnés de la terre*. Paris: François Maspero, 1961.

Green, M. M. *Igbo Village Affairs*. New York: Praeger, 1964.

Hafkin, N. J. and Edna G. Bay, ed. *Women in Africa: Studies in Social and Economic Change*. Stanford: Stanford University Press, 1976.

Horton, Robin. "African Traditional Thought and Western Science." *Africa* 37 (1967): 150-181.

——. "Types of Spirit Possession in Kalabari Religion." In *Spirit Mediumship and Society in Africa*, ed., John Beattie and John Middleton. New York: Africana Publishing Corp., 1969.

Jackson, Michael. 1983. "Thinking Through the Body." *Social Analysis* 14 (1983): 127-149.

Jell-Bahlsen, Sabine. "Names and Naming: Instances from the Oru-Igbo." *Dialectical Anthropology* 13 (1988a): 199-207.

——. "A Murder Case: Igbo Conflict Settlement." *Dialectical Anthropology* 12 (1988b): 359-366.

Lanternari, Vittorio. *Religiose Heilsbewegungen unterdruckter Volker.* Berlin/Germany: Luchterhand, 1960.

Leacock, Eleanor. "Introduction" in F. Engels, *The Origin of the Family, the Private Property and the State.* New York: International Publishers, 1972.

Leith-Ross, Sylvia. *African Women: A Study of the Ibo of Nigeria.* New York: Praeger, 1965.

Lewis, I. M. *Ecstatic Religion.* London: Routledge, 1989.

Lugard, Lord. *The Dual Mandate in Tropical Africa.* London, 1922.

Masquelier, Adeline. "Narratives of Power, Images of Wealth: The Ritual Economy of Bori in the Market." In *Modernity and Its Malcontents: Ritual and Power in Postcolonial Africa,* ed., Jean Comaroff, and John Comaroff. Bloomington: Indiana University Press, 1993.

Mudimbe, V. Y. *The Invention of Africa: Gnosis, Philosophy and the Order of Knowledge.* Bloomington: Indiana University Press, 1988.

Nnaemeka, Obioma. "Bringing African Women into the Classroom: Rethinking Pedagogy and Epistemology." In *Borderwork: Feminist Engagements with Comparative Literature,* ed., Margaret Higonnet. Ithaca: Cornell University Press, 1994:301-318.

———. "Orality and Writing in Africa: Perspectives on Gender and Power." Paper presented at a Rockefeller seminar, Center for Advanced Feminist Studies, University of Minnesota, April, 1992.

Nwapa, Flora. *Efuru.* London: Heinemann, 1966.

———. *Idu.* London: Heinemann, 1970.

Ortner, Sherry B. "Is Female to Male as Nature to Culture? In *Woman, Culture and Society.* ed., Michelle Zimbalist Rosaldo and Louise Lamphere. Stanford, Calif.: Stanford University Press, 1974: 67-86.

Price, Sally. *Primitive Art in Civilized Places.* Bloomington: Indiana University Press, 1991.

Rapp, Rayna Reiter, ed. *Toward an Anthropology of Women.* New York: Monthly Review Press, 1975.

Rodney, Walter. *How Europe Underdeveloped Africa.* Dar-es-Salaam: Tanzania Publishing House, 1972.

Rogers, S. "Anti-Colonial Protest in Africa: A Female Strategy Reconsidered." *Heresies* 3.1 (1980): 22-25.

Schmoll, Pamela, G. "Black Stomachs, Beautiful Stones: Soul Eating among the Hausa in Niger." In *Modernity and Its Malcontents: Ritual and Power in Postcolonial Africa,* ed., Jean Comaroff and John Comaroff. Chicago: University of Chicago Press, 1993.

Sudarkasa, Niara. "Female Employment and Family Organization in West Africa." In *The Black Woman Cross-Culturally,* ed., Filomina Chioma Steady. Cambridge, Mass.: Schenkman, 1981: 49-64.

Uchendu, Victor. *The Igbo Speaking Peoples of Southeastern Nigeria.* New York: Holt, Rinehart & Winston, 1973.

Van Allen, Judith. "'Sitting on a Man': Colonialism and the Lost Political Institutions of Igbo Women." *Canadian Journal of African Studies* 6.2 (1972):165-181.

———. "'Aba Riots' or 'Igbo Women's War'? Ideology, Stratification, and the Invisibility of Women." *Women in Africa: Studies in Social and Economic Change.* ed., Nancy Hafkin and Edna Bay. Stanford, Calif.: Stanford

University Press, 1976:59-85.

FILMS

Jell-Bahlsen, Sabine. *Owu: Chidi Joins the Okoroshi Secret Society.* New York and Gottingen/Germany: Institut f.d. wissenschaftlichen Film. Watertown, Mass: DER, 1994.

―――. *Mammy Water: In Search of the Water Spirits in Nigeria.* Berkeley: University of California Extension Media Center, 1991.

―――. *Divine Earth-Divine Water, Part 2: Annual Sacrifice to the Earth Goddess, Ani.* New York.

―――. and Georg Jell. *Eze Nwata: The Small King.* New York, 1983.

An Appraisal of Feminism in the Socio-Political Development of Nigeria

Glo Chukukere

INTRODUCTION

THE NIGERIAN WOMAN IS A CONUNDRUM. HER SITUATION cuts across various strata of a society in which her position reflects both that of a victim and that of a victimizer. Issues affecting her are as complex as the multifarious roles she is called upon to play.[1] These variables determine her reaction to the "woman question." In general terms, however, oppression of the Nigerian woman is an invariable constant; a part of the global dilemma—ageless, systematic, and deep-rooted. Truly embedded within the economic, cultural, political, social, and ideological structures of society, women's oppression has attracted global attention and become the subject of numerous investigations. Several charters of the United Nations are aimed at eliminating all forms of discrimination against women. The year 1975 was, for example, recognized as the International Women's Year, and 1976–1985 as the Decade for Women. As a signatory to the 1979 United Nations Convention for Elimination of all Form of Discrimination Against Women, Nigeria has surged ahead to improve the lot of women in all its ramifications. The establishment of the Better Life Program and the Commission for Women by the Babangida administration, the vigorous functioning of the various organs of government concerned with women, the proliferation of women organizations, all point to a positive, dynamic, and result-oriented course for women in this country. Yet, the mere mention of feminism or Women's Liberation draws anger and rejection from a majority of the menfolk and disassociation from even those women who, by the virtue of their positions and exalted lifestyles, embody the very tenets of this movement.[2] The following typical responses reflect the current social dilemma:

(1) "The word liberation doesn't arise here at all because we were never in any form of bondage."[3]

(2) "Please don't confuse Nigerian women with that nonsense."

(3) "Feminism is for developed countries like America and Great Britain. Our women here are all right....no problem."

(4) "I believe the lot of Nigerian women could be greatly improved, but I am not a feminist.... I don't like that word...."

Sensitive to this confusion arising out of prejudice and misunderstanding, it is pertinent to examine why people generally shy away from feminism and Women's Liberation. What indeed is feminism? Is there a Nigerian brand of it? In order to address these and other issues effectively, this paper will examine the socio-cultural and political attitudes of Nigerians towards women, their responses to the folkloric version of Women's Liberation Movement, patriarchal control, and the social antipathy towards forms of feminism from the Western world.

The genesis and history of feminism need not detain us. As a subject of intense research, feminism has enjoyed global attention. Its definition is shaped by one's training, ideology, social and cultural location, and race. Whether in the context of precapitalist/capitalist socio-economic formation, Marxist/Socialist perspective (where class with gender intersect in analysis), or, indeed, that of Black Feminism which argues for a much more integrative approach to the understanding of the multiple systems of oppression,[4] feminism or womanism is, simply put, the theory of the woman's point of view. Its quintessential method, particularly at the inception of

the second wave of feminism in the West, is the consciousness raising of existing conditions—in the past and present—and of future
possibilities. In practice, feminism addresses the socio-political and
cultural inequities in women's lives and seeks positive ways of
improvement. Thus, when Nigeria's First Lady, Maryam Babangida,
articulates the objectives of the Better Life Program, which embody
the vision of assisting women to harness their creative energy for
concrete and achievable goals in education, agriculture, health, and
politics, she is speaking to feminism.[5] Or, when the society directs
its searchlight on exploring ways of empowering the Nigerian
woman, it is feminism that is receiving attention, albeit the Nigerian
brand of it! According to Eno Irukwu, the National Coordinator of
the Better Life Program, "our women need power and authority to
act—to break loose from the shackles that have kept them down for
years.... Empowerment will equip and release women to fully participate in development activities of the nation."[6]

Given the concerted efforts by Nigerian society to dismantle the
socio-political structures that impede the woman's full integration
in nation-building, it is a paradox of sorts that the same society is
simultaneously rejecting, in theory, what it champions in practice.
This dilemma in accepting the legitimacy of the Women's
Liberation Movement as a concept is easily traceable to several factors, namely the social, moral, and ideological differences between
Black feminism (or even what Alice Walker calls womanism) and
the Western brand of the Women's Liberation Movement.

In Nigeria, women enjoy constitutional rights that are still
denied Western women. As an offshoot of the Civil Rights
Movement of the 1960s in the United States, the Women's
Liberation Movement fought along the lines of development,
health, education, and employment of women. There were also the
issues of equal pay for comparable work, securing of abortion rights,
and wages for domestic chores for those nursing mothers who could
not afford to work. These issues do not reflect the burden of the
Nigerian woman, who has never been marginalized in the same way
as her Western counterpart. Nigerian women have historically held
substantial economic powers, whether through agriculture, petty-
trading, or wholesale business enterprises. Also, the polygynous
nature of households, together with extended family relationships,
enable women to realize their dreams despite maternal responsibilities. Thus, the question of the Nigerian woman's right to work
is not at issue, although an improvement in the conditions under
which she functions is most desirable.

Poor and biased press reporting, particularly the tendency to equate liberation with female sexuality on display or promiscuity, creates a bad image for feminism. As a result, the most responsible and respectable members of the society distance themselves from the concept. Equally repugnant are manifestations of radical feminism in the West whose extreme liberties include sexual freedom and separatism. This extremism took an original turn in the late '60s and early '70s when women began to discard their brassieres, earrings, and panty-girdles in a bid to be as free as men. Elizabeth Obadina captures the essence of this obnoxious segment of an otherwise noble movement:

> [Some] of the women who organize themselves in the mainstream WLM in the West seek to live apart from men, seeking emotional, sexual and domestic satisfaction from other women. They are radical feminists amongst whom a woman who chooses to share her life with a man, especially if that relationship is a happy monogamous one, finds herself an oddity; someone who must be saved from selling her soul down the river of male chauvinism and oppression.[7]

No doubt, such direction for the feminist movement will encounter popular resistance in Nigeria as a result of the social regard for matrimony and general responsible behavior. Indeed, when this radical feminist perspective found an ally among prostitutes who brazenly called on the Nigerian Government to formally recognize their Union, Nigerian Union of Prostitutes (NUP), the outraged public immediately countered with derogatory articles and provocative cartoons, one of which read "Money for hand; back for ground."[8] This bizarre turn and an absence of a sharp positive focus on feminism compelled the Vice Chancellor of the University of Benin, Professor Grace Alele Williams, to make clear the distinction between warped and realistic Nigerian feminism. When asked if she belonged to the Women's Liberation Movement, she responded thus: "Not to the group that shouts boisterously of what women should have or shouldn't have, but to that group that can demonstrate the extra ability to merit certain positions, that sits down to plan a better life for women."[9]

Global sisterhood as propounded by Western feminists has received severe knocks in Nigeria, as there is precious little link between our experiences and those of most women in the West. First, racism holds back solidarity between the two movements. Although the history of oppression of the African woman started before colonialism, it was colonialism that reshaped it in new and more insidious dimensions. This is why the African feminism with which Nigerian women closely identify cannot afford the Western separatist agenda, as the liberation of women in Africa is linked to that of the entire continent from colonial and neocolonial structures. Western schools of feminism, such as Marxist, Socialist, and radical are part of the history of those countries' political development and reflect their concerns with class contradictions. This scenario is not exactly the case in Africa, in general, and Nigeria, in particular. For Nigerian women, ours is an anti-colonial, non-separatist movement. Women's problems cannot be neatly divorced from other related issues which plague society at large, because the liberation of women is an index of a liberated society. Furthermore, Western feminists are inevitably part of the continued colonial and neocolonial exploitation of Africa, and would need to address the issues of their complicity in the history of the oppression of the black race before a meeting of minds is possible. Indeed, the issues of race and cultural allegiances create most conflicts between African and European/American models of feminism.

Apart from racism, Western feminism has proven unable to handle adequately issues that affect the black woman. According to Fatima Babiker, the attitude of certain Western feminists is as follows:

> ...just a new and alternative kind of imperialism...[their] literature suffers from a number of weaknesses. They generalize....talk about Third World women as if women are the same all over the place....[and fail] to acknowledge the areas in which women have gained power....[thus making] them invisible.[10]

In view of these contradictions in orientation, grasp, and practice of feminism, there is a crying need for us in Nigeria to redefine concepts such as feminism, Women's Liberation Movement, womanism, and any such terms as they affect us. The imposition of Western feminism with its distinct socio-political and cultural allegiances cannot serve Nigeria well. The same goes for the great harm done by the bad press given to the extreme versions of feminism that are gaining ground in our country, Nigeria.

The concepts feminism and Women's Liberation have neither found currency in the average Nigerian woman's vocabulary nor constituted the impetus for collective action. Yet in her daily existence, she faces the gender inequities of life under patriarchy. In her own ways she struggles to make a meaningful existence and, where necessary, joins other women to fight for women's rights. The Nigerian woman knows herself and is aware of her present and expected responsibilities to society. Through various support groups and her own personal efforts, her full integration into the socio-political landscape of her country has become a realizable vision for her. She has experienced consciousness raising, especially with regard to her oppression and the recognition of the potential heights she can attain despite all odds. She knows that society needs to be transformed for the good of all—men and women—and that women are the key agents to make this dream a reality. Thus, the average Nigerian woman is a feminist of sorts in practice, even if not necessarily in theoretical formulations. In light of the Nigerian woman's experience historically and her future possibilities, it is possible to extrapolate a theoretical framework for understanding Nigerian women's activism as well as the supportive Nigerian structures that have worked together for female emancipation.

NIGERIAN FEMINISM OR WOMANISM

First, Nigerian feminism or womanism is not antagonistic to Nigerian men, but recognizes a communality of struggle with them to overthrow imperialism and unjust systems in order to create a just and equitable society for all. It does challenge men to accept salient facts about women's subjugation in society and to work towards the eradication of stultifying norms.

Second, Nigerian feminism examines the society with a view to accepting institutions which are of value to women while rejecting those that are inimical to their socio-political development. For example, motherhood and wifehood are highly respected but should not be made obligatory. Nigerian feminism does not simply import Western women's agenda on monogamy; it is equally aware of some utility and positive aspects of polygamy (e.g., childcare and sharing of household responsibilities, sisterhood, and emotional support).[11] This vantage point forestalls total condemnation of polygamy, although women are often angered by the men's excesses that are disrespectful of and detrimental to their wives.

Third, Nigerian feminism places a high value on women in aid of themselves and as ends in themselves. It rejects the cultural images of women as incompetent, petty, irresponsible, and weak—stereotypes that are subtly encouraged to persist through patriarchal influences. Contrarily, it affirms the woman's capacities to be strong, capable, self-reliant, and ethical. These qualities, when allowed to bloom, enable women to control their own political, social, economic, and personal destinies. Feminism rejects the societal tendency to categorize human qualities or determine and valorize capabilities according to sex and gender.

Fourth, Nigerian feminism accepts that some belief systems and attitudes regarding women in our culture are false because they are based on myth, ignorance, and fear. Therefore, it seeks to replace myth with reality, ignorance with true knowledge. It recognizes that women themselves must be in the vanguard of this revolutionary process to ensure actualization of their dreams.

Finally, Nigerian feminism is womanism—a nonviolent, non-confrontational concept which places a high value on disciplined freedom, self-determination, and the ability of women to produce maximum results through cooperative endeavors.

NIGERIAN WOMEN IN HISTORY: THE PAST AND THE PRESENT

Nigerian feminism recognizes that the history of women in Nigeria did not start with the colonial and postcolonial era. Accordingly, it examines precolonial societies and their socio-political structures to unearth roles that women played in antiquity. Revised historical records reveal Nigerian precolonial women as competent warriors, rulers, and co-administrators with their menfolk. In the old Borno Empire, the Magira or the head of the palace women, held incredible powers, had her full complement of assistants, and was often the semi-final arbiter in difficult cases. Her position was the link between the harem and general state organizations, enabling her to influence state matters.[12] The legendary powers of Queen Amina of Zazzau are often dismissed by condescending masculinist historiography as mere folktale or myth. However, her remarkable successes in war in her thirty-four-year reign ensured her a place in Sultan Bello's *Kano Chronicle or Infag al-Maisuri*. *The Chronicle* states that Zaria under Amina conquered all the towns as far as Kwararafa and Nupe. Every town paid tribute to her. The Sarkin Nupe sent 40 eunuchs and 10,000 kolanuts to her. She first had eunuchs and kolanuts in Hausaland.[13]

Although traditional Igbo women did not enjoy individual political power proportional to that of Queen Amina, yet collectively they exerted strong political influence in spite of the patrilineal nature of their societies. Through their association of *mitiri* or *mikiri* (a probable adulteration of meeting), their interests were protected while redress was effectively sought for injustices against them. The Aba Women's War of 1929 is a typical example.[14] In Yoruba areas, women chiefs wielded considerable political, ritual, and religious powers over their subjects. The Egbe Iyalode of Oyo and Iyalode of Ibadan are important historical figures. Other groups of palace women much respected include the Ayabas of Oyo Kingdom, the Magira (Queen Mother), Gumsu (first wife of the King), and Magara (King's elder sister) in the Kanuri Kingdom. These women, individually and collectively, nurtured the kings' sons and wielded tremendous influence over the entire women and general populace of their respective kingdoms.[15]

In more recent times, powerful figures such as Lady Yinka Abayomi (who founded the Women's Party of 1944), Funmilayo Kuti, Margaret Ekpo, and Hajiya Gambo Sawaba, formed women's wings of political parties that fought for independence and, through their collective actions, championed better living standards for their fellow Nigerian women.

In terms of economic activities, there was in traditional times no polarization of roles whereby women were restricted to the home by their maternal duties while the men sustained the family. Unlike the West, where women were restricted to the home mostly as mothers and homemakers, the Nigerian woman participated in agriculture, crafts, and trade, effectively supplementing the family income.[16] However, it must be noted that in spite of these commendable roles, the status of the traditional woman remained relatively lower than that of her male counterpart, especially in light of criteria such as power, wealth, and status that are usually employed in stratification analysis.

THE CONTEMPORARY ERA

In contemporary times, modernization has proved both a blessing and a curse for the Nigerian woman. Monogamous marriages with the privilege of choice, formal educational, careers leading to better job prospects, expanded commercial activities, and family planning facilities are some of the enduring benefits of modernization. Paradoxically, however, modernization has led to the exacerbation of the socio-economic gap between male and female (e.g., in the field of agriculture). It has been argued that the relative loss of economic status of the woman is a product of colonialism. For instance, in farming, Europeans promoted cash cropping and the idea of cultivation as a man's job; consequently, Nigerian men were taught new and improved methods of agriculture and given necessary farming equipment while women, who do most of the subsistence farming, were relegated to the background. This writer has argued elsewhere that in politics and education, the story is not much different.[17]

In spite of these glaring inequities, women have sought to compete favorably with their male counterparts in all spheres of endeavor. Noteworthy successes have been recorded although the situation is far from ideal. Women have proliferated in the professions and, during the First and Second Republics, made inroads into politics. In addition to the two senators in the First Republic, the Second Republic saw Franca Afegbua in the Senate and several other women in the House of Representatives. But it is in the past years of the military interregnum that women have taken a great leap forward. Responding to the ideals of the United Nations Decade for Women, the Nigerian government has made genuine efforts to integrate women in the socio-political affairs of the country. Women have been appointed as commissioners in all state cabinets, directors general and deputy governors in Lagos and Kaduna States. Although hard-core feminists may dismiss these as tokenism, yet one must not lose sight of the well-intentioned approach of the Babangida administration. In current transition politics women have boldly emerged on the scene, but with minimal results. There are, however, two civilian deputy governors, three local government chairmen, two secretaries to civilian state governments, and a handful of female legislators. Gender barriers—social norms, poor planning, and severe financial constraints—have been identified as factors limiting women's effective participation in Third Republic politics.[18]

In the popular parlance that power is never given but taken, women have emerged on the geo-political and socio-economic scene determined to mobilize themselves for effective participation in the growth of the country. The level of women's social consciousness and awareness of their roles is evidenced by the numerous organs of government and private associations that seek not only to liberate and center women but also empower them in all areas of human endeavor. Nigerian women now realize that their marginalization is due to their lack of education and economic power which in turn determines their lack of political power.

Above all, the importance and role of women, especially in the rural sector, has received a commendable boost through the establishment of the Better Life Programme inaugurated and chaired by the wife of the President, Maryam Babangida. At the launching of the program in Abuja in 1987, Maryam Babangida recognized that with the right assistance rural women can go from a situation of triple disadvantage (as poor, as women, and, sometimes, as single heads of households) to one in which their contributions will have a multiplier effect from the micro-level to the macro-level, where their impact will affect future generations. According to Maryam Babangida,

> The Better Life Programme has become a major focal point for mobilizing rural women for self development and political awareness in the entire Federation.... It has ....motivated (them) to take positive steps towards solving their own problems through self-help efforts and seeking support of designated government agencies.... Noticeable achievements have been made in Health...Agriculture...Education....Social Welfare....and Co-operatives....[19]

As a people-oriented model of development, the Better Life Programme is a radical shift from the conventional development intervention that functions on the macro-economic and quantitative level to an engagement that is rooted in (wo)man-based qualitative strategy.[20] Thus, by creating awareness, raising the consciousness of rural women, and improving the socio-economic standard of their lives, Maryam Babangida has aligned herself with the mainstream of the struggle for the total eradication of the marginalization of Nigerian Women. This engagement goes to the core of Nigerian feminism.

PROBLEMS CONFRONTING NIGERIAN WOMEN

It would be erroneous to claim that the problems of Nigerian women are over. Far from it. Certain inequities established since time immemorial and reinforced through male- dominated structures, still persist in spite of the various instruments of the United Nations on discrimination against women and in spite of concerted efforts by the government, public-spirited individuals, and various organizations to improve women's lot. Women have least access to food, health and education, while their contributions to the development of society are hardly acknowledged. The woman's roles as mother (child- bearer and child-rearer) are given secondary status and occasionally brought to bear against her employment opportunities.

Her attempts to penetrate the political arena have met with minimal success as a result of the unwritten laws which favor men in terms of raising funds for campaigns. Financial constraints which equally cripple her ambition to compete favorably with men include, for example, colossal sums of registration fees for aspiring political candidates, especially at the presidential level—amounts often beyond the means of the few female aspirants.

Other related economic matters include lack of access to credit, especially for rural women. Development funds or grants are shared out to men, bypassing women—who form the bulk of rural farmers! Banks often ask for the consent of a husband before granting loans to women, thereby eliminating widows, spinsters and unmarried mothers from the running. Inheritance laws and land tenure discriminate against women, denying them legal ownership and, with it, any access to credit. Jadesola Akande has recently decried the pitiable state of the widow who is left "in the unhappy position of returning as a destitute to her own family because she cannot inherit any part of her husband's estate."[21] In the alternative, she may remain with her husband's family to be remarried to one of the kinsmen or made to suffer untold humiliation on the suspicion that she is responsible for her husband's death.

Other specific forms of the general oppression of the Nigerian woman include disease, poverty, child marriage, and scant access to educational opportunities. Attempts to address the "woman question" through academic research and other avenues of discussions and activities are often met with derision and outright hostility. This perhaps led the First Lady to challenge Academia to go into research to increase understanding of the plight of rural women and the impact which the Better Life Programme could have on them.[22]

Perhaps two of the most important areas that Nigerian feminism must address are taxation and the family. The prospect of tax relief for the Nigerian woman may have received a blow with the 1992 budget, which has abolished the wife's allowance. To some, this shows continued injustice against women while others believe that it now puts men and women at par, as most women are ignorant of this benefit. In truth, tax relief for children continues to be earned by men even in cases where women shoulder most family responsibilities. Consequently, women pay more tax. Single mothers, divorcees, and widows especially suffer; the same goes for those whose husbands are abroad, out of work, or serving jail terms. The increase in personal allowance, although conciliatory, is not enough replacement for children's allowance. Housewives equally suffer from the withdrawal of wife's allowance if they are unemployed when their working husbands lose this benefit.

Molara Ogundipe-Leslie has identified the family, especially marriage, as the social structure that most oppresses the Nigerian woman.[23] According to her, a woman, as wife, has a lower status than she had as a daughter or sister in her lineage. She is over-worked as wife, childbearer, and homemaker. Her significance increases with her ability to bear children, especially sons, who enjoy greater importance than daughters. A childless woman is anathe-ma in Nigeria's social landscape; an unmarried mother, a divorcee, or old spinster is marginalized. Indeed, no matter the level of edu-cation, relations between the husband and wife are based on an unequal power relation in which the woman expects orders and gives, in return, total obedience. The man's prerogative to com-mand his wife sometimes leads to physical abuse.

Decades of internalization of expected social and cultural norms has prevented women from overturning debilitating social conventions. Women are thus their own worst enemies; often being the first to criticize any concerted efforts to change the status quo. Women, afraid of being labeled social renegades and radical femi-nists, lapse into fatalist acceptance of male dominance and claim that if it was good enough for their mothers, it is good enough for them. Men may not be as much woman's enemy as women them-selves are when bound by a slave mentality and unable and unwill-ing to act in a positive manner to improve their lot.[24]

FUTURE POSSIBILITIES

Nigerian feminists believe that there is an urgent need to address oppressive structures in the society. Although the principal tenets of feminism have been enshrined in the Nigerian Constitution, the average Nigerian woman still hovers at the periphery of patriarchal space. Feminism's first task in Nigeria is to demystify the concept of liberation for the Nigerian woman in isolation and effectively link it to the liberation of the entire society. Nigerian feminism or womanism is about the fundamental human rights of women in all areas of life—public and private.[25] According to Charles Fourier, "the change in a historical epoch can always be determined by women's progress towards freedom.... The degree of emancipation of woman is the natural measure of general emancipation."[26]

Women must continue to meet, discuss, and learn from each other's experiences. Knowledge of individual experiences will lead to group consciousness. The Better Life Programme, other national bodies such as the newly created National Commission for Women, National Council for Women Societies (NCWS), Women In Nigeria (WIN), the Moslem Women Organization, and numerous other associations of a professional, social, and cultural nature which have recently proliferated on the Nigerian landscape, are all well equipped to play leadership roles in this direction. Grassroots reorientation and education are necessary ingredients for total female emancipation. Consciousness raising and increased awareness of human rights among women will ultimately lead to their empowerment. The accomplishment of this goal requires the concerted effort and collaboration of all Nigerian women. The militant stance of the Western feminist agenda has no place in the Nigerian context. Men are not necessarily the enemy; women are also their own worst enemies. Genuine co-operation and dialogue between women and men will transform women's problems into society's problems—which requires the entire society's involvement in the quest for solutions. These are some of the future goals of feminism in Nigeria.

CONCLUSION

The issue of women in Nigeria is a vast and complex one. This paper attempts to link the sociopolitical development of women in Nigeria to feminism or womanism. For, if truly feminism implies a female-oriented consciousness, then there is no doubt that the decades of women's concern for women's issues in Nigeria is feminist in its direction. In rewriting their own histories, Nigerian women have discovered that women in traditional societies held admirable economic, social, and political powers, not commensurate with those of their male counterparts but near enough. In other areas, they suffered and continue to suffer severe handicaps. Therefore, all women in Nigeria, particularly the feminists among them, hold the key to regaining lost prerogatives and creating new, dynamic, and enduring ones for our society. Feminism will change the woman's sense of herself as an unimportant and secondary figure who walks miles behind her male counterpart. A true feminist agenda will help to enfranchise women, returning them to powerful policy-making positions and institutions so that their numerical strength will match their contributions to society. It will give them access to economic independence, reverse the masculinist perspectives in politics and education, and reaffirm in society the quest for harmony, peace and humane living. This is true feminism as it ought to be; more importantly, this is the Nigerian brand of it.

NOTES

1. Sule Bello has argued that the term feminism is essentially akin to professional and other interest groups which work largely to consolidate their own self-interests, in opposition to that of women in general. In precolonial times, women belonged to various classes and fought accordingly against the destruction and for preservation of their respective interest groups. Some of these are market women associations and women of the aristocracy. See her "Problems of Theory and Practice in Women's Liberation Movements," in *Women in Nigeria Today* (London: Zed Press, 1985), pp. 23-27. Also see Molara Ogundipe-Leslie, "Women in Nigeria," ibid., p. 21.

2. Glo Chukukere, "Female Roles in West Africa," *Introductory Readings in the Humanities and Social Sciences* (Onitsha: University Publishing Company, 1988), p. 195.

3. Violet Arene, "Might Has Become Right," *Sunday Vanguard*, January 26, 1992, p. 11.

4. Maggie Humm, *The Dictionary of Feminist Theory* (Worcester: Billing and Sons Ltd., 1989), pp. 74-75.

5. Tajudeen Kareem, "Amazons against Hunger," *The Guardian*, July 25, 1991, p. 11.

6. Yinka Oduwole, "Exploring Ways of Empowering Women," *The Guardian*, March 11, 1992, p. 27.

7. Chukukere, *op. cit.*, p. 196.

8. Elizabeth Obadina, "How Relevant is the Western Women's Liberation Movement for Nigeria," *Women in Nigeria Today*, p. 138.

9. Ewaen Osarenren, "Women Liberation Movement: The Misunderstood Lot," Sunday Concord, June 5, 1986, p. 12.

10. Fatima Babiker, et al., "African Feminism," *Spare Rib* 197 (December 1988-January 1989):16-17.

11. Buchi Emecheta raised this point at an African Studies Association Meeting in 1984 in California. Also note the contribution of some Ibadan business women and traders who sanctioned polygamy because it released them from household chores to pursue their businesses. See Ogundipe-Leslie, *op. cit.*, p. 123.

12. For a fuller discussion of this and other areas in which women in antiquity, especially those of the aristocracy, held powers, see Halina D. Mohammed, "Women in Nigeria History: Examples from Borno Empire, Nupeland, and Igboland," in *Women in Nigeria Today*, pp. 45-50.

13. *Ibid*, p. 46.

14. One such method of seeking redress was known as "sitting on a man," a process whereby members gathered at the culprit's residence to castigate him with songs and derogatory mechanisms until the offender relented. See Judith Van Allen "Sitting on a Man: Colonialism and the Lost Political Institutions of Igbo Women" *Canadian Journal of African Studies* 6.2 (1972):165-181. This is an original interpretation of the 1929 Women's War especially in terms of traditional Igbo political structures.

15. Mallam Wushishi, "Nigerian Women: 1992 and Beyond," *Daily Times*, January 22, 1992, p. 32.

16. See Lambo, "Socio Economic Changes and Its Influences on the Family, with Special Emphasis on the Role of Women: A Socio-Psychological Evaluation," Ibadan, 1969, pp. 30-35. Barbara Rogers, *The Domestication of Women: Discrimination in Developing Societies*, (London: Tavistock Publications, 1980), pp. 12-20.
17. Glo Chukukere, "Female Roles in West Africa," in Chukukere, ed., *Introductory Readings*, chapter 12.
18. For a more detailed discussion of the factors responsible for the Nigerian women's poor showing in the Third Republic transition politics, see Angela Agoawike and Funke Fayemi, "Mobilizing Women for Effective Campaigns and Election," *Daily Times*, Thursday, March 12, 1992, p. 13.
19. Maryam Babangida, "The Role of Women In National Development." Excerpts of an address by the First Lady of Nigeria, Mrs. Maryam Babangida, at the African Caribbean Pacific/European Economic Community (ACP/EEC) Joint Assembly in Luxembourg, September 26, 1990, in *Sunday Concord*, October 7, 1990, p. 21.
20. Ibid.
21. J. Akande quoted by Keji Daodu, "Global Attention to Rural Women," *National Concord*, February 25, 1992, p. 5.
22. Maryam Babangida threw this challenge to Nigerian institutions on the occasion of being awarded a Doctorate Degree (*Honoris Causa*) by the University of Nigeria, Nsukka, March 1992.
23. Ogundipe-Leslie, *op. cit.*, p. 123.
24. See Aluko and Alfa, *Women in Nigeria Today*, p. 167
25. Ogundipe-Leslie, *op. cit.*, p. 122.
26. Charles Fourier, cited by Marx and Engels, *The Holy Family* (Moscow: Progress Publishers, 1975), p. 230.

WORKS CITED

Agoawike, Angela., and Funke Fayemi. "Mobilizing Women for Effective Campaigns and Election." *Daily Times* (March 12, 1992): 13.

Aluko, Grace B., and Mary O. Alfa. "Marriage and Family." *Women in Nigeria Today*. Ed. Editorial Committee. London: Zed Press, 1985: 163-173.

Arene, Violet. "Might Has Become Right." *Sunday Vanguard* (January 26, 1992): 11.

Babangida, Maryam. "The Role of Women In National Development." *Sunday Concord* (October 7, 1990): 21.

Babiker, Fatima, et al. "African Feminism." *Spare Rib* 197 (December 1988-January 1989): 16-17.

Bello, Sule. "Problems of Theory and Practice in Women's Liberation Movements." In*Women in Nigeria Today*, ed., Editorial Committee. London: Zed Press, 1985: 23-27.

Chukukere, Glo. "Female Roles in West Africa." In *Introductory Readings in the Humanities and Social Sciences*, ed. Glo Chukukere. Onitsha: University Publishing Company, 1988.

Daodu, Keji. "Global Attention to Rural Women." *National Concord* (February 25, 1992): 5.

Humm, Maggie. *The Dictionary of Feminist Theory.* Worcester: Billing and Sons Ltd., 1989: 74-75.

Kareem, Tajudeen. "Amazons against Hunger." *The Guardian* (July 25, 1991): 11.

Lambo, "Socio Economic Changes and Its Influences on the Family, with Special Emphasis on the Role of Women: A Socio-Psychological Evaluation." *Ibadan* (1969): 30-35.

Marx, Karl, and F. Engels. *The Holy Family.* Moscow: Progress Publishers, 1975.

Mohammed, Halina D. "Women in Nigerian History: Examples from Borno Empire, Nupeland and Igboland." In *Women in Nigeria Today,* ed., Editorial Committee. London: Zed Press, 1985: 45-51.

Obadina, Elizabeth. "How Relevant is the Western Women's Liberation Movement for

Nigeria." In *Women in Nigeria Today,* ed., Editorial Committee. London: Zed Press, 1985: 138-142.

Oduwole, Yinka. "Exploring Ways of Empowering Women." *The Guardian* (March 11, 1992): 27.

Ogundipe-Leslie, Molara. "Women in Nigeria." In *Women in Nigeria Today,* ed., Editorial Committee. London: Zed Press, 1985: 119-131.

Osarenren, Ewaen. "Women Liberation Movement: The Misunderstood Lot," *Sunday Concord* (June 5, 1986): 12.

Rogers, Barbara. *The Domestication of Women: Discrimination in Developing Societies.* London: Tavistock Publications, 1980.

Van Allen, Judith. "'Sitting on a Man': Colonialism and the Lost Political Institutions of Igbo Women" *Canadian Journal of African Studies* 6.2 (1972): 165-181.

Wushishi, Mallam. "Nigerian Women: 1992 and Beyond." *Daily Times* (January 22, 1992): 32.

AFRICANA WOMANISM

CLENORA HUDSON-WEEMS

> Feminism. You know how we feel about that embarrassing
> Western philosophy? The destroyer of homes. Imported
> mainly from America to ruin nice African women.
> —Ama Ata Aidoo, 1986

CENTRAL TO THE SPIRIT OF AFRICANANS (CONTINENTAL Africans and Africans in the diaspora) regarding feminism in the Africana community is the above quotation by internationally acclaimed African novelist and critic, Ama Ata Aidoo. One of today's most controversial issues in both the academy and the broader community is the role of the Africana woman within the context of the modem feminist movement. Both men and women are debating this issue, particularly as it relates to Africana women in their efforts to remain authentic in their existence, such as prioritizing their needs even if the needs are not of primary concern for the dominant culture. The ever-present question remains the same: what is the relationship between an Africana woman and her family, her community, and her career in today's society that emphasizes—in the midst of oppression, human suffering, and death— the empowerment of women and individualism over human dignity and rights?

While many academicians uncritically adopt feminism in its established theoretical concept based on the notion that gender is primary in women's struggle in the patriarchal system, most Africana women in general do not identify with the concept in its entirety and thus cannot see themselves as feminists. Granted, the prioritizing of female empowerment and gender issues may be jus-

tifiable for those women who have not been plagued by powerlessness based on ethnic differences; however, that is certainly not the
case for those who are Africana women. Those Africana women who
do adopt some form of feminism do so because of feminism's theoretical and methodological legitimacy in the academy and their
desire to be a legitimate part of the academic community. Moreover,
they adopt feminism because of the absence of a suitable framework for their individual needs as Africana women. But while some
have accepted the label, more and more Africana women today—
in the academy and in the community—are reassessing the historical realities and the agenda for the modern feminist movement.
These women are concluding that feminist terminology does not
accurately reflect their reality or their struggle.[1] Hence, feminism—
even qualified as Black feminism, which relates to African-American
women in particular—is extremely problematic as a label for the
true Africana woman and invites much debate and controversy
among today's scholars and women in general.

It should be noted here that there is another form of feminism
that is closely identified with Africana women around the world.
While African feminism is a bit less problematic for Africana women
than is feminism in general, it is more closely akin to Africana womanism. According to African literary critic Rose Acholonu, in a
paper she presented in July 1992 at the first international conference on Women in Africa and the African Diaspora: Bridges across
Activism and the Academy, Nsukka, Nigeria:

> The negative hues of the American and European radical
> feminism have succeeded in alienating even the fair-mind-
> ed Africans from the concept. The sad result is that today
> [the] majority of Africans (including successful female writ-
> ers) tend to disassociate themselves from it.[2]

Hence, in spite of the accuracy of Filomina Chioma Steady in her
astute assessment of the struggle and reality of Africana women (*The
Black Woman Cross-Culturally*), the very terminology "African feminism"
is problematic, as it inevitably suggests an alignment with feminism, a
concept that has been alien to the plight of Africana women from its
inception. This is particularly the case in reference to racism and clas-
sism, which are prevailing obstacles in the lives of Africana people, a
reality that the theorist herself recognizes. According to Steady:

> Regardless of one's position, the implications of the femi-
> nist movement for the black woman are complex.... Several

factors set the black woman apart as having a different order of priorities. She is oppressed not simply because of her sex but ostensibly because of her race and, for the majority, essentially because of their class. Women belong to different socioeconomic groups and do not represent a universal category. Because the majority of black women are poor, there is likely to be some alienation from the middle-class aspect of the women's movement which perceives feminism as an attack on men rather than on a system which thrives on inequality (23-24).

In an essay, "African Feminism: A Worldwide Perspective" (Terborg-Penn et al., 1987), Steady asserts that

> For the majority of black women poverty is a way of life. For the majority of black women also racism has been the most important obstacle in the acquisition of the basic needs for survival. Through the manipulation of racism, the world economic institutions have produced a situation which negatively affects black people, particularly black women.... What we have, then, is not a simple issue of sex or class differences but a situation which, because of the racial factor, is castlike in character on both a national and global scale. (18-19)

It becomes apparent, then, that neither the terms Black feminism nor African feminism are sufficient to label women of such complex realities as Africana women, particularly as both terms, through their very names, align themselves with feminism.

Why not feminism for Africana women? To begin with, the true history of feminism, its origins and its participants, reveals its blatant racist background, thereby establishing its incompatibility with Africana women. Feminism, earlier called the Woman's Suffrage Movement in the United States, started when a group of liberal, white women, whose concerns then were for the abolition of slavery and equal rights for all people regardless of race, class, and sex, dominated the scene among women on the national level during the first half of the nineteenth century. At the time of the Civil War, such leaders as Susan B. Anthony and Elizabeth Cady Stanton held the universalist philosophy on the natural rights of women to full citizenship, which included the right to vote. However, in 1870 the Fifteenth Amendment to the Constitution of the United States ratified the voting rights of Africana men, leaving women, white women in particular, and their desire for the same rights, unaddressed. Middle-class white women were naturally disappointed, for they had assumed that their efforts toward securing full citizenship for Africana people would ultimately benefit them, too, in their desire for full citizenship as voting citizens. The result was a racist reaction to the Amendment and towards Africanans in particular. Thus, from the 1880s on, an organized movement among white women shifted the pendulum to a radically conservative posture on the part of white women in general.

In 1890 the National American Woman Suffrage Association (NAWSA) was founded by northern white women, but "southern women were also vigorously courted by that group" (Giddings, 81), epitomizing the growing race chauvinism of the late nineteenth century. The organization, which brought together the National Woman Suffrage Association and the American Woman Suffrage Association, departed from Susan B. Anthony's original women's suffrage posture. They asserted that the vote for women should be utilized chiefly by middle-class white women, who could aid their husbands in preserving the virtues of the Republic from the threat of unqualified and biological inferiors (Africana men) who, with the power of the vote, could gain a political foothold in the American system. For example, staunch conservative suffragist leader Carrie Chapman Catt and other women of her persuasion insisted on strong Anglo-Saxon values and white supremacy. They were interested in banding with white men to secure the vote for pure whites, excluding not only Africanans but white immigrants as well. Historians Peter Carrol and David Noble quoted Catt in *The Free and the Unfree* as saying that "there is but one way to avert the danger. Cut off the vote of the slums and give it to [white] women." She continued that middle-class white men must recognize "the usefulness of woman suffrage as a counterbalance to the foreign vote, and as a means of legally preserving white supremacy in the South" (296). These suffragists felt that because Africana people (Africana men in particular, with their new status as voters) were members of an inferior race, they should not be granted the right to vote in advance of the female "half" of the dominant group. Thus, while the disappointment of being left out in the area of gaining full citizenship—i.e., voting rights—for white women was well-founded, their hostility and racist, antagonistic feelings toward Africanans in general cannot be dismissed lightly.

Feminism, a term conceptualized and adopted by white women, involves an agenda that was designed to meet the needs and demands of that particular group. For this reason, it is quite plausible for white women to identify with feminism and the feminist movement. Having said that, the fact remains that placing all women's history under white women's history, thereby giving the latter the definitive position, is problematic. In fact, it demonstrates the ultimate in racist arrogance and domination to suggest that authentic activity of women resides with white women. Hence, Africana women activists in America, in particular, such as Sojourner Truth (militant abolition spokesperson and universal suffragist), Harriet Tubman (Underground Railroad conductor who spent her lifetime aiding Africana slaves, both male and female, in their escape to the North for freedom), and Ida B. Wells (anti-lynching crusader during the early twentieth century), can be considered *pre*feminists, despite the fact that the activities of these Africana women did not focus exclusively on women's issues. In view of the activities of early Africana women such as those mentioned above and countless other unsung Africana heroines, what white feminists have done in reality was to take the life-style and techniques of Africana women activists and used them as models or blueprints for the framework of their theory, and then name, define, and legitimize it as the only real substantive movement for women. Hence, when they define a feminist and feminist activity, they are, in fact, identifying with independent Africana women, women they both emulated and envied. Such women they have come in contact with from the beginning of American slavery, all the way up to the modern Civil Rights Movement with such Africana women activists as Mamie Till Mobley, the mother of Emmett Louis Till,[3] and Rosa Parks, the mother of the Modern Civil Rights Movement. Therefore, when Africana women come along and embrace feminism, appending it to their identity as Black feminists or African feminists, they are in reality duplicating the duplicate.

Africana womanism is a term I coined and defined in 1987 after nearly two years of publicly debating the importance of self-naming for Africana women. Why the term *"Africana Womanism"*? Upon concluding that the term "Black Womanism" was not quite the terminology to include the total meaning desired for this concept, I decided that *"Africana Womanism,"* a natural evolution in naming, was the ideal terminology for two basic reasons. The first part of the coinage, *Africana*, identifies the ethnicity of the woman being considered, and this reference to her ethnicity, establishing her cultural identity, relates directly to her ancestry and land base: Africa. The second part of the term, *Womanism*, recalls Sojourner Truth's powerful impromptu speech "And Ain't I a Woman," one in which she battles with the dominant alienating forces in her life as a struggling Africana woman, questioning the accepted idea of womanhood. Without question, she is the flip side of the coin, the co-partner in the struggle for her people, one who, unlike the white woman, has received no special privileges in American society. But there is another crucial issue that accounts for the use of the term woman(ism). The term "woman," and by extension "womanism," is far more appropriate than "female" ("feminism") because of one major distinction—only a female of the human race can be a woman. "Female," on the other hand, can refer to a member of the animal or plant kingdom as well as to a member of the human race. Furthermore, in electronic and mechanical terminology, there is a female counterbalance to the male correlative. Hence, terminology derived from the word "woman" is more suitable and more specific when naming a group of the human race—in a word, more "human."

The Africana womanist is not to be confused with Alice Walker's "womanist" as presented in her collection of essays entitled *In Search of Our Mothers' Gardens*. According to Walker, a womanist is:

> A black feminist or feminist of color...who loves other women, sexually and/or nonsexual. Appreciates and prefers women's culture....[and who] sometimes loves individual men, sexually and/or nonsexually. Committed to survival and wholeness of entire people, male and female.... Womanist is to feminist as purple to lavender. (xii, xii)

Clearly the interest here is almost exclusively in the woman: *her* sexuality and *her* culture. The culminating definition, "womanist is to feminist as purple to lavender," firmly establishes the author's concept of the affinity between the womanist and the feminist. There is hardly any differentiation, only a slight shade of difference in color. The Africana womanist, on the other hand, is significantly different from the mainstream feminist, particularly in her perspective on and approach to issues in society. This is to be expected, for obviously their historical realities and present stance in society are not the same. Africana women and white women come from different segments of society and, thus, feminism as an ideology is not equally applicable to both.

Neither an outgrowth nor an addendum to feminism, *Africana womanism is not* black feminism, African feminism, or Walker's womanism that some Africana women have come to embrace. *Africana womanism is* an ideology created and designed for all women of African descent. It is grounded in *African* culture and, therefore, it necessarily focuses on the unique experiences, struggles, needs, and desires of Africana women. It critically addresses the dynamics of the conflict between the mainstream feminist, the black feminist, the African feminist, and the Africana womanist. The conclusion is that Africana womanism and its agenda are unique and separate from both white feminism and Black feminism; moreover, to the extent of naming in particular, Africana womanism differs from African feminism.

Clearly there is a need for a separate and distinct identity for the Africana woman and her movement. Some white women acknowledge that the feminist movement was not designed with the Africana woman in mind. For example, white feminist Catherine Clinton asserts that "feminism primarily appealed to educated and middle-class white women, rather than black and white working-class women" (Clinton 1987:63). Steady, in her article entitled "African Feminism: A Worldwide Perspective" (Terborg-Penn *et al.*, 1987), admits that:

> Various schools of thought, perspectives, and ideological proclivities have influenced the study of feminism. Few studies have dealt with the issue of racism, since the dominant voice of the feminist movement has been that of the white female. The issue of racism can become threatening, for it identifies white feminists as possible participants in the oppression of blacks. (3)

Africana men and women do not accept the idea of Africana women as feminists. There is a general consensus in the Africana community that the feminist movement, by and large, is the white woman's movement for two reasons. First, the Africana woman does not see the man as her primary enemy as does the white feminist, who is carrying out an age-old battle with her white male counterpart for subjugating her as his property. Africana men have never had the same institutionalized power to oppress Africana women as white men have had to oppress white women. According to the Africana sociologist, Clyde Franklin II, "Black men are relatively powerless in this country, and their attempts at domination, aggression, and the like, while sacrificing humanity, are ludicrous" (Franklin II 1986: 112). Joyce Ladner, another Africana sociologist, succinctly articulates the dynamics of the relationship between Africana men and women and does not view the former as the enemy of the latter :

"Black women do not perceive their enemy to be black men, but rather the enemy is considered to be oppressive forces in the larger society which subjugate black men, women and children" (Ladner 1972: 277-78).

Since Africana women never have been considered the property of their male counterparts, Africana women and men alike dismiss the primacy of gender issues in their reality, and thus dismiss the feminist movement as a viable framework for their chief concerns. Instead, they hold to the opinion that those Africana women who embrace the feminist movement are mere assimilationists or sellouts who, in the final analysis, have no true commitment to their culture or their people, particularly as it relates to the historical and current collective struggle of Africana men and women.

Second, Africana women reject the feminist movement because of their apprehension and distrust of white organizations. In fact, white organized groups in general, such as the Communist Party and the National Organization for Women, have never been able to galvanize the majority of Africana people. On the whole, Africanans are grassroots people who depend on the support and confidence of their communities and who, based on historical instances of betrayal, are necessarily suspicious of organizations founded, operated, and controlled by whites. In general, Africanans focus on tangible things that can offer an amelioration of or exit from oppression, which are of utmost importance for survival in the Africana community. Those Africana intellectuals who insist on identifying with organizations that offer them neither leadership nor high visibility generally subordinate their blackness to the comfort of being accepted by white intellectuals. Unfortunately for those Africana intellectuals, philosophy and scholarship take precedence even over self-identity, and they seem to be satisfied with merely belonging to a white group.

Having established that the major problem with the African feminist is that of naming, what is the major problem with the black feminist? Briefly stated, the black feminist is an Africana woman who has adopted the agenda of the feminist movement to some degree in that she, like the white feminist, perceives gender issues to be most critical in her quest for empowerment and selfhood. On the outskirts of feminist activity, Black feminists possess neither power nor leadership in the movement. Black feminist bell hooks obviously realizes this, as she makes a call for Africana women to move "from margin to center" of the feminist movement in her book entitled *Feminist Theory: From Margin to Center.* Receiving recognition as heralds of feminism by way of legitimating the movement through their identification with it, black feminists are frequently delegated by white feminists as the voice of Africana women. However, this peripheral promotion of black feminists is only transient, as they will never be afforded the same level of importance as white feminists enjoy. It is quite obvious, for example, that bell hooks will never be elevated to the same status as either Betty Friedan or Gloria Steinem. At best, she and her fellow black feminists are given only temporary recognition as representatives and spokespersons for Africana people in general and Africana women in particular. Black feminists advance an agenda that is in direct contravention to that in the Africana community, thereby demonstrating a certain lack of African-centered historical and contemporary perspective. Although white feminists contend that the movement is a panacea for the problems of Africana women, they have been unsuccessful in galvanizing the majority of Africana women as feminists. In fact, there is no existing group of white women controlling the majority of Africana women to the extent of directing and dictating the latter's thought and action.

While Africana women do, in fact, have some legitimate concerns regarding Africana men, these concerns must be addressed within the context of African culture. Problems must not be resolved using an alien framework (e.g., feminism) but must be resolved from within an endemic theoretical construct—*Africana Womanism.* It appears that many Africana women who become black feminists (or who are inclined more in that direction) base their decisions upon either naiveté about the history and ramifications of feminism or on negative experiences with Africana men. For example, because there are some Africana women who pride themselves on being economically independent (which was the way of life for Africana women long before the advent of feminism) and because one of the chief tenets of feminism in the larger society is that a woman is economically independent, many Africana women unthinkingly respond positively to the notion of being a feminist. To be sure, Africana women have always been, by necessity, independent and responsible co-workers and decision-makers. But while this naiveté can be easily corrected, negative personal experiences cannot be rectified so readily.

True, one's personal experiences are valid ways of determining one's world view; however, the resulting generalization that many black feminists share—that all or most Africana men are less worthy than women—is based upon intellectual laziness, which requires effortless rationalization. By the same analysis, it is easy for some people to believe that all white people or all people of any race or sex form a homogenous group, and it is difficult for them to treat people as individuals. This is important because, in reality, relationships are based on individual particularities rather than on an overriding group characteristic. For example, an Africana brother having a bad experience with an Africana woman might conclude that all Africana women are undesirable, thus castigating this entire group of people. A classic example of gross exaggeration based not on facts but on polemics or limited personal experiences, is Michelle Wallace's book entitled *Black Macho and the Myth of the Super Woman* (1980). In this book, the author makes a serious attack on Africana men by categorizing them as super macho men who physically and mentally abuse Africana women. It is apparent that the author's personal negative experiences with Africana men, which she relates throughout the book, influenced her ideology. The tragedy is that her book, which was endorsed in different ways by the many feminists listed in the Acknowledgments, received such wide exposure that it consequently influenced the thoughts of an entire generation, thereby representing a watershed in the development of modern black feminist thought.

If one considers the collective plight of Africana people globally, it becomes clear that we cannot afford the luxury, if you will, of being consumed by gender issues. A supreme paradigm of the need for Africana women to prioritize the struggle for human dignity and parity is presented by South African woman activist, Ruth Mompati. In her heart-rending stories of unimaginable racial atrocities heaped upon innocent children, as well as upon men and women, Mompati asserts the following:

> The South African woman, faced with the above situation, finds the order of her priorities in her struggle for human dignity and her rights as a woman dictated by the general political struggle of her people as a whole. The national liberation of the black South African is a prerequisite to her own liberation and emancipation as a woman and a worker. The process of struggle for national liberation has been accompanied by the politicizing of both men and women. This has kept the women's struggle from degenerating into a sexist struggle that would divorce women's position in society from the political, social, and economic development of the society as a whole. From the South African

women who together with their men seek to liberate their
country, come an appeal to friends and supporters to raise
their voices on their behalf. (Ntiri 1982:112-13)

Overall, "human discrimination transcends sex discrimination....the
costs of human suffering are high when compared to a component,
sex obstacle" (Ibid.: 6). Furthermore, according to Steady in *The
Black Woman Cross-Culturally*:

for the black woman in a racist society, racial factors, rather
than sexual ones, operate more consistently in making her
a target for discrimination and marginalization. This
becomes apparent when the "family" is viewed as a unit of
analysis. Regardless of differential access to resources by
both men and women, white males and females, as members of family groups, share a proportionately higher quan-
tity of the earth's resources than do black males and females.
There is a great difference between discrimination by privilege and protection, and discrimination by deprivation and
exclusion. (27-28)

Steady's assessment here speaks directly to the source of discrimination that Africana women suffer at the hands of a racist system.
There is the oppression of the South African woman who must serve
as maid and nurse to the white household with minimum wage earn-
ings, the Caribbean woman in London who is the ignored secretary, and the Senegalese or African worker in France who is despised
and unwanted. There is the Nigerian subsistence farmer, such as
the Ibo woman in Enugu and Nsukka, who farms every day for minimum wages, and the female Brazilian factory worker who is the
lowest on the totem pole. Clearly, the problems of these women are
not inflicted upon them solely because they are women. They are
victimized first and foremost because they are black; they are further victimized because they are women living in a white male-dominated society.

The problems of Africana women, including physical brutality,
sexual harassment, and female subjugation in general, perpetrated
both within and outside the race, ultimately have to be solved on a
collective basis *within Africana communities*. Africana people must
eliminate racist influences in their lives first, with the realization that
they can neither afford nor tolerate any form of female subjugation. Along those same lines, Ntiri summarizes Mompati's position
that sexism "is basically a secondary problem which arises out of

race, class and economic prejudices"(5).

Because one of the main tensions between Africana men and women in the United States involves employment and economic opportunity, Africanans frequently fall into a short - sighted perception of things. For example, it is not a question of more jobs for Africana women versus more jobs for Africana men, a situation that too frequently promotes gender competition. Rather, it is a question of *more jobs for Africanans in general.* These jobs are generated primarily by white people, and most Africanans depend on sources other than those supplied by Africana people. *The real challenge for Africana men and women is how to create more economic opportunities within Africana communities.* Many people talk about the need for enhanced Africana economic empowerment. If our real goal in life is to be achieved—that is, the survival of our entire race as a primary concern for Africana women—it will have to come from Africana men *and* women working together. If Africana men and women are fighting within the community, they are ultimately defeating themselves on all fronts.

Perhaps because of all the indisputable problems and turmoil heaped upon the Africana community, much of which is racially grounded, Africanans frequently fail to *look closely at available options* to determine if those options are, in fact, sufficiently workable. Rather than *create other options for themselves,* Africanans ally with white privileged-class phenomena, such as feminism. On the other hand, when a group takes control over its struggle, tailoring it to meet its collective needs and demands, the group is almost always successful. When success in one's goals is realized, it makes for a more peaceful reality for all concerned, and one is more inclined to a wholesome and amicable relationship with others, knowing that the concerns of the people are respected and met. As Africana Womanism—rather than feminism, black feminism, African feminism, or "mere" womanism—is a conceivable alternative for the Africana woman in her collective struggle with the entire community, it enhances future possibilities for the dignity of Africana people and the humanity of all. In short, the reclamation of Africana women via properly identifying our own collective struggle and acting upon it is a key step toward human harmony and survival.

NOTES

1. For many reasons, many white women as well as African women have become disenchanted with feminism.
2. Rose Acholonu presented a paper entitled "Love and the Feminist Utopia in the African Novel" at the first international conference on Women in Africa and the African Diaspora: Bridges across Activism and the Academy, Nsukka, Nigeria, July 13–18, 1992.
3. Emmett Louis "Bobo" Till was the 14-year-old Africana Chicago youth who was lynched in 1955 in Money, Mississippi for whistling at a 21-year-old white woman. For a detailed explanation of Till's importance to the Modern Civil Rights Movement, read Clenora Hudson's (Hudson-Weems's) 1988 doctoral dissertation entitled "Emmett Till: The Impetus for the Modern Civil Rights Movement" and "Emmett Till: The Sacrificial Lamb of the Civil Rights Movement."

WORKS CITED

Acholonu, Rose. "Love and the Feminist Utopia in the African Novel." Paper presented at the first international conference on Women in Africa and the African Diaspora: Bridges across Activism and the Academy, Nsukka, Nigeria, July 13–18, 1992.

Aidoo, Ama Ata. "Unwelcomed Pals and Decorative Slaves or Glimpses of Women as Writers and Characters in Contemporary African Literatures." In *Literature and Society: Selected Essays on African Literature*, ed., Ernest Emenyonu. Oguta: Zim Pan African Publishers, 1989: 1-19.

Carroll, Peter N., and David W. Noble. *The Free and the Unfree: A New History of the United States*. New York: Penguin Books, 1977.

Clinton, Catherine. "Women Break New Ground." *The Underside of American History*, vol. 2, ed., Thomas R. Fraizer. New York: Harcourt Brace Jovanovich, 1987: 62-83.

Franklin, Clyde, II. "Black Male—Black Female Conflict: Individually Caused and Culturally Nurtured." *The Black Family: Essays and Studies*, ed., Robert Staples. Belmont, Calif.: Wadsworth Press, 1986: 106-113.

Giddings, Paula. *When and Where I Enter: The Impact of Black Women on Race and Sex in America*. New York: Bantam, 1984.

hooks, bell. *Feminist Theory: From Margin to Center*. Boston: Southend, 1984.

Hudson, Clenora. "Emmett Till: The Impetus for the Modern Civil Rights Movement." Ph. D. dissertation, University of Iowa, 1988.

Ladner, Joyce. *Tomorrow's Tomorrow: The Black Woman*. Garden City, N.Y.: Anchor, 1972.

Mompati, Ruth. "Women and Life under Apartheid." In *One is Not a Woman, One Becomes: The African Woman in a Transitional Society*, ed., Daphne Williams Ntiri. Troy, Mich.: Bedford Publishers, 1982: 108-113.

Ntiri, Daphne Williams, ed. *One is Not a Woman, One Becomes: The African Woman in a Transitional Society*. Troy, Mich.: Bedford Publishers, 1982.

Steady, Filomina Chioma, ed. *The Black Woman Cross-Culturally*. Cambridge, Mass.: Schenkman, 1981.

——."The Black Woman Cross-Culturally: An Overview." In *The Black*

Woman Cross-Culturally. Cambridge, Mass.: Schenkman, 1981.

——. "African Feminism: A Worldwide Perspective." In*Women in Africa and the African Diaspora*, ed., Rosalyn Terborg-Penn, Sharon Harley, and Andrea Benton Rushing. Washington, DC: Howard University Press, 1987: 3-24.

Walker, Alice. *In Search of Our Mothers' Gardens.* San Diego: Harcourt, 1983.

Wallace, Michele. *Black Macho and the Myth of the Superwoman.* New York: Warner, 1980.

North American Feminisms/Global Feminisms[1]— Contradictory or Complementary?

Angela Miles

INTRODUCTION

"Western"/"white"/"first world"[2] feminism[3] is criticized by some these days as: (1) narrowly focused on gender oppression without due attention to class, race, colonial, and other oppressions; (2) presuming white, middle-class women's reality is every woman's reality; and (3) accepting the patriarchal myth that industrialization and urbanization have meant increased equality and liberty for women and that "third world" women are, therefore, more oppressed and their liberation will involve moving closer in condition to "first world" women.[4]

There are, of course, feminists in North America who: (1) accept uncritically the simple, ethnocentric and industrial notion of "progress"; (2) see women's struggle more as a struggle to be admitted into existing structures than to transform them; and (3) on this erroneous basis, make invalid presumptions about the greater powerlessness and oppression of women elsewhere in the world. However, feminisms in North America, like feminisms everywhere, are enormously diverse.

In this paper I will examine forms of North American feminisms shaped by much broader transformative visions and principles which they share with feminisms around the world; and I will illustrate the ways these diverse feminisms are both built by and build women's global struggles across large colonial, class, and race differences, against all these forms of power as well as patriarchal power.

ASSIMILATIONIST AND TRANSFORMATIVE FEMINISIMS IN NORTH AMERICA

I have argued elsewhere[5] that, for all their diversity, North American feminisms can usefully be understood to fall into two main tendencies which I have called "assimilationist" and "transformative." The assimilationist tendency bases the case for women's equality on women's sameness with men. In doing so, these feminists fail to posit any alternative female associated values to the dominant androcentric values. They are thus restricted to essentially limited pressure-group politics.[6] Their politics challenges women's exclusion from dominant structures and definitions of humanity without challenging the nature of these structures and definitions. The mainstream media and many critics of "Western"/"white"/ "first world" feminisms generally presume (or at least speak as if) this tendency is the whole of feminism in North America.[7] But this is to overlook forms of *transformative feminism* that also flourish.

Transformative feminisms go beyond simply claiming women's equality/sameness with men to affirm *both* women's equality with and differences from men. This allows them to use diverse women's specific work, life experiences, concerns, and values as resources to challenge dominant male presumptions and structures and definitions of humanity. As early as 1971, a Canadian feminist expressed the twin goals of access and transformation:

> Our goal must be to obtain full human status for women in every area of human activity. And this is not to accept the present "human activity" realm of the male. Values in the male realm, today, are firmly rooted in the evils of power, dominance and oppression. We must look for a broader and deeper definition of human life.[8]

Transformative feminists' refusal of the apparent logical contradiction between women's equality and difference from men is part of their general refusal of Western patriarchal industrial dualism. These feminists refuse the hierarchical and separatist logic which constructs the world as a series of oppositions, privileging the male-associated side over the female-associated side, and feeding such binaries as ends/means; reason/emotion; society/nature; individual/community; political/personal, self/other, public/private, mental/ manual, mind/body, spirit/flesh.

In transformative feminisms, holistic visions of the world and integrative values are posed in opposition to dualistic logic and separatist values; women and women's work of human and social reproduction are made visible and moved from the margins to the center of visions of social organization and value; individualism and competition are challenged in the name of cooperation, care, nurture, and community; sustaining life is emphasized over making profits; scientific dualism and Western science's claim to universal and superior knowledge is abandoned, thus allowing the valorization and integration of diverse and devalued knowledges (for instance, of women and tribal and indigenous peoples); and diversity is affirmed as a resource. In this process *everything* is redefined: production, progress, development, wealth, to name just a few concepts relevant to this topic.

Feminists of color and lesbian feminists, both white and women of color, have played a central role in the development and strengthening of transformative feminist politics in North America.[9] However it is not restricted to these groups. All the generally recognized strands of feminist radicalism in North America have both assimilative and transformative tendencies. Socialist, black, lesbian, and radical feminisms, for instance, all come in both forms. And Western transformative feminisms, in all these varieties and more, are important potential allies for "third world" feminists and activists who are resisting the same dualistic and exploitative relationships.

TRANSFORMATIVE FEMINISMS IN THE "FIRST WORLD" AND THE "TWO THIRDS WORLD"

Transformative feminists from all parts[10] of the world challenge the dominations of class, race, and colonialism as well as gender; they present feminist perspectives on the whole of society and not just selected "women's issues"; and they reject the assumptions and value judgments underlying the "modernization" project which is being imposed by the West to the detriment of the whole of nature and most of the world's people in all regions.[11]

Transformative feminists everywhere share the view that the existing world system is in crisis on all levels in all parts of both "third" and "first" worlds and that this is reflected in ecological, economic, social, cultural, and ethical breakdown. This system is neither sustainable nor desirable. The unequal, competitive, profit-based, individualistic market relations at its core are exploitative and destructive. "Development" is essentially a violent process of establishing and protecting these relationships (in both "first" and "third" worlds). The economic "growth" that is the acknowledged aim of this "development" is actually the expansion of the market and production-for-exchange at the expense of production-for-use. It (1) removes the means of subsistence from individuals and communities; (2) institutionalizes men's dependence on wages and women's dependence on men; (3) fuels the concentration of wealth and power in fewer and fewer hands, ultimately those of a few non-accountable transnational corporations. It has historically depended on military conquest and control of nature, women, and traditional cultures and communities, and continues to do so.

Today, "first world" feminist criticisms of patriarchal industrial "progress," growth, production, consumption, and profit parallel "third world" feminist criticisms of "development" guided by the same profit-centered, instrumental values. Transformative feminists all over the world not only resist the worst consequences of modernization and "development," but work towards totally different, equal, cooperative, life-sustaining, communal forms of social and economic organization. They make this struggle in the name of both women's equality and women-associated, women-affirming values.[12] U. S. feminists Barbara Ehrenreich and Deirdre English, for instance, in their book *For Her Own Good: One Hundred Years of the Experts' Advice to Women* declared:

> We refuse to remain on the margins of society, and we refuse to enter that society on its own terms.... The human values that women were assigned to preserve [must] become the organizing principles of society. The vision that is implicit in feminism [is] a society organized around human needs.... There are no human alternatives. The Market, with its financial abstractions, deformed science, and obsession with dead things must be pushed back to the margins. And the "womanly" values of community and caring must rise to the center as the only *human* principles.[13]

Vandana Shiva from India argues similarly in her book *Staying Alive: Women, Ecology and Development* that:

> The recovery of the feminine principle allows a transcendence and transformation of patriarchal foundations of maldevelopment. It allows a redefinition of growth and productivity as categories linked to the production, not the destruction of life. It is thus simultaneously an ecological and a feminist political project which legitimises the way of knowing and being that creates wealth by enhancing life and diversity, and which delegitimises the knowledge and practice of a culture of death as the basis for capital accumulation.[14]

The international "third world" feminist group DAWN (Development Alternatives with Women for a New Era) also views women's values and activities as the key to a more human world in the book, *Development, Crises, and Alternative Visions: Third World Women's Perspectives:*

> We want a world where inequality based on class, gender, and race is absent from every country, and from the relationships between countries. We want a world where basic needs become basic rights and where poverty and all forms of violence are eliminated. Each person will have the opportunity to develop her or his full potential and creativity, and women's values of nurturance and solidarity will characterize human relationships.... We want a world where all institutions are open to participatory democratic processes, where women share in determining priorities and making decisions.[15]

These shared values and visions[16] mean that "third world" feminists can expect significant support from transformative Western feminists in their resistance to the destruction being imposed on their communities in the name of "modernization" and "development," and that transformative feminisms in the West will be significantly broadened and strengthened by these links.

"WOMEN IN DEVELOPMENT" AND TRANSFORMATIVE FEMINISMS

In our divided world, most "third world"/"first world" interaction is still through unequal "development" relationships of "donor" and "recipient." Donor nations and multi-national agencies have, for some ten to fifteen years now, been providing money and introducing guidelines to encourage and require women's increasing participation in "development." This has been partly a response to feminist pressure and has, on occasion, provided support for women in development agencies, both in the North and the South, and at the grassroots. It has also provided valuable experiences of struggle from which women have learned a great deal about the limits of "development." However, "Women in Development" (WID) and "Gender and Development" (GAD) initiatives are, by definition, largely restricted to change within "development" and are designed to reform rather than transcend the process. It is crucial not to confuse these (often important but nevertheless limited) WID and GAD initiatives with autonomous transformative feminist practice.

In my more paranoid moments I suspect that one of the reasons for the surprisingly quick economic response of the development industry to demands for attention to women is precisely because WID and GAD do potentially displace/disrupt/interrupt political connections among autonomous women's groups and activists in "third" and "first" worlds. Relations of donor and recipient are fostered instead. WID and GAD relationships are between "third world" and "first world" women in development agencies or between these women and activists and/or grassroots women from the *South*. By definition they exclude activists from the *North*. These connections among women may be useful to feminists concerned to build autonomous and equal relationships. However, the general exclusion of "first world" feminists active in their own communities undermines the reciprocal, movement to movement, connections which are the hallmark of global feminisms.

The unequal discourse of development that shapes and contains WID and GAD relationships means that they cannot provide an adequate frame for the development of political sisterhood/solidarity. On the contrary, if they are understood by "third world" women to reflect the whole of Western feminisms, these WID and GAD relationships can mask the existence of transformative feminisms in the "first world" and impede the development of global solidarity/sisterhood. When this occurs, the necessary and difficult process of building political relations among "first world" and "third world" movement counterparts is supplanted by suspiciously well-funded relations between women in the development industry in North and South and between these women and some activists in the South.

The realm of "development" and "aid" is an important area of practice. Transformative feminists around the world are struggling to change the definitions and structures of the "development industry." But this is only one among many arenas of international practice. Health-care workers, publishers, disabled women, trade unionists, adult educators, Women's Studies teachers, lesbians, filmmakers, judges, Christian women, Muslim women, indigenous women—to name just a few—are building autonomous regional and international networks. Political links are being forged in resistance to (among other things) reproductive technologies, militarism, external debt and structural adjustment policies, environmental destruction, sex tourism, violence against women, and religious fundamentalism in all its forms.[17]

In the process it is becoming clear that what we call "development issues" in the "third world," such as housing, education, health, child care, and poverty, are called "social issues" in the "first world." These are not qualitatively different phenomena as "development" definitions imply, but shared political issues that constitute a potential basis for common political struggle. Global feminisms are the result of this common struggle grounded in diverse local realities. They supersede unequal "development" relationships by building equal and authentic[18] international and regional political relationships among activists in every area of practice. Caribbean feminist Peggy Antrobus describes the ways that broader and deeper analyses are supporting new understandings for all women which enable "global sisterhood...(to) eliminate notions of the rich and powerful helping the poor":

> Just as I have finally come to the issue of Peace out of an acknowledgment of the implications of the economic, social and political cost of the arms race for developing countries, my sisters of the North may begin to understand how the issue of Development affects and is affected by their life styles: And we may all come to accept a new interpretation of Equality as the basis for a global sisterhood which eliminates notions of the rich and powerful helping the poor and powerless. We inhabit one World and no person is an island—we are all part

of the mainland of our planet—Equality, Development and
Peace are as important to the women and countries of the
North as they are for the women and countries of the South.[19]
[Equality, Development and Peace are the themes of the
United Nations Decade for Women 1975–85]

It is clear from this quotation that dialogue and networking among
diverse women is key to the mutual learning that reveals common
interests and sustains a common struggle.

"TWO THIRDS WORLD"/"FIRST WORLD" DIALOGUE

In fact, transformative feminists are criticizing industrialism/mod-
ernization/ "development"/capitalism from both the "developed"
and "developing" ends of the process. Sharing observations and
experiences from these different locations in the same international system of exploitation is an important resource in developing feminist theory and practice in both contexts. "First world" feminists
reveal the hollowness of liberal, urban, modern promises of equality in marriage, the work force, and sexual relations. "Third world"
feminists describe the negative impact on people in general and
women in particular of processes which increasingly shape their
countries and communities to the requirements of "growth" and
production for profit and the market, and they report on the costs
of the structural adjustment policies of the World Bank, the
International Monetary Fund (IMF), and Western nations. "First
world" women let their "third world" sisters know that in "developed"
nations female poverty and economic dependence, wife beating, and
violence against women in general persist, while the invisibility of
women's work is aggravated. "Third world" women challenge the
ethnocentrism of the convenient patriarchal myth that "modernization" has generated unproblematic "progress" for women and
that women in "developed" nations necessarily enjoy freedom and
status envied by women elsewhere. "Third World" women point out,
to the contrary, that the introduction of market economies and the
undermining of traditional practices are generally done in ways
which disadvantage women; they insist, moreover, that "first world"
feminists recognize and resist the role their own governments and
corporations have historically played—and continue to play—in the
exploitation and destruction of "third world" communities and peoples and that they acknowledge the extent to which levels of consumption in the North depend on this exploitation.

Women all over the world also learn a great deal about their own personal situations from dialogue with women in different circumstances. One of the most powerful ways that patriarchal ideological mystifications of a culture can be revealed is through questions about a country's or community's practices and beliefs by women who have not been raised with them. "Third world" women's questions about romance and Western marriage may reveal to "first world" women the unfounded presumptions they/we often make, for instance, that couples share an economic status and that the power and economic interests of the man and woman are the same. In dialogue across cultures, it appears that patterns of relationships, behaviors, and customs—in all communities—that are so taken for granted as to be invisible and seen as natural are revealed as social constructions that can be challenged and changed or honored and built upon.

Diversity is a resource not only because different experiences can provide space for questions unthinkable to those born and raised in a culture and so increase awareness, but also because activism among diverse groups of women forces issues of race and class and colonialism to be raised and dealt with among feminists. The argument here, that transformative feminisms provide a frame which can enable sisterhood/solidarity to be built among women across these deep divisions should not be read to suggest that women in all groups are likely to develop the same insights and make the same contributions. Obviously working-class women, women of color, lesbian women, and "third world" women have particularly important roles to play in the development of full feminist politics which can address these dominations as well as gender domination.[20]

The tensions and difficulties of working across differences are great, and not all feminisms can sustain this project. The description, here, of possibilities and achievements is grounded in my study of and participation in an actual women's movement, but it should not be read to suggest that feminists effortlessly or often achieve this kind of mutual learning. I intend merely to show that the principles shared by transformative feminists make this mutual learning and, therefore political growth and solidarity, possible.

MULTI-CENTERED MOVEMENT

Transformative feminisms are not, of course, identical feminisms, because the shape of feminist issues and practice will always depend

on context.[21] They do, however, have common perspectives in the broadest sense. The principles they share include:
(1) A commitment to take nothing for granted, to question everything:

> Today we no longer say: "give us more jobs, more rights, consider us your 'equals' or even allow us to compete with you better." But rather: Let us re-examine the whole question, all questions. Let us take nothing for granted. Let us not only re-define ourselves, our role, our image—but also the kind of society we want to live in. (Madhu Kishwar and Ruth Vanita, Indian feminists)[22]

(2) A presumption to struggle on all fronts and resist all dominations:

> To accept the existence of class, race, ethnicity and generational differences among women and to devise multiple fronts of struggle in order to eliminate domination in any of its forms is what gives feminism its vitality. By broadening the concept of political, to include all spheres of power from the 'natural' state of hierarchies to the power of language to the ensemble of intra-household relations and showing how these institutions perpetuate the ideologies of domination, feminism brings a new vision and breadth to social movements. (Alya Baffoun, an African feminist)[23]

(3) An understanding of feminism as a perspective on the whole of society, not just women:

> Many of us believe that everything in the world concerns women because everything affects us. Since feminists seek the removal of all forms of inequality, domination and oppression through the creation of a just social and economic order, nationally and internationally, all issues are women's issues. There is and has to be a women's point of view on all issues and feminists seek to integrate the feminist perspective in all spheres of personal and national life. Women must therefore take a position on everything whether it is nuclear warfare, war between two countries, ethnic and communal conflict, political, economic and development policies, human rights and civil liberties or environmental issues. (Kamla Bhasin and Nighat Said Khan, Indian feminists)[24]

(4) A belief in the difficult project of developing sisterhood/ solidarity across the deep divisions among women—a point argued explicitly in the statements below by feminists from Africa, Asia, and North America:

(a) Some of you may ask is it possible to talk of all women as one? Is a rural woman's situation the same as say a typist's or a Permanent Secretary's? Of course not. There are many factors dividing us. But if you look at the nature of our oppression, our sex does determine our situation in a very fundamental way. As women we all carry a double burden. As women we all have to be concerned about reproductive rights. As women we face situations which men do not have to face; e.g., sexual harassment at work. As women our role as homemakers gets trivialised and unacknowledged, and our reproductive role is portrayed as our biggest liability. These are some of the issues we face as women. (Fatma Alloo, Chairperson of the Tanzanian Media Women's Association [TAMWA][25]

(b) But is it possible to talk of women as an undifferentiated mass? Isn't life very different for a tribal woman, a Dalit woman in rural India, a factory worker, a clerk, a doctor, a university student, a middle-class or working-class housewife, an air hostess, a woman in purdah, or a common prostitute? Yes, there are a lot of factors dividing women from each other—class, caste, religion, race, education (or the lack of it), one's field of work (in the house or out of it), and many other complex historical forces. Yet if we look at the nature and basis of women's oppression, we discover that our sex determines our common predicament in a very fundamental way. (Madhu Kishwar and Ruth Vanita, editors of *Manushi*, an Indian feminist journal)[26]

(c) The power of the father: a familial social, ideological, political system in which men by force, direct pressure or through ritual, tradition, law and language, customs, etiquette, education and the division of labor, determine what part women shall and shall not play, and in which the female is everywhere subsumed under the male...Under patriarchy, I may live in purdah or drive a truck...I may serve my husband his early morning coffee within the clay walls of a Berber village or march in an academic procession, what-

ever my status or situation, my derived economic class, or
my sexual preference, I live under the power of the fathers,
and I have access only to so much privilege, or influence as
the patriarchy is willing to accede to me, and only for so
long as I will pay the price of male approval. (Adrienne Rich,
U. S. feminist poet and writer)[27]

Feminism's difficult but exhilarating political challenge is to build
sisterhood/ solidarity across differences, using the differences as
resources in developing shared critiques and visions. This deeply
radical and inclusive challenge to all systems of oppression is only
possible for feminists who are powerfully and autonomously women-
identified and share women-centered and women-positive visions.
Although this is not widely understood, and at first may seem para-
doxical, it is feminists' deep commitment to women and uncompromising critique of patriarchal power that enables them to
participate fully in anti- racist, anti-colonial, and anti-capitalist struggles, and to affirm diverse cultures.

U. S. feminists Adrienne Rich and Marilyn Frye have both shown
convincingly that deep understanding of one's condition as a
woman and a full break with patriarchal values and ideologies necessarily involves, for white middle-class feminists, disloyalty to the
class and race power of the men they are attached to.[28] Marie-Aimée
Hélie-Lucas, Algerian feminist and founder/member of the international network, Women Living Under Muslim Laws, has written
about the ways her identification with and autonomous commitment to women enabled her to break with enforced forms of absolute loyalty to partial male-defined forms of resistance to these
powers.[29]

For feminists all over the world, this is far from being an aban-
donment of their various cultures and communities. On the contrary, the affirmation of women is the ground on which diverse
women claim their place in defining their own communities and
struggles.[30] This autonomous participation by women is a potential
strength for groups and communities resisting colonial and capitalist oppression. For the transformative assertion of non-dualistic
female-associated values and work—such as cooperation, care, nurture, and community—espoused by these feminists is a necessary
part of any successful resistance to exploitation and the dominant,
separatist worldview:

The women's movement too can have an ethic drawn from
women's daily lives. At its deepest it is not an effort to play

"catch up" with the competitive, aggressive "dog-eat-dog" spirit of the dominant system. It is, rather, an attempt to convert men and the system to the sense of responsibility and nurturance, openness, and rejection of hierarchy that are part of our vision. (DAWN)[31]

This vision also means that transformative feminists are supportive of and available for alliance with all those who are making a holistic challenge. For progressive change will involve drawing on the resources of many non-dualistic, non-hierarchical knowledges which have been denied and destroyed by the colonial and patriarchal imposition of dualistic competitive values and structures on indigenous peoples as well as women:

> Mother Earth, women and colonized cultures. It is from these fringes that we are beginning to discern the economic, political and cultural mechanisms that have allowed a parochial science to dominate and how mechanisms of power and violence can be eliminated for a degendered, humanly inclusive knowledge. (Vandana Shiva)[32]

Autonomously defined social movements emerging today among numerous groups around the world are making new forms of political struggle possible. We can hope, today, to create for the first time, multi-centered social movement, where the articulation of diverse and particular (Afro-centric, native, female, and other) identities and voices enriches rather than displaces universal, life-centered values and visions, where no single group can claim to be the norm or the center, and the specific experiences of any and all groups can illuminate the universal condition and contribute to general struggle.[33]

Today, women around the world are claiming equal humanity with men without feeling the need to base that claim on their putative "sameness" with men; they are rejecting male definitions of cultures and communities as part of their increasingly active commitment to these communities; and they are affirming their commonality with other women at the same time as they also explore their differences from them. These dialectical feminist politics are absolutely central to emerging possibilities for new forms of multi-centered global movement. Their presence in both North and South is mutually reinforcing and gives hope for the future.

NOTES

1. The term "global feminism" is sometimes read to imply a presumption or vision of a single, monolithic politics for all the worlds' women, and is rejected on these grounds. The plural term "global feminisms," used in the title of this paper, refers to diverse feminisms around the world with global understandings/perspectives/concerns.

2. Here there are no really satisfactory solutions to the question of terminology. The terms "first world" and "third world" have been read by some as uncritically reflecting colonial categories. I have nevertheless chosen to use mainly this terminology as the best of a bad lot. I do this because most "third world" feminists I have spoken to and/or read use this terminology. Also, because I prefer terms which reflect real and continuing relations of domination and resistance over other terms (such as the geographical designations "North" and "South") which do not. It should be clear from the argument to follow why I consider "developed," "underdeveloped," and "developing" to be particularly inappropriate— even offensive—terms." In Section headings I have substituted the term "two thirds world" for "third world" to force attention to what might otherwise be a taken-for-granted terminology, to interrupt any tendency to read "first world" and "third world" as implying orders of importance, and to remind the reader of "third world" nations' predominance in both population and land mass.

3. The focus of this paper is on women's autonomous and women positive activism, whether or not it is self-defined as feminist. In places I mention both feminists and autonomous women activists, in others I simply refer to feminists. However, my intention is inclusive in all cases.

4. See, for instance, the Introduction and some of the articles in Chandra Mohanty, Ann Russo, and Lourdes Torres, eds., *Third World Women and the Politics of Feminism* (Bloomington: Indiana University Press, 1991).

5. See, for instance, "Integrative Feminism," *Fireweed: A Feminist Quarterly* 19 (Summer/Fall 1984); "Feminism, Equality, and Liberation," *Canadian Journal of Women and the Law* 1.1(1985); *Feminist Radicalism in the 1980s* (Montreal: New World Perspectives, 1985).

6. Alain Touraine in his book *The Post-Industrial Society* (New York: Random House, 1971) develops the distinction between the partial politics of a pressure group, which offers no alternative rationality to the dominant rationality, and the full politics of a social movement which challenges the whole of society on the basis of an articulated alternative rationality.

7. "Third world" feminist and feminist-sympathetic critiques of "Western" feminist ethnocentrism need to be carefully distinguished from the widespread non-feminist and anti-feminist critiques. Feminist and feminist-sympathetic criticisms, though often angry and sometimes despairing, are made in a spirit of mutual learning with the aim of contributing to the kind of dialogue that will deepen global feminist understanding and analysis and enable the development of alliances. Non-feminist and anti-feminist critiques generally fail to recognize feminism's oppositional role in the West and deny any possibility of political alliance by dis-

missing all feminisms as simply and necessarily a part of the exploitative Western modernizing/colonizing process. Indian feminists have noted, for instance, that: "(There) is considerable false propaganda against feminists and feminism. The media for example, which is controlled to a large extent by men, has been responsible for a widespread misrepresentation of feminists as 'bra-burning,' 'man- hating,' 'family-destroying' women. This propaganda is reinforced by other forces and groups that see the emancipation and liberation of women as a threat, with the result that feminists in our countries are attacked and dismissed as 'middle class,' 'westernized' and 'rootless' women" (Kamla Bhasin and Nighat Said Khan, *Some Questions on Feminism and Its Relevance in South Asia*, 1986, p. 1). Diverse feminists in the "third world" categorically reject these attacks as reflecting a blatant and politically self-serving double standard: "'Feminism' or 'women's liberation' is branded an imperialist, cultural-domination ploy and therefore anti-African. Of course, this is clearly an African, sexist view, a mechanism of scapegoating women as traitors to African values." African feminist resistance to this patronizing and sexist intimidation is loud and eloquent: "In spite of evidences [of African women's traditional power] which are supported by oral traditional and social structures, present attempts by African women to recover equality and freedom are ridiculed by male power and interpreted as a mere 'mechanistic mimesis' and as contamination from the West. The rationale behind this is as absurd as asserting that black slaves who were exploited in the 19th century in America had never been free people in their own societies and that in trying to free themselves from slavery they were merely identifying themselves with white people" (Alya Baffoun, "The Future of Feminism in Africa," *AAWORD Newsletter* 2/3 (1985): 4.

8. Dorothy, "Position Paper of a Feminist on the Report of the Royal Commission on the Status of Women in Canada and the National Ad Hoc Committee on the Status of Women," in *The New Feminist* 2.2 (1971): 3.

9. See, for instance, Cherrie Moraga and Gloria Anzaldua, eds., *This Bridge Called My Back: Writings by Radical Women of Color* (Watertown, Mass.: Persephone Press, 1981); Barbara Smith, ed., *Home Girls: A Black Feminist Anthology* (New York: Kitchen Table, 1983); Paula Gunn Allen, *The Sacred Hoop: Recovering the Feminine in American Indian Traditions* (Boston: Beacon Press, 1986).

10. See note 2 about this "Two Thirds World" terminology.

11. For a study of these feminisms around the world see my *Integrative Feminisms: Building Global Visions 1960s to 1990s* (Routledge, 1996).

12. For "first world" feminist sources illustrating these global transformative perspectives see: Charlotte Bunch, *Passionate Politics: Feminist Theory in Action* (New York: St. Martin's Press, 1987); Cynthia Enloe, *Bananas, Bases and Beaches: Making Feminist Sense of International Politics* (London: Pandora, 1989); Maria Mies, *Patriarchy and Accumulation on a World Scale: Women in the International Division of Labour* (London: Zed Books, 1986); Swasti Mitter, *Common Fate, Common Bond* (London: Pluto Press, 1986); Marilyn Waring, *If Women Counted: A New Feminist Economics* (New York:

Harper and Row, 1988). For "third world" transformative resistance to "development" see: Anita Anand, "Rethinking Women and Development," *Women in Development, a Resource Guide for Organization and Action,* ISIS (1983); The Association of African Women on Research and Development (AAWORD), "The Dakar Declaration on Another Development With Women," *Development Dialogue* 1/2 (1981); Kamla Bhasin, Nighat Said Khan, and Ritu Menon, "Women and Development? or Development of Women?" Paper presented at the Third International Interdisciplinary Congress on Women, Dublin Ireland 1977; *The Nairobi Manifesto,* presented by African women at the United Nations "End of the Decade Conference," Nairobi, Kenya (1985), published in AAWORD in *Nairobi '85* (n.d.) Occassional Paper Series No. 3, pp. 1-5; Rosiska Darcy de Oliviera and Thais Corral, eds. *Terra Femina,* Brazil: IDAC and REDEH (1992); Achola O. Pala, "Definitions of Women and Development: An African Perspective." Signs 3.1(1977): 9- 13; Gita Sen and Caren Grown, *Development, Crises, and Alternative Visions,* (New York: Monthly Review Press, 1987); Vandana Shiva, *Staying Alive: Women, Ecology and Development* (London: Zed Books, 1989).

13. Barbara Ehrenreich and Deirdre English, *For Her Own Good: 150 Years of the Experts' Advice to Women* (New York: Anchor Press, 1979), p. 342.

14. Vandana Shiva, *op. cit.,* p. 13.

15. Gita Sen and Caren Grown, *op. cit.,* pp. 80 - 81.

16. It is important to note here that I am not suggesting that feminist struggles are the same around the world or even from one neighborhood or institution to the next. They are, in fact, as diverse as the conditions under which women find themselves. Nevertheless, shared principles of approach and values can be identified

17. The World Women's Congress for a Healthy Planet, held in Miami in November 1991, is an example of feminism's increasing capacity for international dialogue and political initiative. Five days of dialogue among 1500 women from 84 different countries produced consensus on women's/feminist perspectives and positions for the United Nations Conference on Environment and Development (UNCED). These were published as the *Women's Action Agenda 21* which makes clear the connections between race, colonial, class and gender oppression and the need to revalue women, indigenous peoples, and nature that I have identified as hallmarks of transformative feminisms. Examples of the kind of networking and dialogue that this conference built on include events such as the United Nations Decade for Women Conferences in 1975, 1980, and 1985, particularly the closing one in 1985 in Nairobi; International Tribunal on Crimes Against Women, 1976; International Workshop on Feminist Ideology and Structure, Bangkok, June 1979; Latin American Feminist Encuentros held every two years since 1981; Dakar Conference On Another Development with Women, 1982; Tribunal on Reproductive Rights, Amsterdam, 1984; Female Circumcision: Strategies to Bring About Change, Somalia,1988; Trafficking in Women Internationally, Conference in October 1988 in New York; Women, Peace and the Environment Conference, Moscow, June 1989; Commonwealth Women's Conference, Toronto 1991; Women

in Africa and the African Diaspora: Bridges Across Activism and the Academy, Nsukka, Nigeria, July 1992. International networks such as Development Alternatives with Women for a New Era (DAWN); International Network of Women Living Under Muslim Laws; Women Against Fundamentalism; Greenham Common Peace Network; Feminist International Network of Resistance to Reproductive Technologies and Genetic Engineering (FINRRAGE); Disabled Women's Network; Coalition Against Trafficking in Women; Sisterwatch; Grassroots Organizations Operating Together for Sisterhood (GROOTS); Women, Environment and Development Network; regional networks such as Asian and Pacific Centre for Women and Development; Asian Women's Research and Action Network; Association of African Women on Research and Development (AAWORD); Health Network of Latin American and Caribbean Women; Caribbean Association for Research and Action (CAFRA); Asian Indigenous Women's Network.

18. Authentic political relationships are always mutual and dynamic; participants are not equal at all times but they are always active and respectful and the learning/leadership roles shift.

19. Peggy Antrobus, *Equality, Development and Peace: A Second Look at the Goals of the UN Decade for Women* (Women and Development Unit, University of the West Indies, 1983), p. 19.

20. For statements by women in these and other groups about the particular importance of their contributions to feminist analysis and politics and the importance of solidarity beyond their groups see: Kamla Bhasin and Nighat Said Khan, *Some Questions on Feminism and Its Relevance in South Asia* (New Delhi: Kali for Women Press, 1984); Charlotte Bunch, "Not for Lesbians Only," in Bunch, 1975, op. cit., pp. 174-181; "Combahee River Collective Statement," in Barbara Smith, ed., *Home Girls: A Black Feminist Anthology* (New York: Kitchen Table Press, 1983), pp. 272-282; Paula Gunn Allen, *The Sacred Hoop: Recovering the Feminine in American Indian Traditions* (Boston: Beacon Press, 1986); Maria Meis, *op. cit.*; Cherrie Moraga and Gloria Anzaldua, eds., *op. cit.*: Gita Sen and Caren Grown, *op. cit.*; Vandana Shiva, *op. cit.*

21. Women at the Dakar Conference on Another Development with Women made a similar point in their Declaration: "Feminism is international in defining as its aim the liberation of women from all types of oppression and in providing solidarity among women of all countries; it is national in stating its priorities and strategies in accordance with particular cultural and socio-economic conditions (AAWORD, *op. cit.*, p. 15).

22. Madhu Kishwar and Ruth Vanita, *In Search of Answers: Indian Women's Voices from Manushi* (London: Zed Books, 1984), pp. 244–245.

23. Alya Baffoun, "The Future of Feminism in Africa," *Association of African Women on Research and Development Newsletter* 2.3 (1985): 3.

24. Kamla Bhasin and Nighat Said Khan, *op. cit.*, p. 12.

25. Fatma Alloo, "The Need for a Women's Magazine," *Sauti Ya Siti* 1 (March 1988): 2.

26. Kishwar and Vanita *op. cit.*, p. 242.

27. Adrienne Rich, *Of Woman Born: Motherhood as Experience and Institution* (New York: Norton, 1976), pp. 57-58.

28. Adrienne Rich, "Disloyal to Civilization: Feminism, Racism, and Gynephobia," *Chrysalis* 7 (1978): 9-27, and Marilyn Frye, "On Being White," *Trouble and Strife* 4 (Winter 1984): 11-16.

29. Marie-Aimée Hélie-Lucas, "Women's Struggles and Strategies in the Rise of Fundamentalism in the Muslim World: From Entryism to Internationalism," in Haleh Afshar ed., *Women in the Middle East: Perceptions, Realities and Struggles for Liberation* (London: MacMillan, 1993), pp. 206-242.

30. The following statement by Nieto Gomez, a Chicana feminist in the United States, illustrates the important connection between women's expression of their own interests and values and ability to play an active role in defining their own culture and community: "The aggregate cultural values we [Chicanas] share as women can also work to our benefit if we choose to scrutinize our cultural traditions, isolate the positive attributes and interpret them for the benefit of women. It's unreal that *Hispañas* have been browbeaten for so long about our so-called conservative (meaning reactionary) culture. It's also unreal that we have let men interpret our culture only as those practices and attitudes that determine who does the dishes around the house. We as women also have the right to interpret and define the philosophical and religious traditions beneficial to us within our culture, and which we have inherited as our tradition" (cited by Alma M. Garcia, "The Development of Chicana Feminist Discourse," in Carol DuBois and Vicki L. Ruiz, eds., *Unequal Sisters: A Multi -Cultural Reader in U. S. Women's History* (New York: Routledge, 1990), pp. 422-423. Members of the Circle of Concerned African Women Theologians also speak about their delicate and necessarily complex relationship to both African culture and Christianity as they denounce the patriarchal aspects of each while simultaneously claiming a newly active and transformative role as women within both; see: Judith Ann Diers, "Freeing Liberation Theology," *Ms* (July/August 1992): 74-75.

31. Gita Sen and Caren Grown, *op. cit.,* pp. 72-73.

32. Vandana Shiva, *op. cit.,* p. 21. See also: Paula Gunn Allen *op. cit.,* and Maria Meis, *op. cit.*

33. This, of course, depends on the existence of diverse movements whose visions and values are capable of these alliances and the broadening and learning that they require and make possible: anti-colonial, anti-racist, and socialist struggles that respect feminisms which are anti-colonial, anti-racist, and anti-capitalist.

WORKS CITED

African Association of Women on Research and Development (AAWORD). *The Nairobi Manifesto.* Presented by African Women at the United Nations End of the Decade Conference, Nairobi, Kenya, 1985.

——. *AAWORD in Nairobi '85.* Occasional Paper Series 3 (n. d.): 1-5.

Antrobus, Peggy. "Equality, Development and Peace: A Second Look at the Goals of the UN Decade for Women." Address to the Associated Country

Women of the World, Vancouver, British Columbia (June 18-29), 1983.

Allen, Paula Gunn. *The Sacred Hoop: Recovering the Feminine in American Indian Traditions*. Boston: Beacon Press, 1986.

Alloo, Fatma. "The Need for a Women's Magazine." *Sauti Ya Siti* 1 (1988): 1-2.

Anand, Anita. "Rethinking Women and Development." *Women in Development, A Resource Guide for Organization and Action. ISIS International* (1983): 5-11.

Baffoun, Alya. "Future of Feminism in Africa." *Echo, AAWORD Newsletter* 2/3 (1985): 4-6.

Bhasin, Kamla. "Asian Women against Mal-development." *Fenix 00* (1990): 22-26. . "Alternative and Sustainable Development." *Convergence* 25.2 (1992): 26-35.

Bhasin, Kamla and Nighat Said Khan. *Some Questions About Feminism and Its Relevance in South Asia*. New Delhi: Kali for Women Press, 1986.

Bunch, Charlotte. "Not for Lesbians Only." *Quest: A Feminist Quarterly* 2.2 (1975): 50- 56. Also in *Passionate Politics, Feminist Theory in Action: Essays 1968-1986*. New York: St. Martin's Press, 1987: 174-181.

———. *Passionate Politics, Feminist Theory in Action: Essays 1968-1986*. New York: St. Martin's Press, 1987.

Combahee River Collective. "A Black Feminist Statement." In *Capitalist Patriarchy and the Case for Socialist Feminism*, ed., Zillah R. Eisenstein. New York: Monthly Review Press, 1979. 259-291. Also in *Home Girls: A Black Feminist Anthology*, ed., Barbara Smith. New York: Kitchen Table Press, 1983: 272-282.

Development Dialogue. "The Dakar Declaration on Another Development with Women." 1.2 (1982): 11-16.

Diers, Judith Ann. "Freeing Liberation Theology." *Ms* (July/August 1992): 74-75.

Dorothy. "Position Paper of a Feminist on the Report of the Royal Commission on the Status of Women in Canada and on the National Ad Hoc Committee on the Status of Women." *The New Feminist* 2.2 (1971): 2-6.

Ehrenreich, Barbara and Deidre English. *For Her Own Good: 150 Years of the Experts' Advice to Women*. New York: Anchor Press/Doubleday, 1978.

Enloe, Cynthia H. *Bananas, Beaches and Bases: Making Feminist Sense of International Politics*. London: Pandora, 1989.

Frye, Marilyn. "On Being White: Toward a Feminist Understanding of Race and Race Supremacy." In *The Politics of Reality: Essays in Feminist Theory*. Trumansburg: The Crossing Press, 1983: 110-127.

Garcia, Alma M. "The Development of Chicana Feminist Discourse." *Unequal Sisters: A Multi-Cultural Reader in U. S. Women's History*, ed., Carol DuBois and Vicki L. Ruis. New York: Routledge, 1990: 422-423.

Hélie-Lucas, Marie-Aimée. "Women's Struggles and Strategies in the Rise of Fundamentalism in the Muslim World: From Entryism to Internationalism." In *Women in the Middle East: Perceptions, Realities and Struggles for Liberation*. London: MacMillan, 1993: 206-242.

Kishwar, Madhu and Ruth Vanita, ed. *In Search of Answers: Indian Women's Voices from Manushi*. London: Zed Books, 1984.

Mies, Maria. *Patriarchy and the Accumulation of Capital on a World Scale: Women in the International Division of Labour.* London: Zed Books, 1986.

Miles, Angela. "Integrative Feminism." *Fireweed: A Feminist Quarterly* 19 (Summer/Fall, 1984): 55-81.

——."Feminism, Equality and Liberation." *Canadian Journal of Women and the Law* 1.1 (1985): 42-68.

——. *Feminist Radicalism in the 1980s.* Montreal: New World Perspectives, 1985.

____. *Integrative Feminisms: Building Global Visions, 1960s to 1990s.* New York: Routledge, 1996.

Mitter, Swasti. *Common Fate, Common Bond.* London: Pluto Press, 1986.

Moraga, Cherrie and Gloria Anzaldua, ed. *This Bridge Called My Back: Writings by Radical Women of Color.* Watertown, Mass.: Persephone Press, 1981.

Oliviera, Rosiska Darcy de and Thais Corral, ed. *Terra Femina.* Brazil: IDAC (Institute of Cultural Action) and REDEH (Network in Defense of Human Species), May/June, 1992.

Pala, Achola O. "Definitions of Women and Development: An African Perspective." *Signs* 3.1 (1977): 9-13.

Rich, Adrienne. *Of Women Born: Motherhood as Experience and Institution.* New York: W. W. Norton, 1976.

——. "Disloyal to Civilization: Feminism, Racism, and Gynephobia." *Chrysalis* 7(1978): 9-27. Also in *On Lies, Secrets and Silences: Selected Prose, 1966–1978.* New York: W. W. Norton, 1979. 275-310.

Sen, Gita and Caren Grown. *Development, Crises, and Alternative Visions: Third World Women's Perspectives.* New York: Monthly Review Press, 1987.

Shiva, Vandana. *Staying Alive: Women, Ecology and Development.* London: Zed Books, 1989.

Smith, Barbara, ed. *Home Girls: A Black Feminist Anthology.* New York: Kitchen Table Press, 1983.

Touraine, Alain. *The Post-Industrial Society: Tomorrow's Social History: Classes, Conflicts and Culture in the Programmed Society,* trans., Leonard F. X. Mayhew. New York: Random House, 1971.

Waring, Marilyn. *If Women Counted: A New Feminist Economics.* San Francisco: Harper and Row, 1988.

World Women's Congress for a Healthy Planet. *Official Report Including Women's Action Agenda 21 and Findings of the Tribunals.* New York: Women's Environment and Development Organization (WEDO), 1991.

THE GAP BETWEEN GENDER RESEARCH AND ACTIVISM IN UGANDA

DEBORAH KASENTE

FOR PURPOSES OF THIS PAPER, GENDER RESEARCH REFERS to those studies which address issues related to the situation and position of women as compared with that of men in society. The paper was written after a comprehensive survey of the research materials available in major research centers in Uganda, one of which is the former National Research Council known since 1990 as Uganda National Council for Science and Technology. Some of the functions of this Council are to draw national research priorities, control research done in the country, and disseminate research findings. Additionally, the following units were visited and their officials interviewed concerning trends, constraints, and future plans for research in gender issues: Makerere Institute of Social Research at Makerere University; Center for Basic Research (new and privately owned); and the new Ministry of Women, Culture and Youth.

Owing to a history of civil strife in Uganda between 1971 and 1986 and lack of commitment to gender issues prior to the 1985 Nairobi conference to conclude the International Women's Decade, most of the gender research findings available are post-1985. In almost all fields, the scattered studies done prior to 1985 were conducted mostly by academicians in fulfillment of degree or other academic requirements (White, Ilokot, Mackenzie, Cheffe, Kasente [a], Tamale , Atiku , Maleche [a & b]. However, even during that period, there were a few academicians who carried out gender sensitive studies : (Perlman, Tadria, Perlman, Tibuligwa, Ayuru). Much of the gender research done is fairly recent and this seems to be the case in many other countries (Casimiro, Liberman, and Osario). The change in the nature of gender research since 1986 can be attributed to two factors: the awareness raised by the 1985 UN Nairobi conference, and the change of government in Uganda. The new government that came into power in 1986 established a Women in Development Program with official mandate to integrate women in the development process. This created a demand for baseline data on the situation of women, especially women in the rural area where 90% of the population lives.

A number of studies have since been carried out both by academicians and by international and local non-governmental organizations to respond to the demand for baseline data. Most of this research and government programs are funded by donor agencies (UNICEF, 1988 & 1989, UNFPA, USAID, Friedrich Ebert Foundation) who have deemed it necessary to inform the policy interventions of the new government. In spite of the presence of such studies, records at the research centers reveal that the research scene is still mainly dominated by academicians from Makerere University and other professional institutions, and the focus is still largely on women (Muhereza, Kabuzi, Kyamureku, Matovu, Lubowa-Nanono, Katusabe, Katahoire, Seruwagi-Nalunga, Bantebya, Buregyeya, Kisamba-Mugerwa, Musoke, Mwaka, Naamara, Ndugwa, Kampikaho [a], Kwesiga, Ankrah).

The 1980s also saw the emergence of a number of foreign researchers working alone or collaborating with Ugandan researchers. Except in a few cases (Boyd), most of these externally initiated research activities responded to the needs and interests of foreign research centers and funding agencies and not to the priorities of Uganda research centers (Bond, Darwish, Dimock).

Most of the studies conducted after 1986 have been situation studies geared towards informing policy making in the short term. Because such studies are aimed at guiding policy making, they have necessarily tended to concentrate more on quantitative than qualitative aspects. Zimbabwe has recorded similar trends after the war (Gaidzanwa). Very few longitudinal gender studies have been done because they tend to be both expensive and span long periods of time. There have been limited academic gender studies; most of the existing studies merely fulfill requirements for post-graduate degrees. Because the Women's Studies Program at Makerere

University (post-graduate level)was established only in 1990, the relatively few academic studies on gender issues are still in progress.

Although a number of researchers have been on record advocating for participatory methods (Zirabamuzale), most of the studies referred to earlier have tended to use the traditional methods of the questionnaire, structured and unstructured interviews, and secondary data. However, there have been a few anthropological studies emphasizing participant and non-participant observation (Tadria). There is evidence that many of the on-going studies are beginning to emphasize qualitative methods in gender studies more than the earlier studies (Kasente, Obbo). It may be that this trend has been influenced by the evidence that shows how policy interventions resulting from simple situations studies have tended to produce intended as well as unforeseen and sometimes negative consequences.

It is important to point out the fact that this study is by no means an exhaustive survey of all gender research going on in Uganda. So much has been going on since 1986, in many disciplines, that any attempt to categorize neatly could easily create a distorted picture. It is equally important not to create an impression that all researchers on women and gender issues in Uganda form a monolith. Different research institutions and individual researchers have differing levels of commitment to the issues of gender. Mbilinyi raised an important issue by pointing out one of the major problems in contemporary gender research in Uganda: "Elite African women are able to monopolize research opportunities and funding, and many follow the conceptual approaches established by Western liberal scholars." What may be different in Uganda is that there are a number of independent and institution-affiliated male researchers in gender. What may not be disputed is that many of the research projects are commissioned and funded by donor agencies who control the conceptual approaches to suit their development policy and strategies. This could be partly responsible for the evident lack of theoretical direction in the gender research reviewed. Most of the research officers interviewed shared the view that although a lot of research on women and gender issues was being done, there was a general lack of coordination based on conceptual frameworks defined in terms of Ugandan reality.

One hopes that the Women's Studies Program at Makerere University will be fully supported to develop conceptual and analytical frameworks based on authentic knowledge of the dynamics of Ugandan society. In the literature surveyed, except in very few studies (Tadria), there is evidence that detailed attention has not been paid to the historical and cultural gender practices. In addition to studies done in Uganda, studies carried out in other countries of Africa also point to this major weakness (Stamp, Pala).

Although the available data are criticized for lacking theoretical and analytical frameworks, it must be said that a lot of material is now available that portrays which groups of men and women are more disadvantaged in the development process, thus making it possible to promote strategies and programs targeted at the disadvantaged groups. This was definitely not the case in the mid-1980s. The impact and sustainability of such development programs, however, still need to be systematically assessed to see whether they meet the objectives for which they were set up.

Perhaps one of the saddest aspects of gender research in Uganda and many other countries in Africa is that in spite of the concerted efforts being made by researches in the area of gender (and other areas), most of the findings remain inaccessible—both to policy planners and to the local population for whom these findings have great relevance. Mwaka and Kasente point out some of the constraints that lead to the problem of inaccessibility:

(1) Most of the research findings are published in a form that is not easily retrievable for a large audience.

(2) Research results (in the form of theses and dissertations) at Makerere University and other institutions cannot be easily accessed by policy makers who would benefit from the data and recommendations contained in such theses.

(3) The various research projects done by individuals are not coordinated and research projects on women are spontaneous and lack a practical, purposeful approach. The research results are therefore seen as an end in themselves rather than as a means to an end.

(4) Some of the existing research lacks concrete policy-oriented conclusions.

(5) Because of the lack of an organized, professional documentation system, some important gender concerns are not covered while others are over-researched.

The research officers in the Ministry of Women in Development admitted that the Ministry did not have the power to control research projects or their findings unless such projects were funded by the Ministry. The research officer at the National Research Center, through which all research must be channeled, said that the Council had the mandate but lacked the human and material resources to control or disseminate research findings. It is reported that most of the researchers deposit their proposals with the Council just to get clearance to have access to subjects of research. Although researchers are required to deposit their reports with the Council after the completion of their research, most of them fail to do so, with the result that it is difficult and sometimes impossible to have access to data in report form without tracking down individual researchers. Many of the researchers interviewed said that they would like to communicate their findings to the population researched, but they did not do so because the funding for research did not cover expenses for the dissemination of information. Sometimes, funding agencies fund the dissemination of research findings through workshops and seminars. Experience has shown that attendance at such workshops is usually disappointingly low. Only those with resources (transportation, accommodation, etc.) and technical interest in such findings bother to attend.

This may all sound as if lack of funds is the main problem, but I share Stamp's view that a major problem—i. e., the dynamics of the relationship between the researcher and the researched—has not been adequately investigated. In most cases, research is done in rural areas among the poor. The channels of dissemination of information to these rural people have not been systematically developed. Many researchers have complained of lack of cooperation from the researched. This is an area that has not been carefully studied. A number of studies show that researchers tend to look for information from chiefs, clan leaders, opinion leaders, and heads of households—mostly men. Apart from the fact that the rural people, especially women, work all day and do not have the time or confidence to talk to well-dressed town people, they have also not lost sight of the fact that many people who seek information regard them as ignorant and usually bypass them to get information from the "important" people in the village. It is possible that even those who seek close collaboration with the rural poor may be met with passive response, given what the researched (rural poor) have experienced in the past. There is also the issue of the discomfort of the rural poor *vis-à-vis* urban strangers to whom they may have nothing presentable to offer as expected culturally.

The main problem with gender research in Uganda is not lack of researched material, but rather the existence of materials which are fragmented, uncoordinated, dispersed, and buried in documents that fail to cross the boundary between one area of expertise and another. Furthermore, sometimes one discovers that some of the materials have little or no relevance to Ugandan reality.

The conceptual and methodological preoccupations in gender studies in Uganda have already started showing awareness to some of the problems pointed out in this paper. There is an observable shift from focusing on women only to a focus on gender. Some funding agencies show tendencies of flexibility by funding areas identified by the country's needs, but the top-down approach in development studies and funding is still very prevalent.

What remains a big problem is the lack of developed frameworks based on gender systems specific to Uganda's historical and cultural practices rather than on Western knowledge. One way of solving this problem would be to tap the insights of rural women and men who have themselves struggled with the questions being investigated. This calls for participatory research and evaluations that require the active involvement of the researched and avoid treating them as docile, ignorant subjects. Such active involvement of the researched will address the complaint raised by a women's group I visited in Mpigi District who gave the following reason for their lack of enthusiasm in responding to researchers: "We are tired of endless flow of interrogators who all seem to ask the same questions one after the other and never come back to give [us] anything even after [we] have told them all [our] problems" (translated from Luganda, a local language).

As more and more researchers shift from the top-down approach, one hopes the gap between the researcher and the researched will be gradually eliminated. Repackaging findings in usable form for relevant audiences remains a big challenge to the research centers, the funders, and the researchers themselves. Most materials still exist in the form of conference proceedings, research reports, theses etc. Some effort is being made in this area, but progress is very slow. Some disaggregated data on gender are beginning to appear, but they are still scattered in different locations in Government Ministries, research centers and development agencies. Dissemination is also beginning to show slow improvement with the attempts to discuss some of the studies in local workshops and publish conference papers for the literate audience. As the rate of illiteracy is still very high in Uganda, dissemination of information to the local population should take advantage of the local government channels of communication which are fairly well developed and do not necessarily depend on the written word only. For gender studies to be meaningful to the targeted population in Uganda, researchers are faced with the challenge of charting a course—theoretical and practical—that is tailored to the reality and interests of Uganda.

WORKS CITED

Alum, J. M. "An Appraisal of the Women Movement's Efforts in the Realization of Gender Equity." Unpublished.

Ankrah E. M. "Human Immunodeficiency Virus (HIV) Infection: Perception of Risk of HIV Infection for Women of Child Bearing Age in Uganda." Unpublished.

Atiku, J. *Rural Women and Children in Uganda. A Study of the Situation in West Nile, Nebbi, Arua and Moyo Districts.* Kampala: UNICEF, 1984.

Ayuru, R. "The Role of Women in Agriculture with Special Reference to Uganda." Paper presented at the Makerere Institute of Social Research, Kampala, 1984.

Bantebya, G. "The Role of Women in Petty Commodity Production." Unpublished.

Bond, V. "Banyarwanda Women in a Rural Settlement." Unpublished.

Boyd, R. "Empowerment of Women in Contemporary Uganda : Real or Symbolic?" Unpublished.

Buregyeya, E. "Women's Human Rights in Ankole Uganda since 1970." Unpublished.

Casimiro, I., G. Liberman, and Osario. "The Status of Women's Studies in Africa: Research on Women and Gender in Mozambique." Document presented at the African Studies Association annual meeting workshop on the Status of Women's Studies in Africa, St. Louis, Missouri, 1991.

Chaffe, J. "Behavior and Attitude of Women towards Work and Family in Uganda." Unpublished.

Dimock, R. E. D. "The Role of the Church Missionary Society in Uganda and Tanzania 1890s-1939 with Special Reference to Women's Education." Unpublished.

Friedrich Ebert Foundation. *Women's Status, Participation and Initiatives in the Development of the Uganda Economy.* Kampala, 1990.

Gaidzanwa, R. B. "Women's Studies and Research on Women in Southern Africa : The Zimbabwe Case Paper presented at the ASA Conference in St. Louis, Nov. 1991.

Ilokot, E. "Wastage of Girls in Uganda Primary Schools." Unpublished.

Kabuzi, R. "Status and Condition of Women in Uganda." Unpublished.

Kampikaho A. (a). "Maternal Mortality Excluding Abortion Mortality in Kampala Hospitals Case Control Study : A Comparison Between Those Who Die and Those Who Survive." Unpublished.

_____. (b). "Culture and Women's Rights in Uganda." Unpublished.

_____. (c). "The Problem of School Girls Drop-out in Upper Primary Classes : The Uganda Situation." Unpublished.

Kasente, D. H. (a). "Guidance Needs for Adolescent Girls in Kampala Secondary Schools." Unpublished.

_____. (b) "Performance of the Uganda Women's Tree Planting Movement." Unpublished.

_____.(c). "Factors Influencing Gender Differences in Access to Post Secondary Institutions in Uganda." Unpublished.

Katongole-Mbidde. "Heterosexual Transmission of HIV Infection." Unpublished.

Katusabe, M. G. "The Relationship between School Administration and School Drop-out among Girls in Selected Primary Schools in Kabarole District." Unpublished.

Katahoire, A. "The Emerging Role of Non-formal Education in Uganda as a Means of Equipping Women with Skills for Employment." Unpublished.

Kisamba-Mugerwa. "A Multi-centre Study on Patterns of Contraceptive Use and the Health of Women in Kenya, Uganda, Zambia, Swaziland and Mauritius." Unpublished.

Kulubya, C. "Upward Mobility of Women to High Level Executive Positions in Selected Areas of Uganda Public and Private Enterprise." Unpublished.

Kwesiga, J. C. "The Participation of Women in Higher Education in Uganda." Unpublished.

Kyamureku, P. K. "Women in the Professions: A Case Study in Uganda." Unpublished.

Lubowa-Nanono, M. "African Women in Literature and Drama and their Role in Management." Unpublished.

Mackenzie. D. T. "Domestic Service and its Place in the Occupational Structure." Unpublished.

Maleche, A. J. (a). "A Study of Wastage in Primary Schools in Uganda." Paper presented at the Makerere Institute of Social Research Kampala, 1960.

——. (b). "Sociological and Psychological Factors Hindering or Favouring the Education of African Women in Uganda." Unpublished.

Matovu, N. "A Comparative Study of the Effectiveness of the Laws of Succession in Relation to Ugandan Women in Selected Districts." Unpublished.

Mbilinyi, M. "Research Priorities in Women's Studies in Eastern Africa." *Women's Studies International Forum* 7.4 (1984): 289-300.

Muhereza, E. D. "Women's Organisations in Uganda and the Struggle for Women's Liberation and Development." Unpublished.

Murari-Muhwezi. "Education and the Reproduction of Gender Inequalities." Unpublished.

Musoke, M. G. "Women in the Professions: Challenges and Prospects of Careerism in Uganda since Independence." Unpublished.

Mwaka, V. M., and D. H. Kasente. "The Status of Women's Studies in Uganda." Paper presented at the conference on the status of Women's Studies in Africa, Columbus, Ohio, Nov. 1991.

Mwaka, V. M. "Socio-economic and Fertility Behaviour of Women Heads of Household in the Luwero Triangle." Unpublished.

Naamara, "A Case Control Study to Determine the Relationship Between Pregnancy and HIV Infection." Unpublished.

Ndugwa, C. M., Coulter Kataaha, and Hart. "A Longitudinal Study of Infants Born to HIV Positive Ugandan Mothers to Investigate the Response to Immunisation and Long Term Prognosis." Unpublished.

Pala, A. "Definitions of Women and Development: An African Perspective." *Signs* 3.1(1977): 9-13.

Perlman, M. L. "Some Aspects of Marriage Stability in Toro Traditional Ways of Marriage." Paper presented at the Makerere Institute of Social Research Kampala, 1960.

Stamp, P. *Technology, Gender and Power in Africa.* IDRC, Canada, 1989.

Tadria, H. M. "The Changing Structure of the Division of Labour and Resource Control in Buganda since 1900." Unpublished.

Tamale, N. N. "Sex-role Identification: Intelligence and Academic Attainment of Senior Girls in Uganda." Unpublished.

UNFPA. *A Report on the Baseline Survey of the Situation of Women in the Eight Pilot Districts.* Kampala: Ministry of Women in Development, 1991.

UNICEF. *Uganda Women's Needs Assessment Survey.* UNICEF, Kampala, 1988.

___ *Children and Women in Uganda* : A Situation Analysis. UNICEF, Kampala, 1989.

USAID. *Uganda Education Sector Review.* USAID, Kampala, 1990.

Wangoola, A. L. "A Simple Guide to the Law of Divorce in Uganda." Unpublished.

White, C. D. "The Role of Women in Ugandan Politics." Unpublished.

Zirabamuzaale, C. "Towards Action Oriented Research Leading to Concrete Community Development Programmes." Paper presented at a Women in Development Workshop, Mukono, Uganda, 1989.

CHALLENGES FOR THE INCLUSION OF GENDER ISSUES IN SOCIAL SCIENCE RESEARCH AND PLANNING

P. L. MAHOLTRA

YOUR EXCELLENCY THE FIRST LADY OF NIGERIA, ESTEEMED members of the Government of Nigeria, conference organizers, distinguished scholars, committed practitioners and activists from across the African continent and the African diaspora, representatives from other United Nations Organizations, on behalf of the Director-General of UNESCO, Dr. Frederico Mayor, I wish to extend to you warm greetings on the occasion of this first international conference on Women in African and the African Diaspora: Bridges Across Activism and the Academy and to express to you the particular interest of UNESCO in the original and crucial themes that will be examined during this meeting.

This conference serves as a unique opportunity for networking between women academicians and activists from Africa and the African diaspora on recent knowledge and practice concerning women's rights and gender issues. It will provide a forum to discuss new paradigms and innovative ways of addressing current global crises at local, national, regional, and international levels as well as to consider how women may maintain or gain a place in the transition and change processes underway in many countries. Having long been kept on the periphery of policy making, women are most likely to have a more critical and fresh approach and provide new perspectives on development models and strategies that often have been taken for granted, despite the evidences of insufficiency or failure.

The present economic crisis has had the most severe impact on developing countries and on the most vulnerable and poor groups within these societies, i.e., groups in which women and children predominate. Furthermore, due to gender hierarchies within the family and discrimination faced within the wider society, women and girls are most often the first to bear the brunt of penury, increasingly scarce resources, environmental deterioration, inadequate nutrition and health, and multifold tasks of unpaid labor. Their resistance and the strategies they have devised for fending for themselves and their families are noteworthy and merit our attention and support.

In the past, women researchers in various countries and regions were frequently isolated, unable to exchange findings, and thus often forced to reinvent the wheel before proceeding to further analysis. Research on the specific situation and problems of women and on gender relations has likewise had difficulty in becoming accepted as a legitimate academic pursuit within the scientific establishment in practically every country of the world. Despite this, and as witnessed by the present conference, theoretical and applied scientific research in different disciplines and within an inter-disciplinary framework has now finally gained a small foothold within the academy. Taking into account the discrimination experienced by women in many societal contexts, these research pursuits undertaken from the academy or by independent women's research centers and associations have frequently aspired to encompass an action-oriented function and to bring to public attention the hitherto unheard voices and demands of poor rural and urban women. In view of the current crises in values, societal theories, paradigms, and development models, and the fact that analyzing the situation of women is akin to taking the pulse of the health of the society, this research is now being considered increasingly imperative and urgent.

Despite considerable knowledge and research that has now been produced and accumulated by the academic community, as well as the applied research commissioned by governmental bodies or donor agencies, it is surprising how little of this knowledge has actually been consulted or used by planners and policymakers as part of setting priorities and as a means to direct social change in favor of women. Researchers and professors within the academic community, from research associations as well as women's and human rights groups may well wish to direct efforts towards preparing some user-friendly documentation and information on new development paradigms and on women's conditions, needs, and aspirations for policymakers and planners, in order to sensitize them to some of the issues at hand and to put pressure on them to bring about necessary changes in society.

Research on gender issues in the academy has been closely linked to the needs of women's organizations and women's collective grassroots action and has often emerged as a result of these movements. In addition to popularizing research findings for use by women in the wider society, it is hoped that women researchers and professors within the academy can also reach out and share some of their explorations of new frontiers of knowledge on societal processes and gender issues with colleagues in schools and adult education as well as in teacher-training colleges. It is hoped that in this manner the message of social justice and gender equity can begin to be incorporated into teaching materials and spread to new generations.

UNESCO programs for the advancement of women focus on studies and action in the social sciences and education, as well as in science, technology, culture, and the media, with particular reference to the needs of rural women. I would like to draw your attention to the fact that in terms of the status of women, Africa and the least developed countries figure among the Organization's highest priorities. As part of UNESCO's work in the Social Sciences, some support has been provided for networking of specialists, research institutes, and scientific non-governmental organizations in different regions and internationally, in particular through preparing some directories of researchers and institutes concerned with gender issues and through joint research projects on identified priority themes. A few meetings have been convened to exchange information concerning university teaching and research programs on women, including a Sub-Regional Seminar on Curriculum Development Research and Training in Women's Studies in Higher Education in Southern Africa organized in cooperation with the University of Zimbabwe in Harare in September 1987.

UNESCO looks forward with interest to the stimulating discussions that will take place at this meeting and intends to study what possibilities there may be of contributing to some of the future follow-up action, particularly in the African context. We wish you every success in your deliberations and in the fruitful outcome of this conference.

SINGING IN PRISON: WOMEN WRITERS AND THE DISCOURSE OF RESISTANCE

PAMELA RYAN

> From being an art of unbearable sensations punishment has
> become an economy of suspended rights.
> —Michel Foucault[1]

THIS PAPER FOCUSES ON THE THEME OF RESISTANCE IN THE writing of so-called "Third World women." As the quotation above suggests, the specific type of resistance I discuss is political in origin and punishable by imprisonment. There is, however, implicit in my discussion, another kind of resistance, my own, to the idea that in writing a paper one has to adopt a particular strain of critical discourse. Like Jane Tompkins, I also discover "two voices inside me:"[2] one which fearfully pays homage to the literary-critical establishment by ensuring that I use the "correct" discourse, show that I am familiar with the most recent theoretical terminology, and demonstrate that I am up-to-date with my references; and the other which feels more comfortable communicating my feelings. These two voices engage in a continual dialogue throughout my discussion.

In my first voice, I must interrogate the phrase "Third World women" in terms other than "universal sisterhood," trying to avoid creating a fictional monolith of a heterogeneous group of women bound together by geographical location, race, class, and gender. In their introduction to *Third World Women and the Politics of Feminism* (1991) Mohanty, Russo and Torres use the term "Third World," even though it is maligned and contested, preferring it to "postcolonial." Mohanty admits that it is just as difficult to erect a monolithic structure called Third World feminism as it is to speak of a "singular entity called 'Western feminism.'" She sees Third World women's writing in terms of oppositional strategies of an "imagined community" of writers who collaborate across divisive boundaries in the common struggle against forms of hegemony and domination.[3] As a white South African feminist, I find this a particularly comforting stance (second voice speaking) since I have frequently experienced guilt and anxiety over my subject-position *vis-à-vis* the black women writers whose work I write about. Mohanty elaborates on this common context of struggle which supersedes bonds of color, religion, and history and pits itself against "specific exploitative structures and systems."[4]

However, despite the comforting notion that one is part of a collaborative effort, there is no room for complacency for white feminists who must maintain their vigilance in regard to appropriating black women writers. Several writers have addressed themselves to this problem. While Ashcroft et al. ascribe to "a radical appropriation which can achieve a genuinely transformative and interventionist criticism,"[5] Mohanty focuses on the "political implications of *analytic* strategies" by Western feminists. Mohanty discusses the problem of appropriation, emphasizing in particular the production by Western feminists of the "Third World Woman" as a "singular monolithic subject."[6] Mohanty makes a distinction between "woman" (which is "a cultural and ideological composite constructed through diverse representational discourses") and "women" (who are real, material, and historical subjects). The dangers are that white feminists tend to colonize the material and historical heterogeneity of black women in a number of ways, either by adding to their curriculum vitae yet another article on black women (as I am doing) or reducing the *variety* of discourses *by* black women to a monolithic construct, thus conveniently negating the complexity and the conflicts which are part of the lives of women of different language and culture groups, classes, and social positions. Ifi Amadiume endorses Mohanty's view and exposes the limitations in the idea of global sisterhood. She deplores the arrogance and imperialism of white, Western feminists who embark on research programs on African women, in total ignorance of their very subjects' knowledge and social positions:

> Once, in a seminar, I asked a young white woman why she was studying social anthropology. She replied that she was hoping to go to Zimbabwe, and she felt she could help women there by advising them how to organize. The Black women in the audience gasped in astonishment. Here was someone scarcely past girlhood, who had just started university and had never fought a war in her life. She was planning to go to Africa to teach female veterans of a liberation struggle how to organize! This is the kind of arrogant, if not absurd attitude we encounter repeatedly. It makes one think: better the distant armchair anthropologists than these "sisters."[7]

Radhakrishnan offers a solution to this problem of appropriation by suggesting that white women in South Africa, who are in a dominant position but who are also feminists involved in the struggle against hegemonic forms of institutionalized power structures, should be in the process of "de-authorizing" themselves. Black women in South Africa are "emerging revolutionary subjects" who need to affirm and legitimate their subject positions, so that we have a situation where "the dominant position requires acts of self-deconstruction [and] the subordinate position entails collective self-construction."[8] While I am uncomfortable with the words "dominant" and "subordinate," preferring Collins's[9] idea of a non-hierarchical model which does away with such binary oppositions as dominant/subordinate, I acknowledge that this is useful advice. However supportive a white feminist might be of her black "sister," she is not an historical inhabitant of a black woman's subject position and needs to maintain a rigorous interrogation of her *own* subject position while listening to black women articulate *their* situation. Gayatri Spivak describes the condition which emerges when "basically benevolent impulses" become translated into "a ravenous hunger for Third World literary texts."[10] She has also recently spoken of the need to *work for* the subaltern rather than "speak for" her (New Nation Conference, Johannesburg, December 1991).

Black women in South Africa are beginning to voice their differences from white women and their growing dissent from the cultural traditions which bind them to their past, as Winnie Mandela explains:

Looking at our struggle in this country, the black woman has had to struggle a great deal, not only from a political angle. One has had to fight the male domination in a much more complex sense. We have the cultural clash where a black woman must emerge as a politician against the traditional background of a woman's place being at home! Of course most cultures are like that. But with us it's not only pronounced by law. We are permanent minors by law. So for a woman to emerge as an individual, as a politician in this context, is not very easy.[11]

White women who have previously belonged to distinct, separate groups (Black Sash, Women's Bureau, National Council) and to academic units such as Women's Studies, and who have always been sympathetic to the struggle while perhaps hesitant to intrude on behalf of black women, have now joined together with black women's organizations in a common cause—the National Coalition for the Women's Charter. It is in this context of negotiation and cooperation that, following Cherryl Walker (1990), I tentatively suggest new areas for consideration when writing about women's resistance texts in South Africa.

Walker shows how an "over-concern with the correctness of one's theoretical position" in relation to the politics of race and gender has led to a reluctance on the part of feminist theorists and critics to enter into current debates. She explains how this sense of constraint

...is a concern which can lead to a restrictive reluctance to question the authority of respected texts, even where these have little or nothing to say about gender; the construction of an adequate theory of gender requires not simply rigour but critical imagination and a willingness to rethink many of the assumptions of social theory as well. One cannot bend gender to fit the mould created by existing theories of class and race; issues like sexuality, the ordering and control of female fertility, patriarchal relations within the family, and sexual violence cannot be adequately accommodated in gender-blind theories.[12]

It is on this basis of a willingness to rethink old assumptions and to retain a vigilant awareness of gender in my reading of resistance texts that I offer the following analysis in which I focus on Caesarina Kona Makhoere's *No Child's Play*.[13]

Apartheid rule in South Africa instituted a set of conditions in which political ideologies have overruled gender considerations. It has been common for black women activists and writers to excuse the patriarchal conduct of black men out of sympathy for their plight under white domination and out of a common loyalty to the struggle. Thus Caesarina Makhoere can make excuses for her father's betrayal of her which resulted in her being imprisoned for five years. In *No Child's Play* Makhoere explains, almost matter-of-factly, that her father was a policeman, that is, a member of the most hated and despised institution in South Africa. She describes him as a gentle man, respected by his community. Yet when he betrays his daughter, she says: "Even today I don't really blame him for everything that happened to me. He never deliberately tried to hurt me or my mother. He was trapped and could not help pointing out where I was hiding when I was on the run."[14]

It is the "really" that is the slip in the discourse. Although she portrays her father's weaknesses and his inability to articulate his reasons for sending his daughter to prison, Makhoere refuses to criticize him openly. Instead, she allows the reader to witness her mother's condemnation of him when he tries to bully one of his son's into joining the police force. The son runs away from home rather than join and the mother blames her husband for trying to force his will on the family. By implicit comparison, Makhoere's mother is shown as a stronger and more caring person, and her father as a cowardly and authoritarian patriarch. Overt criticism of the father is subsumed within the safer agenda of the oppressive apartheid institutions which force him into compliance, even to the point where he would allow his own daughter to go to prison.

Similarly, no mention is made of the father of the child Makhoere has when she is sixteen years old. The bold statement "I became a mother"[15] implies independent agency on the part of the young girl. No blame is apportioned to the father of the child—we are not even told his name—but once again the suggestion is that it is the apartheid regime that is to blame. Makhoere describes how her mother was forced to enter domestic service, spending most of her time "slaving for them."[16] Without proper guidance, says Makhoere, the children did whatever they liked. This is a common thread connecting the narratives and autobiographies of black women in South Africa: there is usually early pregnancy and childbirth, with little or no help from the father, and no blame from the mother who is left to raise the child (see also Sindiwe Magona's *To My Children's Children* and *Living, Loving and Lying Awake at Night*).[17]

I am not suggesting that Makhoere does not support women in her narrative. On the contrary, her account of her time in prison is full of explicit praise for her fellow women prisoners ("the pillars of the struggle have always been the women, even though we were never given the accolades we deserved"),[18] but she is caught in the traditional patterns of family and social interaction which do not allow her to criticize men to whom she is bonded in a familial way. It is certainly important for us to remember—and to keep being reminded by writers of the resistance—that oppressive regimes like to enforce hierarchized and rigid distinctions between colonizers and colonized, and between races and classes; it is also equally important that we take into account that colonial states make use of already existing patriarchal structures and enlist already existing social and gender inequalities in the service of their own hegemonic practices. This is evident in property rights (which are granted to men and not women), marriage laws (which empower men and not women), the patriarchal household (in which the head of the house may beat his wife and rule over his daughters)—all these are eminently suitable to the enforcement of colonial ideology. As Mohanty says, "racist ideology has the hegemonic capacity to define the terms whereby people understand themselves and their world."[19]

Black women in South Africa have traditionally been both the agents of resistance and the supporters of their menfolk. They have expressed their opposition to the legitimized forms of colonial rule by organized demonstrations, liberation struggles, or by aligning themselves with such military structures as *Umkhonto We Sizwe*, the military wing of the African National Congress. Women's growing political consciousness and sense of identity can also be observed in their everyday lives. The thoughts and feelings of domestic and factory workers, for example, have been given voice in such texts as Jacklyn Cock's *Maids and Madams* and Obery's *Vukani Makhosikzi*.[20] While Mohanty challenges the idea that simply being a woman or being poor or black is sufficient grounds to assume a politicized oppositional identity, Patricia Hill Collins shows how resistance need not be organized along institutionalized lines. According to Collins, who describes the situation of African-American women whose socio-political conditions are very similar to those of black women in South Africa, black women's activist tradition has occurred along two primary lines. The first is the creation of female spheres of influence within existing structures of oppression, because direct confrontation is neither possible nor preferred. These oppressive institutions are opposed by a subtle undermining of the way they operate. The second option consists of institutional transformation consisting of direct challenges in the form of trade unions, boycotts, marches, sit-ins, and so on.[21] Domestic workers frequently engage in the first type of resistance as is evident in the stories told by Sindiwe Magona in her book *Living, Loving and Lying Awake at Night.*[22] Domestic workers assume servile and deferential roles, gratefully accepting old clothes in lieu of payment, adopting a child-like pose in front of their employers, and so on. Meanwhile, they create a space for resistance in their shared stories about their "medems." As Collins says, they act in servile ways but refuse to relinquish control over their self-defini-tion: "While they pretend to be mules and mammies and thus appear to conform to institutional rules they resist by creating their own self-definitions and self-valuations in the safe spaces they cre-ate among one another."[23]

Collins refers to Cannon's discussion of the contradiction in being a valued person in a devalued occupation. This is particular-ly evident in Magona's stories of domestic workers who discuss their employers in their time off and who create a moral system of indi-vidual worth in their discussions with each other.[24] The production of self-consciousness and self-worth as an oppositional stance—which is part of Radhakrishnan's plan for authorizing the subal-tern—is also effected through the act of writing. There is, of course, an important corollary here which I have discussed in another paper [25] and that is the necessity of having space and time in which to write and to articulate a conscientized and politicized identity. The social conditions of production of the black woman writer have not been conducive to writing novels (as Tlali has suggested in an interview with Cecily Lockett),[26] and certainly black women's silence may, in part, be attributed to their harsh living conditions. But there is also another important reason why South African black women "have not had time to dream." Bell hooks explains in her Introduction to *Ain't I a Woman* (1981) that black women's silence in America was "the silence of the oppressed—that profound silence engendered by resignation and acceptance of one's lot."[27] In South African texts by black women this resignation and acceptance are more characteristic of older women such as Frances Baard (1986), whose life story, as told to Barbie Schreiner, is remarkable for its understated sense of suffering and humility. From the description of her arrest in the middle of the night when she had to leave her children and not see them again for another 10 years, to her account of the year she spent in solitary confinement, Baard's control of tone and her sense of endurance defy the imagination. To spend a year without anything to read (she was refused a bible), no one to talk to, and nothing to see (her cell was below ground level), would drive lesser mortals to madness. Baard's faith and her strong spirit help her to survive:

> I think they were trying to kill me somehow, but my spirit was too strong.... I spent that whole year, a little bit of exercise sometimes, and then just sit and sit, and no-one to talk to, and nothing to read, and I try to look out of the window and watch the cars go past. Day after day with nothing to do. And so a whole year went by. And then after that year they took me to court now for my case.[28]

Baard's humility and sense of restraint make for an interesting comparison with Caesarina Makhoere, who comes from a younger generation of activists. She also undergoes solitary confinement under similar conditions—no reading material, one stinking pot in the room, half an hour for exercising, and nothing to see but a gray wall through the window. Makhoere does not simply endure passively. She goes out of her way to resist and antagonize, and she wins most of her battles. She describes how she likes to sing and how singing kept her sane. Singing was prohibited in this prison, but she sang anyway even when threatened by the station commander. This act of singing as a symbol of her resistance is only one of a number of strategies Makhoere adopts to assert a sense of self-worth. She organizes hunger strikes to protest against the inedible food; she refuses to wear the ridiculous prison garb with the iniquitous *doek* (a symbol of servility for black women) given out to black prisoners; she refuses to perform the compulsory daily parade. When something in prison life seems anachronistic or unjust, Makhoere rebels. She ends her book with a validation of her behavior and a testimony to the combined resources of her comrades in prison: "We learned some lessons in their prisons. They thought they could attack us: they failed. We first learned that we could win against them. Even with nothing; even with only our hands and our comradeship and our determination, we could defeat them."[29]

Norma Kitson, a white activist, is also arrested by the security police. Her account of her experience in *Where Sixpence Lives* [30] is just as horrifying as the testimony of the two previous writers, but it is obvious that white prisoners are treated differently from black detainees. On her first night in prison Kitson starts vomiting from the smell of the "broken stinking loo" in her cell. Within hours a frightened doctor enters the cell and transfers Kitson to the hospital as a suspected appendicitis case. Such collusion from a basically sympathetic doctor would be unthinkable for the black detainees. When Kitson is transferred back to jail, her cell mate, Pixie, is on hunger strike. Kitson cannot understand why she is doing this and tries to persuade her to eat. Pixie has to tell Kitson sternly that she is not to join forces with the oppressors in trying to undermine her effort to resist. The sense of immediate understanding and support, evident in Makhoere's text for hunger strikers, is missing here because Kitson has not been brought up with a sense of community. I do not intend to diminish in any way Kitson's part in the struggle. She was brutally interrogated, on one occasion being held out of a high building by her ankles, and her courage in continuing with her resistance despite intimidation is obvious from her account in *Where Sixpence Lives*. Analysis, however, must take into account the significant differences in socio-economic background between Kitson and Makhoere, differences which play themselves out in their texts. One major difference between privileged white activists and oppressed black women as revealed in their testimonies[31] is the latter's stated aim to communicate a communal ethos, whereas white women tend to record the consciousness of an individual. Both kinds of testimony are important in creating a self-conscious political identity. Yet, as Mohanty points out, the mere record of experience is not in itself of interest or significance; more important is how that experience is recorded and how it is received.

This point brings me back to the issue of mutual collaboration between writer and critic in postcolonial cultures. White feminist critics have to move away from responses of denial and guilt (which promote immobilization and passivity) toward responsibility, action, and mutual exchange with women of color; we have to act as responsible feminist critics when we analyze texts of resistance by responding to the inherent subversive indicators that operate in the text. Life stories, narratives and testimonials can serve several functions at once. They can record the past (which may have been destroyed or forgotten) as Sindiwe Magona does in *For My Children's Children*; they can incorporate images and events which undermine the hegemonic recording of history as is most strongly evident in the praise poems *(imbongi)* and oral poems recorded and translated by Jeff Opland in his book *Words That Circle Words*,[32] in which the teller can be openly subversive because he or she knows that certain white onlookers will not understand the language in which the praise poem is articulated; or they can create a communal political consciousness in the mode of Miriam Tlali's stories. Testimonials by black South African writers often set out to record a past way of life as a reminder for future generations. Ellen Kuzwayo's *Call Me Woman* (1985) and Miriam Tlali's stories and novels are written in the mode of testifying to the black women's experience of living under a repressive, racist regime, while Sindiwe Magona wishes to preserve the memory of a pastoral existence in the Transkei.

There is yet another dimension to an analysis of the discourse of resistance, one which enters the realm of psychoanalysis: the problem of domination and the role of gender. In what ways do women resist authority and domination and what analyses of power are most useful to deconstruct the oversimplified idea that women are simply victims of male abuse. In her book *The Bonds of Love*,[33] Jessica Benjamin (1988) analyzes the structures of domination and submission from a psychoanalytical framework, showing how it is necessary to avoid seeing the problem of domination and submission simply as a "drama of female vulnerability victimized by male aggression."[34] Benjamin refers also to the weakness of radical politics in which it has tended "to idealize the oppressed" as if their politics and culture were untouched by the system of domination, and as if people did not participate in their own submission.[35] Audre Lorde (1984) suggests much the same thing when she says that "the true focus of revolutionary change is never merely the oppressive situations which we seek to escape, but that piece of the oppressor which is planted deep within each of us."[36]

Patricia Hill Collins (1990: 225) also suggests new ways of thinking about the politics of power when she talks about "the matrix of domination," a means whereby the critic can escape from thinking in terms of binary oppositions such as black/white, master/slave, oppressor/oppressed.[37] Feminists who are attracted by postmodernist forms of knowledge and who are repelled by essentialist notions of the self, identity, woman, and so on, have articulated the need to expunge binary thinking from our various epistemologies. The term "matrix" is ideally suited to such a new way of regarding systems of domination, since it comes from the Latin word for womb and denotes a place in which something is developed or a substance between cells. A matrix, then, is neither one thing nor the other, but a space in between. Collins suggests replacing "additive models of oppression with interlocking ones."[38] By this she means rejecting those models which are rooted in "either/or" dichotomies and which emanate from Eurocentric masculinist thinking, and replacing them with the assumption that (for example) race, class, and gender belong to interconnected and interlocking systems of oppression. This, she says, indicates a paradigm shift which applies to other oppressions such as sexual orientation, religion, age, and ethnicity. Such a paradigm shift from dichotomous thinking to inter-connectedness affects all knowledge systems that involve the "other."

Instead of an "either/or" situation, Collins advocates the "both/and" position. For example, "white women are penalized by their gender but privileged by their race."[39] In addition, the matrix of domination excludes one-dimensional tropes of domination such as the idea that domination operates from the top down by "forc-ing and controlling unwilling victims to bend to the will of more powerful superiors."[40] It includes the idea of sustained resistance by victims who refuse to allow themselves to be dominated and who reverse the movement back up the scale. Caesarina Makhoere, for instance, by consistently analyzing the psychology of her oppres-sors, assumes superiority over them and enters the matrix of dom-ination by making her oppressors her political and moral inferiors. Taken almost at random from her book is this passage:

> I never did work again. From March 1979 until my release, I never again touched their prison work. I am not a prison-er, I am not a slave; I am just on holiday because they have decided to take me away from my public life. They thought they were going to work me; I made them work thorough-ly instead. Everyone who thought of me during my impris-onment ended up shivering, because they thought I was a very difficult person to control. Which of course I was; you cannot just make life easy for them. I told myself and I told them that I was not in prison to work for them. They took on that employment, which was to look after me. So they worked for me. And I made sure that when they got their salaries they felt that they had really earned that money, in a very difficult manner. [41]

"I am not a prisoner, I am not a slave." With these words, Makhoere redefines herself, empowers herself, and reverses the process of domination. Collins explains this phenomenon as follows: "domi-nation operates not only by structuring power from the top down but by simultaneously annexing the power as energy of those on the bottom for its own ends."[42]

By altering the pattern of power relations from a hierarchical, vertical model to a more fluid model of interrelatedness, we can begin to analyze the dynamics of domination and resistance in new ways and, as Collins says, we can give women the conceptual tools to resist oppression.[43] When we shift our analysis from a one-dimensional paradigm of domination to multiple systems of oppression, we acknowledge that we belong simultaneously to multiple dominant groups and multiple subordinate groups.[44] This takes Radhakrishnan's ideas a step further, since this more dynamic and flexible paradigm is a transformative model which is a means of empowering the oppressed. In Collins's view, empowerment means that we reject those dimensions of knowledge that perpetuate objectification and dehumanization. In this regard, *No Child's Play* is an empowering text since it refuses to acknowledge any interaction that dehumanizes or objectifies the individual. Makhoere insists on being a fully human subject.

Singing in prison becomes another transformative metaphor in Makhoere's text.[45] Much more than a token of resistance, it is a sign of her personhood, a means of communication, the sound of solidarity, and a message of hope. Singing occurs again near the end of Makhoere's text when it is expressly forbidden in Pretoria Prison. When the authorities tell her that singing ("the only freedom I was left with") is a punishable offense, she becomes angry and *she sings louder than before*. As she says, "One needs strong lungs for the struggle ahead, after all—VICTORY IS CERTAIN."[46] The singing is extended from the lone voice to a choir of solidarity as the prisoners teach each other political songs: "Some days the prison walls just echoed defiance, back and forth; oppression or no oppression, exploitation or no exploitation, imprisonment or no imprisonment, *a luta continua*, until final victory."[47]

Into the hegemony of prison regulations and male domination, Makhoere inserts a self that will not be cowed. Her singing brings down, symbolically, the walls of the prison. In forcing the prison staff to recognize her as a human subject, Makhoere breaks the cycle of domination in which subjugation by the master ensures the dehumanization of the slave. She replaces the closed structure of subjugation and submission with the principles of self-determination, individual power, and freedom. In Benjamin's terminology, Makhoere *alters the paradigm of power* to make a space in which the mutual recognition of subjects can compete with the relationship of domination.[48]

NOTES

1. Michel Foucault, *Discipline and Punish: The Birth of the Prison*, translated by Alan Sheridan (Harmondsworth: Penguin, 1977).
2. Jane Tompkins, "Me and My Shadow," *New Literary History* 19 (1987): 169.
3. Chandra Mohanty, Ann Russo, and Lourdes Torres, eds., *Third World Women and the Politics of Feminism* (Bloomington: Indiana University Press, 1991), p. 4.
4. Ibid., p. 4.
5. Bill Ashcroft, Gareth Griffiths and Helen Tiffin, *The Empire Writes Back: Theory and Practice in Post-Colonial Literatures* (London and New York: Methuen, 1989), p. 180.
6. Chandra Mohanty, "Under Western Eyes: Feminist Scholarship and Colonial Discourse," *Boundary* 2, 12/ 3, 13 (1984): 335.
7. Ifi Amadiume, *Male Daughters, Female Husbands: Gender and Sex in an African Society* (London: Zed books, 1987), p. 7.
8. Radhakrishnan, "Negotiating Subject Positions in an Uneven World," in Linda Kauffman, ed., *Feminism and Institutions* (Oxford: Blackwell, 1989), p. 277.
9. Patricia Collins, *Black Feminist Thought* (Boston: Unwin Hyman, 1990).
10. Gayatri Spivak, *In Other Worlds: Essays in Cultural Politics* (New York: Methuen, 1987), p. 253.
11. Winnie Mandela, *Part of My Soul Went With Him* (London: Norton, 1985), pp. 83–4.
12. Cherryl Walker, *Women and Gender in Southern Africa to 1945* (Cape Town: David Philip, 1990), p. 314.
13. Caesarina Kona Makhoere, *No Child's Play* (London: The Women's Press, 1988).
14. Ibid., p. 1.
15. Ibid., p. 2.
16. Ibid. p. 2.
17. Sindiwe Magona, *To My Children's Children* (Cape Town: David Philip, 1990) and *Living, Loving and Lying Awake at Night* (Cape Town: David Philip, 1991) .
18. Makhoere, ibid., p.18.
19. Mohanty, 1991, op. cit., p. 27.
20. Jacklyn Cock, *Maids and Madams* (Johannesburg: Ravan, 1984). Vukani Makhosikasi, *South African Women Speak* (London: Catholic Institute for International Relations, 1985).
21. Patricia Collins, op. cit., pp.141-2.
22. Op. cit.
23. Collins, op. cit., p.142.
24. Katie Cannon, *Black Womanist Ethics* (Atlanta: Scholars Press, 1988).
25. Pamela Ryan, "Black Women Do Not Have Time to Dream: The Politics of Time and Space," AUETSA papers (Stellenbosch, 1990); forthcoming in *Tulsa Studies in Women and Literature*, Summer, 1992.
26. Cecily Lockett, "Interview with Miriam Tlali," in *Between the Lines*, Craig Mackenzie, and Cherry Clayton, eds. (Grahamstown: National English

Literary Museum, 1989).

27. bell hooks, *Ain't I a Woman* (Boston: South End Press, 1981), p. 1.

28. Frances Baard, *My Spirit is Not Banned* (Harare: Zimbabwe Publishing House, 1986), p. 74.

29. Makhoere, op. cit., pp.120 - 1.

30. Norma Kitson, *Where Sixpence Lives* (London: Hogarth Press, 1987).

31. I use the word "testimony" as it is explained in John Beverley's article "The Margin at the Center: On Testimonio (Testimonial Narrative)" (Modern Fiction Studies 35 [Spring 1989]). Testimonio is discussed as resistance literature by Beverley, who defines it as "a... narrative in book or pamphlet... form, told in the first-person by a narrator who is also the real protagonist or witness of the events he or she recounts, and whose unit of narration is usually a 'life' or a significant life experience" (pp. 12-13). Beverley's explication of testimonio demonstrates that it is primarily an act of bearing witness with an urgency to communicate "a problem of repression, poverty, subalternity, imprisonment... and so on" (p. 14); moreover, it is "concerned with sincerity rather than with literariness" (p. 14). Following Beverley, therefore, I distinguish testimony from autobiography, as a resistance narrative whose author may or may not be literate, and which is concerned with a "problematic collective social situation" (p. 15). I therefore differentiate myself from the comment made by Gitahi Gititi that *No Child's Play* is not "necessarily most remarkable for stylistic power or clarity of ideological enunciation" ("Self and Society in Testimonial Literature: Caesarina Kona Makhoere's No Child's Play, in Prison Under Apartheid," *Current Writing* 3 [1991]: 42-49), but endorse her statement that it is "remarkable for its articulation of anger" (p. 43).

32. Jeff Opland, *Words That Circle Words* (Johannesburg: Ad Donker, forthcoming).

33. Jessica Benjamin, *The Bonds of Love* (New York, Pantheon Books, 1988).

34. Ibid., p. 9.

35. Ibid., p. 9.

36. Audre Lorde, *Sister Outsider* (New York, 1984), p. 123.

37. Patricia Collins, op. cit., p. 225.

38. Ibid., p. 225.

39. Ibid., p. 225.

40. Ibid., p. 227.

41. Makoere, op. cit., pp. 45-6.

42. Collins, op. cit., pp. 227-8.

43. Ibid., p. 228.

44. Ibid. p. 230.

45. Singing also occurs in prison liteature by male authors, for example, Hugh Lewin's *Bandiet: Seven Years in South African Prison* (London: Heinemann Educational Books, 1983).

46. Makhoere, op. cit., p. 95.

47. Ibid., p. 97.

48. Benjamin, op. cit., p. 220.

WORKS CITED

Amadiume, Ifi. *Male Daughters, Female Husbands: Gender and Sex in an African Society*. London: Zed books, 1987.

Ashcroft, Bill, Gareth Griffiths, and Helen Tiffin. *The Empire Writes Back: Theory and Practice in Post-Colonial Literatures*. New York: Methuen, 1989.

Baard, Frances. *My Spirit is Not Banned*. Harare: Zimbabwe Publishing House, 1986.

Benjamin, Jessica. *The Bonds of Love*. New York, Pantheon Books, 1988.

Beverley, John. "The Margin at the Center: On Testimonio (Testimonial Narrative)." *Modern Fiction Studies* 35 (Spring 1989): 11-28.

Cannon, Katie. *Black Womanist Ethics*. Atlanta: Scholars Press, 1988.

Cock, Jacklyn. *Maids and Madams*. Johannesburg: Ravan, 1984.

Collins, Patricia Hill. *Black Feminist Thought*. Boston: Unwin Hyman, 1990.

Foucault, Michel. *Discipline and Punish: The Birth of the Prison*. Trans. Alan Sheridan. Harmondsworth: Penguin, 1977.

Gititi, Gitahi. "Self and Society in Testimonial Literature: Caesarina Kona Makhoere's *No Child's Play: In Prison Under Apartheid*." *Current Writing* 3 (1991): 42-49.

hooks, bell. *Ain't I a Woman*. Boston: South End Press, 1981.

Kitson, Norma. *Where Sixpence Lives*. London: Hogarth Press, 1987.

Lewin, Hugh. *Bandiet: Seven Years in South African Prison*. Cape Town: D. Philip, 1989.

Lockett, Cecily. "Interview with Miriam Tlali." In *Between the Lines*, ed., Craig Mackenzie and Cherry Clayton. Grahamstown: National English Literary Museum, 1989: 69-85.

Lorde, Audre. *Sister Outsider*. Trumansburg: Crossing Press, 1984.

Magona, Sindiwe. *To My Children's Children*. Cape Town: David Philip, 1990.

_____ *Living, Loving and Lying Awake at Night*. Cape Town: David Philip, 1991.

Makhoere, Caesarina Kona. *No Child's Play: In Prison under Apartheid*. London: The Women's Press, 1988.

Makhosikasi, Vukani. *South African Women Speak*. London: Catholic Institute for International Relations, 1985.

Mandela, Winnie. *Part of My Soul Went With Him*, ed., Anne Benjamin. New York: W. W. Norton, 1984.

Mohanty, Chandra, Ann Russo, and Lourdes Torres, ed. *Third World Women and the Politics of Feminism*. Bloomington: Indiana University Press, 1991.

Mohanty, Chandra. "Under Western Eyes: Feminist Scholarship and Colonial Discourses." *Boundary* 2.12/3.13 (1984): 333-358; *Feminist Review* 30 (1988): 61-88.

Opland, Jeff. *Words That Circle Words*. Johannesburg: Ad Donker (forthcoming).

Radhakrishnan, R. "Negotiating Subject Positions in an Uneven World." *Feminism and Institutions*, ed., Linda Kauffman. Oxford: Blackwell, 1989: 276-290.

Ryan, Pamela. "Black Women Do Not Have Time to Dream: The Politics of Time and Space." *AUETSA papers*. Stellenbosch, 1990. Forthcoming in *Tulsa Studies in Women and Literature* (Summer, 1992).

Spivak, Gayatri. *In Other Worlds: Essays in Cultural Politics*. New York:

Methuen, 1987.

Tompkins, Jane. "Me and My Shadow." *New Literary History* 19 (1987): 169-178.

Walker, Cherryl. *Women and Gender in Southern Africa to 1945.* Cape Town: David Philip, 1990.

II
WOMEN ORGANIZING FOR CHANGE

CLOSING THE GAP—ACTIVISM AND ACADEMIA IN SOUTH AFRICA: TOWARDS A WOMEN'S MOVEMENT

GERTRUDE FESTER

PREAMBLE

THIS PAPER WAS PREPARED FOR THE FIRST INTERNATIONAL conference on Women in Africa and the African Diaspora, held in Nsukka, Nigeria, in July, 1992. It thus reflects the South African situation at that time. Since then, however, events have changed dramatically. At the time of writing, the negotiations at CODESA (Convention for a Democratic South Africa) which commenced mid-1990 were fragile and eventually broke down. I will attempt to summarize the events from July 1992 to July 1994.

Due to the commitment of the parties involved, negotiations in the form of what became known as the Multi-Party Talks resumed at Kempton Park in early 1993. The broadest range of parties and political movements participated. The participation of women at those talks created a debate. On February 22, 1993 the African National Congress proposed that one out of every two delegates be a woman. This proposal was not accepted as only three parties (the

ANC, the South African Communist Party, and the South African Indian Congress) supported the proposal. Some parties gave reasons for not supporting such a move. According to them it would be tokenism and women would feel further marginalized if they were there and could not participate meaningfully. However, in March 1993, under pressure from the women's lobby at Kempton Park, the negotiating council agreed to appoint an additional delegate to the negotiating team of each party/organization. The agreement stipulated that one of the delegates had to be a woman with full speaking status.

Research on women's participation at the Multi-Party Talks confirmed that the women's participation had long-term impact even though "affirmative action programs may suffer from an initial period where problems are all too evident"(*Agenda* 20 [1994]:19). Another outcome was that male delegates had been gender-sensitized and "some men began to correct the use of gender-insensitive language by other male delegates."

The Multi-Party Talks had various tasks: an interim Constitution had to be drawn up; a Transitional Executive Council (TEC) had to be formed which would direct events during the transitional period and election dates, and conditions around elections had to be decided. The Transitional Executive Council had various sub-councils, such as defense, local government, finance and (because of the vociferous women's lobby) a sub-council on women. These sub-councils had various powers and the one on women could make recommendations on the budget and legislation; other sub-councils had to promote the full participation of women in the electoral and transitional processes, etc. The TEC instituted the Independent Electoral Commission (IEC) which had to oversee the electoral process as well as conduct voter education and assess whether the elections had been free and fair.

During the drawing up of the interim constitution there were many very contentious issues. One attracting a lot of attention and lobbying was the Equality Clause: "No person shall be unfairly discriminated against, directly or indirectly, and without derogating, which states that all people are equal and that no one can be discriminated against on grounds of race, gender, religion, sexual orientation, location and physical disabilities" (Chapter 3:8). Apparently this is the only constitution in the world that categorically states that people cannot be discriminated against on the grounds of their sexual orientation. What, however, made this equality clause problematic was the reference to gender. The CONTRALESA (Congress of

Traditional Leaders) delegates wanted the Equality Clause to be subjected to customary law. According to customary law, women are not
allowed to inherit property, cannot become chiefs, widows are subjected to the authority of their eldest sons and in some cases had to
become the wives of their brothers-in-law (in other words, perpetual
minors). Women lobbied and protested nationally against this. The
Gender Advocacy Project sent each woman delegate a fax urging
them to vote against the CONTRALESA proposal. Women from rural
areas protested outside the Multi-Party Talks. Eventually the constitution was amended so that customary law was subjected to the
Equality Clause. This was, indeed, a triumph for women.

The Women's National Coalition continued their campaign to
collect demands from women throughout the country. It is claimed
that two million women have been consulted for their demands.
Despite this major achievement, the campaign has been very
uneven. In some areas the bridge between the researchers and grassroots was narrowed considerably as a meaningful working relationship became established between them. This, however, was not
always the case. Many of the regions were dominated by white
and/or academic/middle-class women. Even though some of the
aims of the Women's National Coalition (WNC) were to mobilize
women and enhance women's organizational capacity, these aims
were not achieved at all. Yet, one cannot underestimate the important development to which the WNC contributed. The campaign
had lots of media coverage and women's demands for equal participation are definitely on the national agenda. The Women's
Charter which resulted from this campaign touches on all aspects
of women's lives.

The election fever had meanwhile escalated throughout the
country. Unfortunately, so did the violence in the Natal region and
the PWV region (area surrounding Johannesburg). All organs of
society including non-governmental organizations (NGOs) and
churches embarked on voter-education programs. This was particularly challenging as there is a high rate of illiteracy in South Africa
and at least eleven languages are spoken in the country. The
Women's College researched the gender-sensitivity of these programs and it was discovered that no program targeted women and
the context of their lives specifically. International observers and
monitors poured into the country and an atmosphere of intense
excitement as well as apprehension prevailed.

But not everyone was excited about the elections. A new alliance
was formed by former antagonists; white and black extreme right

organizations and political parties formed the Freedom Alliance. They boycotted the elections as their demands had not been acceded to. Some of their demands were: more power for the provinces, a 'Volkstaat' or homeland for white Afrikaners, and that the Zulu king's sovereignty and power be constitutionalized. Violence continued between supporters of the African National Congress (ANC) who supported the elections and the Inkatha Freedom Party (IFP) of Mangosuthu Buthulezi. It must be noted, however, that many of the IFP members wanted to participate in the elections. Tensions were particularly high in the homelands, so-called countries or "ethnic enclaves" in line with the apartheid policy (e.g., Kwazulu—although the whole of Natal province was affected by violence—and Bophuthatswana). The white rightist AWB (Afrikaner Weerstandbeweging—the Afrikaner Resistance Movement) vowed that they would sabotage the elections.

Many political parties mushroomed. This was especially contentious as many of the initiators of these parties have been politically apathetic in the past. Accusations of political opportunism on their part were met by retorts that it was in the spirit of democracy that they had been formed. There were also rumors that some of these new parties had been funded by the Nationalist Party (current ruling party that legislated apartheid) and/or other reactionary forces in order to split the vote and prevent an overwhelming ANC majority. There were 26 parties altogether, nineteen contested nationally. Amongst these new parties were two Christian parties, two women's parties, two Muslim parties, a Portuguese party, Soccer Party, KISS (Keep it Straight and Simple) Party, and Green Party. There was also a deep concern that these many parties would confuse the voters, the majority of whom were voting for the first time. The high level of illiteracy would also compound this problem.

Nationally, the tension was aggravating. The civil servants in Bophutswana were striking because of their concern for their pension. The future of the homeland was unclear as the leader, Lucas Mangope, was adamant that they were not going to participate in the elections. This could mean that the region would not be incorporated into the new South Africa. As the strikes increased, the homeland became completely ungovernable. The white rightist AWB entered to support the homeland government but had to leave in humiliation when it was told it had not been invited. Two AWB soldiers were fatally wounded, allegedly by Bophutatswana soldiers. South African soldiers entered to salvage the situation. Two administrators were appointed by the Transitional Executive Council to run the homeland and the former leader had to resign. Immediately, voter education started in the region.

The Freedom Front, a major partner in the Freedom Alliance, decided to participate in the elections. The white right was now completely fragmented. Deadlines for registration were continuously postponed as more parties which earlier had refused to participate registered to participate. Meetings continued between ANC leader Nelson Mandela, South African Government leader De Klerk, and Inkatha Freedom Party leader Mangosuthu Buthelezi. Once more power was given to the regions, Buthulezi insisted that the double ballot be introduced—one for regional government and one for national government. It was in the interest of a free election and future peace that it was agreed that there would be a double ballot. The IFP thus joined on the eve of the elections. The ballot papers had already been printed. A sticker with the name of the IFP had therefore to be added to all the ballot papers.

The days of the election eventually dawned: April 26–28, 1994. People were queuing from the early hours of the morning. There was indeed a celebration of democracy. People walked for miles and some stood for up to ten hours in queues without a murmur. In the Western Cape it started storming. A white electoral officer was astonished that people remained in their queues, no one bothered to seek shelter. An old woman stated that she had waited eighty years for that moment and a few drops of rain were not going to stop her. During those few days, not a single incident of violence was reported. The Independent Electoral Commission did not expect so many millions to turn up at the voting stations. There was no way of assessing numbers as there was no voters' roll. Many polling stations ran out of ballot papers after only a few hours of voting. Yet the people stood and waited. Even after it was explained to them that new ballot forms were being printed and would only be available the following day, they stood patiently.

A truly festive atmosphere reigned in some areas. There were singing, dancing, crying; kiosks, where food was sold, appeared suddenly. In the rural areas there were major problems. People waited for an entire day and yet the ballot forms were still not delivered. There were reports of false polling stations in Kwazulu-Natal. Other reports claimed incidence of intimidation, once again especially in the rural areas. Farm workers, on being interviewed, claimed they voted for whom their bosses had told them to vote for. Others claimed that the presiding electoral officers told them whom to vote for; they did not know that they had a choice. Illiterate people claimed that officers made their crosses even before they had indicated whom they wanted to vote for. The complaints were numerous and the IEC had to deal with all of them. After all the investigations, Judge Kriegler from the IEC pronounced the elections "substantially free and fair." The elections were an astounding victory for the African National Congress nationally. In the provinces, there were ANC majorities in seven provinces with the exception of two, the Western Province where there was a National Party majority and in Kwazulu-Natal with an Inkatha Freedom Party majority.

Because the ANC took a policy decision to increase the number of women at decision-making levels, at least one third of the prospective members of the national and provincial legislatures are women. Unfortunately, at the time of this presentation, this was not reflected in the top echelons of power where there were only one woman cabinet minister and two deputy-ministers. The women's parliamentary caucus had already been meeting and they intended to lobby for more powerful positions for women. People outside of parliament were committed to building a strong civil society. The Women's National Coalition (WNC) had decided to continue its work with the intention of focusing on the following:

(1) to empower women and strengthen their public voice by mobilizing and reinforcing women's organizations to secure the objectives of the Women's Charter;

(2) to play a leading role mobilizing women in NGOs to secure their effective participation in the 4th World Women's Congress in Beijing in 1995;

(3) to further research on women's issues;

(4) other areas of work include lobbying, advocacy, monitoring and ensuring the effective participation of women in the Reconstruction and Development Program of the Government.

Some of the challenges of the WNC would be to facilitate communication between the leaders of the WNC and grassroots women as well as empower them. Neither of these was achieved in the first two years of the coalition's existence. It was also of grave concern that at the moment the majority of the newly elected National Committee was comprised of white women. Regional representatives still had to be elected, but the fact that these white members had already been elected would give them extra experience, hence more power. In any coalition, those that are involved must strategize so that power is not concentrated in the hands of a small group.

This is the challenge facing South African women. The Women's National Coalition should not only reflect the majority of women's interests but also the diversity of the female population especially at the executive level.

The interim constitution is, as I have already mentioned, fairly progressive. Women must ensure that they are adequately represented on the committee that will draft the new constitution. South Africans may have achieved what many say is a political miracle. The implementation of these new rights and powers, especially for women, is still to come; therein lies the real challenge.

THE WAAD PAPER

This paper is an attempt by a black[1] woman activist[2] with some academic training to address the activism/academy question. My claiming activist status does not mean that I am either anti-academy or trying to imply that this paper may not fulfill the demands of academia. I will try to illustrate the demands on women activists' lives and the everyday experiences and problems that we have had with academicians. I want to emphasize, however, that as activists we have not had only negative experiences. Working hand in hand with academicians has enhanced our contribution to the struggle for the liberation of women and, in my view, helped academicians to sharpen their analytical tools. Because South Africa differs so vastly from region to region and my experience is limited largely to the Western Cape, this paper will focus on the Western Cape region.

Secondly, I would like elaborate on the methodology used in constructing this paper. One of the weaknesses of academicians is that many of them (and I'm specifically referring to South African women academicians) write about women without interviewing them, without using any primary data whatsoever. Of course one understands that there are often limitations of time, money, etc. Many academicians are either so entrenched in their written culture or find collecting data so time-consuming that they do not see the need to verify their readings about certain women even when those women live in the same city. I intend to use this paper as a sort of corrective and will therefore make extensive use of women's speeches as well as organizational pamphlets and documentation.

In South Africa, which is notorious for its apartheid/segregationist policies, the societal fragmentation is starkly reflected in the women's movements. I want to emphasize the plural (movements) because there is no way that we can speak of a women's movement.

In fact there may even be some critics who would argue that there are no women's movements because the movements are not feminist enough. I will comment on this and elaborate on the concept of feminism later. The activism/academy dichotomy which is the focus of this conference is less harshly experienced by the majority of South African women because of the other major contradictions in their lives. It is common knowledge and it is well-documented[3] that women do not form a homogeneous group. Apartheid and its concomitant exploitation and oppression of black people in general and of African women in particular have aggravated the divisions amongst women and the conditions of African working-class and rural women.[4] Ethnicity was reinforced and/or revived through the Bantustan policies. Cultural practices which over the years may have disappeared were recreated. The apartheid ideology had a profound effect on race and ethnic consciousness.

Apartheid also impacted what was acknowledged as the main site of struggle. Because national oppression was so severe and black men and women were oppressed, black women and men became allies against the oppressors. The debate over whether women's liberation was contradictory or complementary to national liberation has still not been resolved for many. In fact, because of the crises in this period of negotiations many women's organizations vacillated between different programs of action. This, I think, is an unconscious alignment with "national" issues. It is not that "women's" issues are subordinated, but more time is spent on responding to national mandates and activities. Women's organizations are less consistently proactive with regard to women's issues.

Not only is this ambivalence experienced at an organizational level but also at a personal level. In a workshop held at CACE (Centre for Continuing Adult Education) at the University of the Western Cape in October 1990, participants were broken up in small groups and asked to reflect on oppressive gender experiences. When a white woman described her fear and anguish on being robbed by a man, black women immediately asked whether the man was black. The black women promptly attempted through race and class analysis to justify this action. It was also conceded that race loyalty/consciousness was stronger than gender and class consciousness. Other divisions comprise religious groups, lesbians, the disabled, radical feminists, and language groups. What I found interesting in Hansson (1991) is that she used South African race divisions for black women, but she divided white women into official language groups (i.e., English and Afrikaans), in the same way the South African government had done with its divide-and-rule policy: all blacks were divided into ethnic groups whereas white ethnic divisions were minimized despite large numbers of immigrants speaking Greek, Portuguese, German, etc.

Because of the central role the liberation struggle plays in the lives of the majority of women, women were divided according to liberation ideologies. It was surprising that women academicians hardly mention this very important and often insurmountable division. As an ANC WL[5] activist, my experience is that this ideological division permeates everything. With the launch of the National Women's Coalition, this division has been temporarily overcome. How successful this liaison is to be will eventually be proved by history. I will elaborate on the National Coalition later.

In order to analyze the activism/academy gap it is important to attempt to conceptualize what we mean by these terms, as was made clear to me when I interviewed women very many of whom had different interpretations of the word. According to the Twentieth Century Chambers Dictionary, "activism" refers to "a philosophy of creative will, especially practical idealism of Rudolf Eucken; a policy of vigorous action" and an "activist" is "a believer in the philosophy of activism; one who supports policy of vigorous action; one who plays a special part in advancing a project or in strengthening the hold of political ideas." "Academy" refers to "Plato's school of philosophy; a higher, would-be higher, or specialized school or university; a society for the promotion of arts and science; purely theoretical arguments." Many women interviewed saw themselves as combining the above two extremes. Comrade Ray Alexander, prolific writer and an ANC and SACP member, definitely saw herself as an activist, although to the average activist she was seen as an academician. A social anthropologist saw herself as combining the two. She has been a campaigner for improved working conditions for all women staff, in an attempt to get away from the academic, administrative, and maintenance divide. Many activists think that only mainstream activists can be called activists.

I feel it is imperative that I raise some of the problems and demands of being an activist at this (presumably) largely academic gathering. I am also wondering, because of the focus of the conference, to what extent the organizers have attempted to ensure that the voice of activists will be heard here and to what extent they have been successful. As a woman activist for more than a decade in a period of extreme state repression, violence, and intense mass action, I knew there was no way that even the most realistic program of action could be adhered to. Activities that had to be sacrificed because of responses to crises included education and training programs and a task whose urgency was apparent to us but which we never succeeded in executing—the documentation of our struggle. Very seldom could we be pro-active; our activities were largely reactive. During the state of emergency the police had draconian powers. Political meetings were prohibited and thousands of people, men, women, and even children as young as nine were detained.

Let me outline other problems. From early 1984 to 1990—and even beyond, to a lesser extent—many of our members were "on the run" from the security police; that means not living in the same place for more than a few days. We disguised ourselves to avoid being recognized and subsequently arrested. We always said that there was too much work to be done outside the prisons and we could not afford the luxury of prison. We rarely used telephones to arrange meetings, but when we did, we used our code. Often there were communication problems when a code was not deciphered correctly. Those of us who had access to cars would change them regularly, swapping with friends. When moving from place to place we always had to check whether we were being followed and if we were, we found ways to outmaneuver our followers. Certain persons had the task of finding "safe" houses and cars. Venues for work or meetings were never known beforehand. We had to meet at a designated place, wait for everyone to arrive, without communicating, of course, and leave for the venue after ten minutes. All of this was not negative. We benefited from the state of emergency in that we had to be punctual otherwise we would miss the checkpoint. There are many other examples that I could outline. But I need to emphasize that we were not only victims of police intimidation and unlimited power. We have many stories to tell about how we, as individuals or collectively as women, intimidated and defied the police. For example, when fifteen of us were arrested for being in an African township without a permit, we made so much noise at the police station, irritated them with our questions and our demands of what our rights were that they released us after a few hours "on bail" which we still have not paid.

Our women's organization is racially mixed and multi-class, but we ensured that the issues taken up were the issues of the most oppressed women: housing, passes, cost of living, demands for troops to get out of the townships.[6] Because of various factors, we have not succeeded in empowering as many women as we should have. Our tasks are many, but the most demanding was responding to political crises. This often resulted in education and training, as important as they are, being sacrificed. Our meetings are often long, as it is imperative that we use translators. To facilitate broad participation, members are encouraged to speak in the language that they are most comfortable in. As English, Xhosa, and Afrikaans are spoken in our region we would, therefore, use these three languages simultaneously. Meetings are often lengthened by repeated explanations, which we do not find problematic as we feel it is important for members to understand the issues discussed. It is because of these practices that many women, who were shy and without confidence initially, now participate actively. Many women leaders on being interviewed about their political growth, admitted that their training ground was in the women's organizations.[7]

Communication is also a big problem. In a technological era when telephones, computers, and cars are taken for granted, we as women's organizations do not have those luxuries as the majority of our members are poor and live in rural and squatter areas. Loudspeakers are used to announce meetings. A whispering chain is used for sensitive areas.[8] We must acknowledge that many activists who are obsessed with meetings confuse "vigorous action" with intellectual debate and discussions. Action is sometimes delayed by mandates, democracy, and bureaucracy. It is imperative that a pragmatic and creative balance between accountability, initiative, and action be found.

It is also interesting that even though some of our members are academicians, very few have ever made their skills available to the organization. In fact, some of them wrote articles about the organization without any consultation. I do not mean that they needed "permission" from the organization, but in their articles they made no reference to the fact that they were members, leading one to wonder why they want to be part of these grassroots organizations. There are also cases where academicians join grassroots women's organizations and that's the end of their participation. One cannot but question their intention and commitment even when one understands that not all members can give total commitment. To aggravate matters, as out of touch as these academicians are with the organization, they state on public platforms that their women's organization does not take up women's issues. What motivates these academicians/white women to join these grassroots and largely black organizations? Yes, there are a few who are committed to changing the conditions of poor women. But, may I also be so bold as to say that many of them seem to be opportunistic feminist aca-

demicians and intellectuals who have used the study of less privileged women for economic and professional advancement. There
is no way in which they are challenging the *status quo*. Their documentation solely lines the book shelves and makes their *curriculum
vitae* more impressive. We are also inundated with requests from
academicians, local and foreign, for interviews. We have always conceded to these requests with the proviso that we get a copy of the
article. In all my experience of hundreds of interviews, I am aware
that it was only the authors[9] of *South African Women Speak* who sent
their draft for us to read. The state of emergency has been used as
a reason for researchers' inability to check the contents of their
work for inaccuracies. It is disconcerting to read distortions about
one's life in the sacrosanct "printed word." A veteran woman activist,
Mama Holo from Nyanga Township, after hearing about the request
for another interview by a specific academicians, had this to say:
"She keeps on interviewing me and writes more and more books
and she buys more pillows. And I still live in the same hovel.
Nothing's changed for me."

I must admit that women academicians also have limitations.
Many have stated that resources are not always readily available for
women-centered research. Within their departments they have to
prove that Women or Gender Studies are academically justified.
The working conditions that plague other women workers—e.g.,
minimal promotion, little recognition of the value of their work,
less salary, temporary posts—affect women academicians as well. It
may not always be easy for them to have some sort of "working relationship" with women's organizations, as they themselves are
marginalized in their place of work. The few academicians who do
have a limited working relationship with activists are often frustrated
because of the inability of activists to respond within deadlines.

Most of the women who are doing research and writing books
are white and/or middle-class. Some do not, because of lack of primary research, interpret black women's experiences accurately.
There have been criticisms by women in squatter areas in Cape
Town about certain assumptions made in texts. Yes, it is easy to ask
why organized squatter women do not write their own histories. The
answer is complex. Many women do not have the skills or confidence to do so. The idea of writing a book is often outside of their
reality, and unless this process is facilitated for them it is unlikely
that they will ever record their stories. As mentioned earlier, most
of the women who are doing research and writing books on women
are white and/or middle-class and the "objects" of their studies are

mostly black and working-class. This arrangement is the subject of a current debate. Walker challenges the criticism of Nkululeko, who asks: "Can an oppressed nation....rely on knowledge produced....by others, no matter how progressive, who are members of the oppressor nation?" Walker responds with the following:

> For one thing, the subjective experience of a condition or situation does not guarantee the ability to reflect critically and analytically upon it, nor does it preclude the problem of bias. For another, which social attributes one chooses to privilege in order to define the boundaries of who is or is not the legitimate "subject-researched," the insider, is in itself a matter of political and intellectual choice: for instance, the assumption that race should be privileged above class or gender, thereby allowing black women, and perhaps, black men to write about both male and female blacks, but debarring all whites, male and female, from writing about blacks, whether of the same class and/or sex or not. (6)

Many black women have voiced their anger at being "research objects" and ask if it means that white and middle-class women are not oppressed in view of the fact that they are always writing about black women's oppression. I see this as academic colonialism. My response to this is: Would it not be better if there were wider consultation or collective writing on these issues? It also seems that if white women are going to continue writing about the oppression of black women and not write about the oppression of white women, is it not emulating the very racism that we're trying to get away from—where white people are doing things "on behalf of" blacks? Would it not be better if there were more facilities for those who have not, because of the political context, had the ability to write their own histories? It is also important for white women to write about their contradictory status: as oppressed women and as oppressors as members of the white community. Black women feel strongly about this because it is when data on white women are incorporated that we will have a complete picture of the oppression of women in South Africa. At the moment there is a wealth of data about black women and very little about white women.

Bazilli (1991) pleads that we learn to share our resources before we can make our priorities work for us. She correctly refers to "our legacy of proprietiness." This is easier said than done. At recent women's conferences[10] there were resolutions about cooperation between academicians and activists as well as access to academic research. As far as I know this has not been done in the Western Cape, and I have not been able to find out whether in fact this happened in other areas. Yes, it is easy to make resolutions, but unless resolutions contain practical ways of implementing them they are seldom or never realized. Or maybe we will once again, ironically at an international conference, realize how non-existent our regional and national networks are and use this forum here, in Nsukka, to facilitate them.

Bazilli (1991: 3) refers to what the Chinese call "speaking bitterness" and appeals for more speaking bitterness and less pettiness. I agree that we need to confront areas of conflict, and racism is one of them. At a recent international Gender and Popular Education Seminar organized by CACE (1992),[11] the agenda was altered to incorporate a workshop on racism after complaints by black participants. It by no means resolved many things but it was a good start in confronting a very complex and delicate issue. Unfortunately, class was not addressed and, because of the integration of gender, race, and class, it is imperative that class be also addressed. Because racism is an emotional issue, it was realized that a workshop was but a start, but those who felt that class needed to be addressed refrained from doing so. I am not sure that this was a wise decision.

At the "Women and Gender in Southern Africa" conference (Durban 1991), the relationship between black and white, academicians and activists, and the marginalization of black women created some intense discussion. This resulted in various responses, some highly critical like that of Desirée Lewis (1992).[12] Bazilli (1991: 3) on the other hand, is quite apologetic, stating that "There is no blame—there is just history." I acknowledge the tremendous work and effort put into the conference by the organizers. But history is not some detached omnipotent force; people are history, people have made and continue to make history, people benefited from or suffered under certain historical conditions, and people have challenged and changed that history. It is no longer productive that we continue planning conferences as they have been in the past. New contact lists must be drawn up. In fact the organizing group should be broadened into a more representative group. Yes, it is difficult and even frustrating, but if we want to stop "objectifying" working-class and black women, they have to be part of the entire process. This process could demystify conferences and empower grassroots women. Maybe I am being too idealistic, but if the women's movements are to be relevant we somehow have to find ways of bringing our theories and praxis closer. Activists or grassroots women are often tired because of their demanding jobs— it's an extra meeting and not part of their wage labor. The same applies to writing papers; it's all extra labor. We could be more creative in conferencing. Many women have important experiences to share. The oral tradition could well be used here.

Many women academicians have done valuable research and work which must be acknowledged and appreciated. In order to include black and working-class women in the writing of their own histories, a more feminist approach must be used. White women/ academicians could empower black women by collaborating with black women to write black women's stories. The entire process of writing could be demystified and the piece of work would emerge as more authentic due to the direct participation of black women. Such a collaborative work will contrast with some published articles consisting mostly of unacknowledged quotations by women whose stories are being written. An exception is Barbie Schreiner, who had fully acknowledged the collective work done in the production of the book, *My Spirit Is Not Banned.* Schreiner interviewed Frances Baard and as part of the sub-title Schreiner included "as told to Barbie Schreiner." When women writers were asked why they did not empower black women to tell their stories and why they, the established writers (incidentally all white), could not just edit the books, the responses were varied: "The publishers asked me to write the book"; "There is no time"; "Yes, but not for this book, the next one maybe"—all very valid answers, but when does affirmative action start? Are we really serious about empowering other women? Whose task is it to initiate or facilitate this process? And, in any case, if these black and working-class women provide the information for the research, why can't they be part of the project as authors and collaborators?

If we are feminists (granted there are different interpretations, but basically feminism concerns the questioning of unequal gender relations and attempting to change them), we have, by implication, some sort of solidarity with women less privileged than ourselves. Changing power and gender relations cannot be isolated from other inequalities. Gender equality can be realized only within a radical social transformation. Feminists should therefore combine theory and praxis. I also question whether one can be a feminist working in isolation without networking with other feminists. In other words, being feminist means using feminist methodology for empowering other women. Since the late 1980s the word feminism has become more frequently used in mass-based organizations, but it is important to add that very many ordinary, grassroots women still find feminism an alienating word, something that "overseas women or white women or educated and rich women worry about." It is a challenge to all of us to propagate a brand of feminism, an indigenous South African feminism, that is relevant to the women of South Africa. But the future for women in South Africa lies in working together, acknowledging our differences and commonality, and devising strategies to achieve our common goals. Because women's issues and demands are marginalized from CODESA,[13] women, ranging from academicians in the universities to activists in the trade unions and liberation movements should stop wasting energies emphasizing only their differences.

Two attempts at forward-looking strategies are the establishment of Women's Studies Units and the formation of Women's Alliances and the National Women's Coalition. Individual women academicians have also structured their work to fulfill the needs of organizations and have felt unhappy about polarizing activism/academy all the time. According to Barbara Klugman, "Many of the women at the conferences are themselves struggling against the elitism of academia. Many have engaged in participatory research at the request of grassroots organizations. Many of these academics are also activists themselves, both in universities and mass based organizations" (Shefer & Mathis, 1991).[14] This view was not broadly accepted. Shireen Hassim, one of the organizers of the "Women and Gender in Southern Africa" conference felt that "Activists wanted a much more subordinate intelligentsia within the women's movement; subordinated to the need to build a political base and accountable to that in their research."[15] Kabeer explains why she agrees with Hassim: "Because research throws up unpopular findings and academics should be free to pursue those and disseminate them" (Shefer & Mathis, 1991).[16]

If the above has been the academicians' experience, they are justified in their caution. On the other hand, many academicians critique organizations without having a full understanding of them. Political organizations would benefit from regular assessment and evaluation. Strategies should then be changed accordingly to increase their effectiveness. Our women's organizations have grown through this process. However, it would be disastrous for a women's movement if this academic/activist schism were to continue or even intensify. The field of Women's Studies could be one way out of this impasse. Dubel outlines the origin of Women's Studies in the North and the way in which it links the feminist/women's activism and academia:

> Women's Studies emerged from a political and social move-
> ment outside the walls of the university. Its concerns were
> thus not strictly academic and its legitimacy depended on
> acceptance by the feminist community as well as the uni-
> versity. Women's Studies was seen to be the academic wing
> of the women's movement; committed to the goals of the
> women's movement [including a critique of "traditional"
> academic standards]. (Dubel 1991)[17]

Women's Studies as a discipline is still in its initial stages in South African universities and it would do well if it, too, could be the "academic wing" of the women's movement. As I mentioned in my introductory paragraph, the work of academicians could be enhanced if they had a good working relationship that is based on true partnership and mutual respect with women's organizations. Consequently, the accuracy of research material could be verified. This working relationship could have obviated the situation whereby, for example, a paper on the history of women's organizations presented at an Anthropology conference in Amsterdam in the mid-1980s contained inaccuracies.[18] Similarly, activism could be informed by sound theoretical analysis accessed by academicians. As deplorable as it sounds, activists sometimes do not have the luxury of time to read; often they cannot even read or write. The "unpopular findings" that Kabeer (Shefer & Mathis 1991) referred to could render their work more effective. Strategies that have been implemented in other struggles could be shared with the women's organizations. That way the women's movements all over the world could learn from the mistakes and successes of women in other countries. The list is endless.

To a certain extent, service organizations or non-governmental organizations (NGOs) consist of both academicians and activists and have succeeded, to a greater or lesser extent, in balancing activism with academia. A weakness in South Africa is the relative isolation in which activists and academicians work. This too is the case with NGOs. Even though they see affirmative action with regard to women as their primary focus, they do not work with women's organizations. We need to redress this imbalance in communication by exchanging strategies and resources. Not only will it facilitate and strengthen our work, but unnecessary duplication would be avoided.

The formation of the National Women's Coalition[19] and region-al Women's Alliances[20] could potentially be vehicles for a vibrant women's movement in South Africa. The affiliates to the Coalition and the Alliances include political women's organizations, trade unions, church women's organizations, business and professional organizations, human rights, lesbian women's organizations, rural and disabled women's organizations, and feminist organizations concentrating on specific issues such as rape and battery. It is, there-fore, a broad cross-section of South African society with its class, race and cultural contradictions and the concomitant implications.

The launch of the National Women's Coalition proved that, despite political differences, women could work together fairly effectively when faced with a task that would benefit all women. The Women's National Coalition's main task is the drawing up of a Women's Charter which would contain women's demands. These demands would be drawn up after consultation with women in all works of life. Various methods would be used to ascertain these demands: from consulting women at their homes and work places to conferences, talk shows on television and radio, and through the distribution of questionnaires. The campaign also aims at raising an awareness amongst women of their situation and consulting them about their problems and demands. A charter will be based on these demands. Women will then lobby to have them included in a bill of rights and the constitution. Research is being done to assess how these rights can best be incorporated into and protect-ed through the judicial system. This campaign, which has already started, is making the working relationship between activists and academicians a reality.

But the women's alliances present many problems. Because of the legacy of apartheid and the divided, exploitative society we've inherited, building a true and meaningful alliance is not an easy task. The alliances/coalition need to be broadened to be truly rep-resentative of the women of South Africa. The challenges for us are enormous. How do we challenge power relations amongst women so that the educated/middle-class/academic/white/urban/confi-dent women do not dominate? How do we ensure that all affiliates participate equally and meaningfully? We have learned from women's experiences in other countries as well as our own the dif-ficulty, if not impossibility, of the concept of "sisterhood." There are inevitably different interest groups. How do we reconcile them? We need to distinguish between our short-term and long-term goals and assess to what extent these are contradictory. What will our strategies and tactics be to realize these goals? As Bazilli said: "No one said it was going to be easy." Maybe if we, as activists and academicians, stop emphasizing our differences and commit ourselves to working together, we will work towards an effective women's movement. It's only when we start appreciating and respecting the others' work and understanding their problems and limitations that we will succeed in our working relationship. It's only in realizing and accepting that our work is complementary and not contradictory that we will benefit.

I have come to realize through writing this paper that a very urgent task has arisen for us activists. If we want our ideas to be used by women academicians, we should be able to facilitate this process. In order to facilitate the documentation of our struggle, women's organizations should see it as their task to either audiotape or videotape all their major activities. A group of women activists and academicians should be commissioned to record contemporary history.

Even though there are mutterings from the apartheid state's president that "Apartheid has been abolished," all the apartheid structures are intact and the lives of ordinary persons have remained the same, if not aggravated. It is also common knowledge that these differences will not disappear overnight. In fact, nothing has been done to redress the evils of the past, except for a few class concessions; the same applies to the position of women. Even though the political climate has changed in the sense that the people's organizations are no longer banned, the demands on women activists have not lessened. In fact, the challenges we as women face have increased. Women have contributed to the changing climate, yet they are not represented substantially in decision-making forums.

The violence currently sweeping our country is a major concern for all. Perhaps one of the greatest tasks that a potential women's movement can take on is to challenge the power-hungry forces and expose those who are instigating the violence. We cannot pretend that apartheid and its lackeys are not largely responsible for the climate of violence. There are many women academicians and women's structures that have influence even within the regime. The time for neutrality is long overdue. One does not need to align oneself with a particular political party. The need for peace and justice is universal and above party politics. In a country that is ravaged by strife and hostility, I cannot but state as a political activist that we live in two worlds. The world of the middle-class/white/academicians is poles apart from the world in which black people are suffering and dying every day, as if black lives were not important. One wonders what the De Klerk regime would have done had the victims been white? Let us leave the ivory tower of objectivity and speak out for peace and justice.

Malibongwe igamalamakhosikasi!
Let the name of women be praised!

NOTES

1. The term black is used in the liberation struggle to refer to all who are disenfranchised. This emerged from the Black Consciousness Movement started by Steve Biko. In the early 1970s the term black was popularly used to refer to all people who could not vote. Hence colored, Indian, and African (the term used by the apartheid state for indigenous black people) people were all called black. But all black people are not equally oppressed. In the apartheid hierarchy, Indian and Colored (of mixed race) people have more privileges than African people (indigenous to Africa); e.g., the Western Cape was designated a Colored Labor Preference area, which meant, according to legislation, that certain unskilled jobs were reserved for colored people only. At the time of writing this paper (early 1992) "black" was predominantly used. Yet in this period of affirmative action and pre-elections it seems "pragmatic" to disaggregate black. As a classified colored, I had easier access to tertiary education than "African" women. My class position has subsequently changed because of my education.
2. For most of my adult life I have been an activist and for the past fifteen years an activist in the Charterist women's movement. The term Charterist refers to organizations which during the time when the African National Congress (ANC) was banned, supported the ANC. The word Charterist is derived from the Freedom Charter which was drawn up by the Congress of the People (ANC, S. A. Indian Congress, Colored People's Congress, and the Congress of Democrats [whites]) in 1955 in Kliptown. It contains the minimum demands for a non-racial South Africa.
3. All the pamphlets published by women's organizations in general and by United Women's Organization and United Women's Congress, outline these different degrees of oppression. All women are oppressed as women and can be raped and abused by men. Yet many white and middle-class women collude with men to oppress African and working-class women. Black working-class women experience greater exploitation than white working-class women. In fact, because of apartheid, many white working-class women do not have a working-class consciousness. SADWU (South African Domestic Workers Union [established November 1, 1886]) and COSATU (Congress of South African Trade Unions) publications emphasize particularly the class oppression. The

report of the Women and Gender in Southern Africa Conference (January 1991) refers to critiques of the use of the concepts such as the triple oppression used by the progressive movement.

4. The conditions of black people's lives in the rural areas differ substantially from their urban counterparts. In many rural areas, feudal relations still exist. The white farmers "own" the workers. They, therefore, often sexually abuse women workers and their daughters.

5. In 1960 the ANC and the Pan Africanist Congress (PAC), which was formed in 1959 by African dissidents in the ANC, were banned. There was a lull in mass above-ground political activity. In the late 1970s six women in the Western Cape together with women in exile, met in Botswana to discuss reviving the United Women's Organization (UWO), which was launched in April 1980. It was the first mass political organization in South Africa after the 1960s lull and a women's organization at that. Many men wanted to join and were annoyed at the women for not including them. They did the catering and child care at UWO general councils. It was the UWO women who initiated the formation of Civics, mixed organizations concerned with housing and rent problems. In April 1986, the UWO merged with the Women's Front Organization to form the United Women's Congress (UWCO). As mentioned before, UWCO supported the ANC and a major campaign was demanding the unbanning thereof. After the unbanning of the ANC, UWCO dissolved to form the ANC Women's League. The PAC attended the Women's Alliance conference in July 1991, at the University of Western Cape. They have not attended since.

6. There has been and still is criticism that these issues are not women's issues. These criticisms were made by middle-class women to whom housing, for example, was not an issue. For the women in our organization who live in squatter areas it is indeed a major concern.

7. Women on the First Western Cape United Democratic Front Regional Executive were all members of United Women's Congress. Cheryl Carolus, a prominent woman leader, states in "The Freedom Charter, 30 Years Later" (Kronin and Suttner, 1985) that her training ground was UWO.

8. A whispering campaign would be used if the message is of a sensitive nature and not for the general public. Person #1 would inform or whisper to person #2 the information to be transmitted. Person #2 will then inform person #3; with person #3 again informing person #4, etc. This process will continue until the entire group that is supposed to be informed has been "whispered" to. Often the links are secret, which means that each person only knows the identity of two persons; the one who informs her and the person whom she in turn informs.

9. Jane Barret, et. al, *Vukani Makhoskasie: South African Women Speak* (London: Catholic Institute for International Relations, 1985).

10. Since 1980 conferences were frequently held outside South Africa, with women from inside the country meeting women in exile. The Malibongwe Conference held in Amsterdam in January 1990 was the most publicized. It was jointly planned by the Dutch Anti-Apartheid Movement and the ANC Women's Section. Among the conferences

recently held inside the country are: South African Council of Churches-Women and the Constitution (Durban, October 1990); ANC Women's Conference at University of Western Cape in December 1990 hosted by Center for Development Studies; Lawyers for Human Rights, Women and the Constitution (Johannesburg, November 1990); Women and Gender in Southern Africa (University of Natal, Jan./Feb. 1991); Gender and Development (Institute for Natural Resources, University of Natal, Pietermaritzburg, March 1992).

11. Seminar on Gender and Popular Education (Center for Continuing Adult Education, University of Western Cape, May 1992).

12. Desirée Lewis, "The Politics of Feminisms in South Africa: Natal University's Women and Gender Conference" (unpublished paper written as a response to the 1991 conference).

13. Main political players ranging from the ANC to the ruling Nationalist Party are engaged in negotiations. It has been boycotted by right-wing movements like the Conservative Party and the more leftist New Unity Movement, Pan Africanist Congress, Azapo (Azanian People's Organization). At the time of writing, negotiations reached a stalemate and the ANC was considering withdrawing.

14. Quoted in Tammy Shefer and Sibylle Mathis, "The Search for Sisterhood," *Work in Progress*, 73.

15. *Ibid.*

16. *Ibid.*

17. Ireen Dubel, "Whither South African Women's Studies?" Paper presented at Women and Gender in Southern Africa Conference, Durban, 1991.

18. The paper dealt with the analysis of women's organizations in the Western Cape. The writer presented the United Women's Congress as a federal structure whereas it was in fact a unitary one. This error produced an inaccurate analysis.

19. The National Women's Coalition was launched in Johannesburg on April 25, 1992. Fifty-six national organizations were represented. The 350 delegates were from a range of organizations across the political spectrum. Some of the organizations are the ANC Women's League, the National Party, Inkatha Freedom Party, COSATU (Congress of South African Trade Unions), Democratic Party, Young Women's Christian Association, The Girl Guides Association, Business and Professional Women, the Rural Women's Movement, and Disabled People of South Africa. The main campaign will draw up the Women's Charter in consultation with women everywhere in South Africa.

20. These are regional coalitions and alliances. Women's Coalition (Pretoria Witwatersrand, Vereeniging-PWV) was launched on August 9, 1991. Women's Charter Alliance of Southern Natal was launched on December 7, 1991 with 44 women's organizations as affiliates. Women's Alliance in the Western Cape was launched on November 24, 1991. The main campaign of the alliances is to do broad consultation with local women for their demands. Western Cape Alliance also has two other projects: (1) the campaign to end violence against women, and (2) the founding of the Women's College. The College will initiate leadership and skills

training courses. If structured courses women want are already being offered by service organizations, women will be referred to them. The Women's College will set up a working relationship with these NGOs to ensure that the courses offered are gender-sensitive.

WORKS CITED

Baard, Frances. *My Spirit Is Not Banned: As Told By Frances Baard to Barbie Schreiner*. Harare: Zimbabwe Publishing House, 1986.

Bazilli, Susan. "Conferencing the Stone." Paper written in response to Women and Gender in Southern Africa Conference, University of Natal, Durban, Jan. 30-Feb. 2, 1991.

Bonnin, Debbie, et al. "Report of the Conference on Women and Gender in Southern Africa." University of Natal, Durban, 1991

Dubel, Ireen. "Whither South African Women's Studies?" Paper prepared for Women and Gender in Southern Africa Conference. University of Natal, Durban, Jan. 30-Feb. 2, 1991.

Federation of South African Women (Western Cape), minutes of meetings.

Hansson, Desirée. "A Patchwork Quilt of Power Relations: A Challenge to 1991South African Feminism." Paper prepared for the International Conference on Women, Law, and Social Control, Montreal, Canada, 1991.

Lewis, Desirée. "The Politics of Feminism in South Africa." Paper written in response to Women and Gender in Southern Africa Conference. University of Natal, Durban Jan. 30-Feb. 2, 1991.

Shefer, Tammy, and Sibylle Mathis. "The Search for Sisterhood." *Work in Progress* 73 (1992): 14-16.

Suttner, Raymond, and Jeremy Cronin. *Thirty Years of the Freedom Charter*. Johannesburg: Ravan Press, 1985.

United Women's Congress, minutes of meetings.

United Women's Organization, minutes of meetings.

Walker, Cherryl, ed. *Women and Gender in Southern Africa*. Cape Town: David Philip, 1990.

INTERVIEWS

Conducted with Ray Alexander, Jenny Schreiner, Nomatyala Hangana, Mildred Lesia, Dorothy Mafacu, Mildred Holo, Lynne Brown, Nonkolisa Samdaka, Rhoda Joemat, and Rhoda Kadalie (November 1991-March 1992).

THE ARAB WOMEN'S SOLIDARITY ASSOCIATION:

THE CONTEXTS OF CONTROVERSY AND THE POLITICS OF VOICE

PETER HITCHCOCK

WHO SPEAKS FOR ARAB WOMEN? THIS QUESTION NOT ONLY flags the dubious qualifications of my own subject position, but is predicated on a complex and problematic history. The answer, "Arab women themselves," while obviously paramount and indeed essential, elides one of the more prominent first principles of contemporary theories of the subject; namely, that there is no unified subject position that might be self-present with its putative voice. This is neither a conundrum nor a simple paean to Derrida and deconstruction, but it is a recognition that the following notes on the contemporary dilemma of AWSA (the Arab Women's Solidarity Association) are predicated on a notion that when one speaks of "Arab women" (even, as here, in solidarity) one is speaking of the multiple and the incommensurate. The danger, of course, is that such a theory of subjectivity colludes with precisely the divide-and-rule rhetoric of those who do not wish to hear "Arab women" in the first place. The challenge is to articulate a notion of political constituency that does not cancel itself out with the subtleties of sliding signifiers, etc. I intend to read the current situation of AWSA as an allegory of the predicament of political voice, as a symptom both of empowerment and as a version of a representational dilemma that threatens to undermine significant forms of political identity.

It comes as little surprise that AWSA emerged as an organization in Egypt in 1982 through the efforts of Nawal el Saadawi, that country's leading feminist: first, because the complex historical conditions of Egypt make it a focus of the Arab world; second, only a woman of el Saadawi's commitment and energy could have envisioned an organization to unify the political claims of Arab women in Africa and West Asia. Clearly, however, there are problems with AWSA's bold steps for collective representation. This is not primarily because the organization's character is defined through its charismatic leader (although Arab feminists, including Leila Ahmed and Marnia Lazreg, have sometimes questioned the centrality accorded to or assumed by el Saadawi in national and international cultural relations[1]), nor indeed because Cairo is AWSA's operational base, but because "Arab" and "woman" do not easily trace the contemporary borders of identity. Note the realm of difference in Magida Salman's definition of the "Arab woman":

> Notwithstanding her condition, whether as a peasant in Algeria, a doctor in Cairo, or a secretary in Beirut, a student in Baghdad, a worker in Syria, or veiled in a Harem in Saudi Arabia, the Arab woman shares with her sisters a common fate: a life of renunciation, of captivity, during which she will have to atone for her sin of having been born a woman in a hyper-male society where the ever-present feminine remains synonymous with shame and threat.[2]

Is the common fate of the doctor in Cairo (who might well be el Saadawi) the same as the worker in Syria? Is the fate of the Algerian peasant the same as the woman in the Saudi Arabian harem? What about the fates which derive from the identities of nation and class? In addition, although Salman correctly states that the Arab family is primarily a Muslim family, where does this leave Arab Christians or Arab Jews? And, last but not least, what of the Arab women of the Diaspora? Are their lives best described as ones of renunciation and captivity? Magida Salman's definition of the "Arab woman" is as good as any other, the common fate she describes as a Lebanese feminist is more common than any other, but this example emphasizes that the identity politics which coalesce around the notion of "Arab woman" depend for their success on a strategic essentialism that cares less for the difference which occurs between "Arab" and "woman" than the specific prescience of their combination. Thus, when AWSA distributed its political agenda to the UN International Conference on Women in Nairobi in 1985 only two of its eight principles make any reference to Arab women: the bulk of its appeal is to international feminism, and international feminism of the "Third World" at that.[3] Clearly, this is at one with the tenor of the Nairobi conference, but this is in stark contrast to AWSA's constitution, in which the term "Arab women" dominates almost every article. Again, the point is not to belittle the *raison d'être* of the organization, but to assess the efficacy and politics of its positioning. To focus on the practical advantages of strategic essentialism we need first not a theory of the subject so much as a sense of AWSA's specific history, and it is to this that we now turn.

The formation of AWSA is not only the latest chapter in feminist activism in Egypt but follows in a strong tradition of radical Egyptian politics. Together these form a discontinuous history which makes AWSA if not inevitable then certainly explicable. Like many other countries in Africa, the modern Egyptian state has developed because of—and despite—the calipers of colonialism and capitalism that have held it, yet the particular character of its nationalist movements has always set it apart from its immediate neighbors. In addition, Egypt's secularism has given its emergent bourgeoisie a decidedly different outlook: on the one hand providing a smoother course for its integration into international capital relations; on the other, suggesting to much of its intelligentsia that different models of development might obtain. The contradictory logic of Nasserism was in part a product of these symptoms, whether one focuses on the early period of resistance to imperialism, the post-Suez moment of state socialism and closer ties to the Soviet Union, or the collapse of centrist policies in the wake of the Six Day War and the later rise of Anwar Sadat.

The relationship of feminism to these broader changes in Egyptian society since the end of the Second World War is instructive. During the period of resistance to British colonialism, feminist sentiment and radical politics flourished in Egypt. Nevertheless, it was difficult to build a national women's movement, both because of prejudice against political participation and because of unequal educational opportunities. Many feminists therefore found themselves allied with the Left, seeing women's liberation within the context of a democratization of society as a whole. The League of Women Students and Graduates of Egypt, created in 1944/45, was a product of this alliance as was the Women's Committee for Popular Resistance, formed in 1951. As Inji Aflatun wrote in 1949 in *We Egyptian Women*, "Woman's participation in the political life of society constitutes an important element in a healthy democratic regime and a prime factor in the evolution and development of this society."[4] Ironically, with the triumph of Nasser the strength and importance of such women's organizations was undermined, the Nasserite regime apparently quelling feminist sentiment (including Islamic feminism), just as it snuffed out communist insurgency (Inji Aflatun herself was arrested for her "communist sympathies" and spent four years in Qanatir jail). Yet, as Kathleen Merriam-Howard has argued, the Nasserite experiment, while generally hostile to feminism, encouraged educational opportunities for women which have provided the seedbed for the subsequent development of a significant feminist consciousness in Egypt.[5] Almost despite itself, the socialist principles which underpinned Nasser's government produced more egalitarian notions of citizenship than before. In reviewing these, Leila Ahmed notes that the National Charter (drafted and approved by the National Congress in 1962) is explicit in its support for women when it states: "Woman must be regarded as equal to man and must, therefore, shed the remaining shackles that impede her free movement, so that she might take a constructive and profound part in the shaping of life."[6]

Like many other blueprints for democracy, however, the assertion of principles does not automatically imply equality in practice. Nevertheless, and Nawal el Saadawi is just one example, radical feminists within the intelligentsia have increasingly taken the new opportunities provided by such principles (particularly in education, and subsequently in the vast labyrinth of government bureaucracy) to create links with their feminist sisters abroad while challenging bourgeois feminists (or what el Saadawi calls the "official opposition") in the urban centers at home. Anwar Sadat's crackdown in 1981 only sharpened the resolve of these activists (including el Saadawi who, like her feminist foremother Aflatun, was incarcerated in Qanatir) and despite repressive government policies the organizational structure of AWSA emerged to protect and promote women's rights.

One can specify this history still further by looking at the organizational aims of AWSA. On one level, it has consistently stressed that women's solidarity be seen in the context of Arab nationalism, a nationalism that guarantees women's individual rights while resisting foreign intervention in the internal affairs of the Arab nation. Clearly, in terms of Egypt, this is a critique not only of the consequences of Sadat's "Open Door" policies and the Camp David Accords but also a challenge to the Mubarak regime, which in general has played off secular and Muslim groups against each other while simultaneously using peace with Israel to garner Western, particularly American, investment and arms. On another level, AWSA has had to define its policy not only in terms of civic law but with respect to the dictates of Islam (or the *"salafi"* movements) since, with the resurgence of fundamentalism, Islam has often stood for a rolling back of women's rights via conservative interpretations of the *Quran* and *sharia*.[7] Between the neo-colonial realities which delimit Arab nationalism and the confines of conservative Islamicism, AWSA has had to navigate the Scylla and Charybdis of the modern Arab state. Indeed, it is precisely the contradictory forces of economic dependency on the West and the ideological underpinnings of Islam that together drive the wedge between "Arab" and "woman" in AWSA's identity politics. Thus, in attempting to disarticulate the contradictions which form this wedge, AWSA has often become the victim of both elements. Two examples may clarify this identity "fix."

The year after AWSA's successful contribution to the Nairobi women's conference, it organized an international Arab women's conference in Cairo. This was some feat because AWSA had been under pressure from the Egyptian Ministry of Social Affairs for protesting the abolition of Personal Status Law No. 44, a major guarantee of women's marriage and divorce rights in Egypt.[8] El Saadawi had received a warning from the Ministry that AWSA's intervention constituted "political activity" under the Law of Association (an accusation that will have special meaning in our second example). Without the support of the Ministry of Social Affairs, AWSA had to seek government approval for the conference from elsewhere, eventually getting recognition from the Ministry of Foreign Affairs (which would have had difficulty refusing since by this time AWSA had consultative status with the UN Economic and Social Council, a major international organization). The question of funding was more complex. The Arab League in Cairo provided its premises for the conference in a major recognition of AWSA's importance to Arab solidarity. Organizational costs were also defrayed by contributions from the Ford Foundation, OXFAM, and the Dutch group,

NOVIB. None of these groups attached conditions, but their donations obviously attracted criticism: simply put, it is much harder to
fault government collusion with the West when your group also
seeks Western funding. I would read this somewhat differently: if
the Ministry of Social Affairs refuses recognition for the conference
based in part on AWSA's prior political activities, then is the Ford
Foundation donation therefore based on politics or on the more
dubious ideology of the politically neutral? The point here is not
to enforce a "political correctness" about organizational funding
but to wonder aloud about the realities of the Arab nation state and
the limitations these set on pan-Arab feminism. The fact that not
one of the Arab or Egyptian organizations approached for funding
provided any underlines that AWSA's internationalism is not just a
matter of intellectual curiosity but a necessity of contemporary feminist politics in the Arab world. The second example will show that,
unfortunately, even internationalism can be compromised by the
masculinist dictates of the international public sphere.

In the report based on AWSA's 1986 conference (and published
in English in the anthology *Women of the Arab World*), the organizers proposed to write and publish a journal on Arab feminism.
Initially blocked by the Egyptian Higher Press Council, ostensibly
on the grounds of insufficient start-up funding, AWSA published
the journal as an internal periodical for organization members, thus
sidestepping the otherwise prohibitive publication codes.
Nevertheless, the journal, *al-Noon* (the Arabic letter N, but also the
name of an ancient Egyptian goddess of the universe) was threatened with bans almost from its inception in late 1989. Banned from
Egyptian radio and TV and periodically censored in the press, el
Saadawi saw in *al-Noon* an opportunity to write and distribute feminist criticism in an otherwise hostile environment. Yet the restrictions on publication and distribution imposed by the government
undermined *al-Noon*'s national let alone international appeal; until,
that is, the Gulf War. Outraged by foreign intervention in the war,
AWSA began publishing articles critical of the coalition forces and
calling for peace initiatives. *Al-Noon* also praised a group of women
in Saudi Arabia who had defied government and religious sexism
by driving cars through downtown Riyadh. Other articles included
an extensive critique of Shiekh Ben Baz who had suggested that
women in Saudia Arabia should be completely covered in public,
except for one half of one eye. These attacks gained the ire of both
the Saudi Arabian and Egyptian governments. Mubarak's regime
in particular, saw yet another opportunity to bolster its image in the

eyes of the West (it had already joined the coalition and sent troops to the front). Any internal opposition to the Egyptian government and its Saudi ally was seen as a threat to the stability of an otherwise fragile Arab contribution to the coalition forces. Not surprisingly, the government instructed *al-Noon*'s printer to cease producing copies of the "unlicensed" magazine.

Unfazed by government attacks, AWSA formed a delegation which joined other international women's organization representatives on a peace mission to Baghdad in January, 1991 just before the outbreak of war. Although their appeals to Saddam Hussein failed to secure Iraq's withdrawal from Kuwait, the delegation's efforts embarrassed the "peaceful" pretensions of the coalition forces. After the war was out of the way, the Egyptian government moved quickly to complete its crackdown on AWSA's activities. As before, they invoked the law of association, specifically Article 3 of the Statutes of Organizations, forbidding any institution related to the Ministry of Social Affairs from discussing "politics or religion." Under this pretense, the Egyptian chapter of AWSA was dissolved on June 15, 1991. The government went further, however, by suggesting that there were financial irregularities in AWSA's records and therefore urged the confiscation or transferral of AWSA's financial assets to another association, "Women of Islam." (This itself is an interesting and controversial decision given the government's checkered history of relations with Islamic groups.) With little proof and still less argument General Abdel Raouf Abdelrahman, one of Cairo's governors, declared: "The principal reason for dissolving the organization was due to its financial and legal violations.... and not to political considerations."[9]

Since this decision, legal representatives for AWSA have been in and out of court attempting to overturn it. In May of 1992 Cairo's Administrative Court upheld the government's position (surprise, surprise), but AWSA has continued to fight the legality of these maneuvers. Meanwhile, AWSA's operational base in Cairo remains closed. There was an attempt to move the organizational hub to Algeria, but this foundered when the political situation in Algeria itself became unstable. According to el Saadawi, AWSA is currently "nowhere"; however, a communications network is still in place and AWSA members continue to operate despite the machinations of the Egyptian government.[10]

What does this second example tell us about AWSA's political identity? Despite some progressive tendencies in Mubarak's policies, especially in comparison to Sadat, his government will not sanction a more radical voice for Egyptian women if this compromises either Egypt's image in international affairs or its placation of Islamic fundamentalist groups within its borders. Once again, as el Saadawi has noted, "woman is the sacrificial lamb of Arab politics."[11] The government's position on women's organizations is patently absurd: if an Arab feminist association cannot talk about politics or religion, then what is it supposed to discuss? Small wonder that many of these organizations are reduced to supervising charities. The absurdity of the government position, however, goes to the heart of the problematic identity of "Arab women." As our cursory history of recent Egyptian feminism shows, when women embrace pan-Arabism, patriarchal state formations tolerate their protests only so long as they do not intervene in the Arab nation's self-projection to the world. Yet when women seek to become a political force commensurate with their goals of equality and self-representation, this is deemed unconstitutional and a threat to the strategic balance of state and religion. In short, the more Arab, the less woman; the more woman, the less Arab. The context of the controversy, the consequence of what Maria Mies would call "patriarchy and accumulation on a world scale,"[12] determines the false dichotomy inscribed in the political identity, "Arab woman"; but to challenge the structural logic of this dualism appears to court the loss of woman's voice altogether. And of course this dilemma is not the monopoly of AWSA.

The triumph of AWSA in the last decade has been to suggest that the modern state must be made answerable to the conflictual representation of Arab women. In part, one might say that the state, or the Mubarak regime in this example, has exploited the contradictory categories of "Arab" and "woman"; but that, I believe, does it too much justice. The silencing of AWSA is due not just to the malevolent tenacity of a moribund bureaucracy, nor indeed to the tactical "error" of AWSA protesting war, but to the categorical compulsion of the term "Arab woman" itself. By tracing various histories of Arab feminism, it is obvious that patriarchy's silencing of Arab women has depended upon an othering or marginalizing of "Arab woman" as subject. Put another way, AWSA's history can be constructed alongside an itinerary of silence which is compelled not to speak the words, "Arab woman," for this threatens the very logic of patriarchy's own systemic violence. Theory aside, one is not saying that AWSA, merely by attempting to articulate "Arab woman," has brought the contemporary Arab state to crisis. I am suggesting, however, that the apparent incompatibility between these terms reveals the structural compulsions of the state. This places a heavy burden on the politics of voice, and I therefore conclude with a coda to this concept.

AWSA's constitution and activities are a tribute to an Arab feminism that is radically democratic, self-reflexive, and indefatigable. But I would do it a violence very similar to that of the Egyptian state if I proposed that its identity was somehow unitary or in "place." The way AWSA decenters is not by the marginality of its position as such, but by enunciating "Arab woman" it disrupts a whole chain of signification in the political order. Again, one does not have to rely on poststructuralist sophistication to see why this might be so. AWSA dares to suggest that there is a strategic interest in essentializing the subjectivity of Arab women, and that by universalizing their claims to political representation, Arab women in fact resist the ideology of exclusion resplendent in the figure of "universal man" (sic). AWSA constructs the voice of Arab women to "distinguish the necessity of silence."[13] It is precisely patriarchy's necessity to silence that is challenged by the incommensurable claims that emerge in the conjunction of "Arab" and "woman." In that sense we should not be too disheartened by the contingent realities of AWSA, for it is neither the first nor the last voice to disarticulate the mythologies of man. Whether promoting the constitutional rights of women, rethinking attitudes to women's health and planning alternative strategies, articulating a gender-specific body politics, encouraging women's cultural participation through publishing and conference ventures, resisting patriarchal versions of Islam, or attacking sexist employment practices, AWSA has shown that strategies of voice are also strategies of activism. While this might not free AWSA from the concrete dilemma of linking "Arab" and "woman," the history sketched above underlines that politics compels Arab women to fight this "impossibilty" for the possible worlds beyond. Nahid Toubia, a prominent AWSA spokeswoman, has noted, "We are making our voices heard. May the world stop to listen." Indeed, a certain world will have to not only stop but end in order for anyone to listen in peace.

NOTES

1. For a good overview of Leila Ahmed's positions on such arguments see Leila Ahmed, "Feminism and Feminist Movements in the Middle East." *Women and Islam*, Azizah al-Hibri, ed. (Oxford: Pergamon Press, 1982), pp. 153-168, and "Arab Culture and Writing Women's Bodies." *Feminist Issues* 9.1 (Spring 1989): 41-56. Ahmed's view has softened somewhat in

her recent book (see Note 6). See also Marnia Lazreg, "Feminism and Difference: The Perils of Writing as a Woman on Women in Algeria," *Feminist Studies* 14.1 (Spring 1988): 81–107. Neither Ahmed nor Lazreg disputes the significance of el Saadawi's contribution. They do, however, take issue with her tendency to generalize her own subject position, since this runs the risk of obscuring other specific elements and instances of the oppression of Arab women.

2.   Magida Salman, "The Arab Woman" in Khamsin Collective, ed., *Women in the Middle East* (London: Zed Books, 1987), p. 6.

3.   See Appendix 1 to Nahid Toubia, ed. *Women of the Arab World* (London: Zed Press, 1988), pp. 154–155; this book represents the most detailed report on the formation and work of AWSA available in English. It includes some of the papers presented at the AWSA conference in Cairo, 1986. A second AWSA collection, *Al-Fikr al-Arabi al-Muasir wa al-Mara (Contemporary Arab Thought and Women)* was published by their press in 1989. A third collection, tentatively titled "A New Battle in the Liberation of Women" and focusing on AWSA's current legal fight (of which more in due course) was in press as this article was being prepared.

4.   Inji Aflatun, "We Egyptian Women," trans. Michelle Raccagni, in Margot Badran and Miriam Cooke, eds. *Opening the Gates: A Century of Arab Feminist Writing* (Bloomington: Indiana University Press, 1990), pp. 345-351.

5.   Kathleen Merriam-Howard, "Women, Education, and the Professions in Egypt," *Comparative and International Education Society* 23.2 (June 1979): 256-270.

6.   See, Leila Ahmed, *Women and Gender in Islam* (New Haven: Yale University Press, 1992), pp. 209-210. Chapters ten and eleven are particularly enlightening, given the present argument. In addition to the points made here, Ahmed tracks the suppression of Islamic feminism after the Second World War, and the example of Zeinab al-Ghazali is crucial in this regard. Ahmed is clear, however, that al-Ghazali's Islamic feminism is not beyond reproach, even if the government's double standards regarding the same are equally suspicious. For another extensive commentary on the relationship of women and Islam in Egypt see, Sherifa Zuhur, *Revealing Reveiling* (Albany: SUNY Press, 1992).

7.   There has been much debate on this subject. See, for example, papers given by Nawal el Saadawi, Sherif Hetata, Mohamed Husein, and Safia Safwat collected in Institute for African Alternatives, *Islamic Fundamentalism* (London: IFAA Publications, 1990); and Azizah al-Hibri, ed., *Women and Islam* (Oxford: Pergamon Press, 1982). Many of the selections in *Opening the Gates* address this issue and clearly it is the focus of AWSA's publications to date.

8.   For more on the Personal Status Laws, see *Women of the Arab World*.

9.   Quoted in Kim Murphy, "Speaking Her Mind on Women's Rights" *Los Angeles Times*, August 27, 1991, p. 6. Murphy's article was generally supportive of Nawal el Saadawi and AWSA's plight, which earned her a rebuke from the Egyptian ambassador stationed in Ottawa. See Adel Elsafty, "Egyptian Feminist," *Ottawa Citizen*, September 23, 1991, p. A8.

10.   For more on AWSA's recent history and el Saadawi's political activism,

see my interview with el Saadawi, "Living the Struggle,"*Transition* 61 (1993/4): 170-179.
11. Nawal el Saadawi, "The Political Challenges Facing Arab Women at the End of the Twentieth Century" trans. Marilyn Booth in Toubia, *Women of the Arab World*, pp. 8-26.
12. See Maria Mies, *Patriarchy and Accumulation on a World Scale* (London: Zed, 1986). Mies shows how the dictates of capital accumulation overdetermine patriarchal political regimes and the international division of labor.
13. I borrow this phrase from Pierre Macherey in his discussion of the "said" and the "non- said" in literary analysis. While there is no one-to-one correspondence between the literary and the political "voice," Macherey's discussion of the necessity of silence is an important way of understanding the dilemma at issue. See Pierre Macherey, *A Theory of Literary Production*, trans. Geoffrey Wall (London: Routledge, 1978).

WORKS CITED

Aflatun, Inji. "We Egyptian Women." In *Opening the Gates: A Century of Arab Feminist Writing*, trans., Michelle Raccagni, ed., Margot Badran and Miriam Cooke. Bloomington: Indiana University Press, 1990: 345-351.
Ahmed, Leila. "Feminism and Feminist Movements in the Middle East." In *Women and Islam*, ed. Azizah al-Hibri. Oxford: Pergamon Press, 1982: 153-168.
____"Arab Culture and Writing Women's Bodies." *Feminist Issues* 9.1 (Spring 1989): 41-56.
____*Women and Gender in Islam*. New Haven: Yale University Press, 1992.
al-Hibri, Azizah, ed. *Women and Islam*. Oxford: Pergamon Press, 1982.
el Saadawi, Nawal. "The Political Challenges Facing Arab Women at the End of the Twentieth Century." *Women in the Arab World*, trans. Marilyn Booth; ed., Nahid Toubia. London: Zed Press, 1988: 8-26.
Elsafty, Adel. "Egyptian Feminist." *Ottawa Citizen*, September 23, 1991, p. A8.
Hitchcock, Peter. "Living the Struggle." *Transition* 61 (1993/4): 170-179.
Institute for African Alternatives. *Islamic Fundamentalism*. London: IFAA Publications, 1990.
Lazreg, Marnia. "Feminism and Difference: The Perils of Writing as a Woman on Women in Algeria." *Feminist Studies* 14.1 (Spring 1988): 81-107.
Macherey, Pierre. *A Theory of Literary Production*, trans., Geoffrey Wall. London: Routledge, 1978.
Merriam-Howard, Kathleen. "Women, Education, and the Professions in Egypt." *Comparative and International Education Society* 23.2 (June 1979): 256-270.
Mies, Maria. *Patriarchy and Accumulation on a World Scale*. London: Zed, 1986.
Murphy, Kim. "Speaking Her Mind on Women's Rights." *Los Angeles Times* August 27, 1991, World Report: 6.
Salman, Magida. "The Arab Woman." In *Women in the Middle East*, ed., Khamsin Collective. London: Zed Books, 1987.

Toubia, Nahid, ed. *Women of the Arab World*. London: Zed Press, 1988.
Zuhur, Sherifa. *Revealing Reveiling*. Albany: SUNY Press, 1992.

MATERNAL POLITICS IN ORGANIZING BLACK SOUTH AFRICAN WOMEN: THE HISTORICAL LESSONS

JULIA WELLS

"MATERNAL POLITICS" IS A TERM INCREASINGLY USED TO describe a widespread feature of women's political activity. It refers to political movements which are rooted in women's defense of their roles as mothers and protectors of their children. These can be movements which predate the radical feminist critique of motherhood as an oppressive institution or more contemporary movements which take place among women who give motherhood and family responsibilities a high priority. In either case, the fact that such movements develop implies that among many women, in a variety of places and times throughout history, their maternal roles have been the driving force behind public political actions. As Sara Ruddick has put it, "a woman's politics of resistance affirms obligations traditionally assigned to women and calls on the community to respect them" (1989:40).

In the mid-1980s, a group of feminist scholars came together in

New York to compare their research on a variety of women's movements which showed symptoms of a vague commonality related to
motherhood. The cases of the South African women's anti-pass campaigns of the 1950s and the mothers of the Plaza de Mayo in
Argentina (weekly women's demonstrations protesting the disap-
pearances of their children, starting in 1979) stand out as particularly vivid and well-documented examples of maternally-rooted
political movements. Other case studies from India, England, Chile,
El Salvador, and the USA also have contributed to the development
of an understanding of the nature of such movements.[1] Tentatively,
the label "motherist" was applied to signify the most obvious common thread. Yet it was used with some hesitation, partly because of
the vagueness of its meaning and partly because of its anti-feminist
implications. However, a clear pattern of maternal politics slowly
emerged, not as a quantifiable phenomenon which could be measured by the frequency with which protesting women used mother-
centered terminology to articulate their grievances, but as an
analytical concept, distilled from a comprehensive examination of
each case study. As a theoretical approach to understanding
women's political movements, the study of "motherism" or maternal politics is in its infancy (so to speak). Nevertheless, the following broad features describe what such movements tend to have in
common:

(1) They arise in situations in which women perceive their
roles as mothers—ensuring the survival of their children—to be threatened by a socially illegitimate force,
often government actions.

(2) They bring women into the public sphere in a way which
is highly unusual for the particular place and time; conventional roles as homemakers are temporarily abandoned as women take part in demonstrations or other
forms of collective action.

(3) They enjoy exceptionally widespread, often spontaneous popular support, characterized by high levels of
emotion, enthusiasm, and energy.

(4) They often result in the formation of a new organization to deal with the immediate issue, although existing
political groups frequently try to capitalize on and corral the enthusiasm.

(5) They challenge government policies on the moral
grounds that their capacity to function as good moth-

ers has been jeopardized.

(6) They attract members from across traditional social divisions and class boundaries, due to the emotive appeal of their cause, but are not initiated by the poorest of the poor.

(7) They are often relatively short-lived and episodic in character, following a "bubble" pattern of growth and development; for a limited time they are allowed to grow rapidly and are tolerated by authority figures, but this comes to an abrupt end, virtually destroying the movement.

Few such movements contain all of these characteristics, some of which may be only partially applicable. The list provides a general guideline.

Maternal politics are clearly not to be confused with feminism. Women swept up in mother-centered movements are not fighting for their own personal rights as women but for their custodial rights as mothers. Since concepts of the sanctity of motherhood are so deeply entrenched in the social fabric of most societies, this strategy often proves effective where other attempts to generate social change fail. So potent has been the traditional discourse on motherhood that husbands, families, and government officials all tend to acknowledge and respect the heartrending claims of mothers, giving women an unusual amount of political space in which to organize. Significant allies are easily won over, strengthening the political clout of such movements. Nevertheless, these movements must be recognized as limited in scope, duration, and success in achieving their goals and, above all, should not be mistaken for political maturity.

MATERNAL MOVEMENTS IN SOUTH AFRICAN HISTORY

Having described the basic characteristics of motherist movements, we shall now turn to two case studies to see how the historical record relates to this paradigm. The cases are taken from my own research on women's resistance to pass laws.

THE ORANGE FREE STATE—1913

Black women first resisted pass laws in Bloemfontein, then a city of nearly 27,000 people, in May 1913. The resistance was triggered by sharply stepped-up enforcement of old pass laws that had been on the books since 1892.[2] A steady stream of protest documents from the local black community dating back to the 1890s cited a number of complaints: passes leave women vulnerable to unscrupulous constables who physically harassed them; paying for monthly passes was costly, eroding the viability of household budgets; black women had to leave their own families behind to work as domestic servants for whites in order to get a pass; young daughters forced into employment could not be properly supervised, and they returned with unwanted pregnancies.[3] The complaints added up to a constellation of problems all related to state interference in a woman's capacity to run her home and raise her children. However, the history of ineffectual petition protests made it clear to the Bloemfontein women that the new crisis needed new tactics.

Led by the wives and daughters of black clergy and professionals, over 600 Bloemfontein women from all economic strata first organized a mass march into the all-white city center; then they collected all the unwanted passes and flung them at the feet of officers at the location police station. They taunted the police and invited arrest for being without passes. Finally, the police acquiesced and arrested 80 women. The magistrate hearing their case, however, refused to prosecute the town's most reputable black elite housewives, tried to talk them out of continuing the passive resistance and even "forgave" them for breaking the law. Municipal officials tried negotiating with well-known black male political leaders, but the women refused to acknowledge these talks and stepped up their resistance. When policemen became rough in handling crowds of female protesters, women beat and *sjamboked* (whipped) the officers—but were still generally forgiven! Although no details of the magistrate's logic are available, his actions suggest that he personally viewed the women's complaints against passes as legitimate and must have felt this view would be shared by his superiors.

This generosity, however, was short-lived and a harder line was soon taken. Eventually, over a period of 5 to 6 months, hundreds of women were arrested for being passless and imprisoned in towns far away from their communities, unable to receive regular visitors, not allowed to wear shoes in a very cold winter, forced to eat prison rations worse than those of male prisoners, and had to perform hard labor. Upon their release, virtually all required medical attention.

During the resistance, the women formed the Orange Free State Native and Colored Women's Association to help consolidate public support for their campaign. The Association worked with the black-readership newspapers, *Tsala ea Batho,* edited by Solomon

Plaatje in Kimberley, and *The APO* (African Political Organization), edited by Abdul Abdurahman in Cape Town, to solicit funds for medical treatment. It also lobbied Free State whites to exert pressure in Parliament for legislative relief. At one point, white women in Winburg advocated a public march in support of the black pass resisters. Both the white liberal press and the mission press in South Africa championed the women's cause.

In this case, the resistance produced at least partial success. Within four months of its start, government officials from Cape Town visited the Orange Free State and persuaded municipal officials to ease up on enforcement of women's pass laws. The women, however, suspended the campaign in mid-1914 when the all-male-led South African Natives National Congress (later renamed African National Congress) called for a moratorium on political actions during the First World War. Whether or not women felt unwillingly coerced into adopting this policy is not known.

The 1913 Free State case thus reflects the pattern of maternal politics fairly closely. The intensity of commitment, unusual levels of political activity, strong alliance building and government policy challenges are all consistent with the motherist pattern. The women had clear expectations of their roles as mothers, protecting, feeding, housing children and managing family budgets. Interfering and coercive government policies were simply not tolerated.

JOHANNESBURG—1950s

Only after the Nationalist Party came to power in 1948 with its policy of apartheid were passes for African women seriously reintroduced. From the outset, at the first hint of policy changes in 1952, black women overtly linked the pass question to the responsibilities of motherhood. The invitation to the launching of the Federation of South African Women (FSAW) in 1954 was addressed to "the mothers of the nations" (Walker 1982:142). Over the next four years, women in Johannesburg built a campaign around the concerns of mothers. The campaign started with preparations for the drafting of the Freedom Charter at the Congress of Democrats in 1954-55. Women's participation in this African National Congress (ANC) initiative was also urged in strong maternal terms: "We call the housewives and mothers. Let us speak of the fine children that we bear, and of their stunted lives. Let us speak of the many illnesses and deaths, and of the few clinics and schools. Let us speak of the high prices and of the shanty towns."[4]

Following the Congress of Democrats, the next women's function was a "Transvaal Congress of Mothers." Here, a decision to march to the Union Buildings in Pretoria was taken. This marked the start of a long series of women's public marches and demonstrations. Undoubtedly support for this first Pretoria march skyrocketed when, one week before it took place, the government announced its intention to actually start issuing passes for women at the beginning of 1956. The turnout of 2,000 women on October 27, 1955, far exceeded the expectations of the FSAW and ANC Women's League organizers.[5] By the beginning of 1956, a special joint committee of the ANCWL and FSAW had been established to coordinate a national women's anti-pass campaign. Again, their definition of the task at hand was highly mother-centered:

> We women have the greatest force in the world in our hands; it is the courage and determination of mothers to fight for the rights of the children she had born in pain and suffering. There is no power on earth that can prevent the mothers of South Africa, and of the world, from achieving justice for their children, if women organize and go forward, together with their men, on the march to freedom.[6]

The campaign planned and executed for 1956 and 1957 included urging women to refuse to accept passes, numerous local marches to Magistrates and Native Commissioners, special local conferences to promote the campaign and a grand march again to the Union Buildings in Pretoria, this time with support from throughout the nation. The great march took place on 9 August 1956, attended by 20,000, and is still annually commemorated as "Women's Day." Getting women to refuse to take out passes was difficult, but the local demonstrations, dozens of which occurred throughout the country, were well-supported and often quite boisterous and rowdy. In the Transvaal, women convened local anti-pass conferences in Benoni, Pretoria, and Krugersdorp in March 1957. Of all these tactics, the public demonstrations were the most successful. This period represents the peak of participation in public demonstrations in the 1950s.

The onset of pass-issuing in Johannesburg in October 1958, however, provoked a particularly strong maternal response. What started as a march and demonstration to the pass offices, soon turned into a passive resistance exercise, as police arrested large numbers of protesters. Following the initial arrests, women poured into the streets, spontaneously seeking to be arrested also, with the result that within two weeks 2,000 black women sat in jail. The crisis apparently triggered a power struggle among the ANC's male leadership. First, rumors spread that it was against ANC policy for women to seek arrest, which created confusion. Ultimately, the newly-elected Transvaal Provincial Executive of the ANC asserted its sovereignty in the matter, overruling the multi-racial Transvaal Consultative Committee, a structure of the Congress Alliance. This resulted in the decision to pay bail and release the women from jail. FSAW organizer, Hilda Bernstein, recalls that it was at this point that women felt a sudden deflation of enthusiasm in the fight against passes.[6] The assertion of male authority was accepted as politically correct, and the unique energies of this motherist movement quickly dissipated. A few weeks later, an FSAW/ANCWL placard protest failed to draw the anticipated amount of support. Thus, the male leadership from within the ANC and the exercise of state force worked together to defuse women's resistance to passes.

ANALYZING THE CONTEXTS—THEN AND NOW

What has been provided above is largely descriptive of the two historical episodes used to illustrate how maternal politics functioned in South African history. This section will briefly explore how these events fit into the larger historical context and begin to draw out the implications for understanding the present.

Scholars generally agree that up until the early 1960s a prominent feature of the South African economy was persistent shortages of unskilled labor. Hence, a materialist analysis suggests that most of the legislation imposed by the ruling white minority over the black majority was in one way or another designed to control labor supplies, often taking the form of extra-economic coercion. Our two episodes of women's resistance to pass laws must be understood within this context. In the Orange Free State case, white urban dwellers made it very clear that they sought control over the labor power of local black women. "Servants can't be got at any price," they complained.[7] Women were being directly coerced into leaving their own homes to work in those of whites.

The relatively elite women in Bloemfontein who led the resistance could have expected their children to grow up to become teachers, clerks, artisans, small-business owners or court interpreters—as their husbands were. They came from a particularly valued and upwardly-mobile sector of society. In addition to being personally inconvenienced by pass laws, the women resented being deprived of their ability to remain in their homes to provide the necessary nurture and guidance to their children. Without this care, they believed, the bright future might indeed become dim. These elites, in turn, led their less economically advantaged sisters in a very determined campaign.

Straightforward economic pressures for a woman to work outside of her own home were accepted as legitimate, but the extra-economic intrusion of pass laws was not. Confirmation of the "illegitimacy" of pass laws came from the other three provinces outside of the Orange Free State, where no women were required to carry passes. Thus, we see how the labor needs clashed with ideological factors: the women's sense of their own worth and their children's worth, combined with the conviction of the illegitimate nature of passes for women. Together, these forces created a militant reaction.

By the 1950s, the South African social structure had shifted so that labor shortages existed only in certain sectors. White farmers continued to complain of chronic shortages, but the growing industrial sector had little trouble filling its labor requirements, since it paid higher wages. Many urban areas reported shortages of domestic workers, as people moved on into more remunerative employment alternatives. Mine labor needs were largely met by recruitment from outside South Africa's borders. The concept of "influx control" (controlling the number of Africans allowed to live in an urban area by a strict quota system) had been around since the late 1930s, but was enforced quite differently from one urban area to another, according to local supply and demand.

In Johannesburg, we can surmise how these factors influenced women and their levels of participation in the anti-pass campaigns. Despite the strident tone of apartheid rhetoric, policies were designed not to expel all Africans from urban areas, but rather to re-allocate workers from the attractive, better-paying sectors, where there was a surplus, into the unattractive and low-paying sectors, where shortages existed. In a large urban area like Johannesburg, women who were self-employed or independent earners (brewers, seamstresses, laundresses, hawkers, landladies) fell into the category of "surplus labor" by state definitions. They were targeted for removal into rural areas, presumably to help make up the agricultural workforce. Alternatively, forcing them to carry passes might push them into full-time domestic service, a labor-shortage sector in Johannesburg. For such women, the advent of passes clearly spelt doom for their way of life and viability. Consequently, they actively resisted passes.

Full-time housewives from Soweto and professional women formed another category of active participants. Both categories of women were threatened with neither eviction from the city nor a change in their daily jobs. Their motivation was probably similar to that of the elite housewives of Bloemfontein, half a century earlier. The housewives qualified to remain in the urban area on the basis of their husbands' status. Many a Soweto housewife of the late 1950s found herself in her own home for the first time.[8] Life may not have been comfortable, but at least it had recently improved in some ways. For such women, the threat of arbitrary arrest any time of night or day, which came along with passes, haunted them as a nightmare beyond belief. Deprived of the support network of the overcrowded slums from which they had very recently moved, their families would be left utterly in the lurch if the mothers suddenly disappeared. Among them, maternal rhetoric was particularly strong. Both the housewives and professionals again came from that sector which perceived itself as particularly upwardly-mobile in the larger social order, and were, therefore, less willing to accept women's passes as legitimate.

Conversely, sectors of women not known to give hearty support to the 1958 passive resistance effort included factory workers and domestic workers. For them, maintaining their jobs was paramount. The disapproval of white employers was too risky, whether for time off from work for demonstrations and jail, or refusing to obtain a pass. In some parts of South Africa, where possession of passes was the key to obtaining new houses, women cooperated fully, even enthusiastically, with acquiring the document.[10] This is not to say that passes were ever unambiguous for certain women, but that they meant different things in different times and places, depending on a host of factors. These factors clearly include a woman's place in the economy, with the self-employed and lower-middle-class acting as the most enthusiastic supporters of the anti-pass campaign. Another factor was their sense of upward mobility, more for their children than for themselves. Here government interference clashed directly with their expectations.

IMPLICATIONS FOR POLITICAL ORGANIZING

The foregoing discussion has examined some of the most dramatic events in black South African women's resistance history in an attempt to understand the factors which motivate determined political action. It is not intended as an exhaustive survey of all women's

movements, but rather probes two cases in depth to go beyond a
superficial level of understanding. When compared with the more
universal analysis of motherism, a close correlation becomes evident. But what are the lessons and implications?

For the long years of struggle against the apartheid system, the
question of what makes women militant has been particularly
urgent. Many an activist has asked whether or not those earlier levels of women's militancy could not be retrieved and harnessed
afresh in the long, drawn-out struggle. Further, now that white
minority rule has ended, can that intense energy of women be channeled into the much-needed reconstruction and development program or into other uniquely women's concerns? Time and time
again, the stories of old have been told and retold with an aim to
inspire and motivate.

There can be little doubt that the women's tradition of resistance helped secure them a firm place within the liberation struggle. The maintenance of the ANC Women's League through all the
long years of exile, a series of special conferences on women and
women's rights, the inclusion of mandatory female delegates at the
constitutional negotiations, the campaign for a women's charter to
be included as part of the new constitution and the ANC's commitment to a 30% quota of women in its electoral lists all confirm
that women have earned a place in the male-dominated political
order.

But despite these significant gains for women, the implication
of the motherist analysis is that the explosive, spontaneous nature
of the old movements is not a quality that can be invented or orches-
trated at will. Such enthusiasm arises only from the pressures of
complex and interlocking factors. Although these factors may vary
from case to case, the common thread underlying such emotive
movements is a defense of women's capacity to function effectively as mothers and homemakers. Historically, this has come at times
when government policies threatened to destroy the status quo. The
South African motherist movements were not general protests
against inequitable distribution of wealth or racial or gender discrimination. They were reactions against the extremities of the
apartheid policies when they invaded too deeply into their private
worlds. The dehumanizing, at times genocidal, elements of
apartheid touched black women in a unique way. Non-economic
coercion into unwanted, poorly-paid jobs and an artificial ceiling
on upward social mobility stifled women enormously, particularly
their capacity to raise children. Conversely, policies implemented

by a popularly-elected government in South Africa's future should not trigger such reactions. One could expect motherist movements to remain a relic of the apartheid past.

Although motherism cannot be turned on and off at will by political organizations, important lessons remain from this study. In a world where the importance of women's roles as mothers has been under attack from many feminists, the exploration of motherist movements sends a strong signal that in many communities over time, large numbers of women have valued their mothering roles sufficiently to take extraordinary actions in its defense. Such an appreciation should therefore inform all policy formulations. While the intensity of a maternal protest movement cannot be generated by design, a recognition of the driving force behind the movements of the past could ensure women's support and participation in the constructive programs of the future.

NOTES

1. A number of scholars consulted together in an ongoing seminar at the Barnard Center for Research on Women in late 1986 and early 1987 in preparation for a panel on mother-centered movements at the Seventh Berkshire Conference on the History of Women, Wellesley College, Wellesley, Massachusetts, June 19-21, 1987. A selection of related publications includes Argosin et al. (1987a), Frank (1985), and Ruddick (1989).

2. In May 1913, the number of women arrested for pass offenses in Bloemfontein increased 400% over the previous month (Orange Free State Archives, Bloemfontein Criminal Record Book, 1913).

3. As details of this campaign have been published elsewhere, only a brief summary is provided here. For further information, see Julia Wells in Works Cited.

4. Federation of South African Women Papers (FSAW), University of the Witwatersrand, Gubbins Library, Johannesburg. Circular letter, August 25, 1954.

5. Personal interview, Lilian Ngoyi, Johannesburg, September 1977.

6. FSAW, Letter to First National Conference of ANC's Women's League, December 14, 1955.

7. Personal interview, Hilda Bernstein, Harare, March 1990.

8. Bloemfontein Town Council Minute Book, December 1, 1910 (Orange Free State Archives, Bloemfontein).

9. Personal interview, June Mlangeni, Soweto, October 1990.

10. This was the case in Grahamstown, according to research done by Michaela Webster for an Honors Dissertation, Rhodes University, 1994.

WORKS CITED

Argosin, Marjorie, Temma Kaplan, and Teresa Valdez. "The Politics of Spectacle in Chile." *The Barnard Occasional Papers on Women's Issues* 2.3 (Fall, 1987a).

Argosin, Marjorie. "Emerging from the Shadows: Women of Chile." *The Barnard Occasional Papers on Women's Issues* 2.3 (Fall, 1987b).

——. *Scraps of Life Chilean Arpilleras, Chilean Women and the Pinochet Dictatorship*. London: Zed Books, 1987c.

Frank, Dana. "Housewives, Socialists and the Politics of Food: The 1917 New York Cost of Living Protests." *Feminist Studies* 11. 2 (Summer, 1985): 255-285.

Ruddick, Sara. "Maternal Peace Politics and Women's Resistance: The Example of Argentina and Chile." *The Barnard Occasional Papers on Women's Issues* 4.1 (Winter, 1989).

——. *Maternal Thinking: Towards a Politics of Peace*. London: Women's Press, 1989.

Walker, Cherryl. *Women and Resistance in South Africa*. London: Onyx Press, 1992.

Wells, Julia. "The War of Degradation: Black Women's Struggles against Free State Pass Laws, 1913." *Banditry, Rebellion and Social Protest in Africa*, ed., Donald Crummey. London: Heinemann Educational Books, 1985.

——."Why Women Rebel: A Comparative Study of Women's Resistance in Bloemfontein in 1913 and Johannesburg 1958." *Journal of Southern African Studies* (Special Issue on Women) 10.1 (October, 1983): 53-70.

——. *We Have Done with Pleading the Women's 1913 Anti-Pass Campaign*. Johannesburg: Ravan Press, 1991.

——. *We Now Demand!* Johannesburg: University of Witwatersrand Press, 1993.

BUILDING A POWER
ORGANIZATION:
A NETWORK TEAM APPROACH
TO GRASSROOTS ORGANIZING

DÉ BRYANT

INTRODUCTION

THE PROCESS OF SOCIAL CHANGE HAS LONG BEEN A TOPIC of discussion for the intelligentsia—whether or not they profess to have a position about political matters—as well as for citizens beyond the walls of the academy. Unfortunately, these accounts are predominantly anthropological, anecdotal, or biographical. Few empirical analyses of grass-roots collective action have been conducted.

The projects reported here were conducted in two different black neighborhoods in a small US community. They were designed to document the evolution of community cohesiveness as citizens progressed from being isolated individuals to forming a collective. The objective was to create a university-community partnership by conducting a participatory research effort that enabled members of the community to take control of their lives. The second project is an expansion of an earlier work in the same community, building on findings regarding the underlying elements of a sustainable social action.[1]

The role of what Mollenkopf refers to as an entrepreneurial agent, an external agent of change facilitating the action, is central to these studies.[2] The entrepreneur was an Intervention Team composed of members from both the university and the community. The team functioned as the hub of the resource and communication network which brought residents together and later supported the fledgling organization.

The research did not seek to examine intrapsychic characteristics of individuals nor social dynamics in groups. Such micro considerations, while important, have already been studied extensively.[3] Rather, this intervention uses a functionalist approach and systematically examines the mechanics involved in the change process.

SOCIAL CONTEXT FOR THE MODEL

Perhaps most importantly, the project is a seminal model for long-term community development as opposed to knee-jerk programming. The Social Action Project (SOCACT) took a preventative approach. It proposed that a competent and cohesive community can play a significant role in forestalling discord. To accomplish this, citizens are involved in planning that will impact upon their neighborhoods, thus reducing the frustration of feeling that control of their lives is in someone else's hands.

As economic conditions deteriorate in declining urban areas in the US, existing latent tensions may erupt. These confrontations can escalate, consuming vast quantities of human lives and resources as they spiral out of control.[4] Yet public planners and city officials too often use a management-by-crisis approach to the potential for conflict. The results are hastily constructed programs generated under extremely volatile circumstances.[5]

The two projects described here were conducted in Benton Harbor, a community in southwest Michigan. The total population is 44,000, with 98% of city residents being black; the community suffers from an economic downturn and its accompanying urban decline. The two neighborhoods where the projects were conducted have no formal names; yet they are well known to those who live there and call those blocks home. For descriptive purposes they will be called NORTHSIDE, so called because it is on the north side of town, and EASTSIDE, named for being on the east side of town. There are approximately 10 miles between them, and they are apparently quite distant socially as well. Members of the two resource networks that developed did not overlap.

To ensure that the researchers did not impose their perceptions of need onto the neighborhoods, the projects were designed in collaboration with the residents. Their input was used to identify and prioritize the conditions they would most like to change in their respective neighborhoods. This approach of asking people what they need, rather than presuming to know better than they do, is the essence of participatory research.[6]

The first project, NORTHSIDE, consciously focused on race relations, forcing contentious issues to the surface and addressing them in a straightforward manner. The objective was to determine whether people could build a history of working together that might slow the rate of escalation when problems arise in the community. The second study, EASTSIDE, emphasized resource mobilization, using redistribution of information or materials to empower residents. Examining how competent neighborhoods come about was the goal of this study.

THE NETWORK TEAM APPROACH

The network team approach is an adaptation of the pyramid model proposed by some to maximize the impact of a limited number of professionals.[7] The pyramid puts the person with the expertise—clinician, organizer, educator, etc.—at the apex. Information flows down, being used by a steadily increasing number of individuals, until it reaches the base of the pyramid. In contrast, the network model changes the direction of the flow.[8] The professional still plays a central role, but he/she is the nexus of a concentric network. She trains a team of paraprofessionals, who then go out and train others, who will go out in their turn and train the people that they know. Information also comes back to the professional following the same paths originally used for dissemination.

This exchange between professionals and members of the community meets two objectives. First, constant feedback between action carried out in the community and conceptualization of that action can occur. This is, by definition, action research.[9] Second, the reciprocal flow of information places control in the hands of each individual in the network. This self-action works in opposition to dysfunctional reactions such as inertia, learned helplessness, and cognitive rigidity. Through successive approximations, empowerment overcomes failure to attain personal goals and increases participation in issues affecting the community.

INTERVENTION TEAM

A maxim in community psychology is that individuals must work collectively to deal with limiting situations such as poverty, drugs, racism, or a myriad of other social ills. Scholars and activists alike have presented compelling evidence of the importance of a third party in these efforts.[10] This external agent of change is an individual or group that facilitates the goals of an intervention through redefining the problem, identifying new resources, and creating new linkages between individuals or groups.

Members of the intervention team acting as the entrepreneur were active catalysts initiating the intervention after which they moved to more peripheral roles as participants became more knowledgeable. Members of the team were from both the university and the community. They worked directly in the community throughout the research period. Where a neighborhood group became established, the team members attended regular meetings acting as resource people.

On the basis of these functions, team members were clearly predisposed to being activists within their neighborhoods. At first glance this might cause one to wonder whether the findings could be applied to other communities. In the strictest sense, this may be true; each community is unique. At this point it is important to reiterate that the focus of this study is the change process itself. In this context, a cadre of self-described activists is an element common to most communities.

RESOURCE NETWORK

The power of networking has been demonstrated repeatedly in a broad range of writings about social change. For example, Piven & Cloward discuss the rise and fall of poor people's movements seeking social, economic, and political equity.[11] Alliances among key actors in the sociopolitical milieu brought legitimacy, financial support, and political clout. Conversely, the breakdown of these linkages contributed to the steady reduction in effectiveness of concerted pressure for change. Comparable work has been conducted that describes how networks extend the scope of issues at the local level into regional, national, and international arenas.[12]

A resource network has been conceptualized here as a voluntary collaboration among autonomous individuals or groups. The network enables each participant to mobilize needed persons, materials, or services in order to bring about mutually beneficial outcomes. The process by which these exchange relationships develop has been studied in terms of the differences between "strong" and "weak" network links.[13] Weak, loosely knit network links more quickly disseminate information beyond the boundaries of some groups or cliques than do strong, closely knit links. In practical terms, this means that people on the edge of the group—occasional members, marginal people, radicals —may be more effective agents of change than those heavily invested in the group.

This finding is echoed by other theorists and practitioners interested in how information is spread. Rogers and Kincaid, who study the creation and maintenance of networks, find that the exchange relationship is a dynamic process that develops over time.[14] Their analyses shift from the individual to the communication relationship between individuals and back again. The power of this kind of analysis is demonstrated by their study of the diffusion of innovations in Brazil, Nigeria, and India.[15] One study related the communication of innovations to the process of social change; another examined the acceptance of family planning in Korea. Careful attention to who talked to whom and about what yielded even richer data on the spread of new ideas.[16]

Third parties—external agents of change—are powerful influences on the exchange relationship. They may do something as elementary as introducing actors formerly unknown to one another. At another level, they may deliberately redefine the basis for an interaction, reframe the question. The projects described here very consciously press the integral roles of the external agent to its fullest potential.

METHODOLOGY

The research question, "How can the average citizen bring about social change?" is vital in this context of creating effective exchange relationships between the university and the community. A competent community organization, articulate and knowledgeable, can be an effective conduit linking "town and gown." This research seeks to verify how such a collectivity evolves. The progression of any social intervention is in many ways unpredictable. However, as stated previously, some fundamental milestones have been suggested by the literature: (1) existence of an entrepreneurial agent who facilitates the action; (2) creation of linkages along which information and resources flow; and 3) coalescence of identifiable, goal-oriented groups. Milestones as the change process unfolded were monitored using three criteria. First, the manner in which people came together over time to create a functional organization was documented. Functional is defined as being goal-oriented and having a sense of group identity. Second, the extent to which direct contact with the Intervention Team decreased as indigenous leaders became active. Third, networking and resource mobilization were monitored. Characteristics of the network (e.g., key actors, roles, memberships) as well as the type of resources (person, material, services) were documented.

THE INTERVENTION TEAM

Members of the intervention team were recruited on the basis of being acknowledged leaders in their reference group, their awareness of the social and political dynamics within a community, and their experience in working in communities. Personal information was gathered via project-developed questionnaire regarding experience in community organization, conflict resolution, and race relations.

The team was trained on state-of-the-art techniques in community development and social change: grassroots organizing, consultation, advocacy, program development and evaluation. Training also involved guidelines for analyzing and handling problems associated with race relations. Initial sessions were followed by weekly meetings between team members and the principal investigator. "Booster" in-services on specific issues were periodically held to address specific issues as they arose in the course of the intervention.

Team members were instructed on the use of project-developed process logbooks. As the team worked in the field, the log entries generated information about their activities and observations; planning for follow-up activities; and conclusions, speculations, or concerns about the intervention. The logs included a networking report that asked for details about who was contacted, their affiliation, the outcome of the contact, and the respondent's perception of the utility of the contact. People named in these reports were assigned numbers and respondent-contact matrices were constructed using two computer-assisted network analyses.

NETWORK ANALYSIS

Two computer-assisted network analysis programs, NEGOPY and FATCAT, were used to identify the structure and content of the networks that evolved.[17] NEGOPY assigns individuals in the network to a discrete set of categories and detects groups. The category system is discrete because an individual can belong to only one category; thus there are no overlapping groups. The detection of groups is dependent solely on patterns of links between individuals. People in the networks (nodes) name one another as contacts. Hence, NEGOPY answers the question "Who is talking to whom?" in the network.

To enhance identification of groups, the links were weighted. Conventionally, social network research uses frequency of contact to indicate the degree of importance. These studies use as weights the contact's reported utility, the status and content of the communication, and the outcome of the contact. Such indicators were conceptually consistent with the question of impact on a change activity. Strength equations were constructed for NEGOPY to calculate the contact's reported impact on the intervention. NEGOPY was instructed to drop from the calculation links with values lower than 6.0 because such an individual was reported to have been of no use. (See Table 1 for a detailed description of each category and its assigned value.)

FATCAT does contextual analysis ("What are these people talking about?").[18] The goal is to uncover the relationship between two kinds of data: that which describes the individuals in the network and that which describes the connections between individuals. In this way the analysis gives an indication of the types of resources (person, service, material) flowing between members in the network. As with NEGOPY, individuals (nodes) in the communication network were generated using the networking reports from the process logbooks. People named in these reports were assigned numbers and respondent-contact matrices were constructed. FATCAT constructed categorical matrices using variables which described these individuals and their connections (Table 2 lists the categories used).[19]

RESULTS

NETWORK ANALYSIS

In the earlier work, referred to as NORTHSIDE, a network of 42 people was generated using individuals named in the logs.[20] From this information, NEGOPY constructed a network. The largest number of individuals named in the groups had links with strengths of 6.0 and 10.0, with a mean link strength of 8.5. This indicates that most individuals made contacts whose contributions were perceived to be useful. Furthermore, links with greater utility (with strengths of 10.0) led to cooperative outcomes that resulted in either endorsement of the group aims or some kind of partnership. NEGOPYalso measured the connectedness of the overall structure. This measure has a range from 0.0 (a network with no more differentiation than would occur by chance) to 1.0 (a network with relatively small groups of people who selected one another). The network described in this neighborhood measures .60, indicating the presence of several identifiable groups.

Out of the 42 individuals in the network, NEGOPY identified eighteen isolates: people with either no contacts with others or who have links with only one other person in the network. This raises the question of who is really talking to whom in this network if 43% of its participants are isolates? The question is explored further in the EASTSIDE study described later in this section.

The FATCAT contextual analysis of NORTHSIDE affirmed some basic tenets of the field of community psychology. The intervention team acted as the interested third party that helped redefine situations for citizens in the neighborhoods. Homemakers and self-proclaimed activists were equally effective as professional agents of change. People built their network by working outward in radial fashion; that is, beginning with their personal friends and moving to self-help groups, religious or civic clubs, and business connections. Racial cooperation between group members in the network was the result of conscious effort. The influence of such decisions was evident in the high utility ratings assigned to respondents of varying ethnicities.

The EASTSIDE study generated a network of 86 people. Comparable to the NORTHSIDE study, the pattern of making useful contacts appears to be consistent with the earlier work. Where these findings differ from those in NORTHSIDE is that no group was detected. That is, the computer analysis which searched for groups (people who consistently named one another as contacts) found none. Instead the analysis identified dyads (two people who talked to each other) or triads (two people connected through a mutually known third person). In the EASTSIDE study people reported that when they contacted people, they got what they wanted. In this way, the contacts were very useful to attaining goals. However, no partnerships, and therefore no groups, were formed in this neighborhood.[21] The FATCAT contextual analysis in EASTSIDE indicated that age and community role are important factors in how useful a contact had been in getting the person what they wanted. Since the neighborhood is 98% black and 95% single-female head of household, it is given that the network will be black and female. The analysis found that the most effective network members (having the highest utility/outcome ratings) were older black women who were homemakers.[22]

INTERVENTION TEAM

The team fostered the creation of the neighborhood organization represented by Group #1 in NORTHSIDE. According to the log-books, team members facilitated links between members in this group and people in the larger community. As the organization's goals became more clearly defined, team members moved out of its center and acted as boundary people. They functioned within the group yet remained on its fringes, thus becoming its strongest source of new information. Team members brought previously unidentified or unavailable resources to the group.

In EASTSIDE no neighborhood organization formed. Rather, a loosely connected group of individuals became evident in the data. These nodes were type 2 isolates (having only one link) and dyads who functioned outside the boundaries of any group. The litera-ture suggests these conditions indicate an alienated neighborhood hostile to personal growth. Yet according to team logbooks the women were actively involved: going back to school, addressing crime in the neighborhood, providing emotional support and mutual aid.

The team facilitated by linking the network members with peo-ple in the larger society, such as advocacy groups like Welfare Warriors.[23] The team also brought in new information or resources by creating the resource guide for welfare recipients who want to continue their education. The guide is a how-to manual covering everything from financial aid to child care.[24] This information was disseminated through the boundary linkages, comparable to the previous work in NORTHSIDE. The intervention team, acting as the external agent of change, did facilitate the creation of resource and communication networks in both neighborhoods. Their role as boundary people lent significant support to Granovetter's notion of the "strength of weak ties."

In NORTHSIDE members of the team were named as group members, but were the other halves of type 2 isolates; that is, they were the only other person in the network named by a person out-side the group. They had the greatest contact with and access to diverse contacts outside the group by virtue of being of the group, but not enmeshed in it. In EASTSIDE team members were conduits through which information and resources flowed between the women constructing their lives and the agencies or institutions in control of those resources.

DISCUSSION

NETWORK ANALYSIS

The FATCAT and NEGOPY analyses provided valuable information about the nature of the networks that evolved. Several of the individuals (nodes) that were examined in NORTHSIDE connected dissimilar groups, bringing to each information or resources that might not otherwise have been available. Members of the intervention team and resource people were the linkages outside the boundaries of both NORTHSIDE and EASTSIDE. Presumably they were the conduits through which the exchanges occurred between groups in the network.

The conclusion that team members acted as boundary people between the neighborhood and the larger society becomes even more compelling when groups are compared in NORTHSIDE. Groups #2 and #3 have no connections beyond their boundaries; therefore, neither group has access to new information or resources. This may help explain why no formal organization was developed, unlike in Group #1. It could be argued that new information offered by the team lay fallow because Groups #2 and #3 were too insular to accept and process the innovations.

The findings seem to be supported by a similar occurrence in EASTSIDE, which also did not develop an organization. Yet the resources and information brought by the team did not go to waste. The impact of the resources were most evident at the individual level rather than at the community level. They redistributed the "loot and clout" available in the society, but not necessarily accessible to the women of EASTSIDE.[25] Empowerment was happening, but it did not take the shape of an organization.

The FATCAT contextual analysis in NORTHSIDE showed that a cohesive core group was being built as neighbors named neighbors in the network report. Formal and informal agreements solidified links between individuals and groups. Further, the analysis highlighted black-white cooperation. This finding remained solid even when content (Table 2) was tested with race in the analysis. Such an outcome builds a compelling case for focusing on relationship building to foster interracial links prior to a crisis.

The finding that homemakers and self-styled activists were equally effective as agents of change was supported in both NORTH-SIDE and EASTSIDE. The homogeneity of EASTSIDE (predominantly black and female) allowed the examination of other factors which might influence network growth. The role of older black women as activists has been examined by Saegert.[26] She found that these women influenced tenant responses to the empowerment process. Similarly, older black women in EASTSIDE played an important part in the resource network. The end result was that people developed the wherewithal to act on their own behalf.

Yet the EASTSIDE findings raise a further question concerning levels of empowerment. Community psychology has implicitly assumed that true empowerment occurs at the collective level, beginning in neighborhoods and building in increments until change occurs across the society. Hence effective social change is defined as creating organizations and other formal structures.[27] Yet can this be the only route to community empowerment? If sufficient numbers of individuals who compose a community are empowered, can the community therefore become empowered by virtue of their collective presence?

CONCLUSIONS

Findings of the two studies highlight areas needing further study to continue building this model of creating effective long-term interventions. This section describes how future work may respond to these questions.

THE TIME PROBLEM

The network analyses quite successfully charted the links that developed between individuals. The findings supported conventional wisdom and theories about how collectivities form. They also raised questions about how people make decisions about the content of exchanges. That is, "who talks to whom, about what, and why?"

The network that evolved during the initial work in NORTH-SIDE yielded intriguing information. Further analyses might have been even more revealing, but were not conducted. This problem was a function of the research design. The team spent six months in the community; this did not take into account the amount of start-up time needed to break the inertia of a neighborhood. Telephone calls are made and not returned, appointments are arranged and not kept, meetings are set and no one attends. A great deal of time can pass before people actually begin to talk to someone other than the member of the intervention team. Therefore an identifiable network emerged just as data collection ended.

The EASTSIDE project ran for a total of 18 months. Initially the team worked nine months; that milestone was considered a provisional end, at which time the team assessed progress within the neighborhood. Most members of the network were still talking only with the intervention team members, so the model was extended another three months. This assessment was repeated at three month intervals for a maximum of nine additional months. The assumption was that at some point during the period an identifiable organization would emerge. However, no organization ever emerged in EASTSIDE.

THE DEFINITION PROBLEM

Current empowerment theory suggests the action in EASTSIDE was a failure because no organization formed. The women's own words indicate otherwise. The team worked with some of the women using the manual guiding welfare recipients through the labyrinth of barriers to continued education. One woman's sentiments regarding that process are representative of those expressed repeatedly by women in the neighborhood: "I want to get my associates degree. I want to do something for myself and for my kids. I gotta take care of home first before I can even be thinking about them other folks."

The literature proposes that if a neighborhood does not generate a collectivity—a community-based organization (CBO) —it is not empowered. Theory offers several explanations for the lack of such a CBO: the impact of external inhibitory social or political forces, improper use of incentives to motivate people, the dampening effect of a deteriorated physical environment.[28] It is equally possible that residents prioritize individual and community empowerment differently than current social science theory.

If empowerment is defined as accomplishing personal goals, people in both neighborhoods appear to be empowered. Comparing the findings in NORTHSIDE, where an organization formed, and in EASTSIDE, where one did not, the difference seems to be the level at which empowerment occurs. EASTSIDE reported the process at work among individuals; NORTHSIDE reported the formation of an organization. But does this mean individual empowerment is less significant than collective empowerment?

Table 1
Utility-Outcome Codes for Network Analysis

UTILITY: the extent to which respondents rate the usefulness of an individual as a resource to reach identified goals

Value	Description	Definition
0	None at all	This individual was of no use
1	Marginally	This individual was a little useful but only minimally
2	Moderately	This individual facilitated movement toward identified goals
3	Significantly	This individual helped attain a definite milestone
4	Indispensable	This individual was crucial in attaining identified goals

OUTCOME: nature of the agreement between the respondent and the individual/group contacted at the end of a log entry

Value	Description	Definition
1	Referral	Sends member to another source
2	Hostility	Unresolved conflict, competition, outright resistance
3	Neutral/Benign	No apparent hostility, no apparent commitment nor support
4	Cooperation	Agreement to undertake joint ventures defined by either party; veto power retained by group; agreement need not be formalized (e.g., in writing)
5	Formal Endorsement	Supports mission, programs; sends representative; veto power retained by group; agreement formalized (e.g., in writing)
6	Full Partnership	Share equal decision-making power in defining joint ventures; agreement formalized (e.g., in writing)

Table 2
Link and Index Variables for Network Analysis

ROLECOMM: function contact serves in the context of the larger community; identified at time of interaction

Code	Description	Code	Description
0	Isolate	5	Funding Source
1	Religious	6	City Official
2	Businessperson	7	Homemaker
3	Educator/Educatee	8	Social Service Worker
4	Civic Activist	9	Government Worker

ROLEGRP: function of contact in the context of his/her reference group

Code	Description
0	No Group Affiliation
1	Leadership/Autonomous
2	General Membership
3	Affiliated Only

GRPS: description of associations formed through work of Intervention Team and groups contacted through activities to build the resource network

Code	Description	Code	Description
0	No Affiliation	5	Business
1	Religious	6	Government
2	Civic/Activist	7	Self-Help
3	Education	8	Non-Profit
4	Recreation		

Table 3
Strength Distribution Histogram[1]

Strength	Number of Links[2]	
1 - 1	0	
2 - 2	0	
3 - 3	0	
4 - 4	0	
5 - 5	0	
6 - 6	62	xxxxxxxxxxxxxxxxxxxxxxxxxxxxxxx
7 - 7	7	xxx
8 - 8	50	xxxxxxxxxxxxxxxxxxxxxxxxx
9 - 9	1	
10 - 10	66	xxxxxxxxxxxxxxxxxxxxxxxxxxxxxxxxx
11 - 11	4	xx
12 - 12	22	xxxxxxxxxxx
13 - 13	0	
14 - 14	0	
15 - 15	1	

Mean Link Strength = 8.51
Number of Link Components = 213.00

1. Both incoming and outgoing halves of links are counted.

2. Each X represents 2 links.

Something changed in EASTSIDE that the prevailing schools of thought in community psychology cannot accurately map. Empowerment occurred as a result of relationships that were built between individual women rather than through the work of a formalized structure. Writers in the feminist tradition have pointed out that this "women's way of knowing" is as effective as forming organizations to accomplish neighborhood goals.[29]

Looking at networks over time allows us to set aside the assumption that an organization was on the verge of formation when data collection ended. While this assumption would allow the researcher to keep hold of comfortable theories, the conclusions do not reflect realities that clearly exist in communities. Perhaps a more germane question would be to examine the connection between individual and collective empowerment and to ask how they interplay.

NOTES

1. D. C. Bryant, "The Creation of an Interracial Social Action: Examination of the Process." (Unpublished doctoral dissertation, Michigan State University, East Lansing, Mich., 1990).

2. J. H. Mollenkopf, *The Contested City* (Princeton, N.J.: Princeton University Press, (1983).

3. E. Hoffer, *The True Believer: Thoughts on the Nature of Mass Movements*, (New York: Perennial Library, 1966). Hoffer looked at participation in terms of fanaticism, discussing what occurs when political agendas meet religious fervor. Toch and his contemporaries, Turner & Killian, used a more traditional sociological approach to examine theoretical explanations for an individual's social activism. See R. H. Turner and L. M. Killian, *Collective Behavior* (Englewood Cliffs, NJ: Prentice-Hall, 1972); Toch, *The Social Psychology of Social Movements* (New York: Bobbs-Merrill Company, 1965). Chavis and his colleagues use an organizational analysis approach, asking whether strengthening how individuals function in organizations will enhance participation. See D. M. Chavis and A. Wandersman, "Sense of Community in the Urban Environment: A Catalyst for Participation and Community Development," *American Journal of Community Psychology* 18.1 (1990): 55-81.

4. The world witnessed the outcome of long-term tension between poor economic conditions and social injustice recently when Los Angeles erupted into violence. Residents in poor neighborhoods all over the US would tell similar stories. The major difference is that no one has recorded them on video tape for mass media to broadcast into the social consciousness of the nation.

5. A. J. Catanese, *The Politics of Planning and Development* (Beverly Hills: Sage, 1984); E. Marciniak, *Reclaiming the Inner City*, (Washington, D. C.: National Center for Urban Ethnic Affairs, 1986); E. Marciniak, "Reversing Urban Decline: A Report Prepared for the Department of Planning of the City of Chicago," 1981. Excellent examples that examine the relationships between urban planners, politicians, and community activists, they provide case studies from metropolitan areas around the country which emphasize the pitfalls (and disasters) of waiting until a problem has developed to open lines of communication between major stakeholders.

6. Participatory research sees participants as active contributors to the investigation rather than as objects to be manipulated and observed. Research of this nature is difficult to conduct because divergent viewpoints must be synthesized into a feasible project. This is a process that involves much negotiation, consensus building, and open communication. Traditional social science methodologies have been developed using a top-down, expert-subject approach which does not easily lend itself to collaboration. Hence, participatory research is an alternative approach developing new methodologies.

7. J. Rappaport, *Community Psychology: Values, Research, and Action* (New York: Holt, Rinehart, and Winston, 1977). In this his seminal text on community psychology, he addressed the recommendations by the Joint

Commission on Mental Health. The Commission found that there were insufficient Ph. D. psychologists to meet the nation's needs, in general, and the needs of underserved populations, in particular. Rappaport proposed the educational pyramid to spread the impact of the professional (at the apex) across the greatest number of potential clients (at the base). It is interesting to note that this same top-down approach is characteristic of the aid work in developing nations. Korten does a compelling review of this history and proposes what he calls a "fourth generation" of development activity; see *Getting to the 21st Century: Voluntary Action and the Global Agenda* (Hartford, Conn.: Kumarian Press, 1993). Bryant uses this framework to discuss work in a Nigerian community to establish a library ("Responsible to Whom, for What?: The Case of the Village Library," manuscript under review).

8. D. C. Bryant, and G. Mettetal, "Teaching Participatory Research: Empowerment in Students and Communities" (manuscript in preparation). Their writing examines service learning and its utility in teaching participatory research. Several student cases are presented to illustrate how students as well as communities are empowered by this approach to post-secondary education. It is proposed that this empowerment occurs precisely because of the dynamic process at work. Students are participant-observers, not simply observers. They must accurately record information, but then they must also relay it, interpret its impact, and feed that information back into the community.

9. Action research is used in community psychology to transform theory into a tool to bring about social change; that is, it serves both science and practice. The challenge of doing such research is that a balance must be maintained between scientific rigor and social relevance. The researcher has a foot in two worlds—the academic community and the larger society—each of which operates by its own rules. When the requirements of the two conflict, as they often do, the research is caught in between.

10. J. C. Jenkins, "Resource Mobilization Theory and the Study of Social Movements," *Annual Review of Sociology* 9 (1983) 527-553; J. McCarthy, and M. Zald, *The Trend of Social Movements in America: Professionalization and Resource Mobilization* (Morristown, N.J.: General Learning Press, 1973). J. McCarthy, and M. Zald, "Resource Mobilization and Social Movements: A Partial Theory," *American Journal of Sociology* 82.6 (1974): 1212-1241; M. Zald, and R. Asch, "Social Movement Organizations: Growth Decay, and Change," *Social Forces* 44 (1965): 327-341. The authors discuss the professionalization of social movements. They propose that grievances have become secondary in social activism. Rather, citizen participation occurs because of perceived inequities in the distribution of resources. The people who lead such movements are just as likely to do so as a vocation as an avocation. S. B. Sarason, C. F. Carroll, K. Maton, S. Cohen, and E. Lorentz, *Human Services and Resource Networks: Rationale, Possibilities, and Public Policy* (San Francisco: Jossey-Bass Publishers, 1977). Rogers and Kincaid, (1981, *Ibid.*) described how a single influential person may be pivotal in matching resources to needs so that distribution is effective and fair. Similarly, a single personality can prevent information or technology from reaching those in need. Mollenkopf

(1983, *Ibid.*) coined the phrase "entrepreneur" to describe the work of third parties who helped ethnic minorities become politicized in the early 1960s.

11. F. F. Piven, and R. A. Cloward, *Poor People's Movements: How They Succeed, How They Fail* (New York: Vintage Books, 1979).

12. Community-based organizations (CBOs) have long been considered as mainly local. During the 1960s many social movements gained national prominence, but these were mainly viewed as exceptions. Some authors have looked at CBOs as possible mechanism to connect the local and the global. Ignacio, "The Pacific/Asian Coalitions: Origin, Structure, and Program." *Social Casework* 57.3 (1976): 131-135, looked at the local, regional, and national strategies of the Pacific-Asian Coalition. Bryant, ("The Evolution in Canada of the Citizen's Movement Against Nestlé: A Descriptive Study" (unpublished M. A. thesis, Wilfrid Laurier University, Waterloo, Ontario, Canada, 1985) examined the evolution of the Nestlé Boycott from a single local action cell into an international movement.

13. Granovetter's work, "The Strength of Weak Ties," *American Journal of Sociology* 78 (1973): 1360-1380, is most commonly cited in reference to the influence of boundary people. Sarason et al. (1971, *Ibid.*) as well as Sarason and Lorentz (*The Challenge of the Resource Exchange Network: From Concept to Action* (San Francisco: Jossey- Bass, 1979) are additional authors who discuss the role of individuals who are of a group but not *in* the group. The focus relates to moving needed resources through difficult or hostile communities.

14. E. Rogers, and D. Kincaid, *Communications Networks: Toward a Paradigm for Research* (New York: Free Press, 1981).

15. E. M. Rogers, J. J. Ascroft, and N. G. Roling, "Diffusion of Innovations in Brazil, Nigeria, and India," *Research Report* #24, Department of Communications, Michigan State University, East Lansing, 1970. Traditional examinations of social networks have only asked about frequency of contact between members. In each of these studies, researchers also asked about the nature of those contacts: who was talking and how were they regarded in the community?

16. E. Rogers, and F. F. Shoemaker, *Communications of Innovations: A Cross-Cultural Approach* (New York: Free Press, 1971). Examines the role of "stars" in information dissemination.

17. W.D.Richards, "The NEGOPY: Network Analysis Program," Department of Communications, Simon Fraser University, Burnaby, British Columbia, 1989 [Computer assisted network analysis software for PC]. NEGOPY categorizes people (nodes) in the network to describe their link to one another. The links were weighted using these formulas: NORTHSIDE: strength = 2b + c , where b = Utility, and c = Outcome. EASTSIDE: strength = a (b + c + e), where a = Utility, b = Outcome, c = Content-Current, and e = Content-Future Plans.

18. W.D.Richards, "FATCAT-For Thick Data," Department of Communications, Simon Fraser University, Burnaby, British Columbia, 1989 [Computer-assisted network analysis software for PC]. FATCAT uncovers the relationship between two kinds of data generated by the net-

work report: to describe individuals in the network (index variables) and to describe connections between individuals (link variables). The analysis indicates the types of resources (person, service, material) flowing between members in the network (see Table 2). The program constructs categorical matrices using the chi-square test of association. Having established the degree of independence between categories, FATCAT then computes the amount of linkages between individuals that fall into each one. Findings are displayed in a standard cross-tabulation-format table, showing counts and row/column percentages.

19. The first analysis in NORTHSIDE was a 4 x 3 chi-square which asked respondents to rate the utility of people with different roles in the community. Homemakers and activists were identified as being the most useful contacts. Municipal and state government officials were of the least utility (chi-square(42) = 853.547, p is less than.01). The second analysis was a 2 x 8 chi-square that examined the effect of race and content on communication. The highest amount of linkage for both blacks and whites were for cooperative purposes (chi-square(7) = 319.515, p is less than.01). The discrepancy between percentages (87% for blacks and 43% for whites) is because 70% of the people in the network are black. The third analysis was a 7 x 8 chi- square that examined the effects of types of groups and content of communication. Cooperation was the greatest amount of content represented. It fell into two types of groups: civic and self-help. Civic groups requested full partnerships and religious groups relied on friendship ties. Educators both got and gave information or advice; business groups received and sent friendship ties (chi-square(42) = 853.547, p is less than.01.). The fourth analysis was a 2 x 8 chi-square that looked at the effects of individuals' roles in groups and content of communication. Most of the communication was cooperative (chi-square(7) = 132.666, p is less than.01). The content varied among individuals of different roles in the groups. Leaders and autonomous people most often sought cooperation or requested formal endorsement. Communication between general members of the groups focused on cooperation. The last analysis was a 6 x 8 chi-square that examined the effects of outcome and role in the community. All of the full endorsements were accomplished by activists, as were half of the benign outcomes. For their part, homemakers established half the full partnerships between groups in the network. Government officials were responsible for the most referrals. Businesses engaged in cooperative ventures and homemakers created full partnerships (chi-square(35) = 1713.078, p is less than.01).

20. The network constructed in NORTHSIDE contains three groups and has an interconnectiveness score of .60. The network contains 42 nodes, 18 of which were categorized as isolates. Intervention team members were named as members of the group, but were also the other halves of type-2 isolates. Two hundred and fifty-three (253) links were identified. Forty were dropped because their strength value was lower than 6.0, indicating that the interaction had little or no impact toward goal attainment. No unreciprocated links were dropped; instead, 23 markers were added to force reciprocation. A total of 213 links were processed.

21. The network constructed in EASTSIDE contains 89 nodes, 49% of which were categorized as isolates. Intervention team members were named as the other halves of type-2 isolates (a person with only one other link). A total of 392 links were processed.

22. The first FATCAT analysis in EASTSIDE was a 4 x 9 chi-square which asked respondents to rate the utility of people with different roles in the community. Homemakers were identified as being the most useful contacts. Social service workers and businesspersons were of the least utility (chi-square (25) = 35.582,p is less than.01). The second analysis was a 13x9 chi square that examined the effect of age and role in the community on communication; a 13x4 chi - square examined age and utility. It showed the highest amount of linkage for both respondents aged 41-54 (chi-square (10) = 25.939) who were homemakers (chi-square (10) = 38.569, p is less than.01). The final analysis was a 6 x 13 chi-square that examined the effects of age and outcome of communication. It showed that cooperation was the greatest amount of content represented: (chi-square (20) = 38.137, p is less than.01).

23. The Welfare Warriors is a national advocacy group based in Chicago, Illinois, to protect the rights of welfare recipients. Its work includes a newsletter and other services for those who feel they have been treated unfairly by the welfare system.

24. The manual is entitled *Community Resource Guide to Education* and was compiled by Karen Charles under the auspices of the Social Action Project (SOCACT). The guide walks the welfare recipient through the steps involved in returning to school. It includes information about offices to contact, language to use to describe the situation or need, where to acquire needed forms, timelines, and hints for surviving the process. Copies of the guide are available for $10US by writing to the SOCACT address.

25. I. Goldenberg, *Oppression and Social Intervention* (New York: Nelson-Hall, 1978). First coined the term "loot and clout" to describe what a society values and strives to obtain. His hour-glass representation of social functioning illustrates that the goodies that society holds dear are available to all but *accessible* to only a few. This is so because the access channel is the narrowest part of the hour glass and only a select few may pass through. The way is guarded by gatekeepers whose function is to regulate access, decisions which are governed by bureaucratic rules and the values of the gatekeeper.

26. S.Saegert, "Unlikely Leaders, Extreme Circumstances: Older Black Women Building Community Households," *American Journal of Community Psychology* 17.3 (1989): 295-316.

27. The best example is work by Wandersman and his colleagues who have developed the Block Booster Project. It focuses on organizational development in terms of physical structure as well as enhancing relationships between individuals in the organization. Their work, which spans two decades, was most recently summarized in a special issue of the *American Journal of Community Psychology* 18.4 (1990).

28. *Ibid.*

29. M. F. Belenky, B. M. Clinchy, N. R. Golderger, and J. M. Tarule, *Women's*

Ways of Knowing: The Development of Self, Voice, and Mind (New York: Basic Books, 1986). Discusses this term at length as part of an exploration of individuation and self-definition among women. It is applied again in work by Saegert (1989, *Ibid.*) that discusses the role of older black women in community development.

WORKS CITED

Belenky, M. F., B. M. Clinchy, N. R. Golderger, and J. M. Tarule. *Women's Ways of Knowing: The Development of Self, Voice, and Mind.* New York: Basic Books, 1986.

Bryant, D. C. "The Creation of an Interracial Social Action: Examination of the Process." Unpublished Ph. D. dissertation, Michigan State University, East Lansing, Mich, 1990.

——. "The Evolution in Canada of the Citizen's Movement Against Nestlé: A Descriptive Study." Unpublished M. A. thesis, Wilfrid Laurier University, Waterloo, Ontario, Canada, 1985.

——."Responsible to Whom, for What?: The Case of the Village Library." Unpublished.

Bryant, D. C., and Mettetal, G. "Teaching Participatory Research: Empowerment in Students and Communities." Unpublished.

Catanese, A. J. *The Politics of Planning and Development.* Beverly Hills: Sage, 1984.

Charles, Karen. *Community Resource Guide to Education.* Manual produced under the auspices of the Social Action Project (SOCACT), South Bend, Indiana.

Chavis, D. M. and A. Wandersman. "Sense of Community in the Urban Environment: a Catalyst for Participation and Community Development." *American Journal of Community Psychology* 18.1 (1990): 55-81.

Goldenberg, I. *Oppression and Social Intervention.* New York: Nelson-Hall, 1978.

Granovetter, Mark S. "The Strength of Weak Ties." *American Journal of Sociology* 78 (1973): 1360-1380.

Hoffer, E. *The True Believer: Thoughts on the Nature of Mass Movements.* New York: Perennial Library, 1966.

Ignacio, "The Pacific/Asian Coalitions: Origin, Structure, and Program." *Social Casework* 57.3 (1976): 131-135.

Jenkins, J. C. "Resource Mobilization Theory and the Study of Social Movements." *Annual Review of Sociology* 9 (1983): 527-553.

Korten, David. *Getting to the 21st Century: Voluntary Action and the Global Agenda.* Hartford, Conn.: Kumarian Press, 1990.

Marciniak, E. *Reclaiming the Inner City.* Washington, D.C.: National Center for Urban Ethnic Affairs, 1986.

——. "Reversing Urban Decline: A Report Prepared for the Department of Planning of the City of Chicago," 1981.

McCarthy, J. and M. Zald. *The Trend of Social Movements in America: Professionalization and Resource Mobilization.* Morristown, NJ: General

Learning Press, 1973.

——. "Resource Mobilization and Social Movements: A Partial Theory." *American Journal of Sociology* 82.6 (1974): 1212-1241.

Mollenkopf, J. H. *The Contested City*. Princeton, NJ: Princeton University Press, 1983.

Piven, F. F. and R. A. Cloward. *Poor People's Movements: How They Succeed, How They Fail*. New York: Vintage Books, 1979.

Rappaport, J. *Community Psychology: Values, Research, and Action*. New York: Holt, Rinehart, and Winston, 1977.

Richards, W. D. "The NEGOPY Network Analysis Program." [Computer assisted network analysis software for PC]. Burnaby, British Columbia: Department of Communications, Simon Fraser University, 1989.

——."FATCAT-For Thick Data." [Computer assisted network analysis software for PC]. Burnaby: British Columbia: Department of Communications, Simon Fraser University, 1989.

Rogers E. and D. Kincaid. *Communications Networks: Toward a Paradigm for Research*. New York: Free Press, 1981.

Rogers, E. M., J. J. Ascroft, and N. G. Roling. "Diffusion of Innovations in Brazil, Nigeria, and India." *Research Report* #24. East Langsing: Department of Communications, Michigan State University, 1970.

Rogers, E. and F. F. Shoemaker. *Communications of Innovations: A Cross-Cultural Approach*. New York: Free Press, 1971.

Saegert, S. "Unlikely Leaders, Extreme Circumstances: Older Black Women Building Community Households." *American Journal of Community Psychology* 17.3 (1989): 295-316.

Sarason, S. B., C. F. Carroll, K. Maton, S. Cohen, and E. Lorentz. *Human Services and Resource Networks: Rationale, Possibilities, and Public Policy*. San Francisco: Jossey-Bass Publishers, 1977.

Sarason, S. B. and E. Lorentz. *The Challenge of the Resource Exchange Network: From Concept to Action*. San Francisco: Jossey-Bass, 1979.

Toch, Hans. *The Social Psychology of Social Movements*. Indianapolis: Bobbs-Merrill Company, 1965.

Turner, R. H. and L. M. Killian. *Collective Behavior*. Englewood Cliffs, N.J.: Prentice-Hall, 1972.

Wandersman, Abraham, et al. "Citizen Participation, Voluntary Organizations and Community Development: Insights for Empowerment through Research," (Special Section). *American Journal of Community Psychology* 18.1 (1990): 41-151.

Zald, M. and R. Asch. "Social Movement Organizations: Growth Decay, and Change." *Social Forces* 44 (1965): 327-341.

White Women in  Umkhonto We Sizwe, the ANC Army of Liberation: "Traitors" to Race, Class, and Gender

Betty Welz

The African National Congress (ANC) was founded in 1912 as a South African Liberation organization. In 1960 it was banned—declared illegal and unable to operate legally within the country—by the South African Government. Cynics remark that as it is the oldest still-existing liberation organization in the world, it must therefore be the least successful; but to be fair, one must consider the might of the apartheid establishment it was resisting.

In late 1961, after the police shootings in Sharpville that shocked the world, the ANC, in exile, moved away from its hitherto exclusively peaceful policy while its leader, Chief Albert Luthuli, was receiving the Noble Peace Prize in Oslo. In association with the

South African Communist Party (SACP), also banned and in exile, an army of liberation was formed—*Umkhonto we Sizwe*, the Spear of the Nation, known to insiders as "MK." This obviously represented a basic change in tactics, but as the peace-loving, old Chief Luthuli remarked, he had been knocking on the white man's door for so many years to no avail. The MK manifesto of December, 1961, asserted that "the time comes in the life of any nation when there remain only two choices: submit or fight. That time has come for South Africa. We shall not submit and we have no choice but to hit back by all means within our power in defense of our people, our future and our freedom" (MK 1991:18).

It is not the purpose of this paper to chart the history of the MK. This has been done elsewhere, notably by Howard Barrell of Oxford, the leading academic expert on the topic (Barrell, 1990). Suffice it to say that many thousands of young South Africans went into exile to become "part of the glorious army." MK cadres were trained in exile, chiefly in Angola; operations were directed from Lusaka (Zambia) and operatives were sent into the country clandestinely in small groups to carry out acts of sabotage, at first directed solely against nonhuman targets, although later military and police personnel came to be regarded as legitimate targets. It is perhaps useful to note, as academic commentators on "terrorism" have done, that "terrorists" rarely do near the amount of damage, especially in terms of killing, that their training and their material would allow them to do. This would certainly seem to apply to MK. Barrell asserts that "by the end of 1987 MK had trained more than 12,000 guerrillas since the 1967 uprisings.... More than half....had been deployed in the country" (1990: 64). Every year the number of MK-initiated "incidents" inside South Africa increased, and although there was little actual combat in the sense of hand-to-hand fighting, MK's visibility was maintained at a high level owing to some spectacularly successful missions such as the bombing of Sasol, South Africa's huge oil-from-coal plant. The "armed struggle," as it came to be known, was formally suspended in August 1990 to accommodate constitutional negotiations.

The cadres in MK have been overwhelmingly male and black. Precise figures of any sort are difficult to give since in the mistrustful atmosphere of current South African negotiations, MK understandably plays its cards close to its chest. An academic researcher will of necessity be trusted with only a certain amount of information, and there are certain questions to which no answer will be given. There have been a number of black women in MK, although from their own accounts they were by far in the minority (Cock 1991). Jacqueline Molefe's account is fairly typical: "I was recruited when I was 16 or 17.... I finished (the 10th grade)....and went into exile to join MK in 1964.... My brother was with me but I was the only girl out of a big group" (1992). Barrell basically ignores the gender issue, but Cock asserts that about 20% of MK cadres were women (162). White men could probably be counted in dozens, but I have been able to identify only seven white women, five of whom have been made public due to their capture by the South African security forces. It should be noted here that there is a distinction between merely working underground for the ANC (as did Barbara Hogan, who was tried and sentenced in 1983, or Helene Pastoors in 1986) and membership in MK. Although many of those who regard themselves as MK cadres never formally joined or took an oath of loyalty, the distinguishing characteristics would seem to be the acquisition of military skills of whatever sort, including military intelligence, and the adherence to military discipline as expressed in a chain of command. An MK cadre regards herself or himself as a soldier.

Why did so few women join MK? Once we turn our attention to academic work, we encounter the loaded term "terrorism." Discussing a topic such as this is like walking through a linguistic minefield. If terrorism is defined in Alexander's (1978: x) words as "the acts of extralegal violence used intentionally by subnational groups, principally....as a part of a domestic or transitional revolutionary strategy," then MK cadres are "terrorists."

As far back as 1977, Hassel (incidentally, an FBI agent) was moved to analyze "the terrorist....by examining the sociological factors that have led to privileged members of the middle class to become involved in terrorism. Sociological roots of rapid social change are discussed in relation to the current wave of terrorism, which is traced to its roots in the 1960's" (1). He also examined "the attraction for women to the terrorist movements." He remarked that: "some of the terrorists... are the sons and daughters of the privileged who have benefited most from the very society they seek to disrupt," and pointed out that academic research into terrorism and disorder had traced reasons for the rage "of certain deprived groups, particularly urban blacks [in the United States]" (2)—but, he asked, "How does one explain a Bernadine Dohru or an Abbie Hoffman? What would cause these and other members of the white middle class to declare war on the very society that has nurtured them?....Why...do some heirs of the upwardly mobile middle class

engage in violence against and reject the very source of their affluence?" (2). Hassel's answer is that traditional middle-class values
have been undermined by the rapidity of modern social change.
The disaffected youth, in his opinion, "see their affluence in stark
contrast to three-fourths of the world that still live in dire poverty"
(3). With a breathtaking assurance, Hassel writes off such militants
by saying that: "The terrorists themselves are overwhelmingly middle class and college educated.... [Although] most students survive
and even grow through their period of normal [student] rebellion
against parental ideals.... a few still remain intellectually frozen as
rebelling [students, although] most mature and recognize that participation within the system is a much more practical way to create
change" (4). Militants would, of course, not agree but perhaps claim
that most rebellious young people simply settle down to a comfortable way of life and forget the altruism of their youth.

   This is an attempt to explain middle-class involvement in revolutionary movements, but why do women in particular become
involved? Women, although usually proportionately fewer than
men, have often played prominent positions in such movements —
recall Bernadine Race Dohru of the Weather Underground (US),
Ulrike Meinhof, Gudrun Ensslin and Angela Luther of the "Baader-
Meinhoff gang" (West Germany), Leila Khaled of the PLO, Fusako
Shigenobu of the Japanese Red Army, or Thandi Modise, Marion
Sparg, Jenny Schreiner, and Jacqueline Molefe of MK. Hassel
attempts a "with-it" answer:

> The participation of women appears in these movements to
> be an aberrant extension of the legitimate striving of
> women, as represented by the feminist movement, to break
> out of the narrow, structural roles into which they have been
> unfairly forced over the centuries. (8)

He claims that "revolutionary rhetoric" has an obvious appeal "to
those few women who can see no answer other than a resort to violence and terror" (9), and ascribes great weight to what he calls "the
terrorists mystique":

> What other occupation, especially in the work-a-day world
> of middle-class society, offers such adventure, fame, and
> prestige for the idealistic immature university dropout with-
> out the drudgery of study, work and long years of appren-
> ticeship necessary to achieve success on the stodgy
> professional ladder." (10)

What Hassel is doing here is presenting the standard counter argument to (inexplicable) revolutionary involvement, particularly on the part of women.

As Cock points out, "the politics of gender [is] used against....radical....women (dismissed as 'social failures') to discredit them and denigrate their commitment" (ix). Liz Stanley points to:

> ...interesting differences in the reaction of the media and academics to female and male members of the Baader-Meinhof gang: the activities of the women are seen as the product of sexual hang-ups about men in general or of unresolved Oedipal complexes concerning their fathers, while the men are seen as politically motivated revolutionaries. Radical women, almost by definition, are seen as having sexual hang-ups; radical men are radical men. (Stanley and Morley, 147)

This contention is aptly illustrated in the treatment accorded by academicians to white women in MK. My title reflects descriptions of such women as "'traitors' to race, class and gender." How have they been seen as traitors to their race? The best illustration of this comes from the trial of Marion Sparg for arson and treason in 1986. The first white female MK operative brought to trial, Sparg had been responsible for various bombings, including that of the Johannesburg police headquarters, but had brought about no loss of life. She, nonetheless, received the extreme sentence (in South African terms) of 25 years imprisonment. Why such severity? In his judgment, the judge said:

> You are a mature and intelligent woman, 28 years old. You have no previous convictions, you suffered no particular hardship in your life and you have deliberately chosen....to align yourself against the law and order in this country and to espouse the cause of an organization committed to the overthrow the lawful Government of the Republic of South Africa by revolution and acts of terrorism. You may choose to call it acts of war.... You are a dedicated and unrepentant member of *Umkhonto we Sizwe,* the armed section of the ANC. You are dedicated to Marxism and revolution. If a black South African were in your position his or her acts could be understood, although not excused. *The fact that as a white South African you have espoused the cause of revolution I regard as an aggravating feature. "* (Court Papers, emphasis mine)

Sparg's judges (the appeal court confirmed her sentence) would seem to be of the same mind as Hassel, in not attributing sufficient weight to altruism as a motivating force. Sparg's lawyers, in arguing her appeal, claimed:

> The learned judge failed to attach sufficient or any weight to [Sparg's own] evidence and failed to recognize that the sense of powerlessness and frustration which (by implication) his Lordship would allow black South Africans to experience, is equally applicable to a small but growing number of white South Africans. (Court Papers)

From a political point of view, of course, while not impugning the independence of the South African judiciary, it could be argued that an exemplary sentence was required in this case in order to dissuade "a small but growing number of white South Africans" from following in Sparg's footsteps. Sparg's whiteness and her femaleness were the two aspects of her case that featured prominently in the media, especially in newspapers such as *Beeld, The Citizen,* and *The Star.*

Equally, white involvement with either the ANC or the MK has been seen as breaking class ranks, since the class/race categorization is largely conflated in South African society (O'Meara 1982; Marks and Trapido 1987). As Saul explains, this is owing to:

> ...the unique manner in which the structure of racial oppression forged by colonial conquest has interacted with the structure of capitalist exploitation produced by the dramatic transformation of South Africa's economy in this century. There has been considerable debate about the precise form of the interaction, and we shall see that it has implications for any attempt to characterize the composition of the movement (national-cum-racial liberation? class struggle?) that must turn up to oppose the system. Here it bears emphasizing that for extended periods of time in South Africa racial hierarchy and capitalist relations of production have been mutually reinforcing.... For many analysts the term "racial capitalism" has seemed useful.... [We can see a] linkage between racial domination and capitalist exploitation. (211)

It is obvious that cadres in MK (which initially drew its membership from both the ANC and the SACP—a result of the enduring SACP/ANC alliance) would be seen as betraying class interests and would have the full force of hegemonic institutions of capital, such as the courts and the media, brought to bear upon them.

How were white women in MK seen as betraying their gender? (Cock discusses this in the role of women in the South African military.) As Taylor aptly notes,

> The woman terrorist seems to offer challenge to the contemporary stereotype of the woman as caregiver and protector and the notion of the violent woman seems to give rise to both horror and fantasy for Western men...and clearly reflects upon our most deep seated prejudices about gender-appropriate behavior, especially with regard to fighting and aggression. (13)

MK white women have had their femininity used against them or called into question in the courts and by the media. During the trial of Susan Westcott, the State prosecutor pointed out that she had had an abortion and had also had a black lover—two very derogatory assertions in the South African context. Marion Sparg was viciously depicted in the media as having "failed" as a woman. A page of one newspaper described her as "....with a tortured mind....frustrated....weight problem....haunted....consumed by her desperate loneliness....rejected" (*Sunday Times,* November 9, 1986). The unflattering police photographs published in the same issue (one blown up to a third of the broadsheet front page) showed her in leg-irons with the laces of her shoes untied and looking vacant. The "overweight" charge (in so far as it has relevance) is the only one that papers could support by evidence; Sparg's supposed "loneliness" was apparently deduced from two poems she had hand-written as a young school girl. But "unsuccessful women" (and therefore "unfeminine") was the message the press succeeded in communicating. Whatever the perceptions of white women in MK,

> the 'armed struggle' nowadays has little more than a symbolic appeal. This is widely accepted even within the ANC's armed wing—as one *Umkhonto we Sizwe* insurgent was reported to have responded when asked about the armed struggle: "What armed struggle?" In terms of guerrilla attacks attributable to the ANC, and admitted by them, the armed struggle has fallen away to virtually nothing. *Umkhonto's* striking capacity has been dramatically reduced by removal of its camps to Tanzania and by virtually drying up of its traditional Eastern sources of arms. (IRIS 1990b: 71)

But the names of known MK operatives are still revered in the South

African black townships. When asked, at the trial of Susan Westcott and two white MK men, what the township reaction would be to a visit from white MK cadres, a black bishop responded: "Oh, they would be treated as kings and queens" (Court Papers). And it is perhaps appropriate to conclude with a poem (Lockett 1990: 331) by Annemarie Hendrikz, whom I do not know but suspect to be a black South African woman:

> FOR MARION SPARG
> How do you plead?
> Guilty your Honour
> Guilty
> Guilty
> Guilty and proud
> 25 years for you
> Not for treason
> Not for arson
> Not for courage
> nor commitment
> 25 years for aggravating factors
> Woman.
> White.
> Misguided
> By Joe Slovo
> A history
> of obesity
> inability
> to relate socially
> Very aggravating indeed.
> Viva woman
> Beautiful, brave, fat, white
> woman
> Viva!

WORKS CITED

Alexander, Yonah, ed., *International Terrorism*. New York: Praeger, 1976.

Barrel, H. *MK: ANC's Armed Struggle*. London: Penguin, 1990.

Beeld (newspaper). Various issues. Johannesburg.

Becker, J., *Hitler's Children: The Story of the Baader-Meinhof Terrorist Gang*. Philadelphia: Lippincott, 1977.

Cock, Jacklyn. *Colonels and Cadres: War and Gender in South Africa*. Cape Town: Oxford University Press, 1991.

——. *Women and War in South Africa*. London: Open Letters, 1992.

Lockett, Cecily, ed. *Breaking the Silence: A Century of South African Women's Poetry*. Parklands: AD Donker Publisher, 1990.

Marks, Schula and Stanley Trapido, ed. *The Politics of Race, Class, and Nationalism in Twentieth Century South Africa*. London: Longman, 1987.

O'Meara, Patrick and Gwendolen Carter, ed. *International Politics in South Africa*. Bloomington: Indiana University Press, 1982.

——. *South Africa: The Continuing Crisis*. Bloomington: Indiana University Press, 1982.

O'Meara, Patrick, and Phyllis Martin, ed. *Africa*. Bloomington: Indiana University Press, 1986.

Stanley, Liz and Ann Morley. *The Life and Death of Emily Wilding Davison: A Biographical Detective Story*. London: Women's Press, 1988.

Saul, John and Stephen Gelb. *The Crisis in South Africa*. Revised edition. New York: Monthly Review Press, 1986.

The Citizen (newspaper). Various issues. Johannesburg.

III

WEAVING OUR LIVES: THE
PERSONAL IS POLITICAL

CARRYING THE BATON: PERSONAL PERSPECTIVES ON THE MODERN WOMEN'S MOVEMENT IN NIGERIA

IFEYINWA IWERIEBOR

INTRODUCTION

I CANNOT SAY FOR SURE WHY I BECAME A FEMINIST. I am using the term to refer to anyone concerned with ensuring that women are treated equitably. Perhaps it was genetics. The women of my mother's family were reputed to be dynamic and strong-willed. Indeed the family's customary salutation, *Ogbuefi*—literally, "One who has killed a cow"—was inherited from a female ancestor who had achieved sufficient wealth and status to perform what in those days was a remarkable feat of community service. On the other hand, my paternal grandmother was noted for her leadership qualities, underpinned by the imperial and regal confidence of her position as an *Ada* (first daughter) princess.

Perhaps I was affected by the lives of the women around me—hard-working, determined, affectionate, disciplinarian, taking no nonsense from me as a child, and always encouraging me to reach for the sky. In particular, my mother was a major influence. Extremely affectionate (I was her only biological child) but strict, she wanted only one thing of me—that I should choose a good profession, in particular medicine, because it would fulfill three objectives dear to her heart: first, it would enable me to be independent of salaried employment; second, it would enable me to be financially independent of a man; third, the title "Doctor," would enable me be independent of the titles "Mrs." or "Miss" that immediately indicate one's marital status.

Even if I did not end up as a doctor (whether of medicine or of philosophy), the notions of personal independence (whether financial or professional as she suggested, or emotional and intellectual as I was to develop) remained a cornerstone of my life. She did not live long enough to see that women of my generation who did become doctors, still found it necessary to qualify their marital status—a practice I understand intellectually but do not subscribe to. I was therefore quite happy when the title "Ms." surfaced, and have used it ever since I became aware of it in 1973. This was not because I was against marriage. A romantic at heart, I kept my eyes open, like any Mills & Boones heroine, for my tall-dark-handsome stranger, and happily hooked up with him when he showed up. No, it was because I believed and still do, that one's marital status should not be the first point of self-definition.

From my maternal grandmother, I learned how to analyze the multiple jobs of a woman. She had once felt compelled to remark acidly to my grandfather thus, "I am the cook, steward and washerman. And you want me also to be the missus?" He had made the mistake of tapping his walking stick to hasten her preparations for their daily evening stroll, and she felt he had not been sensitive to her dutiful hustling and bustling to make sure things were right in the house before they set off.

Of course, I could not help but be affected by my mother's lifetime search for children. I had come after eight tortuous years of trying to conceive, and she resumed her search some years afterwards, this time for a son. Even though my father had done his best to assure her that it did not matter, she—like her fellow women, custodians of societal values—knew that even if it did not really matter to him *then*, it would one day. In any case, it certainly mattered to *her*, to everyone else, and to society in general. Did this make me feel devalued? As a person, no, definitely not. I enjoyed all the pampering of a long- awaited first born and (for more than a decade) only child. As a girl, the answer is also no, because to my father I was clearly a cherished princess with the sky as my limit, and a source of joy to my mother. While I had longed for siblings for company, I grew used to being alone, and was not lonely. Yet, it gradually dawned on me through my layers of self-absorption, that aspects of my parents' lives might have been easier had I had brothers. This then was the genesis of my interrogation of gender issues.

My ruminations began to surface as a college undergraduate in the Caribbean, against a background of intense intellectual upheaval interrogating race, class, culture, and international politics. I engaged in long, boisterous arguments about the position of women in the "struggle," socialism, slavery, Rastafarianism, Africa past and present. What finally crystallized was that I was immensely satisfied with being biologically female, but extremely dissatisfied with many societal aspects of living as a female in a male-dominated world. My personal experience and shared knowledge of colonialism, imperialism, neo-colonialism, and racism made me interrogate gender matters in a situational context. For example, my mother had told me how Europeans had misinterpreted the fact that African women walked behind men as an example of male oppression, while their own touted custom of "ladies first" was viewed by African women as an invitation to "walk into danger first." This became my subconscious take-off point for analytical thinking—examining societal processes on their own terms.

Back home in Nigeria, first as a national youth corps member and later as a postgraduate student, I eagerly expounded my vigorous views about feminism at every opportunity, wearying friends and acquaintances of both sexes. Some took the easy way out, declaring me too foreign and alienated to be relevant. Others took me seriously enough and battled to the point of verbal exhaustion, whereupon they would cry, "Write! Write! Since you have so much to say, write it down!" I accepted their advice. Talking people to death was no way to sustain friendships.

By the time I eventually commenced my formal career in 1979, as a journalist with the News Agency of Nigeria (NAN), the elections ushering in the Second Republic had been completed. I wrote my first article examining how women had fared in the political process. My editor-in-chief, a very pleasant man, was affronted. Expressing deep disappointment at my gender sectionalism he

declared, "This is not the Women's Agency of Nigeria" and strongly advised me to adopt a broader perspective.

Well, from then on, the battle lines were drawn. I wrote about
a wide range of topics—commerce, politics, the arts, health, science, medicine—but never passed up an opportunity to insert
"women" as a legitimate newsworthy item. Gradually this gained
acceptance. I was given permission to interview some women political office holders and eventually linked up with the leadership of
the National Council of Women's Societies (NCWS). I routinely
wrote about their activities, and they, in turn, expressed appreciation for the publicity. This was my first chance to find out what formal women's organizations did. Hitherto I had been vaguely aware
of women's involvement in ethnic associations and development
unions, but was basically ignorant about anything that constituted
a Nigerian women's movement. My initial journalistic curiosity soon
revealed to me that Nigerian women's organizations were beehives
of activity. Popular perception, however, informed me that this energy was expended on trivia. I begged to differ and have been differing ever since.

My instinct to differ derived, again, from my recollections of my
mother. I had never known her to be frivolous, nor indeed had I
known any frivolous women. My aunties and cousins, schoolmates,
fellow youth corpers, university and work colleagues had all taken
themselves very seriously in whatever they did. Sure, most liked to
dress nicely, but I knew from experience that it took very hard work
to look nice—real discipline and grooming, certainly more than I
cared for. I may not have enjoyed all their topics of discussions
because of ideological differences, but I knew that even what is
termed malicious gossip had its social value. The basic truth was that
I respected myself, I respected human beings; I respected human
beings of the same gender, and that was going to be the basis of my
interrogations. If you respect yourself and your people, you operate
from the premise that there is logic and sense, rhyme and reason in
what they do, even if you disagree with it. That is why, in addition to
being a feminist, I am a nationalist both politically and culturally.
My vague humanism which has been with me since childhood has
also evolved into a belief that if the means of production are socially well-organized, it would be easier to cater to the needs of all people rather than be plagued by the glaring inequalities which require
so much energy to sustain. My training in the natural and social sciences equipped me with skills of objective assessment, invaluable
tools that have served me well in my life, work, and writing. Thus it

was that I was able to discern that, in general, despite the seeming cacophonic multiplicity of women's organizations and their activities, there was direction and commonality of purpose.

MUSINGS ON THEORY

As several writers have pointed out, Nigerian women—and indeed most African women —have been known to form organizations from time immemorial. Substantial and well- known research has been done on women's organizations of the precolonial, colonial, and early independence periods.[1] Some work is going on about current activities of Nigerian women. Some of these that have come my way subscribe to some fashionable trends and viewpoints that concern me.[2] I will summarize a few. One such viewpoint is to compare modern Nigerian women unfavorably with their traditional forebears, in terms of their abilities or success in achieving change. Modern Nigerian women are accused of subscribing to the forces that disunite the country—ethnicity, language, and religion.[3] There is also the oft-repeated allegation that elite women who usually feature in the forefront of the better-known women's organizations have pursued their narrow class interests and have "failed" or "neglected" the masses of impoverished women who form the bulk of Nigeria's womanhood. The corollary, of course, is that elite women living in the lap of urban luxury cannot identify with the suffering rural women, and thus their participation in programs supposedly designed to assist poor women are for show and the appropriation of resources. Other writers exhort modernized elite women to commit class suicide and develop strategic linkages to effectively mobilize the masses for development. While some aspects of such arguments may have some merit, I disagree fundamentally with the notion of a dichotomy between traditional and modern women, or between urban and rural women, or even between elite women and women of the laboring classes. I hold the view that the different categories represent a continuum across time and space and the economy, and that there is a dialectical relationship which can be utilized for the good of all.

Certainly theories of rural-urban dichotomy do not explain my personal experience and knowledge of a Nigeria in which my urban-based parents and relatives spend three- quarters of their lives hammering out schemes to ensure some item of development, be this a school or a hospital to be built or located in their rural towns and villages. Neither do modernization theories explain the origins, evolution, reconstitution, emergence, and operations of the myriad of women's organizations in modern Nigeria. Traditional class analyses do not account for the sisterhood shared by the tasks that bind, nor the commonalities of shared discrimination based solely on gender.

The notion that urban life in a developing economy automatically connotes luxury is a laughable myth easily exploded by any Nigerian urbanite who examines her real existence. Rural women may have to walk long distances to fetch water with pots on their heads, but at least it is a regular routine. Urban women have to cope with the emotional stress of irregular water supply and *still* have to roam around in search of it. The majority still have to carry containers on their heads, while the so-called elite ones with their Mercedes and BMWs find to their chagrin that their fancy cars have rusted through with the constant spills of water from jerrycans they have had to lug about. The same goes for food, cooking fuel, and electricity. Of course, urban women can appreciate the need for rural development, agricultural mechanization, health clinics, wells, and motorable roads. After all, where do the majority of their mothers, aunties, and cousins live? Of course they would like markets cleaned up so they can shop in salubrious surroundings and cooperatives formed if this means they can buy foodstuff cheap. In short, the fashionable theories do not account for the reason urban and rural women have to and do invest in each other.

Similarly, existing economic theories do not explain the nature of women's financial investments in property such as cloth, jewelry, and crockery. Instead these are mocked as examples of compulsive greed or meaningless conspicuous consumption. Likewise, popular models of social psychology cannot accommodate the fact that a woman's economic status cannot be judged by her dress, and in fact, insult the poorer classes of women by expecting them to dress poor. That has never been the African (or at least Nigerian) way, because avant-gardism and fashion aesthetics have never been the exclusive preserve of a privileged class (as is the case in the West, for example). Observers of public functions equate fancy dressing with elitism and wealth. What indeed is quite incredible is the dysfunction in analysis. That the *producers* of exotica such as handwoven cloth would not be expected to have some to wear on important occasions is an amazing flight of rational thinking. The fact that a woman is poor does not mean that she will look poor simply to satisfy some social scientist's presumptions.

Some theories of feminism require a running battle with men.

Any form of compromise is regarded as an acceptance of patriarchy. One of the most significant arenas in which the struggle for gender democracy takes place is the family, particularly the marriage institution. The dominant thinking among Nigerian women is that they are committed to the institution of the family and certainly do not want to have to do without their men. They simply do not want to be mistreated and so are interested in working out guidelines that protect women and eradicate discrimination.

I have come to understand and recognize that a basic tenet of Nigerian and perhaps African feminism is that it is integrationist rather than separatist. In terms of tactics and style, it has utilized negotiation, confrontation, compromise, building on steady gains, advocating the twin paths of merit and quotas. In many cases the style may be considered reformist. The eventual achievements have been revolutionary. In real life, revolutions are not single unilinear explosions, they are continuous multifaceted dimensions of life. I am urban born and bred. By virtue of my inherited status, educational level attained, employment and lifestyle, I belong to the petty bourgeoisie. So what? What does that mean? Does it mean that my life is not part of Nigeria's history? I exist, therefore I am. Simple. I am not a theoretician. However, I hope in the subsequent account of my experiences to suggest that any objective assessment of the modern women's movement in Nigeria has to be based on its own realities, and not that of the past or of other countries or *a priori* assumptions.

THE NATIONAL COUNCIL OF WOMEN'S SOCIETIES (NCWS)

As mentioned earlier, my journalistic coverage of the National Council of Women's Societies (NCWS) was my first contact with a formal women's organization.[4] The national President of the Council then (1980), Mrs. Ifeyinwa Nzeako, was a lawyer. She was pretty, dressed simply, little or no make-up, absolutely professional, extremely articulate. She could easily have been a senior school mate of mine or a young teacher. I also met her then vice-president, Mrs. Hilda Adefarasin, a genteel woman, a nurse I believe, with fine aristocratic features. I also met another active member, Mrs. Emily Imokhuede, who owned an art gallery. She had very pleasant features with a discerning eye. Subsequently, Adefarasin was to head the NCWS for two two-year terms (1984–1988), while Imokhuede took over up to 1992.

I gathered that their concerns at that time were to consolidate the membership of the Council, encourage more and more women's groups to affiliate formally, and make the public aware of its activities. For example, they ran a home for handicapped children and a day-care center in one of the busiest markets in Lagos. They had also been involved in spreading awareness of women's voting rights.[5] I saw them as women who were aware and proud (not conceited) of their personal achievements—academically and professionally. They knew they represented role models and were determined to make full use of their status to uplift the condition of women in any way they could and contribute their quota to the country's development.

At this point I would like to comment briefly on perceptions about the modern Nigerian or even African elite. In precolonial societies, elite status carried the responsibility of *noblesse oblige.* However, in contemporary times, the elite status has been criminalized. This view was first espoused by colonialist socio-political thought, which sought to drive wedges between the elite and other sectors of the society, so as to undermine a potentially united anti-colonial and nationalist front. It has continued to be propagated by neo-colonialist thought and is uncritically re-echoed by many Africanist and African writers. As such, the African elite has been made to feel anxious, illegitimate and apologetic. Its validity depends on the extent to which it can be seen to commit class suicide, rather than its potential to build and inspire. Against this background, female members of the elite who are activists have to choose and select strategies and tactics very carefully. At every stage in Nigeria's history since colonialism, the balance of power or complementarity between the sexes has had to confront its own dilemmas of social, political, and economic change.

These NCWS ladies were aware of the tricky path they trod. As formally educated women, they were subject to accusations of being ignorant of culture. As elites, they were accused of being incapable of relating to the masses. As urbanites, they were supposedly living in the lap of luxury at the expense of rural women. As Lagosians, they were considered too far removed from the realities of the rest of Nigeria. As women whose working environment (unlike that of the traditional women farmers and traders) was not child-friendly and child-tolerant, or as women who opted for monogamy and nuclear families and therefore had lost access to family child-care support, they were easy targets for accusations that they were responsible for child delinquency and crime increase. Sensitive to allegations that women organizing for change are out to overthrow or disrupt the family, one of the major tactics chosen by the NCWS has been to constantly avow its loyalty to the family and acceptance of the structure that posits the man as the head.

However, this has to be understood against the background of a common social philosophy among most Nigerian communities—i. e., that leadership is consensual and not authoritarian. Hence, the accepted family structure is not as undemocratic as many Western or European-influenced prisms of thought perceive it. Regarding men as family heads is not tantamount to viewing women as inferior beings and hapless victims suffocating at the bottom of the totem pole. Rather, the concept posited by the NCWS of women as "necks" reflects the notion of women as essential pivots, controlling direction, without which the man's leadership is useless, empty, and vain.

Hence, Ifeyinwa Nzeako and her generation had good reasons for choosing the notion of support for the family as a framework and focus for action. However, in my mind, this did not and does not mean that they were automatically conservative and submissive to patriarchy. It was simply a frame of reference which had its own potential to be successfully used to mobilize for change and criticize discriminatory policies. For instance, when informed that some state governments had refused to implement the Federal Government's policy of giving housing allowances to women public servants, Nzeako, rather than quarrel about the gender inequality of fringe benefits, issued a statement pointing out that this policy hurt the family, depriving it of the adequate space that could be provided with the benefit of two incomes. The NCWS however did at times succumb to the pressures which made it a self-defensive group of elite women. Not having the confidence that women's issues were legitimate enough to justify a celebration of International Women's Day, it recommended to the government, in 1983, that the name of the day be changed to Family Day. It took five years of efforts by a new generation of non-apologetic radical feminists to reverse this decision. The compromise was, of course, Nigerian style. A separate day was selected to venerate the Family and in 1988 Women's Day was returned to Nigerian Women.

BIAWAZO AND CONCERNED WOMEN

Women living in megalopolises like Lagos are often criticized for being ignorant of what happens in other parts of Nigeria. What is hardly brought out is that the very cosmopolitanism of a large city has made many urban women leaders aware of the need for unity among Nigerians. This was in fact one of the rationales the NCWS had for constantly attempting to expand its membership and encourage other women's groups to affiliate with it. It appeared to some that the NCWS was not active enough in this regard, and a new group, *BIAWAZO*, emerged in mid 1980 to address this issue specifically. I became aware of this cosmopolitan drive for national unity when, at a memorial service for my late mother, an old friend of hers who had last seen me as a little girl turned up. A veteran journalist and former grassroots politician in the first Republic, she pounced on me and insisted I got involved in the formation of a new women's group. Its purpose was to bring women of all ethnic groups and social classes together for the common good. Its founding members formulated the name *Biawazo* from the words meaning "come," in Ibo *(bia)*, Yoruba *(wa)*, and Hausa *(zo)* —Nigeria's three most widely spoken languages. BIAWAZO's early meetings were held at the residence of Lady Onikan Abayomi, a veteran nationalist politician from the pre-independence era, and founder of Nigeria's first woman's political party.

Lady Abayomi was to host the formation of another group I became aware of, a year or so later. There had been some crisis (I forget what now) and a large number of ladies had congregated at her place to decide what they should do about it. They proceeded to form an association which they decided to call "Concerned Women," because as several individuals adamantly insisted, unlike many women in existing organizations (by implication, the NCWS), they were concerned about what was happening in the country. These ladies were mostly elite, middle-class women, professionals, teachers, market women, representatives of religious bodies and so on. Their average age ranged from about 30 to 55. Of course, by then Lady Abayomi was in her eighties and a few of her age-mates were still active with her in this business of forming associations for various reasons.

What was also interesting to note was that the NCWS always sent representatives to these founding meetings, keeping track of new associations, informing them about the NCWS, and inviting them to affiliate. Since the prime *raison d'être* of these groups was to accomplish tasks the Council had not been able to, several of their members would frequently express the wish to distance themselves from the Council and pursue their goals untrammeled. This inevitably led to debates about duplicating efforts, working together, speaking with one voice, independence of action, and so on and so forth.

From what I can discern in a decade of close observation, the NCWS has had to work hard to convince women's groups around Nigeria to work within an umbrella organization. It has had to learn to accommodate the diverse and sometimes competing needs and desires, aims, objectives, and class interests of women across the country. Many of its leaders who came from a background of community service and philanthropic social welfarism found themselves faced with an unprecedented avalanche of widely differing ideological perspectives thrown up by the surging changes taking place at the social, economic, educational, communication, and infrastructural levels in the three decades since independence. NCWS has never had the luxury of taking its self-declared leadership (or rather spokeswomanship) of Nigerian women for granted. On those occasions that it does not demonstrate a capacity to be truly representative or relevant, it has been effectively bypassed by even its own affiliates. It would seem, therefore, that the generality of Nigerian women prefer an arrangement that allows for independence of thought and action, and at the same time, have available to them channels for unity of purpose and action whenever necessary. Like many other interests in Nigeria, a balance is constantly being negotiated between fissiparous tendencies which dissipate energies, and over-streamlining which can lead to stagnation and rigidity.

The National Council of Women's Societies faced its greatest challenges in the 1980s. First, in 1982, an ideologically radical feminist group called Women in Nigeria (WIN) emerged, and has managed for twelve years to pursue an independent line of action which has pushed the struggle for women's equality to greater heights. A serious religious challenge came in the mid-1980s from the Federation of Muslim Women Associations of Nigeria (FOMWAN), which also conspicuously refrained from affiliating with the Council. By the late 1980s, women from the northern parts of the country had become quite vociferous about inserting their own agendas and concerns into NCWS mainstream thought and action, and by 1993, for the first time in the Council's history, the National President is a northern-based northerner, Alhaja Laila Dogonyaro, a veteran activist and politician. She was succeeded in 1995 by another northerner, this time a Christian from a minority ethnic group, Mrs

Amina Sambo. In the meantime rural and local government women's groups have continued to use their own initiatives in pursuing their own goals, quite independently of any umbrella or even conscientizing vanguard.

As a career journalist and (later) free-lance writer, my primary responsibility has been to report as much as I know about what is going on. As a feminist, I had a duty to contribute to the process of legitimizing women's concerns in mainstream media consciousness. I also had to consciously work to combat pervading negative images of women that are bandied about. As a professional, I had to do this as objectively as possible, regardless of my own personal opinions and ideologies. As a nationalist Nigerian concerned with unity and progress, I have striven to provide information, promote understanding where differences exist, and facilitate consensus rather than exacerbate conflict.

THE NIGERIAN ASSOCIATION OF MEDIA WOMEN (NAMW)

In June, 1981, the Nigerian Association of Media Women (NAMW) was established. Its numerous objectives included breaking out of the "pots, pans and panties" syndrome that women journalists had been confined to, advocating for professional development in terms of training opportunities and promotions, combating discrimination in the work-place, and correcting negative images of women by and in the media. The association opted to affiliate with the NCWS from the onset.

Prior to the founding conference, I had felt isolated professionally, since at that time there were only four of us women in the editorial department of NAN, one in each section —Features, Reportorial, News Desk, and Library. I had since my marriage transferred from Lagos to the branch office in Ilorin, where even though I had the status of being the Head, and my male colleagues were very collegial, I still missed female company. The founding conference was an invigorating experience, as one was exposed to media women of all professional disciplines, managerial levels, generations, and outlooks. Ideas generated in the course of my personal ruminations found vindication in the chorus of shared experiences, and I was both titillated to meet with some who shared my feminist views and gratified to know that some of my perspectives merited appreciation and approval by some senior and more experienced colleagues. There were inevitable disagreements and ideological battles, but above all, I learned a great deal. There was so much I had been ignorant about, and the conference enhanced my professionalism and catalyzed the expansion of my knowledge base.

Eventually I was given the task of founding a chapter of NAMW in Kwara State, where I lived. The prospect of recruiting fellow women into a professionally activist organization was challenging. Tentatively, I visited the various media houses in Ilorin and made my sales pitch. I was encouraged by the positive response of my fellow women, most of whom I had never met before. A few became very active and formed the core. Within months, in May 1982, we elected an executive and launched the Kwara Chapter. The ceremony was presided over by the Lagos-based National President, Mrs. Eno Irukwu, a veteran broadcaster and (at the time) a deputy director with the Federal Radio Corporation of Nigeria (FRCN).

Most of us were middle-level professionals—journalists, producers, newscasters, public relations officers. About half of us were married with children, the rest were single. Being in Ilorin, a medium sized city, we acquired a visibility and salience which would have been drowned in a megapolis like Lagos. We established linkages with all the women's groups we could, in particular the local branch of the NCWS, the Kwara Women's Association, the newly established groups like the Women's Wing of the Nigerian Labour Congress (NLC), and Women in Nigeria (WIN). We also maintained contact with prominent women in education and the public service, and with women members and executives of related organizations such as the Nigerian Institute of Public Relations (NIPR).

The reaction of male colleagues was a mixture of collegiality, amusement and suspicion. Top managers, such as the General Manager of Radio Kwara, Alhaji R. K. Yusuf, and the editor of the *Nigerian Herald*, Alhaji Sule Raji, were very supportive. The latter welcomed the coming-of-age of media women and suggested a few areas he thought we should address. Some male colleagues questioned the rationale of what they considered a separatist movement splintering the professional ranks for unnecessary gender reasons. Others teased us, reiterating that the terms "newsmen" or "gentlemen of the press" were the only acceptable generic terms for members of our profession, ridiculing the notion of media *women*.

These arguments hardly ever got acrimonious, and as long as we got adequate press coverage for our activities, we did not mind. We organized seminars, fashion and cultural exhibitions featuring works by women, patronized women photographers, and eventually started a cyclostyled newsletter called *Kwara Women's Voice*. In it we compiled news reports of the women's activities we knew about, conducted interviews with prominent women in the state, politicians, labor leaders, officers of professional organizations and so on. We wrote commentaries, reviews, and poetry. Then, in news-agency style, we issued the newsletter to the mainstream media. They in turn published what they considered newsworthy, with the result that there was a marked increase in publicity on and awareness of women's activities. NCWS was very appreciative of the publicity and was particularly impressed with our supportive role (like the donation from our sale of stickers) during the celebration of its 25th anniversary in 1983.

In our bid to remain socially relevant, we launched in 1984 our own local chapter of the government's program of the "War Against Indiscipline" and used the occasion to link up with children, some of whom performed plays on the theme of discipline. During the 1985 national debate on the IMF Loan, the Kwara chapter of the NAMW hosted a forum attended by a wide variety of women's groups, including Women in Banking, which provided us with useful insights into how foreign exchange manipulations were ruining the economy. Needless to say, we joined the rest of the country in issuing a resounding "no" to taking the loan.

All the monies used for our activities came from donations made at fund-raisers, from mostly private sources, membership dues, voluntary contributions from individual members, and sales of our newsletters. We frequently used the hall at the Officers' Mess of the Nigerian Police Force, taking advantage of the generous favorable discounts the police gave as a matter of policy to women's organizations; a philanthropic subsidy based on their perception of women as "poor." We also used the Press Center of the Nigerian Union of Journalists (NUJ), which was located in the main town (as opposed to the Police Mess which was in the Government Reserved Area). This was strategic for two reasons. It meant we maintained organizational links with a trade union to which many of us belonged, thus assuring the mostly male membership of our intention to work *with* and not against them. It was also psychologically more accessible to people—particularly women—with whom we wished to work, but who might otherwise feel too alienated to attend functions in an elitist location.

At the national level, the significance of the NAMW became apparent when in 1987, the wife of the President, Mrs. Maryam Babangida, set up her initial "kitchen cabinet" (the "M Team"), forerunner of the Better Life for Rural Women Committee. This was composed partially of representatives of various women's organizations. NAMW was the only one which had two representatives, both the National President (Mrs. Irukwu) and Secretary (Mrs. Therese Nweke). It was speculated that this representation was because of NAMW's potential to facilitate press coverage. Both went on to be active members of the Better Life Committee. Mrs. Irukwu in particular was very visible in the coordinating role of mistress of ceremonies, in which capacity she constantly exhorted women to participate in national development or politics, attend literacy classes, form cooperatives, or utilize opportunities for credit facilities. She was later appointed to the Nigerian Electoral Commission (NEC).

For various reasons, especially the inability of the national leadership to renew its mandate or hand over to successors, the NAMW declined. A related association, the Nigerian Association of Women Journalists (NAWOJ), was established in 1989 by the NUJ in a partial attempt to fill the vacuum. However, its activities up till 1991, when I left Nigeria, did not seem to me to reflect a professional perspective. It seemed to spend a lot of its energy donating funds to various underprivileged groups such as handicapped children or motherless baby homes, i.e., social welfarist activity. Furthermore, because it is limited to journalists it does not have the umbrella-type appeal the NAMW does, embracing women in all branches of media and communication. Periodically, various state chapters of the NAMW that have experienced a resurgence of interest have seized the initiative to host national conferences of the association. The last time I attended such a meeting was in 1991 in Kaduna. The membership of NAMW had become even more diverse, in keeping with ongoing expansions in the communications industry.

In Kwara State the NAMW also underwent a decline for a number of reasons. Lacking direction from the national body, many members decided to devote more attention to other organizations such as the Nigerian Institute of Public Relations (NIPR), WIN, FOMWAN, or NAWOJ. Still others opted to work within the NUJ, rising to executive positions and helping to make it more sensitive to the needs of women members. Others left town or became more engrossed in domestic matters. There were even some personal problems among members which proved to be distractions.

WOMEN IN NIGERIA (WIN)

In the first quarter of 1982, I received an invitation to attend a conference on Women in Nigeria at Ahmadu Bello University (ABU), Zaria. The convener was Ayesha Imam, a sociology lecturer specializing in media matters, whom I had met at the 1981 founding conference of the NAMW. Indeed, she had been elected a national publicity secretary of the organization. We had noticed that we had a lot in common in terms of feminist and even radical views, but had not seen each other since. If I had found meeting fellow media women exciting, meeting fellow radical and even socialist-oriented feminists was a heady experience. Absolutely exhilarating. I was virtually breathless with anticipation for the three days of the conference. For the first time in my life I was in a group of intellectual women and men, mostly academicians, but many professionals like myself, who were of the radical persuasion. As a postgraduate student at the University of Ibadan in 1978 I had attended an historic conference on "Radical Perspectives on Literature." Thrilling as that had been, the unrealized perspective of women's issues had irked and disappointed me. The ABU conference represented for me, therefore, a definitive advancement of Nigerian radical political thought.

We were able to explore women's issues in theoretical terms, interrogating it in class, nationalist, cultural, and religious frameworks. What was most thrilling was that Nigeria was the centerpiece of our discussions. For once, I was with people who could talk as much as I. I felt like the proverbial "Ugly Duckling" who became a beautiful swan, surrounded by fellow swans delighted to welcome her. With mind soaring, I forayed into as many intellectual frays as I liked. In fact, I came away with my brain so packed with information I thought it would burst. There were innumerable ideological tendencies, vigorous and even acrimonious disagreements, but overall, one view dominated. This was lucidly expressed by Bene Madunagu, a biologist with the University of Calabar and well-known radical political activist. She observed that it had become historically necessary for a movement to emerge that could pose concrete alternatives to the oppression of women in particular, while recognizing that this could not be eliminated without the gaining of control of economic, political, and social affairs by Nigeria's toiling people.[6] It was resolved to form such a movement, which, because of serious doubts about the ability of the NCWS to provide appropriate leadership or support, would not affiliate with the

Council. Again, I was given the responsibility for starting a branch
in Kwara State. This time, I was at a loss as to where to start. With
NAMW, I knew where to find media women (that was easy, they were
in the media). Where on earth did one find radical women? Where
could one host a meeting?

With my media connections, I sent out public announcements.
My carefully crafted words did not attract much of a crowd, but right
on cue a representative of the NCWS arrived. I was in a dilemma.
In Zaria, the NCWS was projected as a bourgeois, elitist, conservative group, but did the ladies I knew in Ilorin fit this image? One of
my first self- imposed tasks as feminist, journalist, and researcher
had been to interview the president of the Kwara Branch of the
NCWS, Chief (Mrs.) Ayo Bello. I had been impressed with her pio-
neering spirit, and her account of women's activities and achievements in Kwara State. For example, the Kwara Women's Association
had raised money to donate a block to the Government Maternity
in Ilorin. They had begged from door to door of business estab-
lishments, plaited hair, and danced in the streets. What did "elitist"
and "bourgeois" *mean* in this case? And the lady standing patiently
in front of me, old enough to be my auntie if not my mother? A
caterer with the then Kwara College of Technology (now Kwara
Polytechnic), she was asking me politely about the meeting I had
convened. I made up my mind. Stereotypes did not matter here.
Here was a fellow woman in the women's movement. The least I
could do was to provide information. So I told her all I knew. I even
told her that WIN specifically did not want to affiliate with the
NCWS because of serious ideological differences. The most current
disagreement at that time was over the call for support of the government's austerity measures, made by Mrs. Beatrice Ekwueme, wife
of the Vice-President, and Matron of the Council. She had actually urged women to dissuade their husbands from striking against
the measures, which were expected to cause economic hardships.
The second was the NCWS proposal to rename Women's Day
(March 8) Family Day, a move WIN disagreed with. The perspectives I raised seemed to be provoking some thought. She expressed
the opinion that some issues probably required more discussion,
and observed that many decisions were taken in Lagos and then
conveyed to the branch offices. We parted. Her name was Chief
(Mrs.) Teresa Akobe-Ajibolu. She was later to serve as state secretary and from 1986 to 1990 as state president of the NCWS.

Eventually, I met a lady lecturing in Languages at the University
of Ilorin, Ms. Yetunde Laniran. She had heard about WIN and want-

ed to join. She was the ideal partner I needed. We were soon joined by a fellow member of the NAMW, Ms. Ladi Abdulazeez, a features journalist and arts critic with the *Herald*. With their vigor and connections a viable and virile branch was soon on its way. I say virile deliberately. A sizable proportion of our membership was male!

Male membership of WIN has often been a source of curiosity. Even though the philosophical tendencies of Nigerian feminism have been integrationist, the vast majority of women's movements have been and are all-female, and have run courses separate from and parallel to their male counterparts. Male involvement in such cases is usually limited to support from the sidelines. One of the reasons for WIN's uniqueness lies in the fact that it is primarily a women-oriented group rather than a female one. While other female activist associations may have evolved to a point of being concerned with broader social issues, WIN has from its inception been involved with the entire spectrum of national matters while paying particular attention to women's concerns. Its holistic perspective enables it to accommodate anyone who is interested in agendas that ensure equitable treatment of women. Some men are concerned about their mothers, sisters, wives, and daughters, either personally or politically. WIN provides them with a forum for thought and action. In terms of the ramifications of Nigerian feminist ideology, the presence of men in WIN encourages dialogue which enables both sexes to see the other's point of view, and clear up a lot of misconceptions and preconceptions on both sides. At the practical level, having men as allies in a male-dominated world has been found to be an excellent strategy for advancing the cause of women's liberation. Over the twelve years of WIN's existence, careful thought has been given and deliberate action has been taken to avoid or minimize the potential twin problems of male domination of WIN and exploitation of male footsoldiers by the women.

In 1984, I drove with Yetunde to Port Harcourt in Rivers State to attend the WIN Annual General Meeting on Education. It is pertinent to comment on the evolution of Nigeria's infrastructure at that time. Convoluted as it may have seemed, the various National Development Plans were being implemented, especially with regards to roads. Thus it was possible by 1984 for me, a woman, to drive virtually the length and breadth of Nigeria in my Subaru hatchback. Of course I was not alone in this. Even when using public transportation, the extensive linkages by road, rail, and air made it possible for us, modern professionals operating a five-day work-week, to hastily attend meetings all over the country. This was a communications revolution in Nigeria's socio-economic history, which has more ramifications than can be discussed here. Suffice it to say that it greatly facilitated the pan-Nigerianization of social, political, and professional activism.

In Port Harcourt, I was elected National Publicity Secretary, while Yetunde was elected Kwara Branch Coordinator. We boldly contested with other branches to host the 1985 Conference. It was on a theme I had suggested—"Women in Rural Areas." Since 1982, I had joined the Agricultural & Rural Management Training Institute (ARMTI) as the Public & Staff Relations Officer. In the course of my duties, I had been exposed to discussions on women and agricultural matters, and felt that WIN could effectively address this issue in all its ramifications. Many members had come to this conclusion independently, and the topic was chosen. Indeed, the recommendations emanating from this conference, which were presented to the nation's First Lady, are believed to be the genesis of the "Better Life Program for Rural Dwellers," even though WIN has criticized what it considers to be the negative aspects of the program.[7]

I soon found out that holding a national post was no joke. As the local chairperson of NAMW, or even state coordinator for WIN, I had some control over the demands on my time. Now I was swept up in a whirlwind of action. Ayesha Imam, the National Coordinating Secretary, was a veritable tornado of memos, instructions, and reports. Altine Muhammed, a lecturer of Architecture in ABU, was the epitome of guillotine-like efficiency. Hannatu Omole, a hospital matron in Zaria, was crisp and business-like as Financial Secretary. The Membership Secretary, Arlene Enabulele, a researcher with the Center for Social, Cultural & Environmental Research (CENSCER), Benin, was cool and critical.

I should comment briefly about WIN's leadership structure. We eschewed the traditional or conventional structure that vested one position, such as the president or chairperson, with overwhelming power and responsibility, and opted for collective leadership, which was replicated at the state-branch and chapter levels. The names of the posts reflected areas of prime but not sole responsibility. Efforts were made to ensure that executive members came from a variety of states to make for genuine nationwide representativeness. The fact that any executive member was accorded the right to speak on behalf of the organization enabled swift and effective responses in different parts of the country. It also meant that WIN had to be sure that its members were sufficiently grounded in its philosophy to handle positively the responsibility of diffused power. This called for continuous education and conscientization through a balance between decentralization and centralization. The supreme decision-making body was the Annual General Meeting (AGM) of all members, while the National Coordinating Council, comprising the National Executive Committee and the coordinators of all state branches, was to meet quarterly. The National Executive Committee served as the nerve center, meeting as often as eight to twelve times a year.

The 1984-86 executive had three members living in Zaria, Kaduna State, in the north central part of Nigeria, one member in Benin, Bendel State, in the mid-west, and in Ilorin, Kwara State, in the western middle belt region, who were able to develop communication infrastructure across hundreds of miles. If I was not being hauled off somewhere, I was hosting meetings under siege-like conditions. There are no words to describe the intensity and urgency of WIN meetings. In our attempts to be thorough, to be democratic, to make sure everyone knew what everyone was doing, to ensure that no one was hijacking the organization for personal or career reasons, to jealously guard our constantly challenged freedom from compromise, we had to make elaborate reports and discuss extensively. Suddenly I was inundated with information and required to express an opinion about the group's finances, auditors' reports, publishing contracts, investigations by the National Security Organization (NSO), cross-activities with other progressive groups, details of what was happening in each state branch, both with WIN members and other women's groups.

In my capacity as publicity secretary, I was confronted with the responsibility of having to be up-to-date with government pronouncements and current developments of all sectors of society, in order to assess their impact on women and to issue virtual running commentary on behalf of the organization. Most importantly, I had to come to terms with the fact that, with my name on communiqués, I had to avoid romantic knee-jerk anti- governmental adventurism. So I had to be absolutely sure of my facts and learned to craft statements which used language firm and focused enough to convey our seriousness, yet without abusing the subject or providing an opening for red-herring attacks.

The story and achievements of WIN belong elsewhere.[8] Suffice it to say that WIN contributed immensely to the conscientization of women (and men) in modern Nigeria. Many of the issues it has addressed, such as education, rural development, "Women's Day," and political representation, have received some attention from the government and its agencies. WIN's fearless, unwavering condemnation of anti-women and anti-people policies, its championing of popular causes, and solidarity with the progressive forces, have made it an indelible part of Nigeria's history. Its publications represent some of the most concentrated collections of modern Nigerian radical, nationalist, feminist thought. I am proud to have been able to be a tiny part of this.

By this time my husband was studying in the U. S. A. and I was mother of two small children whom I frequently had to drag about with me on my travels. My job was hectic and involved a lot of traveling. Combining a career, motherhood, single-handedly running a household of relations and in-laws, as well as activism required a lot of adrenaline. As I look back, I can see that I thrived only by the grace of God. Emotionally, I enjoyed the support of my husband, who not only had encouraged my intellectual pursuits, but understood the inevitability of my activism in feminist affairs.

STRADDLING THE FENCE

At the end of 1984, at the annual general meeting of the Kwara Branch of the NCWS, I had, unbeknownst to me, been selected in abstensia to be the Newsletter Editor. This was in recognition for the role I had played as a free-lance journalist and member of NAMW in publicizing their activities. Thus, the beginning of 1985 saw me in the ironic position of holding executive positions in two organizations that were supposed to be at loggerheads. On a personal level, I did not find it a contradiction, as I could locate myself at the convergence of their respective tangential paths. Since neither was an underground movement, there were no secrets to spy about. All I needed to do was to don my different hats, Nyerere style,[9] at appropriate times.

My participation in meetings of the NCWS (where occasionally I doubled as publicity secretary, because the lady holding that post that year was ailing) enabled me to see how women of a different generation and clime operated. Their self-identities had less to do with class than with their occupations, areas of origin, religion, and commonalities of interests as women, mothers, and wives. Ideologically they, like the national body, subscribed to the family-oriented framework of analysis, with its corollaries of security, peace, and progress. This led them to take action guided by perspectives that represented vestiges of traditional Nigerian political thought which I had not known much about. For instance, during the 1985 confrontation between the Nigerian Medical Association (NMA) and the Buhari military regime, officials and members of the University of Ilorin branch of the Academic Staff Union of Universities (ASUU) who wished to express solidarity with the NMA were detained by the NSO. In the characteristic approach of Nigerian civil activism, the local ASUU vice-president launched an appeal to all people and organizations, urging women and women's groups to intervene as "mothers," while traditional and religious leaders on the other hand, were expected to act as "fathers."

Chief (Mrs.) Ayo Bello summoned an emergency meeting of the NCWS to discuss the situation and plan of action. Many of the ladies, from organizations such as the Sewing Women's Association, Domestic Science Association, Muslim Women's Association, Market Women's Association, Offa Women's Development Association, and so on and so forth, were initially not fully aware of the details, which I helped to outline for them. After deliberations, they girded their wrappers anew and adjusted their headties, and voiced the following opinion: "Our task as mothers is to ensure that there is peace, and prevent any outbreak of violence. Kwara State, in particular, is well known for being peaceful. Even during the civil war, people ran here seeking haven. So far, this matter has not erupted into violence elsewhere, and we certainly won't allow it to start here." (This was in apparent reference to the belief that since the tough no. 2 man in the regime, Major-General Tunde Idiagbon, hailed from Kwara, the local ASUU's actions were likely to be interpreted as "bearding the lion in its den," which had the potential of attracting severe repercussions from the state, provoking a civil strife). They continued, " if these lecturers continue to be detained, ASUU will go on strike. That means that our childre who are university students will suffer. All the fees we have paid will be wasted. This matter must be resolved peacefully. The government should release the lecturers, and pay the doctors what they want—they deserve it. They (the NMA and ASUU), in turn, should apologize to the government. One should not quarrel with one's father, and the government is our father." They then appointed delegates to convey their recommendations to the Kwara State Governor, and mandated me to inform the media. There was no doubt that their intervention contributed to the release of the lecturers a couple of days later, and ASUU included the NCWS in its subsequent "thank you" tour.

CONCLUSION

The above represents a small part of my experience within the Nigerian women's movement during the 1980s. While it does not begin to approximate the myriad variety and synergy of women's activities in Nigeria, it gives some insight into some of the operating options of frameworks for thought and action. Fundamentally it challenges a popular notion that modern Nigerian women are self-centered or only pursue narrow class or ethnic interests. Such centrifugal notions ignore the political, economic, and infrastructural developments that have become independent and weighty centripetal forces catalyzing a pan-Nigerianization of hitherto unimagined dimensions.

Social groups and development unions have continued to proliferate, while the emergence of activist professional associations of media women, women lawyers, accountants, etc., or ideologically radical feminists represent the results of Nigeria's educational investments of a quarter of a century. The literacy rate for adult Nigerian women, for instance, has leaped from 6% in 1981[10] to 39.5%.[11] This can have nothing short of a revolutionary impact on the way women think of or perceive themselves. The convoluted, continuous evolution, with all its contradictions and challenges from without and within umbrella groups, reflects the growth of the women's movement in a pan-Nigerian direction. This has been greatly enhanced by the intervention of the government and its agencies. Conventional theories that preach against government involvement in civil society on the grounds that it automatically undermines, weakens, and corrupts, do not explain the dynamics of struggle, change, and progress in a country like Nigeria. People do not struggle for the joy of struggling in perpetuity. For Nigerian women the slogan is not "The struggle continues!" but rather "The struggle must achieve results!"

One of the achievements of modern Nigerian women has been to make their governments, whether civilian or military, more sensitive to women's needs. Any government policy that promotes women's interests has been as a result of unrelenting agitation from all classes and interests of women who have used different styles of mobilization. The proliferation of women's agencies is a visible testimony to their efforts.

Now, through the National Women's Commission, women's groups should be getting regular subventions which would enable them function without the constant humiliation of begging for funds. The Better Life for Rural Women Program is able to put tax-payers' resources at the disposal of the women who bear the brunt of food production for the country. The bulk of the credit facilities provided by the People's Bank has gone to women. It is the height of romanticism to imagine that even collectively women would be able to mobilize that scale of resources on their own. It is even exploitative to expect them to. What is a government for if it does not serve its people? If these agencies are found wanting by virtue of inefficiency, misdirection, or misappropriation of resources, then the struggle is to put them on the right track.

The struggle is by no means over. According to Fanon, each generation must determine its role and play it. Nigerian women played their roles in the pre-colonial period. They contributed their energy to the anti-colonial, nationalist, and independence struggles. With respect to the primary challenge of the post-independence era—nation building—against a background of neo-colonialism, and even re-colonization, modern Nigerian women have carried the baton, have risen to the task, and are running their own race.

I know...I am one of them.

NOTES

1. Nina E. Mba, *Nigerian Women Mobilized: Women's Political Activity in Southern Nigeria, 1900–1965* (Berkeley: Institute of International Studies, University of California, 1982); Judith Van Allen, "'Sitting on a Man': Colonialism and the Lost Political Institutions of Igbo Women," *Canadian Journal of African Studies*, 6.2(1972): 165-181; P. K. Uchendu, *The Role of Nigerian Women in Politics, Past and Present* (Enugu: Fourth Dimension Publishing Co., 1993).
2. Dennis A. Itavyar and Stella N. Obiajunwa, *The State and Women in Nigeria* (Jos: Jos University Press Limited, 1992); O. I. Aina, "Mobilizing Nigerian Women for National Development: The Role of the Female Elites," *African Economic History* 21(1993): 1-20; several unpublished articles, and numerous expressed opinions.
3. Aina, p. 17
4. For an account of the formation of the NCWS, see Mba 1982, pp. 187-192.
5. Ifeyinwa Elumeze, "Women's Organizations: Just Lace and Grace?" *NAN Features Bulletin*, 1980.
6. Bene E. Madunagu, "Contemporary Positions and Experiences of Women," *Women in Nigeria Today* (London: Zed Books, 1985), pp. 136-137.
7. Ayesha Imam, "The Dynamics of WINing: An Analysis of Women in Nigeria," *Women in Nigeria: The First Ten Years*, Elsbeth Robson, ed. (Zaria: WIN, 1993), pp. 30 and 36.

8. Elsbeth Robson, ed., *Women in Nigeria: The First Ten Years* (Zaria: WIN, 1993).
9. In 1974, President Julius Nyerere of Tanzania attracted some controversy when he visited Jamaica in his dual capacity as head of state and political party leader.
10. Ifeyinwa Iweriebor, "The Role of Nigerian Women in National Development since Independence," in *NIigeria—The First 25 Years*, Uma Eleazu ed. (Lagos: Infodata Ltd.; Ibadan: Heinemann, 1988), p. 329.
11. General Sani Abacha (Nigerian Head of State), quoted in "Government Unfolds Plans to Boost Literacy Levels," *The Guardian*, December 16, 1993, p. 5.

WORKS CITED

Abacha, Sani. Quoted in "Government Unfolds Plans to Boost Literacy Levels." *The Guardian*. December 16, 1993.

Aina, Olabisi I. "Mobilizing Nigerian Women for National Development: The Role of the Female Elites." *African Economic History* 21(1993): 1-20.

Elumeze, Ifeyinwa. "Women's Organizations: Just Lace and Grace?" *NAN Features Bulletin*, 1980.

Imam, Ayesha. "The Dynamics of WINing: An Analysis of Women in Nigeria." In*Women in Nigeria: The First Ten Years*, ed., Elsbeth Robson. Zaria: WIN, 1993: 20-44.

Itavyar, Dennis A. and Stella N. Obiajunwa. *The State and Women in Nigeria.* Jos: Jos University Press, 1992.

Iweriebor, Ifeyinwa."The Role of Nigerian Women in National Development Since Independence." In *Nigeria—The First 25 Years*, ed., Uma Eleazu. Lagos: Infodata Ltd.; Ibadan: Heinemann, 1988: 325-336.

Madunagu, Bene E. "Contemporary Positions and Experiences of Women." In *Women in Nigeria Today*, ed., Editorial Committee. London: Zed Books, 1985: 132-137.

Mba, Nina E. *Nigerian Women Mobilized: Women's Political Activity in Southern Nigeria, 1900–1965.* Berkeley: Institute of International Studies, University of California, 1982.

Robson, Elsbeth, ed. *Women in Nigeria: The First Ten Years.* Zaria: WIN, 1993.

Uchendu, Patrick K. *The Role of Nigerian Women in Politics, Past and Present.* Enugu: Fourth Dimension, 1993.

Van Allen, Judith. "'Sitting on a Man': Colonialism and the Lost Political Institutions of Igbo Women." *Canadian Journal of African Studies* 6.2(1972): 165-181.

ADJUSTMENT AND ASSIMILATION IN TANZANIA: A PERSONAL EXPERIENCE

JAMIILA CUSHNIE-MNYANGA

INTRODUCTION

INVASIONS

IT IS CRYSTAL CLEAR TO PEOPLE OF AFRICAN DESCENT that the *his*-story we learned in schools and were graded upon is wrong. We are even marginalized in the history of our continent. We were taught the *his*-story of people like Francis Drake, David Livingstone, Christopher Columbus, and Marco Polo. The African child born abroad can neither name a king or a queen that is part of Africa's history, nor identify two rivers on the continent. The then colonial master never saw any reason for us to know our history, since he honestly believed that we did not have a history. So when will the black peoples' *our*-story get written? When will reparation be assessed and children of the future given a correct account of their origins? The slave trade and colonialism, inhuman invasions of unimaginable proportions, intervened most viciously to shape the destinies of people of African descent. Of all the innumerable consequences of these collisions, I will bring up for scrutiny the radical changes they made in women's lives in Africa and the diaspora.

WOMEN/DEFEMINIZATION

In the New World, African women were forced to breed new crops of slaves and thereby reduce the expense and danger of crossing the Atlantic. The forced pairing of men and women for reproduction was, in fact, one of the earliest manifestations of sexual harassment. Once the woman showed signs of pregnancy, the liaison between her and the would-be father of the child stopped. In many instances, the man might be sent on loan to other farms or plantations to service other female slaves. Unlike their sisters still on the continent, women slaves in the diaspora never had the chance to create meaningful and lasting relationships. Thus, the separation of men from their families and relationships has its roots in slavery.

Perhaps this is where the course for the Caribbean woman was set. On the one hand, she was to become hard of heart, strong in nature, fearless, no-nonsense, tolerant til provoked, determined, strict, a stickler for principle, willful at times, spiteful with a mouthful of words. On the other hand, she was most loving, jealous, sex object/temptress, loyal, true, and a friend to the end. She embodied all the basics for creating a matrifocal system that continues in much of the islands today. Over the years, a hierarchy began to establish itself. On the one hand, those who aped the master's voice and were very good mimics eventually found a place in the big house. On the other hand, a brigade of the servant class was created: butlers, chefs, nannies, housepersons, bodyguards, valets, yardboys, kitchenhands, and even wet nurses.

Forced mating still went on, with white men forcing themselves on black women. The women had no choice and, in no time, little mulatto children became very much a part of the scenery, thus initiating the hierarchization of different shades of black skin. It is widely believed that this gross interference in the lives of women in the Caribbean has created an indelible pattern in the island whereby women do not grant men the type of respect their African counterparts would give their men.

One good aspect of what we of the diaspora managed to salvage is the determination to carry on our cultural tradition of being strong, and keeping ourselves together in crises. Thus, our matrifocal system is not an accident. It came about as a result of hundreds of years of oppression, silencing of women, and lack of commitment on the part of our menfolk that produced generations of fathers who cared less about their responsibility. Women became mothers and fathers of their children, judges, doctors, talebearers, financial agents; they were everything. Women's self-determination and self- sufficiency made it imperative for them to participate in and even lead the rebellion to gain control of their country in the fight for independence. In spite of centuries of attempts to make us forget or scorn our origins, we grew up questioning everything we have come to know and being cautious of the government in colonial and postcolonial times. It is out of the foregoing background that I became who I am.

BREAKING DOWN THE BARRIERS

SELF

At fifteen, I left the Caribbean to join my mother in the United Kingdom. From the early 1900s to late 1970s, several thousands of my people had made such an exodus in search of a better life. I often feel that in my case it was the onset of the search for identity. In my teenage years, I read avidly about my people's past as slaves. *Roots* (released long after I had read books such as *Seize the Time, Soul on Ice, Black Skin White Mask, Sex and Race, If they Came in the Morning,* and *Things Fall Apart*) had left an indelible impression on my mind; it empowered me to probe more into my past that was distorted in the textbooks I read at school in Jamaica. I tried to educate my mother about these historical distortions, but she did not want to hear of it. She belonged to the class of blacks in the United Kingdom who still believed the tales of Africa we learned in the Caribbean; tales about Africans who lived in trees. "What will you gain by trying to claim relationship with them?" my mother would ask. When I became acquainted with a few Nigerians, Ghanaians, and Sierra Leonians, I discovered that they too knew little about us in the diaspora.

THE JOURNEY

My desire to be independent of the life of the black bourgeoisie lived by my mother led me to get married at seventeen. In fact, the marriage earned me another mother—my mother-in-law! After many years of intense competition between my mother-in-law and myself for the attention of my husband, we all came to the point where he had to make the ultimate choice; he chose his mother over me and our three children. We separated hoping to get back together, but it never happened; we divorced instead. I was ready to start a new life. I told myself that I would go to Africa. I never knew specifically where in Africa I would settle. But I was determined to go and look at the Africa that is chiseled in my head; the one I felt was inside my soul when the Creator first placed my forebears on earth. I had no idea of the exact location in Africa my forebears came from. Should I go from one corner of Africa to another asking kings, elders, and statesmen where I came from? Who will receive us, lost sons and daughters? Who will create my birthright to a specific nation? The first place in Africa I set foot on was Morocco. I thought I would feel automatically at home. Eyebrows were raised at my entry into and exit from places. I never saw a friendly face smile at me. I later learned the meaning of the raised eye-brows: "How dare you, a woman at that, walk about all by yourself in an Islamic state?" Different values, culture, and philosophy! It appeared quite hostile to me. How minimal my Caribbean education was in matters of religion and cultures!

"Whatever does an Islamic state mean?" I asked myself. I later learned about this new religion, Islam. I learned to separate Arabism from the tenets of Islam. I became a Muslim. Although I had been observing, recording, and researching Islam since 1972, it took years before I actually accepted that I wanted no other purpose in my life than to dedicate myself to the belief in one Creator, Allah. I decided to go to Jamaica to tell my folks. This was in 1979. It was hard trying to explain to my mother, father, and siblings that I had accepted Islam. My mother ended all relationship with me. My father said I was old enough to know what was good for me. My grandmother replied that she was currently watching the movie "Roots" on television, and as far as she was concerned, not everything we learned in Jamaica was the truth. I left her with joy in my heart. The day I was leaving she whispered: "Come see my things." The things turned out to be burial clothing, those with which she would be laid in state. She further added: "In our youth, the leaders showed us how to equip ourselves, to avoid knocking on every door in search of a shroud." I was advised to follow this rule of preparedness; she bade me to go in peace with my God.

My grandmother had advised me to remarry because, according to her, all men are not the same. Coming back to the U. K. in 1980 had a new feeling for me. I began to put my life back on track. The first step was to grant custody of my children to their father because he told me that the house was in his name and the law would want me to show how I could support my children in rented accommodations. Gearing myself for a new life, without my children, I decided that I would travel to see the vastness of the world. Instead, I was to be drawn by fate into marriage with a Tanzanian.

LIFE IN TANZANIA

I arrived in Tanzania twenty-two months after my husband had gotten there. Because I had wanted to complete my courses in Journalism, Youth Leadership, and Drama, I did not travel with him when he did. I arrived in the country to find before the first week was over that he had four wives already: one traditional, one that was married in the registry, plus two as concubines! My decision to leave came when I found out that he was a Christian, not a Muslim as he had claimed in the U. K. With no knowledge of Kiswahili, I managed to find a job with the local English-speaking daily paper. I lived in lodgings til I found a room. I wanted to leave, but was this not Africa? I was determined to get a divorce and move to another area. I discovered that if Jamaica is a matrifocal society, Tanzania is 100% patriarchal.

PATRIARCHAL SYSTEM

My petition for a divorce got lost again, after I had filed it more than thrice. The immigration service then began to hassle me with the warning that I could not work in view of the fact that I had a dependent status. I went from courts to lawyers, advisers, and welfare workers—all men—and was given a run-around by everybody. I was exhausted, with neither funds nor job. In a state of desperation, I went up to the Justice Ministry, refused any delaying tactics and went into the Justice Minister's office determined to be heard. I expressed the gravity of my situation and made the following issues clear to him: (a) I had no source of income and according to the law I was a dependent; (b) If I didn't work, how could I exist?; (c) Why was my petition repeatedly removed from my file?; (d) What services were open to women in my case?; and (e) I would not leave without a divorce because I needed to take my life back! I was condescendingly listened to and given special permission to continue in my job. The whole exercise, however, taught me that women in Tanzania were exceptionally vulnerable. I began to probe and discovered that there were not many provisions in the law in the early 1980s that favored women. Taken from a religious point of view, women were also without many of their basic rights. According to Islam, I was entitled to free myself from my marriage. On the basis of such an entitlement, an Islamic organization supported me for a few months.

The local party offices were afraid that my husband would come and make trouble. I found a few women under similar circumstances and this compelled me to begin a one-woman campaign for women's causes. My case eventually got heard. I refused to take any alimony and devoted my time and energy to fighting for the rights of women. In view of the fact that I grew up in a matrifocal society, I had to reorient my thinking if I were to survive in my adoptive home, where politically and culturally everything is seen and valorized from a male perspective.

According to the 1988 census, more than half of the 23 million people living in Tanzania were women. Although equal rights exist in the law, women are still excluded from full participation in the political and economic life of the country. Ninety percent of the country's food consumption is produced locally and predominantly by women. The country depends more on agriculture than on the industrial sector. Women needed to be trained and provided with the appropriate technological skills and equipment in order to increase food production. Women here have a tendency to keep a low profile, be seen and not heard, and this is a big area of concern for me. As a woman living among my people, I know that my duty lies in helping to create a better society for us all, men and women.

LIVING WITH THE PEOPLE

It was not easy finding a job and a place to live in, interact with the people, build community, and also create a platform from which to lobby for change. With the stigma of divorce and being single in a society where even women themselves look down on a spinster, single mother, or divorcée, I joined any women's group that catered to my beliefs. In order to be fully functional, I quickly and seriously learned the Tanzanian culture and national language. I came to respect several aspects of life here and dedicated myself to the task of creating the awareness my sisters needed in order to liberate themselves from cultural constraints. After some time, I secured a good job in addition to freelancing for the media. I soon heard of a group meeting which I attended with a Tanzanian sister who grew up in the United States. Several meetings later, a group of us founded what was to become the Tanzania Media Women's Association (TAMWA), the first of its kind in Tanzania. Our objectives are:

(1) To be the voice of the voiceless through publications.

(2) Promote the development of Third World women through train-

ing, linkages, and lobbying governments.

(3) Provide a forum for the exchange of ideas and technical skills.

(4) Provide consciousness-raising through days of action.

(5) Conduct Research and compile documentation.

We have managed to get most of our activities off the ground. We are very well regarded in the various government ministries. We have managed to acquire and maintain a very efficient office, and have continued to meet our objectives. We are work-oriented and conscientious. It is fortunate that through my efforts to bond in sisterhood with this group, I have been accepted as a militant member who is committed to change.

AWAY FROM URBAN LIFE

My second husband's job made us settle in the northern part of Tanzania. After I had spent all my life in urban areas, the first two years of living in rural Tanzania was exceptionally hard on me. Forced at times to cope with no running water (I had to join the water march to a nearby well), no charcoal or electricity (I had to procure my bundle of contraband fuelwood), I found village life very different and taxing. When the water or the electricity was restored, my immediate problem was over, but what of my sisters for whom this is a way of life?

I rallied and lobbied with these rural, illiterate, and semi-literate villagers for change and liaised with the women leaders to find ways to improve the lot of the people living in our district. My engagement in this area became part of my outreach work for our association, TAMWA. In TAMWA, I don't feel as though I am an outsider; I feel a part of a team. Some are more educated or assertive, it is true, but we all blend as a team.

Because of my background, I am aware that I am invariably the one to adapt to the patriarchal system in Tanzania. I am criticized by many sisters for my views; I am appreciated by several for my attitude. I am baffled and unenthused by the way the majority of sisters are open and up front in discussions regarding male issues, but are not ready to teach their sons the art of understanding women. I am amazed by how little wholesome affection exists among women. I strongly feel that unless African women love each other as we do our work, we as activists will see our work continuously undermined. It is true, however, that we as campaigners for women's rights have moved in leaps and bounds over the past twenty years. Activities at the Nairobi Conference included the tabling of the 1985 *Forward-Looking Strategies* for implementation. One important issue here in Tanzania right now is the mobilization against violence against women and children.

As a black woman from the diaspora, I have been concentrating my efforts on the uplift of rural women. My activism is not limited by geographical boundaries. I feel very strongly for Africa as a whole and want very much to see some effort at educating Africans on the issue of the diaspora, through films, news items, or curricular changes in school to reflect profound knowledge of the black world, not limited to the knowledge of the colonizers as was the case with colonial education.

NORTH-SOUTH RELATIONS

Another concern we here in Tanzania have is the condition under which we are funded by international agencies, particularly in view of the international agencies' interference in the affairs of African NGOs. The international NGOs claim autonomy from their respective countries, but cry foul should we demand the same. Our relationship with these agencies and organizations is one-sided; they come to Africa and carry out their work freely but limit what we can do if we go to their country. We, as activists, have to look at ways to address the issue before the real donor fatigue sets in.

On a personal note, I have remarried. I am sensitive to several marital issues. My husband, a Muslim, is supportive, from an Islamic point of view, of some of the issues— such as women acquiring education and being active in community development—that relate to the emancipation of women.

OVERALL DIASPORA ISSUES

It is most troubling that African states are not harmonious in creating a unified Africa that will make the OAU work better. It is true that the many religious and ethnic conflicts in Africa adversely affect the unity of the continent. We have to work very hard not only for the unity of Africa but also the unity of Africa and the African diaspora. We have to remember that the super powers are super only because they mobilize as one.

My paper is certainly the personal experience of an activist, but it is from real life experiences that we can learn in order to better understand the nature and scope of the work we have to do. I hope that the deliberations at the WAAD conference will include the following resolutions:

(1) To respond to the debt crisis of the Third World through this forum.

(2) To acknowledge via debate the question of reparation and how to contribute to it.

(3) To challenge the dominance of foreign NGOs to the detriment of the autonomy of our own local NGOs.

(5) To empower each other through networking.

(6) To support each other economically.

THE DEVELOPMENT OF A SISTERHOOD IN MEMPHIS, TENNESSEE

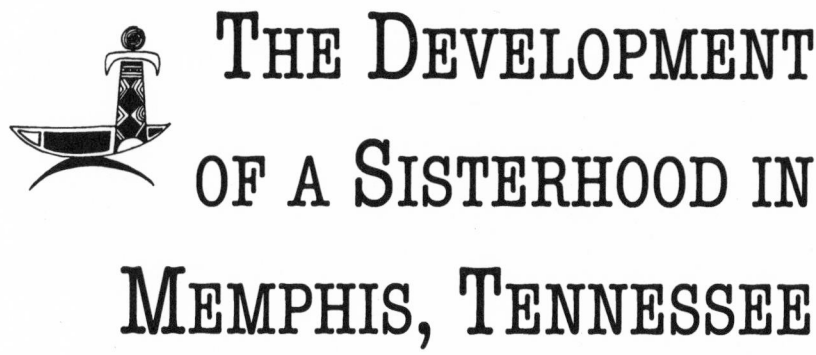

FEMI AJANAKU AND NKECHI AJANAKU

AFTER MARTIN LUTHER KING'S DEATH IN 1968, A GROUP of college students led by a newly graduated law student was formed in Memphis. Reflections on events of the sixties had revealed to these students a need to question not only the lack of civil rights but also the lack of family and community relationships governed by African American needs. With this perspective, they decided to make a commitment to the African American community by using their newly acquired skills and education to sew and distribute *dashiki*-style clothing in the group-owned shop, The Black Arcade. A chartered organization, the Ghetto Development Corporation, was also created to write and define the group's philosophy and to secure funding.

By 1970, these activities expanded to a factory production of African clothes, jewelry, and ceramics in a youth-development program administered with a federal War on Poverty grant. The number of Black Arcade outlets increased and sold these items along with records and books. All participants were urged to wear natural hair styles and African clothes at the work site and to put a part of their salaries into a collective saving fund to ensure continuation after the federal funds were depleted. There was resistance to African culture and economic development creativity from the older, established African American community leadership as well as problems within the core group due to the prevailing negative attitudes and information about Africa. These responses along with internal conflicts split the group into different factions during the subsequent years between 1971 and 1974, thus pointing to a need to focus on the African American family as well as individual psychology.

In 1974, after all the splintered ventures had failed, the first nucleus group of the Ajanaku family emerged as members struggled through developing a healthy process to build more productive relationships which would have to be worked on twenty-four hours a day without interruption by those who did not have an appreciation for searching in African traditions for solutions to our community problems. A need to have a social family where all members shared the same last name and principles prompted a brother from Nigeria to propose the name Ajanaku to the group that would capture a sense of "fighting on for the liberation of African people the world over until victory or death."

Although the unfledged Ajanaku family members had an intellectual awareness that they were making a total flip, there was no placenta to nourish this new growth because old friends, relatives, and former members questioned and criticized these new family relationships. So in 1974, two women, two men, and two children set up residence in a semi-solated area of Durham, North Carolina. Updates with invitations to join this process in Durham were sent to the people who had been involved in Memphis. By the late spring of 1975, the size of the group had more than quadrupled with an internal administrative process governing the group as a social family and by mid-summer this population had grown to over twenty-five adults and twenty children. That fall the base (headquarters) was moved back to Memphis.

The Sisterhood evolved as part of this social family, first as a physical section in the living quarters and then as a psychological sanctuary where women could develop a value for their minds and creative potential in order to influence the external society as well as the internal group. When the laws of the Ajanaku family were written in the summer of 1975, the Sisterhood was recognized as one of the three main divisions of the family including the Brotherhood and the Childrenhood. In compliance with the laws, women who joined the family had to make a commitment to the social family and Sisterhood laws. This paper examines from an African feminist sociological perspective the relationships and actions of various members of the Sisterhood from 1975 to 1985.

AFRICAN FEMINIST THEORY

Over the last two decades, African American feminists have discussed the need for an appropriate framework and methodology to address the complexity of activism within the African American sisterhood (Gloria Hull, et al., 1982; bell hooks, 1989; Vivian Gordon, 1987). Other scholars (Deborah King, 1987 and 1989; Patricia Hill Collins, 1989 and 1990) have developed a sociological theoretical framework that addresses specific concepts and assumptions based on explanatory models of the African American experience. Even in organizational participation, African American women's ideological foundations are examined as an interpretation, a response, and a challenge to multiple realities of ethnicity, class, and gender oppression. Additionally, King and Collins both assert that the African American feminist scholar has to meet the challenge to locate and validate the core issues in the activism of women who are not considered to be intellectuals.

Feminist methodology is employed to make assertions that the African American feminist cannot be intimidated by standards that are barriers to locating obscure voices. According to the emerging dialogue of methodological techniques among African American social scientists that Collins describes as a "distinctive" methodology (Collins, 1990: xiii), the social scientist must take advantage of being an insider and assume the authority to locate the knowledge production sites, and then validate them based on the contours of the research subject's epistemology. An excellent example of this unity of theory and method is Scott's study of African American women's life strategies (Kesho Yvonne Scott, 1991). Her analysis that includes her aunt, the mother of a friend, herself, and her daughters, is an interplay between the researcher's subjective and objective knowledge of her sources.

The authors of this paper were members of the Ajanaku sisterhood during the ten-year period being highlighted, although at present we are marginal participants for various reasons that will be discussed further in the paper. This paper grew out of our recollections, some biographical notes, phone conversations, and personal letters between us and other women. We wish to maintain the anonymity of some uncirculated notes. We also used letters, newspaper clippings, magazine articles, personal minutes of lectures and meetings, programs and announcements, and other mementoes in our personal files.

The following questions helped to shape our recollections of the sisterhood during this time period: How did we internalize the laws? Which activities did we remember the most? What were the strengths and weaknesses of this experiment? How has our time in the Ajanaku family shaped our lives today? We are cognizant of the fact that our immersion in a subjective process of collecting empirical data gives us as observers difficulty in recognizing our setting as a social laboratory with objective measurements. However, we assert that measurable outcomes exist from experiences created and imposed upon each sister by the environment, both physical and social.

AJANAKU FAMILY STRUCTURE

The four components of the family that developed—"administration," "the brotherhood," "the sisterhood" and " the childrenhood"—were guided by the Laws of the Ajanaku family. These laws were written in the summer of 1975 by asking all members, including the children, to write down what laws the group was living by. This was possible because specific roles for man/woman relationships were attributed to gender; whereas men would plan, command, organize, investigate, define, defend, and create, women would initiate, stimulate, criticize, regulate, navigate, and analyze. Individually and collectively, both genders had the responsibility to help educate, procreate, and execute orders. Moreover, principles and values that produced these laws had come into being as a result of daily meetings and discussions of relationships and behavior within the group.

The completed document, titled "The Introductory Laws and Processes of the Ajanaku Family," had sixteen main sections. Section two states that "policy and laws are formulated through the dynamics of the general organizing process—meetings, discussions, analysis, etc. and are FINALIZED and DECIDED by ADMINISTRATION." Administration consisted of the Head of the Family, the General Administrator; Sisterhood Administrator and Brotherhood Administrator. In this hierarchy, a sister held the second highest position with the power to order or direct members to a particular action. One might be ordered to assume a certain posture regarding relations with other family members or go to a particular place to work. The other sections elaborate on how the family is organized; the principles that all members live by, the specific laws for the sisterhood and brotherhood, child protection, and an objective agenda for effecting productive communications between members. This paper focuses on the laws that pertain to the sisterhood.

THE SISTERHOOD

Section four of the Ajanaku laws states that the theme of the family is "Sisterhood is the Key" with the rationale that the sisterhood's internal needs direct and regulate the brotherhood's provision of external security. Section six describes the method of organizing nuclear family units within the larger Ajanaku Family as one to withdraw sisters from "the slave marriage premise of inside winner woman with good legal and legitimate children and the outside woman with illegal and illegitimate bastard children." The intent of this objective was to equalize all women and children in the entire African American family because both legal and illegal relationships created situations that isolated both women and their particular children from each other and cut off the father's full protection and support.

Specific sisterhood laws supported this equality of all women by structuring a polygamous marriage unit with at least two sisters and making all sisters collective mothers of all the children. The process of learning to work past one's upbringing and to accept a new way of personal relationships was a difficult process. This difficulty is articulated by a sister upon entering a marriage unit: "The realization that the man could care for not only you but another woman was a sobering feeling." One got over this feeling of not being singularly special by becoming committed to the growth and development of other sisters. Additionally, Ajanaku men brought women who were attracted to them, physically or mentally, to sisterhood orientation meetings because they could expect to have relationships with only those women who were committed to the sisterhood laws. After marriage had occurred, any sister who had problems was expected to bring them to sisterhood meetings for discussion. The power of the sisterhood in the family is specifically addressed under the administration section of laws which states: "The SISTERHOOD has the FINAL say in ALL political matters affecting the AJANAKU SISTERHOOD." The position of the Queen Mother was created as a symbol of this authority but was not functional until the 1980s.

SISTERHOOD ACTIVITIES

Activities in which sisters were engaged are reviewed in order to show some connections between individual internalization of laws and family roles. These activities are organized under the following themes: educational and intellectual, economic, cultural, personal growth, and recollections.

EDUCATIONAL AND INTELLECTUAL

As an objective arm of the social family, the Ajanaku African American Research Institute provided evidence that there were systematic ways and means to resolve any issue or dilemma. The Research Institute was a part of the chartered association for commercial, cultural, and educational community development. Persons interested in any of these aspects of grassroots community development but not interested in making a total commitment to live within the confines of the laws were considered extended family members. The extended family members and base (nuclear) members both participated in writing position papers and attending meetings and social functions.

The Institute was also the body that wrote and disseminated the data accumulated by the social family members' daily process of analyzing and adjusting behavior and relationships. Specific strategies to program ourselves with positive messages were constantly employed. To counter the negative scripts in our minds, tapes of speeches and music were made in Durham. When Malcolm X's speeches were not playing, the Ojays were singing "Ship Ahoy." Nina Simone's "I Wish I Knew How It Felt To Be Free" was inspirational because it was about freedom and one particular sister was frequently asked to sing this song when the tape was not available. When on the road, in the evenings as we made jewelry for the next day, we would sing our new freedom songs to the people we met. The head of the family wrote a poem, "African Heritage House," about Queen Nzinga that the little sisters would recite on special occasions. The children formed into a group and sang on several occasions and even had a weekly radio show hosted by Nkechi Ajanaku. The favorite song about the Sisterhood was "Dada Sermatema, My Sisters, I Am Talking about Y'all." Queen Mother Washiri Ajanaku wrote a song titled "African Women, See How High They Fly." By 1985 the weekly sisterhood meeting began with a round of "I love you (name), indeed I do and I hope you love me too" exchanged between sisterhood members.

In all activities, one main objective was to educate everyone about Ajanaku; the corporate, religious, educational, and political leaders on every point of the continuum. Negotiating for Nkosi Ajanaku, the head of the family, became one of the major responsibilities for the Sisterhood. A team was trained to meet and give orientation meetings to persons before they met with the head of the family. When the Ajanaku Sisterhood was organizing the African American Women's Republican Federation, Marilou Awiakta, Cherokee feminist poet and writer, spoke at our luncheon meeting. She told us that it was a Cherokee tradition that the women, as representatives of their particular chief, negotiated with the chiefs of other tribes regarding important matters. Their position was that women negotiated war and other potentially volatile situations from a life-promoting, soft, and non-threatening posture. The Ajanaku Sisterhood's charge of negotiating for the head of the family seemed to grow from the same rationale.

We took trips out of Memphis to meet with state officials, mayors of other cities, a bishop in a national religious denomination. Representatives of national corporations, state and federal governments came to Memphis after a sisterhood representative might have negotiated for months by telephone. One sister remembers that she learned to use the representation of Nkosi as a leverage in negotiating on a first hand basis with people, especially European American males, without feeling intimidation. Additionally, we had an objective force outside the sisterhood, a male figure to hold up "vis-à-vis the external world" as expressed in the laws.

At the same time we became the primary teachers of the new paradigm without any feeling of guilt, shame, or blame about the past; we were responsible for the present and the future. A new concept of ethnicity was developed as a strategy for responsibility and accountability through community education. Black, white, and other references to color were substituted by ethnic terms and a positive recognition of culture and creativity. One sister says that proclaiming our ethnicity produced a unique feeling of being able to relate to other ethnicities on an equal human basis.

This responsibility of also educating the European family and changing the relationship between the African and European American Sisterhoods is evidenced by a letter from Nkechi to Gloria Steinem (Nkechi Ajanaku, 1982). This leading feminist was told that keeping her father's last name was an "edification of the sexual contract within the context of the nuclear Anglo-Saxon marriage contract" and also the basis for the power relations between

European American women and African women. Steinem never responded, but we had numerous meetings with other European American women in Memphis who were active in politics, education, and voluntary associations. These meetings were productive in that primary dialogue was established. Another result was that one European American woman joined and lived with the Ajanaku sisterhood for a short time in 1985.

ECONOMIC

The economic base for the family was the selling of hand-dipped incense, hand-crafted jewelry, and literature door-to-door in the African American community. This was to serve two purposes; to have a mobile dissemination of cultural items and information and to have an image of Africa constantly presented in the community, since we had no control over the media and educational institutions.

In Durham it became apparent that the market place should be maintained by the sisters. The sisters were more knowledgeable than the brothers in the area of pricing hand-crafted items for sale (we knew how much milk and diapers cost!). Later, in Memphis, the sisterhood helped expand the original economic base of incense and jewelry sales to include copying, notary, and secretarial services, selling fruits and vegetables from door to door, and handling about 20 paper-delivery routes.

The sisterhood managed the bookkeeping and customer service for the paper routes that were serviced by all family members including the children and some extended family members as well. The door-to-door collections to over 2,000 customers provided access into homes, especially in the integrated neighborhoods of middle-income professionals that might not have been receptive to the items we usually sold door-to-door in apartment complexes and public housing. A beneficial outcome was our ability to build relationships with the senior citizens in our own low-income African American community. The elders began to trust us after asking us everything they had always wanted to know about us and, in turn, shared the history of the community, herbal remedies, food, and household items.

Some of the Ajanaku Institute's thrust in the larger community's economic development had a specific sisterhood agenda, such as the formation in 1989 of Fifty Sisters Economic Development Group as part of the Economic Development Committee of the NAACP. The objective was to use this women's group to help organize a group of 100 brothers for the construction of an African Oasis that would consist of a hotel, a convention center, and an African Import Center. A companion to the aforementioned project was the "30,000 Homes" program that was designed to make the grassroots sisters aware of all the resources that could be tapped if they were well-organized. Much of the talent in the public housing community was channeled into consumer boards to sanction residential management for building crowded and ill-planned projects rather than constructing the type of homes needed by individual families. Our research had shown that this energy could be better used to provide community-controlled jobs by making commitment to buy from the sisterhood the items that were used daily in a household such as bread, rice, soap, bathroom paper, and hair-care products. This commitment would become an investment into larger projects that could provide the women in the housing projects and sub-standard housing with adequate housing as well as incomes. These economic development plans were never realized, but they afforded Ajanaku women the opportunity to work with other groups as a collective body.

CULTURAL

Taking African names was a responsibility assumed by all members of the Ajanaku family, including the children. On the road, every one who did not have a name was given one. Also, whenever we met persons from the Motherland, we wrote down the meanings of their names and asked them for some of their favorite names. When our oldest children enrolled in public schools, the sisterhood approached the school board administrators for support on the issue of using the children's African names in the classroom. While the support was given, it was not consistently followed at the classroom level and we decided it was a burden for the children to be called by their slave names. The need to change from "slave names" to "legal" African names afforded the group an opportunity to create the best and most expeditious way to go into the courts as a group and change names. The ease with which we were able to use the court system and legally change our names was due to the leader's legal training. This undertaking was a huge success as well as a manifestation of our personal values and convictions regarding lifestyle change based on African culture. "I really felt born again, this time as an African woman" is one response to the occasion. Also, when people responded to our African names with "What is your real name?" they were shown our driver's permits.

This change to African names gave birth to several other projects. The "Community Clinic Workshop" helped persons petition for a legal name change. Members of the sisterhood personally accompanied persons to court appearances, especially members of the Nation of Islam who were changing to religious names. A sister artist who was not a core member but was inspired by our commitment to name change created the "Name Certificate." Another sister, who left the core family but remained an extended family member, published the *Ajanaku African Name Book* in 1981. The sisterhood was responsible for the first public Kwanzaa celebrations in Memphis. For several years, Nia, the day of purpose, was highlighted as Sisterhood Day during which prominent women outside the family were honored at a ceremony by Queen Asante Waa.

Personal Growth

All sisters were given responsibilities upon joining the sisterhood. Some of the acquired skills included jewelry-making, sewing, typing, marketing and soliciting, and analyzing human behavior. Also, as relationships were tested and observed, it became apparent that the women would have to fuse their bonds and internal strength in order for the growth of the African family in America to acquire some semblance of order and eventual freedom. The sisterhood learned to rigorously court, sequester, and protect, for instance, a new sister who might be hesitant to give her baby to the family to care for. At the same time, a veteran sister might need this same attention if a deeper layer of slavery surfaced during the daily process. Sisterhood meetings sometimes were scheduled every day and involved vocabulary development as well as reading books and articles aloud. Sisters shared responsibility for each other's individual and collective success, which could range from pronouncing a word to producing a position paper.

The various projects afforded the sisterhood opportunities to learn about systems and linkages in the society. For one project, research was conducted about the rice fields, the types of rice, the packaging, and the existing relationships between landowners and supermarket chains. Relationships were formed with small rice farmers in the mid-south area who were interested in becoming part of the economic development projects. One sister researched chemicals while learning the pest-extermination business.

All Ajanaku sisters were highly visible members of our community and sometimes were officers of various organizations as well as members of city and county citizen committees. Two sisters were selected as members of the Leadership Memphis classes; one served as an officer of the school parent/teacher association, and another as an officer in a community democratic club. In a magazine feature on the Ajanaku family in 1982, Washiri Ajanaku gave the main part of the interview about the family (Tom Martin, 1982). On Martin Luther King's birthday in 1985, a color picture of a woman in dreadlocks who was standing in front of a sign that read "Ajanaku Sisterhood" appeared on the front page of the morning paper (Leroy Williams, Jr., 1985). The picture appeared with an article about Washiri's experiences in the 1960s' sit-in movement.

RECOLLECTIONS

Only one of the authors took part in the first extended sisterhood trip. We remember that the original plan was to have a sisterhood trip to Nigeria, but it never materialized even though we obtained our passports and shots for our visas. Three of us left Durham in an old station wagon with a broken back window, packed with a sewing machine, clothes, incense and jewelry-production tools and supplies. We had to stop and pick up another sister in a nearby city and also allow one sister to obtain a driver's permit.

The trip gave us the opportunity to learn about many things as we internalized our laws. On the third day, we pulled into a small city and called the cousin of an Ajanaku family member to see if we could spend the night in their home. We were told to come in the evening. However, after we were there for a while they informed us that we could not spend the night. With no other contact or money for a motel room we drove around until we found a place to park the car and sleep for the night. People were still up so we got out to sell our products and also see if we could find someone who would allow us to spend the night. One sister who was having a party invited us in and allowed us to stay a couple of days. We were starting to meet the unknown sisterhood remnants that had been pulled off into the isolated slave units across the nation by following our law of "Do the Don't." This simply meant we had to get past our fears of rejection and use new expressions or actions when reaching out for the hidden dimensions of humanity.

By the time the trip ended two months later, we had picked up more sisters although we had to give bus tickets to those who could not continue with us. We had been in numerous projects (public housing developments) in cities ranging from Durham, Columbus (Ohio), Detroit, and Louisville to Jackson (Mississippi), Baton

Rogue, and New Orleans. Sisters in a Muslim community welcomed us in Columbus, Ohio. We learned about our history from Sister Dara in New Orleans as she told us about the activities in the 1920s and 1930s of the Universal Association of Ethiopian Women with Queen Mother Audrey Moore.

The potential to expound and develop the concept of the Ajanaku Family was amplified in collective sisterhood negotiating and organizing sessions. All sisters who were involved in these very intellectually charged sessions reported that these were very intense experiences, although recollections vary in detail. Some found the intensity threatening and overwhelming. One sister is still humored about the time the president of an African American college put the group out of his office. Two sisters, Kanika and Monifa, who lived on the process for short periods at different times between 1975 and 1981, have concluded that the process is a hoax to establish male authority by exploiting women's talents and energies (Letter from Kanika and Monifa Ajanaku to Washiri Ajanaku, 1991). Despite the negative moments, the general intent was to locate the benefits in every interaction; this is the "conjunctive plus" in Ajanaku terms.

One sister remembers that she had sole responsibility for providing clothes for a team of three women every day while simultaneously providing the meals for the entire family during a campaign in 1976 to disseminate "The Model Memphis Plan," one of the first public papers explaining the Ajanaku position on race relations in Memphis. At several other times, she was in charge of a team of brothers and sisters during extended trips to sell Ajanaku products in various cities. Her first-time experience as a college student was just another execution of an Ajanaku order. She was confident of the support of the other family members who had attended college. One sister mentioned that she never felt the issue of skin color was resolved even though it was consciously addressed in the Sisterhood. Another sister felt that darker-skinned children suffered color discrimination in the process from members who had not internalized the beauty of African features and, consequently, favored lighter-skinned ones. It was difficult to hear a person outside the community ask those with lighter skin tones, "Why do you mess up yourself with those nappy dreadlocks?" but tragic when a member of the family reflected this same attitude. We recall the time that we saw a physical change in a particular person's face and posture due to the love and attention heaped upon them. How pretty everyone looks after an affirmation! We were aware that skin color is part of complex social and psychological issues and were ready to work at it every day.

One sister said she had learned that the very people who laugh the loudest at your "strangeness" will admit after having a chance to know you that they are working on their own acceptance of African culture. For example, a woman at her job had asked her to take down her dreadlocks and change her hairstyle but she refused. By the next year, this same woman divulged that she might try wearing dreadlocks if only her boss would let her. Of course, the Ajanaku sister had been wearing her locks in different styles and positions so that the other woman had become familiar with the flexibility that was invisible at first. We had different recollections of people who were critical in the early years coming back years later to borrow African clothes or ask for help in planning receptions with an African theme.

At one point in the 1980s, everyone started wearing three badges with the picture of Nkosi, the head of the family, and the following inscriptions, respectively: "I Love Africa," "Ajanaku Economic Development," and "Ajanaku African American Research Institute." One woman commented one day about the "I love Africa" button by asking the following question: "Isn't it redundant for you to be wearing that?" My response came with a smile: "Of course, that's the objective!" Each one of us can also remember the times that we were not sure of displaying our African creativity but feel we made it to this point by having each other through times of self-doubt. We have had to remember Nkosi's directive to "monitor your selves, go inward to assess all the facts concerning all issues" ("Notes," 1980). For example, when a conversation among sisters showed signs of becoming acrimonious, one solution would be to take a deep breath and say "Sisterhood is the Key."

CONCLUSION

Although the population of the sisterhood changed, due to many sisters who joined the family but left for various reasons, there was a core of four sisters who remained for eight to ten years. In 1985, this core consisted of six sisters who were working on the National African American Women's Sisterhood Network when the head of the family decided that the sisterhood should again be extended geographically and politically. The Queen Mother was dispatched to Atlanta to renew contacts from the civil rights movement. One author was dispatched to Knoxville, in eastern Tennessee, to work with the African American caucus in the Tennessee Legislature and is still in the city pursuing a degree in clinical psychology. Three other sisters were directed by the Ajanaku administration to pursue graduate work. Since that time, one sister who entered as a freshman is currently working on a Master's degree in Education, another (one of the authors) has just completed the course work for a Ph.D. in Sociology, and the third is currently enrolled in Law School.

The Ajanaku sisterhood has been empowered by the strict adherence to the laws and ideology governing the organization. Perceptions about cultural identity, issues related to skin color and beauty were scrutinized and positions modified within the sisterhood through daily meetings and activities. The outside community, at first an entity from which to protect ourselves, became a vehicle for internalizing our laws and a source of scattered data for strengthening the process. These circular dynamics developed due to the fact that the sisterhood, a body of varied perspectives, was in a solid position to maintain a continuous posture of objectivity.

There has been little comment up to this point about the weaknesses of the process or the sisterhood. This does not mean that weaknesses did not exist, but we saw any weakness in the individual or the process as only an uncompleted part of the growth process—something to be worked on collectively. Strategies might change, the population of the group might change, but each person had to assume primary responsibility for the internalization of the family laws. Each personal decision to join the family was challenged from several directions. Women who have had the best results from this period had the time to internalize the laws and came to appreciate their relationship to the larger society. While this paper has provided a small glimpse of the activities and relationships that occurred during this time, the greater value is the potential to highlight several aspects of African American women's activism. As an integral part of the process of documenting subjective experiences and developing objective positions, one sees that an invaluable experience was gained via grassroots, bottom-of-the-barrel economic and educational development. For when one has the opportunity to work intensively and exclusively in depressed and aberrant conditions, struggling to maintain a sense of objectivity and strict adherence to academic standards, the hands-on acquired skills are habitual and long lasting.

Most important is the full circle from activism to the academy that these activities represent. The impetus for the first involvement in the 1960s and 1970s was the lack of linkages between the academy and the community of origin. Relevant connections were formed with those scholars who remained in institutions and by the 1980s, there were contexts being discussed that could frame and analyze the Ajanaku experience. Through the Ajanaku experiences we have glimpsed unwritten women's history and can point to isolated knowledge-production sites throughout the African American community. It would be significant to undertake more in-depth, structured, individual and group interviews and identify the core themes of individual and collective experiences. For example, we realized that we do not have answers to some questions, such as why the sisterhood trip to Nigeria never took place although tremendous efforts were made. We also did not elaborate on the issue of motherhood in the family. Our questions have sparked general responses which led us to recollect or seek more specific details in our archives and from other persons who were in administrative positions. As authors, we have relied considerably on individual recollections. More specific questions developed from this paper will provide a fuller analysis of an era of shared life with our sisters.

POSTSCRIPT

Presently, there is little communication between base members and extended family members. Sisters who live at the base were invited on December 26, 1992 by extended sisterhood members (authors included) to discuss the future of the sisterhood. There were concerns that the original intent of the sisterhood had been violated by the head of the family and that sisters and children, residing at the base, were potential victims. The majority of these sisters did not join the family until the late 1980s and the majority of the extended Sisterhood members had been a part of the earliest formation of the family. Although the headquarters are still in Memphis, most of the Ajanaku family base members, along with the head of the family, moved to Atlanta in early 1993 and are working under an organization called Future America. More analysis of the recollections in this paper have led to additional questions, recollections, and analyses. The process that we have shared has provided us with a clear picture of the strengths and weaknesses of group living. Some of these strengths were addressed in the paper. We suspect that the weakest part of the experience has been the effect on children of the taboo placed on biological relationships by the Ajanaku family: mothers and fathers had to deny complete ownership of their biological children but when mothers left the base they assumed responsibility of the children more often than the fathers who left.

The support and network system in the extended Ajanaku Family Sisterhood is strong and the authors are in the process of working with other extended family members to publish more detailed analyses of the Ajanaku experience and philosophy.

WORKS CITED

Ajanaku Family. *Introductory Laws and Processes of the Ajanaku Family,* Memphis, 1975.

Ajanaku, Nkechi. Letter to Gloria Steinem. September 23, 1982.

Ajanaku, Kanika and Monifa Ajanaku. Letter to Washiri Ajanaku. November 11, 1991.

Collins, Patricia Hill. "The Social Construction of Black Feminist Thought." *Signs* 14. 4 (1989): 745-773.

———. *Black Feminist Thought: Knowledge, Consciousness, and the Politics of Empowerment.* Boston: Unwin Hyman, 1990.

Gordon, Vivian. *Black Women, Feminism and Black Liberation: Which Way?* Chicago: Third World Press, 1987.

hooks, bell. *Talking Back.* Boston: South End Press, 1989.

Hull, Gloria, Patricia Bell Scott, and Barbara Smith, ed. *All the Women Are White, All the Blacks Are Men, But Some of Us Are Brave.* Old Westbury: The Feminist Press, 1982.

King, Deborah K. "Race, Class and Gender Salience in Black Women's Womanist Consciousness." Typescript, 1987.

———. "Multiple Jeopardy, Multiple Consciousness: The Context of a Black Feminist Ideology." *Signs* 14.1 (1989): 43-73.

Leroy, William, Jr. "King 'Stirred up the World': Aide's Birthday Wish—Stir on." The *Commercial Appeal* (January 15, 1985): A1, A6.

"Notes from Economic Development Sub-Committee Meeting." Memphis, Tenn., September 6, 1980.

Scott, Kesho Yvonne. *The Habit of Surviving: Black Women's Strategies for Life.* New Brunswick: Rutgers University Press, 1991.

Tom, Martin. "The Ajanakus: In Search of an African American Identity." *Memphis* 1982: 34.

IV
POSTSCRIPT

THIS WOMEN'S STUDIES BUSINESS: BEYOND POLITICS AND HISTORY (THOUGHTS ON THE FIRST WAAD CONFERENCE)

OBIOMA NNAEMEKA

PREAMBLE: THIS WOMEN'S STUDIES BUSINESS

> In our world, divide and conquer must become define and empower.... *I urge each one of us here to reach down into that place of knowledge inside herself and touch that terror and loathing of any difference that lives there. See whose face it wears.* Then the personal as the political can begin to illuminate all our choices.
> —Audre Lorde, *Sister Outsider*, 113

AS WE ENGAGE IN OUR WORK IN THE WOMEN'S MOVEMENT and in feminist scholarship,[1] some of us from the so-called Third World are caught in our ambivalence. Faced with the contradictions in the Movement and in feminist agendas, we vacillate between hope and despair. We are frustrated and debilitated by the agendas even as we are encouraged by their possibilities. The "hopes and impediments"[2] of the feminist movement and of its offshoot, Women's Studies, are captured by two oppositional moments in the history of the second wave of the Women's Movement. These two periods, separated roughly by a couple of decades, allegorize the complexities and problematics of feminist engagement. The title of Robin Morgan's book, *Sisterhood is Global,* which captures the spirit of the 1960s and 1970s, was greeted on the one hand with enthusiasm and hope and on the other with the cynicism that is engendered by feminist exclusions. The mythology of sisterhood was not lost on many of us, although some of us were either too naive or too lazy to probe the reality that the mythology of sisterhood mystifies. The spirit and radical questioning of the 1980s— generated by the "women of color movement"—is captured by the title of another book, *When and Where I Enter,* by Paula Giddings. That title encapsulates three important elements in feminist debates—history/time (when); location/space (where); and subjectivity/agency (I).

The history of the feminist movement and feminist scholarship brings to mind wars and revolutions, particularly the aftermath of wars and revolutions. The French Revolution ended the monarchy but it also ushered in one of the most bloody moments in French history as the revolutionaries fought among themselves. Coming closer home to Africa, examples abound: the "revolutionaries" that got rid of Siyad Barre in Somalia emerged as power-hungry "warlords"; in Liberia, Johnson and Taylor eliminated Samuel Doe but continued the blood bath. Revolutions and wars have the potential of breeding more wars and revolutions. Shifting power relations compel those who fought *against* power to fight *for* power and in the process construct, legitimize, and enforce new power paradigms that mimic the oppressive ones they fought so hard to eliminate.

The challenge to feminist scholarship to abandon the analysis of women's lives based solely on the commonality of sex and replace it with a more inclusive methodology that recognizes the intersection of differences compelled feminist scholarship to widen its horizon, explore its possibilities, and gain a new lease on life. Unfortunately, the politics of feminism allows at best only the awareness of differences while impeding the evolution of feminism into a political gesture that is grounded in the commonality of struggle at the intersection of differences. The preoccupation with the intersection of categories of difference—race, class, ethnicity, etc.—fails to take into account the boundaries that exist within each category. In assessing the feminist challenge and the challenges of feminism, I, an African woman from Igboland, think of "when and where I enter," both in the larger feminist movement and the women-of-color variant. Victims of the Big Sister syndrome that permeates the larger feminist movement and the women-of-color/Third World women configuration, African women are marginalized as knowledge producers.[3] In the women's movement, the overall attitude towards African women generates reactions similar to Chinua Achebe's "We're not anybody's junior brothers" given in response to Albert Schweitzer's statement: "The traditional attitude of Europe or the West is that Africa is a continent of children. A man as powerful and enlightened as Albert Schweitzer was still able to say, 'the black people are my brothers—but my junior brothers'" (Moyers, 1989: 335). As will be discussed later, it was in this spirit that Nigerians and other Africans opposed the demand by a few[4] African-American participants at the first international conference on Women in Africa and the African Diaspora (WAAD) that whites be excluded from the conference—a demand that was issued as an order without any consultation with their Nigerian hosts. Undoubtedly, it was not only the nature of the demand but the unilateral manner in which it was made that provoked the opposition.

Events at WAAD point to the complexity of the issues raised above, particularly the challenges of engaging from seemingly similar but radically different locations. Those events led me to rethink issues related to inclusion and exclusion, (feminist) politics, hope and despair, power and powerlessness, voice, and history, as well as to contextualize "this Women's Studies business"—business as an industry (with attendant corporate mentality of pursuit of gain and power, survival of the fittest, and fight for preeminence), but also business as issue, politics, or problem (what is called *palaver* or *wahala* in Nigeria).[5] Often, the control and management of information undergird claims of voice, authority, and legitimacy. Successful careers have been built on studies about Africa and African women by "experts" who either refuse to listen to the voices of Africa/African women or only listen long enough to appropriate, reshape, and misleadingly articulate what they heard. Such external and internal experts remind me of colonialism and its infamous descendant, neocolonialism. Colonialism, in its most insidious form, indigenized oppression and exploitation by creating an indigenous elite within the former colonies. Thus, the profound violence of the neocolonialist state emanates from the collaboration between outsiders and a few insiders to crush the majority of insiders. This paradigm is replicated in what I call *neofeminism*, the precarious alliance between feminist insiders and feminist outsiders to generate and control knowledge about the totality of African women.

For me, convening the first WAAD conference was a very difficult but extremely rewarding experience in terms of intellectual growth. It brought home to me, sometimes in a most brutal way, what I already knew about feminist exclusions. By opening up new geographies and fascinating horizons of knowledge for me, the WAAD experience was like earning a Ph. D. in Women's Studies! The myriad of issues and debates in Women's Studies and feminist scholarship—agency, exclusion, sisterhood, voice, authenticity, authority, turfism, power, oppression, violence, racism, sexism, imperialism, etc.—were etched in relief. The foregoing provides the context for examining the following details of conference organizing and points to the conclusion of this paper with its emphasis on the relationship between politics and history.

THE CONFERENCE

I have tried to learn my anger's usefulness to me, as well as its limitations....what you hear in my voice is fury, not suffering. Anger, not moral authority. There is a difference.
—(Audre Lorde, *Sister Outsider*, 131-32)

RATIONALE AND FOCUS

In convening this conference, I was motivated by the following concerns:
(1) The commodification of African women in Women's Studies and feminist scholarship and their marginalization in the process of gathering, articulating, and disseminating knowledge.
(2) The marginalization of the African space as a legitimate location for global debates about Africa and peoples of African descent.
(3) The need for a thorough re-examination of the urban/rural, research/activism, and African Continent/African Diaspora relationships.
The bilingual (French and English) conference materials sent to everyone who requested them specified all aspects of the conference—conceptualization, focus, modalities for participation, etc. Conference announcements clearly stated that the conference was

open to activists and scholars working on women in African and the African Diaspora. As the conference announcement indicated, the conference was *about* women in Africa and the African Diaspora and not exclusively *for* black women:

> In view of the foregoing, I am convening an international conference in July 1992. The conference will address issues affecting women everywhere but specifically women in Africa and the African Diaspora. *Activists and scholars inside and outside Africa* will have the opportunity to share their experiences and work, and plan collaborative work. There will be sessions in which academic papers in all disciplines will be presented and discussed. Workshops will be organized to address a wide range of issues—from curriculum development to leadership and organizing, from cooperatives and social change to creativity and indigenous technology. Issues relating to rural women and rural development will be specifically addressed. The presence of rural women at the conference will provide the opportunity for dialogue and plan of action. Representatives of the numerous Women's Studies centers and projects, women's organizations and groups that are operating all over Africa will be invited to share their activities and experiences with other participants. This will be a golden opportunity for *men and women* who are interested in or are doing research on women in Africa and the African Diaspora to see things first hand and up close. [emphasis added]

The composition of the organizing committee—six black women (from Africa and the Diaspora), two white women, one black man, and one white man—symbolized this spirit of inclusion. The regional representatives were of different races; the local planning committee was almost all black (it had one white member) and almost all female (it had one male member); the city and institutional representatives (Nigeria) were all black and of both sexes. Men and whites sent in proposals and requests for participation according to the spirit and letter of the conference and they were invited accordingly. The conference was not planned to exclude whites and men, but the identity of the key players in the organization left no one in doubt as to who was in charge—*black women.*

Furthermore, by not targeting one specific concern, the first WAAD conference served as a forum for discussing all aspects of the lives of women in Africa and the African Diaspora and in the process allowed the participants to determine the focus and agenda of subsequent meetings, thus ensuring that women in Africa and the African Diaspora, not any group or agency, determine their own priorities. I reasoned that participants would be better served if given the freedom to choose and discuss what they considered important to them without feeling constrained by the imposition of thematic limits. This arrangement was chosen above others partly because of the often-voiced but usually ignored charges by African women that issues discussed and projects initiated and executed on their behalf are not necessarily those of primary importance to them.

ORGANIZATION

It took two years (1990–1992) to organize the conference. I sent out the first "call for action" in February 1990 and by the end of May I had received over 180 proposals. I contacted a few friends and colleagues committed to issues and research on women in Africa and the African Diaspora to join me as members of a ten-person organizing committee. Due to funding difficulties, it was not possible for the committee to meet regularly as a body. Our telephone conversations were supplemented by periodic briefings on the status of conference planning.

Unfunded for the two years it took to organize it, the conference was sustained by the benevolence of a network of national and regional volunteers that spanned more than forty countries in all continents. In the host country, Nigeria, a local organizing committee was set up. It was first chaired by Edith Ihekweazu, who unfortunately died before the conference was held, and subsequently by Julie Okpala. In addition to the local planning committee, a network of representatives in Nigeria's major cities and tertiary institutions was put in place. Institutional, city, national, and regional representatives were responsible for disseminating information and coordinating activities in their respective geographical areas. The Nigerian federal and state governments as well as all the national and state commissions for women and Better Life Programs were contacted. During the two-year period, state governments in Nigeria were changed twice and more states were created. With every change, fresh letters and information packets were sent to the new occupants of state government houses and all new directors of women's commissions and chairpersons of the Better Life Program! African governments were contacted through their foreign missions in Washington, D. C. Conference materials were sent to Women's

Studies programs and women's centers and agencies in Africa—
such as WODORC (Nigeria), FEMNET (Kenya), CACE (South
Africa), TAMWA (Tanzania), SFPA (Sudan), WAU (Botswana),
GILLBT (Ghana), AALAE (Kenya), MUSASA (Zimbabwe),
AAWORD (Senegal), Center for Human Rights (Gambia), etc.—
and outside Africa (Britain, Brazil, Costa Rica, the Netherlands,
Germany, Sweden, Spain, Italy, France, Switzerland, Australia, India,
Pakistan, the Caribbean, the Philippines, Belgium, Guyana,
Malaysia, Mexico, Panama, Portugal, Russia, Bangladesh, Surinam,
Finland, etc.). I travelled to Senegal to meet with the Director of
AAWORD and hold discussions with CODESRIA. I travelled to
Nigeria five times at my own expense to meet with the local orga-
nizing committee and city/institutional representatives.

FUNDING

Funding difficulties presented the biggest challenge. The conference did not receive funding until June 1992, after over two years
of planning and organizing and just a month before the event took
place. I am grateful to the College of Wooster, particularly Dean
Yvonne Williams, for supporting the project. Without the secretarial help, as well as photocopying and mailing privileges the College
provided, the project would not have survived the critical initial
stages. Our able secretaries, Dale Catteau, Ardis Gillund and Carol
Boreman, worked tirelessly to keep up with the daily influx of proposals and letters. My Diaspora sisters and colleagues Martha Banks
and Annetta Jefferson gave unreservedly of their support and
encouragement. When I moved to the University of Minnesota,
Minneapolis in 1991, my friends rallied round to give their unalloyed support. Carolann Dickinson and Lehn Benjamin spent innumerable nights and weekends typing and assembling conference
materials. Susan Geiger, Janet Spector, and Michael Mbabuike stood
by me all the way, giving advice and working tirelessly to contact
funding sources at their own expense. When I was broke, Catherine
Bicknell came to my rescue with financial assistance. Throughout,
my sons, Ike and Uche, remained pillars of strength by working tirelessly for the conference and giving unreservedly of their emotional
support.

The numerous funding rejections I received were accompanied
by reviewers' reports, some of which are pertinent to the concerns
I expressed earlier:

(1) "...the proposal expressed the intention of holding the conference at Abuja, but also mentioned Women's Studies programs

at Ibadan and African Studies programs at Nsukka.... Nothing unique about these locations."

(2) "...meeting in Nigeria of researchers and activists, is this scholarship?"

(3) "This is a conference that looks more like a conference in social engineering than humanistic research. As a non-specialist, I can identify people whose research and teaching are directly related to the conference themes but who are not involved. And this does not build my confidence. By what criteria were individuals selected?"

(4) "I think the idea of the conference is generally good...the conference has attracted a lot of attention, and as I look at the names and locations that people show, I was struck that most of these were home addresses. I didn't see many of them coming from the more well-known Women's Studies programs."

(5) "First, I have a comment and then a question. The document you assembled is impressive. I cannot believe that anyone can set up such a complex global network without funding. My question is, why Nigeria?" (The latter comment and question are from the female Director of an international agency who called after receiving my funding request packet).

These "experts" and "non-experts" expressed concerns mainly about two issues—location and participants. They expressed concerns about *where* we should debate issues concerning women in Africa and the African Diaspora and *who* should raise their voices in the debate. According to these reviewers, Abuja, Ibadan, and Nsukka are not unique and researchers and activists meeting in Nigeria is not scholarship. I would bet that if they meet in "unique" places like Brussels or London, it *would* be deemed "scholarship"! The insistence on work address as a criterion for determining legitimate participants would automatically eliminate most rural participants whose workplaces (farms) do not have addresses. Furthermore, a majority of self-employed women whose home address is the same as their work address would be equally excluded. It is disturbing to see a conference *on* African women with hundreds of contributors *from* Africa devalued because many participants are not from "the more well-known Women's Studies programs" (in the West, of course). The truth of the matter is that most of the original, innovative, and meaningful work about African women is generated *in Africa by Africans* and not in those so-called "more well-known Women's Studies programs" outside Africa where the same old information about Africa and African women is packaged, repackaged, and recycled *ad infinitum*. In effect, these spurious reasons for funding denials coupled with the fact that I already had hundreds of accepted proposals in my hands made me more determined than ever, although at great personal cost, not to abandon the project.

The foregoing raises concerns about the feminist exclusionary strategy that I call "gate-keeping" in which foreign and local "gate-keepers" and self-proclaimed "experts" on African women "collaborate" to review, construct, generate, manage, and circulate knowledge about African women. Usually, the "gate-keepers" in Africa provide the raw data that are reshaped and disseminated by their gate-keeping foreign "collaborators." Without examining, and if necessary questioning, the way their data have been used, the African "gate-keepers" collect more data while awaiting the arrival of the next plane ticket for their routine travels to world capitals.[6] No wonder then that these African "gate- keepers" are those who are *always* invited to Western cities, conferences, workshops, etc., where issues about (rural) African women are discussed in cozy five-star hotels.

The thorny issue of the creation and legitimating of "authentic" African voices ("gate-keepers") in Women's Studies and feminist scholarship was vigorously debated at the WAAD conference. The African "gate-keepers" are usually older and more established scholars who are pioneers in the study of African women. Admittedly, these scholars have made their mark and must be applauded for their contributions and accomplishments. However, this does not justify their coronation as eternal custodians of "truths" about African women. What is more important, the prominent roles often played by the older scholars/"gate-keepers" in the governments of their respective countries raise concerns about loyalty, allegiance, and conflict of interest. It is doubtful that the politics and policies of compromised spokespersons for African governments (legitimate and illegitimate) are always in the interest of other categories of women. It would be more productive to periodically recycle the contingent of African "stars" to include mid-career African female academicians and activists who have different or new (even if not necessarily the most popular) perspectives and ideas to offer.[7] As rightly noted by one participant, the research and concerns of beginning and mid-career African academicians articulated at the WAAD conference were not always the run-of-the-mill concerns that proliferate Women's Studies scholarship on African women:

The conference's strength was due to the input of many African participants who could attend because of its location in Africa. Their presence, both in panel presentations, workshops, plenary sessions and discussions, was strongly felt and very important for everyone. I was particularly thrilled with the work of some younger scholars who were educated in Nigeria, had not been abroad, but have done real fieldwork in their own country instead. Their reports were a refreshing departure from the work of older African scholars trained and educated in Europe and the U. S. A.[8]

In Spring of 1992, the funding situation changed drastically, with funding coming from the MacArthur Foundation and some international agencies—the Swedish International Development Authority (SIDA), the International Development Research Center (IDRC), Ottawa, Canada; and the Swedish Agency for Research Cooperation with Developing Countries (SAREC). The timely intervention of funders changed drastically the nature and outcome of the conference. Due to the late arrival of funding, African grantees were refunded their travel expenses when they got to Nigeria and African participants who could not afford the registration fee received a waiver. No African participant was denied participation because he/she could not pay the registration fee. Without the intervention of our generous sponsors, many African participants could not have attended.

Considering the timing of funding (Spring 1992), it is inaccurate for some to charge that whites were allowed to participate because the conference was funded by white agencies. *Funding came in too late—two years into the planning of the conference and one month before the conference took place—for funding conditionalities to influence organizational decisions in any way.* By Spring 1992, the conference was to take place with or without funding. Obviously, the timely intervention of our kind sponsors made it possible for us to have a bigger and more successful conference, and for that I am most grateful. However, all the decisions made before, during, and after the conference were *in no way* influenced by any of the conference sponsors.

TRAVEL

Travel arrangements constituted the sore spot in the conference planning. By the time I discovered that the conference "travel agent" misrepresented himself, he and his partner had already collected thousands of dollars from participants, thus making it impos-

sible for me to change agents. As late as a week before the conference, I was still in the United States because the "travel agent" had
not issued tickets to participants. The day I finally left for Lagos, I
was on the same flight with nine other participants. On arriving
Lagos, we discovered that our luggage (including the box with
copies of the conference program) was not on the flight. With only
a few days to the conference, we started drawing up another program. We succeeded in producing daily programs the first couple
of days and a complete program soon after. The worst was yet to
come at the end of the conference with the cancellation of the flight
back to the United States.

LOCATION

The conference was held in Nsukka, a small rural town in southeastern Nigeria. The choice of location encouraged the participation of rural women and those working in the Better Life Program
for rural dwellers. Furthermore, the choice of Nsukka made a statement against the usual practice of holding women in development
conferences in five-star hotels in African capitals that are priced out
of the reach of most Africans and very far removed from the rural
women who are discussed interminably. Due to the huge turnout
at the conference, some participants stayed in Enugu, a city about
40 miles south of Nsukka, and commuted to the conference site.

Many participants enjoyed the rural setting and thought it was
a brilliant idea that Nsukka was chosen as the conference site.[9] As
expected, there were complaints ranging from the serious to the
ridiculous. I remember vividly one such complaint. One of our foreign participants complained endlessly about the unavailability of
wake-up calls at our Nsukka hotel. Unswayed by my lengthy reasons
for our lack of privilege, she persisted in her complaints. By the
third day, frustrated by my powerlessness to wean this sister from
technological dependency, I proposed the two options most likely
to be available in our small town: (1) If she wanted to wake up at
4:00 a.m., I would get the rooster, but (2) if she wanted to be woken
up at 6:00 a.m., I would summon the town crier! She got the message.

Organizing an international conference of the magnitude of
WAAD '92 and locating it in a small rural town in Africa was, to be
sure, a daring undertaking. Although the difficulties—ranging from
logistics to transportation and communication—were many and
daunting, they should not preclude Africa as a stage for international meetings on Africa or African women. At WAAD the diffi-

culties were many, but we prevailed. The benefits of choosing Africa as a location far outweighed the difficulties. In view of the fact that the majority of Africans cannot afford to travel outside their respective countries, and are not "stars"/"gate-keepers" whose participation is usually sponsored, they are unable to bring their immense contributions to international gatherings. Maureen Malowany's contribution to the "Forum" section addresses the issue of funding African participants and keeping the WAAD conference in Africa. A post-conference report from one of the participants sums up the general feeling about the caliber of African women who attended the conference:

> With summer, Nsukka and Nigeria on my mind, I think of you. As the days, weeks and months roll by, I think and feel, although differently. At Nsukka, I cried because I hated your decision to permit the participation of white women. I shed tears of hate. As I write this, I cry but I shed tears of love and admiration for you and your courage. You had the courage to make tough choices. Your strength and vision made me read again my copy of Judith Van Allen's work on the 1929 "Igbo Women's War." Surely, you and the other intelligent Igbo women I met come from a long tradition of strong, beautiful black women. I hold you in the highest esteem...Thank you for putting together such a monumental project.

How would this and other participants have gained this insight if they had not come to Igboland?

JULY 12-22

I was at the Lagos airport on July 12 to welcome participants from the United States. For most of the African-American participants, particularly those who were making their maiden voyage to Africa, the trip to Nigeria was a personal and emotional one; for me, welcoming them to Nigeria was very moving. Some came with their mothers. In the arrival hall of the Muritala Mohammed International Airport, Lagos, one of the African-American sisters came up to me, hugged me, and said "Thank you, I feel I am somebody." With tears in our eyes, in that moment of embrace, we both felt the weight of history; our history that went separate ways because of the intervention of other histories—histories of slavery, colonization, and imperialism.

We travelled by air from Lagos to Enugu and by road to Nsukka, the conference site. Travelling difficulties are exemplified by the journey from Lagos to Enugu. Enugu is an hour by air from Lagos but the journey from Lagos to Enugu took a whole day. We did not leave Lagos until evening because an aircraft had to be negotiated and renegotiated. We arrived Nsukka very late at night. At the opening ceremony the next day, presided over by the wife of the Enugu State Governor, Dr. Dorothy Nwodo, there were over 700 participants from 43 countries representing all continents. Later that day, Professor Martin Ijere presented one of the three keynote addresses of the conference ("The Imperative of Women's Leadership in the Socioeconomic Life of a Nation"), at the end of which one of the major controversies of the conference took root. I was busy with arrangements for newly arrived participants and was not present at Professor Ijere's presentation. The crisis erupted when an African-American woman demanded during the question-and-answer session that white participants be barred from the conference.

The bilingual conference materials that were disseminated all over the globe clearly stated the scope of issues to be discussed, modalities for participation, and categories of participants. As a conference planned for scholars, activists, and others interested in or working on women in Africa and the African Diaspora, WAAD was not organized to promote race and gender exclusions. Some of those who opposed the participation of whites argued that whites had no business participating in a conference billed as "Women in Africa." To insist that "Women in Africa" is synonymous with "black Women" ignores the fact that in Africa *today* there are whites who are *citizens* of some African countries by virtue of birth, marriage, or naturalization.[10] Obviously, the demand that whites not speak at the WAAD conference failed to recognize that in *contemporary* Africa, "women in Africa" means women of different races. The issue of racism is a very important one that must be addressed unequivocally and vigorously, as was the case with many papers presented at the conference. Most participants saw the issue as an impetus for debate and action and not as a weapon for excluding and silencing others. What is more important, the WAAD conference was a historic and truly global event of monumental proportions that should not be defined by the race controversy that occurred. Far larger than the race controversy, the conference raised many crucial issues that need urgent attention and serious debate. This volume of WAAD conference papers offers a glimpse into the complexity and import of the event and stands as a small tribute to those who participated in the meeting.

On the whole, there were three major controversies at the conference—two were political and the third was ideological—and all three were exclusionary: (1) the exclusion of whites, (2) the objection to the presence of men, and (3) the fight among feminists, womanists, and Africana womanists for ascendancy. The controversies that exploded and the tensions that mounted sent participants crying and scurrying for cover in their little corners.

When the news of the controversy over the participation of whites reached me, I first viewed the videotape of the plenary session where the incident occurred to better assess what happened and determine a line of action. A couple of hours later, I summoned a meeting of some women from our host country, Nigeria, to seek their advice on how best to handle the situation. Some of the women at the meeting were disappointed by the African-American woman's intervention on the following grounds: they felt that the African-American (1) was trying to sabotage the big event that was taking place in their corner of the planet; (2) had no right to dictate who should or should not speak on Nigerian soil; (3) showed disregard by failing to consult either the convener or Nigerians, her hosts, before issuing her order in the full assembly. As I pointed out at our meeting, I did not ascribe much importance to the first reason because big events are not always good events; bad big events should not be allowed to occur. I found the second and third reasons compelling, considering my previously noted concerns about feminist exclusions and imperial arrogance. Moreover, there was something unusual about the demand by the small group of protesting African-Americans and the tactics eventually employed for its implementation. Many of us are familiar with instances of displeased conference participants staging a protest walkout. What was unusual at the WAAD conference was the insistence of displeased participants that they stay while ordering other participants to walk out. When their demand was not met, they resorted to all sorts of tactics from shouting down and intimidating white participants, to walking up to them to demand what right they had to be in Nigeria,[11] to forcing them to leave panel presentations and ordering them to go to the back of the bus.

As I listened to the Nigerian women at our meeting, I was haunted by the pain I saw on the African-American woman's face in the video I had watched earlier in the day. I felt and still feel that pain. I also empathized with the disappointment and frustration of our Nigerian hosts, particularly in view of the *enormous* personal sacrifice they made in what turned out to be a thankless job.[12] The picture of that pain and the frustration in those voices stood between me and sleep. Still feeling the debilitating effects of a sleepless night, I headed to the assembly hall the following morning resolved to find a prompt and just solution to the problem. I declared an open microphone session at the general assembly and prefaced the session with few comments by noting that I was one of the few people in the auditorium who could identify with all factions involved in the crisis. As I told the Nigerians at our meeting the previous day, Africans (excluding South Africans, for example), who have spent all their lives in Africa and have not been exposed to racism on a daily basis, are sometimes naive about the violence of racism. I had felt that violence not in Nigeria but in Europe and the United States. I pleaded with the African participants to show more understanding to our African-American sisters for whom racism is a painful reality on a daily basis. I also urged the African-Americans to extend the same understanding, tolerance, and spirit of cooperation to others.

Shortly before the meeting, I saw two South Africans, one black and the other white, holding each other and crying. On talking to them, I found out that they co-authored their conference paper. The white woman was crying because she felt she should withdraw for the sake of peace. The black woman was crying because she would also withdraw if her friend and collaborator withdrew. The case of these South Africans epitomized the complexity of the problem that faced us. Bi-racial groups of presenters from the United States found themselves in a similar situation. Two Americans, one black and the other white, co-authored their two presentations.[13] An African-American professor attended the conference with two of her white students who collaborated to produce their presentation.[14] There was another bi-racial group from California. Given this scenario, how could we, black women, exclude white participants without excluding some of our own sisters? Doesn't it matter that we exclude and hurt some of our own in our relentless effort to exclude and hurt others? In effect, the demand by a handful of African-Americans that whites be barred could have led to the exclusion of some African-Americans as well. After a couple of hours of listening to participants' views on the matter, I suggested we bring the open microphone session to closure by proposing a cultural solution to the political issue. I reminded the participants what the Nsukka man, who broke the kola nut during the opening ceremony the previous day, said in Igbo, "*Obialu be onye abiagbunaya, onaba nkpunkpu apunaya*" ("May my guests not come to crush me and when they leave, may they not leave with a hunchback"). In Igboland, where the conference was held, there is an understood pact between host and guest that is rooted in mutual respect and protection. The Igbo see it as their responsibility to protect their guests regardless of gender, class, color, creed, or national origin: "[Igbo] tradition asserts that a friendly visitor is never rejected, 'pushed out in the rain'" (Okpala and Ohuche).[15] If the dissenting group of African-American sisters had first, upon arriving in Nigeria, familiarized themselves with their new environment by talking to their hosts, they would probably not have made their demand (certainly not in the unilateral, non-consultatory manner it was made); and when they made it, they would have understood why Nigerians did not support them for insisting that "their guests" be sent away ("pushed out in the rain").[16]

During the open microphone session, the leader of the Namibian delegation, Ms. Gawanas, raised an objection to the exclusion of white participants. According to her, as the head of a government delegation that had a white woman as one of its members, she had no right to exclude a government delegate from the conference. A Bulgarian-born Nigerian citizen denounced the demand that whites be excluded from participation. According to her, she was married to a Nigerian, has lived in Nigeria for twelve years, and resented the idea that an African-American woman who had been in Nigeria for only a day would demand that she, a Nigerian citizen, not speak in Nigeria. She was promptly shouted down by some African-Americans. At that point, another Nigerian woman, angered by the disrespect shown to the Bulgarian-born Nigerian, shouted back at the protesters: "No one, black or white, has the right to insult our wife." In all likelihood, the Nigerian woman that spoke these words did not know the Bulgarian-born Nigerian personally. But so long as the Bulgarian is married to a Nigerian, she is "our wife" and must be respected. In Igboland, that is the law of the land (omenani).

Obviously, what emerged was a clash of perspectives—on the one hand, the perspective of live-and-let-live, inclusion, accommodation, negotiation, and balance, and on the other hand, the perspective that is based on color, difference, and separatism. Linked to this clash of perspectives are important identitarian questions regarding the fluidity and complexity of identity-formation and their implications for social engagement. Our Nigerian hosts saw beyond the seemingly immutable black/white binary by collapsing the conflictive elements to allow the emergence of a third identitarian category ("guest") upon which they acted. Identity politics that permanently resists border-crossings is troubling and should be challenged: "I do challenge the notion 'I am, therefore I resist!'

That is, I challenge the idea that simply being a woman, or being poor or black or Latino, is sufficient ground to assume a politicized oppositional identity" (Mohanty, 1991: 33).

I ended the session by noting that so long as we were in Igboland, the laws of the land *(omenani)* would prevail. This cultural solution to a political problem did not resolve the issue for some; the majority, however, went ahead with the business of the conference. Unfortunately, the thick cloud of hurt, suspicion, and intolerance that this episode generated hung tragically over us and refused to dissipate. The whole episode was most taxing and debilitating, as energy and time needed for overall conference operations were spent on crisis management, the nature and intensity of which were not anticipated. The next day, the South African delegation, after long deliberations, read a statement recommending that everyone, black or white, be allowed to present his/her paper.[17]

A closer look at the specific statements made by some of the African-American women who spearheaded the move to ban white participants will shed some light on the resistance against the move. A Nigerian reacted vehemently against what she overheard: "Let us teach our African sisters how to deal with them white folks." The first African-American to demand that whites be excluded stated unequivocally: "I am sick and tired of white women telling me how I feel." She is correct; no one can adequately articulate another person's pain. In actuality, some of the white participants expressed the same view in their conference papers: "However supportive a white feminist might be of her black 'sister,' she is not an historical inhabitant of a black woman's subject position and needs to maintain a rigorous interrogation of *her* own subject position while listening to black women articulate *their* situation" (199). However, the African-American sister's claim that white women were in charge of the conference is inaccurate. Black women were in charge of the conference. *I* was in charge of the conference; *the local planning committee* was in charge of the conference.

The other African-American in the forefront of the controversy said: "Go and tell George Bush to let our people go. Most of our men are in jail from New York to Los Angeles." Of course, the unprecedented incarceration of black males in the United States must be of concern to people of African descent everywhere. Each time I watch the videotape of the controversy, I am saddened by the pain on the faces of my Diaspora sisters as well as the pain on the faces of Nigerian women as they reacted against what they considered an unfair, unilateral demand by those who, within twenty-four hours of arriving in Nigeria, had positioned themselves to (1) dictate to Nigerians who should or should not speak on Nigeria soil, (2) silence a Nigerian citizen on Nigerian soil because she is white, (3) insist on the exclusion of an official delegate of an African government because she is white, (4) claim the world begins in New York and ends in Los Angeles, (5) forget that George Bush was not the president of most participants. It was equally important for participants to know how women live under other presidents with names such as Robert Mugabe, Ibrahim Babangida, Jerry Rawlings, and Abdou Diouf. The conference was about America in so far as it is part of the African Diaspora; but the conference was not about America *exclusively*. Some Nigerians, who felt the insurgent group of African-Americans issued their orders as Americans, reacted against what they perceived as an American take-over[18] or, as one African-American participant put it:

> I had traveled, not only with my mother, but with my European American business partner and research colleague; we had two presentations scheduled which were designed, in large part, to demonstrate the benefits of building bridges. Our research and our life work has been dedicated to improving health conditions for all people, but with a special focus on issues faced by African American women. The idea that we had traveled so far to be told that *our* work was not welcome was nearly unbearable. In those terrible moments, I saw a side of the Ugly American that I had hoped I had left behind for a week.[19]

Obviously, as noted by one participant, in this controversy Africans watched as the center talked to the center.[20] It would have been easy for me to ask white participants to withdraw. However, the easy way is not always the right and just way. White and male participants as activists and researchers came because of the scope and objectives of the conferences *as defined in the conference literature;* they had the right to share the space with other participants. The path that most of the participants and I took was a difficult and painful one but I am convinced it was the right one. As an African-American participant stated in her post conference report,

> What was affirming about those few days was that we chose life. It was painful and messy and demanded much from some of us. We are all shaped from first breath by racial allegiances

and historical prejudices. It is hard to negotiate from those places within ourselves. But we did. And we not only survived, we were victorious. If we could do it, we can show people in our own little corners of the world how to do the same.[21]

My main concern was less about the possible sabotage of two years of hard work and more about the possibility of African and African Diaspora women losing a rare opportunity to discuss their issues *on their own terms* with a truly international audience *on African soil.* Many participants were frustrated that the controversy made white women the focus of a conference on women in Africa and the African Diaspora. It is ironic that the attempt to marginalize and exclude the handful of white participants made them more visible and central.

There is a lot to be learned from the WAAD controversy. First, the controversy sketched in stark relief the complexity and hetero-geneity of the category "woman"/"black woman." Black women crossed, negotiated, and renegotiated boundaries (political, ideo-logical, theoretical, etc.) individually and collectively. Most Nigerian participants were against the exclusion of whites, some were neu-tral; some African-Americans opposed the participation of whites, others insisted otherwise.The same lack of unanimity was evident among participants from southern Africa. Second, the controversy reminded us in a most brutal way that all is not well, and that the violence of racism touches all black people wherever they may be. However, in order for our protest to be meaningful and political, it must be strategically relevant; strategic not only in terms of plan-ning/logistics but also in terms of choosing the appropriate loca-tion and moment. We cannot abandon dialogue for insurgency unless we have proven the inefficacy of the former. Dialogue remains the most effective mode of conflict resolution. Finally, we should not confuse political engagement with posturing or grand-standing. The achievement of real and lasting social change depends less on the amount of energy we invest and more on how our energy is used:

> Too often, we pour the energy needed for recognizing and exploring difference into pretending those differences are insurmountable barriers, or that they do not exist at all. This results in a voluntary isolation, or false and treacherous con-nections. Either way, we do not develop tools for using human difference as a springboard for creative change with-in our lives. We speak not of human difference, but of human deviance. (Lorde 115-16)

Another controversial issue was raised as an ideological question but degenerated into a squabble over terminology. The controversy erupted at the end of the second keynote address, delivered by the Ghanaian writer Ama Ata Aidoo. Aidoo's paper touched on many issues related to the African woman. Feminism was, at best, peripheral to her presentation. However, during the question-and-answer session, the first and only question that dominated the discussion came from an African-American who urged other participants to abandon *feminism* (which she labeled a white women's movement) and embrace *Africana womanism* (which she considered more appropriate for the analysis of black women's experiences). Different configurations of groups with opposing and sometimes unclear allegiances evolved. The womanists, feminists, and Africana womanists battled for authenticity, legitimacy, and supremacy while the majority of African women were caught in the middle, watching in utter amazement. At some point during the heated argument, a Queen Mother from Ghana, Nana Apeadu, and an African-American, Kathleen Geathers, denounced the disruptive and diversionary debate, pointing out that we should debate the important issues raised in Aidoo's paper and not waste time on an irrelevant argument over terminology. Similar to Martin Ijere's keynote address that was shoved aside by the controversy over the unilateral demand for the exclusion of whites, Aidoo's important paper on African women was hijacked, renamed, and left undiscussed. Such silencing of African women and issues of importance to them in international forums causes great concern. The non-interest of most African participants in the squabble over terminology was an indication that they were more concerned with "*doing* their struggles" (performance) and less concerned with "*naming* their struggles" (rhetoric). At the end, the majority of the participants thought it more prudent and productive to be just *human beings* and move ahead with the business of the day.

Many foreign participants resented the presence of male presenters, but African women saw it differently. African women observed that they have worked collaboratively with male scholars who are genuinely committed to research on African women, and with male activists who are partners in the struggle for societal transformation. The divergent views on the participation of men show that Women's Studies and feminist scholarship and engagement operate differently in different cultures. The all-female Women's Studies classroom that is the norm in the US, for example, may configure differently in other parts of the world. The sex-based and

race-based exclusionary practices in Western feminist engagement
are neither the only way nor necessarily the right way. In fact, often,
such exclusionary practices have less to do with philosophical or
ideological beliefs and differences and more with turfism, visibility, and power struggle. In addition to practicing inclusive feminism
(what I call *negofeminism*—the feminism of negotiation, accommodation, and compromise; no ego feminism),[22] African feminists
resist being sidetracked by unnecessary rhetorical squabbles from
what they have *to do*. Feminist education and growth will thrive on
a global cross-fertilization of ideas in which African feminists have
a crucial role.

Other issues of the conference were debated in a less contentious atmosphere. Each day of the conference week, there were
about a dozen concurrent sessions and two workshops in which dis-
ciplinary and interdisciplinary issues were discussed. Many rural
women[23] took part in the activities, especially the workshops and
the event at the Enugu stadium. An African-American participant
condemned the absence of lesbian issues on the program. Many
African participants, mostly younger academics, spoke vigorously
for the need to address woman-on-woman abuse/violence and suggested that the issue be placed on the agenda in future WAAD meetings. The conference prioritized health and education and,
consequently, chose health and human rights as the theme of the
second WAAD conference to be held in Indianapolis, U. S. A., in
October 1998. The focus would be on health not only as a physical
or medical question but, in a broader sense, as a social issue thus
allowing participants to debate physical health issues in their relatedness to the economy, education, human rights, the environment,
the arts, and global interdependence. For example, the campaign
against female circumcision in Africa and the Arab world could be
discussed simultaneously as a health issue, an economic issue, and
a human rights question.

THE BETTER LIFE PROGRAM FOR THE RURAL WOMAN

That the meeting at Nsukka was more than a conference was pri-
marily due to the generosity and involvement of the governments
and Better Life Programs of Anambra and Enugu States.
Representatives of the Better Life Program from other states—Oyo,
Ondo, Lagos, Rivers, Ogun, Osun, Bauchi, Kano, Imo, Cross River,
Benue, Abia, and Akwa Ibom attended. The delegation from Cross
River State came with gifts for our foreign guests. Conference par-
ticipants spent the week-end following the conference in Enugu

and Awka as guests of the governments of Enugu and Anambra States. On Saturday, the Enugu State Better Life Program staged a big event at the Enugu stadium in which busloads of rural women from all local government areas in Enugu State participated. Besides the numerous activities that were organized at the stadium, the Governor's wife and Chairperson of the Better Life Program, Dr. Dorothy Nwodo, took participants on a tour of self-help projects designed by and for rural women. The evening ended with a sumptuous dinner and spectacular entertainment at the State House sponsored by the Governor, Dr. Okwesileze Nwodo, and his wife. The following day we travelled to Awka, the Anambra State capital, at the invitation of the Governor and his wife, Dr. and Mrs. C. Ezeife. In addition to offering us a wonderful dinner and rich entertainment at the Awka State House, the Governor's wife and Chairperson of the Anambra State Better Life Program, Mrs. Njideka Ezeife, took us on a tour of numerous women's development projects in nearby villages. For participants, our visits to Enugu and Anambra were the high points of the WAAD conference. Unfortunately, due to infrequent flight operations between Nigeria and some regions of Africa, many African participants—especially those from southern Africa—left Nigeria before the weekend and were unable to participate in the wonderful activities organized by the Anambra and Enugu State Governments. I am most grateful to Anambra and Enugu States for providing the cultural context for our discussions of African women's experiences.

PROCEEDINGS

Out of the 572 abstracts that were submitted, 340 were accepted. It took me three years to compile and edit the conference proceedings of 247 papers and workshop reports. The task entailed the retyping of thousands of pages because most of the papers (particularly those from Africa) were not on diskettes and the hard copies either scanned poorly or did not scan at all. The conference generated a book of abstracts (493 pp.) and a ten-volume proceedings categorized as follows (see "Conference Proceedings [Contents]" in the Appendix):

Vol. I: Addresses, Keynote Speeches, and Reflections (173 pp.)
Vol. II: Rethinking Feminisms and Power (505 pp.)
Vol. III: Health, Human Rights, the Environment (388 pp.)
Vol. IV: Art, Literature and Film (501 pp.)
Vol. V: Art, Literature and Film (395 pp.)

Vol. VI: Agriculture and Rural Development (384 pp.)
Vol. VII: The Academy, Education and the Media (403 pp.)
Vol. VIII: Labor and the Economy (323 pp.)
Vol. IX: Culture and Society (359 pp.)
Vol. X: Religion and Society (324 pp.)

The conference generated a body of knowledge that is unique in
its originality. The editorial process affirmed for me the view I
have expressed repeatedly in many circles that original work on
Africa and African Women is done *in Africa*. The problem has been
the inadequate dissemination of such original works. Hopefully,
the publication of some of the conference materials will contribute
in some way to redressing this problem. For me, compiling and
editing the proceedings was a labor of love and a professional
imperative.

VIDEOTAPES

In addition to the proceedings, the thirteen videotapes generated
by the conference underscore the uniqueness and import of the
meeting. Apart from capturing the controversies that erupted at
the conference, the videotapes hold vivid memories of important
discussions of the issues of the conference as well as the participants'
involvement in rural development projects and activities in two
Nigerian states (Enugu and Anambra). When funds are available,
a sixty-minute documentary of the conference will be produced.

ASSOCIATION OF AFRICAN WOMEN SCHOLARS (AAWS)

The Association of African Women's Scholar (AAWS) with membership open to African men and women was established to encourage, coordinate, and document research on African women as well
as establish a strong network of African female and male scholars,
policy-makers, and activists inside and outside Africa and encour-
age/sustain their strong involvement in African affairs (see
"Association of African Women Scholars [AAWS]" in Appendix for
details).

Undoubtedly, the first international conference on Women in
Africa and the African Diaspora was a monumental task and a historic event that left no participant untouched, albeit differently.
Given the numerous obstacles that militated against the project, it
was an achievement for all of us that the conference not only took
place but also accomplished most of its goals. At the conference,
the issue of language was raised but not fully addressed. Conference
documents were in two European languages, English and French.

It was wonderful to hear the rural woman from Namibia deliver her presentation in her indigenous language and the Nigerian rural women address participants in Igbo during the event at the Enugu stadium. In order to expand the range of participants, serious thought should be given to the use of vernacular languages in addition to European languages. Although we did not have simultaneous translation facilities at Nsukka, we still managed to accommodate, to some degree, participants who did not speak English or French. In future, more attention should be paid to regional specificities by encouraging participants to draw up and submit regional agendas for inclusion in the program. To foster bonds between participants from Africa and the African Diaspora, I proposed that in future conferences, instead of putting participants up in hotels, arrangements could be made for families in host countries to host foreign and national participants.

CONCLUSION: BEYOND POLITICS AND HISTORY

We have chosen each other
and the edge of each other's battles
the war is the same
if we lose
someday women's blood will congeal
upon a dead planet
if we win
there is no telling
we seek beyond history
for a new and more possible meeting.
(Audre Lorde, *Sister Outsider*, 123)

During the controversies that erupted at the WAAD conference, I thought about Audre Lorde, about her work which stands as a beacon for many feminists, scholars and activists committed to societal transformation. Audre Lorde was an institution in the sense that her whole life was a cathedral of learning from which some of us learned and continue to learn. This powerful black warrior spoke, wrote, and fought vehemently against racism anywhere it reared its ugly head—from the Western hemisphere to Cape Town—without being paralyzed by it. She taught us to go beyond without relinquishing; to fashion the new without forgetting the old. She went beyond the facile and unimaginative injunction from some black intellectuals that blacks need to transcend race. How can one transcend with leaving oneself behind? Audre Lorde knew how to *transcend with race.* Audre Lorde was angry, very angry, and justifiably so:

> My response to racism is anger. That anger has eaten clefts into my living only when it remained unspoken, useless to anyone. It has also served me in classrooms without light or learning, where the work and history of Black women was less than a vapor. It has served me as fire in the ice zone of uncomprehending eyes of white women who see in my experience and the experience of my people only new reasons for fear or guilt. And my anger is no excuse for not dealing with your blindness, no reason to withdraw from the results of your own actions. (Lorde 131)

However, Lorde did not allow her intense anger against racism to paralyze and preclude her from forming alliances across differences in her commitment to societal transformation. Therein lies her power and the change it wrought: "But anger expressed and translated into action in the service of our vision and our future is a liberating and strengthening act of clarification, for it is in the painful process of this translation that we identify who are our allies with whom we have grave differences, and who are our genuine enemies" (127). Who knows what she would have told us if she had been present at WAAD '92 where the advocacy of all sorts of exclusions and politics—sexual, racial, feminist—reigned supreme.

Some of the participants who advocated the exclusion of whites argued that we, black women, need our space. I totally agree. In fact, such a space was built into the organization of the conference. African women looked forward to meeting, hosting, and having private moments with their sisters from the Diaspora. Unfortunately, the controversy that exploded in our faces on the *first day* of the conference diverted our attention and sapped our energies. Despite these difficulties, we still succeeded in carving out a space for ourselves before the conference ended; and for some of us, that was a high point of the conference. Indeed, I had proposed in my bilingual introduction to the conference that one of the outcomes of the conference would be the formation of an organization of women in Africa and the African Diaspora. Certainly, we, as black women, need our space. However, we should not see that space as an end in itself but as a means to an end. We should not quarantine ourselves in a space whose comfort may eventually prove lethargic. Our ability to use our space as a tool for refashioning self and society will depend on our willingness to open the doors of our space to allow it to project into and intersect with other spaces. Identity politics must be seen not as an end but as a rest-stop to refuel and reenergize for our long, inevitable journey with other identities and destinies. Furthermore, we must not forget that people have crossed boundaries of race, gender, class, ethnicity, etc., in their fight against oppressive conditions to which others were victims. The exclusion of partners in struggle on the basis of difference undermines us all:

> Significant contributions to other emancipation movements have been made by thinkers who were not themselves members of the group to be emancipated. Marx and Engels were not members of the proletariat. There are whites in our own nation as well as in South Africa and other racist regimes who have been willing and able to think in antiracist ways— indeed, they have been lynched, exiled, and banned for their antiracist writings. Gentiles in Europe and the United States have argued for and suffered because of their defenses of Jewish freedoms. So it would be historically unusual if the list of contributors to women's emancipation alone excluded by fiat all members of the "oppressor group" from its ranks. (Harding 11)[24]

Most importantly, one of my major objectives in convening the conference was to provide a meeting ground for African women and their sisters in the Diaspora. Evidently, the events at the conference foregrounded the need to address the Continent/Diaspora issue. One of the African-American participants, Deborah Plant, states succinctly the complexity of the issue and the urgent need for dialogue:

> This historic conference pointed up the fundamental need for a dialogue between continental and diasporic Africans which addresses each group's different histories and geopolitical situations. By unmasking the presumption of categorical unity based on skin color, the dynamics of the conference underscored the need for a greater awareness of and respect for cultural differences among black people. It also made clear the dearth of information black people all over the globe have of one another and the need to be better informed. The political fallout generated by clashes of "race" and sex challenges black women to consider the irony of silencing black men at women's conferences while white women are allowed to speak. The intense and con-

flictual events of this conference promise to give birth to more productive and progressive dialogue in the future. As the past never stays at bay, chickens and roosters have come home to roost. Theories of gender, sex class, race, nationality, and culture defied containment in facile intellectual abstractions as Africa's Diaspora looked home, as those more apparently oppressed looked to those who have the "privilege" of formal education and material acquisitions, and as women looked at one another with uneasy, distrustful eye. (456-57)

As people of African descent, our attention should not be solely on how blacks in Africa and those in the African Diaspora are *related with* each another, but also on how they *relate to* each other. Education on both sides of the Atlantic is the key to better understanding and relationship.[25] It is not sufficient to say that we *need* this education; *we must be open and willing to imbibe such an education.* It is ironic that, at the WAAD conference, some of those who advocated the rejection of feminism because it is white and proposed instead womanism/Africana womanism that is grounded in African culture failed to appreciate and accommodate the African culture of inclusion, mutuality, and negotiation as articulated by their Nigerian hosts.[26] It is important to examine the ways in which the politics of color and location have been used not only to promote racism but also to separate and "territorize" Africans in Africa and the African Diaspora with the result that they continue to speak this language of separation even today, at least until moments of crisis and rejection compel the search for and claims of affinities from both sides of the Atlantic as a measure of expediency. Audre Lorde wonders who is served by the distortions and separation:

> Hatred is the fury of those who do not share our goals, and its object is death and destruction. Anger is a grief of distortions between peers, and its object is change.... It implies peers meeting upon a common basis to examine difference, and to alter those distortions which history has created around our difference. For it is those distortions which separate us. And we must ask ourselves: Who profits from all this? (129)

The experience of Africans in the United States is instructive. When European immigrants landed/land in the United States, they were/are bestowed the identity that is linked to geography—Irish

Americans, Italian Americans, Polish Americans, etc.[27] On the contrary, when Africans landed/land on the American shores, they were/are collectively color-coded —Negroes, blacks; they came from *nowhere*. Of course they came from *somewhere*! They came from *different* parts of Africa, to be precise, but the homogenization of Africa in the Western imagination and discourses and the arrogant denial of the humanity of the slaves contributed to this way of naming.

The construction of the slaves' "from nowhere" identity (their "from nowhereness," if you will) served not only to justify the inhumanity of slavery but also has implications for the different ways in which Africans on the continent and those in the Diaspora individually and collectively name themselves. Consequently, "blacks" is used in the United States to mean African-Americans exclusively,[28] and "Africans" is used by those on the continent to name themselves exclusively. These different identity claims and compartmentalization limit the scope not only of African Studies (in Africa) and Black Studies (in the United States) but radically influence the scholarship on women of African descent that is produced on the Continent and in the Diaspora respectively. For the type of mutual education I mentioned above to occur, African Studies should be the center-piece (or a strong component, at least) of Black Studies in the African Diaspora,[29] and African Diaspora Studies should be a strong component of African Studies in Africa. This mutual learning and cross-fertilization is not always the case on campuses in the United States where African Studies Programs and African American or Black Studies Programs are often polarized in terms of orientation, governance, and exchange (intellectual and cultural), and in Africa where African Diaspora Studies are minimal or non-existent in school curricula. The result is that Africans on both sides of the Atlantic are either uneducated or miseducated about each other; in other words, they are *mis*educated because they are *un*educated about each other. Since the era of transatlantic slavery, there have been Africans on both sides of the Atlantic whose knowledge of one another is nebulous at best and distorted at worst. Fortunately, many have worked and continue to work for meaningful ways to articulate our affinities.[30] In a way, at the core of the controversy at the WAAD conference was less a lack of awareness of race matters[31] on the part of Africans and more an index of different ways of naming and identity claims that are based on color or geography—on the one hand is the racial (color) reasoning of exclusion, and on the other hand is the locational/Igboland (cultural, if you will) reasoning of inclusion.

As I recall the events of the conference, thoughts of feminist politics and imperialist history of violence and domination pass through my mind. I think of the beautiful line that touches on the relationship between freedom and history: "Our struggle is also the struggle of memory against forgetting."[32] All oppressed peoples must not forget. We cannot afford the risk of historical amnesia, however momentary it may be; neither can we afford to fall victim to historical paralysis. History has a way of intervening in the present in order to either strengthen or cripple it for the future. Frantz Fanon stated it more succinctly: "Use the past with the intention of opening the future, as an initiation to action and as a basis for hope." Maya Angelou, in her inaugural poem, "On the Pulse of Morning," intones the "wrenching pain" of history with hope in her voice (Angelou 1993). The inevitability of the fusion of destinies that is highlighted in Maya Angelou's poem is vividly captured in Cheikh Hamidou Kane's *Ambiguous Adventure*, a powerful fictional evocation of the collision of individual and collective histories. The processes of the collision and/or interpenetration of destinies challenge separate existence by producing what I call the "third term."[33] The inseparability of destinies is even more pertinent in our time with the collapse of ideological walls, massive global immigration and great strides in technological advancement. In Kane's novel, the father of the protagonist, Samba Diallo, sees in the collision between Africa and the West not so much the necessity of a fusion as the end of history epitomized in the inevitability of this first son of the earth—the hybrid, the "third term":

> Every hour that passes brings a supplement of ignition to the crucible in which the world is being fused. We have not had the same past, you and ourselves, but we shall have, strictly, the same future. *The era of separate destinies has run its course.* In that sense, the end of the world has indeed come for every one of us, because no one can any longer live by the simple carrying out of what he himself is. But from our long and varied ripenings a son will be born to the world: the first son of the earth; the only one, also. (79-80; emphasis added)

Although Samba Diallo's father is fundamentally concerned about the positioning of the architects of the New World Order, he is prepared to pledge his son, Samba, not as a passive observer, but as an active partner in constructing the edifice: "My son is the pledge of that [future]. He will contribute to its building. It is my wish that he contribute, not as a stranger come from distant regions, but as an artisan responsible for the destinies of the citadel" (80).

Our goal should not be to exclude other architects, but rather to pledge ourselves and our sons and daughters and, in the process, take our places as active participants with other architects in the construction of the edifice. Historical consciousness is a necessary ingredient for social change; however, *paralyzing* historical consciousness constitutes an impediment to the type of active participation Samba's father envisages for his son. We must not forget, but we must also not allow ourselves to be enslaved and paralyzed by history. The tears that were shed at the WAAD conference will be meaningful and political only when we do not allow them to blur our vision, but rather use them to see clearly into the future. We cannot forget our pain because by forgetting our pain we depoliticize our struggles; our engagement becomes political in the context of our pain. From our "geographies of pain,"[34] we must not forget that the contexture of our engagement/battlefield/war is similar even though the textures of our struggles/battles may be different. The theme of the WAAD conference points to the need for bridge-building, but as one of the participants, Chioma Opara, argues, the way in which we wage our war and fight our battles may or may not produce a "universal ridge" that will make a bridge unnecessary:

> The moral of the WAAD controversy may be summed up thus: There could be several bridges across activism and the academy but not a single one has been constructed across the ridges of culture, creed and race tinctured with deep seated rancor and strife. Not until these ridges are leveled can that yawning hiatus be bridged. The axis of true feminism should be sisterly love that rises above differences, discrimination and resentment. Surely, that unalloyed love hinged on tolerance, equity and forgiveness would overcome retrogressive stereotyping and aim at a universal ridge which would have no need for a bridge.[35]

We can challenge those who exclude us without learning from them how to exclude. We must have the courage to dialogue. We must have the political and moral will to see the good in difference and use it. Audre Lorde taught us a lot in this regard:

> Difference is that raw and powerful connection from which our personal power is forged.... Without community there

is no liberation, only the most vulnerable and temporary armistice between an individual and her oppressor. But community must not mean a shedding of our differences, nor the pathetic pretense that these differences do not exist. (112)

A note one of the participants handed me on the last day of the conference reminds me of the good in difference and the benefit of collective action grounded in mutual respect: "....For it is your words which feed my passion for justice and it is your wisdom that challenges me. It is your spirit which feeds my spirit, teaching me respect, and your strength and vision that give me hope. Yes, I have *followed you, only to walk by your side*....my sister, my friend" [emphasis added]. Yes, our pain must not diminish our passion for justice. Our faith in possibilities will clear our vision, deepen mutual respect, and give us hope as we *follow each other walking side-by-side.*

NOTES

1. This paper was delivered as a keynote address at the African Studies Association Women's Caucus luncheon, Seattle, Washington, November 1992.
2. Chinua Achebe, *Hopes and Impediments* (London: Heinemann, 1988).
3. Many anthologies on Third World women published in the US (edited either by white feminists or feminists of color) follow the same pattern in assembling contributions/contributors—Asian women speak for Asian women; Latin American women speak for Latin American women; Middle-eastern women speak for Middle-eastern women; everyone, except African women, speaks *about, for,* and sometimes *against* African women. The marginalization of African women, particularly those working *in Africa*, is cause for legitimate concern. Most of the original and relevant research on African women is done *in Africa* and the marginalization of the important work done on the continent diminishes what is produced outside the continent. The inclusion of voices from the African continent should be seen as a question of relevance and necessity, not as an issue of representation or tokenism. Such voices are crucial not only in debates about Africa but also in discussions of global issues.
4. It is important to stress that African-American participants did not oppose *en bloc* the participation of whites. In actuality, the majority of the African-Americans steered clear of the controversy and participated fully in the conference through paper presentations, panel discussions, and networking. The perspectives they brought into discussions animated panel sessions and informal meetings.
5. For concerns about Women's Studies as an industry, see Obioma Nnaemeka, "Bringing African Women into the Classroom: Rethinking

Pedagogy and Epistemology," in Margaret Higonnet, ed., *Borderwork: Feminist Engagements with Comparative Literature* (Ithaca: Cornell University Press, 1994, pp. 301-318. Also, for a good analysis of the controversies surrounding the relationship between minority discourses, market forces, and institutionalization, see Leslie Bow, "'For Every Gesture of Loyalty, There Doesn't Have to Be a Betrayal': Asian American Criticism and the Politics of Locality," in Judith Roof and Robyn Wiegman, eds., *Who Can Speak?* (Urbana: University of Illinois Press, 1995), pp. 30-55.

6. See Yash Tandon, "Foreign NGOs, Uses and Abuses: An African Perspective," *IFDA Dossier* 81(1991):67-78, for an analysis of the unequal power relations between foreign and African NGOs that undergird what he calls "informational accountability."

7. During my search for funding, one organization in Britain informed me that it targets mid-career African women scholars and professionals for a substantial portion of its financial awards. Attention to this category of recipients is a step in the right direction.

8. See Sabine Jell-Bahlsen in this volume (p. 433).

9. See Lumka Funani in this volume (p. 413).

10. See also Okpala and Ohuche in "Forum." If nativism and territorial claims are pushed to their limits, only Aborigines would live in Australia, blacks in Africa and Native Americans in the United States; but as we all know, this is not the case. Equally problematic is the often debated issue of "nativism" in the authentication of knowledge claims, articulation, and dissemination. Ros Posel addressed this issue by noting that "this leads to what de Reuck calls "radical conceptual solipsism". In other words, the only proper subject of my own investigation is myself" ("'Alien Researchers?' White Feminists Writing about the Past of Black Women" in *Proceedings of the First International Conference on Women in Africa and the African Diaspora: Bridges across Activism and the Academy*. Nsukka, Nigeria, July 13-18, 1992, Vol. II, p. 393).

11. See Maria Olaussen in this volume.

12. It is important to address the context in which Nigerians faced the demand on *the first day* of the conference to get rid of white participants. Putting together a conference of the magnitude of WAAD without funding was most daunting, frustrating, and debilitating; it required immense commitment and extreme personal sacrifice. I flew to Nigeria five times at my own expense and during those visits, I was humbled and overwhelmed by the unbelievable sacrifices—from walking many miles without food to taking risky trips in dilapidated public transportation at their own expense—made by the members of the local organizing committee (the backbone of the conference). I remember one such trip that I took with the chairperson of the local organizing committee, Dr. Julie Okpala. We travelled to Abuja to discuss with the President's wife, Mrs. Babangida, the possibility of subsidized and free accommodations for conference participants. By the time we left the State House after 6: 00 p. m., we were faced with the possibility of spending the night in Abuja. Unable to afford the $200-a-night hotel room at the Abuja hotel, we took a taxi and travelled all night from Abuja to Nsukka in what

turned out to be the most eventful trip of our lives. I also remember a member of the local organizing committee breaking down in tears out of exhaustion on the second day of the conference when I pleaded with her to travel back to Enugu for a third time in the same day. Exhausted by what they saw as a thankless job, our Nigerians hosts were not willing to accept the unilateral demand that some of their guests be sent away ("pushed out in the rain").

13. See Martha Banks in this volume.

14. See Dé Bryant in this volume. For her one-week stay in Nigeria, Professor Bryant succeeded in starting a linkage program between a high school in Aba, Imo State, and African American youth in Michigan who collected and shipped books and other educational materials for the Aba High School library. Professor Bryant has returned to Nigeria a couple of times since the WAAD conference to continue her work on the project. It is doubtful that her presenting a paper as a member of a bi-racial group undermines her racial allegiance and commitment to the African Continent/African Diaspora relationship.

15. See also Chimalum Nwankwo and Chioma Opara in this volume.

16. It is revealing that virtually all the African-Americans who led the campaign for the exclusion of whites were making their maiden voyage to Africa. The African-Americans who had either been to or lived/worked in Africa before the WAAD conference watched from the sideline. Obviously, they knew the terrain and how to respond to it.

17. See the Appendix for the full text of the statement by the South African delegation. In actuality, those at the center of the controversy over race/racism would have benefited from the numerous well-written and well-articulated papers from South Africans (blacks, coloreds, and whites). Many of the papers (see Fester, Weltz, Ryan, etc.) document the commitment of white and colored women (as members of the ANC, in general, and *Umkhonto We Sizwe*, in particular) to the liberation struggle in apartheid South Africa. Some of these women were present at the conference and we should not have dismissed them without listening to them; they too had important stories to tell.

18. Global meetings such as Copenhagen '80, Nairobi '85, and Beijing '95 can be *truly global* only when issues and concerns from all regions of the world are given *equal* time, attention, and exposure. The two key words of the theme of the 1985 UN Women's conference in Nairobi ("equality" and "peace") should not be seen in isolation from each other, but rather in their relatedness. Peace comes with equality. When we work for equality, we will be rewarded with the peace of equality—that is, the peace that equality brings. Inequality inscribes insurgency at our individual and collective borders. What was truly heroic and historic at the WAAD conference was that the majority of the participants—blacks *and* whites, women *and* men, South *and* North—spoke with one global voice against another take-over of an international conference.

19. See Martha Banks in this volume (p. 390).

20. See Maria Olaussen in this volume.

21. See Dé Bryant in this volume (p. 405).

22. See Obioma Nnaemeka, "Feminism, Rebellious Women and Cultural

Boundaries: Rereading Flora Nwapa and Her Compatriots," *Research in African Literatures* 26.2 (1995):106-109.

23. It is interesting to note that in spite of the representation and participation of rural women in conference activities in Nsukka, Enugu, and Awka, some foreign participants still complained that rural women did not show. I imagine some of them came to Africa looking for "Africa" in Africa and were disoriented and frustrated when they did not find "it." Obviously, the rural women were unrecognizable because they came fully clothed, not half-naked or wearing raffia skirts and *jigida* (waist beads) with mounds of loads on their heads and babies strapped to their backs! The busloads of rural women from Igboland appeared as they normally would—fully and decently clothed.

24. See also Betty Welz in this volume for the involvement of white women in *Umkhonto We Sizwe*, the ANC Army of Liberation.

25. See Kathleen Geathers and Gloria Braxton in this volume.

26. See the contributions to the "Forum" by Chimalum Nwankwo, Chioma Opara, Julie Okpala, and Elsie Ohuche for discussion of mutual respect and sharing that govern the guest/host relationship in Igboland. This was demonstrated by our Nigerian hosts, who had next to nothing but were very willing and eager to share the little they had with their guests.

27. The struggle by African-Americans to replace "Negro" with "African-American" is not a mere rhetorical question. It is a question of affirmation and agency (the agency of self- naming); it is a necessity. The same old way of naming immigrants in the US persists even today where the identity of many non-European immigrants groups (like their European counterparts)—Cuban Americans, Chinese Americans, Korean Americans, Japanese Americans, Mexican Americans, etc.—is linked to *somewhere*.

28. See Carole Boyce Davies, *Black Women, Writing, and Identity* (London: Routledge, 1994), pp. 7-9 for the use of the category "black" in the United States and Britain. See also Gertrude Fester in this volume for its use in South Africa.

29. With due respect to some critiques of Molefi Asante's work, one must give him credit for insisting on the need and relevance of centering African Studies in African-American scholarship.

30. Randall Robinson's extraordinary work in the areas of democratization and human rights needs special mention. In the recent past, many attempts have been made to establish linkages between Africans in Africa and Africans in the Diaspora (the United States, in particular). However, a disproportionate amount of energy and attention is focused on the economic and political arenas. The creation of economic ties between Africans in Africa and Africans in the African Diaspora is certainly an important one. However, for the ongoing economic and political missions to Africa from our brothers and sisters in the Diaspora to be solid and long-lasting, they need to be grounded in cultural and educational missions.

31. See Chioma Opara in this volume.

32. Cited in bell hooks, *Yearning: Race, Gender, and Cultural Politics.* (Boston: South End Press, 1990), p. 147.

33. See Obioma Nnaemeka, "Marginality as the Third Term: A Reading of Cheikh Hamidou Kane's *Ambiguous Adventure*," in Leonard Podis and Yakubu Saaka, eds., *Challenging Hierarchies: Issues and Themes in Post-Colonial Literature* (New York: Peter Lang [forthcoming]).

34. See Françoise Lionnet, "Geographies of Pain: Captive Bodies and Violent Acts in the Fictions of Gayl Jones, Bessie Head and Myriam Warner-Vieyra," in Obioma Nnaemeka, ed., *The Politics of (M)Othering: Womanhood, Identity, and Resistance in African Literature* (London: Routledge, 1997), pp. 205-227. See also Rubin Patterson, *Foreign Aid after the Cold War: The Dynamics of Multipolar Economic Competition* (Trenton, N.J.: Africa World Press, 1997).

35. See Chioma Opara in this volume (p. 427).

WORKS CITED

Achebe, Chinua. *Hopes and Impediments*. London: Heinemann, 1988.

Angelou, Maya. *On the Pulse of Morning*. New York: Random House, 1993.

Bow, Leslie. "'For Every Gesture of Loyalty, There Doesn't Have to Be a Betrayal': Asian American Criticism and the Politics of Locality." *Who Can Speak?*, ed., Judith Roof and Robyn Wiegman. Urbana: University of Illinois Press, 1995.

Davies, Carol Boyce. *Black Women, Writing, and Identity*. London: Routledge, 1994.

Giddings, Paula. *When and Where I Enter*. New York: W. Morrow, 1984.

hooks, bell. *Yearning: Race, Gender, and Cultural Politics*. Boston: South End Press, 1990.

Lionnet, Françoise. "Geographies of Pain: Captive Bodies and Violent Acts in the Fictions of Gayl Jones, Bessie Head and Myriam Warner-Vieyra." *The Politics of (M)Othering: Womanhood, Identity, and Resistance in African Literature*, ed., Obioma Nnaemeka, London: Routledge, 1997. 205-227.

Lorde, Audre. *Sister Outsider*. Trumansburg, NY: Crossing Press, 1984.

Mohanty, Chandra Talpade. "Introduction: Cartographies of Struggle, Third World Women and the Politics of Feminism." *Third World Women and the Politics of Feminism*, ed., Chandra Talpade Mohanty, Ann Russo, and Lourdes Torres. Bloomington: Indiana University Press, 1991.

Morgan, Robin. *Sisterhood Is Global*. New York: Anchor Books/Doubleday, 1984.

Moyers, Bill. *A World of Ideas*, ed., Betty Sue Flowers. New York: Doubleday, 1989.

Nnaemeka, Obioma. "Bringing African Women into the Classroom: Rethinking Pedagogy and Epistemology." *Borderwork: Feminist Engagements with Comparative Literature*, ed., Margaret Higonnet. Ithaca: Cornell University Press, 1994: 301-318.

——. "Feminism, Rebellious Women and Cultural Boundaries: Rereading Flora Nwapa and Her Compatriots," *Research in African Literatures* 26.2 (1995): 80-113.

——. "Marginality as the Third Term: A Reading of Cheikh Hamidou Kane's *Ambiguous Adventure*." *Challenging Hierarchies: Issues and Themes in Post-*

Colonial Literature, ed., Leonard Podis and Yakubu Saaka. New York: Peter Lang, (forthcoming).

Patterson, Rubin. *Foreign Aid after the Cold War: The Dynamics of Multipolar Economic Competition*. Trenton, N.J.: Africa World Press, 1997.

Posel, Ros. "'Alien Researchers?' White Feminists Writing about the Past of Black Women" in *Proceedings of the First International Conference on Women in Africa and the African Diaspora: Bridges across Activism and the Academy*. Nsukka, Nigeria, July 13-18, 1992, Vol. II, pp. 391-403.

Tandon, Yash. "Foreign NGOs, Uses and Abuses: An African Perspective." *IFDA Dossier* 81(1991): 67-78.

V
FORUM

Bridges Across Activism and the Academy: One Psychologist's Perspective[1]

Martha Banks (U. S. A.)

WHEN DR. OBIOMA NNAEMEKA FIRST TOLD ME THAT SHE was convening a conference on "Women in Africa and the African Diaspora: Bridges Across Activism and the Academy," I was ecstatic. I saw an opportunity to visit the continent of my ancestors and share that visit with my mother, a retired social worker. As is the case with many other conferences that interest me, I also saw an opportunity to learn and share research with feminist professionals. For many personal and professional reasons, I have a long-standing thirst for international and multicultural perspectives.

As the buses entered the campus of the University of Nigeria at Nsukka, I eagerly pulled out my new camcorder to capture some of the drama of the opening of the conference. I was impressed with the obviously international crowd of attendees and overwhelmed as I listened to conversations in languages that I could not identify. As was the case when I had toured Europe as a choral singer 20 years earlier, I felt humbled by my foreign status. There was a big difference, however. In Nsukka, I felt comfortable.

The opening ceremonies were impressive. There was a wonderful formality in the introductions of the dignitaries, the conference organizers, and the welcoming university officials. The music of young recorder players and a professional piper added a thrill to the proceedings. Dr. Nnaemeka's opening address, with many acknowledgments and tributes, confirmed that this historic conference would be one of the most important I would ever attend.

As the afternoon began, we were entertained by local dancers. Speeches were followed by a protest from a small group of mostly

African-American and African-British women who objected to the presence and participation of European and European American women. With a total lack of sensitivity to Nigerian protocol, they questioned the pivotal roles of men in the conference. My ecstasy was quickly dashed and replaced by anger and sadness. I had traveled, not only with my mother, but with my European American business partner and research colleague; we had two presentations scheduled which were designed, in large part, to demonstrate the benefits of building bridges. Our research and our life work has been dedicated to improving health conditions for all people, but with a special focus on issues faced by African American women. The idea that we had traveled so far to be told that our work was not welcome was nearly unbearable. In those terrible moments, I saw a side of the Ugly American that I had hoped I had left behind for a week.

Although I like to think of myself as open-minded, I had much difficulty listening to the arguments of participants who would close doors on sharing and developing understanding. I reflected on my knowledge of "Black" psychology with its roots in the communal philosophy of Kemet. Why did some of the African American women believe that *they* spoke in African voices when their divisiveness was more reflective of European competition than African cooperation? I found myself struggling (as I had with "Colored," "Negro," "Afro-American," "Third World," and "Black") with the term "African American"; this is clearly a racial name, not necessarily built on cultural roots, understanding, or identity. As they spoke, I saw other women involved in the same identity struggle, asking "If we are not African and we are not (European) American, then who are we?" I was most relieved when Dr. Nnaemeka took a poll of our hosts, the Nigerian women, and announced that the conference would proceed as originally planned. All accepted papers were to be delivered.

The paper sessions were very inspiring. It was clear that the conference committee had thoroughly screened the proposed papers and included presentations which were pragmatic and thought-provoking. The Nigerian women, in particular, engaged in discussions during the question-and-answer periods in such a way that ideas were clarified. Most importantly, the assumptions of researchers were challenged so that all participants left with a better understanding of the limitations of national, as opposed to global, interpretations. For example, a presentation of the negative aspects of clitoridectomy led to a lively discussion of the economic, political, religious, and clinical aspects of the issue. Although I gained a lot of information from the formal presentations, I learned far more from the discussions.

Another powerful dynamic in the conference was an intensely personal one. Throughout the conference, African women stopped me to ask if the silver-haired woman with me was my mother; they were always delighted when I introduced her. The quiet, yet profound, respect for the elderly was heartwarming for both of us. It was the kind of respect my mother had learned to expect when she grew up in St. Vincent in the West Indies and of which she has been deprived for most of the nearly 50 years she has lived in the United States.

To Dr. Obioma Nnaemeka I shall always owe a debt of gratitude. Her convening of the historic conference will have a positive impact on the understanding of women from around the world. Many of the bridges span more than activism and the academy—they brought together, for all too brief a time, sisters at heart.

NOTES

1. A previous version of this article was solicited and submitted for publication in the newsletter of the Women's Caucus of the African Studies Association and was published in the *Psychology of Black Women Newsletter* (Winter, 1993).

THINKING IGBO, THINKING AFRICAN

CHIMALUM NWANKWO (NIGERIA)

IN THE DIM HISTORY OF IGBO COUNTRY, THE PEOPLE WHO identified their roots with Omambala, Enugu, Isu Abame, Aro, and so on returned to their ancestral homes periodically in large masses at either festival time or a specially appointed time. When they did, there were always distinctions, ritual-based and underogatory, between those who lived abroad and those who lived at home. Among the Aro, even today, those who lived abroad, in distant outposts, humbly accepted the appellation of *Aro uzo* (the Aro who live abroad) and those at home, in the ancestral base, affirmed a gentle superiority as people of *Aro uno* (the Aro who live at home). There were no misunderstandings about this. It was something based on closeness with the earth, with *omenana* (tradition), with the cumulative and accumulating knowledge and mastery of all the rites and rituals of communal identification with the total Aro cosmos.

It was clear that those who were at home as *Aro uno* knew more about the standards of Aro culture, the mores and values unvitiated by time and distance. The groves were there with them. The shrines were there with them. The cenotaphs of icons and heroes and deities were there along with the memorial festivals and the rituals which affirmed their origins and assured their perpetuation for posterity. That these home-bred were in steady consonance and amity with their physical and metaphysical habitat gave them the prerogative of dictating critical calendars for mytho-spiritual events like the *Ikeji* (New Yam festival) involving the reunion of all the people and the ancestral spirits.

The people of *Aro uzo* had and still have their own versions of the *Ikeji* but they either took their calendrical directives from aboriginal ritual or firmly established and maintained their own festivals with their own new rules and regulations. The two never mixed. When they did, mutuality or commonality was refereed or protected by distance. But if *Aro uzo* ever submitted or submits to a home-based communion, there was never and has never been a doubt about whose system and whose rules would prevail. This is the logic of reunions in all meaningful rituals and festivals on this planet. It is so in Tibet, in Jerusalem, in Mecca, as it is in New Orleans and Rio de Janeiro and numerous other such stations on this planet. The custodians of the culture always led and will always lead by virtue of proximity.

At the WAAD conference, I watched with sadness certain female participants, specifically from the United States, attempt with unabashed and immodest vigor to subvert that sacred pattern of order. With very ugly emotionality, they challenged the organizers of the conference for inviting certain participants and allowing them "hijack the helms" of the proceedings. These nationalists were so righteously deep in their indignation that they did not notice the astonishment on the faces of their largely Igbo hosts. They missed the fact that up to the moment of their outbursts, none of the so-called "hijackers" had featured in any visible or meaningful manner in the proceedings of the conference. They missed the significance of the breaking of the tell-tale *kola* which all readers of African Literature have encountered in Chinua Achebe's celebrated *Things Fall Apart.* They missed the Igbo live-and-let-live enshrined in the proverb of the perching of the eagle and the hawk. They missed the fact that the dynamo of their emotions was powered by the imperial plague of their blameless circumstances. I still wonder today whether they did not miss the kernel of the wily Igbo proverb which Professor Obioma Nnaemeka pulled out urgently from an improvised diplomatic bag : *Obialu be m abiagbune m, o na-ana mkpukpu apunaya* (May my guest not kill me with a visit, so that he or she may not be afflicted at departure with a hunched back!)

How does one communicate the spiritual and political implications of that proverb? How does one explain to an obtuse alien consciousness that, of all the major African ethnic groups, the Igbo are the only group without a martial history of empire and that despite that lack there is probably an Igbo chief doing business quietly right now from an igloo in the Tundra! And how does one explain that when Igbo people gather even today, that it is still a democratic haven: the retarded citizen and the "village idiot" enjoy equal speaking time and space with the high and the mighty. The audience always knows what to pay heed to and what to discard and, by and large, mutual respect is mass property. In Igbo country, the lunatic is welcome in all homes and is sheltered as long as time permits, barring any flare of lunacy.

When I thought the conference had survived the initial challenge from the irate sisters, there were periodic flares of a different sort which terribly threatened my elastic Igbo patience. Groups of African-American women walked up to me repeatedly to complain about everything from the bad roads and deplorable hotel circumstances to things as distant from my control and expertise as an English Professor as the inability to call home from their rooms. Fearing that the attraction could be my shining bald head, I momentarily acquired a hat for disguise but these complaints did not stop. Then and now in retrospect, I wondered and still wonder what an American of any ethnic extraction would tell me if I accosted him/her and rudely laid bare all the frustrations of living in a land in which everything about me is either insufferably funny, strange, outlandish, uncouth, and of course, invariably culturally askew or inappropriate. I wonder....

I wonder if we all ever attempt, in our sober moments, to contemplate *how* serviceable and enduring bridges are erected; what makes spans sit on the shoulders of embankments. And I wonder whether any one has contemplated weighing the dangers or indeed making that choice between living in the belly of the killer whale or in the precarious environs of its fins. Unless our reflections run in such veins, it remains most unlikely that we shall understand certain happenings which some observers are likely to characterize as uncharitable and (in the parlance of those who hold the global yam and the knife of dispensation)...uncivilized.

Many observers found it difficult to understand why, at a certain convention in London in 1988, courageous African women closed their doors to any alien participation in their discussion of the problems of African women. Those women were wary of the selfishness and arrogance of certain kinds of "foreign aid." Many observers also found it difficult to understand the discomfort and irritation of most African men and some women who were present during certain sessions at the WAAD conference. The boundaries between guests and hosts were being recklessly trampled. But other attendant issues and questions also remained quite clear and simple. In all matters affecting the destiny of anything African, whether it is the celebrated, phony thousand Africas of Appiah or Mudimbe or in the old nebulous one battered out of shape, form, and meaning by the cultural and economic legerdemain of intractable evil forces from all over this planet, all attitudes converge: Africa is the school kid's clay, available for the desultory and perfunctory fingers of clowns and gurus. For now and the future, the scare and the great tragedy lie in the cynocephalic humility with which too many Africans accept this condition. Thanks to the imponderable ravage of the continent by a cold war which flamed red hot in this continent, African intellectuals are groveling like migrant laborers all over the world.

The predominant spirit at the WAAD tells me that the answers to the problems of the black world are sitting there in the laps of the black world. From what I have tried to explain in the relationship between the people of *Aro uno* and those of *Aro uzo*, it ought to be clear that the builders of bridges must all surrender their shoulders like two equal embankments. Charity, we all know, never begins abroad. Any other conduct or practice merely fits into the programs of the guru or the clown who periodically stretches and yawns, and looks toward the African continent for the cure of his/her *ennui*.

FUNDING AFRICAN PARTICIPANTS

MAUREEN MALOWANY (CANADA)

LIKE MANY OTHER WOMEN WHO ATTENDED THE FIRST WAAD Conference, my Batik bag travels everywhere with me—to other research sites, conferences, seminars, libraries—in and out of Africa. It is a beautiful reminder of that fraught gathering of women (and some men), of many tears, of friends met and kept, of visits to homes of many women in Nsukka, thanks to the hospitality and generosity of our hosts. Women associated with the University of Nsukka were keen to discuss their academic and personal lives, their local, regional and national political elections. There was as much excitement outside the conference as within. I am sure the women of Nsukka continue to engage in the complexity of Nigerian political life. From the first day of the conference and, it would seem, throughout those days and now years following its closing, we continue to be engaged in the issues raised on that first day of the conference regarding exclusion and racism. For this public and published forum I would like to address two other concerns that have to do both with the 1992 Conference and the planned "WAAD 2" for 1998.

Many women have stated how the experience of meeting so many African women from a variety of backgrounds, nation states, interests—talking about themselves or other African women, both in Africa and the Diaspora—profoundly affected our thinking, our work, our activism; this is now commonplace. But perhaps this representative body should be more closely examined. I could not help but feel terrific loss at the conference with the absence of those African women who could not come to Nsukka in 1992. They faced layers of constraints: some political, others geopolitical, but overriding all was a lack of money.

In her welcoming address, Obioma told us of specific women

who had planned to attend but, in the end, could not be there. There were hundreds of others we didn't even know—or who themselves did not know the conference was being held—who also were unable to attend. After the conference, when friends in Cairo told me they watched reports on the conference on Egyptian television, I wondered how Egyptian women, unrepresented, felt as they watched us attend a conference that should have included them.

When the women from Namibia arrived after grueling days of traveling, we cheered and I thought again of those women who were not there—from Ethiopia, Côte d'Ivoire, Burkina Faso, Zambia, Mozambique. As I listened to the women from Southern Africa talk of missed connections, layovers in countries too expensive to visit, inability to buy local currencies—the problems of those who did indeed arrive—I wondered if I could not have helped. Many women from North America, including myself, were going on to other ports, vacations in nearby African countries or European countries on their way home. Perhaps that "extra" money could have allowed for the presence of more African women. The spirit and commitment expressed by so many women visiting Nsukka surely would have supported such a funding proposal. I felt uncomfortably privileged to be there.

Economic difficulties across that large continent of Africa have not ameliorated. Today in Nigeria many of the women who came from the north of that country might not have the transportation available, or affordably so, to attend a second conference held in their own country. I was not always convinced that the day-to-day expense of life in Nigeria for ordinary people was appreciated by conference attendees as we stayed in hotels economically out of reach for most Nigerians. And we thus applaud even more the warm hospitality offered to us by the women and their families of Nsukka who kept much of this hidden from our eyes and video cameras.

For the coming conference I ask us all to consider some type of 'twinning' program whereby women who have the means (or whose institutions have the means) to permit attendance at "WAAD 2" might provide assistance to women of all parts of Africa to attend also. There was such a dearth of African women from francophone Africa that this must surely be rectified. I would strongly suggest that WAAD stay within Africa and be organized in Dakar or Ouagadougou. Both of these cities possess the infrastructure to host international conferences. Both cities would benefit from the monies spent by organizers and participants. All of us would benefit from the experience of being in this region of Africa.

To Obioma I offer my assistance—long distance—and to any other women who care to work on the preparation or funding proposals for "WAAD 2." Please keep the conference in Africa. Let us please assist all women of Africa to attend.

"So Why Theorize about the Brontes?"[1]: African Women Writers and English Literature in Finland

Maria Olaussen (Finland)

At the very beginning of the Nsukka conference I was rather abruptly approached by an African American delegate and asked about the topic of my paper. She also wanted to know why I attended the conference and my reason for, as she put it, doing "research on African women." I was rather taken aback by her abrupt manner but took this as another American way of starting a conversation. So I explained that I teach English literature at a university in Finland and that some of this literature is written by African women. Our conversation stopped at this point which I again found rather puzzling. There was definitely something wrong with my way of handling the situation. I tried to ask her about her paper but by then she had again rushed off and was now asking another white woman the same questions. At this point I realized that this was not an instance of small-talk gone wrong. I also understood that "why" here meant "with what right."

Studying English Literature in a small, relatively wealthy but geographically and culturally marginal country in Western Europe very often means trying to cover up one's marginality. It is often only when I leave Finland that I actually have to confront my geographical location and start to think about where it is I am standing in relation to the texts I am studying. In a way this should be quite easy. In the English departments in Finland we study cultures and literatures written in English language and all the cultures we meet are foreign cultures. Some of them are admittedly more foreign to us than others.

At this point I want to stress that I am well aware of the fact that this particular relation to the English language is quite unusual in the world today. Not all non-English members of English departments are in a position where they can make this very clear distinction between a language not my own and a culture not my own. I have on several occasions been puzzled by the fact that works originally not written in English are taught in translation in some English departments. An Egyptian colleague once told me that he teaches Strindberg in the English department! We teach Strindberg in Comparative Literature and in the Swedish department but definitely not in the English department. My colleague did not understand my confusion. It is only later that I have come to understand that for a writer to make it in the English department the writer has to be "a great writer." On a different occasion I was invited to a British Council course on the New Literatures in English. This course was specifically designed for people teaching English literature overseas. Participants from all over the world met in Oxford in April. The daffodils were in full bloom. The most fascinating thing about people's reactions to the daffodils was the way you could tell exactly how far removed from the center someone was by the way they discussed the daffodils. Ironically enough, those of us who had not grown up with Wordsworth and who had studied his poetry secure in our own cultural traditions, were the ones who knew that we were supposed to handle this matter with care. We were also closest to the center and, together with those of our colleagues from other parts of the world who for some other reason also had access to the newest books and the newest theories, we knew that we were not supposed to enjoy the daffodils. It is only through incidents like these that I have come to think about my particular position in relation to the texts I study and teach.

Why—with what right and for what reasons—do I study the texts by African women? It is for the same reason and with the same justification or lack of justification that I "theorize about the Brontës." I try to understand foreign cultures. I would argue that we in the English departments in Finland are all fairly secure about the fact that we study foreign cultures in a foreign language. We are quite happy to "theorize about the Brontës" and we certainly do not ask ourselves why. At least not until we read that now the Americans are asking themselves and each other this question. What happens next is typical of the margins. Suddenly the students are blaming themselves for the racism in the United States. They do not discuss racism in Finland or white supremacy in other forms. The students think they are white Americans (at least until they have visited the United States) and they see themselves as being directly involved in American race relations.

Naturally, we no longer theorize about the Brontës. We read Alice Walker, Toni Morrison, Ama Ata Aidoo, Flora Nwapa, and Bessie Head. And I have to admit that we are doing this not because we suddenly realized that we had been terribly Eurocentric up till now. It is not because we suddenly understood that there are all these other people who also use the English language and who have developed different kinds of English literatures. It is because the center realized this that we also suddenly came to the same insight and started changing the syllabus. I am not saying that I would rather not have been "told" this. There are of course people who would happily use this as an argument against any changes in the departments. But this would only mean imitating the preferences of the center twenty years ago; that is, we would continue to see only a limited part of the English-speaking world and read only texts by white men. I am very happy about the way things have developed and fascinated by the new cultures that I now encounter. But I would find it very dishonest to claim that we in our English department decided that we wanted to study black American women, African, and Indian writers. We did only what we always do, we imitated the center. The idea was great but it was not our own.

It was with an awareness of these power relations that I followed the discussion at the Nsukka conference about whether white women should speak at the conference. I followed the discussion from the side because it was very clear to me that here was a matter of the center discussing with itself and leaving the margins as an audience. This is not to say that I didn't understand and sympathize with the arguments. It is a fact that white people have used their position of power over black people to theorize about them and by so doing fortify their position. I can understand the symbolic significance of not letting white women speak. What I found rather astonishing was the total lack of awareness on the part of some delegates that they are now the ones in power. The Nigerian women did not bring up the issue, neither did the South Africans. The center spoke and "told" the margins not to let the ones in power speak, no matter what they had to say. There is a powerful contradiction in this attitude (I also find a certain contradiction in my feelings towards it). I want to listen to arguments no matter who is speaking. But I also want to analyze the reasons behind the fact that it is this particular voice I now hear. Where is that person located that I can hear her voice so clearly? Are there other voices? And where am I located—might that be the reason why I can suddenly hear new voices?

It was important for me to be able to go to Nigeria. Living in a wealthy country naturally doesn't mean having personal wealth. It means having access to facilities and funding. As everyone knows, funding agencies have their rules and regulations and one of them is generally that persons attending a conference can get access to funding only if they contribute to the conference. Discussing my research at a conference means having an opportunity to listen to other opinions. It does not mean telling other people what to think. The ideas behind the "white women" discussion at the Nsukka conference were not only a total disregard for the real power relations present (i.e., the inability on the part of some Americans to see themselves as the rich and powerful ones that they in fact are); it was also a misunderstanding of the nature of academic work and the purpose of a conference presentation.

The Nsukka conference was important for my work. I was able to meet Flora Nwapa and Ama Ata Aidoo and many other African women. I could discuss my work on Bessie Head with others interested in her work. On my return I was able to introduce the work of African women writers to groups inside and outside the university. And, I repeat, I am happy about the way English Studies are developing but I am also very well aware of the fact that this development is—to use the well-known title of a novel by Bessie Head— a question of power.

NOTES

1. Here I borrow Alice Walker's well-known question (*In Search of Our Mothers Gardens*, New York, 1983) to Patricia Meyer Spacks who felt she did not want to construct theories about experiences she had not had and so left out black women's writing entirely from her book, *The Female Imagination*.

REFLECTIONS ON NSUKKA '92

DÉ BRYANT (U. S. A.)

THE CONFERENCE WAS WELL WORTH THE WORK IT TOOK
to get there. The whole week was filled with new people to meet,
places to go, and foods to eat. It was a conference with over 700 people from 43 different countries. They came from points all around
the globe; they came in waves for the first three days. That meant
at breakfast every day there were new faces, additional languages,
and ever more stunning clothes. We got into some great conversations even if communication wasn't always "a piece of tart," to quote
one of my fellow conference attendees.

Actual sessions were held at the University of Nigeria, Nsukka
(UNN). I can only begin to tell you all the fascinating topics that
were covered in those few short days. My students and I split up and
attended different sessions to get maximum coverage and still we
missed an awful lot. The sessions ran concurrently, so you're forced
to choose what to leave in and what to leave out. It was really tough
sometimes. Over two hundred papers were presented. In between
the sessions, there were all manner of other activities to occupy the
mind and delight the senses. Every day brought a different troupe
of dancers, artists, and chanters. It quickly became apparent that a
custom of the area was to press money on the foreheads of the
dancers, usually the females, while they perform. I am told that this
is in appreciation of the degree of talent and/or enthusiasm the
dancer displays. It is like tipping; the amount of money pressed to
the forehead is in proportion to the talent and/or enthusiasm. Folks,
let me tell you, there was a lot of enthusiasm in that hall those days!

A mini-market materialized on the conference site about the
second day. I suspect the word got out that there was a group of
folks there who were anxious to spend money. It was good in a way,
as the inflated prices supported the local economy (It was interest-

ing to note just how high those prices crept as the days passed). In my later travel I realized that these vendors had made a killing, by Nigerian standards. I believe it's called "charging what the market will bear."

A little gadget called camcorder has changed the face of living today. At any given moment you could see at least twenty of them going. Now instead of flashes going off in the faces of the dancers and speakers, there's the whirl of video cameras. All around us, I saw otherwise normal people with great, black growths extended from the sides of their faces! What was most notable about the video-tapers was that they kept ducking and diving and dodging their way through the action. (A few of those tapes can only be viewed after a dose of dramamine!)

The conference had a severe rough spot. During the open mike at the end of the first day a woman from the U. S. strode to the front. She asked forgiveness from her ancestors, those present, and progeny yet unborn. I knew something was coming. She claimed to represent a faction of those attending, then started a discussion that split the conference into camps: Black Women and White Women and Who's Zooming Who. The *mêlée* raged for two days. I won't go into all the bloody details but here's the gist of it:

(1) Whether white women should be allowed at the conference to present. "Who are they to tell us about us?"

(2) Whether white women should be allowed at the conference at all. "Who invited them to a black women's conference?"

(3) Whether conference organizers misrepresented the purpose of the conference by naming it "Women in Africa and the African Diaspora."

(4) Whether conference organizers had allowed themselves to be swayed by white (financial) supporters and had lost their blackness.

The bad situation got worse as the hours ticked by. Major falling outs occurred around all the conference locations far into the night and through the next day—people yelling at each other, people crying, people storming out of rooms, people refusing to breathe the same air, people offering to pull out, people being ordered to pull out, people wondering if they should pull out; black women consoling black women, black women consoling white women, black and white women consoling each other; conference organizers explaining, conference organizers refusing to explain. Caucuses of white women, caucuses of black women, caucuses of sessions, people being turned away from sessions, etc.

For myself, I was taken aback by two factors: the interpretation of the purpose of the conference and the ferocity of the attacks. So I started asking questions to find out if I was indeed absolutely uninformed. It soon became clear that the vortex of the storm was a group of 20 to 25 black women from the U. S. They had come to the conference to "find themselves" and to return to the motherland; we were caught up in their frustration and rage at being unable to do either. They had succeeded in disrupting the conference because they hit all the switches each of us carries in his/her head when it comes to dealing with racial issues. Their malignancy spawned other malignancies and so the disease spread for those two days.

By the early morning plenary of the third day there was emotional and psychological blood on the streets. Events had long since deteriorated beyond being just uncomfortable, they were downright murderous. Bringing people in contact with racism—their own and the society's—is a vital part of healing and change. That's one thing. What was happening at that conference was a bloodletting, pure and simple. That's something entirely different.

I am still processing what happened that caused things to change. In retrospect, I believe it was a series of events rather than one major turning point. The conference convener, Obioma Nnaemeka, reiterated her position that the conference was not intended to be a pilgrimage; it was to discuss ways to bridge the gaps between those who know and those who need to know. Nigerians spoke out against the very notion that people invited to their country should be ordered to leave at all, much less ordered to do so by Americans. The protests got louder and louder from the majority of us who were appalled by the violence and hatred of the past few days. The volatile group of Americans that sparked the whole conflagration began to burn itself out.

The community began to look for ways to heal itself, with people coming together in twos and threes or in small groups to search for resolution. By the end of the third day a semblance of order and calm had returned to the conference. With a few notable exceptions, people were once again going to sessions and sitting together at breakfast and going about their business. Don't misunderstand me. The wounds of the previous three days were still there; no one was pretending that nothing happened. The hurts continued to have an impact on how people related to one another for the remainder of the conference. Rather than denial, people were trying to find common ground again in order to accomplish the work that had brought us to that place: building bridges.

As I look back on those few days I feel two emotions equally balanced one with the other. First is a deep sadness about the degree of carnage that I witnessed. Martin Luther King, Jr. told us that as long as one of us is oppressed, then all of us are oppressed. I agree. I believe it's just as destructive when black people act on their hatred as it is when white people act on theirs. Over and over again I heard things like, "It's about time they see what it's like," "Let them cry; black people have been crying for generations," and "They need to be crying; they know they'll go home and do some black person wrong all the same." I have to tell you that the comment that grieved me the most to hear was, "Good. I like to see white people hurt." I hear it still when I tell people here what happened. "Good. I like to see white people hurt." My response to that is simple: may I never become so angry and bitter that I can honestly enjoy watching another person's agony. To do so would mean I have a hole in my soul through which all that is humane and just and good is leaking out. If that day arrives, I will have become what I have committed my life to overcoming: the oppressor.

In reflecting on those days, I also feel affirmation. Think of it! For 72 hours we at the conference were a microcosm of our world today. Ethnic tensions soared, tempers flared, nationalism raged. People divided into camps and factions with boundaries designed as much to keep members inside as they were to keep others outside. The air was thick with position statements, mandates, resolutions, and even ultimatums. Diplomats and representatives shuttled back and forth making proposals and counter-proposals. A silent majority shifted restlessly, watchful but remaining detached, as the major stakeholders engaged one another.

As with any conflict, there was a time when the outcome hung absolutely in the balance. Life or death. Sounds melodramatic, but isn't that the end result of everything? The things we do in life, to varying degrees, give birth or bring death. To a very great extent, we choose which it will be. We can face the tough questions and make the hard choices, or not. We can embrace the pain that accompanies growth, or not. We can give up things precious to us because we recognize they no longer serve us well....or not. We can give up the "safety" of the familiar for something greater yet unknown, or not.

What was affirming about those few days was that we chose life. It was painful and messy and demanded much from some of us. We are all shaped from first breath by racial allegiances and historical prejudices. It is hard to negotiate from those places within ourselves.

But we did. And we not only survived, we were victorious. If we could do it, we can show people in our own little corners of the world how to do the same.

Some of you may be wondering how I handled the situation in terms of our presentation. In case I didn't mention it, I am an African American and my two students are white. Did they present their papers? Absolutely. Didn't I consider that a betrayal of my brothers and sisters? Absolutely not. Doesn't that mean I sold out to the "Europeans," betraying my blackness? Those of you who know me well already know the answer to that question. At the risk of redundancy, I'll repeat myself: Absolutely not.

I realize that some of you reading this are already disagreeing with me. I accept that. I will say again as I have said before that my enemies are called "injustice," "oppression," "hatred," "evil." I have found them equally, albeit in different guises, among all races. I therefore look for their counterparts equally among all races. After these nearly forty years on earth, I am not so naive as to deny that racism lives....and kills. Nor will I play Pollyanna and say that everything will be alright if we just all lo-o-o-ove one another. It's a cold, mean jungle out there and my fellow human is the biggest predator afoot. I know that. I accept that. I refuse to accept that it has to be this way for all time.

As I do the work that I do, I've surrounded myself with the rainbow of people that I have because I refuse to inherit the hatred. If I don't claim it as a birthright, I will not leave it as a legacy. That will be my contribution to helping "the arch of the universe always bend toward justice." They are unpopular beliefs among some, but I still own them. And they own me.

THE NIGERIA CONFERENCE REVISITED

LUMKA FUNANI (SOUTH AFRICA)

I WAS BROWSING AROUND IN THE FLEA MARKET AND ALSO came for a fitting of my African dress at the dress-maker's. I wanted to use the toilet, I could not find it anywhere. All I could do to relieve myself was to keep passing wind. At this stage I cared not at all whether my brothers and sisters heard this or smelt *iqaqa pole-cat* until I got to the dress-maker's premises.

"Could I please use your 'ladies,' I'll greet later" met with the young woman dropping everything and coming to my rescue. By this stage my hand was pressing frantically on my back to prevent an accident. She asked as she was accompanying me to the toilet, "will you manage our toilet?" "Yes, why not?" I was ahead of her, I walked pass the toilets—conquered in my mind by colonialism even in this environment. The young woman called me back and pointed at the toilets. I looked around in search of the toilets; she pointed at them the second time—flat stones with small round holes (no walls, no pillars, nothing) surrounded only by the strong smell of old strong urine. The word privacy does not exist here: any one could see me, big lizards and *qabentulo* were running around me. They kept on lifting and lowering their heads, also able to see what I was doing. I was squatting, at the same time trying to measure visually the small round hole so that I would not miss it, thus I kept up an impossible position on my haunches needing to keep looking between my legs.

Just at that time the issue of what divided us at the Nigeria WAAD conference as black South African sisters from our white counterparts, that divided us as African sisters among ourselves and us from Afro-American sisters filled my mind. Whilst we were fighting amongst ourselves, *sinyolana*, pointing fingers at one another, our white South African counterparts were cushioned, relaxed, enjoying their breakfast, maybe saying "How stupid those black folks are."

The question in my mind was how many of those white folks (sisters) would have been able to adjust to this environment? Peristalsis had pushed the fecal matter to a point of no return but there is always what is called compensation that could lead to impacted feces: maybe they would prefer to suffer the latter. I had little problem with this kind of environment because it was not new to me but part of typical African suffering, oppression.

CONFERENCE IN CONFLICT

The question that tore the conference apart was "Should white women present papers about black women's experiences?" This question was raised by an Afro-American. Before this question was addressed, the next question was asked, "What do American women know about the struggle in Africa?" What was not looked at was the significance of the issues themselves, the misguided focus was on who was raising the issues instead.

Black American women at the conference said 'No' to white women reading papers about black women's experiences. African women supported black American women except for the supporters of the conference organizer, Obioma Nnaemeka; i.e., Nigerian women and amazingly South African women, the most oppressed. The belief is that one can talk only from experience; i.e., when one has lived such experience. I am referring to a life where one has no choice of withdrawal because there is this home and no other home, these parents and no other parents, this food or no other food to prevent starvation, this dress to put on or no other dress to cover one's nakedness, this school or no school, this colonialist education or no education.

I cannot emphasize adequately how I used to envy *abe-lungu* (whites) whom I would only see when I was sent to Sterkspruit in Herschel, our small town with only one dirt road. What I did not know was how much these whites were losing out on 'stress tolerance mechanisms' and how badly this would affect them later. I have also discovered the meaning of my life in terms of my strength acquired through suffering. Only a few whites can match me in this regard. When our white counterparts claim to *know* the black women's experience because they have done research in these areas, we have to question the meaning of their 'knowing.'

LIVED KNOWLEDGE

Collecting data, analyzing and reporting them is not the same as living them! Academicians who research in black areas have academic achievement as their main goal—here is nothing ethically binding on them. They have the choice to withdraw, which in actual fact they often do when the situation gets uncomfortable and unfavorable. They can cool off and go back some other time if they so wish. A few examples come to mind from my childhood experience as a black woman. Our school was about twenty kilometers from our village; there were no buses and no taxis to our school, so we had to walk. There was a big river that had to be crossed, summer and winter. This river never went dry and we had to walk across it regardless of the conditions. Herschel has extreme conditions. In summer the river crossing might have been pleasurable because it helped us to cool off, but in winter, by the time one had walked across the almost frozen river, one's feet would have lost sensation, the pain penetrating through to the bone marrow. The crossing stones incidentally were used only by males, just another incident of the sexist oppression of women. Even the snow would not stop us from walking to school. At this stage we could not leave for any other life: we were rooted like trees and woven like veins in Herschel. And a white colleague could claim she had lived such an experience!

It is legitimate and justifiable for only black women to protest for what we so broadly and confidently know about our suffering. This is a descriptive presentation of the way the native lives; a phenomenology, an object of thought and reflection. And the thinking and reflecting subject is no other than the native herself. The colonist/white person cannot strike back with mere academic "knowledge." The colonist curriculum included needle-work, sewing, knitting Western clothing to make us good mothers. It was not aimed at cultivating an independent, constructive, critical mind. What was learned at school had very little to do with helping to criticize daily torments, our living conditions. Most often it was an escape from our misery. What do we blame? Colonialism for our being a conquered people!

One pregnant black woman who was in labor started bleeding at 9 p. m. in the rural areas of Mdambona in Herschel. She went to the Health Clinic, the so-called health clinic had no telephone, no walkie-talkie, no transport, no blood, no house in the neighborhood had a telephone; the mother hospital was very far from the clinic. The nurse woke up the next door neighbor who took the woman to the plaas. When they got there, *die ou man* did not respond to the calls for assistance. The nurse and the man had to walk to the hospital to fetch an ambulance. By the time the ambulance arrived at the clinic, the patient was gasping, she was successfully resuscitated but the baby died. Which white woman can claim to have lived that painful and traumatic experience? Even though the nurse had participated in the black family's experience of helplessness, panic, mental and physical fatigue, she could not claim to have lived that experience. There are specific areas of abrasion which only black women can enter, touch, live with and inside of, and from which they emerge strong.

TIME TO TALK FOR OURSELVES

The forums for sharing ideas and researched work have been created, but black experiences cannot be. African women have been dumb for years about their own experiences, leaving their white counterparts to talk for them, but I feel the time has come for us, as African women, to stand and talk for ourselves in this foreign tongue, English, and through interpreters, get a real sense of our sisters' experience. Let us be ready to take the risk for what we believe is correct. There are issues that are not negotiable. Who even among black women can claim to know the pain and trauma of other African women who are mutilated by clitoridectomy?

When the issue of the participation of white women was raised, South African women met, but the woman who brought South Africans, black and white, together was Euro-African, colored. She is also amongst those who cannot fully know the African experience. Furthermore, the white women about whom the debate was raging, instead of allowing the black women to reach their own conclusions, dominated the argument by virtue of their whiteness and, therefore, greater degree of articulateness.

The Euro-African woman imposed on the meeting the ANC political philosophy which is non-discriminatory and, therefore, supportive of the argument that white women should participate. The counter argument was that each situation should determine how issues are handled. Political organizational philosophy cannot be imposed without critical analysis of circumstances. Yes, the conflict at the WAAD conference was a political question, but it was raised outside of the ANC paradigm as such and within different political groupings of women.

JOINT STATEMENT

The consensus reads as follows and it is offered verbatim:

> South African participants deliberated privately on whether white South Africans should be afforded the opportunity to read their papers during the conference. After a careful examination of the problem, the following observations were made:
>
> (1) That due to the effects of the policy of racial classification in South Africa, women stand in different positions and are accorded different statuses depending on their race and class. The group articulated advantages and disadvantages that go with each position. For instance, it was noted that white women over a long period of time had access to resources such as computers, electricity, offices, international networks, which are essential in the act of contending knowledge and writing.
>
> (2) That it is imperative for feminist and all other progressive scholars to move towards the transformation of the practices of male and Western hegemony which has a history of being discriminatory. The trend should be to begin to create a space for, and to facilitate the visibility of women who previously have been discriminated against.
>
> (3) That academicians in particular have to move beyond rhetoric which are often made in international conferences about and on behalf of black women. A specific suggestion was that they should devise strategies which will close the gap between academics and activism by facilitating the oppressed women's need to articulate their own stories.
>
> (4) That a significant number of white scholars have made a tremendous contribution in the transformation of society.
>
> (Conclusion:) Taking into consideration political developments in South Africa and also realizing the inherent contradictions in this issue, the group suggests that all South Africans, irrespective of race, should be allowed to participate in the conference.

Objections to the consensus were seen to be unscientific. I never compromise my principles; in fact I did not. To paraphrase Es'kia Mphahlele: Comes a time when you do not care to shut the door anymore when its been flung open so many, many times in the painful south. Comes a time when you want the heat to stay on in the ego center so you can hear the voices. Feel the push and pull, so you don't forget, not ever, who you are, whence you came. How real, how to meet the tyranny of time and place and memory that keep bearing down on you so you feel the pulse of every minute of your growth and decline and wear and tear, so you hear your soul and body like a clock ticking, so you leave your fingerprints on everything you touch in fact and fiction, so there is little else to do but to define and redefine yourself.

One can easily establish the connections between black peoples all over the world, and capture the general mood, the yearning and militancy to assert a Pan-African identity. Our white counterparts can speak to two audiences, each from a different black area and project a set of revolutionary assumptions that do not in fact apply equally to both.

WHAT DOES DIASPORA MEAN?

Diaspora from the Greek means a forced dispersion that is a prelude to complete exile. It is only the oppressed who are in the Diaspora, and being in Diaspora (exile) is painful. Diaspora provides a concept which is used to interpret the experiences (often bitter experiences) of people who have been driven out of their native land and forced to be homeless through slavery and imperialism.

COMPLEX CONTRADICTION

Relations between people in the Diaspora and those in their ancestral homelands are complex and full of dialectical contradictions. First, there is anger, bitterness, and remorse among the exiles, and often among people at home as well, over the weakness that permitted the dispersion to occur. Second, there is conflict when the dominant hosts attempt to justify the subordinate status of the exiles and the latter, in turn, refuse to accept the status thrust upon them. Not infrequently, the dominant groups display contempt for the homelands of their victims and the latter feel constrained to defend the countries from which they or their ancestors came. Third, there is often an acrimonious debate among the exiles themselves, and between them and their host and ancestral communities. A corollary is the issue of what effect a return will have on those exiles still in Diaspora.

In a case like that conference, you need an intimate familiarity with the world you depict; you need a locale, its smell, its taste, its texture. You can arrive at an ideological position in the end which has implications for the whole of the black world. As African women, we wanted a cultural milieu in which the conference would have relevance to us in terms of our Diaspora. The most thoughtful and recommendable step taken by the convener, Obioma Nnaemeka, was to have the conference held at Nsukka, a remote town in Nigeria. When people (particularly those who claim "knowledge" of the average black experience) were complaining about the venue (that it was too rural), transportation, communication, accommodation, etc., it was important to point out to them that conferences held in glittery towns would be inappropriate for this context of black Diaspora.

I do not dispute the fact that a solution from white women would be implicit in a correct historical evaluation, just as given medical remedies are indicated or contra-indicated by a correct diagnosis of a patient's condition and an accurate case history. The purpose of this conference from its theme was to bring African women together to explore further the nature of their exploitation, rather than to satisfy the "standards" set by our oppressors and their spokespeople in the academic world. All the bitterness arises from the poverty which is the fundamental result of the policy of apartheid and its various forms of discrimination —economic, spiritual, educational, social, emotional, etc. We need our own space to explore our own realities, first, before we can make this space available to others.

THE NIGERIA CONFERENCE

FIDELIA FOUCHÉ (SOUTH AFRICA)

I WISH TO COMMENT ON THE VIEWS EXPRESSED BY LUMKA Funani in her article, "The Nigeria Conference Revisited" (*Agenda* 15, 1992). Funani's article is a response to a question raised by an Afro-American woman at the conference on Women in Africa and the African Diaspora held in Nigeria during July 1992. This question which "tore the conference apart was 'should white women present papers on black women's experiences?'" (63) Funani's conclusion is essentially that white women should be excluded from black women's conferences, for "we need our own space to explore our own realities, first, before we can make this space available to others" (68). She blames the bitterness between white and black women on the policy of apartheid with its various kinds of discrimination. For me, the question is whether, in principle, the cure for apartheid can be more apartheid?

There have justifiably been accusations that some white academic women have researched black women with little insight and sensitivity, exploited their findings and, therefore, their subjects of research for their own academic prestige. But it is also true that other white women writers, some of them academicians, have sensitively articulated the experience of black women, often acting as the mouthpiece of black women, and thereby helped prevent the forgetting of that experience or the delaying of its accessibility to others.

I can cite, for example, *Side by Side* by Helen Joseph, *My Spirit Is Not Banned* as told by Frances Baard to Barbara Schreiner, *Lives of Courage* by Diana Russell, *Maids and Madams* by Jacky Cock, *Flashes in Her Soul: The Life of Jabu Ndlovu* by Jean Fairbairn, *A Snake in Ice Water* edited by Barbara Schreiner, *The Women of Phokeng* by Belinda Bozzolli. Helen Joseph describes the black women who were her friends and associates in the struggle and the writers/compilers of other works recount the experiences of individual women or record interviews with them.

FRIENDSHIP AND RESPECT

The charge that these writings are illegitimate generalizations about "third world women" and objectifications of them by first world feminists cannot, therefore, be leveled. Nor can they be seen as showing a patronizing "colonial" approach. While apartheid separated people from each other and helped create insensitive and patronizing white women, it did not wholly succeed in stamping out the friendships and mutual respect that have existed between white and black women. Nor did it always prevent black and white women's pursuit of common goals. A blanket condemnation of white women by black women is, therefore, as inaccurate and unfair as white women's facile generalizations about black women.

COMMONALITIES OF EXPERIENCE

But people's experience does not only differ; there is also commonality of human experience which Funani seems to overlook. Nobody, however privileged and pampered, is completely insulated against cold, exhaustion, discomfort, pain, and the ordinary miseries that afflict human beings. By analogy, with our own experience of cold we can gain access to the experience of barefoot children crossing an icy river; although we have not literally felt "the pain penetrating through to the bone marrow" (65). We can in imagination feel enough to fuel our indignation about others' sufferings that will lead us to take action on their behalf or, better still, to join forces with them.

Black and White: We Are One, Sustained by Sisterly Love

Julie Okpala* and Elsie Ogbanna-Ohuche (Nigeria)

THE WAAD CONFERENCE TOOK OFF HAPPILY ON MONDAY, July 13, 1992, with the arrival of hundreds of participants from over 42 countries representing all continents. The warm reception accorded the visitors synchronized with the bright, dry Nsukka weather that was unusual to rainy July in Nsukka. The beautiful, green, rolling hills of Nsukka seemed to join in giving the participants a typical Igbo welcome. Activities marking the opening ceremony and the first day were punctuated by hugs, laughter, and pleasantries among participants, irrespective of color and nationality.

The happy and joyous atmosphere among the participants continued until the evening of the first day, when a controversy exploded in our faces. By the second day, it was observed that some black women from the Diaspora were gathering in small groups of threes, fours, and fives. They were talking in low tones and their voices were grave. The issue of their discussion was not known. Also, some white participants were seen in similar small groups either talking or sobbing. With this uneasy atmosphere, it became clear that there was a problem. The organizers made quick inquiries and found out that a group of African Americans felt that the conference was for Africans in Africa and the Diaspora and should not include whites.

The organizers of the conference felt that this was an issue for immediate open and free discussion for peace to be restored. The convener, Obioma Nnaemeka, initiated an open microphone session during which various views were expressed by the Africans in Africa, those from the Diaspora, and whites. The Africans in the Diaspora argued that the conference was, for them, like a home-

* Dr. Julie Okpala was the chair of the local organizing committee.

coming; a return to their roots away from their current domicile where they felt unaccepted, dehumanized, and segregated, unable to enjoy the benefits and privileges of the developed world. They further argued that the inclusion of whites in the conference was an indication that their kindred in Africa neither understood nor appreciated the emotional turbulence they have been experiencing in foreign lands. They also criticized the membership of the organizing committee which they said was predominantly whites. The presence of the whites, they insisted, was emotionally disturbing and a menace to their peace of mind here in their own home. Consequently, they threatened to discontinue their participation in the conference if the whites were allowed to stay on. At this juncture, it became obvious that if the problem was not addressed and resolved, the conference would be thrown into disarray and might even end prematurely.

The whites, on their part, appealed for peace and argued that their presence and participation in the conference was an indication of their genuine interest and true spirit of sisterhood. After all, they argued, many whites have extended hands of fellowship to blacks in marriages and have participated in the fight against apartheid and the oppression of blacks in other parts of the world. Some whites, according to them, have even sacrificed their lives for the emancipation of blacks. They therefore rested their argument on the plea that not all whites should be condemned as racist.

Most Nigerians and African participants felt that the whites should be allowed to participate for two main reasons: First, the conference was *on* Women in Africa and the African Diaspora not *for* Women in Africa and the African Diaspora. Hence, it was an open conference for all interested men and women—irrespective of race, class, ethnicity, religious persuasion, and national origin—to come together and brainstorm on issues related to women of African descent, with a view to making suggestions for their empowerment and the improvement of their lives. After all, many whites are in Nigeria and many other countries on humanitarian assignment. There are whites who are wives/husbands of blacks. In terms of conceptualization, the conference was rooted in the spirit of oneness of humanity. Secondly, they also argued that pushing out the whites, their visitors, from the conference was contrary to the Igbo tradition. This tradition asserts that a friendly visitor is never rejected ("pushed out in the rain").

The convener of the conference dispelled the accusation that she involved only whites in the committee by showing that the organizing committee was predominantly black and the local organizing committee was entirely black. She also explained the openness with which she advertised the conference as an invitation to researchers, activists, and all interested parties, irrespective of gender or race. Those who expressed an interest were invited. She pleaded with all to work as one because despite color or nationality, problems faced by one group, directly or indirectly, affect other groups.

Various participants—men and women, black and white—further expressed the view that although blacks have been oppressed and aggrieved, a dialogue between the oppressor and the oppressed was the best approach to finding a lasting solution to the conflict. Arguments from the various parties dragged on for over two hours and finally almost everybody broke down—Africans in Africa were crying, Africans from the Diaspora were sobbing, whites were weeping. It dawned on many of us (black and white) that we needed each other for meaningful and peaceful coexistence. There was absolute calm and suddenly a chorus, "The More We Are Together the Happier We Shall Be," was raised from somewhere by a black. The conflict was resolved by a decision to allow white participants to present their papers; some of the earlier happy and cordial atmosphere was restored and the conference continued to a happy, successful, and fruitful end. The lesson learnt from this highly emotional incident is clear—dialoguing is a necessary strategy for conflict resolution.

We would like to conclude by stating that since the inception of the University of Nigeria, Nsukka, the first indigenous university in Nigeria, in October 1960, there has not been any event/conference that attracted such a large population of black and white participants. Happy memories of the conference linger on and will continue to linger for quite a long time to come. The successful organization and management of the conference left a yearning, a wish on the lips of participants for yet another such conference—a repeat performance.

BUILDING OR BURNING BRIDGES? A REPORT FROM THE 1992 WOMEN IN AFRICA AND THE AFRICAN DIASPORA CONFERENCE

DONNA FLYNN (U. S. A.)

I ATTENDED THE FIRST INTERNATIONAL CONFERENCE ON Women in Africa and the African Diaspora, held in Nsukka, Nigeria. The theme of the conference was "Bridges across Activism and the Academy." The WAAD conference was convened by Obioma Nnaemeka, of the Department of French and Women's Studies Program at Indiana University, Indianapolis. She and her co-planners succeeded in an extraordinary effort to bring scholars and activists together to share experiences and to collaborate on plans of action addressing issues of women in Africa and the Diaspora.

Issues concerning women and rural development received particular emphasis. Indeed, the site of the five-day conference at the University of Nigeria, Nsukka (a small rural town) enabled rural African women, scholars, and activists to attend; participants who could not afford to travel to more distant and more expensive urban centers. Attendees presented over 200 papers on topics ranging from grassroots development cooperative in Nigeria to concerns of low-income black single mothers in the United States. The conference was highlighted by keynote speeches from distinguished writers such as Flora Nwapa and Ama Ata Aidoò.

The conference got off to a shaky start, however, when on the first afternoon a small group of African-American women demanded that all white participants, like myself, withdraw from presenting papers. Representing activist groups and universities throughout the United States, they apparently had the mistaken belief that this conference *about* black women was also restricted to participation *by* black women. They were surprised and angered to discover that about a fifth of the participants were white. While the argument that black women need to speak for themselves carries both historical and political force, their attempt to appropriate the WAAD conference as a political forum to achieve this end was unfortunate. The conference organizers had carefully developed and presented the meeting as a global, multi-national, and multi-racial assembly, with the organizing committee itself composed of black and white men and women. The challenge they offered was not only to the white women at the conference, but to the work of the organizing committee itself.

To give all participants a chance to express views on the issue of race and open conference participation, the organizers provided an open microphone on the second day of the session. Many African-American women came to the podium to express strong opinions on both sides of the call for excluding whites from the conference (oddly enough, objection to male participants—black and white—were never raised). Tensions ran high. One white woman expressed frustration at being told that after more than twenty years in Nigeria, she had less right to speak of African women than a black woman who had never before visited Africa. She found herself interrupted by an African-American woman who stood up in the audience to condemn her position and disrupt her remarks.

After hours of discussion, a suggestion was made that conference participants vote on the proposed separatist agenda. As conference chair, Dr. Obioma Nnaemeka tactfully used her executive authority to overrule the suggested vote to preserve the clear intention of the organizing committee: "We are all preaching accommodation. We are all preaching toleration....we are going to accommodate all visitors." Before ending the open session, it was agreed that a special session be held towards the end of the week to provide African Diaspora women and African women a forum to discuss among themselves concerns of black women around the world.

The display of American racial politics at the WAAD conference gave all participants a firsthand glimpse of our domestic turbulence that had only increased in intensity since the Rodney King verdict. It also presented an embarrassing example of American arrogance and self-righteousness that threatened to dominate the entire conference and to destroy the very "global bridges" that were the thematic centerpiece of the gathering.

After the initial reverberations of the proposed racial exclusion had been settled, most participants either privately or publicly expressed their support for the multi-racial nature of the conference. The efforts of the smaller group to create color lines back-fired; the exclusionists created friction between themselves and other African-American women, African women, and white women. The reaffirmation of multiculturalism was perhaps climaxed by a public statement made by a coalition of South African and Namibian participants, black and white, which affirmed their support for women of all colors to present papers. One Namibian sister drew loud applause when she declared that "we want to construct a society of South Africans, a society of Namibians, and not to dehumanize others the way others have dehumanized us."

The event at the WAAD conference also demonstrated again how issues of culture can cross-cut issues of race. One consequence of the actions of those demanding exclusion on the basis of race was how their disregard for the announced format of the conference placed their Igbo hostesses and hosts in an awkward position. Many Nigerian participants were clearly embarrassed by the confrontational attitude of the outspoken Americans; others were frustrated at having the racial issue dominate the first half of the conference while they had more immediate problems to discuss, such as rural women's health issues or small business loan programs. On several occasions, Nigerian women approached me and some other white participants to apologize for the discord created by my fellow Americans and to ensure that we were enjoying our visit to their country. We all learned from an Igbo proverb, cited by Dr. Obioma Nnaemeka in a plea for increased cultural sensitivity: "If you invite guests, may your guests not come to crush you, and when they leave, may they not leave with a hunchback."

The anger directed towards powerful, if not hegemonic, discourses that are fashioned and maintained by the white interests was justifiably voiced. This anger and frustration, indeed, drew new attention to the need for black women to speak for themselves. But the attempt of this group of women to, in their own words, "draw the battle line" between black and white was a serious misjudgment in the context of this conference. Their conclusion that WAAD was an arm of the white hegemonic power structure was myopic; it was a meeting of women and men, black and white, who shared concerns and interests in issues related to black women in Africa and elsewhere in the world.

In Search of Common Ground

Gloria Braxton (U. S. A.)

DURING A RECENT PRESENTATION AT THE NIGERIAN National Center for Women Development in the Federal Capital of Abuja, I was vividly reminded of the most pervasive controversy that dominated the very historic gathering at the 1992 Nsukka Women in Africa and the African Diaspora Conference. I was asked to share my thoughts on the challenge of the Beijing Conference as it related to the significance of African American women. I was struck that Nigerian women would be interested in such a subject and astonished when about forty women attended the session which resulted in a very lively and stimulating discussion. I was overwhelmed with the opportunity to once again express my feelings about the significance of increased understanding and cooperation between African women and African women born and raised in other parts of the world. Thus, it was during this discussion in Abuja that I realized that the reasons I felt that the Beijing Conference posed significant challenges related in part to the feelings I harbored as I departed the Nsukka Conference in 1992.

The most significant discussion centered around the presence, participation, and perceived domination of women of European descent at the Nsukka Conference. Although the tactic employed by the dissenting groups was not one I would have employed, the questions raised by these pungent voices were consequential. With the initial questions raised by African women living in the Diaspora, especially South African women living in Europe, followed by other African women living in Europe and America, very real and potent issues did not receive the singular attention that many expected would dominate the discussions at the conference.

What is the significance of race and class in the struggle to empower African women at home and abroad? What is the nature of their oppression? Are coalition strategies empowering for African women? Do African women have a feminine consciousness similar to women of European descent? Is it a legitimate concern for African women to meet and discuss issues without the watchful eye of their European-descended counterparts? Does the very nature of the difference between the struggles of women of European descent and African descent mean that different (and/or separate) strategies must be employed and different (and/or separate) goals must be established? Will the resolution of problems in Africa promote the effective solution to problems of African women in the Diaspora? Can African women born and raised in America identify with the problems and issues African women face, such that cultural and historical diversities can serve as unifying forces in the struggle for universal empowerment? While some of these questions were addressed in one way or another, it was felt that they should have been discussed only among those the conference was perceived to be by and for.

The problems of African women born and raised within Western culture, especially African American women, are too frequently addressed in the same manner as the problems of women of American European descent. Thus, there has always been a repudiation of African American women's issues and the role they can play in the struggle for empowerment of all African women. The fact that African American women participated in the 1985 Nairobi Conference in large numbers signifies that they believed kinship with African women to be a significant force to foster a greater sense of sisterhood.

For most of the African American participants at the Nsukka Conference, this was their maiden trip to Africa. Most had anxiously anticipated the experience for many months and, however romantically depicted, genuinely expected a void to be filled by interacting and learning from their African sisters. Most were not prepared to share this precious time and hopes with American women of European descent who they believed felt no particular kinship to them, and who for the most part, were representatives of the social, economic, and political problems prevalent back in America. In the United States, African American women are viewed as an appendage to European women, resulting in a misguided and contrived image. Thus, the few African American dissidents were reacting to these realities rather than the mere presence of these women at the conference.

For me, the issue that the controversy stressed related to the development of a sustained relationship between women in Africa and the African Diaspora. In American society, sex and class discrimination are accompanied by flagrant racism. The class and racism factors, particularly, prevent any type of functional coalition-building. However, as in Africa, African women born and raised in America have always worked and this, more than anything else, has shaped their experience in the United States. In fact, it is that work experience that makes an important difference between the struggle of women of European descent and women of African descent. This further prevents the development of a sense of an all-inclusive sisterhood and prospects for coalition-building.

The most serious problem for African women at home and abroad is the lack of focus on developing an ideological paradigm that encompasses their historical and material realities within the overarching global system. Various authors continue to call for a global liberationist ideology that is based on a total reconstruction of existing social structure and the concomitant institutions, attitudes, and knowledge that must accompany such a process.

Filomina Steady, in one of the most notable attempts to address the lack of dialogue and cooperation between African women and African women in the Diaspora, calls for the development of an African feminist theory that encompasses a worldwide perspective (*The Black Woman Cross-Culturally*, 1981). Steady argued that this ideology must be developed by African women and African women in the Diaspora. This means that research must be dominated by ourselves and that this research must be proactive rather than reactive.

If a global liberationist ideology is to form the basis for strategic action by African women on the continent and African women in the Diaspora, this will necessitate conducting more studies of a cross-cultural, comparative nature. Research conducted by scholars from the dominant culture has focused on comparing African American women with white women, white men, and black men. However, the historical realities of slavery, colonialism, and the pre and post industrial society support the fact that African American women have more in common with African women and other women of the non-industrialized world than they do with those of the dominant culture. There is the definite need for continental African women and African women living in the Diaspora to study and analyze the relationship that existed in precolonial and preindustrial Africa, the impact of slavery and colonialism on that society, and how this has changed the traditional role of men and women. Only then can we know and understand that strategies must emanate from a common ground and established goals for the development of African peoples throughout the world.

The effort to recast the study of the status and roles of women in indigenous precolonial African societies has important implications for the study of the roles the descendants of these women came to play in the American context. It is common knowledge that Africans brought with them beliefs and values, varying degrees of knowledge of their political, economic, technological, religion, artistic, recreational and familial organizations, and other societal groupings that came to dominate the life and culture of Africans abroad. Given this context, it is claimed that in order to understand the roles that African American women came to play in America, it is necessary to understand the tradition of female independence and responsibility within a family.

Most importantly, comparative research on African women in Africa and in the Diaspora must be more proactive rather then reactive. This is to say that research activities must lead to the active, effective participation by those involved. Reactive research is research for research's sake and is engaged in for the fulfillment of the dominant group's goals and objectives. The questions raised, approaches advanced, and methodologies employed are antithetical to the growth and development of African people. Therefore, African women have little to gain by following the dictates of the dominant culture for a research agenda and strategy of action.

African women must launch their own Development Decade and organize a second Nsukka Conference. The burden of responsibility is to become leaders in the establishment of a "growth-oriented" research agenda and this must be assumed by indigenous African women and African women born and raised in the Diaspora. Proactive research dictates that African women both on the continent and in the Diaspora must exude positive energy, enlarging and magnifying, causing our circles of influence and responsibility to expand. The research agenda must have a utilitarian purpose, an empowering purpose that moves beyond the bounds of the academy and into the lives of African communities and the myriad of organizations, groups, and individuals who will provide the leadership for the growth and development of African peoples throughout the world. Only then can the dream envisioned by the Nsukka Conference evolve full circle.

BRIDGES AND RIDGES

CHIOMA OPARA (NIGERIA)

THE CONFERENCE ON "WOMEN IN AFRICA AND THE AFRICAN Diaspora: Bridges across Activism and the Academy" started brilliantly with the multilingual convener, Professor Obioma Nnaemeka, eloquently welcoming the participants to the Nigerian ridge in the true African tradition. The conference was the first of its type in Nigeria, perhaps in all Africa.

What was obvious at the opening was the fact that most of the participants were not resident in Nigeria. This could be attributed to the belated confirmation of the venue. As a conference coordinator in Port Harcourt , Rivers State of Nigeria, I had been severally confronted with inquiries about date and venue which I could not answer. Ineffective means of communication within the country was also a formidable factor to be reckoned with. When the can of worms was opened by the emotive rendition of the South African sister backed up by the African American sisters' advocacy of a vote against white participation in the conference, it was crystal clear that a *mêlée* was imminent.

It is salient to point out here that, much as Professor Nnaemeka has been resident in the United States, she belongs with the Nigerian ridge: a ridge formed and molded by varied cultural beliefs which colonialism and Westernization could not eradicate. One of those deep "Nigerian ridge" beliefs is that it is crass infamy to shoo off one's guest. The unwilling host is culturally expected to hear his or her overbearing guest out before reacting.

The next question then arises: were the white participants really our guests? Was the conference supposed to be *for* or *on* black women? That apparently had not been clearly defined. Since their abstracts and papers had been accepted and not rejected, they fell under the category of guests according to the Nigerian ridge definition. Our black Diaspora sisters did not seem to agree with us. Not only did they decide to boycott panels with white participants, they unequivocally stated that they had been betrayed by the conciliatory stance of the convener. At this moment there was a brief lapse into quibbles and some of the shattered white participants wept openly. Theirs appeared to be a ridge of the minority. The atmosphere was as tense as it was belligerent.

Our black South African and American sisters were visibly smarting under the turn of events. Given their debilitating ridge of racism, they felt it was the opportune moment to get back at the oppressors. This time it should be BLACKS ONLY! The Nigerian ridge was mediating not because the throes of apartheid were lost on it, but mainly because many a hostess realized that a *faux pas* in the course of the conference could result in a fiasco. May it be reiterated that the Nigerian citizen is not insensitive to the menace of racism. The average Nigerian has identified with the struggle of the black South African. Theirs is a familiar ridge, though not experiential. If my impression of overwhelming white dominance and apparent black diffidence during my recent visit to *new* South Africa is anything to go by, I can imagine what life was like in South Africa under apartheid.

Clearly, these women, weighed down by traumatic experiences, were loath to extend a hand of fellowship and share with their oppressors on a more wholesome ridge. The tenets of female solidarity that transcends color could not be piped to our psychologically battered sisters. Who would blame them? Perhaps the whites should have *sincerely* apologized and promised to be votaries of peace in a non-racist society. Perhaps there should have been a special healing forum to vent pent-up feelings amicably and to sort out the antagonism and resentment while ensuring that the roof did not fall over our heads.

May I suggest that in future adequate measures should be taken to set out the scope and limitation of participation when organizing a conference of this nature. The moral of the WAAD controversy may be summed up thus: There could be several bridges across activism and the academy, but not a single one has been constructed across the ridges of culture, creed, and race tinctured with deep-seated rancor and strife. Not until these ridges are leveled can that yawning hiatus be bridged. The axis of true feminism should be sisterly love that rises above differences, discrimination, and resentment. Surely that unalloyed love hinged on tolerance, equity, and forgiveness would overcome retrogressive stereotyping and aim at a universal ridge which would have no need for a bridge.

The 1992 WAAD Conference: Some Thoughts

Liz Dimock (Australia)

I AM WRITING TO THANK YOU FOR YOUR PART IN THE organization of the WAAD conference. It was an enormous undertaking and one for which I think you were not given enough recognition, or indeed thanks, at the time. Our departure from the hotel on Sunday morning after the conference was unfortunate. We left under a cloud of mistrust with the hotel management, and our farewell to you and to Julie Okpala was not made in the best of circumstances. This was also true for other groups departing.

I want to say now how very much I enjoyed the conference. It was not what I had expected and I suppose my expectation in some way reflects my Australian perspective. Australia's involvement in Africa is very marginal and mainly concerned with advisory and technical assistance in economic matters and to a lesser extent in a mediating role in political issues.

I was expecting the development of the rural woman to be the central theme, and was therefore delighted to see a marked focus on Nigerian rural women. I learned a great deal from various papers about the Better Life Program and from the visit to rural projects in Enugu and Anambra States. It was disappointing that there were so few aid workers from agencies that work in Africa at the conference. I sensed also that there was not a lot of communication between representatives of other African countries and the Nigerians. Do you think that was the case? Or was it going on behind the scenes? It would seem valuable that these ideas be communicated to other African countries. From a theoretical viewpoint, however, and using Chandra Mohanty's thesis in particular, the heterogeneity of African culture should warn against making assumptions about the usefulness of the Nigerian experience to other parts of Africa. I was really impressed by Nigerian women's assertion of the needs of rural women and by the programs that they have set in motion. But here too the oppositional structures— elite/urban/educated and poor/rural/under-educated —caution one against championing the Better Life Program without knowing much more about it. The gap between discourse and practice is one that I find difficult to overcome.

What I had been completely unprepared for were the political agendas of groups of participants. This too reflects my own marginality from feminist and racial politics of the United States. I have been aware of these in my reading, but I have never before come across them in practice. The WAAD conference was the first international conference I have attended. My core interest is African studies, only secondarily women's studies. At conferences in Australia, I reckon to be able to enter discussion with any or all participants. Not so at Nsukka. One entered a conversation not knowing what progress you would make and whether you would be rebuked or verbally assaulted. This was extremely interesting and sent me scurrying back to read bell hooks in more detail to gain further insight into a big problem. And it really does seem to be a problem; for if you cannot have dialogue how can issues be resolved?

One of my criticisms of postmodern discourse is that it is reductionist. I like Chandra Mohanty's plea for specificity and the recognition of women's agency. And I sympathize with the protest against center/margin, self/other, subject/object dichotomies and the imperialism of these language structures. They are elitist and exclusive and one does not need to be poor or black or any social category to have a sense of exclusion. The use of "center" and "margin" to describe feminist discourse is in itself so arrogant and provokes a backlash which is clearly very bitter for the vocal African Americans at the conference. What was good about Nsukka was the way in which the conference centralized West African, more specifically Nigerian, and even more, Ibo culture.

It was marvelous to hear women like Flora Nwapa and Ama Ata Aidoo. Their writings illustrate the centrality of the African woman as subject, with all their problems as women exacerbated by the problems of other cultures that are imposed on them. I do hope that the African American women who were so vocal in the early days of the conference gained something from mixing with the Africans. There was a certain sadness in the way that they were unable to let their hosts offer their hospitality unreservedly and there appeared to be tensions between them that there should not have been. I never did find out how that special session for African American women to meet Nigerian women went. Was it a healing occasion?

You were in a difficult situation throughout the conference, and I felt great sympathy for your position as you attempted to bring together all the disparate strands. You did a marvelous job and the choice of Nigeria for the location of the first Women in Africa conference was excellent.

One of the asides of the conference for me was finding out about Women's Studies in Nigeria. I have to write a report for AIDAB (Australian International Development Agency Bureau), an offshoot of Foreign Affairs, which gave me funding to attend. In the light of current financial crises in Nigerian universities, one of my recommendations will be that funding should be given to provide Nigerian women in Women's Studies departments short-term teaching contracts in Australian universities. I hope this does not sound imperialist, colonizing, patronizing, condescending! I see this as of dual benefit—in giving Nigerians access to resources which are so sadly lacking in their own universities, and in bringing to Women's Studies courses in Australian universities a genuine African perspective. Don't you think that would be a worthwhile exercise?

I hope that my comments are of some interest to you. You will, I am sure, be pleased to have feedback on the conference. I expect there is some naiveté in what I have written. Please excuse me if that is so; as I said above, much of the dissension was new to me. I am not sure what further expectations I should have about materials coming out of the conference, but there are a few things that I would like to have. I am listing them on a separate sheet, and will ask you to send me what you can from the list. The most significant items are keynote addresses by Flora Nwapa and Ama Ata Aidoo.

Many, many thanks, Obioma, for your effort in putting the conference together. I hope that you have been able to have a holiday since it ended. It would be interesting to know what your own thoughts are about it retrospectively, but I am sure that you will not have time to write in the midst of your busy life. Would it be possible to do a common letter to send to people who express such an interest? I expect you have had a number of letters since arriving back in the U. S.

REFLECTIONS ON THE 1992 WAAD CONFERENCE

MARIE UMEH (U. S. A./NIGERIA)

THE 1992 WOMEN IN AFRICA AND THE AFRICAN DIASPORA international conference held at the University of Nigeria, Nsukka was copacetic. Professor Obioma Nnaemeka and her committee members' energetic organization was awesome. It was a great conference—very intellectually stimulating and culturally rewarding. The extras (banquets with governors and ministers of State, tours of the Better Life for Women projects and fairs, cultural dances, masquerades, exhibitions of books, paintings, artifacts, African cloth, etc.) were quite exhilarating.

The breadth and scope of the program was most impressive. The papers read and the theories and ideas disseminated by scholars such as 'Zulu Sofola, Clenora Hudson- Weems, Chimalum Nwankwo, Femi Ojo-Ade and many others were comprehensive in their coverage of black women's struggle for empowerment and resistance against the injustices of gender imbalance. It was indeed a thoroughly intellectually stimulating exercise. I grew in more ways than one and I am convinced that it was one of the best conferences I've attended in my life.

As an African-American married to a Nigerian and who formerly lived in Nigeria for many years, going to Nigeria to attend the conference was like attending a family reunion with many in-laws (Governor and Mrs. Emeka Ezeife), colleagues (Ifeoma Okoye and Rose Acholonu), and former students from the Anambra State University of Technology and the Anambra State College of Education, who gave me a warm welcome.

Another feat of the conference was assembling authors and scholars whom I have read, taught about and admired. I was thrilled to meet for the first time the talented poet and dramatist, Ama Ata Aidoo, one of the keynote speakers. Equally important was my reacquaintance with stars such as Flora Nwapa, Gloria Chukukere, Kema Chikwe, Obi Maduakor, and Tanure Ojaide, to name only a few of our great writers of international repute, who presented sterling and innovative papers.

Besides satisfying the intellectual thirst of many of the conference participants, the WAAD conference rejuvenated the African-Americans' connection to Africa. Many of us reveled in seeing our own (fellow blacks) striding in the halls of power. Many of us discarded our perms in favor of braiding and weaving our hair the Nigerian way. Many of us purchased African cloth and ready-made outfits displayed at a fashion show in Enugu, because it represented embracing Nigerian culture, belonging to and identifying with a lost cultural heritage. The indigenes of Igbo country were distinctively wonderful. They were friendly, cheerful, and industrious. They welcomed their foreign visitors with open arms. When I needed to hire a car to visit in a distant village the family of a friend who was studying at Fordham University in New York, the transport manager at the University of Nigeria, Nsukka, saw to it that I reached my destination with an experienced driver and in a good, strong car which took me out-of-state and back to Nsukka in the same day. Additionally, the empowerment the conference instilled in many of the participants could not have been achieved outside of Africa. Coming home seemed to give us the confidence to air our views with confidence and competence, knowing people would listen and understand where you were coming from, even if there were different points of view. For example, the fuss over creating a distinct African term, instead of African women using the Western term "feminism," to articulate the black African woman's quest for female empowerment in the halls of power, divided many of us. Some scholars argued that the word "feminism" reflects all women's struggle for equality in their respective societies, while others insisted that language is culture and Western culture is totally different from African culture. However, it was a healthy and necessary discussion. In fact, nothing was lost by the debate and the tacky situation was handled tactfully by the conference convener, Professor Obioma Nnaemeka. Nevertheless, I'm sure Molara Ogundipe-Leslie's new term, STIWANISM (Social Transformation Including Women in Africa), to reflect the African woman's struggle for social equality in male-dominated societies was created to end this debate and allow women and men to apply their energies to more important issues.

In conclusion, the WAAD conference was a success. All of us who attended left Nigeria more enriched, more fulfilled, more knowledgeable than when we arrived on its embracing shores.

WAAD Conference at ASA

Sabine Jell-Bahlsen (Germany)

At the 1993 ASA Women's Caucus luncheon in Boston, Professor Abena Busia delivered an address in which she made references to Professor Obioma Nnaemeka's speech, "This Women's Studies Business: Beyond Politics and History," to the same forum the previous year in Seattle. Professor Busia's address concentrated on the part of Professor Nnaemeka's speech that touched on the 1992 first international conference on Women in Africa and the African Diaspora which she organized and convened in Nsukka, Nigeria. As a participant in the Nsukka WAAD conference, I wish to make some brief remarks on Professor Busia's response.

First of all, I want to express my gratitude to the convener of WAAD '92, Dr. Obioma Nnaemeka, for inviting me to the fantastic Nsukka conference. I feel very strongly that the conference, planned for researchers and activists of all continents, shapes, and complexions, was too important and significant an event to be belittled by disputes introduced from other parts of the world. This conference had some of the best discussions I have ever witnessed in a conference. It was much more productive than the many similar events that I have attended in America. The conference's strength was due to the input of the many African participants who could attend because of its location in Africa. Their presence in panel presentations, workshops, plenary sessions, and discussions was strongly felt and important for everyone. I was particularly thrilled with the work of some younger scholars who were educated in Nigeria, have not been abroad, but have done real fieldwork in their own country instead. Their reports were a refreshing departure from the work of older African scholars trained and educated in Europe and the U. S. A. Secondly, Dr. Busia did not attend the conference in Nigeria. Her speech was based on hearsay and second-hand information from others about an event they had or had not attended. Thirdly, in my view, Dr. Busia's speech is full of misrepresentations of an event in which she never participated.

It is important to stress the fact that *some, not all,* African-American participants demanded the exclusion of white participants. In fact, those that demanded exclusion were in the minority. Professor Nnaemeka stressed this point in her 1992 ASA keynote address delivered at the Women's Caucus luncheon which I attended. It is equally important to highlight an incident that occurred at the plenary session where Ama Ata Aidoo, the respected writer from Ghana, presented a keynote. Ama Ata Aidoo had barely finished her speech, when an African American woman (one of the insurgents) rudely stormed to the front, grabbed the microphone, and started yelling about how inappropriate was the word "feminism" used by Ama Ata Aidoo in her speech, and offered "Africana womanism" as a terminology that captures more appropriately the black woman's experience. I remember my anger and disgust as I sat there in the audience close to the podium watching this show of disrespect. The African American said that it was an issue of terminology. In my view, it was more an issue of style than that of terminology. I personally feel that Ama Ata Aidoo is someone who deserves a lot of respect from all women. Of course one can challenge a speaker's concepts and words, but the issue here is *how.* In my home country, we call this type of behavior "to pull down someone's pants." It was again an issue of style that made the demand (no consultation with the organizers and our Nigerian hosts) by some African American participants for the exclusion of whites most objectionable to the majority of the Nigerian participants (our hosts).

In her speech, Abena Busia blows out of proportion the presence of Europeans and European-Americans at the conference. In my recollection, there were about 800 participants from all around the world (every continent was represented). Among them, was one Indian woman and some Europeans. Being from Europe myself, I remember meeting a total of seven (7), one was African-British, three from the Scandinavia, one German-American, one British, and one Australian. There were some European- Americans, but I did not meet all of them. I had brought one European-American student, who quickly made friends with an African-American student. On the other hand, I was very happy to meet so many Nigerians, Africans from other countries, and African-Americans with whom I am still in touch. As one of the few Europeans present, I did *not* feel *entitled* to be there or to present a paper, as Busia claims in her speech. I did, however, feel invited. Speaking of entitlement, it is Abena Busia who, in her speech, *feels entitled* to speak for African-American women as she *felt entitled* to speak for Flora Nwapa in another occasion.

At the end of the open microphone session in which participants aired their views on the controversy over the exclusion or inclusion of white presenters, it was agreed that all participants should present their papers. I did. The Africans and the African-Americans who attended my presentation applauded at the end of my presentation which was followed by a very lively and constructive discussion.

The tactics used by some African-Americans to intimidate and abuse white participants were appalling. I have never experienced that kind of hostility from an African, or from an African-American fully conversant and in harmony with the African culture. By contrast, the African Americans who claimed to be Africans constantly complained about African time and food, and cried for "spaghetti and meat balls."

Unfortunately, these American issues are taking up a disproportionate amount of time and space in our work, and pulling us away from serious reflections on the Nsukka conference and its important lessons. The Nsukka experience is much too valuable to be vitiated by all this politics. I still carry my conference bag around and hold it dearly. Thank you and all the best, Obioma. MMIRI DI EGWU!

CROSS-ATLANTIC WOMANISM(S): AN AFRICAN AMERICAN WOMAN'S REFLECTIONS ON THE WOMEN IN AFRICA AND THE AFRICAN DIASPORA CONFERENCE, 1992

JANE SPLAWN (U. S. A.)

THE FIRST INTERNATIONAL CONFERENCE ON "WOMEN IN Africa and the African Diaspora: Bridges Across Activism and the Academy," held at Nsukka, Nigeria, July 13-18, 1992, came as a result of a tremendous effort in planning: paper submissions were selected from participants from all continents. The "bigness" of the project was apparent from the initial "call for action": papers on issues from black women's health and law, to literature, art, and film were invited. However, our sense of the immensity of the project could not have been more acute than when we gathered at JFK International Airport, New York, on July 11 and July 15, respectively, to embark on the final leg of the two years of planning and preparation. For some of us, the conference provided our first opportunity to go to Africa, and with this, sometimes, came attendant expectations—we wanted *this* conference, held at *this* location to be special; but we were not always sure what was required of *us* to make it so.

African-American participants, for the most part, wanted to *connect* with our sisters in Africa and other parts of the diaspora, but we were not always able to view issues of concern to other black women beyond the lens of an African-American perspective. One instance that comes to mind took place at the Lagos airport: after hours of our waiting in line for our tickets and flight to be confirmed, the line suddenly moved forward as a white woman's ticket was processed. "Uh ugh, not here," a black American woman conferee was heard to say, "we're not going to let that kind of thing happen here." The black American woman's frustration with encountering white racial privilege in Africa speaks to one of many similar kinds of oppression black people experience on both sides of the Atlantic.

Even the place of the migration of black women on the eastern side of the Atlantic, as Carole Boyce Davies tersely argues in *Black Women, Writing and Identity: Migrations of the Subject* (1994), is crucial in determining our subject positions. Our sisters from the West Indies, some of whom had migrated to Canada and England, frequently reminded us that the sign "black woman" does not signify black American woman—a position echoed across the Atlantic two years later at MIT's historic "Defending Our Name: Black Women in the Academy" conference.

Perhaps in no one area was the shift in subjectivity more acute than in the area of language. Our francophone sisters from Africa, Canada, and the West Indies let us anglophone black women know that their voices were often silenced when our voices were privileged, sometimes issuing a more stern corrective to us than their translations given in English suggested. Toward the later part of the week when I arrived at the conference, dual announcements in both French and English were made at the "Open Forum," where all conferees convened before the concurrent sessions to discuss issues, strategies, and other concerns to us. In the session in which I delivered a paper, synopses of papers were collectively given by conferees in either French or English.

A more "thorny" issue for me came as a result of my travel experience in Nigeria. Travel in the Third World *is* hard from a Western perspective. However, even as I sighed from the lack of cool air circulating, long lines, less than sanitary public bathrooms, etc., I could not help noting that travel conditions seemed even more debilitating for Nigerians, some of whom I gathered from conversations while waiting in line, had traveled hundreds of miles by car the night before in the hopes of making that night's flight—often to be turned away.

Furthermore, I am somewhat unresolved about the way many African Americans consumed African goods while there. The value of the *naira* (Nigerian currency) had been reduced to one-tenth of its value in 1984—eight years prior to the conference. Savvy American travelers could purchase a lot of Nigerian consumable with a hundred American dollars. I was at times repulsed by black American conferees who literally loaded huge sections of tourist vans, etc. with various purchases, and even more so by conferees on tour who became indignant with working-class Nigerian vendors over what amounted to a difference of coins in American currency. The experience was equally exasperating for some of us when we were substantially overcharged for services in the larger cities like Lagos.

Perhaps, as black women in Africa and the African Diaspora, we brought to the conference a certain desire invested in more specific aims. Severe changes in the economic reality of many middle-class Nigerians—now faced with the erosion of governmental funding to do such things as study abroad—created a desire in some Nigerians to seek African-American mediators to help facilitate the matriculation of their daughters and sons. The power wielded by most African-American participants in our colleges and universities, however, proved insufficient for us to act as effective go-betweens for some prospective students from Nigeria.

Finally, we need to consider the significance of why we as individuals came together to take part in "Women in Africa and the African Diaspora." The desire to be participants in an historic dialogue with our black women sisters across the Atlantic drew many, if not most, of us to Nsukka. The desire expressed in our choices to participate is significant—where will that same desire take us from here?

Self-Naming and Self-Definition: An Agenda for Survival

Clenora Hudson-Weems (U. S. A.)

> Women who are calling themselves black feminists need another word that describes what their concerns are. Black feminism is not a word that describes the plight of black women. (Julia Hare, 15)

TERMINOLOGY IS CRITICAL TO DEFINITION, SINCE WORDS are loaded with meaning. Therefore, when you name a particular thing, you are simultaneously giving it meaning. The African term for proper naming is *nommo,* a powerful and empowering concept. In African cosmology, *nommo* evokes existence, which carries with it the total package. Since Africana people have long been denied the authority of defining self, as inferred in the words of Toni Morrison's narrator in *Beloved*—to the effect that definitions belonged to the definers, not the defined—it is important to seize control over these determining factors now, lest we risk eternal degradation, isolation, and annihilation.

For nearly a decade, I have been actively working on naming and defining, via identifying and refining an African-centered paradigm for women of African descent. In observing the traditional role, character, and activity of this collective group, identified by their common African ancestry, I concluded during the early stages of my research that the phenomenon I named and defined as Africana womanism had long been in existence, dating back to the rich legacy of African womanhood. Therefore, I did not create the phenomenon in and of itself, but rather observed Africana women, documented our reality, and refined a paradigm relative to who we are, what we do, and what we believe in as a people. Society, however, has failed to recognized the operational existence of this long-lived phenomenon and has instead chosen to name and define Africana women within the constructs of a Eurocentric perspective—feminism—indeed, a reality outside of Africana women's historical and cultural context. They have told us where we fit into the scheme of things, without regard for our historical and cultural realities. This obtrusive practice of naming and defining us, rather than respecting our acts of self-authentication, is part of the legacy of European domination. Thus, Africana people will have to actively reclaim our sense of identity. Bob Bender, Professor of English and Women Studies at the University of Missouri-Columbia, asserts that naming is important, and one of the problems with being named by some other group is that you are not who you want to be. Until you have the right to give a name to yourself and to what you are doing, you have no power whatsoever. Africana womanism is a fine idea (*Mizzou Weekly*, 7).

The agenda of Africana women, then, must be one designed from an endemic perspective, shaped by the dictates of their past and present cultural reality. Indeed, no one can be accurately defined outside of one's historical and cultural context. Thus, it is imperative that we set an authentic agenda with our own established priorities. In short, we create our "own criteria for assessing [our] realities, both in thought and in action" (*Africana Womanism*, 50).

Africana womanism is a family-centered rather than a female-centered perspective. By necessity, we are concerned first and foremost with ridding society of racism, a problem which invariably affects our entire family, our total existence. In a follow-up newspaper article highlighting the impact of Africana womanism on the International Conference on Women of Africa and the African Diaspora, held at the University of Nigeria, Nsukka (July 1992), it was stated that "[Africana] womanists do not believe in bra-burning. They believe in womanhood, the family, and society. Their struggle is to enhance these attributes, not repudiate them....The Africana man and woman have always been complementary partners and if there is to be an African[a] economic empowerment and survival, both of them have to work together like they've always done" (Agoawike, 1). The notion of prioritizing the triple plight of Africana women—race, class, and gender—is the differentiating factor between women of African descent and those of the dominant culture, who place gender issues as their number-one priority.

Since the Nigeria conference of 1992, I have continued to speak on Africana womanism throughout the United States and the Caribbean, consistently emphasizing how crucial it is to properly name and define ourslves in order to ensure a proper handling of the critical issues threatening our existence as a people. It is impor-

tant to note that "When the black feminist buys the white terminology (feminism), she also buys its agenda" (*Africana Womanism*,
40). Africana womanism insists that the identity of Africana women
is inextricably connected to the destiny of Africana people: "We (of
the African Diaspora) are not playing with gender issues—we are
dealing with real-life issues which don't exclude gender but deal
with securing and empowering our people" (Fuentez, 3).

Just recently, I pointed out the consequence of subsuming our
priorities under those of the dominant culture. For example, feminists consider female empowerment their top priority. Observe the
inapplicability of their priority for women of African descent in the
case of the recent position on Affirmative Action set-asides. The question had been raised as to how (white) feminists would respond to
the increasing attacks upon Affirmative Action, since they had benefited more as women than blacks, who were the originally intended
beneficiaries of this program. My response was an historically based,
matter-of- fact position, that they would be taken care of, since they
are, after all, members of the dominant culture. Predictably, in June
1995, the Supreme Court ruled that racially determined Affirmative
Action set-asides were unconstitutional; those based upon gender
equality were not. Hence, a woman of African descent—a racially
defined category—would still be burdened with the yoke of racism:
"Even if she does overcome the battle of sexism through a collective
struggle of all women, she will still be left with the battle of racism
facing both her family and herself" (*Africana Womanism*, 59). In other
words, when the *white* feminist realizes all of her demands and has
been properly placed in high level positions in the workplace, the
black woman will still be black and at the bottom. The black woman,
then, who has sacrificed the priority of race for Africana people in
favor of a gender-specific priority, finds herself back to square one—
unresolved, unrealized, and clearly unprotected.

With this glaring revelation, it should be evident that we as Africana
people must decide for ourselves who we are and what our agenda
need be. Africana people must engage in identifying our own demands,
beginning with self-naming and self-definition, so that we can better
focus on what it will take for us to realize total human parity; indeed,
the first giant step toward harmony and survival among all.

WORKS CITED

Agoawike, Angela. "Beyond 'Bra-Burning': [Africana] Womanism as
    Alternative for the Africana Women." *Nigeria Daily Times*, July 27, 1992.
Bender, Bob. "Reassessing Roles." *Mizzou Weekly*, October 27, 1993.
Fuentez, Tania. "Africana Womanism Tied to the Destiny of a People." *The*

Daily News(Virgin Islands), June 2, 1994.

Hare, Julia. *Feminism in Black and White.* Quoted in Mary-Christine Philip. *Black Issues in Higher Education,* March 11, 1993, pp. 12-17.

Hudson-Weems, Clenora. *Africana Womanism: Reclaiming Ourselves.* Third revised edition. Troy, Mich.: Bedford Publishers, 1995.

Morrison, Toni. *Beloved.* New York: Alfred A. Knopf, 1987.

African Culture And Womanhood: The Issue Of Single- Parenthood

Protus Kemdirim (Nigeria)

INTRODUCTION

THE FIRST INTERNATIONAL CONFERENCE ON WOMEN IN Africa and the African Diaspora (WAAD Conference) held in Nsukka, Nigeria (July 13-18, 1992) was a huge success. For one thing, it provided the opportunity for women in Africa and the African Diaspora as well as whites to discuss and understand issues affecting women in developing nations. According to the convener and chairperson of the organizing committee, Dr. Obioma Nnaemeka, and as reflected by the conference theme, "Bridges Across Activism and the Academy," the purpose of the conference was to provide the space for researchers, activists, and all those interested in issues related to women in Africa and the African Diaspora to discuss their work with a view to identifying common grounds for the promotion and enhancement of womanhood.

This short piece is my contribution to one of the major issues of debate and controversy that pervaded that historic gathering of academics, researchers, activists, and field workers from all parts of the globe. It is the issue of single woman parent,[1] with specific reference to the extent to which this societal entity is permissible in the Nigerian culture. Even though there are indeed cultural norms and attitudes that not only discriminate against women but also militate against or completely eliminate their inalienable right to avail themselves of the opportunities of modern science and technology, the empowerment of women is well entrenched in African tradition and culture. As a matter of fact, the African woman is culturally empowered in several sectors at once: religion (priestly roles), the economy (commerce and trading), agriculture (farming and fishing), medicine (as herbalists and midwives), environment (maintenance of the compound, streets, and markets), and family life (child bearing and rearing). Although the African society is hierarchically structured, the places and roles of women are recognized and respected.

STATUS OF CHILDREN IN AFRICAN CULTURES

Let us examine womanhood in African culture with specific reference to bearing children for the continuity of the lineage without going into the merits and demerits of the various forms of marriage (monogamy, polygamy, levirate, and early marriages) as they affect women in Africa. To begin with, it is important to stress the diversity of African culture, and the importance of children to families. Indeed, these two factors are significantly crucial in determining the status of children in various African cultures. In fact, looking at the culture, it is obvious that what may be seen and regarded as taboo and as therefore unacceptable in one African society may well qualify as sacred and edifying in another. For example, in Ogoniland in southern Nigeria, it is culturally permissible for the first daughter not to marry but stay permanently at home and bear children for the father who is not blessed with a male child. This practice is however abhorred by other Nigerian ethnic groups, such as the Efiks, for whom it is a taboo. The point we are making is that, in Africa, the legitimate status of a child or an offspring is not necessarily provided or determined by marriage as contracted in native law and custom. In some African societies, no child is illegitimate. Even in societies where the issue of illegitimacy exists, there are mechanisms for legitimizing a child in the culture. For example, among the Krobo people of eastern Ghana, legitimacy is effected through the ritual called *lapomi*.

To buttress the fact that the issue of illegitimate children is not generally a feature of African cultures, let us consider what may be called symbolic marriages. In such marriages the parties, who may be a man and a woman, or a woman and a woman, are not properly married to each other in the legal sense of the word. Yet the offspring are recognized and accepted in the society as legitimate. Such marriages come in various forms:

(1) The woman is fertile while the man is impotent. The woman bears children from any man of her choice in the name of her legitimate husband.

(2) A single woman is married to a deity. She bears children for the deity through any man of her choice.[2]

(3) The only daughter who has lost both parents or her father may decide not to marry; she stays in the family and bears children in the name of her dead father.

(4) A widow too old to bear children or who has no male children or whose only male child is a celibate priest may marry another woman who bears children through any man of her choice in the name of the widow's deceased husband.

(5) A widow can marry one of her deceased husband's relatives and continue to bear children in the name of her deceased husband (leviratical marriage). She may also decide to marry from outside the family, in which case, the man of her choice would be required to perform some ritual sacrifices.

It is worthy of note that these relationships are recognized in different African cultures as marriages and as providing both a permanent and legitimate status for the offspring. The very concept of illegitimacy is alien to such cultures. But, it may be asked, what about a young girl who gets pregnant before marriage? Of course there is no gainsaying that in some African cultures a child born out of wedlock is looked down upon. It seems to me, however, that this negative attitude derives more from the need to maintain public morality than concerns about illegitimacy. There are cases where men who have no male child surreptitiously encourage any of their daughters to bear a male child for them. Such a child is accorded the same recognition as any other child in the society. As a matter of fact, in the cultures we are familiar with, no child is ever thought of as useless; such a thought itself constitutes a taboo. On the contrary, in Africa a child is thought of as wealth, as a gift from God and as such every effort is made not only to have a child in the family but to sustain, educate and protect him/her. This is the tradition.

CONCLUSION

Strictly speaking, the WAAD conference was extremely rewarding because it generated lively and healthy debates, controversies, and revelations. It was a great learning experience for participants from inside and outside Africa. Many lessons were learned; for example, it was shown that African cultures are not entirely negative towards women. On the contrary, there are aspects of African cultures which ensure women's empowerment. Furthermore, there was an emphasis on the immense diversity in African and the need for researchers to be mindful of specificity in their analyses. It was also pointed out that the importance of children creates room in African cultures for the acceptance of various forms of marriage. Furthermore, the issue of a child being legitimate or not is not very much discussed; rather, mechanisms are put in place through which children are legitimized and equally recognized.

NOTES

1. The issue of single-parenthood apparently sparked off a big controversy that almost destroyed the appreciable quiet and accommodating spirit that characterized the conference. This followed the inadvertent use of the word "bastard" by an African participant in his speech.
2. This was the practice among the people of Ukehe, Enugu State, Nigeria, where a section of the town is peopled by sons and daughters of a deity called *Efuru*. The practice was however stopped in 1978 when the then government of Anambra State destroyed the shrine of the deity and thus ended the deity's obnoxious custom of marrying any girl of her choice.

THOUGHTS ON THE 1992 WAAD CONFERENCE

KATHLEEN GEATHERS (U. S. A.)

THE CONFERENCE ON AFRICAN WOMEN AND WOMEN OF African descent throughout the Diaspora was a excellent idea. It was an opportunity for women with a common ancestral background that had been split asunder by the African Slave Trade, to come together, reach out to each other, learn from each other, and establish bonds of friendship.

For generations, there has been effective brainwashing about each group on both sides of the Atlantic, with only negative stories being told, resulting in suspicion and distrust. On both sides of the Atlantic, each group encountered their foreign sisters and brothers who exercised feelings of superiority over the other. On the American side, we were led to believe that the African is very primitive, wears scant clothing, has a bone through his/her nose, and holds a spear. Some Africans believed that their American sisters thought they had a monopoly on education, and were there to "teach" the African without recognizing the vast fund of knowledge the African possessed. This conference provided the opportunity for these fallacies to be dispelled.

The African is not ignorant, in fact many speak several languages fluently. They are writers, lecturers, teachers, scientists, and are contributors to the entire spectrum of the arts, such as song, dance, and carving. Yet, there are many people in Africa who, like their American sisters and brothers, do not enjoy a decent standard of living, although Africa is rich in natural resources. I hope that one day African peoples will exploit their own resources and use the proceeds to raise the standard of living for all the members of their societies.

While I have traveled to all parts of Africa for more than twenty years, nothing has excited me more than the prospect of getting together at Nsukka with my African sisters and learning about cultural practices I have missed. Some good African cultural practices, such as the communal responsibility for every child and the respect for elders, need to be reinstituted in African American society, while those that are oppressive to women, such as female circumcision and the isolation of widows, must be addressed. African American cultural patterns may differ somewhat from those of Africa, although many create the same pain as experienced by our African sisters. The cultural pattern of male domination persists in both societies in which many men refuse to see us as mature adults, able to make decisions about ourselves and our bodies (thus, the abortion debate goes on endlessly in the United States).

Power over women exists because women did not define their roles in the social order and for a long time they have accepted passively their lot in life. It is now time for women throughout the diaspora to cease being willing victims and grab the power which was illegally taken from them and used to keep them in a servile state. This correction of the imbalance of power can be achieved only if we deal with basics such as equal opportunities for education, jobs with equal pay, child care, health care, and quality care for the elderly. When we occupy powerful decision-making positions, these things will be accomplished and there will no longer be a need for labels such as "feminist," or "womanist," as had been debated in the conference. The accomplishment of our goals will surely earn us respectability as equal members of the human race.

The WAAD conference was a cultural awakening. On both sides of the Atlantic, we wanted a stop to the violence against women, whether clothed in the mask of culture or otherwise. We wanted to be treated as equals. Much work was involved in executing such a conference, although some areas still need improvement. The workshops as listed were interesting and were directed by capable leaders; however, there were too many panelists, with the result that the time allotted for questions and discussions was inadequate. Another factor which was troubling was the conducting of workshops simultaneously with the Assembly. Not knowing that workshops were proceeding as scheduled, I missed some very interesting sessions.

One of the things I have learned about struggle is that "timing" is crucial. Struggle is always fraught with danger; however, in America, while women are still struggling for rights and some men are still opposing them, this opposition does not deter us in our determination. I could not help but wonder if the African woman has reached the point in "timing" where she can aggressively pursue her rights without self endangerment? At any rate, she is aware that she deserves more. Change always begins with awareness, action follows later. Perhaps this conference is the forerunner of change not only for the African woman, but also for her American sisters.

I hope that all of us, on both sides of the Atlantic, will reach out to our economically and educationally deprived sisters. It is difficult to get a response from them because they feel unwanted by and distrustful of us. I know how hard one has to work to gain their confidence; in my role as chair of the Greater Cleveland Chapter of Women for Racial and Economic Equality, I am constantly reaching out to women in all walks of life. I receive many promises, but few are able to follow through and attend meetings. Nevertheless, we should persist in our efforts on both sides of the Atlantic to let them know we care.

We all struggle against oppression. Colonialism and white racism have lingering effects on all of us. However, the African American woman encounters discrimination every day both overtly and covertly; as for example, when she is passed over for promotions in favor of a white person whom she has trained, or when a company believes a lie told by a white woman while discrediting the truth told by an African American woman. Therefore, when some of the African American women arrived in Nigeria and saw white women in key roles in what was expected to be a conference about and by African women and those of African descent, they were indignant, disappointed, and some were even angry ("They had traveled all the way to the mother country to meet the oppressor from back home"). The tension caused by white presence cast a pall over the conference, but if used wisely it could provide a valuable learning experience for each group. What the white woman encountered in her position as a minority should have given her great pause, as this is what African American women encounter frequently. What the African woman learned was that her experience and outlook is different from that of her slave descendant sisters; nevertheless, both groups must work to throw off the lingering effects of colonialism.

Sexism was also a problem. In the opening session, men dominated the platform—which many feminists, including this writer, found appalling. This is not an anti-male statement, but in a woman's conference, women are well equipped to carry out functions. We need and want male support, just as we would be supportive of men in an all-male conference if our input was needed; however, I am sure they would not allow us to occupy prominent positions in their event.

The conference left me feeling optimistic because it meant that the divisions which separated us for so long are in the process of being overcome. If we continue to work to build bridges which have been needed for such a long time, then our combined strength can be utilized to improve the lot of African women, not only in Africa, but throughout the Diaspora.

THE WAAD CONFERENCE AND BEYOND: A LOOK AT AFRICANA WOMANISM

DAPHNE NTIRI (SIERRA LEONE)

WOMEN TODAY ARE ACTIVELY LOOKING FOR TOOLS TO HELP increase emancipation in their lives and in their combined roles as workers and homemakers. Personally, my search slowed down following the WAAD conference at the University of Nigeria, Nsukka, Nigeria in July, 1992. I had attended the conference because of my interest in expanding my knowledge base on women's studies and programs. I am a product of the 1970s university research programs that recruited graduate women students from various states and countries to benefit from the splurge of resources made available during that decade. It was also the United Nations Decade to promote the cause of women all around the world. Before the Nsukka experience, most of the theories I was familiar with were grounded in feminism. However, the discussions about Africana womanism at the WAAD conference brought new insights and a renewed vision in a new-found source of empowerment and status-building for women that has remained with me ever since.

Africana womanism, as theorized by Clenora Hudson-Weems in *Africana Womanism: Reclaiming Ourselves,* gave new meaning to the many distorted images of black women in the literature and provided answers to the ideological predicament that many black women like myself find themselves in. The philosophy she advocates is simple:

> It is an ideology created and designed for all women of African descent. It is grounded in our culture and therefore

it necessarily focuses on the unique experiences, struggles and desires of Africana women. It critically addresses the dynamics of the conflict between the mainstream feminist, the black feminist, the African feminist and the Africana womanist. (11)

The primary goal of the Africana womanist, whether she is in the West or in a Third World society remains one of survival :

The Africana womanist, focusing on her particular circumstances, comes from an entirely different perspective, one which embraces the concept of collectivism for the entire family in its overall liberation struggle for survival, thereby resolving the question of her place in the venue of women's issues. (42)

This goal is tied to the Africana women's common destiny wherever they may be as they engage in self-naming and self-definition. Access to social and economic opportunities at all levels has been historically denied to the Africana woman. It is therefore that past that is marked by the realities of the hegemony and ethnocentrism of Western cultures and the accompanying atrocities of slavery, colonialism, and oppression that sets the tone for the ongoing discourse in Africana womanism. The identity question that this discourse raises is pertinent to black people in Africa and the Diaspora. In the case of the African American, phases of new consciousness have arisen and continue to combine the political, social, and economic realities of African Diaspora life. For women, in particular, a philosophy like Africana womanism becomes critical and receives a warm reception from the field. Its purpose is multifunctional as it serves as the conceptual tool which harnesses the transformative energies and strategies embedded in Africana women's rise from oppression. For me, it has become a part of my teaching and practice. Because I share the vision of Hudson-Weems's philosophy, I have incorporated many of its key elements in my work and presentations. Hudson-Weems has also adopted my edited volume, *One is Not a Woman, One Becomes: The African Woman in A Transitonal Society*, as a companion text to *Africana Womanism*. What is laudable about Hudson-Weems's contribution is the creation of measures for assessing our own realities in thought and action. She states that "the true Africana womanist is family-centered in concert with males in struggle and genuine in sisterhood." She is also strong mentally and physically, male-compatible, spiritual, respectful of elders, and believes in mothering and nurturing. The 1992 WAAD conference at Nsukka opened up extraordinary opportunities for networking and collaboration. Back in the United States, I have been engaged in healthy and productive exchanges and engagements regarding the Africana woman with several other colleagues at other academic institutions. We have shared mutually benefiting inter- campus lectureships. Furthermore, Dr. Hudson-Weems and I have both shared the platform on Africana womanism in several conferences including panels for two consecutive years at the Third World Conference Foundation (TWCF) in Chicago; in the recent past, at the First Civil Rights Conference at LeMoyne-Owens College in Memphis Tennessee (August 1995) and at The Association for African Life and History (ASALH) in Philadelphia, Pennsylvania in October, 1996. Another faculty member, Alma Vinyard of Clark Atlanta University (where this theory has also been tested in the classroom) was also a participant in the WAAD conference. She participated on a panel on Africana womanism with me in the First Civil Rights Conference in Memphis, Tennessee (July, 1995).

WORKS CITED

Hudson-Weems, Clenora. *Africana Womanism: Reclaiming Ourselves*. Third revised edition. Troy, Mich.: Bedford Publishers, 1995

Ntiri, Daphne Williams. *One Is Not a Woman, One Becomes: The African Woman in a Transitional Society*. Troy, Mich.: Bedford Publishers, 1983

THE FIRST INTERNATIONAL CONFERENCE ON WOMEN IN AFRICA AND THE AFRICAN DIASPORA: A VIEW FROM THE U. S. A.

DEBORAH PLANT (U. S. A.)

THE FIRST INTERNATIONAL CONFERENCE ON WOMEN IN Africa and the African Diaspora: Bridges Across Activism and the Academy was held 13-18 July, 1992, in Nsukka, Nigeria. Dr. Obioma Nnaemeka, of Indiana University at Indianapolis, organized and convened the conference. Over forty countries were represented and approximately 800 conferees were in attendance. Papers, panels, and workshops covering a wide range of themes and multiplicity of disciplines were represented. And cultural events were organized by several state Governors to honor the attendees.

The Ghanaian novelist Ama Ata Aidoo was a keynote speaker at the conference. Before Aidoo made her presentation, she took issue with two matters: One matter was that of the invariable confusion and distraction created at women's conferences by the disturbing statements and comments of one or two men. For example, one man stated before a full audience that a child of a woman, who has not the benefit of a marriage to a man, must necessarily become an idiot. The other matter addressed the need for direct participation in conferences by rural African women and African women who do not speak European languages. Although some conference participants met with rural Nigerian women who worked with the government's Better Life Program, a program designed to support and promote the industry of rural women, there was no time given over to significant dialogue and discussion.

That African women "are not as free and equal as African men would like you to believe," was a major point in Ama Aidoo's keynote address. The conception of African women as "the root of all evil" still obtains in contemporary African society, and men continue to "use gender and biology to judge women's efforts and capabilities." The men are groomed for leadership positions in government while the women struggle against the impact of government policies which undermine and erode their capabilities to produce and provide for themselves and their families. Aidoo depicted clearly the oppressive state of affairs which keeps African women and children uneducated and impoverished even as it keeps Africa bound under the tyranny of imperialist and neocolonialist politics.

"We Africans should take charge of our land, its wealth, our lives, and the burden of our own development," Aidoo stated. She called upon African women to take an active part in the struggle for Africa's independence and in the forging of Africa's future direction. In order to do so, Aidoo advocated "emancipatory education" for African women. She bade those who had received formal education to resist tokenism and complacency. And she emphasized the need for African women to wake up from their "collective amnesia." Aidoo recalled leaders and warrior queens like Yaa Asantewa, Cleopatra, and Nzinga. She recalled Dahomey's women soldiers and the participation of women in the Mau Mau movement which liberated Kenya from British colonialism. She recalled the present struggle of the people of Azania (South Africa) and the women who fight side by side with the men. Aidoo's roll call of women of antiquity and those of modern and contemporary Africa served to reawaken their proven capabilities and to encourage contemporary African women to resume their responsibilities of leadership. For, she noted, "men have monopolized leadership positions in Africa over the last 500 years.... If they alone could save us, they would have done so by now.... It is high time African women moved on to center stage with or without any one's encouragement, because some of us are convinced that in our hands lies, perhaps, the last possible hope for ourselves and for everyone else on this continent and in the world."

Another issue Ama Ata Aidoo addressed was whether Black women should embrace the term "feminism" to describe the global African women's ideology. Adioo stated that she was a feminist and that "every woman and man should be a feminist," especially if they believed in and supported African people's independence and autonomy. After a spirited rallying of opinions, in which novelist Flora Nwapa and dramatist 'Zulu Sofola also participated, Aidoo retracted her statement and determined she had to reconsider her opinion. Aidoo's discussion of the terminology stemmed from African women's debate over the issue. Her point of departure was Alice Walker's proposal that the term "womanist" be substituted for "feminist." However, Aidoo's resolve to reconsider her stance was due to the discussion of another alternative term, that of "Africana womanism." Clenora Hudson-Weems, advocator of Africana womanism, emphasized that the embracing of a particular term was also the embracing of a particular philosophy. Having described feminism as a concept derived from and informed by the classist, racist, and sexist politics of the privileged white women of post-Civil War America, Hudson-Weems advocated the rejection of "feminism" by Black women. She urged them to consider Africana womanism as a concept and philosophy which was more inclusive than Walker's "womanism" and more historically and culturally significant than white women's "feminism." At the center of Africana womanism was the Black woman. Although it was proposed that a referendum be drawn up stating the Black women's decision to embrace Africana womanism, this action was not taken.

That sufficient time was not given over to the discussion of this matter was but one point of contention which surfaced at the conference. Another controversial and divisive issue was the participation of white women as co-organizers of a conference on black women and as presenters of papers. Other matters with which conference participants took issue were the lack of time and space allowed for dialogue between continental and diasporic African women; no discussion of issues relevant to lesbian women; accommodations in Nigeria (many women would have welcomed the opportunity of staying with Nigerian families); and problematic management of travel arrangements.

Women of the African diaspora, nevertheless, managed to build bridges with each other as well as with their continental sisters. Out of snatches of discourse came an awareness of the commonalities of experience and feeling among black women all over the Diaspora and a realization of the differences of experience and feeling between continental and diasporic sisters. The gap resulting from these apparently unexpected differences was bridged somewhat and hurt feelings were somewhat healed as sisters from the continent enacted the traditional Welcome Home ritual for their sisters in the Diaspora.

This historic conference pointed up the fundamental need for a dialogue between continental and diasporic Africans which addresses each group's different histories and geopolitical situations. By unmasking the presumption of categorical unity based on skin color, the dynamics of the conference underscored the need for a greater awareness of and respect for cultural differences among black people. It also made clear the dearth of information black people all over the globe have of one another and the need to be better informed. The political fallout generated by clashes of "race" and sex challenges black women to consider the irony of silencing black men at women's conferences while white women are allowed to speak. The intense and conflictual events of this conference promise to give birth to more productive and progressive dialogue in the future. As the past never stands at bay, chickens and roosters have come home to roost. Theories of gender, sex class, race, nationality, and culture defied containment in facile intellectual abstractions as Africa's Diaspora looked home, as those more apparently oppressed looked to those who have the "privilege" of formal education and material acquisitions, and as women looked at one another with uneasy, distrustful eye. These are but few of the issues generated by the First WAAD conference which black women must (re)consider as they continue to occupy center stage in the struggle for emancipation, independence, and autonomy for themselves and others.

VI
APPENDIX

COMMUNIQUÉ

WOMEN FROM ALL OVER AFRICA, THE AFRICAN DIASPORA and other parts of the globe gathered in Nsukka, Nigeria (July 13-18, 1992) to discuss a wide range of issues which affect them. After days of deliberation and debate, the Conference took note of the following:

(1) There are still laws that discriminate against women in all spheres, particularly in employment;

(2) The conflict between customary and general laws pertaining to some countries leave women with an uncertain status;

(3) The plight of rural women should be seriously taken into account as it relates to their own role in development;

(4) The majority of women living in rural areas are illiterate and are not trained in specific skills;

(5) The high mortality rate of women and children as well as the effects of AIDS on women still remain serious problems;

(6) Violence against women has become a matter of concern in all our societies as it dehumanizes the female person and serves as a means of social control. Also, violence must refer to physical, mental, and psychological violence against women;

(7) Women who are involved in small businesses are denied marketing opportunities and access to credit facilities and lack managerial and financial skills;

(8) The movement of migrant laborers affects family life and leaves women with added responsibilities;

(9) Women must acknowledge the differences both in terms of concepts and substance amongst them, find ways to accommodate such,

and find solutions;

(10) There is a lack of women-centered literature on women;

(1) In every employment situation, women be judged on their tested abilities to perform rather than be denied job opportunities because they are women; and that labor laws that are favorable to women be enacted.

(2) All laws which discriminate against women be abolished in line with the 1981 UN Convention on the Elimination of Discrimination against Women;

(3) Rural women be given the opportunity at conferences and seminars to raise their own concerns in the language of their choice;

(4) Literacy programs and training in specific skills be provided to rural women to enable them to participate fully and meaningfully in the development process;

(5) Access to credit and managerial skills development be extended to women involved in small businesses;

(6) All women should have access to health care and participate in primary health-care programs. The health of women should be comprehensive and paramount;

(7) Women must develop strategies and create alliance and cooperation for a common cause by

(a) providing and expanding support systems of women at the family, community, national and international levels;

(b) raising the consciousness of women and men on gender issues using both formal and informal educational settings or cultural and social gatherings;

(8) Women must share information through building national and international networks which could also serve as communication channels;

(9) Women should be allowed to draw up their own priorities and agenda according to their own specific experiences;

(10) Research should be participatory and should involve the community at all levels. Such research should be put to the use of the communities that have educated the researchers on issues.

(11) Women should use all means at their disposal to pressure decision makers and people responsible for policy implementation to put women's issues on the national agendas and governmental development plans.

AMENDMENTS TO THE COMMUNIQUÉ

This conference notes that:

(1) Colonial, racist, class, and gender oppression and injustices against the majority of women in Africa and the African Diaspora are still continuing and;

(2) Women and men must be educated on gender issues and be encouraged to deal with gender inequalities;

AND THIS CONFERENCE RESOLVES THAT:

Women in Africa and of African descent need their own space in order to challenge and combat these injustices suffered by women.

ASSOCIATION OF AFRICAN WOMEN SCHOLARS (AAWS)

Obioma Nnaemeka (President), Helen Mugambi
(Vice-President), Pamela Smith (Secretary)
Omofolabo Ajayi-Soyinka (Treasurer),
Opportune Zongo (Publicity Secretary)
Address: Women's Studies Program, CA 001C, Indiana University
425 University Boulevard, Indianapolis, IN 46202, U. S. A.
Phone: (317)278-2038 or (317)274-0062 (messages),
Fax: (317)274-2347
E-mail: nnaemeka@iupui.edu

MEMBERSHIP

Membership of the organization is open to African women and men (academicians, independent scholars, activists, students, and policy makers) everywhere committed to engendering and promoting scholarship in all disciplines in African Women's Studies

AIMS & OBJECTIVES

(1) To promote and encourage scholarship on AFRICAN WOMEN in African Studies;
(2) To forge intellectual links and network with scholars, activists, and policy makers inside and outside Africa; and
(3) To participate actively in continental and global debate on issues specifically relevant or related to African women.

FUNCTIONS OF THE ORGANIZATION

(1) Organize and sponsor conferences and other forms of scholarly interchange;

(2) Encourage and undertake consortial/collaborative projects;

(3) Institute a refereed journal—Journal of African Women's Studies (JAWS)—to promote and disseminate scholarly research on African women;

(4) Facilitate faculty and student exchanges;

(5) Create a communications network via cyberspace for the pooling and dissemination of resource information, including but not limited to works in progress, dissertations, new studies, research updates, pedagogy;

(6) Create, establish, and/or carry out any other functions and activities which may from time to time arise and are considered to be incidental and conducive to the realization of the above objectives; and

(7) Establish a Research and Documentation Unit which will produce an African Women's Bibliography Series on a biennial basis.

AAWS DISCUSSION GROUP ON THE INTERNET

The discussion group is open to members and non-members. Requests to join can be made on the internet through LISTSERV@LISTSERV.IUPUI.EDU by sending the following message: SUBSCRIBE AFWOSCHO

ASSOCIATION OF AFRICAN WOMEN SCHOLARS (AAWS)
REGISTRATION FORM

Name_____

Address_____

_____

City_____ State_____Zip Code _____

Country _____

Institutional Affiliation_____

Title _____

Rank _____

Field/Discipline_____

Research/Activist

    Interests_____

Telephone(work)_____(home)_____

Fax _____

E-mail_____

ANNUAL DUES

Income over $35, 000	$ 40
Income from $15-$35,000	$ 30
Income below $15,000	$ 15
Students (resident outside Africa)	$ 10
African students studying in Africa	$ 5
Other residents in Africa	$ 10
Institutional Member	$ 100
Life Member*	$1000

(*One-time payment or 4 annual
installments of $250)

AAWS dues are for one calender year. Above dues apply to North America and overseas surface mail. For overseas air-mail add $10. Make checks payable to Association of African Women Scholars. Members not resident in the United States should pay by money order or check in US dollars drawn on a US bank. Send checks to:

Omofolabo Ajayi-Soyinka
Treasurer, AAWS
Women's Studies Program
The University of Kansas
Lawrence, KS 66045
U. S. A.

STATEMENT FROM THE SOUTH AFRICAN DELEGATION REGARDING THE REQUEST BY SOME PARTICIPANTS THAT WHITES BE EXCLUDED FROM PRESENTING PAPERS AT THE WAAD CONFERENCE

SOUTH AFRICAN PARTICIPANTS DELIBERATED PRIVATELY on whether white South Africans should be afforded the opportunity to read their papers during the conference. After a careful examination of the problem, the following observations were made:

(1) Due to the Policy of Racial Classification in South Africa, women stand in different positions and are accorded different statuses depending on one's race and class. The group articulated the advantages and disadvantages that go with being in each position. For instance, it was noted that white women have over a long period of time had access to resources—such as computers, electricity, offices, and international networks—which are essential in knowledge acquisition, research, and writing.

(2) It is imperative for feminists and all other progressive scholars to move towards the transformation of the patriarchal practices and Western hegemony which have a history of being discriminatory. The trend should be to begin to create space for, and to facilitate the visibility of women who previously have been discriminated against.

(3) Academicians in particular have to move beyond rhetoric which is often made in international conferences about and on behalf of black women. A specific suggestion was that they should devise strategies which will close the gap between academicians and activists by facilitating the oppressed women's need to articulate their own stories.

(4) A significant number of white scholars have made a tremendous contribution in the transformation of society.

CONCLUSION

Taking into consideration political developments in South Africa and also realizing inherent contradictions in this issue, the group suggests that all South Africans, irrespective of race, should be permitted to participate fully in this conference.

ACRONYMS

AALAE	African Association for Literacy and Adult Education
AAWORD	Association of African Women on Research and Development
AAWS	Association of African Women Scholars
AIDAB	Australian International Development Agency Bureau
AMRU	Associacao Mozambicana da Mulher Rural
ANC	African National Congress
ANCWL	African National Congress Women's League
ASA	African Studies Association
ASUU	Academic Staff Union of Universities
AWB	Afrikaner Weerstandbeweging (Afrikaner Resistance Movement)
AWSA	Arab Women's Solidarity Association)
AWU	Abeokuta Women's Union
BLP	Be , Life Program
BWIP	Bla.. Women in Publishing
CACE	Centre for Continuing Adult Education
CAFRA	Caribbean Association for Research and Action
CODESA	Convention for a Democratic South Africa
CONTRALESA	Congress of Traditional Leaders
COSATU	Congress of South African Trade Unions
DAWN	Development Alternatives with Women for a New Era
ECOWAS	Economic Community of West African States
FOMWAN	Federation of Muslim Women Associations of Nigeria
FSAW	Federation of South African Women

GAD	Gender and Development
GILLBT	Ghana Institute of Linguistic Literacy and Translation
GROOTS	Grassroots Organizations Operating Together for Sisterhood
IDRC	International Development Research Center
IEC	Independent Electoral Commission
IFP	Inkatha Freedom Party
IMF	International Monetary Fund
IWHC	International Women's Health Coalition
KISS	Keep it Straight and Simple (Party)
MWA	Muslim Women's Association
MWA	Market Women's Association
NAFE	National Association of Executive Females
NAMW	Nigerian Association of Media Women
NANWB	National Association of Nigerian Women in Business
NAWOJ	Nigerian Association of Women Journalists
NAWSA	National American Woman Suffrage Association
NCWS	National Council of Women's Societies
NGO	Non Governmental Organization
NIPR	Nigerian Institute of Public Relations
NLC	Nigerian Labour Congress
NMA	Nigerian Medical Association
NSO	National Security Organization
NUJ	Nigerian Union of Journalists
OISE	Ontario Institute for Studies in Education
PAC	Pan Africanist Congress
SACP	South African Communist Party
SADWU	South African Domestic Workers Union
SAIC	South African Indian Congress
SAREC	Swedish Agency for Research Cooperation with Developing Countries
SFPA	Sudan Family Planning Association
SIDA	Swedish International Development Authority
SWA	Sewing Women's Association
TAMWA	Tanzania Media Women's Association
TEC	Transitional Executive Council
UAWL	Ugadan Association of Women Lawyers
UNCW	Uganda National Council of Women
UWO	United Women's Organization

UWCO	United Women's Congress
WAAD	(First international conference on) Women in Africa and African Diaspora
WAG	Women's Action Group
WAND	Women's Association for National Development (Sierra Leone)
WEDO	Women's Environment and Development Organization
WFO	Women's Front Organization
WID	Women in Development
WIN	Women in Nigeria
WLM	Women's Liberation Movement
WNC	Women's National Coalition

 # SELECTED BIBLIOGRAPHY

Abrahams, Peter. *A Wreath for Udoma*. New York: Alfred Knopf, 1956.

Achebe, Chinua. *Anthills of the Savannah*. New York: Anchor, 1987.

———. *Hopes and Impediments*. London: Heinemann, 1988.

——. *Things Fall Apart*. London: Heinemann, 1958.

Achebe, Chinwe. *The World of the Ogbanje*. Enugu: Fourth Dimension Publishers, 1987.

Acholonu, Catherine. *The Igbo Roots of Olaudah Equiano*. Owerri: Afa Publications, 1989.

———. *The Trial of the Beautiful Ones*. Owerri: Totan Publishers, 1988.

Acholonu, Rose. "Love and the Feminist Utopia in the African Novel." Paper presented at the first international conference on Women in Africa and the African Diaspora: Bridges across Activism and the Academy, Nsukka, Nigeria, July 13-18, 1992.

Adiele, Eunice E. "Widowhood Practices in Igboland: An Examination of the Role of Christian Churches." *Proceedings of the First International Conference on Women in Africa and the African Diaspora: Bridges across Activism and the Academy*. Nsukka, Nigeria, July 13-18, 1992, Vol. IX: 49-62.

Afigbo, Adiele. "Women in Nigerian History." In *Women in the Nigerian Economy*, ed., Martin Ijere. Enugu: Acena Publishers, 1991: 22-40.

———. "Widowhood Practices in Africa: A Preliminary Survey and Analysis." *Proceedings of the First International Conference on Women in Africa and the African Diaspora: Bridges across Activism and the Academy*. Nsukka, Nigeria, July 13-18, 1992, Vol. IX: 63-94.

Aflatun, Inji. "We Egyptian Women." In *Opening the Gates: A Century of Arab Feminist Writing*, trans., Michelle Raccagni, ed., Margot Badran and Miriam Cooke. Bloomington: Indiana University Press, 1990: 345-351.

Ahmed, Leila. "Feminism and Feminist Movements in the Middle East." In *Women and Islam*, ed., Azizah al-Hibri. Oxford: Pergamon Press, 1982: 153-168.

——. "Arab Culture and Writing Women's Bodies." *Feminist Issues* 9.1 (Spring 1989): 41-56.

——. *Women and Gender in Islam*. New Haven: Yale University Press, 1992.

Aidoo, Ama Ata. "Unwelcomed Pals and Decorative Slaves or Glimpses of Women as Writers and Characters in Contemporary African Literatures." In *Literature and Society: Selected Essays on African Literature*, ed., Ernest Emenyonu. Oguta: Zim Pan African Publishers, 1989: 1-19.

Aina, Olabisi I. "Mobilizing Nigerian Women for National Development: The Role of the Female Elites." *African Economic History* 21 (1993): 1-20.

Akpan, Ekwere, O. and Violetta L. Ekpo. *The IgboWomen's War of 1929: A Popular Uprising in South Eastern Nigeria (Preliminary Study)*. Calabar: The Government Printer, 1988.

Al-Hibri, Azizah, ed. *Women and Islam*. Oxford: Pergamon Press, 1982.

Allen, Paula Gunn. *The Sacred Hoop: Recovering the Feminine in American Indian Traditions*. Boston: Beacon Press, 1986.

Alloo, Fatma. "The Need for a Women's Magazine." *Sauti Ya Siti* 1 (1988): 1-2.

Aluko, Grace B. and Mary O. Alfa. "Marriage and Family." In *Women in Nigeria Today*, ed., Editorial Committee. London: Zed Press, 1985: 163-173.

Amadi, Elechi. *The Concubine*. London: Heinemann, 1966.

Amadiume, Ifi. *Male Daughters, Female Husbands: Gender and Sex in an African Society*. London: Zed Books, 1987.

Anand, Anita. "Rethinking Women and Development." *Women in Development, A Resource Guide for Organization and Action. ISIS International* (1983): 5-11.

Angelou, Maya. *On the Pulse of Morning*. New York: Random House, 1993.

Appaport, J. *Community Psychology: Values, Research, and Action*. New York: Holt, Rinehart, and Winston, 1977.

Arene, Violet. "Might Has Become Right." *Sunday Vanguard* (January 26, 1992): 11.

Argosin, Marjorie, Temma Kaplan, and Teresa Valdez. "The Politics of Spectacle in Chile." *The Barnard Occasional Papers on Women's Issues* 2.3 (Fall, 1987).

Argosin, Marjorie. "Emerging from the Shadows: Women of Chile." *The Barnard Occasional Papers on Women's Issues* 2.3 (Fall, 1987).

——. *Scraps of Life: Chilean Arpilleras, Chilean Women and the Pinochet Dictatorship* London: Zed Books, 1987.

Arnfred, Signe. "Women in Mozambique: Gender Struggle and Gender Politics." *Review of African Political Economy* 41 (Sept. 1988): 5-16.

Ashcroft, Bill, Gareth Griffiths, and Helen Tiffin. *The Empire Writes Back: Theory and Practice in Post-Colonial Literatures*. New York: Methuen, 1989.

Atiku, J. *Rural Women and Children in Uganda. A Study of the Situation in West Nile, Nebbi, Arua and Moyo Districts*. Kampala: UNICEF, 1984.

Awe, Bolanle. "The Iyalode in the Traditional Yoruba Political System." In *Sexual Stratification: A Cross-Cultural View*, ed., Alice Schlegel. New York: Columbia University Press, 1977: 144-159.

Azikiwe, Uche. "Widowhood Practices in Nigeria: The Case of Afikpo Community." *Proceedings of the First International Conference on Women in Africa and the African Diaspora: Bridges across Activism and the Academy*. Nsukka, Nigeria, July 13-18, 1992, Vol. IX: 205-216.

Baard, Frances. *My Spirit Is Not Banned: As Told By Frances Baard To Barbie Schreiner*. Harare: Zimbabwe Publishing House, 1986.

Babangida, Maryam. "The Role of Women In National Development." *Sunday Concord* (October 7, 1990): 21.

Babiker, Fatima, et al. "African Feminism." *Spare Rib* 197 (December 1988-January 1989): 16-17.

Baffoun, Alya. "Future of Feminism in Africa." *Echo, AAWORD Newsletter* 2/3 (1985): 4-6.

Bamgboye, David. *Space Science And National Development: An Inaugural Lecture.* Ilorin: University of Ilorin Press, 1987.

Barrel, H. *MK: ANC's Armed Struggle.* London: Penguin, 1990.

Barrios de Chungara, Domitila. *Let Me Speak!: Testimony of Domitila, a Woman of the Bolivian Mines,* trans., Victoria Ortiz. New York: Monthly Review Press, 1978.

Bazilli, Susan. "Conferencing the Stone." Paper written in response to Women and Gender in Southern Africa Conference. University of Natal, Durban, Jan. 30-Feb. 2, 1991.

Belenky, M. F., B. M. Clinchy, N. R. Golderger, and J. M. Tarule. *Women's Ways of Knowing: The Development of Self, Voice, and Mind.* New York: Basic Books, 1986.

Bello, Sule. "Problems of Theory and Practice in Women's Liberation Movements." *Women in Nigeria Today,* ed., Editorial Committee. London: Zed Press, 1985: 23-27.

Benjamin, Jessica. *The Bonds of Love.* New York, Pantheon Books, 1988.

Berger, Iris. "Rebels or Status-Seekers? Women as Spirit Mediums in East Africa." In *Women in Africa: Studies in Social and Economic Change,* ed., Nancy J. Hafkin and Edna G. Bay. Stanford, Calif.: Stanford University Press, 1976: 157-181.

Beverley, John. "The Margin at the Center: On Testimonio (Testimonial Narrative)." *Modern Fiction Studies* 35 (Spring 1989): 11-28.

Bhasin, Kamla. "Asian Women against Mal-development." *Fenix* 00 (1990): 22-26.

———. "Alternative and Sustainable Development." *Convergence* 25.2 (1992): 26-35.

Bhasin, Kamla, and Nighat Said Khan. *Some Questions about Feminism and Its Relevance in South Asia.* New Delhi: Kali for Women Press, 1986.

Boone, Sylvia. A. *Radiance from the Waters: Ideals of Feminine Beauty in Mende Art.* New Haven: Yale University Press, 1986.

Bow, Leslie. "'For Every Gesture of Loyalty, There Doesn't Have to Be a Betrayal': Asian American Criticism and the Politics of Locality." In *Who Can Speak?* ed., Judith Roof and Robyn Wiegman. Urbana: University of Illinois Press, 1995.

Bryant, D. C. "The Creation of an Interracial Social Action: Examination of the Process." Unpublished Ph. D. dissertation, Michigan State University, East Lansing, Mich, 1990.

———. "The Evolution in Canada of the Citizen's Movement Against Nestlé: A Descriptive Study." Unpublished M. A. thesis, Wilfrid Laurier University, Waterloo, Ontario, Canada, 1985.

Bunch, Charlotte. "Not for Lesbians Only." *Quest: A Feminist Quarterly* 2.2 (1975): 50-56.

————. *Passionate Politics, Feminist Theory in Action: Essays 1968-1986*. New York: St. Martin's Press, 1987.

————. "Prospects for Global Feminism." In *Feminist Frameworks*, third edition, ed., Alison M. Jaggar and Paula S. Rothenberg. New York: McGraw-Hill, 1993: 249-252.

Cannon, Katie. *Black Womanist Ethics*. Atlanta: Scholars Press, 1988.

Carroll, Peter N. and David W. Noble. *The Free and the Unfree: A New History of the United States*. New York: Penguin Books, 1977.

Catafygioutou-Topping, Eva. "Mourning for Hypatia." *The Greek American* 8.10 (March 16, 1991): 13.

Catanese, A. J. *The Politics of Planning and Development*. Beverly Hills, Calif.: Sage, 1984.

Chavis, D. M. and A. Wandersman. "Sense of Community in the Urban Environment: A Catalyst for Participation and Community Development." *American Journal of Community Psychology* 18.1 (1990): 55-81.

Chukukere, Glo. "Female Roles in West Africa." In *Introductory Readings in the Humanities and Social Sciences*. Onitsha: University Publishing Company, 1988.

Clifford, James. *Writing Culture: The Poetics and Politics of Fieldwork*. Berkeley: University of California Press, 1986.

Clinton, Catherine. "Women Break New Ground." In *The Underside of American History*, vol. 2, ed., Thomas R. Fraizer. New York: Harcourt Brace Jovanovich, 1987: 62-83.

Cock, Jacklyn. *Colonels and Cadres: War and Gender in South Africa*. Cape Town: Oxford University Press, 1991.

————. *Women and War in South Africa*. London: Open Letters, 1992.

Collins, Patricia Hill. *Black Feminist Thought: Knowledge, Consciousness, and the Politics of Empowerment*. Boston: Unwin Hyman, 1990.

Comaroff, Jean and John Comaroff, eds. *Modernity and Its Malcontents: Ritual and Power in Postcolonial Africa*. Chicago: University of Chicago Press, 1993.

Combahee River Collective. "A Black Feminist Statement." In *Capitalist Patriarchy and the Case for Socialist Feminism*, ed., Zillah R. Eisenstein. New York: Monthly Review Press, 1979: 259-291.

Daodu, Keji. "Global Attention to Rural Women." *National Concord* (February 25, 1992): 5.

Davies, Carol Boyce. *Black Women, Writing, and Identity*. London: Routledge, 1994.

de Beauvoir, Simone. "Women and Creativity." In *French Feminist Thought*, ed., Toril Moi. London: Basil Blackwell, 1987: 17-32.

Development Dialogue. "The Dakar Declaration on Another Development with Women." 1.2 (1982): 11-16.

Diers, Judith Ann. "Freeing Liberation Theology." *Ms* (July/August 1992): 74-75.

Dill, Bonnie T. "Race, Class and Gender: Prospects for an All-Inclusive Sisterhood." *Feminist Studies* 9 (Sept. 1983): 131-150.

Diop, Cheikh Anta. *Cultural Unity of Black Africa*. Chicago: Third World Press, 1978.

Dorothy. "Position Paper of a Feminist on the Report of the Royal Commission on the Status of Women in Canada and on the National Ad Hoc Committee on the Status of Women." *The New Feminist* 2.2 (1971): 2-6.

Dubel, Ireen. "Whither South African Women's Studies?" Paper prepared for Women and Gender in Southern Africa Conference. University of Natal, Durban Jan. 30-Feb. 2, 1991.

Ehrenreich, Barbara and Deidre English. *For Her Own Good: 150 Years of the Experts' Advice to Women.* New York: Anchor Press/Doubleday, 1978.

Ehusani, G. O. *An Afro-Christian Vision "OZOVEHE."* Washington, D. C.: University Press of America, 1991.

Ekwensi, Cyprain. *Jagua Nana.* London: Hutchinson, 1961.

El Saadawi, Nawal. "The Political Challenges Facing Arab Women at the End of the Twentieth Century." In *Women in the Arab World*, trans. Marilyn Booth; ed., Nahid Toubia. London: Zed Press, 1988: 8-26.

Elsafty, Adel. "Egyptian Feminist." *Ottawa Citizen*, September 23, 1991, p. A8.

Enloe, Cynthia H. *Bananas, Beaches and Bases: Making Feminist Sense of International Politics.* London: Pandora, 1989.

Evans-Pritchard, E. *Social Anthropology.* London: Routledge, 1951.

Fanon, François. *Les Damnés de la terre.* Paris: François Maspero, 1961.

Foucault, Michel. *Discipline and Punish: The Birth of the Prison*, trans., Alan Sheridan. Harmondsworth: Penguin, 1977.

Frank, Dana. "Housewives, Socialists and the Politics of Food: The 1917 New York Cost of Living Protests." *Feminist Studies* 11. 2 (Summer, 1985): 255-285.

Franklin, Clyde II. "Black Male—Black Female Conflict: Individually Caused and Culturally Nurtured." In *The Black family: Essays and Studies*, ed., Robert Staples. Belmont: Calif.: Wadsworth Press, 1986: 106-113.

Garcia, Alma M. "The Development of Chicana Feminist Discourse." In *Unequal Sisters: A Multi-Cultural Reader in U. S. Women's History*, ed., Carol DuBois and Vicki L. Ruis. New York: Routledge, 1990: 422-423.

Giddings, Paula. *When and Where I Enter: The Impact of Black Women on Race and Sex in America.* New York: Bantam, 1984.

Gilligan, Carol. *In a Different Voice.* Cambridge: Harvard University Press, 1982.

Gititi, Gitahi. "Self and Society in Testimonial Literature: Caesarina Kona Makhoere's *No Child's Play: In Prison under Apartheid.*" *Current Writing* 3 (1991): 42-49.

Goldenberg, I. *Oppression and Social Intervention.* New York: Nelson-Hall, 1978.

Gordon, Vivian. *Black Women, Feminism, and Black Liberation: Which Way?* Chicago: Third World Press, 1987.

Granovetter, Mark S. "The Strength of Weak Ties." *American Journal of Sociology* 78 (1973): 1360-1380.

Green, M. M. *Igbo Village Affairs.* New York: Praeger, 1964.

Hafkin, N. J. and Edna G. Bay, eds. *Women in Africa: Studies in Social and Economic Change.* Stanford, Calif.: Stanford University Press, 1976.

Hansson, Desirée. "A Patchwork Quilt of Power Relations: A Challenge to 1991 South African Feminism." Paper prepared for the International Conference on Women, Law, and Social Control, Montreal, Canada, 1991.

Hélie-Lucas, Marie-Aimée. "Women's Struggles and Strategies in the Rise of Fundamentalism in the Muslim World: From Entryism to Internationalism." In *Women in the Middle East: Perceptions, Realities and Struggles for Liberation.* London: MacMillan, 1993: 206-242.

Hilda, Bernstein. *For Their Triumphs and for Their Tears: Women in Apartheid South Africa,* third edition. London: International Defence and Aid Fund for Southern Africa, 1985.

Hitchcock, Peter. "Living the Struggle." *Transition* 61 (1993/4): 170-179.

Hoffer, E. *The True Believer: Thoughts on the Nature of Mass Movements.* New York: Perennial Library, 1966.

Hollis, Patricia. *Women in Public: The Women's Movement 1850-1900.* London: George Allen and Unwin, 1979.

hooks, bell. *Feminist Theory: From Margin to Center.* Boston: Southend, 1984.

———. *Ain't I a Woman.* Boston: South End Press, 1981.

———. *Yearning: Race, Gender, and Cultural Politics.* Boston: South End Press, 1990.

———. *Talking Back: Thinking Feminist, Thinking Black.* Boston: South End Press, 1989.

———. "Black Women and Feminism." *Feminist Frontiers III,* ed., Laurel Richardson and Verta Taylor. New York: McGraw-Hill, 1993: 499-507.

Horton, Robin. "African Traditional Thought and Western Science." *Africa* 37 (1967): 150-181.

———. "Types of Spirit Possession in Kalabari Religion." In *Spirit Mediumship and Society in Africa,* ed., John Beattie and John Middleton. New York: Africana Publishing Corp., 1969.

Hull, Gloria, Patricia Bell Scott, and Barbara Smith, eds. *All the Women Are White, All the Blacks Are Men, But Some of Us Are Brave.* Old Westbury: The Feminist Press, 1982.

Humm, Maggie. *The Dictionary of Feminist Theory.* Worcester: Billing and Sons Ltd., 1989: 74-75.

Imam, Ayesha. "The Dynamics of WINing: An Analysis of Women in Nigeria." *Women in Nigeria: The First Ten* Years, ed., Elsbeth Robson. Zaria: WIN, 1993: 20-44.

Ingnacio, "The Pacific/Asian Coalitions: Origin, Structure, and Program." *Social Casework* 57.3 (1976): 131-135.

Institute for African Alternatives. *Islamic Fundamentalism.* London: IFAA Publications, 1990.

Itavyar, Dennis A. and Stella N. Obiajunwa. *The State and Women in Nigeria.* Jos: Jos University Press, 1992.

Iweriebor, Ifeyinwa."The Role of Nigerian Women in National Development Since Independence." In *Nigeria—The First 25* Years, ed., Uma Eleazu. Lagos: Infodata Ltd.; Ibadan: Heinemann, 1988: 325-336.

Jackson, Michael. 1983. "Thinking through the Body." *Social Analysis* 14 (1983): 127-149.

Jell-Bahlsen, Sabine. "Names and Naming: Instances from the Oru-Igbo." *Dialectical Anthropology* 13 (1988a): 199-207.

——. "A Murder Case: Igbo Conflict Settlement." *Dialectical Anthropology* 12 (1988b): 359-366.

Jenkins, J. C. Resource Mobilization Theory and the Study of Social Movements. *Annual Review of Sociology* 9 (1983): 527-553.

King, Deborah K. "Multiple Jeopardy, Multiple Consciousness: The Context of a Black Feminist Ideology." *Signs* 14.1 (1989): 43-73.

Kishwar, Madhu and Ruth Vanita, eds. *In Search of Answers: Indian Women's Voices from Manushi.* London: Zed Books, 1984.

Korten, David. *Getting to the 21st Century: Voluntary Action and the Global Agenda.* Hartford, Conn.: Kumarian Press, 1990.

Ladner, Joyce. *Tomorrow's Tomorrow: The Black Woman.* Garden City, N.Y.: Anchor, 1972.

Lanternari, Vittorio. *Religiose Heilsbewegungen unterdruckter Volker.* Berlin/Germany: Luchterhand, 1960.

Lazreg, Marnia. "Feminism and Difference: The Perils of Writing as a Woman on Women in Algeria." *Feminist Studies* 14.1 (Spring 1988): 81-107.

Leacock, Eleanor. "Introduction" in F. Engels, *The Origin of the Family, the Private Property and the State.* New York: International Publishers, 1972.

Leander, Birgitta, ed. *Cultures: Dialogue Between Peoples of the World.* Vol.VIII, No. 4. Paris: UNESCO, 1982.

Leith-Ross, Sylvia. *African Women: A Study of the Ibo of Nigeria.* New York: Praeger, 1965.

Leroy, William, Jr. "King 'Stirred up the World': Aide's Birthday Wish— Stir on." *The Commercial Appeal* (January 15, 1985): A1, A6.

Lewin, Hugh. *Bandiet: Seven Years in South African Prison.* Cape Town: D. Philip, 1989.

Lewis, Desirée. "The Politics of Feminism in South Africa." Paper written in response to Women and Gender in Southern Africa Conference. University of Natal, Durban, Jan. 30-Feb. 2, 1991.

Lewis, I. M. *Ecstatic Religion.* London: Routledge, 1989.

Liking, Werewere. "An African Woman Speaks out against African Filmmakers," trans., Christopher Winks. *Black Renaissace/Renaissance Noire* 1.1 (1996): 170-177.

Lionnet, Françoise. "Geographies of Pain: Captive Bodies and Violent Acts in the Fictions of Gayl Jones, Bessie Head and Myriam Warner-Vieyra." In *The Politics of (M)Othering: Womanhood, Identity, and Resistance in African Literature,* ed., Obioma Nnaemeka, London: Routledge, 1997: 205-227.

Lockett, Cecily, ed. *Breaking the Silence: A Century of South African Women's Poetry.* Parklands: AD Donker Publisher, 1990.

——. "Interview with Miriam Tlali." In *Between the Lines,* ed., Craig Mackenzie and Cherry Clayton. Grahamstown: National English Literary Museum, 1989: 69-85.

Lorde, Audre. *Sister Outsider.* Trumansburg: Crossing Press, 1981.

Lugard, Lord. *The Dual Mandate in Tropical Africa.* London, 1922.

MacDonald, Gayle. "Feminist Teaching Techniques for the Committed but Exhausted." *Atlantis* 15.1 (Fall/Autumn 1989): 145-152.

Macherey, Pierre. *A Theory of Literary Production*, trans., Geoffrey Wall. London: Routledge, 1978.

Mackenzie, Craig, and Cherry Clayton, eds., *Between the Lines*. Grahamstown: National English Literary Museum, 1989.

McCarthy, J. and M. Zald. *The Trend of Social Movements in America: Professionalization and Resource Mobilization*. Morristown, N.J.: General Learning Press, 1973.

———. "Resource Mobilization and Social Movements: A Partial Theory." *American Journal of Sociology* 82.6 (1974): 1212-1241.

Madunagu, Bene E. "Contemporary Positions and Experiences of Women." In *Women in Nigeria Today*, ed., Editorial Committee. London: Zed Books, 1985: 132-137.

Magona, Sindiwe. *To My Children's Children*. Cape Town: David Philip, 1990.

———. *Living, Loving and Lying Awake at Night*. Cape Town: David Philip, 1991.

Makhoere, Caesarina Kona. *No Child's Play: In Prison under Apartheid*. London: The Women's Press, 1988.

Mandela, Winnie. *Part of My Soul Went With Him*, ed., Anne Benjamin. New York: W. W. Norton, 1984.

Marciniak, E. *Reclaiming the Inner City*. Washington, D.C.: National Center for Urban Ethnic Affairs, 1986.

Marks, Schula and Stanley Trapido, eds. *The Politics of Race, Class, and Nationalism in Twentieth Century South Africa*. London: Longman, 1987.

Marx, Karl and F. Engels. *The Holy Family*. Moscow: Progress Publishers, 1975.

Masquelier, Adeline. "Narratives of Power, Images of Wealth: The Ritual Economy of Bori in the Market." In *Modernity and Its Malcontents: Ritual and Power in Postcolonial Africa*, ed., Jean Comaroff and John Comaroff. Bloomington: Indiana University Press, 1993.

Mba, Nina E. *Nigerian Women Mobilized: Women's Political Activity in Southern Nigeria, 1900-1965*. Berkeley: Institute of International Studies, University of California, 1982.

Mbilinyi, M. "Research Priorities in Women's Studies in Eastern Africa." *Women's Studies International Forum* 7.4 (1984): 289-300.

Mbuende, Elizabeth. "The Namibian Woman's Plight." *SAPEM* (August 1990): 19-21.

McFadden, Patricia. "The Condition of Women in Southern Africa: Challenges for the 1990s." *SAPEM* (August 1990): 3-9.

Merriam-Howard, Kathleen. "Women, Education, and the Professions in Egypt." *Comparative and International Education Society* 23.2 (June 1979): 256-270.

Mies, Maria. *Patriarchy and the Accumulation of Capital on a World Scale: Women in the International Division of Labour*. London: Zed Books, 1986.

Miles, Angela. "Integrative Feminism." *Fireweed: A Feminist Quarterly* 19 (Summer/Fall, 1984): 55-81.

———. "Feminism, Equality and Liberation." *Canadian Journal of Women and the Law* 1.1 (1985): 42-68.

———. *Feminist Radicalism in the 1980s*. Montreal: New World Perspectives, 1985.

———. *Integrative Feminisms: Building Global Visions, 1960s to 1990s.* New York: Routledge, 1996.

Mitter, Swasti. *Common Fate, Common Bond.* London: Pluto Press, 1986.

Mohammed, Halina D. "Women in Nigerian History: Examples from Borno Empire, Nupeland and Igboland." In *Women in Nigeria Today*, ed., Editorial Committee. London: Zed Press, 1985: 45-51.

Mohanty, Chandra, Ann Russo, and Lourdes Torres, eds. *Third World Women and the Politics of Feminism.* Bloomington: Indiana University Press, 1991.

Mohanty, Chandra. "Under Western Eyes: Feminist Scholarship and Colonial Discourses." *Boundary* 2.12/3.13 (1984): 333-358; *Feminist Review* 30 (1988): 61-88.

———. "Introduction: Cartographies of Struggle, Third World Women and the Politics of Feminism." In *Third World Women and the Politics of Feminism*, ed., Chandra Talpade Mohanty, Ann Russo, and Lourdes Torres. Bloomington: Indiana University Press, 1991.

Mollenkopf, J. H. *The Contested City.* Princeton, NJ: Princeton University Press, 1983.

Mompati, Ruth. "Women and Life under Apartheid." In *One is Not a Woman, One Becomes: The African Woman in a Transitional Society*, ed., Daphne Williams Ntiri. Troy, Mich: Bedford Publishers, 1982: 108-113.

Moraga, Cherrie and Gloria Anzaldua, eds. *This Bridge Called My Back: Writings by Radical Women of Color.* Watertown, Mass.: Persephone Press, 1981.

Morgan, Robin. *Sisterhood Is Global.* New York: Anchor Books/Doubleday, 1984.

Mudimbe, V. Y. *The Invention of Africa: Gnosis, Philosophy and the Order of Knowledge.* Bloomington: Indiana University Press, 1988.

Murphy, Kim. "Speaking Her Mind on Women's Rights." *Los Angeles Times*, August 27, 1991, World Report: 6.

Mustapha, A. R. "On Combating Women's Exploitation and Oppression in Nigeria." In *Women in Nigeria Today*, ed., Editorial Committee. London: Zed Books, 1985: 241-246.

Mwaka, V. M. and D. H. Kasente. "The Status of Women's Studies in Uganda." Paper presented at the conference on the status of Women's Studies in Africa, Columbus, Ohio, November 1991.

Nnaemeka, Obioma. "Urban Spaces, Women's Places: Polygamy as Sign in Mariama Bâ's Novels." *The Politics of (M)Othering: Womanhood, Identity and Resistance in African Literature*, ed., Obioma Nnaemeka. London: Routledge, 1997: 162-191.

———. "Development, Cultural Forces, and Women's Achievements in Africa." *Law and Policy* (forthcoming).

———. "Bringing African Women into the Classroom: Rethinking Pedagogy and Epistemology." *Borderwork: Feminist Engagements with Comparative Literature*, ed, Margaret Higonnet. Ithaca: Cornell University Press, 1994: 301-318.

———. "Feminism, Rebellious Women and Cultural Boundaries: Rereading Flora Nwapa and Her Compatriots," *Research in African Literatures* 26.2 (1995): 80-113.

——. "Marginality as the Third Term: A Reading of Cheikh Hamidou Kane's *Ambiguous Adventure*." In *Challenging Hierarchies: Issues and Themes in Post-Colonial Literature*, ed., Leonard Podis and Yakubu Saaka. New York: Peter Lang (forthcoming).

Ntiri, Daphne Williams, ed. *One is Not a Woman, One Becomes: The African Woman in a Transitional Society*. Troy, Mich: Bedford Publishers, 1982.

Nwapa, Flora. *Efuru*. London: Heinemann, 1966.

——. *Idu*. London: Heinemann, 1970.

——. *This Is Lagos and Other Stories*. Enugu: Nwankwo-Ifejika, 1971.

——. *Never Again*. Enugu: Nwamife, 1975; Trenton, N.J.: Africa World Press, 1992.

——. *Wives at War and Other Stories*. Enugu: Tana Press, 1980; Trenton, N.J.: Africa World Press, 1992.

——. *One Is Enough*. Enugu: Tana Press, 1981; Trenton, N.J.: Africa World Press, 1992.

——. *Women Are Different*. Enugu: Tana Press, 1986; Trenton, N.J.: Africa World Press, 1992.

——. *Cassava Song and Rice Song*. Enugu: Tana Press, 1986.

Obadina, Elizabeth. "How Relevant is the Western Women's Liberation Movement for Nigeria?" In *Women in Nigeria Today*, ed., Editorial Committee. London: Zed Press, 1985: 138-142.

Obbo, Christine. *African Women: Their Struggle for Economic Independence*. London: Zed Press, 1980.

Oduwole, Yinka. "Exploring Ways of Empowering Women." *The Guardian* (March 11, 1992): 27.

Ogundipe-Leslie, Molara. "Women in Nigeria." In *Women in Nigeria Today*, ed., Editorial Committee. London: Zed Press, 1985: 119-131.

Okojie, Christiana E. E."Widowhood Practices and Sociocultural Restrictions on Women's Behavior in Edo and Delta States of Nigeria." *Proceedings of the First International Conference on Women in Africa and the African Diaspora: Bridges across Activism and the Academy*. Nsukka, Nigeria, July 13-18, 1992, Vol. X: 175-197.

Okonjo, Kamene. "The Dual-Sex Political System in Operation: Igbo Women and Community Politics in Midwestern Nigeria." In *Women in Africa: Studies in Social and Economic Change*, ed., Nancy J. Hafkin and Edna G. Bay. Stanford, Calif.: Stanford University Press, 1976: 45-85.

Oluwole, Sophie B. "Feminism in Africa." Paper presented at the international conference on Feminism in Africa. Lagos, May 30-June 2, 1994.

O'Meara, Patrick, and Gwendolen Carter, eds. *International Politics in South Africa*. Bloomington: Indiana University Press, 1982.

——. *South Africa: The Continuing Crisis*. Bloomington: Indiana University Press, 1982.

O'Meara, Patrick, and Phyllis Martin, eds. *Africa*. Bloominton: Indiana University Press, 1986.

Opland, Jeff. *Words that Circle Words*. Johannesburg: Ad Donker (forthcoming).

Ortner, Sherry B. "Is Female to Male as Nature to Culture? In *Woman, Culture and Society*, ed., Michelle Zimbalist Rosaldo and Louise Lamphere. Stanford, Calif.: Stanford University Press, 1974: 67-86.

Osarenren, Ewaen. "Women Liberation Movement: The Misunderstood Lot," *Sunday Concord* (June 5, 1986): 12.

Pala, Achola O. "Definitions of Women and Development: An African Perspective." *Signs* 3.1 (1977): 9-13.

Piven, F. F. and R. A. Cloward. *Poor People's Movements: How They Succeed, How They Fail.* New York: Vintage Books, 1979.

Pope, Alexander. *Rape of the Lock.* London: Lane, 1902.

Price, Sally. *Primitive Art in Civilized Places.* Bloomington: Indiana University Press, 1991.

Radhakrishnan, R. "Negotiating Subject Positions in an Uneven World." *Feminism and Institutions,* ed., Linda Kauffman. Oxford: Blackwell, 1989: 276-290.

Rapp, Rayna Reiter, ed. *Toward an Anthropology of Women.* New York: Monthly Review Press, 1975.

Rich, Adrienne. *Of Woman Born: Motherhood as Experience and Institution.* New York: W. W. Norton, 1976.

———. "Disloyal to Civilization: Feminism, Racism, and Gynephobia." *Chrysalis* 7 (1978): 9-27. Also in *On Lies, Secrets and Silences: Selected Prose, 1966-1978.* New York: W. W. Norton, 1979. 275-310.

———. "Compulsory Heterosexuality and Lesbian Existence." *Feminist Frontiers III.* Third Edition. Ed. Laurel Richardson and Venta Taylor. New York: McGraw-Hill, 1993: 158-179.

Robson, Elsbeth, ed. *Women in Nigeria: The First Ten* Years. Zaria: WIN, 1993.

Rodney, Walter. *How Europe Underdeveloped Africa.* Dar-es-Salaam: Tanzania Publishing House, 1972.

Rogers, Barbara. *The Domestication of Women: Discrimination in Developing Societies.* London: Tavistock Publications, 1980.

Rogers E. and D. Kincaid. *Communications Networks: Toward a Paradigm for Research.* New York: Free Press, 1981.

Rogers, E. and F. F. Shoemaker. *Communications of Innovations: A Cross-Cultural Approach.* New York: Free Press, 1971.

Rogers, E. M., J. J. Ascroft, and N. G. Roling. "Diffusion of Innovations in Brazil, Nigeria, and India." *Research Report* #24. East Langsing: Department of Communications, Michigan State University, 1970.

Rogers, S. "Anti-Colonial Protest in Africa: A Female Strategy Reconsidered." *Heresies* 3.1 (1980): 22-25.

Rowbotham, Sheila. *Hidden from History: Rediscovering Women in History from the Seventeenth Century to the Present.* New York: Vintage Books, 1976.

Ruddick, Sara. "Maternal Peace Politics and Women's Resistance: The Example of Argentina and Chile." *The Barnard Occasional Papers on Women's Issues* 4.1 (Winter, 1989).

Salman, Magida. "The Arab Woman." In *Women in the Middle East,* ed., Khamsin Collective. London: Zed Books, 1987.

Sarason, S. B., C. F. Carroll, K. Maton, S. Cohen, and E. Lorentz. *Human Services and Resource Networks: Rationale, Possibilities, and Public Policy.* San Francisco: Jossey-Bass Publishers, 1977.

Sarason, S. B. and E. Lorentz. *The Challenge of the Resource Exchange Network: From Concept to Action.* San Francisco: Jossey-Bass, 1979.

Saul, John and Stephen Gelb. *The Crisis in South Africa*, revised edition. New York: Monthly Review Press, 1986.

Schipper, Mineke. *Source of All Evil—African Proverbs and Sayings on Women*. Chicago: Ivan R. Dee, 1991.

Schmoll, Pamela, G. "Black Stomachs, Beautiful Stones: Soul Eating among the Hausa in Niger." In *Modernity and Its Malcontents: Ritual and Power in Postcolonial Africa*, ed., Jean Comaroff and John Comaroff. Chicago: University of Chicago Press, 1993.

Scott, Kesho Yvonne. The *Habit of Surviving: Black Women's Strategies for Life*. New Brunswick: Rutgers University Press, 1991.

Sembène, Ousmane. *God's Bits of Wood*, trans., Francis Price. Garden City, N.Y.: Anchor Books, 1970.

Sen, Gita and Caren Grown. *Development, Crises, and Alternative Visions: Third World Women's Perspectives*. New York: Monthly Review Press, 1987.

Shakespeare, William. *Antony and Cleopatra*. Cambridge: Cambridge University Press, 1950.

Shefer, Tammy, and Sibylle Mathis. "The Search for Sisterhood." *Work in Progress* 73 (1992): 14-16.

Shiva, Vandana. *Staying Alive: Women, Ecology and Development*. London: Zed Books, 1989.

Smith, Barbara, ed. *Home Girls: A Black Feminist Anthology*. New York: Kitchen Table Press, 1983.

Soyinka, Wole. *The Interpreters*. New York: Africana Publishing Corp., 1972.

Spivak, Gayatri. *In Other Worlds: Essays in Cultural Politics*. New York: Methuen, 1987.

Stamp, P. *Technology, Gender, and Power in Africa*. IDRC, Ottawa: Canada, 1989.

Stanley, Liz and Ann Morley. *The Life and Death of Emily Wilding Davison: A Biographical Detective Story*. London: Women's Press, 1988.

Steady, F. C. "African Feminism: A Worldwide Perspective." In *Women in Africa and the African* Diaspora, ed., Rosalyn Terborg-Penn, Sharon Harley, and Andrea Benton Rushing. Washington, D. C.: Howard University Press, 1987: 3-24.

——. ed. *The Black Woman Cross-Culturally*. Cambridge, Mass.: Schenkman, 1981.

——. "The Black Woman Cross-Culturally: An Overview." In *The Black Woman Cross-Culturally*. Cambridge, Mass.: Schenkman, 1981.

Sudarkasa, Niara. "Female Employment and Family Organization in West Africa." In *The Black Woman Cross-Culturally*, ed., Filomina Chioma Steady. Cambridge, Mass.: Schenkman, 1981: 49-64.

——. "The Studies of Women in Indigenous Africa and the African Diaspora." In *Women in African and the African Diaspora*, ed., Rosalyn Terborg-Penn, Sharon Harley, and Andrea Benton Rushing. Washington, D. C.: Howard University Press, 1987: 25-42.

Suttner, Raymond and Jeremy Cronin. *Thirty Years of the Freedom Charter*. Johannesburg: Ravan Press, 1985.

Tandon, Yash. "Foreign NGOs, Uses and Abuses: An African Perspective." *IFDA Dossier* 81(1991): 67-78.

Tiano, Susan. "The Separation of Women's Remuneration and Household Work: Theoretical Perspectives on Women in Development." *Working Paper No. 2.* Michigan: Office of Women in International Development, Michigan State University, 1981.

Toch, Hans. *The Social Psychology of Social Movements.* Indianapolis: Bobbs-Merrill Company, 1965.

Tompkins, Jane. "Me and My Shadow." *New Literary History* 19 (1987): 169-178.

Toubia, Nahid, ed. *Women of the Arab World.* London: Zed Press, 1988.

Touraine, Alain. *The Post-Industrial Society: Tomorrow's Social History: Classes, Conflicts and Culture in the Programmed Society,* trans., Leonard F. X. Mayhew. New York: Random House, 1971.

Turner, R. H. and L. M. Killian. *Collective Behavior.* Englewood Cliffs, N.J.: Prentice-Hall, 1972.

Uchendu, Patrick K. *The Role of Nigerian Women in Politics: Past and Present.* Enugu: Fourth Dimension, 1993.

Uchendu, Victor. *The Igbo Speaking Peoples of Southeastern Nigeria.* New York: Holt, Rinehart & Winston, 1973.

UNFPA. *A Report on the Baseline Survey of the Situation of Women in the Eight Pilot Districts.* Kampala: Ministry of Women in Development, 1991.

UNICEF. *Children and Women in Uganda : A Situation Analysis.* UNICEF, Kampala, 1989.

USAID. *Uganda Education Sector Review.* USAID, Kampala, 1990.

Van Allen, Judith. "Aba Riots or Igbo Women's War?: Ideology, Stratification, and the Invisibility of Women." In *Women in Africa: Studies in Social and Economic Change,* ed., Nancy J. Hafkin and Edna G. Bay. Stanford: Stanford University Press, 1976: 59-86.

——. "'Sitting on a Man': Colonialism and the Lost Political Institutions of Igbo Women." *Canadian Journal of African Studies* 6.2 (1972): 165-181.

van Sertima, Ivan, ed. *Black Women in Antiquity.* New Brunswick, N.J.: Transaction Books, 1984.

Walker, Alice. *In Search of Our Mothers' Gardens.* San Diego: Harcourt, 1983.

Walker, Cherryl, ed. *Women and Gender in Southern Africa.* Cape Town: David Philip, 1990.

——. *Women and Resistance in South Africa.* London: Onyx Press, 1992.

——. *We Have Done with Pleading: The Women's 1913 Anti-Pass Campaign.* Johannesburg: Ravan Press, 1991.

——. *We Now Demand!* Johannesburg: University of Witwatersrand Press, 1993.

Wallace, Michele. *Black Macho and the Myth of the Superwoman.* New York: Warner, 1980.

Wandersman, Abraham, et al. "Citizen Participation, Voluntary Organizations and Community Development: Insights for Empowerment through Research," (Special Section). *American Journal of Community Psychology* 18.1 (1990): 41-151.

Waring, Marilyn. *If Women Counted: A New Feminist Economics.* San Francisco: Harper and Row, 1988.

Wa Thiong'o, Ngugi. *Petals of Blood.* New York: Dutton, 1978.

Wells, Julia. "The War of Degradation: Black Women's Struggles Against Free State Pass Laws, 1913." In *Banditry, Rebellion and Social Protest in Africa*, ed., Donald Crummey. London: Heinemann Educational Books, 1985.

Wolfe, Leslie R., and Jennifer Tucker. "Feminism Lives: Building a Multicultural Women's Movement in the United States." In *The Challenge of Local Feminisms*, ed., Amrita Basu. Boulder: Westview Press, 1995: 435-462.

Wright, Richard. "Blueprint for Negro Writing." *The Black Aesthetics*, ed., Addison Gayle, Jr. New York: Doubleday, 1971.

Wushishi, Mallam. "Nigerian Women: 1992 and Beyond." *Daily Times* (January 22, 1992): 32.

Zald, M. and R. Asch. "Social Movement Organizations: Growth Decay, and Change." *Social Forces* 44 (1965): 327-341.

Zuhur, Sherifa. *Revealing Reveiling*. Albany: SUNY Press, 1992.

NOTES ON CONTRIBUTORS

Ama Ata Aidoo, a former minister of education in Ghana and distinguished visiting professor of English at Oberlin College, is the author of two novels, *Changes* and *Our Sister Killjoy or Reflections from a Black-Eyed Squint*; a play, *Anowa*; a book of poetry, *Someone Talking to Sometime*; and a collection of short stories, *No Sweetness Here*.

Olabisi Aina is a lecturer in the Department of Sociology/ Anthropology and one of the coordinators of the Women's Studies Program at Obafemi Awolowo University, Ile-Ife, Nigeria. Her research interests are Industrial Sociology and Women's Studies. She and Simi Afonja recently co-edited the book, *Nigerian Women and Social Change* and are currently working on a book titled *Women in Third World Agriculture*.

Femi Ajanaku is an assistant professor of sociology at LeMoyne-Owen College in Memphis, Tennessee. She received her Ph. D. in 1993 from Howard University, with a concentration in African American women in racial/ethnic relations and social demography. She has conducted research on African American women's participation US organizations of the 1970s and 1980s.

Nkechi Ajanaku, who considers herself an inner city cultural environmentalist, resides in Knoxville, Tenn. and is currently an education coordinator for Project 2000, Inc. She is also a co-producer of the five-year-old Kuumba Festival of Knoxville and chair of the African American Appalachian Arts, Inc.

Martha Banks is a research neuropsychologist who holds several offices in the American Psychological Association. She is a retired clinician with numerous publications and presentations on family psychology, women's health issues, and neuropsychological concerns for African-Americans.

Gloria Braxton, an Atlanta University Ph. D., is director of the Center for International Development Programs for the Southern University System in Baton Rouge, Louisiana. Her research has focused primarily on the constraints to economic and political participation of African rural women.

Dé Bryant, an activist-scholar, is Associate Professor of Psychology at Indiana University, South Bend. She received her Ph. D. from Michigan State University, East Lansing. For over a decade she has been the director of Social Action project and community psychologist for the MSU-Benton Harbor Project and in 1992 initiated a collaborative project between youths in Michigan and a high school in Aba, Nigeria. She has published articles on community-based organizations, philanthropy, and technology in developing nations.

Glo Chukukere taught at the Institute of Management and Technology, Enugu, Nigeria. She holds an M.A. from the University of Birmingham and a Ph.D. from the University of Lagos. She has held positions in women's organizations in Nigeria and was the first editor of *Erulu*. Her publications include an edited volume, *Introductory Readings in the Humanities and Social Sciences,* and articles in scholarly journals and edited volumes.

Jamiila Cushnie-Mnyanga, originally from Kingston, Jamaica, now resides in Tanzania where she is involved with women's and activist organizations. She is the founder of the first Black youth hostel, Nottinghill, London. In Tanzania, she has worked for community development with organizations such as the Tanzanian Media Women's Association (TAMWA) and UDANANDA (Art and Culture for Empowerment).

Liz Dimock, lives in Melbourne, Australia, where she has worked on development issues under the auspices of Australian international agencies.

Gertrude Fester has been an anti-apartheid and women's rights activist for most of her life. She has had various executive positions in the United Women's Organization and the United Women's Congress. She was detained in 1988 and charged with treason and terrorism for furthering the aims of the African National Congress but charges were dropped in 1990 after the ANC was unbanned. She was a candidate for the ANC National Assembly during the past elections. She is a member of the steering committee of the Women's College and teaches English and Drama at Hewat College of Education.

Donna Flynn is currently visiting assistant professor in the Department of Anthropology at the College of William and Mary in Williamsburg, Virginia. Her work is on intersections of gender and ritual with processes of transborder trade and smuggling in West Africa.

Fidelia Fouché lectured in philosophy at the University of Natal, Pietermaritzburg, until the end of 1994. In the mid-eighties she initiated the introduction of Gender Studies at the University.
She has been actively involved in the Black Sash, a women's human rights organization. Her article, "Overcoming Sisterhood Myths," was published in *Transformation* in 1994.

Lumka Funani is the national director of Planned Parenthood Association of South Africa. She holds an M. A. from Medunsa University and diplomas in general nursing and midwifery. Her publications include *Circumcision among the Ama-Xhosa* and numerous articles on women's health.

Kathleen Geathers is a retired psychiatric social worker and family therapist. Social activist and organizer of the Greater Cleveland Coalition for a Clean Environment and the Greater Cleveland Chapter of Women for Racial and Economic Equality, Geathers is a world traveller, lecturer, and singer.

Peter Hitchcock is associate arofessor of English and cultural studies at Baruch College, CUNY. He is the author of *Working Class Fiction in Theory and Practice* (1989) and *Dialogics of the Oppressed* (1993). He has also published articles in journals such as *Research in African Literatures, Cultural Studies, Critical Texts, Transition, Third Text, and Modern Fiction Studies.*

Clenora Hudson-Weems is associate professor of English at the University of Missouri-Columbia. She co-authored Toni Morrison and is the author of *Africana Womanism: Reclaiming Ourselves and Emmett Till: The Sacrificial Lamb of the Civil Rights Movement.* Her publications have appeared in *Phylon, CLA Journal, Journal of Black Studies, The Western Journal of Black Studies,* and *Umoja: Scholarly Journal of Black Studies.*

Ifeyinwa Iweriebor is a New York-based freelance editor and consultant on women's issues. A member of the National Association of Executive Females (NAFE) and Black Women in Publishing (BWIP), she had been involved with the Nigerian Association of Media Women (NAMW), the Nigerian Institute of Public Relations (NIPR), and activist women's group such as Women in Nigeria (WIN) and the National Council of Women's Societies (NCWS).

Sabine Jell-Bahlsen received her Ph. D in anthropology from the New School for Social Research in New York. Her published articles appear in such journals as *Research in African Literatures, Dialectical Anthropology, and Commission on Visual Anthropology Review.* Her ethnographic documentary films, *Mammy Water: In Search of the Water Spirits in Nigeria; Owu: Chidi Joins the Okoroshi Secret Society;* and *Tubali: Hausa Architecture of Northern Nigeria* are produced in close collaboration with local communities and co-producers in Nigeria. She is currently a research affiliate of the Architectural Heritage Center of Papua New Guinea University of Technology.

Deborah Kasente received an M. Ed. from Makerere University where she is currently a lecturer in the Women's Studies Program. She represented Uganda Association of University Women at the 1985 UN conference in Nairobi. She has published articles on women in development with a focus on education.

Protus Kemdirim teaches Christian theology and research method in the Department of Religious Studies at the University of Port Harcourt, Nigeria. He holds a diploma in philosophy, and a Ph. D in religion from the University of Nigeria, Nsukka. He has written extensively on feminist studies. He is also the author of *Foundations of Christian Religious and Moral Education.* Dr. Kemdirim is the secretary general of the Catholic Theological Association of Nigeria. (CATHAN) His publications have appeared in scholarly journals including *Mission Studies, Africa Review, CIWA Journal of Inculturation, and Bulletin of Ecumenical Studies.*

P. L. Maholtra is a director of UNESCO and is based in Lagos, Nigeria.

Maureen Malowany is a Ph. D. student in African history at McGill University, Montréal, Canada. She hold diplomas in anthropology and education. In the 1960s, she worked in Nairobi, Kenya.

Angela Miles holds a Ph. D. from the University of Toronto and is a Professor in the Department of Education, Ontario Institute for Studies in Education (OISE), Toronto. A much-published feminist scholar, Miles has written on feminist and international women's issues. In addition to publishing chapters in books and articles in scholarly journals such as *Women's Studies International Quarterly; Fireweed: A Feminist Quarterly; Canadian Journal of Political and Social Theory; and Canadian Journal of Women and the Law*, she has authored and edited three books, *Integrative Feminisms: Building Global Visions, 1960s to 1990s, Feminism: From Pressure to Politics, and Feminist Radicalism in the 1980s*.

Obioma Nnaemeka is associate professor of French, women's studies, and African American studies at Indiana University, Indianapolis. A former Rockefeller humanist-in-residence (University of Minnesota) and Edith Kreeger Wolf distinguished visiting professor (Northwestern University, Evanston), Nnaemeka is the current president of the Association of African Women Scholars. Her numerous publications include the editorship of *The Politics of (M)Othering*, (London: Routledge, 1997), as well as authorship of chapters in anthologies and articles in scholarly journals such as Feminist Issues, Signs, Law and Policy, Western Journal of Black Studies and Research in African Literatures.

Daphne Ntiri is associate professor of social science, Interdisciplinary Studies Program, Wayne State University, Detroit, Michigan. A native of Sierra Leone, she has served as UNESCO consultant in Dakar, Senegal, and Kismayo, Somalia, and presently directs several programs on Adult Literacy at Wayne State University and in Detroit. She is author of several publications on adult literacy and women's studies.

Chimalum Nwankwo, Nigerian poet and critic is an associate professor of English at North Carolina State University, Raleigh. His numerous publicatons include a critical work, *Toward the Kingdom* *of Woman & Man: The Works of Ngugi wa Thiong'o; The Tumpet Parable* (a play); *Feet of the Limping Dancers* (poems) and the Association of Nigerian Authors prize-winning collection of poems, *Toward the Aerial Zone.* A new poetry volume, Voices from Water, is in press.

Flora Nwapa (1931-1993) was Africa's pioneer female novelist and publisher. She is well known for her novels (*Efuru, Idu, Never Again, One Is Enough, and Women Are Different*), short stories (*This Is Lagos and Other Stories, and Wives at War and Other Stories*), and children's literature (*Emeka-Driver's Guard, Mammy Water, The Adventures of Deke, Journey to Space, The Miracle Kittens, etc.*). She combined her writing career with other responsibilities as the founder and publisher of Tana Press and full lectureship schedule inside and outside Africa.

Elsie Ogbonna-Ohuche received a Ph. D. in English from the University of Nigeria where she teaches in the Division of general Studies. She has written on gender and language.

Julie Okpala is chair of the Department of Education at the University of Nigeria, Nsukka. She has published extensively in the field of education. Her current research focuses on environmental issues.

Maria Olaussen works at the Department of English, Abo Akademi University, Finland. She is the author of *Three Types of Feminist Criticism* and *Jean Rhys's Wide Sargasso Sea* (1992) and *Forceful Creation in Harsh Terrain: Place and Identity in Three Novels by Bessie Head* (forthcoming).

Chioma Opara received a Ph. D. from the University of Ibadan, Nigeria. She is a senior lecturer at the Rivers State University of Science and Technology, Port Harcourt, Nigeria, where she lectures in French and literature. Her area of research is African feminist literature. Her numerous publications appear in anthologies and in journals such as *Journal of Pedagogy and Development; Review of English and Literary Studies; Ogele: Journal of the Social Sciences and Humanities;* and *Nka: A Journal of the Arts.*

Deborah Plant is associate professor of Africana studies at University of South Florida. Her publications have appeared in scholarly journals including *Research in African Literatures.* Her book *Every Tub Must Sit on Its Own Bottom: The Philosophy and Politics of Zora Neale Hurston*

(1995) is published by the University of Illinois Press, Urbana.

Pamela Ryan teaches English and women's studies at the University of South Africa. She has published articles relating to feminist theory and South African women writers and is presently working on a book entitled *An Introduction to Women's Studies in South Africa.*

'Zulu Sofola (1935-1995), Nigeria's first published and foremost female playwright, was at her death a professor of drama and head of the performing arts department at the University of Ilorin, Nigeria. She was a member of the executive council of the Association of Nigerian Authors. Her over a dozen plays include: *Wedlock of the Gods; The Operators; Memories in the Moonlight; The Showers and Lost Dream; Queen Omu-Ako of Oligbo; Lost Dreams; Wizard of Law; Old Wines Are Tasty; Disturbed Peace of Christmas; King Emene; The Love of Life; The Sweet Trap;* and *Song of a Maiden.*

Jane Splawn is adjunct professor of humanities at Indiana University, Kokomo. Currently, she is completing a book on black women's drama and ritual and continues to teach and conduct research on 19th- and 20th-century African American women's literature.

Marie Umeh teaches literature of the African world, Western literature, and writing composition in the Department of English at John Jay College of Criminal Justice, CUNY. She is the editor of *Emerging Perspectives on Buchi Emecheta* and *Emerging Perspectives on Flora Nwapa* (both published by Africa World Press, Trenton, NJ). Her essays have appeared in anthologies and journals in Africa, Europe and the United States.

Julia Wells has published widely on the history of black women's resistance to pass laws in South Africa. She obtained her Ph. D from Columbia University in 1982, lectured at the University of Zimbabwe for three years, and now teaches women's history in Africa at Rhodes University, Grahamstown, South Africa.

Betty Welz is a senior lecturer in the Department of Sociology at the University of South Africa, Pretoria. She is working for an M. Phil. at the London School of Economics on forensic sociology in South Africa. She is a founding member and past secretary of the Association for Sociology in South Africa and an executive committee member of the Women's Studies Center at the University of South Africa.

INDEX